The Cambridge Handbook of the Learning Sciences

Learning sciences is an interdisciplinary field that studies teaching and learning. The sciences of learning include cognitive science, educational psychology, computer science, anthropology, sociology, neuroscience, and other fields. *The Cambridge Handbook of the Learning Sciences* shows how educators can use the learning sciences to design more effective learning environments, including school classrooms and informal settings such as science centers or after-school clubs, online distance learning, and computer-based tutoring software. The chapters in this handbook describe exciting new classroom environments, based on the latest science about how children learn. *CHLS* is a true handbook: readers can use it to design the schools of the future – schools that will prepare graduates to participate in a global society that is increasingly based on knowledge and innovation.

R. Keith Sawyer is Associate Professor of Education at Washington University in St. Louis. He received his Ph.D. in Psychology at the University of Chicago and his S.B. in Computer Science at the Massachusetts Institute of Technology. He studies creativity, collaboration, and learning. Dr. Sawyer has written or edited eight books. His most recent book is *Explaining Creativity: The Science of Human Innovation* (2006).

The Cambridge Handbook of the Learning Sciences

Edited by

R. Keith Sawyer
Washington University

CAMBRIDGE UNIVERSITY PRESS
Cambridge, New York, Melbourne, Madrid, Cape Town, Singapore, São Paulo, Delhi

Cambridge University Press
32 Avenue of the Americas, New York, NY 10013-2473, USA

www.cambridge.org
Information on this title: www.cambridge.org/9780521607773

First published 2006
Reprinted 2009 (twice)

Printed in the United States of America

A catalog record for this publication is available from the British Library.

Library of Congress Cataloging in Publication Data

The Cambridge handbook of the learning sciences / edited by R. Keith Sawyer.
    p.   cm.
Includes bibliographical references and index.
ISBN-13: 978-0-521-84554-0 (hardcover)
ISBN-10: 0-521-84554-8 (hardcover)
ISBN-13: 978-0-521-60777-3 (pbk.)
ISBN-10: 0-521-60777-9 (pbk.)
1. Learning, Psychology of.   2. Cognitive learning.   3. Learning – Social aspects.
I. Sawyer, R. Keith (Robert Keith)   II. Title.
LB1060.C35   2006
370.15'23 – dc22   2005036463

ISBN 978-0-521-84554-0 hardback
ISBN 978-0-521-60777-3 paperback

In memory of three learning sciences pioneers:
Ann Brown, Robbie Case, and Jan Hawkins

Contents

Preface

R. Keith Sawyer

Learning sciences is an interdisciplinary field that studies teaching and learning. Learning scientists study learning in a variety of settings, including not only the more formal learning of school classrooms but also the informal learning that takes place at home, on the job, and among peers. The goal of the learning sciences is to better understand the cognitive and social processes that result in the most effective learning, and to use this knowledge to redesign classrooms and other learning environments so that people learn more deeply and more effectively. The sciences of learning include cognitive science, educational psychology, computer science, anthropology, sociology, information sciences, neurosciences, education, design studies, instructional design, and other fields. In the late 1980s, researchers in these fields who were studying learning realized that they needed to develop new scientific approaches that went beyond what their own individual disciplines could offer, and they began to collaborate with other disciplines. Learning sciences was born in 1991, when the first international conference was held, and the *Journal of the Learning Sciences* was first published.

Learning sciences researchers have generated an impressive body of scholarship since 1991, and it's time to share the research with the rest of the world – education researchers, teachers, administrators, policy makers, consultants, and software designers. This handbook is your introduction to an exciting new approach to reforming education and schools, an approach that builds on the learning sciences to design new learning environments that help people learn more deeply and more effectively.

Learning sciences researchers often refer to themselves as a community because sometimes it seems like everybody knows everybody else; only a few hundred scholars attend the professional meetings that are held each year. This is a relatively small group in the context of education research; the American Educational Research Association claims more than ten thousand members. But the learning sciences community is growing, and it is beginning to have an impact on education far beyond its size. Between 2003 and 2006, the National

Science Foundation funded nearly $100 million in grants to accelerate the development of the learning sciences. More and more people are realizing that the approaches emerging from the learning sciences community have great potential to contribute to improving education.

The National Research Council report *How People Learn* (Bransford, Brown, & Cocking, 2000) was the first overview of the new sciences of learning. That book provided an accessible introduction to the learning sciences for a broad audience. The *Cambridge Handbook of the Learning Sciences* (CHLS) picks up where this NRC report left off: CHLS shows how educators can use the learning sciences to design more effective learning environments, including school classrooms, and informal settings such as science centers or after-school clubs, online distance learning, and computer-based tutoring software. The chapters in CHLS describe exciting new classroom environments, based on the latest science about how children learn. These classroom environments combine new curricular materials, new collaborative activities, support for teachers, and innovative educational software, often using the unique advantages of the Internet to extend learning beyond the walls of the school. CHLS is a true handbook in that readers can use it to design the schools of the future – schools that are based on learning sciences research and that draw on the full potential of computer and Internet technology to improve our students' experiences. The learning sciences are supporting deep links between formal schooling and the many other learning institutions available to students – libraries, science centers and history museums, after-school clubs, online activities that can be accessed from home, and even collaborations between students and working professionals.

Many of the cutting-edge classrooms described here make use of advanced computer technology – but not just for technology's sake. Learning scientists are well aware that computers have generally failed teachers and students; that they are, in Larry Cuban's (2001) famous words, "oversold and underused." Learning scientists have discovered that computers only benefit learning when they take into account what we know about how children learn, and when they are designed to be closely integrated with teacher and student interactions in the classroom. This handbook will introduce you to the best of this new educational software. But computer software is only one component of this handbook; various chapters propose new teaching strategies, alternative ways of bringing students together in collaborating groups, and new forms of curriculum that cross traditional grades and disciplines. Some chapters even propose radical new ways of thinking about schooling and learning.

The thirty-four chapters of the CHLS are organized into six parts.

In my own Introduction and Conclusion, I explain why the learning sciences are important not only to education but to our entire society. The major advanced nations and the entire global economy are rapidly changing. In these two chapters, I draw on a large body of recent scholarship that describes the mismatch between the schools we have today and the demands of the knowledge age. Because the learning sciences are discovering how to teach the deep knowledge, skills, and attitudes required in the knowledge society, they are positioned to provide the blueprint for the schools of the future.

Part I, Foundations, introduces the reader to many of the big ideas that have been most influential throughout the learning sciences.

Part II, Methodologies, describes the unique research approaches used by learning scientists to study and to design new learning environments. Experiments are an important research methodology, but they are typically not useful in designing and engineering classrooms, and learning scientists have developed a variety of new methodological tools.

Part III, The Nature of Knowledge, presents new research on the kinds of deep knowledge that support expert activity. Learning scientists are not simply trying to help students memorize textbook facts better, because memorizing isolated facts and step-by-step procedures is not enough in today's knowledge society. Instead, learning scientists study how to help students understand underlying explanations and causes and how to solve complex, real-world problems.

Part IV, Making Knowledge Visible, shows how learning scientists are using these new discoveries about the nature of knowledge to design classroom activities that help students learn by making visible the deep knowledge they need to learn – often with sophisticated computer displays.

Part V, Learning Together, emphasizes the important role of collaboration in learning. A wide range of educational research has found that collaboration contributes to learning. Unlike an older generation of educational software, where each student worked in isolation at his or her own computer, the advent of the Internet and of wireless handheld devices supports students in learning collaborations, so that computers bring students together instead of pulling them apart.

Part VI, Learning Environments, tackles the real-world problems that face any educational reform – teacher professional development, equity for all students, and scaling up innovations throughout school districts and ultimately, throughout the country.

A book like *CHLS* is a massive undertaking; more than sixty authors have contributed, and many other members of the learning sciences community have participated indirectly, by reading and commenting on chapter drafts. As with any professional community, the knowledge that emerges is collectively created by all of the participants. Many important scholars whose names do not appear as authors nonetheless have contributed to the collective endeavor of the learning sciences. While editing this handbook, I have discovered that the members of this professional community are deeply aware that they are each only one participant in a broad community of practice, and that the knowledge generated cannot be considered to be owned or possessed

by any one researcher. By sharing openly and working collaboratively, learning sciences researchers have made great strides in less than two decades. I hope that *CHLS* functions as a resource that will allow a significant expansion of this community of practice, allowing everyone involved with education to tap into these new findings and begin the task of designing the schools of the future.

I have many people to thank for their contributions to this project. Philip Laughlin, my editor at Cambridge University Press, was the original visionary who saw that readers needed a book like this, and I thank him for his support throughout the project. I am particularly grateful to the four advisory board members. They have gone far beyond the call of duty, in devoting their time and energy, responding vigorously whenever I asked them for help concerning issues that arose during the project.

I am grateful for the support I received from Washington University. While working on the handbook, I was partially supported by the St. Louis Center for Inquiry in Science Teaching and Learning (CISTL) and by the Washington University Department of Education. This support was due to the efforts of Jere Confrey, project director at CISTL, and to Bill Tate, Chair of the Department of Education. During the spring 2005 semester, students in a doctoral seminar at Washington University read many of the early drafts of these chapters, and their suggestions were extremely helpful. During final editing in the summer of 2005, Stacy DeZutter provided invaluable editorial assistance, also with support from CISTL.

And of course, I am grateful to each of the authors for the hard work they invested. It was a true pleasure to work with such a deeply professional group of scholars, with everyone delivering their chapters "on time and under budget," as they say. I am particularly grateful that the authors were willing to respond to my suggestions – in many cases I offered detailed comments, and many authors invested a significant amount of time writing a second draft. Having worked so closely with these scholars, I have a deeper understanding of why the learning sciences is having such a significant impact on education.

expressed in this publication are those of the authors and do not necessarily reflect the views of the National Science Foundation.

Acknowledgments

Janet Kolodner provided valuable feedback on an earlier draft of the first half of this Preface.

Editing of this handbook was supported by the National Science Foundation under Award No. ESI-0227619. Any opinions, findings, and conclusions or recommendations

References

Bransford, J. D., Brown, A. L., & Cocking, R. R. (Eds.). (2000). *How people learn: Brain, mind, experience, and school.* Washington, DC: National Academy Press.

Cuban, L. (2001). *Oversold and underused: Computers in the classroom.* Cambridge, MA: Harvard University Press.

Contributors

Editorial Board

ALLAN COLLINS
Northwestern University
School of Education and Social Policy
2120 Campus Drive
Evanston, IL 60208
a-collins@northwestern.edu

JERE CONFREY
Washington University
Department of Education
Campus Box 1183
St. Louis, MO 63130
jconfrey@wustl.edu

JANET L. KOLODNER
Georgia Institute of Technology
College of Computing
801 Atlantic Drive
Atlanta GA 30332-0280
janet.kolodner@cc.gatech.edu

MARLENE SCARDAMALIA
Ontario Institute for Studies in Education
252 Bloor Street West
Toronto, Ontario M5S 1V6
Canada
mscardamalia@oise.utoronto.ca

Chapter Contributors

JERRY ANDRIESSEN
Utrecht University
Heidelberglaan 1
Department of Educational Studies
(IPEDON)
Utrecht 3884 CS
J.Andriessen@fss.uu.nl

SASHA BARAB
Indiana University, Learning Sciences
School of Education, #4066
201 North Rose Avenue
Bloomington, IN 47405
sbarab@indiana.edu

BRIGID BARRON
Stanford University
School of Education
485 Lausen Mall
Stanford, CA 94305-3096
barronbj@stanford.edu

PHILIP BELL
University of Washington
Cognitive Studies in Education Program
312F Miller Hall, Box 353600
Seattle, WA 98195
pbell@u.washington.edu

CARL BEREITER
Ontario Institute for Studies in
    Education
252 Bloor Street West
Toronto, ON M5S 1V6
Canada
cbereiter@oise.utoronto.ca

PHYLLIS C. BLUMENFELD
University of Michigan
School of Education, 4124 SEB
Ann Arbor, MI 48109
blumenfe@umich.edu

JOHN D. BRANSFORD
University of Washington
College of Education
Box 353600, 210 Miller Hall
Seattle, WA 98195
bransj@u.washington.edu

AMY BRUCKMAN
Georgia Institute of Technology
College of Computing
85 5th Street
Atlanta, GA 30332-0760
amy.bruckman@cc.gatech.edu

SHARON M. CARVER
Children's School
Carnegie Mellon University
Pittsburgh, PA 15213
scoe@andrew.cmu.edu

PAUL COBB
Vanderbilt University
Department of Teaching and Learning
230 Appleton Place, Box 330
Peabody College
Nashville, TN 37203-5721
paul.cobb@vanderbilt.edu

ALBERT CORBETT
Carnegie Mellon University
Human-Computer Interaction
    Institute
3605 Newell Simon Hall
Pittsburgh, PA 15213
corbett@cmu.edu

ELIZABETH A. DAVIS
University of Michigan
School of Education
610 E. University Ave., Room 1323
Ann Arbor, MI 48109-1259
betsdy@umich.edu

CHRIS DEDE
Harvard University
Technology in Education Program
323 Longfellow Hall
Cambridge, MA 02138
chris_dede@harvard.edu

ANDREA A. DISESSA
University of California
4533 Tolman Hall #1670
Berkeley, CA 94720-1670
disessa@soe.berkeley.edu

DANIEL C. EDELSON
Northwestern University
School of Education and Social
    Policy
2120 Campus Drive
Evanston, IL 60208
d-edelson@northwestern.edu

BARRY J. FISHMAN
University of Michigan
School of Education
610 E. University Ave., 1360B
Ann Arbor, MI 48109-1259
fishman@umich.edu

JAMES G. GREENO
University of Pittsburgh
School of Education
5524 Wesley Posvar Hall
Pittsburgh, PA 15260
jimgrno@pitt.edu

JULIE HEISER
Adobe Systems, Inc.
345 Park Avenue, E-11
San Jose, CA 95110
jheiser@gmail.com

CELIA HOYLES
Institute of Education, University of
    London
20 Bedford Way
London WC1H 0AL
United Kingdom
c.hoyles@ioe.ac.uk

YASMIN B. KAFAI
University of California
Graduate School of Education & Information
    Studies
2331 Moore Hall, Box 951521
Los Angeles, CA 90095-1521
kafai@gseis.ucla.edu

TONI M. KEMPLER
University of Michigan
School of Education
610 E. University Ave., Room 4041
Ann Arbor, MI 48109
tkempler@umich.edu

KENNETH R. KOEDINGER
Carnegie Mellon University
School of Computer Science
3601 Newell-Simon Hall
Pittsburgh, PA 15213-3891
koedinger@cmu.edu

TIMOTHY KOSCHMANN
Southern Illinois University
Department of Medical Education
P. O. Box 19681
Springfield, IL 62794-9681
tkoschmann@siumed.edu

JOSEPH S. KRAJCIK
University of Michigan
School of Education
610 E. University Ave., Room 4109
Ann Arbor, MI 48109-1259
krajcik@umich.edu

PATRICIA KUHL
University of Washington
Box 357988
Seattle, WA 98195
pkkuhl@u.washington.edu

BARBARA G. LADEWSKI
University of Michigan
School of Education
610 E. University Ave., Room 4002
Ann Arbor, MI 48109-1259
ladewski@umich.edu

CAROL D. LEE
Northwestern University
School of Education and Social Policy
Annenberg Hall #331
2120 Campus Drive
Evanston, IL 60208-0001
cdlee@northwestern.edu

RICHARD LEHRER
Vanderbilt University
Department of Teaching and Learning
166 Wyatt Center, Box 330
Peabody College
Nashville, TN 37235
rich.lehrer@Vanderbilt.Edu

MARCIA C. LINN
University of California
Graduate School of Education
4611 Tolman Hall
Berkeley, CA 94720-1670
mclinn@socrates.berkeley.edu

HEIDY MALDONADO
Stanford University
Stanford Center for Innovations in
  Learning
Wallenberg Hall
450 Serra Mall, Building 160
Stanford, CA 94305
heidym@cs.stanford.edu

KAY MCCLAIN
Vanderbilt University
Peabody College, Department of
  Teaching and Learning
230 Appleton Place, Box 330
Nashville, TN 37203-5721
kay.mcclain@vanderbilt.edu

BARBARA MEANS
SRI International
Center for Technology in
  Learning
333 Ravenswood Ave
Menlo Park, CA 94025
barbara.means@sri.com

ANDREW MELTZOFF
University of Washington
Institute for Learning and Brain
  Sciences
Box 357920
Seattle, WA 98195
meltzoff@u.washington.edu

NA'ILAH SUAD NASIR
Stanford University
School of Education
Wallenberg Hall
450 Serra Mall, Building 160
Stanford, CA 94305
nasir@stanford.edu

CATHLEEN NORRIS
University of North Texas
College of Education
Department of Technology and
  Cognition
P.O. Box 311337
Denton, TX 76203
norris@coe.unt.edu

RICHARD NOSS
Institute of Education, University of
    London
London Knowledge Lab
23–29, Emerald Street
London WC1N 3QS
United Kingdom
r.noss@ioe.ac.uk

ANNEMARIE SULLIVAN PALINCSAR
University of Michigan
School of Education
610 E. University Ave., Room 4121
Ann Arbor, MI 48109-1259
annemari@umich.edu

SEYMOUR PAPERT
The Media Laboratory, MIT
Building E15
77 Massachusetts Ave
Cambridge, MA 02139-4307

ROY D. PEA
Stanford University
Stanford Center for Innovations in
    Learning
Wallenberg Hall
450 Serra Mall, Building 160
StanfordCA 94305
roypea@stanford.edu

CHRIS QUINTANA
University of Michigan
School of Education
610 E. University Ave., 1360D SEB
Ann Arbor, MI 48109
quintana@umich.edu

BYRON REEVES
Stanford University
Department of Communication
Building 160, Room 229
Stanford, CA 94305
reeves@stanford.edu

BRIAN J. REISER
Northwestern University
Learning Sciences
Annenberg Hall, 2120 Campus Drive,
    Room 339
Evanston, IL 60208-0001
reiser@northwestern.edu

JEREMY ROSCHELLE
SRI International
Center for Technology in Learning
333 Ravenswood Avenue, BN-376
Menlo Park, CA 94025
jeremy.roschelle@sri.com

ANN S. ROSEBERY
TERC
2067 Massachusetts Avenue
Cambridge, MA 02139
Ann_Rosebery@TERC.edu

NORA H. SABELLI
SRI International
Center for Technology in Learning
333 Ravenswood Avenue
Menlo Park, CA 94025
nora.sabelli@sri.com

R. KEITH SAWYER
Washington University
Department of Education
Campus Box 1183
St. Louis, MO 63130
ksawyer@wustl.edu

ROGER C. SCHANK
Socratic Arts
http://www.socraticarts.com/

LEONA SCHAUBLE
Vanderbilt University
Department of Teaching and Learning
Box 330 Peabody College
Nashville, TN 37203
leona.schauble@vanderbilt.edu

JANET WARD SCHOFIELD
University of Pittsburgh
Professor, Department of Psychology
Senior Scientist, LRDC
3939 O'Hara Street
Pittsburgh, PA 15260
schof@vms.cis.pitt.edu

DANIEL L. SCHWARTZ
Stanford University
School of Education
Stanford, CA 94305-3096
daniel.schwartz@stanford.edu

NAMSOO SHIN
University of Michigan
School of Education
610 E. University Ave., Room 4031
Ann Arbor, MI 48109
namsoo@umich.edu

ELLIOT SOLOWAY
University of Michigan
Department of EECS, College of
    Engineering
2200 Bonisteel, 306 ERB
Ann Arbor, MI 48109
Soloway@Umich.Edu

Nancy Butler Songer
University of Michigan
School of Education
610 E. University Ave., 1323 SEB
Ann Arbor, MI 48109
songer@umich.edu

Gerry Stahl
Drexel University
College of Information Science & Technology
3141 Chestnut Street
Philadelphia, PA 19104
Gerry.Stahl@drexel.edu

Reed Stevens
University of Washington
Educational Psychology
406A Miller Hall
Seattle, WA 98195-3600
reedstev@u.washington.edu

Daniel D. Suthers
University of Hawaii
Information and Computer Sciences
1680 East West Road, POST 309B
Honolulu, HI 96822
suthers@hawaii.edu

Nancy Vye
University of Washington
College of Education
210 Miller Hall, Box 353600
Seattle, WA 98195
nancyvye@u.washington.edu

Beth Warren
TERC
2067 Massachusetts Avenue
Cambridge, MA 02140
Beth_Warren@terc.edu

CHAPTER 1

Introduction

The New Science of Learning

R. Keith Sawyer

By the twentieth century, all major industrialized countries offered formal schooling to all of their children. When these schools took shape in the nineteenth and twentieth centuries, scientists didn't know very much about how people learn. Even by the 1920s, when schools began to become the large bureaucratic institutions that we know today, there still was no sustained study of how people learn. As a result, the schools we have today were designed around commonsense assumptions that had never been tested scientifically:

- Knowledge is a collection of *facts* about the world and *procedures* for how to solve problems. Facts are statements like "The earth is tilted on its axis by 23.45 degrees" and procedures are step-by-step instructions like how to do multidigit addition by carrying to the next column.
- The goal of schooling is to get these facts and procedures into the student's head. People are considered to be educated when they possess a large collection of these facts and procedures.

- Teachers know these facts and procedures, and their job is to transmit them to students.
- Simpler facts and procedures should be learned first, followed by progressively more complex facts and procedures. The definitions of "simplicity" and "complexity" and the proper sequencing of material were determined either by teachers, by textbook authors, or by asking expert adults like mathematicians, scientists, or historians – not by studying how children actually learn.
- The way to determine the success of schooling is to test students to see how many of these facts and procedures they have acquired.

This traditional vision of schooling is known as *instructionism* (Papert, 1993). Instructionism prepared students for the industrialized economy of the early twentieth century. But the world today is much more technologically complex and economically competitive, and instructionism is increasingly failing to educate our students to participate in this new kind of society. Economists and organizational theorists have reached a consensus that today we are living in a knowledge economy, an economy that is built on knowledge work (Bereiter, 2002; Drucker, 1993). In the knowledge economy, memorization of facts and procedures is not enough for success. Educated graduates need a deep conceptual understanding of complex concepts, and the ability to work with them creatively to generate new ideas, new theories, new products, and new knowledge. They need to be able to critically evaluate what they read, to be able to express themselves clearly both verbally and in writing, and to be able to understand scientific and mathematical thinking. They need to learn integrated and usable knowledge, rather than the sets of compartmentalized and decontextualized facts emphasized by instructionism. They need to be able to take responsibility for their own continuing, lifelong learning. These abilities are important to the economy, to the continued success of participatory democracy, and to living a fulfilling, meaningful life. Instructionism is particularly ill-suited to the education of creative professionals who can develop new knowledge and continually further their own understanding; instructionism is an anachronism in the modern innovation economy.

Beginning in the 1970s, a new science of learning was born – based in research emerging from psychology, computer science, philosophy, sociology, and other scientific disciplines. As they closely studied children's learning, scientists discovered that instructionism was deeply flawed. By the 1990s, after about twenty years of research, learning scientists had reached a consensus on the following basic facts about learning – a consensus that was published by the United States National Research Council (see Bransford, Brown, & Cocking, 2000):

- *The importance of deeper conceptual understanding.* Scientific studies of knowledge workers demonstrate that expert knowledge includes facts and procedures, but simply acquiring those facts and procedures does not prepare a person to perform as a knowledge worker. Factual and procedural knowledge is only useful when a person knows which situations to apply it in, and exactly how to modify it for each new situation. Instructionism results in a kind of learning which is very difficult to use outside of the classroom. When students gain a deeper conceptual understanding, they learn facts and procedures in a much more useful and profound way that transfers to real-world settings.

- *Focusing on learning in addition to teaching.* Students cannot learn deeper conceptual understanding simply from teachers instructing them better. Students can only learn this by actively participating in their own learning. The new science of learning focuses on student learning processes, as well as instructional technique.

- *Creating learning environments.* The job of schools is to help students learn the full range of knowledge required for expert adult performance: facts and procedures, of course, but also the deeper conceptual understanding that will allow them to reason about real-world problems. Learning sciences research has identified the key features of those learning environments that help students learn deeper conceptual understanding.

- *The importance of building on a learner's prior knowledge.* Learners are not empty vessels waiting to be filled. They come to the classroom with preconceptions about how the world works; some of them are basically correct, and some of them are misconceptions. The best way for children to learn is in an environment that builds on their existing knowledge; if teaching does not engage their prior knowledge, students often learn information just well enough to pass the test, and then revert back to their misconceptions outside of the classroom.

- *The importance of reflection.* Students learn better when they express their developing knowledge – either through conversation or by creating papers, reports, or other artifacts – and then are provided with opportunities to reflectively analyze their state of knowledge.

This handbook is an introduction to this new science of learning, and how researchers are using that science to lay the groundwork for the schools of the future. This new science is called *the learning sciences* because it is an interdisciplinary science: it brings together researchers in psychology, education, computer science, and anthropology, among others, and the collaboration among these disciplines has resulted in new ideas, new methodologies, and new ways of thinking about learning. Many people – parents, teachers, policy makers, and even many educational researchers – are not aware of the important discoveries emerging from the learning sciences. Without knowing about the new science of learning, many people continue to assume that schools should be based on instructionism. Parents and policy makers remember being taught that way, and are often uncomfortable when their children have different learning experiences. Many teachers have spent an entire career mastering the skills required to manage an instructionist classroom, and they understandably have trouble envisioning a different kind of school. The purpose of this handbook is to build on the new science of learning by showing various stakeholders how to design learning environments and classrooms:

- For *teachers*, reading about the new science of learning can help you be more effective in your classrooms.
- For *parents*, reading about the new science of learning can help you to be an informed consumer of schools. The learning sciences explains why and when instructionism fails and which alternative learning environments are based in contemporary science.
- For *administrators*, reading about the new science of learning can help you to lead your school into the twenty-first century.
- For *policy makers*, reading about the new science of learning can help you under-

stand the problems with today's curricula, teacher education programs, and standardized tests, and how to form a vision for the future.

- For *professionals*, reading about the new science of learning can help you understand why many people are so poorly informed about science, technology, international relations, economics, and other knowledge-based disciplines.
- And finally, *education researchers* can learn how their own studies relate to the learning sciences, and can see how to participate in building the schools of the future.

This handbook is the second book that introduces a broad audience to the new science of learning. The first was the NRC report *How People Learn*, first published in 1999 and with an expanded edition published in 2000 (Bransford, Brown, & Cocking, 2000). That book provides a higher-level overview of the learning sciences; this handbook goes into more depth, is more specific about exactly how to reform schools, and describes important work that has taken place since 1999. In particular, this handbook describes how to use the new sciences of learning to design effective learning environments, in classrooms and outside, often taking advantage of new computer technology. Learning sciences is now over twenty years old; the publication of this handbook is a sign that the scientific community has reached a consensus about some of the most important discoveries about learning. Redesigning schools so that they are based on scientific research is a mammoth undertaking, and it will require the participation of all of the groups that read this book: teachers, parents, school leaders, policy makers, and education researchers.

The Goals of Education and the Nature of Knowledge

The traditional role of educational research has been to tell educators how to achieve

Table 1.1. Deep Learning Versus Traditional Classroom Practices

Learning Knowledge Deeply *(Findings from Cognitive Science)*	*Traditional Classroom Practices* *(Instructionism)*
Deep learning requires that learners relate new ideas and concepts to previous knowledge and experience.	Learners treat course material as unrelated to what they already know.
Deep learning requires that learners integrate their knowledge into interrelated conceptual systems.	Learners treat course material as disconnected bits of knowledge.
Deep learning requires that learners look for patterns and underlying principles.	Learners memorize facts and carry out procedures without understanding how or why.
Deep learning requires that learners evaluate new ideas, and relate them to conclusions.	Learners have difficulty making sense of new ideas that are different from what they encountered in the textbook.
Deep learning requires that learners understand the process of dialogue through which knowledge is created, and they examine the logic of an argument critically.	Learners treat facts and procedures as static knowledge, handed down from an all-knowing authority.
Deep learning requires that learners reflect on their own understanding and their own process of learning.	Learners memorize without reflecting on the purpose or on their own learning strategies.

their curriculum objectives, but not to help set those objectives. But when learning scientists went into classrooms, they discovered that schools were not teaching the deep knowledge that underlies intelligent performance. By the 1980s, cognitive scientists had discovered that children retain material better, and are able to generalize it to a broader range of contexts, when they learn deep knowledge rather than surface knowledge, and when they learn how to use that knowledge in real-world social and practical settings (see Table 1.1). The notion of deep learning is explored by each learning sciences researcher in a slightly different way, and most of the chapters in this handbook begin by describing the type of deep knowledge studied.

One of the central underlying themes of the learning sciences is that students learn deeper knowledge when they engage in activities that are similar to the everyday activities of professionals who work in a discipline. Authentic practices are the keystone of many recent educational standards documents in the United States In history, for example, reforms call for learning history by doing historical inquiry rather than memorizing dates and sequences of events: working with primary data sources, and using methods of historical analysis and argumentation that are used by historians (National Center for History in the Schools, 1996). In science, the National Science Education Standards calls for students to engage in the authentic practices of scientific inquiry: constructing explanations and preparing arguments to communicate and justify those explanations (National Research Council, 1996, p. 105).

To better understand how to engage students in authentic practices, many learning sciences reforms are based on studies of professional practice.

- Professionals engage in a process of inquiry, in which they start with a driving question and then use discipline-specific methods to propose hypothetical answers to the question, and to gather and evaluate evidence for and against competing hypotheses (Krajcik & Blumenfeld, this volume; Edelson & Reiser, this volume).

- Professionals use complex representations to communicate with each other during collaboration (as discussed in many of the chapters in Parts 3 and 4).
- Scientists and mathematicians work with concrete, visual models, so students should too (Lehrer & Schauble, this volume).

This focus on authentic practice is based on a new conception of the expert knowledge that underlies knowledge work in today's economy. In the 1980s and 1990s, scientists began to study science itself, and they began to discover that newcomers become members of a discipline by learning how to participate in all of the practices that are central to professional life in that discipline. And, increasingly, cutting-edge work in the sciences is done at the boundaries of disciplines; for this reason, students need to learn the underlying models, mechanisms, and practices that apply across many scientific disciplines, rather than learning in the disconnected and isolated six-week units that are found in instructionist science classrooms – moving from studying the solar system to studying photosynthesis to studying force and motion, without ever learning about connections among these units.

Studies of knowledge workers show that they almost always apply their expertise in complex social settings, with a wide array of technologically advanced tools along with old-fashioned pencil, paper, chalk, and blackboards. These observations have led learning sciences researchers to a *situativity* view of knowledge (Greeno, this volume). "Situativity" means that knowledge is not just a static mental structure inside the learner's head; instead, knowing is a process that involves the person, the tools and other people in the environment, and the activities in which that knowledge is being applied. The situativity perspective moves beyond a transmission and acquisition conception of learning; in addition to acquiring content, what happens during learning is that patterns of participation in collaborative activity change over time (Rogoff, 1990, 1998).

This combined research has led the learning sciences to a focus on how children learn in groups (as discussed in the chapters in Part 5).

Of course, students are not capable of doing exactly the same things as highly trained professionals; when learning scientists talk about engaging students in authentic practices, they are referring to developmentally appropriate versions of the situated and meaningful practices of experts. One of the most important goals of learning sciences research is to identify exactly what practices are appropriate for students to engage in and learn, and how learning environments can be designed that are age-appropriate without losing the authenticity of professional practice.

The Foundations of the Learning Sciences

The learning sciences combines many disciplinary approaches to the study of learning. Scholars in a range of university departments conduct research in the learning sciences – they are found in schools of education, of course, but also in departments of computer science and psychology. I review five early influences – constructivism, cognitive science, educational technology, sociocultural studies, and studies of disciplinary knowledge.

Constructivism

In the 1960s and 1970s, Jean Piaget's writings became widely influential in American education. Before Piaget, most people held to the commonsense belief that children have less knowledge than adults. Piaget argued a radically different theory: although children certainly possess less knowledge than adults, what's even more important to learning is that children's minds contain different knowledge structures than are in adults' minds. In other words, children differ not only in the quantity of knowledge they possess; their knowledge is *qualitatively* different.

By the 1980s, researchers had confirmed this fundamental claim that children think differently from adults. Educational researchers had discovered, for example, that children don't get math problems wrong only because they didn't study hard enough or because they forgot what they read in the textbook – they often got the problems wrong because their minds were thinking about the math problems in a different way than educators expected, and math education wasn't designed to correct these misconceptions. Cognitive scientists began to identify the cognitive characteristics of children's "naïve math" and "naïve physics," and began to accumulate an important body of knowledge about the typical misconceptions that people have about these content areas (diSessa, this volume; Linn, this volume). This body of research allows designers of learning environments to connect learning to students' prior knowledge and misconceptions.

Constructivism explains why students often do not learn deeply by listening to a teacher, or reading from a textbook. Learning sciences research is revealing the deeper underlying bases of how knowledge construction works. To design effective learning environments, one needs a very good understanding of what children know when they come to the classroom. This requires sophisticated research into children's cognitive development, and the learning sciences draws heavily on psychological studies of cognitive development (e.g., Siegler, 1998).

Cognitive Science

Many learning scientists began their careers in the interdisciplinary field known as *cognitive science*. Cognitive science combines experimental investigation of how the mind works (in the tradition of cognitive psychology) with computational modeling of proposed mental processes (in the tradition of artificial intelligence), taking into account what we know from sociology and anthropology about how people use knowledge in everyday settings. Through the 1970s and 1980s, cognitive science did not provide much support to educators, because it focused on laboratory methodologies that removed learners from learning contexts, and because it focused on static knowledge like facts and procedures rather than the processes of thinking and knowing (Kuhn, 1990, p. 1). Around 1990, many key concepts from cognitive science became central in the learning sciences; I discuss representation, expertise, reflection, problem solving, and thinking.

REPRESENTATION

Central to cognitive science is the idea that intelligent behavior is based on *representations* in the mind: "knowledge structures" such as concepts, beliefs, facts, procedures, and models. In the 1970s, cognitive scientists thought of representation in metaphors drawn from computer memory techniques. A central feature of most computer languages is the *pointer*: a way for one memory location to "point to" or "refer to" another location. Building on the primitive notion of a pointer, computer programmers were able to develop hierarchically nested data structures – the highest level structure could contain pointers to simpler, lower level structures. For example, the simplest data structure for a house would contain hundreds of variables, including the type of sink in the kitchen and the color of the couch in the living room. But by using the nested data structures that pointers made possible, a more sophisticated data structure for a house could be constructed that would contain pointers to data structures for each room in the house; and the room data structures would each contain pointers to multiple furniture and fixture data structures. This provided a metaphor for how knowledge might be modularized in the mind, and is an example of the kind of metaphors of human cognition that have emerged from computer science.

THE COGNITIVE BASES OF EXPERTISE

One of the most surprising discoveries of 1970s cognitive science was that everyday behavior was harder to represent computationally than expert behavior. Some of the most successful artificial intelligence (AI) programs simulated expert performance in knowledge-intensive domains like medicine, manufacturing, telecommunications, and finance (Liebowitz, 1998). As a result of these efforts, cognitive science developed a sophisticated understanding of the cognitive bases of expertise. Everyday commonsense behavior remains beyond the abilities of AI computer programs, even as some complex aspects of expert performance in knowledge-intensive domains like medicine have been successfully simulated.

A large body of cognitive science research shows that expertise is based on:

- A large and complex set of representational structures
- A large set of procedures and plans
- The ability to improvisationally apply and adapt those plans to each situation's unique demands
- The ability to reflect on one's own cognitive processes while they are occurring

REFLECTION

Studies of experts show they are better than novices at planning and criticizing their work – both *reflective* activities. For example, when expert writers are asked to describe their thought processes out loud as they write, their talk reveals that they develop goals and plans while writing, and they continually reflect on and modify those goals and plans as they write (Flower & Hayes, 1980). School-age writers don't spend time planning and reflecting (Burtis, Bereiter, Scardamalia, & Tetroe, 1983). Based on these findings, and similar findings regarding other school subjects, learning scientists often conceive of the problem of learning as a problem of transforming novices into experts by developing their ability to reflect on their own thinking in these ways.

Collins and Brown (1988) first suggested that the computer could be used to support reflection (Collins, this volume). Collins and Brown talked about capturing an expert's process, then allowing the student to compare her process to that of the expert. The computer's role was to record the expert's reasoning, making it available whenever it could be useful and to whoever needed it. In this way, the computer was supporting a kind of reflection that was difficult to do without a computer. Since then, several learning sciences projects emphasize computer support for reflection. WISE (Linn, this volume) prompts students to think about evidence and its uses as they are creating a scientific argument. Reciprocal teaching (Palincsar & Brown, 1984) helps students to recognize the questions they need to ask themselves as they are trying to understand something they are reading. Knowledge Forum (Scardamalia & Bereiter, this volume) prompts students to think about their actions and their discussion as they are having knowledge-building conversations. Learning by Design (Kolodner, this volume) integrates reflection into classroom activities.

PROBLEM SOLVING

Cognitive scientists have spent several decades attempting to identify the cognitive bases of problem solving. One of the most persistent theories about problem solving is that it depends on a person having a mental representation of a *problem space* (Newell & Simon, 1972) which contains *beliefs* and *mental representations* – of concepts, specific actions, and the external world. Problem solving is then conceived of as searching through the problem space until the desired *goal state* is reached. Because knowledge work typically requires problem solving, many learning sciences approaches to learning are based on this research. For example, Koedinger's cognitive tutors (this volume) assume that *production rules* are used to move through the problem space, and Kolodner's *case-based reasoning* (this volume) assumes that case lookup and matching algorithms are used.

THINKING

Educators often talk about the importance of higher-order thinking skills, but educational programs that emphasize thinking skills are often not based on scientific research. Instead, they are based on one or another intuitively based taxonomy of thinking skills, with almost no scientific justification of why this specific set of skills should be taught in schools (Kuhn, 1990, p. 2). Beginning in the 1980s and 1990s, cognitive psychologists began to study informal reasoning (Voss, Perkins, & Segal, 1991) – the good and bad reasoning that people engage in everyday, when faced with real-life problems that don't have simple solutions. They also began to study everyday decision making, discovering a wide range of common thinking errors that most people make (Baron, 1985; Kahneman, Slovic, & Tversky, 1982). Also during this time, developmental psychologists began to identify a range of good and bad thinking strategies and how these strategies develop over the lifespan. They extended Piaget's original insight, showing how children's thinking differs from that of adults – information that is absolutely critical to education based on the learning sciences (Dunbar & Klahr, 1989; Kuhn, 1989; Schauble, 1990).

Educational Technology

In the 1950s, B. F. Skinner presented his "teaching machines" and claimed that they made the teacher "out of date" (Skinner, 1954/1968, p. 22). The first educational software was designed in the 1960s and was based on Skinner's behaviorist theories; these systems are known as Computer Assisted Instruction or CAI, and such systems are still in use today. In the 1970s, a few artificial intelligence researchers started working in education, developing automated tutoring systems and other applications (Bobrow & Collins, 1975; Sleeman & Brown, 1982; Wenger, 1987). In the 1980s, cognitive scientists like Roger Schank and Seymour Papert made widely popularized claims that computers would radically transform schools (see Papert, 1980; Schank, this volume).

By the 1990s, a strong consensus had formed among politicians, parents, and the business community that it was essential to get computers into schools (Cuban, 2001). During the 1990s, there was a major push to install computers and the Internet in schools – including federal government programs like E-rate that paid for schools to be connected to the Internet. By 2003, 95 percent of schools were connected to the Internet with high-speed connections, and 93 percent of all classrooms were connected to the Internet. On average, there were 4.4 students for each computer with Internet access; this was a dramatic drop from 12.1 students in 1998, when it was first measured (Parsad & Jones, 2005).

However, the impact of all of this investment has been disappointing. By 2000, no studies had shown that computer use was correlated with improved student performance. When researchers began to look more closely at why computers were having so little impact, they discovered that computer use was not based on the learning sciences; instead, they were being used as quick add-ons to the existing instructional classroom (Cuban, 2001).

Learning scientists emphasize the powerful role that computers can play in transforming all learning. But their vision rejects instructionism and behaviorism and the CAI systems based on it, and presents a new vision of computers in schools. Learning sciences research explains why the promise of computers in schools has not yet been realized; because to date, educational software has been based on instructionist theories, with the computer performing roles that are traditionally performed by the teacher – with the software acting as an expert authority, delivering information to the learner. In contrast, learning sciences suggests that the computer should take on a more facilitating role, helping learners have the kind of experiences that lead to deep learning – for example, helping them to collaborate, or to reflect on their developing knowledge. Many of the chapters in this handbook describe the next generation of educational software, software that is solidly based on the sciences of learning, and that is designed in close collaboration with teachers and schools. Computers are only used as part of overall classroom reform, and only where research shows they will have the most impact. Computer software is central in the learning sciences because the visual and processing power of today's personal computers supports deep learning:

- Computers can represent abstract knowledge in concrete form
- Computer tools can allow learners to articulate their developing knowledge in a visual and verbal way
- Computers can allow learners to manipulate and revise their developing knowledge via the user interface, in a complex process of design that supports simultaneous articulation, reflection, and learning
- Computers support reflection in a combination of visual and verbal modes
- Internet-based networks of learners can share and combine their developing understandings and benefit from the power of collaborative learning

Sociocultural Studies

After the burst of activity associated with 1970s artificial intelligence and cognitive psychology, by the 1980s many of these scholars had begun to realize that their goal – to understand and simulate human intelligence in the computer – was still very far off. The 1980s disillusionment with AI was so severe that it was informally known as "the AI winter." Researchers began to step back and think about why the cognitive sciences had not been more successful. The most influential answer was provided by a group of interrelated approaches including the *sociocultural*, *situative*, and *distributed cognition* approaches (Greeno, this volume; Salomon, 1993). Socioculturalists began with the observation that all intelligent behavior was realized in a complex environment – a human created environment filled with tools and machines, but also a deeply social environment with collaborators and partners. Some of the most important studies in this tradition examined

how children learn in nonschool settings – how children learn their first language or the norms and conventions of their culture; how apprentices learn on the job. Some of the most interesting work along these lines focused on informal learning in non-Western societies without formal schooling (Cole, 1996; Lave, 1988; Rogoff, 1990; Saxe, 1991). Equally influential studies examined the socially distributed nature of knowledge work – including studies of navy ship navigation (Hutchins, 1995), of London Underground control rooms (Heath & Luff, 1991), of office systems (Suchman, 1987), and of air traffic control centers (Hughes et al., 1988). This research revealed that outside of formal schooling, almost all learning occurs in a complex social environment, and learning is hard to understand if one thinks of it as a mental process occurring within the head of an isolated learner.

The sociocultural approach has been widely influential in all of the disciplines participating in the learning sciences:

- Artificial intelligence began to emphasize "distributed cognition" in part because of the rapidly evolving network technologies of the 1980s and 1990s
- Cognitive psychology began to study teamwork, collaboration, group dynamics, and the role of social context in cognitive development
- Education research began to study classroom collaboration, collaborative discourse in student groups, and project teams

The Nature of Knowledge Work

Should we reduce auto emissions because of global warming? Should we allow stem cell research to proceed? Should we teach both evolution and creationism in schools? Today's public debate about such controversial issues shows a glaring lack of knowledge about scientific practice. The U.S. *National Science Education Standards* (National Research Council, 1996) observed that "Americans are confronted increasingly with questions in their lives that require scientific information and scientific ways of thinking for informed decision making" (p. 11).

By the early 1900s, major industrial countries had all realized the important role that science and engineering played in their rapid growth, and many scholars began to analyze the nature of scientific knowledge. In the first half of the twentieth century, philosophers came to a consensus on the nature of scientific knowledge: scientific knowledge consisted of statements about the world, and logical operations that could be applied to those statements. This consensus was known as *logical empiricism* (McGuire, 1992; Suppe, 1974). Logical empiricism combined with behaviorism and traditional classroom practice to form the instructionist approach to education: disciplinary knowledge consisted of facts and procedures, and teaching was thought of as transmitting the facts and procedures to students.

Beginning in the 1960s, sociologists, psychologists, and anthropologists began to study how scientists actually did their work, and they increasingly discovered that scientific knowledge was not simply a body of statements and logical operations. In this new view, scientific knowledge is an understanding about how to go about doing science, combined with deep knowledge of models and explanatory principles connected into an integrated conceptual framework. The practice of science involves experimentation, trial and error, hypothesis testing, debate and argumentation. And science is not a solo endeavor; it involves frequent encounters with peers in the scientific community. Scientists frequently talk about evaluating other scientists' claims, and think about how best to support and present their claims to others.

In this new view, scientific knowledge is situated, practiced, and collaboratively generated. The traditional science classroom, with its lectures and step-by-step lab exercises, completely leaves out these elements of science. But this kind of knowledge would be extremely useful to the general public as they read reports of an experimental drug in the daily paper, as they discuss with their doctor the potential risks of an upcoming surgery, or as they evaluate the health risks of a new development near their neighborhood.

This new view of expert knowledge has been extended beyond science to other forms of knowledge work. For example, literacy scholars have discovered that advanced literacy involves much more than knowing which sounds correspond to which letters; literacy involves knowing how to participate in a complex set of literate practices – like reading a recipe, scanning the classifieds for a specific product, or writing an email to a colleague (Palincsar & Ladewski, this volume). Social science educators have discovered that historians are experts because they know how to engage in the complex practices of historical inquiry and argumentation.

Processes Involved in Learning

The learning sciences are centrally concerned with exactly what is going on in a learning environment, and exactly how it is contributing to improved student performance. The learning environment includes the people in the environment (teachers, learners, and others); the computers in the environment and the roles they play; the architecture and layout of the room and the physical objects in it; and the social and cultural environment. Key questions include: How does learning happen? How do different learning environments contribute to learning, and can we improve the design of learning environments to enhance learning? Some researchers work on specific components of the learning environment – software design, the roles that teachers should play, or specific activities each student performs. Others examine the entire learning environment as a system, and focus on more holistic questions: How much support for the student should come from the teacher, the computer software, or from other students? How can we create a culture where learners feel like a "learning community"? How can we design materials and activities that keep students motivated and sustain their engagement?

How Does Learning Happen? The Transition from Novice to Expert Performance

One of the legacies of early cognitive science research was its close studies of knowledge work. Many artificial intelligence researchers interviewed and observed experts, with the goal of replicating that expert knowledge in a computer program. Before it's possible to simulate expertise in a program, the researcher has to describe in elaborate detail the exact nature of the knowledge underlying that expertise. When these researchers became interested in education, they had to consider a new twist: how do experts acquire their expertise? What are the mental stages that learners go through as they move from novice to expert? This question was the purview of cognitive development research, a group of researchers that combined developmental psychology and cognitive psychology, and cognitive development has been an important foundation for the learning sciences.

Because learning scientists focus on the expert knowledge underlying knowledge work, they study how novices think and what misconceptions they have; then, they design curricula that leverage those misconceptions appropriately so that learners end up at the expert conception in the most efficient way.

How Does Learning Happen? Using Prior Knowledge

One of the most important discoveries guiding learning sciences research is that learning always takes place against a backdrop of existing knowledge. Students don't enter the classroom as empty vessels, waiting to be filled; they enter the classroom with half-formed ideas and misconceptions about how the world works – sometimes called "naïve" physics, math, or biology. Many cognitive developmentalists have studied children's theories about the world, and how children's understanding of the world develops through the preschool and early school years. The basic knowledge about cognitive development that has resulted from this research is absolutely critical to reforming schooling so that it is based on the basic sciences of learning.

Instructionist curricula were developed under the behaviorist assumption that children enter school with empty minds, and the role of school is to fill up those minds with knowledge. Instructionist curricula were designed before the learning sciences discovered how children think and what knowledge structures they bring to the classroom.

Promoting Better Learning: Scaffolding

The learning sciences are based in a foundation of constructivism. The learning sciences have convincingly demonstrated that when children actively participate in constructing their own knowledge, they gain a deeper understanding, more generalizable knowledge, and greater motivation. Learning sciences research has resulted in very specific findings about what support must be provided by the learning environment in order for learners to effectively construct their own knowledge.

To describe the support that promotes deep learning, learning scientists use the term *scaffolding*. Scaffolding is the help given to a learner that is tailored to that learner's needs in achieving his or her goals of the moment. The best scaffolding provides this help in a way that contributes to learning. For example, telling someone how to do something, or doing it for them, may help them accomplish their immediate goal; but it is not good scaffolding because the child does not actively participate in constructing that knowledge. In contrast, effective scaffolding provides prompts and hints that help learners to figure it out on their own. Effective learning environments scaffold students' active construction of knowledge in ways similar to the way that scaffolding supports the construction of a building. When construction workers need to reach higher, additional scaffolding is added, and when the building is complete, the scaffolding can be removed. In effective learning environments, scaffolding is gradually added, modified, and removed according to the needs of the learner, and eventually the scaffolding fades away entirely.

Promoting Better Learning: Externalization and Articulation

The learning sciences have discovered that when learners externalize and articulate their developing knowledge, they learn more effectively (Bransford, Brown, & Cocking, 2000). This is more complex than it might sound, because it's not the case that learners first learn something, and then express it. Instead, the best learning takes place when learners articulate their unformed and still developing understanding, and continue to articulate it throughout the process of learning. Articulating and learning go hand in hand, in a mutually reinforcing feedback loop. In many cases, learners don't actually learn something until they start to articulate it – in other words, while thinking out loud, they learn more rapidly and deeply than studying quietly.

This fascinating phenomenon was first studied in the 1920s by Russian psychologist Lev Vygotsky. In the 1970s, when educational psychologists began to notice the same phenomenon, Vygotsky's writings were increasingly translated into English and other languages, and Vygotsky is now considered one of the foundational theorists of the learning sciences. Vygotsky's explanation for the educational value of articulation is based in a theory of mental development; he argued that all knowledge began as visible social interaction, and then was gradually internalized by the learner to form thought. The exact nature of this internalization process has been widely debated among learning scientists; but regardless of the specifics of one or another explanation, the learning sciences are unified in their belief that collaboration and conversation among learners is critical because it allows learners to benefit from the power of articulation.

One of the most important topics of learning sciences research is how to support students in this ongoing process of articulation, and which forms of articulation are the most beneficial to learning. The learning sciences have discovered that articulation is more effective if it is scaffolded – channeled so that certain kinds of knowledge are articulated, and in a certain form that is most likely to result in useful reflection. Students need help in articulating their developing understandings; they don't yet know how to think about thinking, and they don't yet know how to talk about thinking.

Promoting Better Learning: Reflection

One of the reasons that articulation is so helpful to learning is that it makes possible *reflection* or *metacognition* – thinking about the process of learning and thinking about knowledge. Learning scientists have repeatedly demonstrated the importance of reflection in learning for deeper understanding. Many learning sciences classrooms are designed to foster reflection, and most of them foster reflection by providing students with tools that make it easier for them to articulate their developing understandings. Once students have articulated their developing understandings, learning environments should support them in reflecting on what they have just articulated. One of the most central topics in learning sciences research is how to support students in educationally beneficial reflection.

Promoting Better Learning: Building from Concrete to Abstract Knowledge

One of the most accepted findings of developmental psychologist Jean Piaget is that the natural progression of learning starts with more concrete information and gradually becomes more abstract. Piaget's influence in schools during the 1960s and 1970s led to the widespread use of "manipulatives," blocks and colored bars to be used in math classrooms. Not every important abstract idea that we teach in schools can be represented using colored blocks, but the sophistication of computer graphics allows very abstract concepts to be represented in a visible form.

The learning sciences have taken Piaget's original insight and have developed computer software to visually represent a wide range of types of knowledge. Even very abstract disciplinary practices have been represented visually in the computer; the structure of scientific argument can be represented (Andriessen, this volume), and the step-by-step process of scientific inquiry can be represented (Edelson & Reiser, this volume).

In the process of making the abstract concrete, these systems also scaffold students in the articulation of rather abstract conceptual knowledge; their articulation can be visual or graphic rather than simply verbal, and in many cases, visual and spatial understandings precede verbal understandings and can be used to build verbal understanding (e.g., Schwartz & Heiser, this volume).

A Design Science

As scientists who are focused on creating effective learning environments, learning scientists ask questions like: How can we measure learning? How can we determine which learning environments work best? How can we analyze a learning environment, identify the innovations that work well, and separate out those features that need additional improvement? In other words, how can we marshal all of our scientific knowledge to design the most effective learning environments? These questions are fundamental to scientific research in education (Shavelson & Towne, 2002).

The gold standard of scientific methodology is the *experimental design*, in which students are randomly assigned to different learning environments. Many education studies are also quasi-experimental – rather than randomly assigning students to environments, they identify two existing classrooms that seem to be identical in every way, and use one teaching method in one classroom, a different teaching method in another classroom, and analyze which students learn more and better (Shavelson & Towne, 2002). Experimental and quasi-experimental designs can provide educators and policy makers with important information about the relative merits of different approaches. But they can't tell us very much about why or how a teaching method is working – the minute-by-minute structure of the classroom activity that leads to student learning. If we could study those classroom processes, we would be in a much better position to improve teaching methods by continually revising them. Learning scientists combine a range of methodologies to better understand learning processes. The chapters in this book report on experimental comparisons of classrooms, experiments in cognitive psychology laboratories, studies of social interaction using the methodologies of sociology and anthropology, and a new hybrid methodology known as *design research* (Barab, this volume; Confrey, this volume).

Learning scientists have discovered that deep learning is more likely to occur in complex social and technological environments. To study learning in rich social and technological environments, learning scientists have drawn on ethnography (from anthropology), ethnomethodology and conversation analysis (from sociology), and sociocultural psychology (from developmental psychology). Anthropological methods have been influential since the 1980s, when ethnographers like Lucy Suchman, Ed Hutchins, and Jean Lave began to document exactly how learning takes place within the everyday activities of a community (Hutchins, 1995; Lave, 1988; Scribner & Cole, 1973; Suchman, 1987).

Many learning scientists study the moment-to-moment processes of learning, typically by gathering large amounts of videotape data, and they use a range of methodologies to analyze these videotapes back in the laboratory – a set of methodologies known as *interaction analysis* (Sawyer, this volume). Interaction analysis is used to identify the moment to moment unfolding of three things simultaneously: (1) the relations among learners, their patterns of interaction, and how they change over time; (2) the practices engaged in by the learners – individual and group procedures for solving problems, and how they change over time; and (3) individual learning. Individual learning can only be understood alongside the first two kinds of change.

However, deep knowledge cannot be learned in one class session. As a result, learning scientists also study longer term learning, over the entire school year and even from grade to grade (e.g., Lehrer & Schauble, this volume). During the course of a research study, learning scientists continually shift their focus closer and then farther back, studying the microgenetics of one classroom and then analyzing how that class session contributes to the longer-term development of deeper conceptual understanding.

Learning sciences research is complex and difficult. A typical learning sciences research project takes a minimum of a year, as researchers work closely with teachers and schools to modify the learning environment, allow time for the modification to take effect, and observe how learning emerges over time. Some projects follow learners over several years, or follow a particular teacher's classes for several years as that teacher introduces new activities and software tools to each successive class. And after the years of observation are complete, the hard work just begins, because the researchers have shelves of videotapes – in some cases hundreds of hours – that need to be closely watched, multiple times, and many of them transcribed for even more detailed analysis, including quantitative coding and statistical analysis.

The Emergence of the Field of Learning Sciences

In the 1970s and 1980s, many cognitive scientists were using artificial intelligence technologies to design software that could promote better learning (e.g., Bobrow & Collins, 1975; Sleeman & Brown, 1982). During this period, they initiated the "AI and Education" conferences that are still held today. In 1987, Northwestern University decided to make a

major commitment to this emerging field, and hired cognitive scientist Roger Schank from Yale University to lead what became known as the Institute of the Learning Sciences (ILS). Also in 1987, John Seely Brown and James Greeno were cofounders, along with David Kearns, CEO of Xerox, Corp., of the Institute for Research on Learning. At about the same time, Vanderbilt's Center for Learning and Technology was applying cognitive science to develop technology-based curriculum, and Seymour Papert's Logo group at MIT was building constructivist learning environments on the computer.

In Summer 1989, Roger Schank, Allan Collins, and Andrew Ortony began to discuss the idea of founding a new journal that would focus on applying the cognitive sciences to learning. Janet Kolodner was chosen as the editor of the new journal, and the first issue of the *Journal of the Learning Sciences* was published in January 1991. Also in 1991, the AI and Education conference was held at Northwestern at the ILS, and Schank dubbed it the first International Conference of the Learning Sciences. But the newly formed learning sciences community and the AI and Education community found that they had somewhat different interests. AI and Education researchers continued to design tutoring systems and other educational tools based on AI technologies, while the learning sciences community was more interested in studying learning in real-world learning environments, and in designing software that focused on learners' needs, whether or not AI technology was needed. For example, supporting articulation, reflection, and collaboration required different kinds of technologies than the AI and Education community was considering at that time. After the 1991 conference, the AI community and the learning sciences community parted ways. The second learning sciences conference was held in 1996 and conferences have been held every two years since then, with conferences focusing on computer support for collaborative learning (CSCL) held in the intervening years. In 2002, the International Society of the Learning Sciences (ISLS) was founded, and it is now the organization that plans both the ICSL and the CSCL conferences, provides intellectual support for the *Journal of the Learning Sciences*, and helped to found the *International Journal of Computer Supported Collaborative Learning* (http://www.isls.org).

Conclusion

Since the beginning of the modern institution of schools, there has been debate about whether education is a science or an art. The language of science makes some educators nervous. Everyone can remember the artistry of a great teacher – a teacher who somehow against all odds got every student to perform better than they thought they could. Teachers themselves know how complex their job is – every minute of every hour, a thousand different things are going on, and it can seem so unlikely that the cutting-and-slicing reductionist approach of science could ever help us understand what's happening. The history of scientific approaches to education is not promising; in the past, scientists studied learning in a university laboratory, and then delivered pronouncements from the Ivory Tower that teachers were expected to adopt unquestioningly.

Unlike these previous generations of educational research, learning scientists spend a lot of time in schools – many of us were full-time teachers before we became researchers. And learning scientists are committed to improving classroom teaching and learning – many are in schools every week, working directly with teachers and districts. Some even take time off from university duties and return to the classroom, teaching alongside teachers and learning how to make theories work in the real world. This is a new kind of science, with the goal of providing a sound scientific foundation for education.

Acknowledgements

I am grateful for suggestions, comments, and historical details provided by Janet Kolodner and Roy Pea.

References

Baron, J. (1985). *Rationality and intelligence*. New York: Cambridge.

Bereiter, C. (2002). *Education and mind in the knowledge age*. Mahwah, NJ: Erlbaum.

Bobrow, D. G., & Collins, A. (1975). *Representation and understanding: Studies in cognitive science*. New York: Academic Press.

Bransford, J. D., Brown, A. L., & Cocking, R. R. (Eds.). (2000). *How people learn: Brain, mind, experience, and school*. Washington, DC: National Academy Press.

Burtis, P. J., Bereiter, C., Scardamalia, M., & Tetroe, J. (1983). The development of planning in writing. In B. M. Kroll & G. Wells (Eds.), *Explorations in the development of writing: Theory, research, and practice* (pp. 153–174). New York: Wiley.

Cole, M. (1996). *Cultural psychology: A once and future discipline*. Cambridge: Harvard.

Collins, A., & Brown, J. S. (1988). The computer as a tool for learning through reflection. In H. Mandl & A. Lesgold (Eds.), *Learning issues for intelligent tutoring systems* (pp. 1–18). New York: Springer.

Cuban, L. (2001). *Oversold and underused: Computers in the classroom*. Cambridge, MA: Harvard.

Drucker, P. F. (1993). *Post-capitalist society*. New York: HarperBusiness.

Dunbar, K., & Klahr, D. (1989). Developmental differences in scientific discovery strategies. In D. Klahr & K. Kotovsky (Eds.), *Complex information processing: The impact of Herbert A. Simon* (pp. 109–143). Mahwah, NJ: Erlbaum.

Flower, L., & Hayes, J. R. (1980). The cognition of discovery: Defining a rhetorical problem. *College Composition and Communication, 31,* 21–32.

Heath, C., & Luff, P. (1991). *Collaborative activity and technological design: Task coordination in the London Underground control rooms*. Paper presented at the Proceedings of ECSCW '91.

Hughes, J. A., Shapiro, D. Z., Sharrock, W. W., Anderson, R. J., & Gibbons, S. C. (1988). *The automation of air traffic control* (Final Report SERC/ESRC Grant no. GR/D/86257). Lancaster, UK: Department of Sociology, Lancaster University.

Hutchins, E. (1995). *Cognition in the wild*. Cambridge: MIT Press.

Kahneman, D., Slovic, P., & Tversky, A. (Eds.). (1982). *Judgment under uncertainty: Heuristics and biases.* New York: Cambridge.

Kuhn, D. (1989). Children and adults as intuitive scientists. *Psychological Review, 96,* 674–689.

Kuhn, D. (1990). Introduction. In D. Kuhn (Ed.), *Developmental perspectives on teaching and learning thinking skills* (pp. 1–8). Basel: Karger.

Lave, J. (1988). *Cognition in practice: Mind, mathematics, and culture in everyday life.* New York: Cambridge.

Liebowitz, J. (Ed.). (1998). *The handbook of applied expert systems.* Boca Raton, FL: CRC Press.

McGuire, J. E. (1992). Scientific change: Perspectives and proposals. In M. Salmon, J. Earman, C. Glymour, J. Lennox, P. Machamer, J. McGuire, J. Norton, W. Salmon, & K. Schaffner (Eds.), *Introduction to the philosophy of science* (pp. 132–178). Englewood Cliffs, NJ: Prentice Hall.

National Center for History in the Schools. (1996). *National standards for history.* Los Angeles, CA: National Center for History in the Schools.

National Research Council. (1996). *National science education standards.* Washington, DC: National Academy Press.

Newell, A., & Simon, H. A. (1972). *Human problem solving.* Englewood Cliffs, NJ: Prentice Hall.

Palincsar, A. S., & Brown, A. L. (1984). Reciprocal teaching of comprehension fostering and comprehension monitoring. *Cognition and Instruction, 1*(2), 117–175.

Papert, S. (1980). *Mindstorms: Children, computers, and powerful ideas.* New York: Basic Books.

Papert, S. (1993). *The children's machine: rethinking school in the age of the computer.* New York: BasicBooks.

Parsad, B., & Jones, J. (2005). *Internet access in U.S. public schools and classrooms: 1994–2003* (NCES 2005-015). Washington, DC: National Center for Education Statistics.

Rogoff, B. (1990). *Apprenticeship in thinking: Cognitive development in social context.* New York: Oxford University Press.

Rogoff, B. (1998). Cognition as a collaborative process. In D. Kuhn & R. S. Siegler (Eds.), *Handbook of child psychology, 5th edition, Volume 2: Cognition, perception, and language* (pp. 679–744). New York: Wiley.

Salomon, G. (Ed.). (1993). *Distributed cognitions: Psychological and educational considerations.* New York: Cambridge.

Saxe, G. B. (1991). *Culture and cognitive development: Studies in mathematical understanding.* Hillsdale, NJ: Erlbaum.

Schauble, L. (1990). Belief revision in children: The role of prior knowledge and strategies for generating evidence. *Journal of Experimental Child Psychology, 49,* 31–57.

Scribner, S., & Cole, M. (1973). Cognitive consequences of formal and informal education. *Science, 182*(4112), 553–559.

Shavelson, R. J., & Towne, L. (2002). *Scientific research in education.* Washington, DC: National Academy Press.

Siegler, R. S. (1998). *Children's thinking.* (Third ed.). Upper Saddle River, NJ: Prentice Hall.

Skinner, B. F. (1954/1968). The science of learning and the art of teaching. In B. F. Skinner (Ed.), *The technology of teaching* (pp. 9–28). New York: Appleton-Century-Crofts. (Original work published in 1954 in the *Harvard Educational Review*, Vol. 24, No. 2, pp. 86–97).

Sleeman, D., & Brown, J. S. (Eds.). (1982). *Intelligent tutoring systems.* New York: Academic Press.

Suchman, L. A. (1987). *Plans and situated actions: The problem of human-machine communication.* New York: Cambridge University Press.

Suppe, F. (1974). The search for philosophic understanding of scientific theories. In F. Suppe (Ed.), *The structure of scientific theories* (pp. 3–241). Urbana, IL: University of Illinois Press.

Voss, J. F., Perkins, D. N., & Segal, J. W. (Eds.). (1991). *Informal reasoning and education.* Mahwah, NJ: Erlbaum.

Wenger, E. (1987). *Artificial intelligence and tutoring systems: Computational and cognitive approaches to the communication of knowledge.* San Francisco, CA: Morgan Kaufmann.

Part I
FOUNDATIONS

CHAPTER 2

Foundations and Opportunities for an Interdisciplinary Science of Learning

John D. Bransford, Brigid Barron, Roy D. Pea, Andrew Meltzoff, Patricia Kuhl, Philip Bell, Reed Stevens, Daniel L. Schwartz, Nancy Vye, Byron Reeves, Jeremy Roschelle, and Nora H. Sabelli

In this chapter, we argue that the learning sciences are poised for a "decade of synergy." We focus on several key traditions of theory and research with the potential for mutually influencing one another in ways that can transform how we think about the science of learning, as well as how future educators and scientists are trained.

The three major strands of research that we focus on are: (1) *implicit learning and the brain*, (2) *informal learning*, and (3) *designs for formal learning and beyond*. As Figure 2.1A illustrates, these three areas have mainly operated independently, with researchers attempting to apply their thinking and findings directly to education, and with the links between theory and well-grounded implications for practice often proving tenuous at best.

The goal of integrating insights from these strands in order to create a transformative theory of learning is illustrated in Figure 2.1B. Successful efforts to understand and advance human learning require a simultaneous emphasis on informal and formal learning environments, and on the implicit ways in which people learn in whatever situations they find themselves.

We explore examples of research from each of these three strands. We then suggest ways that the learning sciences might draw on these traditions for creating a more robust understanding of learning, which can inform the design of learning environments that allow all students to succeed in the fast changing world of the twenty-first century (e.g., Darling-Hammond & Bransford, 2005; Vaill, 1996).

Implicit Learning and the Brain

Implicit learning refers to situations in which complex information is acquired effortlessly (without a conscious effort), and the resulting knowledge is difficult to express verbally (e.g., Berry, 1997; Cleeremans, Destrebecqz, & Boyer, 1998; Reber, 1967). Although many types of implicit learning exist, a common process underlies most of them – the rapid, effortless, and untutored detection of patterns of covariation among events (Reber, 1993).

Implicit learning is pervasive across many domains, including influences on social attitudes and stereotypes regarding gender and race (Greenwald, Banaji, Rudman, Farnham et al., 2002), visual pattern learning (Musen & Triesman, 1990), motor response time tasks (Nissen & Bullemer, 1987), syntactic language learning (Reber, 1976), phonetic language learning (Goodsitt, Morgan, & Kuhl, 1993; Kuhl, 2004; Saffran, Aslin, & Newport, 1996), and young children's imitative learning of the tools, artifacts, behaviors, customs, and rituals of their culture (Meltzoff, 1988a; 2005; Rogoff et al., 2003; Tomasello, 1999). Implicit learning has educational and even evolutionary value inasmuch as it enables organisms to adapt to new environments by listening, observing, and interacting with the objects and people encountered there, even in the absence of formal pedagogy or a conscious effort to learn.

What Can Neuroscience Add to the Study of Learning?

Research correlating brain and behavior has a long history, but the 1990s were designated "The Decade of the Brain," and advances took place in neuroscience at an especially rapid pace. Three dominant methods for measuring brain activities are (1) ERPs – event-related potentials – which track changes in the electrically evoked potentials measured on the surface of the scalp; (2) fMRI – which tracks changes in blood flow in the brain; and (3) MEG – which tracks magnetic field changes in the brain over time.

Educators and policy makers rapidly recognized the prospects for education of new neural measures of mental activity. In July 1996, the Education Commission of the States and the Dana Foundation held a conference entitled "Bridging the gap between neuroscience and education," convening leaders from the two fields. Many argued that the gap between the neuron and the classroom was substantial, perhaps a "bridge too far" (Bruer, 1997). Research since that time has begun to close this gap.

There are three reasons to include cognitive neuroscience in the learning sciences. First, a mature science of learning will involve understanding not only that learning occurs but also understanding how and why it occurs. Neuroscience measures reveal the internal mechanisms and biological substrates of learning, and this enriches our understanding of how learning occurs. Second, the combination of fMRI, ERPs, and MEG provide useful information about the temporal unfolding and spatial location of the brain mechanisms involved in learning and memory. Third, because of their sensitivity, neuroscience measures may be helpful in understanding individual differences in learning. Cognitive neuroscientists can peek below the behavioral output to the generators of that behavior; brain and behavioral data taken together will enrich our understanding of learning (Gopnik, Meltzoff, & Kuhl, 1999).

Some Fundamental Brain Findings and Their Implications

It is a common misconception that each individual's brain is entirely formed at birth and that "the brain basis" of behavior reveals fixed aspects of human cognition. Instead, experiences during development have powerful effects on the physical development of the brain itself. A pioneering study of the effects of the environment on brain development was conducted by William Greenough and his colleagues (Greenough, Black, & Wallace, 1987). They studied rats placed in various environments and the effects on synapse formation in the rats' brains. They compared the brains of rats raised in "complex environments," containing toys and obstacles and other rats, with those housed individually or in small cages without toys. They found that rats raised in complex environments performed better on learning tasks, and had 20–25 percent more synapses per neuron in the visual cortex. Brain development is thus "experience-expectant" – evolution has created a neural system that "expects" information from the environment at a particular time, allowing

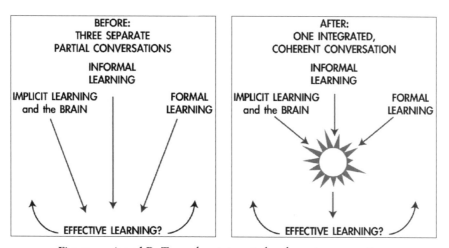

Figure 2.1 A and B. Toward an integrated, coherent conversation.

animals to acquire knowledge that is specific to their own environments when exposed to that information. These experiments suggest that "rich environments" include those that provide numerous opportunities for social interaction, direct physical contact with the environment, and a changing set of objects for play and exploration.

ASSUMPTIONS ABOUT CRITICAL PERIODS
FOR LEARNING

Several brain researchers have hypothesized that humans' brains are preprogrammed to learn certain kinds of knowledge during a limited window of time known as a *critical period*. But the latest brain science is beginning to question this simplistic developmental notion. For example, new brain research shows that the timing of critical periods differs significantly in the visual, auditory, and language systems. Even within different systems, there is emerging evidence that the brain is much more plastic than heretofore assumed, and that the idea of rigid "critical periods" does not hold.

New studies by Kuhl and colleagues explored potential mechanisms underlying critical periods in early language development (e.g., Kuhl, Conboy, Padden, Nelson, et al., 2005; Rivera-Gaxiola et al., 2005). The idea behind the studies relies on the concept of *neural commitment* to language patterns. Kuhl's recent neuropsychological and brain imaging work suggests that lan-

guage acquisition involves the development of neural networks that focus on and code specific properties of the speech signals heard in early infancy, resulting in neural tissue that is dedicated to the analysis of these learned patterns. Kuhl claims that early neural commitment to learned patterns can also constrain future learning; neural networks dedicated to native-language patterns do not detect non-native patterns, and may actually interfere with their analysis (Iverson, Kuhl, Akahane-Yamda, Diesch, et al., 2003; Kuhl, 2004; Zhang, Kuhl, Imada, Kotani, et al., 2005). If the initial coding of native-language patterns interferes with the learning of non-native patterns, because they do not conform to the established "mental filter," then early learning of one's primary language may limit second language learning. By this argument, the "critical period" depends on *experience* as much as time, and is a *process* rather than a strictly timed window of opportunity that is opened and closed by maturation.

The general point is that learning produces neural commitment to the properties of the stimuli we see and hear. Exposure to a specific data set alters the brain by establishing neural connections that commit the brain to processing information in an ideal way for that particular input (e.g., one's first language). Neural commitment functions as a filter that affects future processing (Cheour et al., 1998; Kuhl, 1991; Kuhl, Williams, Lacerda, Stevens, et al., 1992; Näätänen,

Lehtokoski, Lennes, Cheour, et al., 1997), and results in highly efficient processing of learned material (Zhang et al., 2005). The most studied example is *language*, where neural filters affect processing at all levels, making native-language processing highly efficient and foreign-language processing difficult for adults (Strange, 1995). In adulthood, second language learners have to overcome committed brains to develop new networks.

LEARNING IN INFANCY BEFORE NEURAL
COMMITMENT: NEUROPLASTICITY

In a recent illustration of how the brains of infants remain open to developing neural commitments to more than one "mental filter" for language experiences, Kuhl and colleagues tested whether American nine-month-old infants who had never before heard Mandarin Chinese could learn the phonemes of Mandarin by listening to Chinese graduate students play and read to them in Mandarin Chinese (Kuhl, Tsao & Liu., 2003). Nine-month-old American infants listened to four native speakers of Mandarin during twelve sessions in which they read books and played with toys. Then infants were tested with a Mandarin phonetic contrast that does not occur in English to see whether exposure to the foreign language would reverse the usual decline in infants' foreign-language speech perception. Infants learned during these live sessions, compared with a control group that heard only English, and American infants performed at a level statistically equivalent to infants tested in Taiwan who had been listening to Mandarin for eleven months. The study shows how readily young infants learn from natural language exposure at this age.

Children's Implicit Learning from other People: Imitative Learning

Children learn a great deal outside of formal learning settings simply from watching and imitating other people. This is important for the transmission of culture from parents to children and for peer-group learning.

The laboratory study of imitative learning has undergone a recent revolution, revealing that we are the most imitative creatures on the planet, imitating from birth (Meltzoff & Moore, 1977) and learning from imitation beyond other primates such as monkeys and chimpanzees (Povinelli, Reaux, Theall & Giambrone., 2000; Tomasello & Call, 1997; Whiten, 2002).

Recently, the importance of imitative learning has been underscored by the discovery of "mirror neurons" that are activated whether a subject performs an action or sees that action performed by another (e.g., Rizzolatti, Gadiga, Fogassi & Gallese, 2002; Meltzoff & Decety, 2003). Clearly, imitative learning involves more than the presence of mirror neurons, and neuroscientists are trying to determine the special abilities – perhaps uniquely human abilities such as perspective taking and identification with others – that support our proclivity for learning by observing others.

Ample research shows that young children learn a great deal about people and cultural artifacts through imitation, and children are influenced not only by their parents, but also by their peers and what they see on television. For example, one study showed that fourteen-month-old infants learn from and imitate their peers in daycare centers (Hanna & Meltzoff, 1993). Another showed that two-year-olds learn novel actions from watching TV (Meltzoff, 1988b). This is an important finding because young children in Western culture watch a good deal of TV: a Kaiser Foundation report (Rideout, Vanderwater, & Wartella, 2003) indicates that almost 70 percent of children 0–3 years old watch television on a typical day and 58 percent do so *every* day.

The next decade of research in neuroscience will focus on the relationship between behavioral development and brain development. One thing has been established without a doubt – learning experiences help sculpt an individual's brain. Brain development is not a product of biology or culture exclusively, but, more accurately, a complex interaction of both.

Informal Learning

Here we outline the second strand of research, the processes and outcomes of informal learning. *Informal learning* usually takes place outside of school. The important distinction here is not the physical location where learning occurs but, rather, the contrast between informal learning and the explicitly didactic instructional practices that have emerged in Western schooling, which we refer to as formal learning. Informal learning can be pervasive in peer-to-peer interactions within school, and formal learning may take place in noninstitutional settings such as community centers, or during an "instructional moment" when a parent mimics didactic instruction.

Informal learning has been studied in work settings, museums, zoos, aquariums, community centers, sports teams, Girl Scout troops, and among communities without formal schooling (Bransford et al., in press; Hull & Shultz, 2001; Schauble, Leinhardt, & Martin, 1998). We begin with a brief summary of insights from a broad range of researchers who investigate learning out of school and then move to a discussion of why the study of informal learning is a crucial area for the learning sciences.

Cognitive Consequences of Schooling and Contrasts in Learning Settings

In a widely cited *Science* paper, Scribner and Cole (1973) reviewed many comparative cultural studies using cognitive and developmental methodologies to examine thinking and reasoning processes. The distinctions they inferred from the empirical literature between the forms of thinking, acting, and learning in formal education and informal practical life are echoed in later influential writings by Lave (1988), Resnick (1987), and others, right up to today's contemporary research at and across the boundaries of informal and formal learning. Their thesis is that "school represents a specialized set of educational experiences which are discontinuous from those encountered in everyday life and that it requires and pro-

motes ways of learning and thinking which often run counter to those nurtured in practical daily activities." (p. 553). Research from Greenfield and Bruner (1966), Luria (1971), Cole, Gay, Glick, and Sharp (1971) and others was reviewed to reveal the different skills manifest in classification, reasoning, and concept formation performances when individuals had more schooling experience. First, they noted that schooling contributed to *greater facility in abstract reasoning*. Second, they noted that more schooled individuals were distinguished in their *greater use of language* for describing how they are achieving their tasks, as in memory or classification. These findings included adults as well as children.

Scribner and Cole identified three distinctive features of informal learning:

1. Informal learning is person-oriented, or *particularistic*, in that expectations of performance are based on who a person is instead of what he has accomplished;
2. Informal learning *fosters traditionalism* (since the elders are accorded the highest group status); and
3. Informal learning involves *fusing emotional and intellectual domains*. In informal learning, emotional engagement is wrapped together with cognitive involvement, in part because the content of knowledge is inseparable from the personal identity of the teacher.

Scribner and Cole note that informal learning descriptions by anthropologists also describe common mechanisms, e.g., mimesis, identification, and cooperation (Fortes, 1938; referred to as imitation, identification, and empathy by Mead, 1964). They consider these three categories to be subsumed under a general domain they call "observational learning" – in contrast to learning acquired primarily through language (also see Rogoff, Paradise, Mejia Arauz, Correa-Chavez et al., 2003 for a discussion of an orientation toward learning they call "intent participation," which relies heavily on observation of adult activities).

In contrast to informal learning, formal learning is characterized by: (1) the presence of *universalistic* values, criteria, and standards of performance (over the particularism of who is doing the teaching); (2) *language* is the dominant medium of teaching and learning, rather than the richer sensory context of modeling and observation/imitation common to informal learning; and (3) teaching and learning occur *out of context*, with mathematical symbol manipulation a paradigm case.

Importance of Identity and Broader Units of Analyses

The fusion of emotion/intellectual domains and social/identity issues has been rediscovered in newer work focusing on identity formation in informal learning by youth as it relates to their participation in activities (Holland, Lachiotte, Skinner, & Cain, 1998; Nasir & Saxe, 2003), in larger discourses of disciplines (Gee, 1996), and in issues of affective and motivational issues that underlie and catalyze informal learning (Resnick, 1987; Schauble, et al., 1998).

Later work on informal learning explored additional theoretical constructs that analyzed participation structure in informal learning, and the changing nature of participation in culturally valued activities brought about through such arrangements as *scaffolding* (Wood, Bruner & Ross, 1976; Rogoff, 1990; see Pea, 2004 for history), *apprenticeship* learning (Rogoff, 1990), *legitimate peripheral participation* in "communities of practice" (Lave & Wenger, 1991), and *guided participation* (Rogoff, 2003). A crucial aspect of these approaches is the broadened units of analysis they offer: these views move beyond the study of individuals alone to consider how learning occurs within enduring social groups such as families and communities, and they offer up notions of *cultural practice* and *activity* as fundamental units of analysis (Cole, 1996).

Mutual Influence Perspectives on Development

Ethnographic studies of children in their everyday interactions with others have challenged simplistic socialization accounts of child development that focus on the unidirectional influence of adults on children. Such studies are helping social scientists see the ways that children can propel their own development. From an early age, children often take initiative by asking questions, observing, or taking part in ongoing activities (Rogoff, 2003). Children also contribute creatively to ongoing practices with families and peers by introducing or modifying routines and ways of playing (Goodwin, 1997; Corsaro, 1985), creating new vocabulary and forms of talk (Eckert, 1989), and utilizing the tools of their culture in ways unimagined by prior generations. In turn, parents and other caretakers nurture development not only by providing explanations and role models, but through the manner in which they structure time, introduce topics, purchase toys or other materials, and allow children opportunities to participate in ongoing activities (Ash, 2003; Rogoff, 2003).

The complex intertwining of contributions of both the child and his or her caretakers to cognitive development is nicely exemplified in studies of preschooler's scientific knowledge. Crowley & Jacobs (2002) introduced the idea of "islands of expertise" to reflect the fact that young children often develop considerable knowledge about topics of interest before going to school. They provide the example of a boy who became interested in trains after his parents bought him a book on the topic. This book was read repeatedly and multiple conversations about trains followed, supported by trips to museums and viewing videos. Over time he and his parents built up a great deal of shared vocabulary, schemas for train scenarios, knowledge of mechanisms that allow for train travel, and the like. This shared knowledge in turn allowed the family to have rich conversations that included explanations, elaborations, and analogies to related domains.

Peers are also active learning partners and share knowledge about cultural tools, toys, and practices. For example, children share literature and use it to signify and build friendships (Joiner, 1996) and they share knowledge of how to create and learn with new technologies (Barron, 2004; Chandler-Olcott & Mahar, 2003). With age, children expand their social networks, and peers become more important (Hartup, 1996). Friends, and the parents of friends, may offer a space for activities and conversations not available in their own homes. These studies suggest that we have much to learn about the role of informal learning in the development of interest and knowledge on the road to expertise.

Pathways to Expertise

Many children who fail in school demonstrate sophisticated competence in non-school activities. In particular, learners from nondominant cultural or lower SES backgrounds appear to learn resourcefully and productively outside of school, even though they may not do well inside school (e.g., McLaughlin, Irby & Langman, 2001). These asymmetries raise important questions about the design of our school systems and what resources allow for success out of school.

The goal of *understanding potential synergies between contexts* is a new area of research that raises questions about how to cross-pollinate learning opportunities across settings. Studies of when, where, and how learning occurs when people make the choice to learn (Barron, 2004; Barron, 2005) suggest we need more sophisticated developmental studies that help us understand pathways to expertise, as they often seem to involve both informal and formal learning opportunities as people move across the multiple life-spaces they inhabit.

Designs for Formal Learning and Beyond

The third research strand illustrated in Figure 2.1 involves using the learning sciences to create learning environments, and studying the effects of these environments to inform theoretical development. Most research in educational psychology falls within this strand. Recently, several research summaries have become available that describe current understanding of how to design effective learning environments.[1] We focus here on the topic of *adaptive expertise*: expert knowledge that supports continual learning, improvisation, and expansion.

Researchers have explored the nature of the skills and knowledge that underlie expert performance (e.g., Ackerman, 2003; Alexander, 2003; Chi, Glaser, & Farr, 1988; Hatano & Osura, 2003; Lajoie, 2003; NRC, 2000a; Rose, 2004; Sternberg, 2003). This research contributes to an understanding of the ways that knowledge, skills, attitudes, and thinking strategies combine to support effective performances in a wide variety of domains.

One important finding is that experts notice features of situations and problems that escape the attention of novices (Chase & Simon, 1973; Chi, Glaser & Rees, 1982). Berliner (1991, 2001) has demonstrated large differences in noticing by novice versus expert teachers that affect their abilities to rapidly identify problems and opportunities and act upon them. Classic work with chess masters was among the first to demonstrate the role of noticing and pattern recognition in expertise (e.g., Chase & Simon, 1973; deGroot, 1965).

The fact that expertise affects noticing has a number of important educational implications. One is that merely showing novice students videos of experts doing things does not guarantee that the novices notice all the relevant features (e.g., Michael, Klee, Bransford, & Warren, 1993). Second, an emphasis on expertise and noticing suggests that we do not simply learn *from* experience; instead, we also learn *to* experience (e.g., Becker, 1953; Goodwin, 1994; Stevens & Hall, 1998).

Research indicates that experts' knowledge is not simply a list of disconnected facts – it is connected and organized around important ideas of their disciplines, and includes information about the appropriate conditions for applying key concepts and procedures. Such information helps experts know when, why, and how aspects of their vast repertoire of knowledge and skills are relevant in any specific situation.

Adaptive Expertise

Recently, research has begun to differentiate "routine expertise" from "adaptive expertise" (e.g., Alexander, 2003; Hatano & Inagaki, 1986; Hatano & Osuro, 2003). Both routine experts and adaptive experts continue to learn throughout their lifetimes. Routine experts develop a core set of competencies that they apply throughout their lives with greater and greater efficiency. In contrast, adaptive experts are much more likely to evolve their core competencies and continually expand the breadth and depth of their expertise as the need arises or as their interests demand. This often requires them to venture into areas where they must function as "intelligent novices" who often struggle initially in order to learn new things (e.g., Brown, Bransford, Ferrara, & Campione, 1983).

Schwartz, Bransford, and Sears (2005) have suggested that the concept of adaptive expertise involves at least two major dimensions; processes that lead to *innovation* or invention and those that lead to *efficiency* through well-practiced routines (Figure 2.2).

Sometimes these two dimensions are characterized as mutually exclusive ends of a continuum (e.g., high and low road transfer, Salomon & Perkins, 1989), yet because there are different processes involved, they are not necessarily exclusive. Adaptive experts are high on both dimensions (e.g., Gentner, Brem, Ferguson, Markman, et al., 1997; Hatano & Inagaki, 1986; Wineburg, 1998). The representation of adaptive expertise in Figure 2.2 suggests how people can develop expertise that engages the strengths of both efficiency and innovation, so they may continually adapt to change.

We suggest the importance of investigating a third dimension that appears to help drive the development of adaptive expertise: a metacognitive awareness of the distinctive roles and trade-offs of the innovation and efficiency dimensions of expertise, and the active design and creative structuring of one's learning environment in order to support their dual utilities. Hargadon and Sutton's work (2000) investigating "innovation factories" in businesses such as the design firm IDEO foregrounds these features of innovation factories, and their successes in developing adaptive business expertise in solving complex design problems may offer fertile insights for new educational designs.

Assessments of Efficiencies Versus Innovation

We are concerned that most of today's assessments tend to be "efficiency" assessments, sensitive to well-learned routines and schema-driven processing but failing to capture innovation or metacognitive awareness. Nearly all standardized tests are "direct application" and "sequestered problem solving assessments" (SPS), where people have access to what is currently in their heads (Bransford & Schwartz, 1999). The expertise literature indicates that well-established routines and schemas are indeed an important characteristic of expertise – freeing up resources of mind and attention otherwise devoted to basic issues (e.g. beginning readers often have such significant problems with decoding fluency that they cannot attend to the meaning of what they read). The ability to directly and efficiently apply previously acquired skills and knowledge is certainly important in many circumstances, as in car driving or plane flying.

One alternative to a direct application view of learning and transfer is a focus on adaptive expertise that has been called "preparation for future learning" (PFL) (Schwartz & Bransford, 1998; Bransford & Schwartz, 1999; Schwartz & Martin, 2004; Martin & Schwartz, 2005; Spiro, Vispoel, Schmitz, Samarapungavan et al., 1987). Here the focus shifts to assessments of a person's abilities to *learn* in knowledge-rich environments. When organizations hire

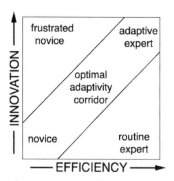

Figure 2.2. Two dimensions of adaptive expertise.

new employees, they want people who can learn, and they expect them to make flexible and competent use of resources to facilitate their learning (e.g. texts, computer programs, social networks of friends, and new colleagues). If people are better prepared for future learning, they will be able to transfer that learning better and faster.

It is important to emphasize that the PFL perspective is different from the *learning-to-learn* literature; the main contrast is that PFL is not principally focused on the existence of a set of general, content-free learning skills. The expertise literature (Chi et al., 1988; NRC, 2000a) shows that strategies and knowledge are highly interdependent; for example, knowing a particular scientific concept can influence the hypotheses that one generates to explain world events. Ideally, assessments of adaptive expertise would include opportunities for people to try out hunches, receive feedback, and attempt to revise based on the feedback. In contrast, typical tests provide few opportunities for feedback and revision – the only option is to provide one's initial thoughts, with no opportunities to test them and revise. Schwartz, Bransford, and Sears (2005) show that assessments of adaptive expertise can reveal the benefits of certain educational experiences, even though those benefits are invisible when standard SPS measures of assessment are used. Many research groups are now exploring innovative ways to measure adaptive expertise (Crawford, Riel & Schlager, 2005; Hatano, 2005; Martin, 2005;

Petrosino, 2005; Schwartz, Blair, Davis, Chang et al., 2005; Walker, 2005).

Research on Instructional Strategies for Achieving Adaptive Expertise

The cognitive sciences have principally focused on how routine expertise is acquired, as people get faster and more accurate at solving recurrent problems. Cognitive theories in this tradition emphasize routinized "scripts," "schemas," "frames" and "procedures" (for definitions and examples, see Anderson & Pearson, 1984; Anderson, 1976; Black & Bower, 1980; Bransford & Johnson, 1972; Minsky, 1986; Schank & Abelson, 1977). These functional structures are important for solving problems efficiently. Much instruction in schools guides students to acquire schemas of particular problem types in order to increase problem solving efficiency by turning nonroutine problems into routine problems. An example involves problem types of the form: *"Jim's parents live 60 miles away. He drove to their house at 60 mph and returned at 40 mph due to fog. What was his average speed?"* Most people simply say 50 mph – not realizing that Jim spends a longer amount of time going the slower speed so the average must be less than 50. There are a variety of problems of this type. When people are helped to acquire schemas that allow them to identify particular problem types, they are much less likely to get tripped up when later encountering similar examples. The acquisition of well-organized and easily accessed procedures, scripts, and schemas is extremely important for effective performance – otherwise people are overly challenged by the attentional demands of many components of task performances (e.g., see Bereiter & Scardamalia, 1993). But experts often need to go beyond such schemas, and have to structure experience in new ways. Adaptive expertise allows people to let go of previously acquired knowledge and skills. Efficiency oriented instruction may thus need to be complemented by different kinds of learning activities.

To increase students' adaptive expertise, learning environments should include activities rich with reflection and metacognition that engage them in (1) "knowledge building" rather than merely "knowledge telling" (Bereiter & Scardamalia, 1989, 1993); (2) systematic inquiry with an emphasis on theory building and disconfirmation (e.g., Karmiloff-Smith & Inhelder, 1974/1975; Krajcik & Blumenfeld, this volume) rather than simply following procedures for how to find some result (e.g. NRC, 2005), and (3) designing "working smart" environments that promote innovation in order to increase efficiency (Vye et al., 1998). Students learn about the general goal of efficiently solving a future set of recurring problems, and are encouraged to prepare for such problems by adopting, adapting, and inventing smart tools to help them work more effectively.

Toward a Synergistic Science of Learning

We have discussed three areas of research that seem well positioned for reciprocal influences: (1) implicit learning and the brain; (2) informal learning; (3) designs for formal learning and beyond. Each of these research traditions has operated relatively independently up to this point. We believe that the coming decade holds great potential for achieving a more robust understanding of learning by synthesizing these three traditions. The learning sciences of the future will embody both neural and behavioral aspects of learning, and must account for implicit, informal, and formal learning activities and outcomes. We do not mean that the research strands will merge into one grand theory that eliminates the unique perspectives each offers, but we do believe that these strands can inform one another and, in the process, create more coherent and useful theories that better illuminate why, how, when, where, and what people learn. A major challenge is to articulate problems in ways that will provide the three approaches with the greatest opportunities for convergence. Fortunately, there are several recent advances in

our understanding of thinking and learning to build on.

One of the major insights about cognitive performance in the last century is the extent to which the local cognitive and social ecology can constrain or support it (Hutchins, 1995; Pea, 1993; Simon, 1996). This distributed, emergent, and ecological view of cognition has made clear that whereas understanding learners and thinkers as independent and self-contained systems is important, it is not adequate for a robust theory of cognition and learning; we need a better theoretical understanding of the dynamics between people and resources in any learning ecology (Barron, 2004). Conceptualizing learning in ecological terms draws our attention to the multiple interacting aspects of a learning environment: the kinds of learning activities, the material and social resources for learning, the roles that learners take on, the knowledge distributed within social networks, and the practices for exchanging information. The ecological perspective explores the relationships between the person and the environment, and the conditions under which they can exert reciprocal influence.

A second major insight is the importance of social aspects of learning as people engage with learning activities, one another, and their identities as learners and doers of particular activities. Many learning scientists refer to this view as the situative perspective (Greeno, this volume).

A third major insight is the important role of cultural practices for learning, and the understanding that arrangements and values for learning are themselves cultural practices (Cole, 1996; Rogoff, 2003; Nasir, Lee, Roseberry, & Warren, this volume). Too infrequently do school-based learning environments capitalize on diverse ways of learning that have arisen from cultural practices.

Together, these three insights suggest an empirical research agenda that will better position us for developing more comprehensive and practical theories of learning. Below, we highlight three areas rich with opportunities for advancing an interdisciplinary theory of learning through collaboration, synergies, and conceptual collisions:

1. *Moving beyond the individual.* All three perspectives have unique ways of investigating units of analysis comprising systems that transcend the individual. These include pairs, small groups, organizational levels of analysis, and tool-mediated learning at each of these system levels. Families, friendships, peer groups, and larger social networks are all units *of* learning as well as significant contexts *for* learning. Each of the three research strands is investigating the mechanisms and outcomes of learning with others. For example, strand 1 has defined an active program of research to specify how and why social interaction is critical for language learning. Studies of social interaction from a sociocultural perspective follow learners across multiple social contexts – such as family, peers, and mentoring relationships – and pay special attention to how resources for learning are taken up, including material resources such as books or computers, but also attitudes and practices surrounding learning. Design-oriented cognitive psychologists are working to specify features of tasks that make it more likely for people to engage in the kinds of interactions that will lead to learning, a topic we know a good deal about from studies of collaboration.

2. *The role of affect in learning.* Though informational resources are important in any learning ecology, affective and motivational resources are also important because they may mediate effort, attention, and a desire to engage in learning. We need a better understanding of the intertwining of affective, relational, and communicative aspects of learning interactions. How do emotional responses mediate learning, and how do they emerge from learning? Research from within strand 1 is beginning to study the brains of adults as they interact, and has located distinct regions associated with competitive versus cooperative activity (Decety, Jackson, Sommerville, Chaminade, et al., 2004). Strand 2 work documents the complex processes of learning in longstanding relationships, and the ways that interactions between people are central for understanding the successful building of collective knowledge or failed attempts at joint work (Barron, 2003). Strand 3 designs experiments to specify the mechanisms underlying persistence and withdrawal of efforts. These areas of investigation can contribute to a better understanding of people's life choices with respect to academic pathways.

3. *Expanding our conception of what is learned.* Most studies of learning have focused on academic content. However, as studies of cognition in action tell us, there is more to expertise than content knowledge. The notion of adaptive expertise reflects this broader conceptualization and raises more questions. Do people learn to interact in more and less productive ways for doing collective work, and does that then change their capacity for learning through collaboration? The area of metacognition is also ripe for expansion – for example, do people become better able to reflect on complex social interactions and recognize when crucial aspects of joint work are not functioning well (such as joint attention or differences uses of terms)? Some have referred to this kind of perception as "professional vision" (Goodwin, 1994; Stevens & Hall, 1998), and define it as being able to see the categories that matter in a community of practice. Recent work on complex organizations also suggests that some environments are better designed for learning and innovation than others (Hargadon & Sutton, 2000). How is it that people become sensitive to their environment, and how do they learn to arrange things for maximum well-being, productivity, and innovation? How do they appropriate and invent new practices of learning? All three strands pursue these kinds of questions and have unique tools for investigating them.

In closing, the ecological, situative, and increasingly cultural approaches characteristic of the learning sciences can help us to understand the biological and embodied aspects of learning and development that shape adaptation. The developmental neuroscience community is helping to articulate how the brain develops in continual interaction with the environment, and how the developing brain influences how later environments are perceived. As a National Academy of Science report (NRC 2000b) suggested, we need a science of learning that works from "Neurons to Neighborhoods."

Acknowledgments

This work was supported by a grant from the National Science Foundation (NSF# 0354453). Any opinions, findings, and conclusions expressed in the paper are those of the authors and do not necessarily reflect the views of the National Science Foundation. Sections of this chapter build on a chapter prepared for the *Handbook of Educational Psychology* (Bransford et al., in press).

Footnote

1. These reports include *How People Learn* (NRC, 2000a), *Knowing What Students Know* (NRC, 2001), *Learning and Understanding* (NRC, 2002), *Learning and Instruction: A SERP Research Agenda* (NRC, 2003), *Internet Environments for Science Education* (Linn, Davis, & Bell, 2004), *How Students Learn* (NRC, 2005), and *Preparing Teachers for a Changing World* (Darling-Hammond & Bransford, 2005).

References

Ackerman, P. (2003). Cognitive ability and non-ability trait determinants of expertise. *Educational Researcher, 32*, 15–20.

Alexander, P. (2003). The development of expertise: The journey from acclimation to proficiency. *Educational Researcher, 32*, 10–14.

Anderson, J. R. (1976). *Language, memory and thought.* Hillsdale, NJ: Erlbaum.

Anderson, R. C., & Pearson, P. D. (1984). A schema-theoretic view of basic processes in reading comprehension. In P. D. Pearson (Ed.), *Handbook of reading research* (pp. 255–291). New York: Longman.

Ash, D. (2003) Dialogic inquiry in life science conversations of family groups in museums. *Journal of Research in Science Teaching, 40*(2), 138–162.

Barron, B. (2003). When smart groups fail. *The Journal of the Learning Sciences, 12*, 307–359.

Barron, B. (2004). Learning ecologies for technological fluency: Gender and experience differences. *Journal of Educational Computing Research, 31*(1), 1–36.

Barron, B. (in press). Knowledge building processes across contexts: A learning ecologies perspective. To appear in *Human Development.*

Becker, H. S. (1953). Becoming a marihuana user. *American Journal of Sociology, 59*, 235–242.

Bereiter, C., & Scardamalia, M. (1989). Intentional learning as a goal of instruction. In L. B. Resnick (Ed.), *Knowing, learning, and instruction: Essays in honor of Robert Glaser* (pp. 361–392). Hillsdale, NJ: Erlbaum.

Bereiter, C., & Scardamalia, M. (1993). *Surpassing ourselves: An inquiry into the nature and implications of expertise.* Chicago, IL: Open Court.

Berliner, D. C. (1991). Educational psychology and pedagogical expertise: New findings and new opportunities for thinking about training. *Educational Psychologist, 26*(2), 145–155.

Berliner, D. C. (2001). Learning about and learning from expert teachers. International. *Journal of Educational Research, 35*(5), 463–468.

Berry, D. C. (1997). *How implicit is implicit learning?* New York: Oxford University Press.

Black, J., & Bower, G. (1980). Story understanding as problem-solving. *Poetics, 9*, 223–250.

Bransford, J. D., & Johnson, M. K. (1972). Contextual prerequisites for understanding: Some investigations of comprehension and recall. *Journal of Verbal Learning and Verbal Behavior, 11*, 717–726.

Bransford, J. D., & Schwartz, D. (1999). Rethinking transfer: A simple proposal with multiple implications. In A. Iran-Nejad & P. D. Pearson (Eds.), *Review of Research in Education* (Vol. 24, pp. 61–100). Washington, DC: American Educational Research Association.

Bransford, J., Vye, N., Stevens, R., Kuhl, P., Schwartz, D., Bell, P., Meltzoff, A., Barron,

B., Pea, R., Reeves, B., Roschelle, J., & Sabelli, N. (in press). Learning theories and education: Toward a decade of synergy. In P. Alexander & P. Winne (Eds.), *Handbook of educational psychology, 2 nd ed.* Mahwah, NJ: Erlbaum.

Brown, A. L., Bransford, J. D., Ferrara, R. A., & Campione, J. C. (1983). Learning, remembering, and understanding. In J. H. Flavell & E. M. Markman (Eds.), *Handbook of child psychology: Cognitive development* (Vol. 3, pp. 77–166). New York, NY: Wiley.

Bruer, J. T. (1997). Education and the brain: A bridge too far. *Educational Researcher, 26,* 4–16.

Chandler-Olcott, K., & Mahar (2003). "Tech-saviness" meets multiliteracies: Exploring adolescent girls' technology-mediated literacy practices. In *Reading Research Quarterly, 38,* 356–385.

Chase, W. G., & Simon, H. A. (1973). Perception in chess. *Cognitive Psychology, 1,* 33–81.

Cheour, M., Ceponiene, R., Lehtokoski, A., Luuk, A., Allik, J., Alho, K., et al. (1998). Development of language-specific phoneme representations in the infant brain. *Nature Neuroscience, 1,* 351–353.

Chi, M. T. H., Glaser, R., & Farr, M. (1988). *The nature of expertise.* Hillsdale, NJ: Erlbaum.

Chi, M. T. H., Glaser, R., & Rees, E. (1982). Expertise in problem solving. In R. J. Sternberg (Ed.), *Advances in the psychology of human intelligence,* (Vol. 1, pp. 1–75). Hillsdale, NJ: Erlbaum.

Cleeremans, A., Destrebecqz, A., & Boyer, M. (1998). Implicit learning: news from the front. *Trends in Cognitive Sciences, 2,* 406–416.

Cole, M. (1996). *Cultural psychology: A once and future discipline.* Cambridge, MA: Harvard University Press.

Cole, M., Gay, J., Glick, J., & Sharp, D. (1971). *The cultural context of learning and thinking.* New York: Basic Books.

Corsaro, W. (1985). *Friendship and peer culture in the early years.* Norwood, NJ: Ablex.

Crawford, V., Riel, M., & Schlager, M. (2005, April). *Characterizing adaptive expertise in biology teachers' reasoning.* Paper presented at the American Educational Research Association Annual Meeting, Montreal, Canada.

Crowley, K., & Jacobs, M. (2002). Islands of expertise and the development of family scientific literacy. In G. Leinhardt, K. Crowley & K. Knutson (Eds.), *Learning conversations in museums.* Mahwah, NJ: Erlbaum.

Darling-Hammond, L., & Bransford, J. D. (2005). *Preparing teachers for a changing world.* Washington, DC: The National Academy Press.

Decety, J., Jackson, P. L., Sommerville, J. A. Chaminade, T., & Meltzoff, A. N. (2004). The neural bases of cooperation and competition: an fMRI investigation. *NeuroImage, 23,* 744–751.

deGroot, A. D. (1965). *Thought and choice in chess.* The Hague, the Netherlands: Mouton.

Eckert, P. (1989). *Jocks and burnouts: Social identity in the high school.* New York: Teachers College Press.

Fortes, M. (1938) Social and psychological aspects of education in Taleland, *Africa,* Suppl., 11(4), 1–64.

Gee, J. P. (1996). *Social linguistics and literacies: Ideology in discourses.* Second Edition. London: Taylor & Francis.

Gentner, D., Brem, S., Ferguson, R. W., Markman, A. B., Levidow, B. B., Wolff, P., & Forbus, K. D. (1997). Analogical reasoning and conceptual change: A case study of Johannes Kepler. *Journal of the Learning Sciences, 6(1),* 3–40.

Goodsitt, J. V., Morgan, J. L., & Kuhl, P. K. (1993). Perceptual strategies in prelingual speech segmentation. *Journal of Child Language, 20,* 229–252.

Goodwin, C. (1994). Professional vision. *American Anthropologist, 96(3),* 606–633.

Goodwin, M. (1997). Children's linguistic and social worlds. *Anthropology Newsletter, 38(4),* 1, 3–4.

Gopnik, A., Meltzoff, A. N., & Kuhl, P. K. (1999). *The scientist in the crib: Minds, brains, and how children learn.* New York: William Morrow.

Greenfield, P. M., & Bruner, J. S. (1966). Culture and cognitive growth. *International Journal of Psychology, 1,* 89–107.

Greenwald, A. G., Banaji, M. R., Rudman, L. A., Farnham, S. D., Nosek, B. A., & Mellott, D. S. (2002). A unified theory of implicit attitudes, stereotypes, self-esteem, and self-concept. *Psychological Review, 109,* 3–25.

Greenough, W. T., Black, J. E., & Wallace, C. S. (1987). Experience and brain development. *Child Development, 58,* 539–559.

Hanna, E., & Meltzoff, A. N. (1993). Peer imitation by toddlers in laboratory, home, and day-care contexts: Implications for social learning and memory. *Developmental Psychology, 29,* 701–710.

Hargadon, A., & Sutton, R. I. (2000, May/June). Building an innovation factory. *Harvard Business Review*, pp. 157–166.

Hartup, W. W. (1996). The company they keep: friendships and their developmental significance. *Child Development*, 67, pp. 1–13.

Hatano, G. (2005, April). *Adaptive expertise.* Paper presented at the American Educational Research Association Annual Meeting, Montreal, Canada.

Hatano, G., & Inagaki, K. (1986). Two courses of expertise. In H. Stevenson, H. Azuma, & K. Hakuta (Eds.), *Child development and education in Japan* (pp. 262–272). New York: Freeman.

Hatano, G., & Osuro, Y. (2003). Commentary: Reconceptualizing school learning using insight from expertise research. *Educational Researcher*, 32, 26–29.

Holland, D., Lachicotte, W., Skinner, D., & Cain, C. (1998). *Identity and agency in cultural worlds.* Cambridge, MA: Harvard University Press.

Hull, G., & Schultz, K. (2001). Literacy and learning out of school. *Review of Educational Research*, 71 (4), 575–611.

Hutchins, E. (1995). *Cognition in the wild.* Cambridge, MA: MIT Press.

Iverson, P., Kuhl, P., Akahane-Yamada R., Diesch, E., Tohkura, Y., Ketterman, A., & Siebert, C. (2003). A perceptual interference account of acquisition difficulties for nonnative phonemes. *Cognition*, 87, B47–B57.

Joiner, M. J. (1996). "Just Girls": Literacy and allegiance in junior high school. *Written Communication*, 13, 93–129.

Karmiloff-Smith, A., & Inhelder, B. (1974) If you want to get ahead, get a theory. *Cognition*, 3 (3), 195–212.

Kuhl, P. K. (1991). Human adults and human infants show a "perceptual magnet effect" for the prototypes of speech categories, monkeys do not. *Perception & Psychophysics*, 50, 93–107.

Kuhl, P. K. (2004). Early language acquisition: Cracking the speech code. *Nature Reviews Neuroscience*, 5, 831–843.

Kuhl, P. K, Conboy, B. T., Padden, D., Nelson, T., & Pruitt, J. C. (2005). Early speech perception and later language development: Implications for the "critical period." *Language Learning and Development*, 1, 237–264.

Kuhl, P. K., Tsao, F.-M., & Liu, H.-M. (2003). Foreign-language experience in infancy: Effects of short-term exposure and social interaction on phonetic learning. *Proceedings of the National Academy of Sciences*, 100, 9096–9101.

Kuhl, P. K., Williams, K. A., Lacerda, F., Stevens, K. N., & Lindblom, B. (1992). Linguistic experience alters phonetic perception in infants by 6 months of age. *Science*, 255, 606–608.

Lajoie, S. (2003). Transitions and trajectories for studies of expertise. *Educational Researcher*, 32, 21–25.

Lave, J. (1988). *Cognition in practice: Mind, mathematics, and culture in everyday life.* Cambridge: Cambridge University Press.

Lave, J., & Wenger, E. (1991). *Situated learning: Legitimate peripheral participation.* Cambridge: Cambridge University Press.

Linn, M. C., Davis, E. A., & Bell, P. (2004). *Internet environments for science education.* Mahwah, NJ: Erlbaum.

Luria, A. R. (1971). Towards the problem of the historical nature of psychological processes. *International Journal of Psychology*, 6, 259–272.

Martin, T. (2005, April). *Measuring preparation for future learning in children's mathematics: Instructional implications.* Paper presented at the American Educational Research Association Annual Meeting, Montreal, Canada.

Martin, T., & Schwartz, D. L. (2005). Physically distributed learning: Adapting and reinterpreting physical environments in the development of fraction concepts. *Cognitive Science*, 29, 587–625.

McLaughlin, M., Irby, M. A., & Langman, J. (2001). Urban sanctuaries: neighborhood organizations in the lives and futures of inner-city youth. San Francisco: Jossey-Bass.

Mead, M. (1964). *Continuities in cultural evolution.* New Haven, CT: Yale University Press.

Meltzoff, A. N. (1988a). Imitation, objects, tools, and the rudiments of language in human ontogeny. *Human Evolution*, 3, 45–64.

Meltzoff, A. N. (1988b). Imitation of televised models by infants. *Child Development*, 59, 1221–1229.

Meltzoff, A. N. (2005). Imitation and other minds: The "like me" hypothesis. In S. Hurley & N. Chater (Eds.), *Perspectives on imitation: From neuroscience to social science* (Vol. 2, pp. 55–77). Cambridge, MA: MIT Press.

Meltzoff, A. N., & Decety, J. (2003). What imitation tells us about social cognition: A rapprochement between developmental psychology and cognitive neuroscience. *Philosophical Transactions of the Royal Society of London, Biological Sciences, 358*, 491–500.

Meltzoff, A. N., & Moore, M. K. (1977). Imitation of facial and manual gestures by human neonates. *Science, 198*, 75–78.

Michael, A. L., Klee, T., Bransford, J. D., & Warren, S. (1993). The transition from theory to therapy: Test of two instructional methods. *Applied Cognitive Psychology, 7*, 139–154.

Minsky, M. (1986). *Society of mind.* New York: Simon & Schuster.

Musen, G., & Triesman, A. (1990). Implicit and explicit memory for visual patterns. *Journal of Experimental Psychology: Learning, Memory, and Cognition, 16*, 127–137.

Nasir, N., & Saxe, G. (2003). Ethnic and academic identities: A cultural practice perspective on emerging tensions and their management in the lives of minority students. *Educational Researcher, 32* (5), 14–18.

Näätänen, R., Lehtokoski, A., Lennes, M., Cheour, M., Huotilainen, M., Iivonen, A., Vainio, M., Alku, P., Ilmoniemi, R. J., Luuk, A., Allik, J., Sinkkonen, J., & Alho, K. (1997). Language-specific phoneme representations revealed by electric and magnetic brain responses. *Nature, 385*, 432–434.

Nissen, M. J., & Bullemer, P. T. (1987). Attentional requirements for learning: Evidence from performance measures. *Cognitive Psychology, 19*, 1–32.

NRC/National Research Council (2000a). *How people learn: Brain, mind, experience, and school (Expanded Edition).* Washington, DC: National Academy Press.

NRC/National Research Council (2000b). *Neurons to neighborhoods.* Washington, DC: National Academy Press.

NRC/National Research Council (2003). *Learning and instruction: A SERP research agenda.* Washington, DC: National Academy Press.

NRC/National Research Council (2005). *How students learn: History, math, and science in the classroom.* Washington, DC: National Academies Press.

Pea, R. D. (1993). Practices of distributed intelligence and designs for education. In G. Salomon (Ed.). *Distributed cognitions.* New York: Cambridge University Press, pp. 47–87.

Pea, R. D. (2004). The social and technological dimensions of "scaffolding" and related theoretical concepts for learning, education and human activity. *The Journal of the Learning Sciences, 13*(3), 423–451.

Petrosino, A. (2005, April). *Measures of adaptive expertise in bioengineering.* Paper presented at the American Educational Research Association Annual Meeting, Montreal, Canada.

Povinelli, D. J., Reaux, J. E., Theall, L. A., & Giambrone, S. (2000). *Folk physics for apes: The chimpanzee's theory of how the world works.* New York: Oxford University Press.

Reber, A. S. (1967). Implicit learning of artifical grammars. *Journal of Verbal Learning and Verbal Behavior, 6*, 855–863.

Reber, A. S. (1976). Implicit learning of synthetic languages: The role of instructional set. *Journal of Experimental Psychology: Human Learning and Memory, 2*, 88–94.

Reber, A. S. (1993). *Implicit learning and tacit knowledge: An essay on the cognitive unconscious.* New York: Oxford University Press.

Resnick, L. (1987). Learning in school and out. *Educational Researcher, 16*(9), 3–21.

Rideout, V. J., Vandewater, E., & Wartella, E. A. (2003, Fall). *Zero to six: Electronic media in the lives of infants, toddlers and preschoolers.* Kaiser Family Foundation Report.

Rivera-Gaxiola, M., Silva-Pereyra, J., & Kuhl, P. K. (2005). Brain potentials to native and nonnative speech contrasts in 7- and 11-month-old American infants. *Developmental Science, 8*, 162–172.

Rizzolatti, G., Fadiga, L., Fogassi, L., & Gallese, V. (2002). From mirror neurons to imitation, facts, and speculations. In A. N. Meltzoff & W. Prinz (Eds.), *The imitative mind: Development, evolution, and brain bases* (pp. 247–266). Cambridge: Cambridge University Press.

Rogoff, B. (1990). *Apprenticeship in thinking: cognitive development in social context.* New York: Oxford University Press.

Rogoff, B. (2003). *The cultural nature of human development.* New York: Oxford University Press.

Rogoff, B., Paradise, R., Mejía Arauz, R., Correa-Chávez, M., & Angelillo, C. (2003). Firsthand learning by intent participation. *Annual Review of Psychology, 54*, 175–203.

Rose, M. (2004). *The mind at work: Valuing the intelligence of the American worker.* New York: Viking.

Saffran, J. R., Aslin, R. N., & Newport, E. L. (1996). Statistical learning by 8-month-old infants. *Science, 274*, 1926–1928.

Salomon, G., & Perkins, D. (1989). Rocky road to transfer: Rethinking mechanisms of a neglected phenomenon. *Educational Psychologist*, 24, 113–142.

Schank R., & Abelson R. (1977). *Scripts, plans, goals and understanding: An inquiry into human knowledge structures*. Hillsdale, NJ: Erlbaum Associates.

Schauble, L., Leinhardt, G., & Martin, L. (1998). Organizing a cumulative research agenda in informal learning contexts. *Journal of Museum Education*, 22 (2 & 3), 3–7.

Scribner, S., & Cole, M. (1973, 9 November). Cognitive consequences of formal and informal education. *Science*, 182, No. 4112, pp. 553–559.

Schwartz, D., Blair, K., Davis, J., Chang, J., & Hartman, K. (2005, April). *Iterative dynamic assessments with feedback to students*. Paper presented at the American Educational Research Association Annual Meeting, Montreal, Canada.

Schwartz, D. L., & Bransford, J. D. (1998). A time for telling. *Cognition & Instruction*, 16 (4), 475–522.

Schwartz, D., Bransford, J., & Sears, D. (2005). Efficiency and innovation in transfer. In J. Mestre (Ed.), *Transfer of learning: Research and perspectives* (pp. 1–52). Greenwich, CT: Information Age Publishing.

Schwartz, D. L., & Martin, T. (2004) Inventing to prepare for learning: The hidden efficiency of original student production in statistics instruction. *Cognition & Instruction*, 22, 129–184.

Simon, H. (1996). *The sciences of the artificial*, 3rd ed. Cambridge, MA: MIT Press.

Spiro, R. J., Vispoel, W. L., Schmitz, J., Samarapungavan, A., & Boeger, A. (1987). Knowledge acquisition for application: Cognitive flexibility and transfer in complex content domains. In B. C. Britton & S. Glynn (Eds.), *Executive control processes in reading* (pp. 177–199). Hillsdale, NJ: Lawrence Erlbaum Associates.

Sternberg, R. (2003). What is an "expert student"? *Educational Researcher*, 32, 5–9.

Stevens, R., & Hall, R. (1998). Disciplined perception: Learning to see in technoscience. In M. Lampert & M. L. Blunk (Eds.), *Talking mathematics in school: Studies of teaching and learning* (pp. 107–149). Cambridge: Cambridge University Press.

Strange, W. (1995). *Speech perception and linguistic experience: Issues in cross-language research*. Timonium, MD: York.

Tomasello, M. (1999). *The cultural origins of human cognition*. Cambridge, MA: Harvard University Press.

Tomasello, M., & Call, J. (1997). *Primate cognition*. New York: Oxford University Press.

Vaill, P. B. (1996). *Learning as a way of being: Strategies for survival in a world of permanent white water*. San Francisco, CA: Jossey-Bass

Vye, N. J., Schwartz, D. L., Bransford, J. D., Barron, B. J., Zech, L., & Cognition and Technology Group at Vanderbilt. (1998). SMART environments that support monitoring, reflection, and revision. In D. Hacker, J. Dunlosky, & A. C. Graesser (Eds.), *Metacognition in educational theory and practice* (pp. 305–346). Mahwah, NJ: Erlbaum.

Walker, J. (2005, April). *Design scenarios as a measure of adaptive understanding*. Paper presented at the American Educational Research Association Annual Meeting, Montreal, Canada.

Whiten, A. (2002). The imitator's representation of the imitated: Ape and child. In A. N. Meltzoff & W. Prinz (Eds.), *The imitative mind: Development, evolution, and brain bases* (pp. 98–121). Cambridge: Cambridge University Press.

Wineburg, S. (1998). Reading Abraham Lincoln: An expert/expert study in the interpretation of historical texts. *Cognitive Science*, 22 (3), 319–346.

Wood, D., Bruner, J., & Ross, G. (1976). The role of tutoring in problem solving. *Journal of child psychology and psychiatry*, 17, 89–100.

Zhang, Y., Kuhl, P. K., Imada, T., Kotani, M., & Tohkura, Y. (2005). Effects of language experience: Neural commitment to language-specific auditory patterns. *NeuroImage*, 26, 703–720.

CHAPTER 3

Constructionism

Yasmin B. Kafai

Learning sciences researchers are unified by their deep commitment to radically transform learning – away from the transmission and acquisition style associated with lectures and quizzes, to a more active, participatory learning style. Perhaps the first scholar to realize that computers provided schools with an opportunity to do so was Seymour Papert, who created the now-famous Logo programming language. Papert, who received two doctorates in mathematics, expanded his career by studying cognitive development with Jean Piaget, the founder of constructivism – one of the theoretical foundations of today's learning sciences. After leaving Piaget's lab in Switzerland, Papert took a faculty position at the Massachusetts Institute of Technology, where he cofounded the Artificial Intelligence Laboratory with Marvin Minsky. In the 1970s, Papert began to expand the psychological insights of Piaget's constructivism into pedagogical principles, providing a template that later influenced many learning sciences researchers.

When Papert's book *Mindstorms* was published in 1980 the term constructionism had

yet to be coined. In this book and subsequent publications he advanced a theory of learning, teaching, and design. Many took the notion of "children, computers and powerful ideas" (to quote the subtitle of his book) as a rather simplistic version of Piagetian discovery learning with the Logo programming language when, in fact, the opposite applied. Constructionism is not constructivism, as Piaget never intended his theory of knowledge development to be a theory of learning and teaching; nor is constructionist learning simply discovery learning and thus opposed to any forms of instruction; and last, in constructionism, people and not computers are seen as the driving force for educational change. Papert's constructionism views learning as building relationships between old and new knowledge, in interactions with others, while creating artifacts of social relevance. Thus any chapter on constructionism needs to begin with a clarification of three issues – constructivism, instructionism, and technocentrism – before delving any further into the theoretical and pedagogical particulars.

Constructionism's close resemblance to Piaget's constructivism often leads to confusion, yet there is a clear distinction between the two:

> [C]onstructionism – the N Word as opposed to the V word – shares constructivism's connotation to learning as building knowledge structures irrespective of the circumstances of learning. It then adds the idea that this happens especially felicitously in a context where the learner is consciously engaged in constructing a public entity whether it's a sand castle on the beach or a theory of the universe. (Papert, 1991, p.1)

Constructionism always has acknowledged its allegiance to Piagetian theory but it is not identical to it. Where constructivism places a primacy on the development of individual and isolated knowledge structures, constructionism focuses on the connected nature of knowledge with its personal and social dimensions. This combination of individual and social aspects in learning is at the heart of many discussions in the learning sciences.

The opposition of constructionism to instructionism often aligns constructionist learning with discovery learning – as learning without curriculum in which the child discovers principles or ideas by him or herself. A common myth associated with constructionism is the idea that all instruction is bad. A closer reading of Papert's original writings clarifies this issue:

> …but teaching without curriculum does not mean spontaneous, free-form classrooms or simply 'leaving the child alone'. It means supporting children as they build their own intellectual structures with materials drawn from the surrounding culture. In this model, educational intervention means changing the culture, planning new constructive elements in it and eliminating noxious ones. (p. 31, 1980/1993)

Constructionism has articulated a more distributed view of instruction, one where learning and teaching are constructed in interactions between the teacher and students as they are engaging in design and discussion of learning artifacts. Furthermore, such learning interactions are not limited to schools alone but extend into community centers and families. How to design learning environments that facilitate collaboration and idea sharing is a key focus of many efforts in the learning sciences.

The Logo programming language has always been closely associated with constructionism, and this has led many to believe that constructionism sees technology as the driving force for how we teach and learn. Yet, as Papert argued, this type of technocentric thinking assigns more importance than is appropriate to technology as an agent of change:

> Does wood produce good houses? If I built a house out of wood and it fell down, would this show that wood does not produce good houses? Do hammers and saws produce good furniture? These questions betray themselves as technocentric questions by ignoring people and elements that only people can introduce: skill, design, and aesthetics. (p. 24, 1987)

Constructionism challenges us to reconsider our notions of learning and teaching. Programming with Logo provided a testing bed for engaging students in problem solving and learning to learn. Moreover, programming in Logo also illustrated conceptually different ways of learning mathematics and science with computers. Many of these challenges to learning and teaching continue to be relevant in the learning sciences, whether or not computers are involved.

The goal of this chapter is, then, to articulate more clearly a constructionist perspective on the nature of knowing, teaching, and learning. In the first part, I review the historical roots of constructionism using Logo as an example and move on to discuss key constructionist ideas around knowledge construction, learning cultures, and the application of knowledge construction to the design of microworlds and construction kits. I then present a case study of software learning through design activities that illustrate the implementation of core constructionist ideas. In conclusion, I address outstanding issues and challenges in constructionism and in the field of the learning sciences.

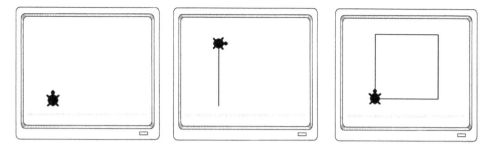

Figure 3.1. The screen shot to the left shows a turtle in starting position ready to be programmed. In the middle screen, the turtle has been programmed to execute the following steps: PEN DOWN FORWARD 10 RIGHT TURN 90. The right screen shows the drawing of a square by having the turtle repeat the commands four times or REPEAT 4 [FORWARD 10 RIGHT TURN 90].

The Historical Roots

In any historical account of constructionism the programming language Logo is the "evocative object" – to use a phrase coined by Sherry Turkle (Turkle, 1995) – for it embodies the issues that fueled many debates about computers in schools in the early 1980s. At that time, the computer was ready to move out of the university laboratories into the world, but computer work was seen as the exclusive domain of adults. Logo was not the first programming language used by children. Basic was prominent in many schools and indeed there was considerable debate about which programming language would be best for schools. But in contrast to Basic, learning with Logo promised to offer more than just learning to program: it included learning about your own thinking and learning, and learning mathematics and science in conceptually new ways. These additions made Logo unlike any other programming language.

The first feature to note about Logo is how learners interacted with the computer: children were writing commands to move a graphical object – called the turtle – on the screen, rather than to manipulate array of numbers or symbols (see Figure 3.1, left). Programming the computer meant programming the turtle. A programmer would give commands for the turtle such as "move forward ten steps and then turn 90 degrees to the right" which in Logo would be "FORWARD 10 RIGHT 90" (see Figure 3.1, middle). The turtle would then move on the screen and thus provide visual feedback on whether or not the program was correct. In addition, the turtle carried a pen with which it could draw, leaving a trace of its steps. The commands "PEN DOWN FORWARD 10 RIGHT 90," executed four times, would result in the drawing of a square on the computer screen (see Figure 3.1, right).

The second feature to note is that the Logo turtle served as a first representative of formal mathematics for children because they could bring to bear their body knowledge on how to move the screen turtle. Consider the following commands, in which the turtle moves one step forward, then moves one degree to the right, and then repeats this procedure 360 times: REPEAT 360 [FORWARD 1 RIGHT 1]. With the pen down, these commands draw a circle on the screen. A child, using his own body, pretending to be the turtle, could execute every single one of these steps. Papert attributed great importance to this feature, which he called *syntonic* learning, because it allowed children to identify with the computational object in multiple ways:

For example, the Turtle circle is body syntonic in that the circle is firmly related to children's sense and knowledge about their own bodies. Or it is ego syntonic in that it is coherent with children's sense of themselves as people with intentions, goals, desires, likes and dislikes. . . . One can also see it as cultural syntonic *in that when drawing the circle, the turtle connects the idea of an angle to the idea of navigation which is closely rooted in children's extracurricular experiences.* (1980/1993, pp. 63–68)

The Logo turtle allowed children to manipulate objects on the screen as they would manipulate them in the physical world. Thus, turtle geometry provided a concrete entrance into the formal world of mathematics and allowed learners to connect their personal experiences to mathematical concepts and operations.

A third and equally important feature of Logo programming is the idea of children learning about their own thinking and learning, called reflection or metacognition. Papert claimed that in learning programming, children learn to articulate procedures, recognize repetition, and "debug" their own thinking when programs don't run as expected: "But thinking about learning by analogy with developing a program is a powerful and accessible way to get started on becoming more articulate about one's debugging strategies and more deliberate about improving them" (p. 23, 1980/1993). Computer programs can become "objects-to-think-with" that help children reflect on their performance in ways similar to experienced learners.

Learning Logo thus combined multiple purposes: learning to program, learning mathematics, and learning to learn. These claims did not remain uncontested. So much has been written about the success or failure of Logo in schools that it's worth providing some background to the debate. In an excellent analysis of the historical context in the United States and in Europe, Richard Noss and Celia Hoyles (1996) identify some of the larger cultural forces at play that led critics to ask certain questions about Logo and not others. In many schools, questions about Logo's learning benefits focused exclusively on the transfer of problem solving skills and less on the benefits of learning mathematics and pedagogical reform ideas. A series of smaller studies conducted by Roy Pea and

Midian Kurland (1984) is often referenced as the sole evidence that learning Logo programming did not produce any transferable effects. These studies had several methodological issues; for example, neglecting to consider the length of time spent learning programming and the type of programs created. These features have now been recognized as instrumental in designing successful programming instruction (Palumbo, 1990) and I discuss them in more detail in a later section on software design for learning. A further problem has been that teachers often adopt Logo but not the pedagogical innovations for learning mathematics and science; and even if they did, many did not receive widespread institutional support in their schools for doing so (Papert, 1991, 1997). Many institutional forces shaped the use of Logo in schools, and the result was often that its constructionist ideas about learning and teaching were the least acknowledged.

Key Ideas in Constructionism

The name "constructionism" brings to mind the metaphor of learning by constructing one own's knowledge, and is often contrasted to the more traditional "instructionism," which favors the metaphor of learning by transmission of knowledge. Although these two metaphors offer a versatile summary, it is worthwhile to unpack the constructionist idea of knowledge construction and examine its individual and social dynamics. We will then move to the notion of learning cultures and address which features of a learning environment promote successful knowledge construction.

Knowledge Construction

The idea of constructing one's own knowledge draws heavily from Piaget's theory of knowledge development and his instrumental insight that children understand the world in fundamentally different ways than adults. He identified two mechanisms, assimilation and accommodation, that explained how children made sense of the world they interacted with and how they integrated these experiences into their understanding. Constructionism builds on these mechanisms, and focuses on the processes that help learners make connections with what they already know. A key aspect in knowledge construction is *appropriation* – how learners make knowledge their own and begin to identify with it. These appropriations go beyond the intellectual and include emotional values.

According to Papert, physical objects play a central role in this knowledge construction process. He coined the term "objects-to-think-with" as an illustration of how objects in the physical and digital world (such as programs, robots, and games) can become objects in the mind that help to construct, examine, and revise connections between old and new knowledge. "Objects-to-think-with" such as the Logo turtle are particularly effective at supporting appropriation, because they facilitate the child's identification with the object, or syntonic learning.

Constructionism further differs from the Piagetian model in equally valuing the concrete and the abstract. In Piaget's stage theory, formal abstraction is seen as the ultimate goal of all knowledge construction, with concrete thinking always associated with younger, less advanced children. Turkle and Papert (1990) instead argue that concrete thought could be just as advanced as abstract thought. The sciences in general, but the computer culture in particular, have tended to value abstract thinking. But in studying programmers, Turkle and Papert discovered that the officially promoted top-down or planning approach was not always superior to a more improvised, more bricoleur-like approach. The bricoleur style is not a stepping stone towards more advanced forms of knowledge construction, but rather is a qualitatively different way of organizing one's planning and problem solving.

In sum, knowledge construction is "the deliberate part of learning [which] consists of making connections between mental entities that already exist; new mental entities seem to come into existence in more subtle ways that escape conscious control. . . . This suggests a strategy to facilitate learning by improving the connectivity in the learning environment, by actions on cultures rather than on individuals" (p. 105, Papert, 1993).

Learning Cultures

The importance of learning cultures was informed by Papert's observations of children's difficulties in understanding and learning mathematics. Piagetian studies indicated that all young children develop their first fundamental mathematical concepts, but many struggle in later school years. In his book *Mindstorms*, Papert offered Brazilian samba schools as one possible image for a learning culture:

> [t]hese are not schools as we know them; they are social clubs with memberships that may range from a few hundred to many thousands. Each club owns a building, a place for dancing and getting together. Members of a samba school go there most weekend evenings to dance, to drink, and to meet their friends. During the year each samba school chooses its theme for the next carnival, the stars are selected, the lyrics are written and rewritten, and the dance is choreographed and practiced. Members of the school range in age from children to grandparents and in ability from novice to professional. But they dance together and as they dance everyone is learning and teaching as well as dancing. Even the stars are there to learn their difficult parts. (1980/1993, p. 178)

Papert's idea of a learning culture has been developed in several directions, from neighborhood centers to virtual worlds. The Computer Clubhouse (Resnick, Rusk, & Cooke, 1998), for instance, is an outside of school learning culture that is located in after school programs and community centers. In these clubhouses, youth convene at their own volition and learn to work with creative software applications to produce digital graphics, music, and videos. Unlike schools, the activities in the clubhouse do not follow a set curriculum, and members are responsible for introducing each other to new activities, with the support of coordinators and mentors. Other examples include multi-user online environments in which community members contribute to the design of various elements of the online world by populating it with objects and houses, such as Bruckman's MOOSE Crossing (this volume).

What stands out in these examples of the samba school, Computer Clubhouse, and MOOSE Crossing is the rich set of interactions between different community members. These instructional interactions are not formulated in the one-directional pathway of traditional classrooms; rather, they draw on apprenticeship models (see also Collins, this volume) in which all members of the community of practice contribute to the larger enterprise (Lave & Wenger, 1991). Although sociocultural researchers emphasize the social dynamics of learning cultures, constructionists focus on how the social context provides opportunities for making connections to what is being learned.

Logo Microworlds and Construction Kits

The programming language Logo provided a programmable object, the turtle, to facilitate learners' constructing relationships with mathematical concepts and their own thinking in the context of programming. *Microworlds* and *construction kits* have expanded on different aspects of Logo to promote learning in mathematics and science. These applications illustrate how the design of computer applications can be driven by constructionist theory.

Microworlds

Microworlds have been described as "a computer-based interactive learning environment where the prerequisites are built into the system and where learners can become the active, constructing architects of their own learning" (Papert, 1980/1993, p. 122). A classic example is the Dynaturtle, a physics environment in which learners can experience Newtonian physics, and also historically important alternatives like Aristotelian physics. Movements and states of turtles can be preprogrammed to respond to certain laws of motion that can be manipulated by the learner. No explicit instruction about the laws is provided in microworlds, unlike in computer-based tutorials or computer-assisted instruction. Learners induce these laws by interacting with a turtle preprogrammed to behave as an object in a frictionless universe.

Further developments have expanded Logo into massively parallel microworlds on the computer; instead of one turtle, now hundreds or even thousands can interact. In StarLogo (Resnick, 1991), a circle would no longer be drawn by one turtle, but instead by dozens of turtles following two simple rules: (1) to keep a specific distance from each other and (2) to repel the group as a whole and move away from other turtles (see Figure 3.2).

This version of Logo connects to another emergent discipline, that of complex system design, which is interested in how complex behavior patterns emerge from interactions between many simple objects. Many natural and human phenomena can be described this way, as Mitchel Resnick argues in his book *Turtles, Termites, and Traffic Jams* (1994). Working with StarLogo offers learners the opportunity to explore the probabilistic patterns in complex interactions in the same way as the turtle in Logo offers learners an opportunity to connect to formal mathematical objects in new ways (Resnick & Wilensky, 1998). StarLogo can provide accessible objects-to-think-with for people to examine emergence in complex systems.

Microworlds are the prototypical constructionist learning environment for the following reasons. First, scientific and mathematical microworlds offer access to ideas and phenomena – such as the frictionless world – that students may not easily encounter in their regular textbooks or classroom lessons. Second, they provide environments that challenge naïve understandings by providing the learner with feedback on their interactions and manipulations. Third, these interactions with the microworld allow the learner to develop personal knowledge that can provide the foundation for more formalized interactions. Last, microworlds create a type

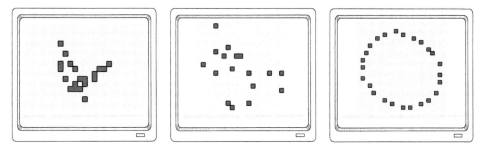

Figure 3.2. These screen shots show a new way to create a circle with StarLogo. No single turtle draws the circle. Rather, the turtles arrange themselves into a circle, based on their interactions with one another. Each turtle follows two simple rules: (1) it tries to keep a certain distance from each of its two "neighbors," and (2) it gently "repels" the group as a whole, trying to move away from the other turtles. With these two rules, the turtles arrange themselves into a circle. (Adapted with permission from the StarLogo Web site at http://education.mit.edu/starlogo/.)

of learning environment in which talking about mathematics (or science) is part of the classroom peer culture. The turtle world in Logo is "a 'place', 'a province of Mathland' where certain kinds of mathematical thinking could hatch and grow with ease. The microworld was an incubator" (Papert, 1980/1993, p. 125). A wide range of microworlds in mathematics and science has been developed since then, and not all of them are Logo-based environments (for more examples of microworlds and further developments see diSessa, 2000; Edwards, 1998; Noss & Hoyles, 1996, this volume).

Construction Kits

LEGO™ building blocks and the programming language Logo were combined to create computationally enhanced construction kits that allow children to explore engineering and architectural design. For example, LEGO™ bricks have been equipped with motors and sensors and a control language to combine the physical and the digital worlds (Resnick & Ocko, 1991). LEGO™/Logo draws on the constructionist tradition of using materials and activities that are already part of children's experiences, but enriches them with computational elements and brings engineering and robotics activities into the classroom and home.

The LEGO™/Logo computational bricks have been employed in a variety of educational contexts, ranging from homes to college classrooms. The Mindstorms robotics competitions, now a part of many high school and college classrooms, specify a goal for the robot, and then give teams a limited amount of time and resources to build a robot out of LEGO™ bricks with motors and sensors; at the end of the time period, the teams test their designs in a competition. One study that followed the students through this process found that this type of combined engineering and programming activity provided the students with hands-on and team experience (Martin, 1996, 2001). In traditional classes college students often have difficulty translating and applying their textbook knowledge into actual robotic design and learning to make distinctions between ideal and real systems.

A further development moves the LEGO™/Logo brick concept into new territory by taking traditional toys such as balls and beads and providing them with computational enhancements (Resnick, 1998). Adding sensors and feedback mechanism to these toys provides them with different interaction possibilities. Providing programmable interfaces lets children not just play with but also design these toys. Another direction is the computational crafts development, which takes traditional craft activities such as origami and uses the computer for the design of materials that can be printed on paper and used for play (Eisenberg, 2003). The design and creation of such polygonic objects gives children experience with different geometry concepts.

The research group around Seymour Papert at the MIT Media Lab, along with many others, has developed, implemented, and examined different examples of constructionist learning cultures and technologies. A more extensive collection of examples and further theoretical papers can be found in two books published by members of the group, *Constructionism* (Harel & Papert, 1991) and *Constructionism in Practice* (Kafai & Resnick, 1996).

Software Design for Learning – A Constructionist Learning Environment

Design activities play a central role in constructionism. They can facilitate knowledge construction, reformulation, and expression in the process of building shareable artifacts such as robots, software, and games. The *Instructional Software Design Project* (hereafter: ISDP; Harel, 1990; Harel & Papert, 1991) provides an example of how students can engage in these processes as they design instructional software to teach fractions to younger students in their schools – a topic that they were learning about in mathematics class. Classroom practices included students writing in notebooks about their software and instructional designs, discussing fraction representations in class, inviting prospective users for feedback sessions, and conducting software review sessions guided by the teacher.

The curricular model of ISDP responded to several of the criticisms of previous Logo research (Palumbo, 1990). First, it situated the daily programming activities in the classroom rather than in a distant computer laboratory visited only once a week. Second, it integrated the learning of programming with other subject matter such as the learning of fractions, rather than keeping programming isolated from the rest of curriculum. Finally, students were asked to create a meaningful artifact, such as an instructional piece of software to teach younger students in their school, rather than to produce small pieces of program code with no authentic purpose.

The analysis of the ISDP outcomes provided compelling evidence of the benefits for both learning fractions and learning programming, especially when compared to two other classes at the same school that either had programming only once a week or daily but without the focus of creating instructional fraction software. In all these comparisons, ISDP students improved significantly – not only in their programming skills but also in their conceptual and procedural understanding of fractions. The instructional software designed by students illustrated personal choices in representations that students created for their learners. Individual interviews also revealed increased metacognitive competence in juggling the multiple demands of learning by design (see Kolodner, this volume). In addition, ISDP students showed increased persistence in debugging Logo programming problems and in their ability to manage the multiple learning demands of software design. The importance of having students create shareable artifacts such as instructional software is one example of the increased attention that the learning sciences are paying to providing authentic learning activities, products, and tools in learning environments. In addition, the provision of an audience other than the teacher for the learning products is another important feature of many learning sciences projects.

Building on the successful design of the first ISDP version, a subsequent version added an apprenticeship component that illustrates how connections across grade levels can help to create a learning culture. Collaborative interactions are a key component of many environments and curricula in the learning sciences. By setting up software design teams rather than individual designers, and composing teams of students with and without prior software design experience, we showed that young designers can bring to bear their previous software design experiences in multiple ways: by initiating and expanding science conversations in groups (Kafai & Ching, 2001), by helping younger inexperienced team members with planning their instructional designs (Marshall, 2000), and by providing

Figure 3.3. Fraction game designs by a girl. The three screen shots showcase Amy's Greek Myths fraction game in which a player has to assemble a map ripped into pieces to finally meet the gods and goddesses of fractions at Mount Olympus. The left screen displays a fraction problem whereas the middle and right screens show game components of Mount Olympus and a meeting with gods and goddesses of fractions.

programming assistance when needed (Ching, 2000).

In a comparison study (Ching, 2000) with software design teams of only inexperienced older and younger students, we found that the quality of collaborative helping interactions also shifted dramatically: teams with experienced software designers provided more collaborative assistance rather than taking over programming tasks, provided room for making mistakes while still monitoring programming activities, and provided more access to computer resources when needed for less experienced members. Our analyses indicated that experience and not age was a decisive factor in how student designers handled programming and collaborative interactions. Apprenticeship, as a model for collaborative interactions, was key in distributing responsibilities in teams and in the classroom with the teacher.

But the most important finding resulted from the analysis of apprenticeship interactions in teams when comparing both setups. Students working with experienced team members were provided with more flexible and collaborative work arrangements. In contrast, students working with older inexperienced students were often put in more supervised activities and not involved in programming activities; their opportunities to develop independent programming skills were largely reduced because older team members directed all their activities, trying to prevent mistakes. These different teams also resulted in different understandings of roles in the projects. Experienced software

designers addressed a much richer set of roles involving planning, helping, teaching, and understanding younger students' concerns and anxieties. These perceptions also change over time, as found in one of the few longitudinal examinations of long-term programming learning (Kafai & Roberts, 2002).

Although instructional software design is safely grounded in school culture, whether it's purchased in the form of commercial software or designed by the students themselves, entertainment media like video games often do not enter the classroom. In a continuation of the ISDP project, a class of ten-year-old children was asked to design and program their own video games. The children met every day over a period of six months to design games by creating their own characters, story lines, game themes, and interactions. Here again, we found benefits in learning programming when compared to other classes not engaged in extended programming (Kafai, 1995).

It is worthwhile to take a closer look at the games created by the students and examine them as microworlds from an instructional and game perspective (Kafai, 1996). The game design activity offered a microworld in which both girls and boys could situate their preferred ideas and fantasies. The most distinctive feature, however, is the degree to which gender differences permeate nearly all aspects of game design. Nearly all the games created by boys featured fantasy contexts, with many characters and violent feedback, when compared to the games designed by girls (see Figures 3.3 and 3.4).

Figure 3.4. Fraction game designs by a boy. Albert designed a haunted house fraction game in which a player explored the different rooms of a house such as the one displayed in the right screen shot. When he opens the treasure chest, a demon jumps out and asks a fraction question (middle screen). A wrong answer choice sends the player to the underworld, eating fried food for the remainder of his life.

Almost all of the boys, for example, created adventure hunts and explorations, whereas the girls' games were more evenly divided among adventure, skill/sport, or teaching. In their choices of game themes and their programming of animation and interactions, the students offered a glimpse into what they found appealing and unappealing in the games and stories they experience through other media. Making a game and its rules allowed the game designers to be in charge and to determine the player's place and role in a virtual world, with all the consequences.

Unlike the microworlds discussed in previous sections, the nature of pedagogical interactions favored by most student designers was that of drill-and-practice. Nearly all games featured multiple-choice questions and expected the prospective learner to provide the answers. There were few constructive elements for learners in these games. We found in follow-up research that children do have models for constructive game activities, but often assume that teaching is about asking questions and learning is about giving answers (Kafai, Franke, Ching, & Shih, 1998).

Under Construction

Constructionism presents a particular combination of individualistic, cognitive processes – with its emphasis on personal appropriation and knowledge construction – and of more social, cultural processes – with its focus on the design of and participation in learning cultures. Microworlds and construction kits have become constructionism's most popular educational software because they combine both cultural and personal aspects. They are cultural because they embody particular disciplinary ideas, and they are personal because they allow for individualized expression of these ideas.

One aspect that deserves further treatment concerns the development of knowledge and its personal connections. I have discussed the importance of connectedness in the process of constructing knowledge, of connecting new ideas to old existing ones, and of facilitating the building of personal relationships with knowledge. Yet in the learning sciences, this aspect is still lacking attention. Learning is often portrayed as a matter of developing disciplinary understanding and practices in the sciences. The learning sciences often build on motivation in their project-based approaches (see Blumenfeld, Kemplar, & Krajcik, this volume) but they do not address "knowledge as desire" as Hans Furth (1987) once articulated in his provocative essay integrating Piagetian and Freudian perspectives to combine cognitive and emotional aspects of learning. Future research needs to expand these combinations of disciplinary practices and interest to develop a better understanding of how learning can tie into the socioemotional personal lives of learners.

The concept of learning cultures has provided a helpful metaphor in designing successful learning environments. Many learning scientists model their learning environments on studies of how professional practice takes place. But in doing this, they necessarily choose one particular model of professional practice, while in most professions, there are multiple approaches in use. For example, many professional programmers use a top-down, more abstract style, and in fact this style is taught in engineering schools. But other successful programmers use a more concrete, bricoleur style. If learning scientists design classrooms based on only one model of professional practice, they risk misrepresenting the full range of successful practices. This has a particular impact on the issue of gender representation in science, mathematics, and engineering, because females often prefer approaches that do not correspond to the officially valued practices in the profession. Research in the sciences has provided ample evidence of nonvalued but equally successful practices as in the case of the Nobel Prize–winner Barbara McClintock (Keller, 1983). The issue at hand is then what kind of images of a learning culture and of practices do we follow and where might we create new ones – especially if we are interested in having learners not just follow the beaten path but create new venues. This is a challenge for the next generation of tools and environments in the learning sciences.

To conclude, in this chapter I examined key aspects of how we can design constructionist learning environments, technologies, and activities that create supportive learning cultures. Microworlds and construction kits illustrated that the design of learning technologies comes wrapped in a theory of mind coupled with disciplinary understanding. Many developments in the learning sciences are influenced by this premise and continue to develop variations on microworlds and construction kits with additional scaffolds to support learners' inquiry, collaboration, and reflection processes (see the chapters in this volume by Edelson & Reiser; Noss & Hoyles; Pea & Maldonado; Stahl, Koschmann, & Suthers). Software design for learning illustrated that

technologies need to be integrated within a larger learning culture. Many curricular efforts in the learning sciences have adopted project-based learning approaches to create motivating and authentic contexts for learners to develop and practice their skills (e.g., Krajcik & Blumenfeld, this volume; Linn; Scardamalia & Bereiter, this volume; Songer, this volume). Constructionist theory challenges us to consider individual and sociocultural aspects in the design and investigation of the learning sciences.

Acknowledgments

The author's work described in the chapter was supported by an EARLY CAREER grant of the National Science Foundation (NSF-9632695). The writing of this chapter was supported in part by a grant of the National Science Foundation (NSF-0325828). The views expressed are those of the author and do not necessarily represent the views of the supporting funding agency or the University of California, Los Angeles.

References

Ching, C. C. (2000). *Apprenticeship, learning and technology: Children as oldtimers and newcomers in the culture of learning through design.* Unpublished doctoral dissertation. University of California, Los Angeles.

diSessa, A. (2000). *Changing minds: Computers, Learning and Literacy.* Cambridge, MA: MIT Press.

Edwards, L. (1998). Embodying mathematics and science: Microworlds as representations. *Journal of Mathematical Behavior, 17*(1), 53–78.

Eisenberg, M. (2003). Mindstuff: Educational technology beyond the computer. *Convergence, 4,* 45–76.

Furth, H. G. (1987). *Knowledge as desire: An essay on Freud and Piaget.* New York: Columbia University Press.

Harel, I. (1990). *Children designers.* Norwood, NJ: Ablex.

Harel, I., & Papert, S. (1991). Software design as a learning environment. *Interactive Learning Environments, 1*(1), 1–30.

Kafai, Y. B. (1995). *Minds in play: Computer game design as a context for children's learning*. Hillsdale, NJ: Lawrence Erlbaum Associates.

Kafai, Y. B. (1996). Gender differences in children's constructions of video games. In Patricia M. Greenfield & Rodney R. Cocking (Eds.), *Interacting with video* (pp. 39–66). Norwood, NJ: Ablex Publishing Corporation.

Kafai, Y. B., & Ching, C. C. (2001). Affordances of collaborative software design planning for elementary students' science talk. *The Journal of the Learning Sciences*, 10(3), 323–363.

Kafai, Y. B., Franke, M., Ching, C., & Shih, J. (1998). Games as interactive learning environments fostering teachers' and students' mathematical thinking. *International Journal of Computers for Mathematical Learning*, 3(2), 149–193.

Kafai, Y. B., & Resnick, M. (1996). *Constructionism in practice*. Mahwah, NJ: Lawrence Erlbaum Associates.

Kafai, Y. B., & Roberts, M. (2002). On becoming junior software designers. In R. Stevens & P. Bell (Eds.), *Proceedings of the Fifth International Conference on the Learning Sciences* (pp. 191–198). Mahwah, NJ: Erlbaum.

Keller, E. F. (1983). *A feeling for the organism: The life and work of Barbara McClintock*. San Francisco: W. H. Freeman.

Lave, J., & Wenger, E. (1991). *Situated learning: Legitimate peripheral participation*. London: Cambridge University Press.

Marshall, S. (2000). *Planning in context: A situated view of children's management of science projects*. Unpublished doctoral dissertation. University of California, Los Angeles.

Martin, F. (1996). Ideal and real systems: A study of notions of control in undergraduates who design robots. In Y. Kafai & M. Resnick (Eds.), *Constructionism in practice* (pp. 255–268). Mahwah, NJ: Lawrence Erlbaum Associates.

Martin, F. (2001). *Robotic Explorations: A Hands-on introduction to engineering*. New York: Prentice Hall.

Noss, R., & Hoyles, C. (1996). *Windows on mathematical meanings: Learning cultures and computers*. Dordrecht: Kuwer Academic Publishers.

Palumbo, D. (1990). Programming language/problem-solving research: A review of relevant issues. *Review of Educational Research*, 45, 65–89.

Papert, S. (1980/1993). *Mindstorms* (2nd ed.). New York: Basic Books.

Papert, S. (1987). Computer criticism versus technocentric thinking. *Educational Researcher*, 16(1), 24–28.

Papert, S. (1991). Situating constructionism. In I. Harel & S. Papert (Eds.), *Constructionism* (pp. 1–14). Hillsdale, NJ: Lawrence Erlbaum Associates.

Papert, S. (1993). *The children's machine: Rethinking school in the age of the computer*. New York: Basic Books.

Papert, S. (1997). Tinkering towards utopia: A century of public school reform. *Journal of the Learning Sciences*, 6(4), 417–427.

Pea, R., & Kurland, M. (1984). On the cognitive effects of learning computer programming. *New Ideas in Psychology*, 2(2), 137–168.

Resnick, M. (1991). New paradigms for computing, new paradigms for thinking. In Y. Kafai & M. Resnick (Eds.), *Constructionism in Practice* (pp. 255–268). Mahwah, NJ: Lawrence Erlbaum Associates.

Resnick, M. (1994). *Turtles, Termites, and Traffic Jams*. Cambridge, MA: MIT Press.

Resnick, M. (1998). Technologies for life long learning. In *Educational Technology, Research & Development*, 46(4), 43–55.

Resnick, M., & Ocko, S. (1991). LEGO/Logo: Learning through and about design. In I. Harel & S. Papert (Eds.), *Constructionism* (pp. 141–150). Hillsdale, NJ: Lawrence Erlbaum Associates.

Resnick, M., Rusk, N., & Cooke, S. (1998). The computer clubhouse: Technological fluency in the inner-city. In D. Schon, B. Sanyal, & W. Mitchell (Eds.), *High Technology and Low Income Communities* (pp. 266–286). Cambridge, MA: MIT Press.

Resnick, M., & Wilensky, U. (1998). Diving into complexity: Developing probabilistic decentralized thinking through role-playing activities. *Journal of the Learning Sciences*, 7(2), 153–172.

Turkle, S. (1995). *Life on the screen: Identity in the age of the Internet*. New York: Simon & Schuster.

Turkle, S., & Papert, S. (1990). Epistemological pluralism and the reevaluation of the concrete. *Signs*, 16(1), 128–157.

CHAPTER 4

Cognitive Apprenticeship

Allan Collins

Throughout most of history, teaching and learning have been based on apprenticeship. Children learned how to speak, grow crops, construct furniture, and make clothes. But they didn't go to school to learn these things; instead, adults in their family and in their communities showed them how, and helped them do it. Even in modern societies, we learn some important things through apprenticeship: we learn our first language from our families, employees learn critical job skills in the first months of a new job, and scientists learn how to conduct world-class research by working side-by-side with senior scientists as part of their doctoral training. But for most other kinds of knowledge, schooling has replaced apprenticeship. The number of students pursuing an education has dramatically increased in the last two centuries, and it gradually became impossible to use apprenticeship on the large scale of modern schools. Apprenticeship requires a very small teacher-to-learner ratio, and this is not realistic in the large educational systems of modern industrial economies.

Even in modern societies, when someone has the resources and a strong desire to learn, they often hire a coach or tutor to teach them by apprenticeship – demonstrating that apprenticeship continues to be more effective even in modern societies. If there were some way to tap into the power of apprenticeship, without incurring the large costs associated with hiring a teacher for every two or three students, it could be a powerful way to improve schools. In the 1970s and 1980s, I was doing research at the intersection of education and new computer technology, and along with many other scholars, I was studying how this new technology could help us to transform schooling. Working with my colleague John Seely Brown, we began to believe that we could develop sophisticated computer-based learning environments that could provide students with apprenticeship-like experiences, providing the type of close attention and immediate response that has always been associated with apprenticeship.

From Traditional to Cognitive Apprenticeship

In her study of a tailor shop in Africa, Lave identified the central features of traditional apprenticeship (Lave, 1988). First, traditional apprenticeship focuses closely on the specific methods for carrying out tasks in a domain. Second, skills are instrumental to the accomplishment of meaningful real-world tasks, and learning is embedded in a social and functional context, unlike schooling, where skills and knowledge are usually abstracted from their use in the world. Apprentices learn domain-specific methods through a combination of what Lave called observation, coaching, and practice. In this sequence of activities, the apprentice repeatedly observes the master and his or her assistants executing (or modeling) the target process, which usually involves a number of different, but interrelated subskills. The apprentice then attempts to execute the process with guidance and help from the master (i.e., coaching). A key aspect of coaching is guided participation: the close responsive support which the master provides to help the novice complete an entire task, even before the novice has acquired every skill required. As the learner masters increasing numbers of the component skills, the master reduces his or her participation, providing fewer hints and less feedback to the learner. Eventually, the master fades away completely, when the apprentice has learned to smoothly execute the whole task.

Of course, most of us think of very traditional trades when we hear the term "apprenticeship" – like shoemaking or farming. John Seely Brown and I realized that the concept of apprenticeship had to be updated to make it relevant to modern subjects like reading, writing, and mathematics. We called this updated concept of apprenticeship "cognitive apprenticeship" to emphasize two issues (Brown, Collins, & Duguid, 1989; Collins, Brown, & Newman, 1989).

First, the term "apprenticeship" emphasized that cognitive apprenticeship was aimed primarily at teaching processes that experts use to handle complex tasks. Like traditional apprenticeship, cognitive apprenticeship emphasizes that knowledge must be used in solving real-world problems. Conceptual knowledge and factual knowledge are learned by being used in a variety of contexts, encouraging both a deeper understanding of the meaning of the concepts and facts themselves, and a rich web of memorable associations between them and the problem solving contexts. This dual focus on expert processes and learning in context are shared by both traditional apprenticeship and cognitive apprenticeship.

Second, "cognitive" emphasizes that the focus is on cognitive skills and processes, rather than physical ones. Traditional apprenticeship evolved to teach domains in which the process of carrying out target skills is externally visible, and thus readily available to both student and teacher for observation, comment, refinement, and correction, and the process bears a relatively transparent relationship to concrete products. But given the way that most subjects are taught and learned in school, teachers cannot make fine adjustments in students' application of skill and knowledge to problems and tasks, because they can't see the cognitive processes that are going on in students' heads. By the same token, students do not usually have access to the cognitive problem solving processes of instructors as a basis for learning through observation and mimicry. Before apprenticeship methods can be applied to learn cognitive skills, the learning environment has to be changed to make these internal thought processes externally visible. Cognitive apprenticeship is designed to bring these cognitive processes into the open, where students can observe, enact, and practice them.

There are two major differences between cognitive apprenticeship and traditional apprenticeship. First, because traditional apprenticeship is set in the workplace, the problems and tasks that are given to learners arise not from pedagogical concerns, but from the demands of the workplace. Because the job selects the tasks for students to practice, traditional apprenticeship is limited in what it can teach. Cognitive apprenticeship differs from traditional apprenticeship in that the tasks and problems are chosen to illustrate the power of certain techniques and methods, to give students practice in applying these methods in diverse settings, and to increase the complexity of tasks slowly, so that component skills and models can be integrated. In short, tasks are sequenced to reflect the changing demands of learning.

Second, whereas traditional apprenticeship emphasizes teaching skills in the context of their use, cognitive apprenticeship emphasizes generalizing knowledge so that it can be used in many different settings. Cognitive apprenticeship extends practice to diverse settings and articulates the common principles, so that students learn how to apply their skills in varied contexts.

A Framework for Cognitive Apprenticeship

Cognitive apprenticeship focuses on four dimensions that constitute any learning environment: content, method, sequencing, and sociology (see Table 4.1, taken from Collins, Hawkins, & Carver, 1991).

Content

Recent cognitive research has begun to differentiate the types of knowledge required for expertise. Of course, experts have to master the explicit concepts, facts, and procedures associated with a specialized area – what researchers call *domain knowledge*. Domain knowledge includes the concepts, facts, and procedures explicitly identified with a particular subject matter. This is the type of knowledge that is generally found in school textbooks, class lectures, and demonstrations. Examples of domain knowledge in reading are vocabulary, syntax, and phonics rules.

Domain knowledge is necessary but not sufficient for expert performance. It provides insufficient clues for many students about how to solve problems and accomplish tasks in a domain. Psychologists have recently been trying to explicate the *tacit knowledge* that supports people's ability to

make use of these concepts, facts, and procedures to solve real-world problems (also see Bransford et al., this volume). I call this second kind of knowledge *strategic knowledge*. Research has identified three kinds of strategic knowledge:

1. *Heuristic strategies* are generally effective techniques and approaches for accomplishing tasks that might be regarded as "tricks of the trade"; they don't always work, but when they do, they are quite helpful. Most heuristics are tacitly acquired by experts through the practice of solving problems. However, there have been noteworthy attempts to address heuristic learning explicitly (Schoenfeld, 1985). In mathematics, a heuristic for solving problems is to try to find a solution for simple cases and see if the solution generalizes.

2. *Control strategies*, or *metacognitive strategies*, control the process of carrying out a task. Control strategies have monitoring, diagnostic, and remedial components; decisions about how to proceed in a task generally depend on an assessment of one's current state relative to one's goals, on an analysis of current difficulties, and on the strategies available for dealing with difficulties. For example, a comprehension monitoring strategy might be to try to state the main point of a section one has just read; if one cannot do so, then it might be best to reread parts of the text.

3. *Learning strategies* are strategies for learning domain knowledge, heuristic strategies, and control strategies. Knowledge about how to learn ranges from general strategies for exploring a new domain to more specific strategies for extending or reconfiguring knowledge in solving problems or carrying out complex tasks. For example, if students want to learn to solve problems better, they need to learn how to relate each step in the example problems worked in textbooks to the principles discussed in the text (Chi, et al., 1989). If students want to write better, they need to learn to analyze others' texts for strengths and weaknesses.

Table 4.1. Principles for Designing Cognitive Apprenticeship Environments

Content	Types of knowledge required for expertise	
	Domain knowledge	subject matter specific concepts, facts, and procedures
	Heuristic strategies	generally applicable techniques for accomplishing tasks
	Control strategies	general approaches for directing one's solution process
	Learning strategies	knowledge about how to learn new concepts, facts, and procedures
Method	Ways to promote the development of expertise	
	Modeling	teacher performs a task so students can observe
	Coaching	teacher observes and facilitates while students perform a task
	Scaffolding	teacher provides supports to help the student perform a task
	Articulation	teacher encourages students to verbalize their knowledge and thinking
	Reflection	teacher enables students to compare their performance with others
	Exploration	teacher invites students to pose and solve their own problems
Sequencing	Keys to ordering learning activities	
	Increasing complexity	meaningful tasks gradually increasing in difficulty
	Increasing diversity	practice in a variety of situations to emphasize broad application
	Global to local skills	focus on conceptualizing the whole task before executing the parts
Sociology	Social characteristics of learning environments	
	Situated learning	students learn in the context of working on realistic tasks
	Community of practice	communication about different ways to accomplish meaningful tasks
	Intrinsic motivation	students set personal goals to seek skills and solutions
	Cooperation	students work together to accomplish their goals

Method

Teaching methods that emphasize apprenticeship give students the opportunity to observe, engage in, and invent or discover expert strategies in context. The six teaching methods associated with cognitive apprenticeship fall roughly into three groups. The first three methods (modeling, coaching, and scaffolding) are the core of traditional apprenticeship. They are designed to help students acquire an integrated set of skills through processes of observation and guided practice. The next two methods (articulation and reflection) are methods designed to help students to focus their observations of expert problem solving and to gain conscious access to (and control of) their own problem solving strategies. The final method (exploration) is aimed at encouraging learner autonomy, not only in carrying out expert problem solving processes but also in defining or formulating the problems to be solved.

1. *Modeling* involves an expert performing a task so that the students can observe and build a conceptual model of the processes that are required to accomplish it. In cognitive domains, this requires the externalization of usually internal processes and activities. For example, a teacher might model the reading process by reading aloud in one voice, while verbalizing her thought processes in another voice (Collins & Smith, 1982). In mathematics, Schoenfeld (1985) models the process of solving problems by having students bring difficult new problems for him to solve in class.

2. *Coaching* consists of observing students while they carry out a task and offering hints, challenges, scaffolding, feedback, modeling, reminders, and new tasks aimed at bringing their performance closer to expert performance. Coaching is related to specific events or problems that arise as the student attempts to accomplish the task. In Palincsar and Brown's (1984) reciprocal teaching of reading, the teacher coaches students while they ask questions, clarify their difficulties, generate summaries, and make predictions.

3. *Scaffolding* refers to the supports the teacher provides to help the student carry out the task. Coaching refers broadly to all the different ways that coaches foster learning, whereas scaffolding refers more narrowly to the supports provided to the learner. These supports can take either the form of suggestions or help, as in Palincsar and Brown's (1984) reciprocal teaching, or they can take the form of physical supports, as with the cue cards used by Scardamalia, Bereiter, and Steinbach (1984) to facilitate writing, or the short skis used to teach downhill skiing (Burton, Brown, & Fischer, 1984). *Fading* involves the gradual removal of supports until students are on their own.

4. *Articulation* includes any method of getting students to explicitly state their knowledge, reasoning, or problem solving processes in a domain. Inquiry teaching (Collins & Stevens, 1983) is a strategy of questioning students to lead them to articulate and refine their understanding. Also, teachers can encourage students to articulate their thoughts as they carry out their problem solving, or have students assume the critic or monitor role in cooperative activities in order to articulate their ideas to other students. For example, an inquiry teacher in reading might question students about why one summary of the text is good but another is poor, in order to get them to formulate an explicit model of a good summary.

5. *Reflection* involves enabling students to compare their own problem solving processes with those of an expert, another student, and ultimately, an internal cognitive model of expertise. Reflection is enhanced by the use of various techniques for reproducing or "replaying" the performances of both expert and novice for comparison. Some form of "abstracted replay," in which the critical features of expert and student performance are highlighted, is desirable (Collins & Brown, 1988). For reading or writing, methods to encourage reflection might consist of recording students as they think out loud and then replaying the tape for comparison with the thinking of experts and other students.

6. *Exploration* involves guiding students to a mode of problem solving on their own. Enabling them to do exploration is critical, if they are to learn how to frame questions or problems that are interesting and that they can solve. Exploration as a method of teaching involves setting general goals for students and then encouraging them to focus on particular subgoals of interest to them, or even to revise the general goals as they come upon something more interesting to pursue. For example, the teacher might send the students to the library to investigate and write about theories as to why the dinosaurs disappeared.

Sequencing

Cognitive apprenticeship provides some principles to guide the sequencing of learning activities.

1. *Increasing complexity* refers to the construction of a sequence of tasks such that more and more of the skills and concepts necessary for expert performance are required (Burton, Brown, & Fischer, 1984; White, 1984). For example, in reading increasing task complexity might consist of progressing from relatively short texts, with simple syntax and concrete description, to texts in which complexly interrelated ideas and the use of abstractions make interpretation more difficult.

2. *Increasing diversity* refers to the construction of a sequence of tasks in which a wider and wider variety of strategies or skills are required. As a skill becomes well learned, it becomes increasingly important that tasks requiring a diversity of skills and strategies be introduced so that the student learns to distinguish the conditions under which they do (and do not) apply. Moreover, as students learn to apply skills to more diverse problems, their strategies acquire a richer net of contextual associations and thus are more readily available for use with unfamiliar or novel problems. For mathematics, task diversity might be attained by intermixing very different types of problems, such as asking students to solve problems that require them to use a combination of algebraic and geometric concepts and techniques.

3. *Global before local skills.* In tailoring (Lave, 1988) apprentices learn to put together a garment from precut pieces before learning to cut out the pieces themselves. The chief effect of this sequencing principle is to allow students to build a conceptual map before attending to the details of the terrain (Norman, 1973). Having a clear conceptual model of the overall activity helps learners make sense of the portion that they are carrying out, thus improving their ability to monitor their own progress and to develop attendant self-correction skills. In algebra, for example, computers might carry out low-level computations – the local skills – so that students can concentrate on the global structure of the task, and the higher order reasoning and strategies required to solve a complex, authentic problem.

Sociology

Tailoring apprentices learn their craft not in a special, segregated learning environment, but in a busy tailoring shop. They are surrounded both by masters and other apprentices, all engaged in the target skills at varying levels of expertise. And they are expected, from the beginning, to engage in activities that contribute directly to the production of actual garments, advancing quickly toward independent skilled production. As a result, apprentices learn skills in the context of their application to real-world problems, within a culture focused on and defined by expert practice. Furthermore, certain aspects of the social organization of apprenticeship encourage productive beliefs about the nature of learning and of expertise that are significant to learners' motivation, confidence, and most importantly, their orientation toward problems that they encounter as they learn. These considerations suggest several characteristics affecting the sociology of learning.

1. *Situated learning.* A critical element in fostering learning is having students carry out tasks and solve problems in an environment that reflects the nature of such tasks in the world (Brown, Collins, & Duguid, 1989; Lave & Wenger, 1991). For example, reading and writing instruction might be situated in the context of students putting together a book on what they learn about science. Dewey created a situated learning environment in his experimental school by having the students design and build a clubhouse (Cuban, 1984), a task that emphasizes arithmetic and planning skills.

2. *Community of practice* refers to the creation of a learning environment in which the participants actively communicate about and engage in the skills involved in expertise (Lave & Wenger, 1991; Wenger, 1998). Such a community leads to a sense of ownership, characterized by personal investment and mutual dependency. It cannot be forced, but it can be fostered by common projects and shared experiences. Activities designed to engender a community of practice for reading might engage students in discussing how they interpret particularly difficult texts.

3. *Intrinsic motivation.* Related to the issue of situated learning and the creation of a community of practice is the need to promote intrinsic motivation for learning.

Lepper and Greene (1979) discuss the importance of creating learning environments in which students perform tasks because they are intrinsically related to a goal of interest to them, rather than for some extrinsic reason, like getting a good grade or pleasing the teacher. In reading and writing, for example, intrinsic motivation might be achieved by having students communicate with students in another part of the world by electronic mail.

4. *Exploiting cooperation* refers to having students work together in a way that fosters cooperative problem solving. Learning through cooperative problem solving is both a powerful motivator and a powerful mechanism for extending learning resources. In reading, activities to exploit cooperation might involve having students break up into pairs, where one student articulates his thinking process while reading, and the other student questions the first student about why he made different inferences.

Themes in Research on Cognitive Apprenticeship

In the years since cognitive apprenticeship was first introduced, there has been extensive research toward developing learning environments that embody many of these principles. Several of these principles have been developed further; in particular, situated learning, communities of practice, communities of learners, scaffolding, articulation, and reflection.

Situated Learning

Goal-based scenarios (Schank et al., 1994, Nowakowski, et al., 1994) embody many of the principles of cognitive apprenticeship. They can be set either in computer-based environments or naturalistic environments. Learners are given real-world tasks and the scaffolding they need to carry out such tasks. For example, in one goal-based scenario learners are asked to advise married

couples as to whether their children are likely to have sickle-cell anemia, a genetically linked disease. In order to advise the couples, learners must find out how different genetic combinations lead to the disease and run tests to determine the parents' genetic makeup. There are scaffolds in the system to support the learners, such as various recorded experts who offer advice. Other goal-based scenarios support learners in a wide variety of challenging tasks, such as putting together a news broadcast, solving an environmental problem, or developing a computer-reservation system. Goal-based scenarios make it possible to embed cognitive skills and knowledge in the kinds of contexts where they are to be used. So people learn not only the basic competencies they will need, but also when and how to apply these competencies.

Video and computer technology has enhanced the ability to create simulation environments where students are learning skills in context. A novel use of video technology is the Jasper series developed by the Cognition and Technology Group (1997) at Vanderbilt University to teach middle-school mathematics. In a series of fifteen to twenty minute videos, students are put into various problem-solving contexts: for example, deciding on a business plan for a school fair or a rescue plan for a wounded eagle. The problems are quite difficult to solve and reflect the complex problem solving and planning that occurs in real life. Middle-school students work in groups for several days to solve each problem. Solving the problems results in a much richer understanding of the underlying mathematical concepts than the traditional school-mathematics problems.

These kinds of situated-learning tasks are different from most school tasks, because school tasks are decontextualized. Imagine learning tennis by being told the rules and practicing the forehand, backhand, and serve without ever playing or seeing a tennis match. If tennis were taught that way, it would be hard to see the point of what you were learning. But in school, students are taught algebra and Shakespeare without being given any idea of how they might be useful in their lives. That is not how a coach would teach you to play tennis. A coach might first show you how to grip and swing the racket, but very soon you would be hitting the ball and playing games. A good coach would have you go back and forth between playing games and working on particular skills – combining global and situated learning with focused local knowledge. The essential idea in situated learning is to tightly couple a focus on accomplishing tasks with a focus on the underlying competencies needed to carry out the tasks.

Communities of Practice

Lave and Wenger (1991; Wenger, 1998) have written extensively about communities of practice and how learning takes place in these contexts. They introduced the notion of *legitimate peripheral participation* to describe the way that apprentices participate in a community of practice. They described four cases of apprenticeship and emphasized how an apprentice's identity derives from becoming part of the community of workers, as they become more central members in the community. They also noted that an apprenticeship relationship can be unproductive for learning, as in the case of the meat cutters they studied, where the apprentices worked in a separate room and were isolated from the working community. Productive apprenticeship depends on opportunities for apprentices to participate legitimately in the community practices that they are learning.

The degree to which people play a central role and are respected by other members of a community determines their sense of identity (Lave & Wenger, 1991). The central roles are those that most directly contribute to the collective activities and knowledge of the community. The motivation to become a more central participant in a community of practice can provide a powerful incentive for learning. Frank Smith (1988) argues that children will learn to read and write if the people they admire read and write. That is, they will want to join the "literacy club" and

will work hard to become members. Learning to read is part of becoming the kind of person they want to become. Identity is central to deep learning.

Wenger (1998) argues that people participate in a variety of communities of practice – at home, at work, at school, and in hobbies. In his view a community of practice is a group of people participating together to carry out different activities, such as garage bands, ham-radio operators, recovering alcoholics, and research scientists. "For individuals, it means that learning is an issue of engaging in and contributing to the practices of their communities. For communities, it means that learning is an issue of refining their practice and ensuring new generations of members. For organizations, it means that learning is an issue of sustaining the interconnected communities of practice through which an organization knows what it knows and thus becomes effective and valuable as an organization" (pp. 7–8).

Communities of Learners

In recent years there has developed a "learning communities" approach to education that builds on Lave and Wenger's (1991) notion of a community of practice. In a learning community the goal is to advance the collective knowledge and in that way to support the growth of individual knowledge (Scardamalia & Bereiter, 1994, this volume). The defining quality of a learning community is that there is a culture of learning, in which everyone is involved in a collective effort of understanding (Brown & Campione, 1996).

There are four characteristics that a learning community must have (Bielaczyc & Collins, 1999): (1) diversity of expertise among its members, who are valued for their contributions and given support to develop; (2) a shared objective of continually advancing the collective knowledge and skills; (3) an emphasis on learning how to learn; and (4) mechanisms for sharing what is learned. It is not necessary that each member assimilate everything that the community knows, but each should know who within the community has relevant expertise to address any problem. This marks a departure from the traditional view of schooling, with its emphasis on individual knowledge and performance, and the expectation that students will acquire the same body of knowledge at the same time.

Brown and Campione (1996) have developed a model they call Fostering a Community of Learners (FCL) for grades 1–8. The FCL approach promotes a diversity of interests and talents, in order to enrich the knowledge of the classroom community as a whole. The focus of FCL classrooms is on the subject areas of biology and ecology, with central topics such as endangered species and food chains and webs. There is an overall structure of students (1) carrying out research on the central topics in small groups where each student specializes in a particular subtopic area, (2) sharing what they learn with other students in their research group and in other groups, and (3) preparing for and participating in some "consequential task" that requires students to combine their individual learning, so that all members in the group come to a deeper understanding of the main topic and subtopics. Teachers orchestrate students' work, and support students when they need help.

In the FCL model there are usually three research cycles per year. A cycle begins with a set of shared materials meant to build a common knowledge base. Students then break into research groups that focus on a specific research topic related to the central topic. For example, if the class is studying food chains, then the class may break into five or six research groups that each focus on a specific aspect of food chains, such as photosynthesis, consumers, energy exchange, and so on. Students research their subtopic as a group and individually, with individuals "majoring" by following their own research agendas within the limits of the subtopic. Students also engage in regular "cross-talk" sessions, where the different groups explain their work to the other groups, ask and answer questions, and refine their understanding. The research activities include reciprocal teaching (Palincsar &

Brown, 1984), guided writing and composing, consultation with subject matter experts outside the classroom, and cross-age tutoring. In the final part of the cycle, students from each of the subtopic groups come together to form a "jigsaw" group (Aronson, 1978) in order to share learning on the various subtopics and to work together on some consequential task. In the jigsaw, all pieces of the puzzle come together to form a complete understanding. The consequential tasks "bring the research cycle to an end, force students to share knowledge across groups, and act as occasions for exhibition and reflection" (Brown & Campione, 1996, p. 303).

A key idea in the learning-communities approach is to advance the collective knowledge of the community, and in that way to help individual students learn. This is directly opposed to the approaches found in most schools, where learning is viewed as an individual pursuit and the goal is to transmit the textbook's and teacher's knowledge to students. The culture of schools often discourages sharing of knowledge – by inhibiting students from talking, working on problems or projects together, and sharing or discussing their ideas. Testing and grading are administered individually. When taking tests, students are prevented from relying on other resources, such as other students, books, or computers. The whole approach is aimed at ensuring that individual students have all the knowledge in their heads that is included in the curriculum. Thus, the learning-community approach is a radical departure from the theory of learning and knowledge underlying schooling.

Scaffolding

Computer-based, interactive learning environments can be designed to offer support to learners in various guises, so that students can tackle complex, difficult tasks. Scaffolding is the support a system provides to learners as they carry out different activities (Wood, Bruner, & Ross, 1976). This can take the form of structured or highly constrained tasks, help systems that give advice when the learner does not know what to do or is confused, guided tours on how to do things, hints when needed, and so on. One form that scaffolding takes is that the system can do many of the low-level chores, such as arithmetic calculations, while the learner concentrates on the higher-level task of deciding what to do. Another form is that the system can provide an overall structure that allows completion of a complex task, guiding students to individual components of the task, and showing them how each component fits into the overall task. Scaffolding helps learners carry out tasks that are beyond their capabilities. Quintana et al. (2004) suggest twenty specific strategies for designing scaffolds to support sense making, inquiry, articulation, and reflection in computer-based learning environments. In most situations, scaffolding naturally *fades* as learners are able to accomplish tasks on their own.

In an analysis of computer-based learning environments, Reiser (2004) points out that most of the work on scaffolding has focused on *structuring* the task for students, in order to make it easier for learners to accomplish the task. But he emphasizes that there is another important role for scaffolding – *problematizing* the student's performance, or explicitly questioning the key content and strategies used during the task, so that students reflect more on their learning. Although this may make the task more difficult, it can facilitate learning.

Bruner based his concept of scaffolding on Vygotsky's (1978) notion of the *zone of proximal development*, which described how adults can support learners to accomplish tasks that they cannot accomplish on their own. Hence, the focus of research on scaffolding (see for example Davis and Miyake, 2004) has been on supporting individuals in their learning. But Kolodner et al. (2003) point out that it is important to scaffold groups as well as individuals. So, for example, in their work teaching science, they first provide students with focused collaboration activities to solve simple problems, which they call "launcher units." Engaging in these activities and reflecting on them helps students to collaborate more effectively and to understand the value of collaboration.

In schools, needing to ask for extra help often implies that the student is inferior, so students are reluctant to ask for help. When scaffolding is provided by computers, it comes without criticism and without others knowing that the student needed help. Computers offer a kind of scaffolding that avoids stigmatization and provides individualized instructional support.

Articulation

In order to abstract learning from particular contexts, it is important to articulate one's thinking and knowledge, so that it becomes available in other contexts. There have been several successful examples of how effective group discussions can be in classrooms. For example, Lampert (Lampert, Rittenhouse, & Crumbaugh, 1996) showed how fifth grade children can form a community of inquiry about important mathematical concepts. She engaged students in discussion of their conjectures and interpretations of each other's reasoning. Techniques of this kind have been successful with even younger children (Cobb & Bauersfeld, 1995) and may partly underlie the success of Japanese mathematical education (Stigler & Hiebert, 1999).

A notable method for fostering articulation in science is the Itakura method developed in Japan (Hatano & Inagaki, 1991). First, students make different predictions about what will happen in a simple experiment, where they are likely to have different expectations. For example, one experiment involves lowering a clay ball into water and predicting what will happen. After students make their initial predictions, they discuss and defend among themselves why they think their predictions are correct. After any revisions in their predictions, the experiment is performed and discussion ensues as to why the result came out the way it did.

Sandoval and Reiser (2004) have developed a computer system called the Biology Guided Inquiry Learning Environment (BGuILE) that supports students in making scientific arguments in the context of population genetics. The system presents the students with a mystery of why many of the finches in the Galapagos Islands died during a period of drought (see Edelson & Reiser, this volume). In order to solve the mystery, students have to analyze extensive data that were collected by scientists and come up with a reasoned conclusion as to why some finches died while others survived. The Explanation Constructor tool in the system prompts the students to put in all the pieces of a sound genetics-based argument, after they have decided what caused the finches to die. Hence, the system scaffolds students to articulate their argument in a much more explicit form than they would normally do.

The Knowledge Forum environment developed by Scardamalia and Bereiter (this volume; 1994) is an environment where students articulate their ideas in writing over a computer network. The model involves students investigating problems in different subject areas over a period of weeks or months. As students work, they enter their ideas and research findings as notes in an online knowledge base. The software scaffolds students in constructing their notes through features such as theory-building scaffolds (e.g., "My Theory," "I Need to Understand") or debate scaffolds (e.g., "Evidence For"). Students can read through the knowledge base, adding text, graphics, questions, links to other notes, and comments on each other's work. When someone has commented on another student's work, the system automatically notifies them about it. The central activity of the community is contributing to the communal knowledge base. Contributions can take the form of (a) *individual notes*, in which students state problems, advance initial theories, summarize what needs to be understood in order to progress on a problem or to improve their theories, provide a drawing or diagram, and so on; (b) *views*, in which students or teachers create graphical organizations of related notes; (c) *build-ons*, which allow students to connect new notes to existing notes; and (d) *"Rise Above It" notes*, which synthesize

notes in the knowledge base. Any of these kinds of contributions can be jointly authored. The goal is to engage students in progressive knowledge building, where they continually develop their understanding through problem identification, research, and community discourse. The emphasis is on progress toward collective goals of understanding, rather than individual learning and performance.

Reflection

Reflection encourages learners to look back on their performance in a situation, and compare their performance to other performances, such as their own previous performances and those of experts. Reflection has received much attention as a vital aspect of the learning process for both children and adults. Schon (1983) describes how systematic reflection on practice is critical for many professionals engaged in complex activities. Designers of learning environments often build supports for reflection into tasks by asking students to discuss and reflect upon the strategies used to guide their actions. Reflection can highlight the critical aspects of a performance and encourage learners to think about what makes for a good performance and how they might improve in the future.

There are three forms that reflection can take, all of which are enhanced by technology: (1) reflection on your process, (2) comparison of your performance to that of others, and (3) comparison of your performance to a set of criteria for evaluating performances:

- *Reflection on your process*: Because technology makes it possible to record performances, people can look back at how they did a task. One useful form of reflection is an "abstracted replay," where the critical decisions made are replayed. A system that teaches complex problem solving could allow learners to compare their decisions in solving a complex problem to an expert solution, so that they can see how they might have done better.

- *Comparison of your performance to that of others*: One of the most effective ways that people learn is by comparing different performances, including their own, to determine what factors lead to success. This is called "perceptual learning" (Bransford et al., 1989). Technology makes it possible to record different performances that learners can then analyze.

- *Comparison of your performance to a set of criteria for evaluating performances*: One of the most effective ways to improve performance is to evaluate how you did with respect to a set of criteria that determine good performance. For example, White and Frederiksen (1998) showed that students who evaluated their performance on projects using a set of eight criteria improved much more than students who carried out the same tasks, but did not reflect on their performance in the same way. In fact this reflection helped the weaker students much more than the stronger students.

The essential way people get better at doing things is by thinking about what they are going to do beforehand, by trying to do what they have planned, and by reflecting back on how well what they did came out. If they can articulate criteria for evaluating what they did, this will help them as they plan what to do on the next cycle. The wide availability of computers and other recording technologies makes performances easier to produce and to reflect on. For example, students can now produce their own news broadcasts, musical performances, or plays, either on audiotape, videotape, or cable television, and send them to other schools or to parents. Furthermore, they can play these back, reflect upon them, and edit them until they are polished. One of the best examples of the use of technology for recording performances has been in Arts Propel (Gardner, 1991) with its cycle of performing, reflecting upon the performance in terms of a set of criteria, and then performing again. Most educational practice has not recognized the power of this learning-cycle approach.

Conclusion

As these examples illustrate, there has been extensive research over the last fifteen years that has incorporated the principles of cognitive apprenticeship in the design of learning environments. As computer-based learning environments become more pervasive, there is likely to be continued development of new ways to embody these principles in their design.

References

Aronson, E. (1978). *The jigsaw classroom*. Beverly Hills, CA: Sage.

Bielaczyc, K., & Collins, A. (1999) Learning communities in classrooms: A reconceptualization of educational practice. In C. M. Reigeluth (Ed.): *Instructional-design theories and models: A new paradigm of instructional theory* (pp. 269–292). Mahwah, NJ: Lawrence Erlbaum Associates.

Bransford, J. D., Franks, J. J., Vye, N. J., & Sherwood, R. D. (1989). New approaches to instruction: Because wisdom can't be told. In S. Vosniadou & A. Ortony (Eds.), *Similarity and analogical reasoning* (pp. 470–497). New York: Cambridge University Press.

Brown, A., & Campione, J. (1996). Psychological theory and the design of innovative learning environments: On procedures, principles, and systems. In L. Schauble & R. Glaser (Eds.) *Innovations in learning: New environments for education* (pp. 289–325). Mahwah, NJ: Lawrence Erlbaum Associates.

Brown, J. S., Collins, A., & Duguid, P. (1989). Situated cognition and the culture of learning. *Educational Researcher*, 18(1), 32–42.

Burton, R., Brown, J. S., & Fischer, G. (1984). Skiing as a model of instruction. In B. Rogoff and J. Lave (Eds.), *Everyday cognition: Its developmental and social context* (pp. 139–150). Cambridge, MA: Harvard University Press.

Chi, M. T. H., Bassok, M., Lewis, M. W., Reimann, P., & Glaser, R. (1989). Self-Explanations: How students study and use examples in learning to solve problems. *Cognitive Science*, 13, 145–182.

Cobb, P., & Bauersfeld, H. (Eds.) (1995). *The emergence of mathematical meaning: Interaction in classroom cultures.* Mahwah, NJ: Lawrence Erlbaum Associates.

Cognition and Technology Group at Vanderbilt (1997). *The Jasper Project: Lessons in curriculum, instruction, assessment, and professional development.* Mahwah, NJ: Lawrence Erlbaum Associates.

Collins, A., & Brown, J. S. (1988). The computer as a tool for learning through reflection. In H. Mandl and A. Lesgold (Eds.), *Learning issues for intelligent tutoring systems* (pp. 1–18). New York: Springer.

Collins, A., Brown, J. S., & Newman, S. E. (1989). Cognitive apprenticeship: Teaching the craft of reading, writing, and mathematics. In L. B. Resnick (Ed.), *Knowing, learning, and instruction: Essays in honor of Robert Glaser* (pp. 453–494). Hillsdale, NJ: Lawrence Erlbaum Associates.

Collins, A., Hawkins, J., & Carver, S. M. (1991). A cognitive apprenticeship for disadvantaged students. In B. Means, C. Chelemer & M. S. Knapp (Eds.) *Teaching advanced skills to at-risk students.* (pp. 216–243). San Francisco: Jossey-Bass.

Collins, A., & Smith, E. E. (1982). Teaching the process of reading comprehension. In D. K. Detterman & R. J. Sternberg (Eds.), *How much and how can intelligence be increased?* (pp. 173–185). Norwood, NJ: Ablex.

Collins, A., & Stevens, A. L. (1983). A cognitive theory of interactive teaching. In C. M. Reigeluth (Ed.), *Instructional design theories and models: An overview* (pp. 247–278). Hillsdale, NJ: Lawrence Erlbaum Associates.

Cuban, L. (1984). *How teachers taught.* New York: Longman.

Davis, E. A., & Miyake, N. (Eds.) (2004). Special issue: Scaffolding. *Journal of the Learning Sciences, 13(3),* 265–451.

Gardner, H. (1991) Assessment in context: The alternative to standardized testing. In B. Gifford & C. O'Connor (Eds.), *Future assessments: Changing views of aptitude, achievement, and instruction* (pp. 77–120). Boston: Kluwer.

Hatano, G., & Inagaki, K. (1991) Sharing cognition through collective comprehension activity. In: L. Resnick, J. Levin, & S. D. Teasley (Eds.), *Perspectives on socially shared cognition* (pp. 331–348). Washington, DC: American Psychological Association.

Kolodner, J. L., Crismond, D., Fasse, B. B., Gray, J. T., Holbrook, J., Ryan, M., & Puntambekar, S. (2003). Problem-based learning meets case-based reasoning in the middle-school science classroom: Putting a Learning-by-Design curriculum into practice. *Journal of the Learning Sciences, 12(4),* 495–548.

Lampert, M., Rittenhouse, P., & Crumbaugh, C. (1996). Agreeing to disagree: Developing sociable mathematical discourse. In D. Olson & N. Torrance (Eds.), *Handbook of education and human development* (pp. 731–764). Oxford: Blackwell's Press.

Lave, J. (1988). The culture of acquisition and the practice of understanding (Report No. IRL88-0007). Palo Alto, CA: Institute for Research on Learning.

Lave, J., & Wenger, E. (1991). *Situated learning: Legitimate peripheral participation.* New York: Cambridge University Press.

Lepper, M. R., & Greene, D. (1979). *The hidden costs of reward.* Hillsdale, NJ: Lawrence Erlbaum Associates.

Norman, D. A. (1973). Memory, knowledge, and the answering of questions. In R. L. Solso (Ed.), *Contemporary issues in cognitive psychology: The Loyola symposium* (pp. 135–165). Washington, DC: Winston.

Nowakowski, A., Campbell, R., Monson, D. Montgomery, J., Moffett, C., Acovelli, M., Schank, R., & Collins, A. (1994). Goal-based scenarios: A new approach to professional education. *Educational Technology, 34(9),* 3–32.

Palincsar, A. S., & Brown, A. L. (1984). Reciprocal teaching of comprehension-fostering and monitoring activities. *Cognition and Instruction, 1(2),* 117–175.

Quintana, C., Reiser, B. J., Davis, E. A., Krajcik, J., Fretz, E., Duncan, R. G., Kyza, E., Edelson, D., & Soloway, E. (2004). A scaffolding design framework fo software to support science inquiry. *Journal of the Learning Sciences, 13(3),* 337–386.

Reiser, B. J. (2004). Scaffolding complex learning: The mechanisms of structuring and problematizing student work. *Journal of the Learning Sciences, 13(3),* 273–304.

Sandoval, W. A., & Reiser, B. J. (2004). Explanation-driven inquiry: Integrating conceptual and epistemic scaffolds for scientific inquiry. *Science Education, 88,* 345–372.

Scardamalia, M., & Bereiter, C. (1994). Computer support for knowledge-building communities. *Journal of the Learning Sciences, 3(3),* 265–283.

Scardamalia, M., Bereiter, C., & Steinbach, R. (1984). Teachability of reflective processes in written composition. *Cognitive Science, 8,* 173–190.

Schank, R. C., Fano, A., Bell, B., & Jona, M. (1994) The design of goal-based scenarios. *Journal of the Learning Sciences, 3*(4), 305–346.

Schoenfeld, A. H. (1985). *Mathematical problem solving.* Orlando, FL: Academic Press.

Schon, D. A. (1983). *The reflective practitioner: How professionals think in action.* New York: Basic Books.

Smith, F. (1988). *Joining the literacy club.* Portsmouth, NH: Heinemann.

Stigler, J., & Hiebert, J. (1999). *The teaching gap: Best ideas from the world's teachers for improving education in the classroom.* New York: Free Press.

Vygotsky, L. S. (1978). *Mind in society: The development of higher mental processes.* (M. Cole, V. John-Steiner, S. Scribner, & E. Souberman, Eds.) Cambridge, MA: Harvard University Press.

Wenger, E. (1998). *Communities of practice: Learning, meaning, and identity.* New York: Cambridge University Press.

White, B. Y. (1984). Designing computer games to help physics students understand Newton's laws of motion. *Cognition and Instruction, 1*(1), 69–108.

White, B. Y., & Frederiksen, J. R. (1998). Inquiry, modeling, and metacognition: Making science accessible to all students. *Cognition and Instruction, 16*(1), 3–118.

Wood, D., Bruner, J., & Ross, G. (1976). The role of tutoring in problem solving. *Journal of Child Psychology and Psychiatry, 17,* 89–100.

CHAPTER 5

Cognitive Tutors

Technology Bringing Learning Sciences to the Classroom

Kenneth R. Koedinger and Albert Corbett

Introduction

Individual tutoring is perhaps the first instructional method. It dates back at least to Socrates and the Socratic method. Although one-to-one tutoring by expert human tutors has been shown to be much more effective than typical one-to-many classroom instruction (Bloom, 1984), it has not been economical to provide every child with an individual tutor. Lectures and books became pervasive in education to spread knowledge at lower cost. However, increasing capabilities of computer hardware and software have been creating new opportunities to bring one-to-one tutoring to more students. Furthermore, computer technology provides an opportunity to systematically incorporate advances in learning sciences into the classroom, to test associated principles of learning, and to best adapt them to the needs of students and teachers.

Early attempts to use computers for instruction included Computer-Aided Instruction (Eberts, 1997) and Intelligent Computer-Aided Instruction or Intelligent Tutoring Systems (Corbett, Koedinger, & Anderson, 1997; Sleeman & Brown, 1982; Wenger, 1987). Computer-based instruction has been shown to be effective in increasing student learning beyond normal classroom instruction (e.g., Kulik & Kulik, 1991), however, not to the level of human tutors (Bloom, 1984). Early attempts at Intelligent Tutoring Systems included mimicking Socratic dialog in teaching electronics troubleshooting, adding intelligent questioning to an existing Computer-Aided Instruction system for learning South American geography, adding tutoring strategies to an existing "expert system" for medical diagnosis, and adding tutoring strategies to an existing educational game for mathematics (Sleeman & Brown, 1982).

In a parallel development that dates back even earlier, cognitive theories of human learning, memory, and problem solving were being implemented as computational models with computers (Newell & Simon, 1972). In the mid-1980s, John R. Anderson and colleagues merged these two strands and introduced a more interdisciplinary approach to Intelligent Tutoring System development and testing (Anderson, Boyle, & Reiser, 1985) that added the discipline of cognitive psychology to the discipline of artificial intelligence that had previously been the prime mover. The Intelligent Tutors emerging from this approach were constructed around computational *cognitive models* of the knowledge students were acquiring and began to be called "*Cognitive Tutors*" (Anderson et al., 1995). These cognitive models represent learner thinking or *cognition* in the domain of interest, whether it is algebra, programming, scientific reasoning, or writing essays. The cognitive model also includes a representation of the kinds of early learner strategies and misconceptions that are steps in the trajectory from novice to expert.

Full-scale Cognitive Tutors have been created to help students learn in a variety of domains including middle and high school mathematics (Koedinger, Anderson, Hadley, & Mark, 1997; Koedinger, 2002), computer programming (Anderson et al., 1995; Mathan & Koedinger, 2003) and college-level genetics (Corbett et al., 2005). Cognitive Tutors typically speed learning or yield greater learning relative to conventional problem-based instruction (Anderson et al., 1995) and approach the effectiveness of good human tutors (Corbett, 2001). The most widely distributed Cognitive Tutor is one for algebra, which is part of a complete course for high school algebra and in 2004–2005 was in use in some 2000 schools across in the United States. As described later in this chapter, students in Cognitive Tutor Algebra I have been shown to score twice as high on end-of-course open-ended problem-solving tests and 15 percent higher on objective tests as students enrolled in a traditional algebra course. A few of these schools are high performing, resource rich suburban schools, but most of them are urban or rural schools, with average teachers and with a relatively large number of economically disadvantaged, minority, or learning disabled students. We estimate that approximately half a million students have used the tutor for a total of about twenty million student-hours.

Cognitive Tutors Provide Aspects of Human Tutoring

Cognitive Tutors support learning by doing, an essential aspect of human tutoring. Learning by doing is the idea of putting students in performance situations whereby the objective concepts and skills can be applied and instruction can be provided in the context of or in response to student needs[1]. Cognitive Tutors accomplish two of the principal tasks characteristic of human tutoring: (1) monitoring the student's *performance* and providing context-specific instruction just when the individual student needs it, and (2) monitoring the student's *learning* and selecting problem-solving activities involving knowledge goals just within the individual student's reach.

This monitoring of students' performance and learning makes use of the cognitive model and two key algorithms, *model tracing* and *knowledge tracing*. In model tracing, the cognitive tutor runs the cognitive model forward step-by-step along with the student to follow the student's individual path through complex problem spaces, providing just-in-time accuracy feedback and context-specific advice. In knowledge tracing, the tutor employs a simple Bayesian method of estimating the student's knowledge and employs this student model to select appropriate problems.

Chapter Overview

In the following section we describe Cognitive Tutors and their foundation in ACT-R theory. Extensive Cognitive Tutor research has served both to validate and modify the ACT-R cognitive architecture model (cf. Anderson & Lebiere, 1998) and we review six general principles of intelligent tutor design that were derived from this theoretical framework (Anderson et al., 1995). Although ACT-R theory provides an important cognitive modeling framework, it does not prescribe course curriculum objectives and activities, it cannot precisely anticipate the prior knowledge that students bring with them to a course or a problem-solving activity, and it cannot prescribe scaffolding

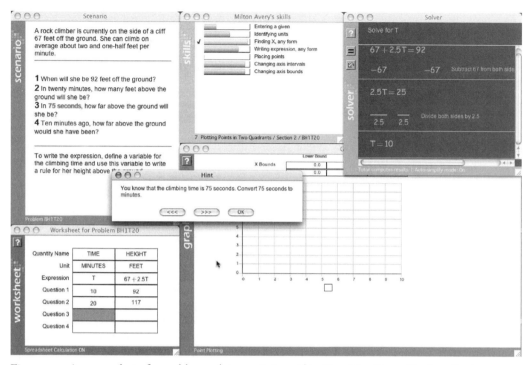

Figure 5.1. A screen shot of a problem-solving activity within Cognitive Tutor Algebra. Students are presented a problem situation and use various tools, like the Worksheet, Grapher, and Solver shown here, to analyze and model the problem situation. As they work, "model tracing" is used to provide just-in-time feedback or on-demand solution-sensitive hints through the Messages window. The results of "knowledge tracing" are displayed in the skills chart in the top center.

activities to help students develop a deep understanding of domain knowledge. In the final section of the chapter, we describe the learning sciences principles and methods that we have employed to address these instructional design questions.

Cognitive Tutor Algebra: A Brief Example

A screen shot of a unit in Cognitive Tutor Algebra is shown in Figure 5.1. Cognitive Tutors tend to have relatively rich graphical user interfaces that provide a workspace in which students can demonstrate a wide variety of problem solving behavior. The workspace changes as students progress through units. The workspace in Figure 5.1 includes a problem scenario window in the upper left where students are presented with a problem situation, often with real facts or data, that they are expected to analyze and model using the tools in the workspace. The tools illustrated in Figure 5.1 are the

Worksheet, Grapher, and Solver. In this unit, the Worksheet has automated features like a spreadsheet. Once students write the algebraic expression for the height "$67+2.5T$" given the time, then the worksheet computes a height value (e.g., 117) when a time value is entered (e.g., 20). In earlier units, the worksheet does not have these automated features, but is more like a table representation on paper and students must demonstrate they can perform the steps on their own. Similarly, the Grapher and Solver tools change as students advance through tutor units. Initially these behave much like blank pieces of paper where students do all the work. Later these tools begin to automate lower level skills, like plotting points or performing arithmetic, and let students focus on acquiring higher-level concepts and skills, like deciding which symbolic function to graph or what algebraic manipulation to perform. As students work, the Cognitive Tutor monitors their performance and may provide just-in-time feedback or on-demand solution-sensitive hints in the hint window. The Cognitive Tutor also monitors student learning, and displays these results in the Skills chart, shown in the top center of Figure 5.1.

It is critical to consider the social context of use of any technology or educational innovation, and Cognitive Tutors are no exception. We have tended to create complete Cognitive Tutor courses whereby we apply learning sciences theory to develop instructional materials, like consumable textbooks, in addition to Cognitive Tutor software. Virtually all schools using our mathematics Cognitive Tutors also use the curriculum and text materials. The typical procedure is to spend two days a week in the computer lab using the Cognitive Tutor software and three days a week in the regular classroom using our text materials. In the classroom, learning is active, student-centered, and focused primarily on learning by doing. Teachers spend less time in whole-group lecture and more time facilitating individual and cooperative problem solving and learning. In the classroom, students often work together in collaborative groups to solve problems similar to those presented by the tutor. Teachers play a key role in helping students to make connections between the computer tools and paper and pencil techniques.

Learning Sciences Theory Behind Cognitive Tutors

Cognitive Tutors are based on the ACT-R theory of learning and performance (Anderson & Lebiere, 1998). The theory distinguishes between implicit performance knowledge, called "procedural knowledge," and explicit verbal knowledge and visual images, called "declarative knowledge." According to ACT-R, performance knowledge can only be learned *by doing*, not by listening or watching. In other words, it is induced from constructive experiences – it cannot be directly placed in our heads. Such performance knowledge is represented in the notation of if-then production rules

that associate internal goals or external perceptual cues with new internal goals and/or external actions. Examples of English versions of production rules are shown in Table 5.1.

Production rules characterize how both advanced and beginning students think or reason in a domain. Students may acquire informal, heuristic, or incorrect patterns of thinking that are different from the concepts and rules that are normatively taught or presented in textbooks. Learning sciences researchers have identified "informal" or "intuitive" forms of thinking that students may learn implicitly and outside of school (cf. Lave, Murtaugh, & de la Rocha, 1984; Resnick, 1987). Production rules can represent such thinking patterns as illustrated by production #1 in Table 5.1, which represents an informal alternative to the formal approach of using algebraic equations like "$8x = 40$" (cf., Koedinger & Nathan, 2004). Production rules can also represent heuristic methods for discovering approaches to solutions (Polya, 1957). Production #2 in Table 5.1 does not suggest any particular operation per se, but characterizes how a good problem solver may think through a plan of action before selecting a particular operation or theorem to apply. Non-traditional strategies can be represented in production rules, as illustrated by #3 in Table 5.1, which characterizes the use of a graphical rather than symbolic strategy for solving an equation.

The if-part of a production rule can help identify when the knowledge students acquire is not at the right level of generality. For instance, production #4 in Table 5.1 is too specific – it shows students how to combine like terms in an equation when coefficients are present (e.g., $2x + 3x \rightarrow 5x$) but not when a coefficient is missing (e.g., $x - 0.2x$). Alternatively, students sometimes acquire productions that are too general. Production #3 in Table 5.1 represents how students may learn to combine numbers by the operator between them (e.g., $2*3 + 4 = x \rightarrow 6 + 4 = x$) without acquiring knowledge that prevents order of operations errors (e.g., $x*3 + 4 = 10 \rightarrow x*7 = 10$).

Table 5.1. Example Production Rules

Production Rules in English	Example of its Application
1. *Correct production possibly acquired implicitly* IF the goal is to find the value of quantity Q and Q divided by Num1 is Num2 THEN find Q by multiplying Num1 and Num2.	To solve "You have some money that you divide evenly among 8 people and each gets 40" find the original amount of money by multiplying 8 and 40.
2. *Correct production that does heuristic planning* IF the goal is to prove two triangles congruent and the triangles share a side THEN check for other corresponding sides or angles that may congruent.	Try to prove triangles ABC and DBC are congruent by checking whether any of the corresponding angles, like BCA and BCD, or any of the corresponding sides, like AB and DB, are congruent.
3. *Correct production for a nontraditional strategy* IF the goal is to solve an equation in x THEN graph the left and right sides of the equation and find the intersection point(s).	Solve equation $\sin x = x^2$ by graphing both $\sin x$ and x^2 and finding where the lines cross.
4. *Correct but overly specific production* IF "$ax + bx$" appears in an expression and $c = a + b$ THEN replace it with "cx"	Works for "$2x + 3x$" but not for "$x + 3x$"
5. *Incorrect, overly general production* IF "Num1 + Num2" appears in an expression THEN replace it with the sum	Leads to order of operations error: "$x * 3 + 4$" is rewritten as "$x * 7$"

The Cognitive Model and Model Tracing in Cognitive Tutors

Developing Cognitive Tutor software involves the use of the ACT-R theory and empirical studies of learners to create a "cognitive model." A cognitive model uses a production system to represent the multiple strategies students might employ as well as their typical student misconceptions. To take a simplified example from an algebra equation solving problem, Figure 5.2 depicts 3 productions that can apply in solving the equation $3(2x + 5) = 9$. The production rule in Strategy 1 distributes (multiplies) "3" across the sum $(2x + 5)$. The production rule in Strategy 2 divides both sides of the equation by "3." The third rule is a "buggy" production that represents a misconception (cf., Matz, 1982) and fails to fully distribute the "3" across the sum $(2x + 5)$.

By representing alternative strategies for the same goal, the Cognitive Tutor can follow different students down different problem solving paths of the students' own choosing, using an algorithm called "model tracing." Model tracing allows the Cogni-tive Tutor to trace each student's problem-solving steps and provide individualized assistance that is just-in-time and sensitive to the students' particular approach to a problem. When a student performs a step, it is compared against the alternative next steps that the cognitive model generates. There are three categories of response. For example, in Figure 5.2, if a student's problem solving action matches either strategy 1 or strategy 2, the tutor highlights the step as correct and the student and tutor move on to the next step. Second, if the student action, like "$6x + 5 = 9$", is matched by a buggy production, the tutor highlights the step as incorrect and presents a feedback message, like "You need to multiply 5 by 3 also." This message is generated from a template attached to the buggy rule, with the variables c and a getting context-specific values from the matching of the production rule to the current situation. Third, if the student performs a problem-solving action that does not match the action of any rule in the cognitive model, the tutor simply flags the action as an error – for instance, by making the text red and italicized.

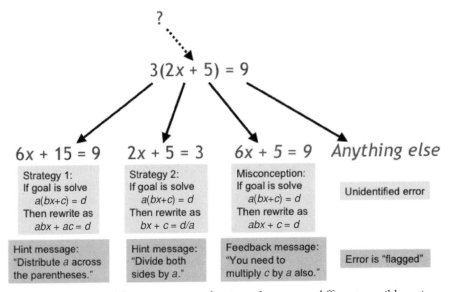

Figure 5.2. How model tracing uses production rules to trace different possible actions students may take. Here the student has reached the state "$3(2x + 5) = 9$". The "?" at the top indicates that these production rules work no matter how the student reached this state. The figure shows how the production rules apply to generate three possible next steps. Attached to the production rules are feedback messages for common errors or next-step hints that students can request if they are stuck.

At any time the student can request a hint (e.g., by clicking on the "?" button shown in figure 5.1). Again the tutor runs the model forward one step, selects one of the model productions that matches, and presents advice text attached to the production. For instance, the hint associated with strategy 1 in Figure 5.2 will say "Distribute 3 across the parentheses" because the production variable a has the value 3 in this case.

Knowledge Tracing in Cognitive Tutors

ACT-R theory holds that knowledge is acquired gradually and the brain essentially keeps statistics on the frequency, recency, and utility of knowledge components including production rules (Anderson & Lebiere, 1998). The Knowledge Tracing algorithm in Cognitive Tutors monitors students' gradual acquisition of production rules across problem-solving activities. At each opportunity to apply a production rule in problem solving, the tutor updates its estimate of the probability the student knows the rule based on whether the student applies the rule correctly. Knowledge Trac-

ing employs a Bayesian update and has been shown to predict students' performance and posttest accuracy (Corbett & Anderson, 1995). These probability estimates are displayed with "skill bars" in the computer tutor interface (see the upper center in Figure 5.1). The Cognitive Tutor uses these estimates to determine when a student is ready to move on to the next section of the curriculum, thus adapting the pacing of instruction to individual student needs. New problems are individually selected for students to provide more instruction and practice on the skills that have not yet been mastered (i.e., the ones for which the estimate is less than 95 percent that the student knows that skill).

Why Production Rule Cognitive Models Are Powerful

A key feature of production rules is that they are *modular*, that is, they represent knowledge components that can be flexibly recombined. It does not matter how a student reached the state of "$3(2x + 5) = 9$" shown in Figure 5.2. It may have been the result, for instance, of translating a story problem into this equation or of simplifying a more complex equation (e.g., "$3(2x + 5) + 10 = 19$") into this form. In any case, the production rule model is always applied to the current state of the problem regardless of how the student reached the current state.

This modularity makes developing Cognitive Tutors more feasible because the production rules can be reused and recombined in different ways to follow students in a potentially infinite variety of problems within a course unit or even across courses (e.g., the equation solving cognitive model is used in the Geometry Cognitive Tutor as well as in Algebra). In addition to facilitating development, modularity is a key scientific claim of ACT-R that yields empirically testable predictions. For instance, knowledge will transfer from a learning activity to an assessment activity to the extent that the kind and number of productions needed in the learning activity are also applicable in the assessment activity (Singley & Anderson, 1989).

Model and Knowledge Tracing Implement Features of Human Tutoring

Model and knowledge tracing algorithms implement key features of human tutoring and apprenticeship training (cf., Bloom, 1984; Collins, Brown, & Newman, 1989; McArthur, Stasz, & Zmuidzinas, 1990; Vygotsky, 1978). The tutor gives the student a task and monitors how well the student is performing the task. Model tracing is a form of such monitoring. When the student strays too far from the tutor's model of desired performance, the tutor may intervene and provide feedback. If the student is stuck, the tutor can provide hints or performance assistance based on his or her own domain expertise. The cognitive model provides the domain expertise or model of desired performance in a Cognitive Tutor. After the student finishes the task, the tutor selects a next task based on the tutor's sense of what the student knows and does not know. Knowledge tracing implements a method for determining, over time, what each student seems to know and not know.

Principles and Methods for Cognitive Tutor Design

Cognitive Tutor Design Principles

In 1995, we published a report on the status of the lessons learned from Cognitive Tutor development (Anderson et al., 1995). We described some general Cognitive Tutor design principles consistent with ACT-R and our research and development experience to that date. Here we review the status of the six most frequently used of those principles. Table 5.2 lists these six principles, slightly rephrased based on our experiences since the 1995 paper. We will briefly describe these principles and then provide more extended examples of two of them.

1. REPRESENT STUDENT COMPETENCE AS A PRODUCTION SET

The principle "represent student competence as a production set" suggests that the instructional designer guides design based on an analysis not of domain content per se, but of the way in which students think about the content. Acquiring competence in a domain is complex, and we tend to be surprisingly unaware of the immense number of details and subtle decision capabilities that we implicitly acquire on the way to expertise (Berry & Dienes, 1993). Complex tasks like reading become second nature to us with time, and we forget – or perhaps are never quite aware of – the learning experiences and resulting knowledge changes that led to such

Table 5.2. Six Instructional Design Principles for Cognitive Tutors

1. Represent student competence as a production set
2. Provide instruction in a problem-solving context
3. Communicate the goal structure underlying the problem solving
4. Promote a correct and general understanding of the problem-solving knowledge
5. Minimize working memory load that is extraneous to learning
6. Provide immediate feedback on errors relative to the model of desired performance

competence. Skinner (1968) estimated that to perform at fourth grade level in math, a student must acquire about twenty-five thousand "chunks" of knowledge (p. 17). Production rules provide a way to represent such chunks of knowledge and decision capabilities.

The *modularity* of production rules in a production set predicts that we can diagnose specific student weaknesses, and focus instructional activities on improving these. The *context-specific* nature of production rules means that instruction cannot be effective if it does not connect knowledge with its contexts of use. Students need true problem-solving experiences to learn the if-part of productions, the conditions for appropriate use of domain principles.

2. PROVIDE INSTRUCTION IN A PROBLEM-SOLVING CONTEXT

A fundamental assumption of ACT-R is that people learn by doing as the brain generalizes from one's explicit and implicit interpretations or "encodings" of one's experiences. It is not the information or even the instructional activities students are given that matter, but how students experience and engage in such information and activities that determines what knowledge they construct from them. Thus, another principle in Anderson et al. (1995) was "provide instruction in a problem-solving context." This principle is consistent with the learning sciences finding that instruction should be *situated* in *authentic* tasks.

3. COMMUNICATE THE GOAL STRUCTURE UNDERLYING THE PROBLEM SOLVING

Among the formidable challenges facing novice problem solvers in complex problem solving is decomposing an initial problem statement into successive subgoals and keeping track of these subgoals (Singley, 1990). The underlying goal structure of a problem solution often remains hidden in traditional problem-solving representations. We have employed two methods for making the goal structure explicit. First, we develop interfaces that make the goal structure visible in the problem-solving interface (Collins

et al., 1989). The most notable examples of this strategy are the geometry proof tutors (Koedinger & Anderson, 1993). A variety of studies have shown that explicit goal-structure scaffolding in the problem-solving interface can speed problem solving even in simple problems (Corbett & Trask, 2000) and result in better learning outcomes in more complex problem solving (Scheines & Sieg, 1994; Singley,1990). Second, the underlying goal structure of the problem can be communicated through help messages. Typically in model tracing tutors, the first level of help is a description of the current goal in the context of the overall problem. Subsequent help messages advise on how to achieve the goal.

4. PROMOTE A CORRECT AND GENERAL UNDERSTANDING OF PROBLEM-SOLVING KNOWLEDGE

In learning to problem solve, students construct production rules based on their own understandings or *encoding* of problem-solving activities and examples. These encodings are often different from those of experts. For example, novices have been shown to encode physics problems based on superficial features of the problems, rather than the underlying physical principles that apply (Chi, Feltovich, & Glaser, 1981). In geometry problem solving, students notoriously will conclude that angles are equal in measure because they look equal rather than because structurally they must be (Aleven & Koedinger, 2002). As illustrated above, students can acquire overly general productions that generate errors in situations different from those in which they were acquired, and overly specific rules that fail to transfer across problem-solving contexts. We have successfully deployed different strategies to help students generate a more general understanding and illustrate one later.

5. MINIMIZE WORKING MEMORY LOAD THAT IS EXTRANEOUS TO LEARNING

It has been documented that errors in complex problem solving can stem from loss of information from working memory

(Anderson & Jeffries, 1988) and that high working memory load or "cognitive load" can impede learning (Sweller, 1988). As a result, we have employed multiple tactics in Cognitive Tutors to reduce such load. Efforts to make the goal structure visible (principle 3) can help reduce working memory load. Another strategy is to simplify problem-solving actions in the interface that are irrelevant to the current learning goals. For example, the equation solver in our mathematics tutor has an auto-arithmetic mode in which students indicate the algebraic operation to perform in each solution step, but they are not required to perform the arithmetic (Ritter & Anderson, 1995).

Similarly, our programming Cognitive Tutors employ structure editors to reduce the working memory load of remembering surface syntax. Littman (1991) reports human tutor behavior that is similar to this strategy. Human tutors do not interrupt students and disrupt their working memory state simply to point out relatively minor errors that have little consequence for the overall problem solution.

6. PROVIDE IMMEDIATE FEEDBACK ON ERRORS RELATIVE TO THE MODEL OF DESIRED PERFORMANCE

Studies have shown that human tutors tend to provide immediate feedback after each problem-solving step (Merrill, Reiser, Ranney & Trafton, 1992), although the feedback may be minimal (Fox, 1991; Lepper et al., 1990) and provided only on "important" errors (Littman, 1991). But these studies don't reveal the relative benefits of immediate feedback. In a study with the Lisp Cognitive Tutor, immediate feedback led to significantly faster learning (Corbett & Anderson, 2001). Not only can immediate feedback make learning more efficient, but it can also be motivating for students (Schofield, 1995). Mathan and Koedinger (2003) demonstrate the benefits of providing immediate feedback, compared to an "intelligent novice" model of desired performance that allows for certain student errors and thus results in more delayed feedback.

Cognitive Tutor Meta-Design Principles

The strengths of ACT-R and the Cognitive Tutor principles are that they are general and can apply in multiple domains. However, these principles beg some higher-level curriculum design questions: What should students be learning? What problem-solving activities support that learning? What relevant knowledge do students bring with them? We need to design Cognitive Tutor activities that not only "work," but work well within the curricular and social context of course objectives, teacher practices, and classroom use. Here we abstract that experience in a set of Cognitive Tutor "Meta-Design" principles.

1. DESIGN WITH INSTRUCTORS AND CLASSROOM USE FROM THE START

An experienced classroom teacher plays many key roles in a Cognitive Tutor development project, contributing hard-won knowledge of the specific learning hurdles students face and of how to help students past those hurdles. An experienced teacher also plays essential roles in integrating Cognitive Tutor activities with other course activities. First, an experienced teacher who is part of the design team will help guide the initial tutor development so that the tutor dovetails with other course activities. Second, an experienced teacher is best positioned to take the technology into the classroom and provide informed observations on situations in which the classroom activities and tutor activities do not mesh.

2. DESIGN THE FULL COURSE EXPERIENCE

We encountered a high-level curriculum compatibility problem in the ANGLE Geometry Proof Project (Koedinger & Anderson, 1993). Between the start of the project and the first classroom piloting, the school district adopted a new curriculum that deemphasized proofs and thus, it became difficult to integrate the tutor into the curriculum. The project teacher who was intimately familiar with the tutor's curriculum objectives was more successful in integrating the tutor into the new curriculum than other teachers, and obtained greater learning effects. In the aftermath of the ANGLE project, we developed the full set of course activities in all our Cognitive Tutor math courses, including the course text and assignments, for two related reasons. First, it spares the classroom teacher from having to figure out how to integrate the Cognitive Tutor activities into the course. Second, it enables us to develop a course that more fully emphasizes problem-based learning throughout.

3. ALL DESIGN PHASES SHOULD BE EMPIRICALLY BASED

The designer should collect student data to guide and test the application of principles, including (a) design experiments that guide initial development, (b) formative evaluations that analyze the successes and failures of problem-solving activities at a fine grain-size, and (c) summative evaluations that examine whether course-level curriculum objectives are being achieved. A spectrum of empirical research methods are available from lower cost, lower reliability to higher cost, higher reliability (e.g., Koedinger, 2002).

Design Research Examples

An important message of this chapter is that we not only need to make progress in better articulating theory and principles, but also in specifying associated empirical and analytic methods that better ensure these principles will be appropriately applied.

The following three sections provide extended examples of each of these three classes of empirical research. The first section describes the use of design studies to guide application of the fifth principle, reduce working memory load. The second section describes the use of design studies to guide application of the fourth principle, promote a general understanding. The third section describes summative evaluations of the Cognitive Tutor Algebra course.

Design Research Guides Reduction of Working Memory Load

In addition to the strategies discussed above to "minimize working memory load," we employed the strategy to design instruction that builds on students' prior knowledge (cf., Bransford, Brown, & Cocking, 1999). When instruction makes connections to what students already know, they need less cognitive load to process, understand, and integrate new knowledge into long-term memory.

How do we know what prior knowledge students have? Sometimes theoretical analysis of domain content is used to predict prior knowledge, under the assumption that smaller component tasks are more likely to tap prior knowledge than larger whole tasks (cf., van Merrienboer, 1997). However, although smaller tasks typically involve fewer knowledge components, they are not always simpler for students. It is not the surface form of tasks that determine how accessible they are to students. Instead, it is the internal mental representations that students acquire and use in task performance that determines what will be simple or not. To identify what prior knowledge students have and which tasks are most likely to tap prior knowledge, it is not enough to analyze the content domain. Instead it is critical to study how students actually perform on tasks – to see student thinking as it really is, not as a content analysis might assume it to be.

Consider the three problems shown here, a story problem, a word problem, and an equation, all with the same underlying quantitative structure and the same solution.

Story Problem:	As a waiter, Ted gets $6 per hour. One night he made $66 in tips and earned a total of $81.90. How many hours did Ted work?
Word Problem:	Starting with some number, if I multiply it by 6 and then add 66, I get 81.90. What number did I start with?
Equation:	$x * 6 + 66 = 81.90$

Table 5.3. Comparisons of Situational and Abstract Problems in Four Content Areas

	Decimal Place Value	Decimal Arith	Fraction Addition	Data Interp-Global
Situation	Show 5 different ways that you can give Ben $4.07. [A place value table was provided.]	You had $8.72. Your grandmother gave you $25 for your birthday. How much money do you have now?	Mrs. Jules bought each of her children a chocolate bar. Jarren ate 1/4 of a chocolate bar and Alicia ate 1/5 of a chocolate bar. How much of a chocolate bar did they eat altogether?	[2 scatterplots given] Do students sell more boxes of candy bars or cookies as the months pass?
% correct	61%	65%	32%	62%
Abstract	List 5 different ways to show the amount 4.07. [Place value table given.]	Add: 8.72 + 25	Add: 1/4 + 1/5	[Scatterplots given] Are there more moops per zog in the left graph or the right graph?
% correct	20%	35%	22%	48%

Which would be most difficult for high school students in a first year algebra course? Nathan and Koedinger (2000) discussed results of surveys of mathematics teachers on a variation of this question. The survey respondents tended to predict that story problems would be most difficult and equations would be easiest. Typical justifications for this prediction include that the story problem requires more reading or that the way the story problem is solved is by translating it to the equation.

In contrast, Koedinger and Nathan (2004) found that students perform best at story and word problems (70 percent and 61 percent, respectively) and worst at the analogous equations (42 percent). Clearly, many students were not solving the story and word problems using equation solving. Instead, they used alternative informal strategies like guess-and-test and "unwinding," working backward from the result, inverting operations to find the unknown starting quantity. Students had difficulty comprehending equations, and even when they did they often had difficulty reliably executing the equation solving strategy.

This result shows that if we want to create instruction that builds on prior knowledge, we should make use of the fact that beginning algebra students have quantitative reasoning skills that can be tapped through verbal or situational contexts. Unlike many textbooks that teach equation solving prior to story problem solving (Nathan, Long, & Alibali, 2002), it may be better to use story problem situations and verbal descriptions first, to help students informally understand quantitative relationships, before moving to more abstract processing of formal representations.

This study illustrates why we advocate the mantra "the student is not like me." We need empirical methods to see past our biases or "expert blind spots" to what students are really like.

Table 5.3 further illustrates why it is important to use empirical methods to determine when and how to employ a principle. Using problem situations to build on prior knowledge and reduce working memory load will not work if those problem situations are not familiar. In our development of Cognitive Tutor Math 6 (Koedinger, 2002), we used a Difficulty Factors Assessment to find which kinds of problem situations make problems easier for students and which kinds do not. Table 5.3 illustrates different content areas in middle school math where we compared concrete story problem situations with abstract context-free problems.

Table 5.3 shows sixth graders' average percent correct on multiple pretest items in each content area. In three of the areas – decimal place value, decimal arithmetic, and fraction addition – the problem situation consistently facilitated performance significantly above the abstract problem. In data analysis, the situation facilitated performance on a global interpretation task, but not on a local interpretation task. In the area of factors and multiples, the situation reduced performance.

Thus, using situations to build on prior knowledge may not be effective for concepts and procedures related to factors and multiples, unless situations can be found that are easier to understand than abstract problems. Although one might still want to use such a problem situation as motivation for learning, given these data it does not appear that such a situation will provide a student with easier, less cognitively taxing access to understanding of the domain content.

Reflection Promotes General Understanding

One well-researched approach to promoting a correct and general encoding is called "self-explanation": students explain to themselves the steps they take in problem solutions (e.g., Chi, de Leeuw, Chiu, & Lavancher, 1994). Aleven and Koedinger (2002) implemented a version of self-explanation in Cognitive Tutor Geometry and experimented with its effectiveness. Figure 5.3 illustrates the "explanation by reference" approach employed. Students provided explanations for problem-solving steps by making reference to geometry rules or reasons in an online glossary. Students could either type the name of the rule or select it from the glossary. This form of explanation is different from the speech-based explanations in most prior experiments on self-explanation, but has the benefit that the explanations can be understood by the computer.

Prior Difficulty Factors Assessments had indicated that students were better able to perform a problem-solving step, like determining that angle ARN in Figure 5.3 is equal to 43.5 degrees, than to explain that step by referring to the "Alternate Interior Angles" rule. One reason for this difference is that students' prior knowledge includes overgeneralized production rules like "if an angle *looks equal* to another, then it is" that can provide correct answers to steps, but cannot provide an understanding of when such steps are justified and why. Such overgeneralized productions may result from shallow encoding and learning. According to Aleven and Koedinger's ACT-R interpretation, self-explanation promotes more general encoding because students think more deliberately, with greater explicit reflection, about the verbal declarative representations of domain rules. This deliberate reflection helps identify key features of the domain rules and thus improves the accuracy of the implicit inductive process of "compiling" (a form of learning) production rules from examples and visual input. Indeed, Aleven and Koedinger (2002) found that students using the self-explanation version of Cognitive Tutor Geometry were not only better able to provide accurate explanations, but learned the domain rules with greater understanding – such that they could better transfer to novel problems, and better avoid shallow inferences like the "looks equal" production illustrated earlier.

Summative Field Study Evaluations and Classroom Observations

We originally assessed Cognitive Tutor Algebra in experimental field studies in city schools in Pittsburgh and Milwaukee, replicated over three different school years. The assessments used in these field studies targeted both (1) higher-order conceptual achievement, as measured by performance assessments of problem solving and representation use, and (2) basic skills achievement, as measured by standardized test items, for instance, from the math SAT. In comparison with traditional algebra classes

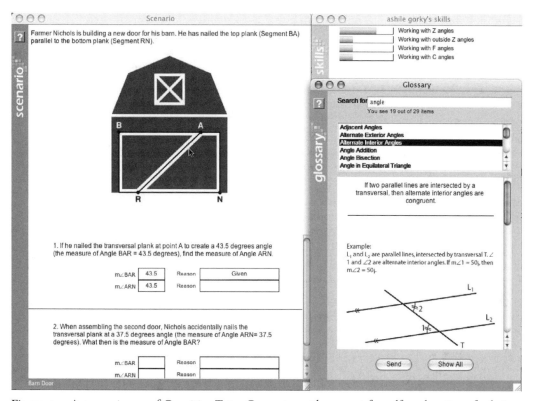

Figure 5.3. A screen image of Cognitive Tutor Geometry with support for self-explanation of solution steps.

at the same and similar schools, we have found that students using Cognitive Tutor Algebra perform 15–25 percent better than control classes on standardized test items and 50–100 percent better on problem solving and representation use (Corbett, Koedinger, & Hadley, 2001; Koedinger et al., 1997; also see http://www.carnegielearning.com/results/reports). More recent studies in other cities have replicated these findings. For example, the Moore (Oklahoma) Independent School District conducted a within-teacher experiment (Morgan & Ritter, 2002). Eight teachers at four junior high schools taught some of their classes using Cognitive Tutor Algebra I and others using their traditional textbook. On the ETS End-of-Course Algebra exam, students taking the Cognitive Tutor curriculum scored significantly higher than control students. Cognitive Tutor students also earned higher course grades and had more positive attitudes towards mathematics.

The deployment of educational technology in the classroom has an impact beyond learning outcomes. Following the observations of Schofield, Evans-Rhodes, and Huber (1990) and Wertheimer (1990), we have also observed the impact of the use of Cognitive Tutor Algebra on changes in classroom social and motivational processes (Corbett et al., 2001). Visitors to these classrooms often comment on how engaged students are. Cognitive Tutor Algebra may enhance student motivation for a number of different reasons. First, authentic problem situations make mathematics more interesting, sensible, or relevant. Second, students on the average would rather be doing than listening, and the incremental achievement and feedback within Cognitive Tutor Algebra problems provide a video-game-like appeal. Third, the safety net provided by the tutor reduces potential for frustration and provides assistance on errors without social stigma. Finally, the longer-term achievement of mastering the mathematics is empowering.

Conclusions and Future Work

Human tutoring is an extremely effective and enjoyable way to learn. But buying one computer per student is a lot more cost effective than hiring a teacher for every student. Before a computer program can function as a tutor, it has to be able to do several key things that human tutors can do: (1) use domain knowledge to solve problems and reason as we want students to do; (2) have knowledge of typical student misconceptions, relevant prior informal knowledge, and learning trajectories; (3) follow student reasoning step by step and understand when and where students reveal a lack of knowledge or understanding; (4) provide appropriate scaffolding, feedback, and assistance to students when they need it and in the context of that need; and (5) adapt instruction to individual student needs based on an ongoing assessment of those needs. The cognitive model, model tracing, and knowledge tracing algorithms of the Cognitive Tutor architecture provide these key behaviors of good tutoring.

Cognitive Tutors and ACT-R are one manifestation of the many advances in cognitive psychology and instructional design made by learning scientists. Cognitive Tutors implement a decidedly simple form of tutoring. More sophisticated tutoring strategies can be imagined (cf. Collins et al., 1989), and some of these strategies, such as natural language tutorial dialog, are being implemented in increasingly practical forms (e.g., Jordan, Rosé, & VanLehn, 2001; Wiemer-Hastings, Wiemer-Hastings, & Graesser, 1999). Experimental studies are testing whether such added sophistication leads to increased student learning (e.g., Aleven, Popescu, & Koedinger, 2003). There is also substantial research on whether even simpler forms of instruction, like worked examples of problem solutions, are as effective or more effective than more complex forms (e.g., Clark & Mayer, 2003).

Cognitive Tutor research is actively advancing along a number of dimensions. A major current research topic is tutoring metacognitive skills in addition to cognitive skills, including self-explanation (Aleven & Koedinger, 2002), error detection and correction (Mathan & Koedinger, 2003), and learning and help-seeking skills (Aleven, McLaren, Roll, & Koedinger, 2004). Cognitive Tutors are also being deployed to support required state testing and school accountability (http://assistment.org) and authoring tools are being created to speed Cognitive Tutor development (http://ctat.pact.cs.cmu.edu). Finally, Cognitive Tutors are being employed as research platforms to allow rigorous experimental tests of learning principles "in vivo," that is, in classrooms with real students and real courses (http://learnlab.org).

Acknowledgments

The National Science Foundation (NSF), Department of Education, and DARPA supported Algebra Cognitive Tutor research. Carnegie Learning, Inc supported Cognitive Tutor Math 6. NSF's Science of Learning Center is supporting the Pittsburgh Science of Learning Center and creation of LearnLab.

Footnote

1. In this chapter we will often refer to such performance situations as "problems" or "problem-solving activities" although we believe that many of the ideas about tutoring expressed in this chapter are relevant to performances that are not usually described as problem solving, like writing an essay, making a scientific discovery, or communicating in a foreign language.

References

Aleven, V., & Koedinger, K. R. (2002). An effective meta-cognitive strategy: Learning by doing and explaining with a computer-based Cognitive Tutor. *Cognitive Science*, 26, 147–179.

Aleven, V., McLaren, B., Roll, I., & Koedinger, K. R. (2004). Toward tutoring help seeking. In Lester, Vicari, & Parguacu (Eds.) *Proceedings of the 7th International Conference on Intelligent Tutoring Systems*, 227–239. Berlin: Springer-Verlag.

Aleven, V., Popescu, O., & Koedinger, K. R. (2003). A tutorial dialog system to support self-explanation: Evaluation and open questions. In U. Hoppe, F. Verdejo, & J. Kay (Eds.), *Artificial Intelligence in Education: Shaping the Future of Learning through Intelligent Technologies, Proceedings of AI-ED 2003* (pp. 39–46). Amsterdam, IOS Press.

Anderson, J. R., Boyle, C. F., & Reiser, B. J. (1985). Intelligent tutoring systems. *Science, 228*, 456–468.

Anderson, J. R., Corbett, A. T., Koedinger, K. R., & Pelletier, R. (1995). Cognitive tutors: Lessons learned. *Journal of the Learning Sciences, 4*(2), 167–207.

Anderson, J. R., & Jeffries, R. (1988). Novice LISP errors: Undetected losses of information from working memory. *Human-Computer Interaction, 1*, 107–131.

Anderson, J. R., & Lebiere, C. (1998). *The atomic components of thought*. Mahwah, NJ: Lawrence Erlbaum Associates.

Berry, D. C., & Dienes, Z. (1993). *Implicit learning: Theoretical and empirical issues*. Hove, UK: Lawrence Erlbaum Associates.

Bloom, B. S. (1984). The 2 sigma problem: The search for methods of group instruction as effective as one-to-one tutoring. *Educational Researcher, 13*, 3–16.

Bransford, J. D., Brown, A. L., & Cocking, R. R. (1999). *How people learn: Brain, mind, experience, and school*. Committee on Developments in the Science of Learning Commission on Behavioral and Social Sciences and Education. National Research Council. Washington, DC: National Academy Press.

Chi, M. T. H., de Leeuw, N., Chiu, M., & Lavancher, C. (1994). Eliciting self-explanations improves understanding. *Cognitive Science, 18*, 439–477.

Chi, M. T. H., Feltovich, P. J., & Glaser, R. (1981). Categorization and representation of physics problems by experts and novices. *Cognitive Science, 5*, 121–152.

Clark, R. C., & Mayer, R. E. (2003). *e-learning and the science of instruction: Proven guidelines for consumers and designers of multimedia learning*. San Francisco: Jossey-Bass.

Collins, A., Brown, J. S., & Newman, S. E. (1989). Cognitive apprenticeship: Teaching the crafts of reading, writing, and mathematics. In L. B. Resnick (Ed.), *Knowing, learning, and instruction: Essays in honor of Robert Glaser* (pp. 453–494). Hillsdale, NJ: Lawrence Erlbaum Associates.

Corbett, A. T. (2001). Cognitive computer tutors: Solving the two-sigma problem. *User Modeling: Proceedings of the Eighth International Conference, UM 2001*, 137–147.

Corbett, A. T., & Anderson, J. R. (1995). Knowledge tracing: Modeling the acquisition of procedural knowledge. *User modeling and user-adapted interaction, 4*, 253–278.

Corbett, A. T., & Anderson, J. R. (2001). Locus of feedback control in computer-based tutoring: Impact on learning rate, achievement and attitudes. *Proceedings of ACM CHI 2001 Conference on Human Factors in Computing Systems*, 245–252.

Corbett, A. T., Koedinger, K. R., & Anderson, J. R. (1997). Intelligent tutoring systems. In M. G. Helander, T. K. Landauer, & P. V. Prabhu, (Eds.), *Handbook of human-computer interaction* (pp. 849–874). Amsterdam: Elsevier.

Corbett, A. T., Koedinger, K. R., & Hadley, W. H. (2001). Cognitive Tutors: From the research classroom to all classrooms. In Goodman, P. S. (Ed.), *Technology-enhanced learning: Opportunities for change* (pp. 235–263). Mahwah, NJ: Lawrence Erlbaum Associates.

Corbett, A. T., MacLaren, B., Kauffman, L., Wagner, A., Jones, E., & Koedinger, K. R. (2005). *Evaluating a genetics cognitive tutor: Modeling and supporting a pedigree analysis task*. Carnegie Mellon University Technical Report.

Corbett, A. T., & Trask, H. (2000). Instructional interventions in computer-based tutoring: Differential impact on learning time and accuracy. *Proceedings of ACM CHI 2000 Conference on Human Factors in Computing Systems*, 97–104.

Eberts, R. E. (1997). Computer-based instruction. In Helander, M. G., Landauer, T. K., & Prabhu, P. V. (Eds.) *Handbook of human-computer interaction* (pp. 825–847). Amsterdam: Elsevier Science B.V.

Fox, B. (1991). Cognitive and interactional aspects of correction in tutoring. In P. Goodyear (Ed.) *Teaching knowledge and intelligent tutoring* (pp. 149–172). Norwood, NJ: Ablex Publishing.

Jordan, P. W., Rosé, C. P., & VanLehn, K. (2001). Tools for authoring tutorial dialogue knowledge. In J. D. Moore, C. L. Redfield, & W. L. Johnson (Eds.), *Artificial Intelligence in Education: AI-ED in the Wired and Wireless Future, Proceedings of AI-ED 2001*. Amsterdam: IOS Press.

Koedinger, K. R. (2002). Toward evidence for instructional design principles: Examples from Cognitive Tutor Math 6. In *Proceedings of PME-NA XXXIII (The North American Chapter of the International Group for the Psychology of Mathematics Education)*.

Koedinger, K. R., & Anderson, J. R. (1993). Effective use of intelligent software in high school math classrooms. In P. Brna, S. Ohlsson and H. Pain (Eds.) *Proceedings of AIED 93 World Conference on Artificial Intelligence in Education*, 241–248. Chesapeake, VA: Associate for the Advancement of Computing in Education.

Koedinger, K. R., Anderson, J. R., Hadley, W. H., & Mark, M. A. (1997). Intelligent tutoring goes to school in the big city. *International Journal of Artificial Intelligence in Education, 8*, 30–43.

Koedinger, K. R., & Nathan, M. J. (2004). The real story behind story problems: Effects of representations on quantitative reasoning. *The Journal of the Learning Sciences, 13* (2), 129–164.

Kulik, C. C., & Kulik, J. A. (1991). Effectiveness of computer-based instruction: An updated analysis. *Computers in Human Behavior, 7*, 75–95.

Lave, J., Murtaugh, M., & de la Rocha, O. (1984). The dialectic of arithmetic in grocery shopping. In B. Rogoff & J. Lave (Eds.), *Everyday Cognition* (pp. 67–94). Cambridge, MA: Harvard University Press.

Lepper, M. R., Aspinwall, L., Mumme, D., & Chabay, R. W. (1990). Self-perception and social perception processes in tutoring: Subtle social control strategies of expert tutors. In J. Olson & M. Zanna (Eds.) *Self inference processes: The sixth Ontario symposium in social psychology* (pp. 217–237). Hillsdale, NJ: Lawrence Erlbaum Associates.

Littman, D. (1991). Tutorial planning schemas. In P. Goodyear (Ed.) *Teaching knowledge and intelligent tutoring*, 107–122. Norwood, NJ: Ablex Publishing.

Mathan, S., & Koedinger, K. R. (2003). Recasting the feedback debate: Benefits of tutoring error detection and correction skills. In Hoppe,

Verdejo, & Kay (Eds.), *Artificial Intelligence in Education, Proceedings of AI-ED 2003* (pp. 13–18). Amsterdam: IOS Press.

Matz, M. (1982). Towards a process model for high school algebra errors. In D. Sleeman and J. S. Brown (Eds.) *Intelligent tutoring systems* (pp. 25–50). New York: Academic Press.

McArthur, D., Stasz, C., & Zmuidzinas, M. (1990). Tutoring techniques in algebra. *Cognition and Instruction, 7*, 197–244.

Merrill, D. C., Reiser, B. J., Ranney, M., & Trafton, G. J. (1992). Effective tutoring techniques: A comparison of human tutors and intelligent tutoring systems. *The Journal of the Learning Sciences, 2*, 277–305.

Morgan, P., & Ritter, S. (2002). *An experimental study of the effects of Cognitive Tutor® Algebra I on student knowledge and attitude*. Pittsburgh, PA: Carnegie Learning Inc. Retrieved April 14, 2005, from http://www.carnegielearning.com/wwc/originalstudy.pdf.

Nathan, M. J., & Koedinger, K. R. (2000). An investigation of teachers' beliefs of students' algebra development. *Cognition and Instruction, 18*(2), 207–235.

Nathan, M. J., Long, S. D., & Alibali, M. W. (2002). Symbol precedence in mathematics textbooks: A corpus analysis. *Discourse Processes, 33*, 1–21.

Newell, A., & Simon, H. A. (1972). *Human problem solving*. Englewood Cliffs, NJ: Prentice Hall.

Polya, G. (1957). *How to solve it: A new aspect of mathematical method*. (2nd ed.). Princeton, NJ: Princeton University Press.

Resnick, L. B. (1987). Learning in school and out. *Educational Researcher, 16*(9), 13–20.

Ritter, S., & Anderson, J. R. (1995). Calculation and strategy in the equation solving tutor. In J. D. Moore & J. F. Lehman (Eds.), *Proceedings of the Seventeenth Annual Conference of the Cognitive Science Society* (pp. 413–418). Hillsdale, NJ: Erlbaum.

Scheines, R., & Sieg, W. (1994). Computer environments for proof construction. *Interactive Learning Environments, 4*, 159–169.

Schofield, J. W. (1995). *Computers and classroom culture*. New York: Cambridge.

Schofield, J. W., Evans-Rhodes, D., & Huber, B. (1990). Artificial intelligence in the classroom. *Social Science Computer Review, 8*(1), 24–41.

Singley, M. K. (1990). The reification of goal structures in a calculus tutor: Effects on problem solving performance. *Interactive Learning Environments, 1*, 102–123.

Singley, M. K., & Anderson, J. R. (1989). *Transfer of cognitive skill*. Hillsdale, NJ: Lawrence Erlbaum Associates.

Skinner, B. F. (1968). *The technology of teaching*. New York: Appleton-Century-Crofts.

Sleeman, D. H., & Brown, J. S. (1982). *Intelligent tutoring systems*. New York: Academic Press.

Sweller, J. (1988). Cognitive load during problem solving: Effects on learning. *Cognitive Science, 12*, 257–285.

van Merrienboer, J. J. G. (1997). *Training complex cognitive skills: A four-component instructional design model for technical training*. Englewood Cliffs, NJ: Educational Technology Publications.

Vygotsky, L. S. (1978). *Mind in society*. Cambridge, MA: Harvard University Press.

Wenger, E. (1987). *Artificial intelligence and tutoring systems: Computational and cognitive approaches to the communication of knowledge*. Los Altos, CA: Morgan Kaufmann.

Wertheimer, R. (1990). The geometry proof tutor: An "intelligent" computer-based tutor in the classroom. *Mathematics Teacher, 83*(4), 308–317.

Wiemer-Hastings, P., Wiemer-Hastings, K., & Graesser, A. C. (1999). Improving an intelligent tutor's comprehension of students with latent semantic analysis. In Lajoie, S. P. and Vivet, M. eds. *Artificial Intelligence in Education, Open Learning Environments: New Computational Technologies to Support Learning, Exploration, and Collaboration, Proceedings of AIED-99*, 535–542. Amsterdam: IOS Press.

CHAPTER 6

Learning in Activity

James G. Greeno

This chapter discusses a program of research in the learning sciences that I call "situative." The defining characteristic of a situative approach is that instead of focusing on individual learners, the main focus of analysis is on *activity systems*: complex social organizations containing learners, teachers, curriculum materials, software tools, and the physical environment. Over the decades, many psychologists have advocated a study of these larger systems (Dewey, 1896, 1929/1958; Lewin, 1935, 1946/1997; Mead, 1934; Vygotsky, 1987), although they remained outside the mainstream of psychology, which instead focused on individuals. Situative analyses include hypotheses about principles of coordination that support communication and reasoning in activity systems, including construction of meaning and understanding.

Other terms for the perspective I refer to as situative include sociocultural psychology (Cole, 1996; Rogoff, 1995), activity theory (Engeström, 1993; 1999), distributed cognition (Hutchins, 1995a), and ecological psychology (Gibson, 1979; Reed, 1996). I use the term "situative" because I was intro-duced to the perspective by scholars who referred to their perspective as situated action (Suchman, 1985), situated cognition (Lave, 1988), or situated learning (Lave & Wenger, 1991). I prefer the term "situative," a modifier of "perspective," "analysis," or "theory," to "situated," used to modify "action," "cognition," or "learning," because the latter adjective invites a misconception: that some instances of action, cognition, or learning are situated and others are not. During the 1980s and 1990s these scholars and others provided analyses in which concepts of cognition and learning are relocated at the level of activity systems. For example, Hutchins (1995b) studied remembering in the activity of flying commercial airplanes and gave an analysis of remembering to change the settings of flaps and slats during a descent as an accomplishment of the activity system of the cockpit, including the two pilots along with instruments and other informational resources. Goodwin (1996) studied perception and comprehension in the activity of managing ground operations at an airport and gave an analysis of perceiving and comprehending conditions at flight gates as an accomplishment of the activity system of the ops room, including several human participants along with telemonitors that provided images of planes at their gates, with interpretation of the images on telemonitors organized by the relevance of information to their practice.

Studies of reasoning and problem solving have been especially influential. Lave, Murtaugh, and della Rosa (1984) analyzed reasoning by grocery shoppers as a process in which their decisions were shaped jointly by their initial goals and preferences along with the objects and symbols in the aisles of the supermarket. Scribner (1984) analyzed problem solving by workers in a dairy warehouse as a process in which their performance of placing requested numbers of items in containers for delivery was jointly determined by the workers' reading of forms showing the numbers needed and the visible numbers of items and open spaces in containers in the situation. The decisions and solutions produced in the shopping and the dairy product-loading systems were generally optimal; that is, the the shoppers generally chose products that had the best unit price, and the dairy product loaders generally filled orders by moving the minimum number of items. When mathematical problems equivalent to those solved by people in everyday activity are given to them in school-like tests, they generally perform poorly, which was documented particularly by Nunes, Schliemann, and Carraher (1993). The strong conclusion is that it is virtually meaningless to ask whether someone has learned a particular topic of mathematics, such as numerical multiplication, without taking into account the kind of activity system in which the person's "knowledge" is to be evaluated. Learning that occurs in one kind of activity system can influence what one does in a different kind of system, but explanations in terms of overlapping aspects of activities in practice are much more promising than explanations in terms of the transfer of knowledge structures that individuals have acquired (e.g., Beach, 1995; Greeno, Smith, & Moore, 1993; Saxe, 1990).

From the situative perspective, all socially organized activities provide opportunities for learning to occur, including learning that is different from what a teacher or designer might wish. We study learning when we choose to focus our observations and analyses on changes over time and experience in people's activities. The study of learning in activity requires us to develop concepts and principles that can explain how and why activities in a setting result in changes in what people can do. Use of the situative perspective in designing learning environments focuses on characteristics of activity systems that can result in learners increasing their capabilities for participation in ways that are valued.

The situative perspective builds on and synthesizes two large research programs in the study of human behavior, both of which emerged as alternatives to behaviorism in the 1960s and 1970s. The first is *cognitive science*; this research focuses on patterns of information that are hypothesized to be recognized or constructed in activity. Generally, this research focuses on individuals, although social interactions can be (and increasingly are) considered as contexts of individual cognition and learning. The second is *interactional studies*; this research focuses on patterns of coordination in groups of individuals engaged in joint action with material and informational systems in their environments. Each of these two research programs has developed a considerable body of empirical findings, theoretical concepts, and methods. Each of them has succeeded in developing concepts and principles that explain significant aspects of learning, and each has played a key role in the formation of the contemporary learning sciences.

Although these two lines of research both provide important scientific knowledge about learning, until very recently they developed mainly in isolation from one another. Research in the individual cognitive perspective has analyzed information structures but has had little to say about the interactions that people have with each other and with technological resources in practice. Research in the interactional approach has analyzed patterns of coordination of activity but has had little to say about the information structures that are involved in the contents of joint activity, for example, what the conversations people have are about. There is much to be learned by continuing both programs energetically. At the same time, it is valuable to develop ways to bring concepts and methods from the two programs together.

I begin by summarizing the individual cognitive and the interactional approaches. They emphasize different aspects of learning, and all of these aspects need to be addressed in the learning sciences. I then sketch two approaches to increasing the connections between research in the individual cognitive and interactional approaches, one that extends the individual cognitive approach to include interaction, the other – the situative approach – that extends the interactional approach to include analyses of information structures. In the rest of the chapter I discuss aspects of situative research, including some key concepts in the analysis of practices in activity, and I present two illustrative examples.

The Individual Cognitive Approach: Focus on Information Structures and Processes

Cognitive scientists focus on the activities of individuals as they answer questions, solve problems, study texts, or respond to stimuli. Most often, they examine performance on experimental tasks or school assessments. Cognitive explanations are models of the processes that individuals use to construct, store, retrieve, and modify patterns of information. These patterns are generally referred to as *information structures*. Concepts and methods for analyzing information structures are the main focus of cognitive science, but have remained in the background in most interactional analyses.

Analyses in the individual cognitive approach study information structures that participants already have learned or com-

prehend in the situation, which are used to engage in the activity, as well as information structures that are constructed in the process of participating in an activity. The cognitivist study of problem solving is an example. Individual problem solvers are hypothesized to have cognitive structures called *problem spaces* that represent the task, including objects of the problem, arrangements of the objects in different states, operators, goals, and strategies. In their activity they construct additional structures of subgoals, evaluations of changes in the problem state, memories of past attempts, and so on (e.g., Newell & Simon, 1972).

The cognitivist study of reading is another example. Cognitive scientists examine reading as a process in which the reader generates mental information structures: inferences, plot connections, characterizations, and overall narrative structures are generated by readers as they read stories. These structures are guided by more general information structures involving grammatical forms and schemata that correspond to patterns of information that can be instantiated with information found in the text (e.g., Kintsch, 1998).

Educational practices informed by the individual cognitive approach emphasize the construction of information structures and procedures that support understanding and reasoning. These approaches include Piaget's work on how children advance by constructing general schemata; curriculum design and development efforts of the 1960s, when experts in mathematics and science designed curricula around the conceptual structures of their subject matter; and curricula and technologies that are based on information-processing models of cognition, such as computer-based tutoring systems (Koedinger & Corbett, this volume).

The Interactional Approach: Focus on Participation Structures and Processes

The study of social interaction includes several disciplinary strands: ethnomethodology, discourse analysis, symbolic interactionism, and sociocultural psychology (compare to "interaction analysis" in Jordan & Henderson, 1995; Sawyer, this volume). This research focuses on how people talk to each other as they plan, evaluate, and coordinate their interactions with the material and technological systems in their environment. The goal is to identify patterns of interaction in which the several components (human and nonhuman) of systems coordinate their behaviors as they participate in their joint activity. Such patterns have been called *participation structures* or *participant structures* (Phillips, 1972).[1] A participation structure describes the distribution of the functional aspects of activity, including agency, authority, accountability, leading and following, initiating, attending, accepting, questioning or challenging, and so on. Participation structures that are characteristic of a community or group are aspects of the community's or group's *practices*, and learning to become more effective in one's participation corresponds to achieving fuller participation in a community's practices (Lave & Wenger, 1991).

The interactional approach focuses its study on the whole activity system, and it leads to conclusions about the principles of coordination of interactive systems. This means that the researcher has to analyze the whole activity system without yet having complete understanding of the individual components – particularly the individual human participants in the system. The tension between the individual cognitive and the interactional approaches thus represents a general difficulty facing scientists who study complex systems: whether to proceed by reduction to study of the components, or by holistic study of the entire system (Sawyer, 2005, Simon, 1969).

Interactional studies have identified important patterns of conversational interaction – patterns of turn taking, opening and closing of topics, and mechanisms of repair in response to apparent misunderstanding have been reported and discussed (Sawyer, this volume; Levinson, 1983). Patterns of differential participation

by different individuals can be analyzed; for example, in some classroom settings, students' contributions almost always respond directly to a question by the teacher (e.g., Bellak et al., 1966; Cazden, 1986; Mehan, 1979), and in others, discourse is arranged so that students also respond to each other's presentations and ideas (e.g., O'Connor & Michaels, 1996; Phillips, 1972).

An important contribution of interactional studies relates to an intuition by many educators that goals for student learning can be informed by aspects of the practices of professional scholars. For example, science education can include goals for students to be able to engage in reasoning, problem solving, and argumentation in ways that reflect practices that scientists have developed – for example, distinguishing hypotheses from evidence (e.g., Kuhn, 1989), inferring specific implications of general principles, and recognizing relations between specific problems and general principles (e.g., Chi, Feltovich, & Glaser, 1981). In pursuing this approach to science education, learning scientists can use results of studies of scientific practice – how scientists do their work and what knowledge and practices are involved in conducting that work. Influential studies of scientific practice were published in the mid-1980s (Latour & Woolgar, 1986; Lynch, 1985). These early interactional studies did not examine information structures in the scientific subject-matter disciplines; in fact, Latour and Woolgar (1986) famously claimed that all of science could be explained in terms of sociocultural factors, with no appeal to cognition. More recent studies have included careful and detailed analyses of the conceptual and empirical contents of scientific practice and development (e.g., Fujimura, 1996; Kitcher, 1993; Nersessian, 1984; 2002).

Including Interaction in Cognitive Analyses

One strategy for unifying individual cognitive and interactional concepts and methods is to work from the cognitive side and extend its reach to include situations involving interaction between more than one person. If an activity system can be decomposed into individuals and their tools, then we can analyze the activity system by reducing it to a study of the individuals and the tools, and then aggregating these explanations back together to form an explanation of the entire activity system. A strategic assumption of the individual cognitive approach is that groups can be explained by reduction to individual study in this way (Sawyer, 2005). However, to study individual learners, researchers create a new kind of activity structure – a laboratory experiment – and because we do not yet know how the properties of individuals depend on the social context, we have to make a *factoring assumption*: that the principles that characterize behavior of the individual research subject do not depend significantly on the rest of the activity system. Without analyzing the activity system as a whole, we risk arriving at conclusions that we think are about the individual, but in fact depend on broader features of the activity system, and thus would not readily generalize from the laboratory to real-world learning environments.

Some research by individual cognitive-science researchers has provided promising findings for the program of extending cognitive principles from individual to group activity. For example, Schwartz (1995), studying performance of middle- and high-school students on tasks involving understanding mechanical or biological systems, found that pairs of students working together included useful abstractions in their conversations more often than was the case for thinking-aloud protocols of individual students. Okada and Simon (1997), studying performance of college students in a simulation of scientific problem solving, also found that pairs of participants outperformed individual participants. The pairs had greater frequencies of generating productive hypotheses to test in the simulation. Dunbar (1995), studying the conversations of biology laboratory groups, found that the participants made productive use of analo-

gies in their joint reasoning. These results indicate that some processes known to be important in reasoning and problem solving by individuals – attending to general features of problem situations, generating hypotheses, constructing analogies – are also significant in reasoning by groups. That some of these processes occur more frequently and, perhaps, more productively in group than in individual performance, could be explained as an effect of the presence of other people as a favorable aspect of the social context.

Other findings, however, indicate that analyses of activity by groups may involve significant processes that are less evident in individual activity. Barron (2003), studying mathematical problem solving by sixth-grade students, concluded that their management of joint attention was an important factor in their success. Sawyer (2003), studying performance by groups performing jazz music and improvisational theater, concluded "that both verbal and musical performance collectively emerge from interactional processes," and that "the analysis of group creativity requires a fundamentally interactional semiotics, one which emphasizes the indexical properties of sign usage" (2003, p. 95). That semiotic interpretation in these improvisational activities is fundamentally indexical has the consequence that understanding meanings and, therefore, the course of a performance requires analysis of the interactional system in a way that goes significantly beyond that of scripted performances and problems that have stable problem spaces.

A Situative Approach: Including Information Structures in Interactional Analyses

Studies in what I call the "situative perspective" use another strategy aimed to bring concepts and methods of cognitive and interactional studies together. In a situative study the main focus of analysis is on performance and learning by an activity system: a collection of people and other systems.

In a situative study, individual cognition is considered in relation to more general patterns of interaction. For example, in inquiry classrooms, students' understandings are shared as they formulate and evaluate questions, and propose and debate alternative meanings of concepts and explanations. Analyses can consider whether the actions of individual students contribute to the class's progress in achieving shared understanding, rather than simply being displays of the understandings they have already constructed cognitively in their prior interactions with textbooks, teachers, and computers.

Developing a situative explanation requires a simultaneous consideration of both the interactive principles of coordination, and the semiotic structures[2] of information that are used in the activity. Such studies include analyses of information structures that are understood, used, and generated by the participants in their joint activity. Those analyses can use many of the concepts and representations that are standard in cognitive science; they differ in that they are based on records of conversation between participants (instead of thinking-aloud protocols of individuals) and they are interpreted as hypotheses about information that is constructed in the participants' conversational common ground, with hypotheses about information that they already shared in their common ground in order to have the conversations we observe. These situative studies, then, bring the individual cognitive and interactional approaches together by providing analyses of interaction in activity systems that include hypotheses about semiotic structures that are the informational contents of the activity. These analyses include representing contributions of the material and technological tools and artifacts of the system. The goal is to understand cognition as the interaction among participants and tools in the context of an activity. For this reason, it is often said that the situative perspective studies *distributed cognition*: problem solving, planning, and reasoning are accomplished by a group of people, working together with complex technological artifacts and with material representations they generate during the task (diagrams, figures, and models).

There is nothing in the situative perspective that precludes analyses on multiple levels simultaneously. Analyses of thinking processes and information structures perceived and constructed by one or more of the individuals participating in a group can be conducted, as can analyses of the ways in which the activity in a system is supported and constrained by the institutional setting of which the activity system is a part. We aspire to progress toward analyses at all of these levels (and others, even studies of brain processes) that can be coordinated with each other, providing different understanding at their several levels of analysis, but also providing understanding of how the concepts and principles at different levels are related to each other.

I propose that analyses in the situative perspective depart from previous work in the cognitive and interactional approaches in three significant ways. I illustrate these with a brief discussion of an example, which comes from a three-minute conversation between a middle school teacher and a student about a draft report that the student had written on behalf of her project group. The class was working on a curriculum unit from the Middle-school Mathematics through Applications Project (MMAP) (Goldman & Moschkovich, 1995; Greeno & MMAP, 1998) called Antarctica, which has the students use a design program called ArchiTech that supports students in designing buildings. Groups of four to five students were working on designing living quarters for four scientists who would have to stay in Antarctica for two years. ArchiTech includes a graphics interface that students use to construct floor plans and to specify details such as the amount of insulation, and average monthly indoor and outdoor temperatures. The program calculates the total cost of the building that they have designed and the projected monthly cost of heating the building, based on their assumptions about temperatures and the amount of insulation and its quality. Their design has to include spaces for work, sleeping, and recreation.

I discuss an episode that involves a special assignment that the teacher gave: find the value of insulation quality, called the "R value," that would minimize the total cost of construction and heating over two years. To solve the task, students kept their designs and temperature assumptions constant, and used the program to calculate the total cost of construction and the monthly heating cost for different R values. The student's group had constructed a table of values with each row showing the construction cost and the two-year heating cost for one R value. In their analysis, they focused on pairs of successive rows in the table, noting how much the construction cost increased and the monthly heating cost decreased from the lower to the higher R value. The R value that they selected as the one that would minimize the total two-year cost was 20 because between R = 10 and R = 20, the increase in construction cost was less than the decrease in heating cost, but between 20 and 30, the increase in construction cost was greater than the decrease in heating cost. The teacher had expected a different form of analysis, in which the total costs (construction plus two years heating) would be calculated for each R value, then allowing a quick identification of the R value that minimized total cost.

In the conversation, the teacher and student successfully constructed a shared understanding of the group's analysis and why it was correct even though it was not what the teacher was expecting. A situative analysis of this episode has two components: an interaction analysis of the conversation, including close attention to its turn taking, responses, and contributions (Sawyer, this volume); and the semiotic structures of information that they constructed in the conversation, which include structures of information represented in the students' table. This latter analysis identified references of symbols to different versions of

the design, each of which had the numerical properties of R value, construction cost, and heating cost represented in a row in the students' table. The meanings of these symbols were constructed as information structures that the teacher and student generated jointly as they achieved a mutual understanding of the group's reasoning in their conversation.

The teacher and student were attuned to several interactional and semiotic practices as well as constraints in the task domain: turn taking conventions, including the expectation that the student would be given a chance to explain the group's reasoning; conventions of constructing and interpreting symbolic representations in numeric tables; regularities in the domain of building design, including the importance of cost; and arithmetic operations, which they used to compare R values. However, at least initially, the teacher was not attuned to the method that the group created to identify the optimal R value, although she followed the student's explanation and became attuned to this reasoning.

Data Are Records of Interaction, Rather Than "Verbal Reports"

One way the situative approach differs from individual cognitive research is in the kind of data that are typically used to infer properties of information structures. In individual cognitive research on problem solving, evidence about information structures is often in the form of thinking-aloud protocols provided by individual subjects. These protocols are then interpreted as providing evidence about the nature of the problem space as represented in the individual's mind, and the processes that the individual used to work in that problem space. A situative approach, in contrast, begins by noting that problem solving often occurs in group settings. When engaged in joint problem solving, participants talk, gesture, and create visible representations for each other as they interact. Using methods of interaction analysis, researchers transcribe the participants' activity, and the transcript provides a group-level analog of the thinking-aloud protocols that are analyzed in studies of problem solving: collaborative discourse is group thinking made visible. The evidence that participants provide each other through their collaborative discourse informs them about their understandings, goals, intentions, and expectations, and it provides evidence to the researcher about semiotic structures that are being generated and used.

How Semiotic Structures Are Generated

The learning sciences are fundamentally concerned with identifying how structures of information are generated and used in learning activities, and with ways that information functions in activity. In an individual cognitive approach, these processes are analyzed at the level of individual mental activities; in the situative approach, they are analyzed at the level of activity systems. If there is more than one person in the system, their conversation is *joint action* that constructs shared information (Clark & Schaefer, 1989). Clark and Wilkes-Gibbs (1986) have shown that reference can be understood as an achievement of joint action, rather than being a property of a symbol itself; the meanings of symbols are often interpreted in relation to problems that emerge in ongoing activity (e.g., Goodwin 1995). Even the referential meaning of a single word is a collaborative achievement that results from representational practice (Clark & Wilkes-Gibbs, 1986).

Researchers in conversation analysis (e.g., Schegloff, 1991) and psycholinguistics (e.g., Clark, 1996) have analyzed ways in which participants in a conversation mutually construct meanings. The conventions whereby symbols are interpreted differ in different cultures. These interpretations are integral components of the ongoing activities that people are engaged in as they participate in activity systems. The situative perspective considers meaning to be a relation between these joint actions of achieving mutual understanding, and the states of affairs or ideas that the participants themselves interpret their statements to be referring to. Material and other informational resources also contribute to the construction of information, in ways investigated in research on distributed cognition (e.g., Hutchins, 1995a) and in social studies of science (e.g., Pickering, 1995).

When researchers shift the analysis of knowledge construction to the level of the activity system, they include explanations about the various participants in the activity, and they analyze ways that individuals are positioned in the participant structures of interaction and how that positioning contributes to generation of information structures.

From Representation to Representational Practice

In the individual cognitive approach, representations are thought to be structures of information that connect concepts with each other in a network of propositions. These networks and concepts are mental objects that are stored in people's memories. In contrast, situativity treats representation as a relation between signs and aspects of situations, resulting from interpretations by people in their activity. The focus shifts to include both representations and *representational practices*.

The emphasis on representation as both mental and socially distributed in practices is a synthesis of cognitive and interactional perspectives. The individual cognitive perspective emphasizes representations of information, and the interactional perspective emphasizes representational practices as distributed across groups of people and across material objects and systems in the environment.

The representations and representational practices analyzed in the situative approach extend the scope of the typical context-free semantic-network representations of cognitive science to include *indexical relations* between a symbol and the context of its use. In a situative analysis, mental states can be considered to be representations, but there should be evidence that the hypothesized representations figure in a functional account of activity that attributes informational functions to those states. In the situative perspective, mental representations are only relevant to the extent that they refer indexically to ongoing activity. Most of the indexical relations that are represented in *semiotic networks* (Greeno & Engle, 1995) are functional in this sense, rather than having interpreted representations inside participant's minds. Researchers need not assume that these functional relations are actually represented in individual learner's minds unless there is evidence of an explicit representation.

Practices in Activity

Situative research focuses on properties of activity systems, especially on principles of coordination between the various components of such systems – the participants, the technological and material tools in the environment, and the informational structures and practices of the participants in the subject-matter domain of their activities.

The situative perspective inherits the assumption of interactional studies that activity is not usually scripted or planned in advance, but has to be negotiated and actively constructed by participants. Decades of research in the interactional tradition have documented that participants expend a great deal of effort coordinating their ongoing interactions, and have documented many cases where interaction breaks down when this coordination effort fails. Given that coordination is such hard work, a major theoretical problem facing situative researchers is to explain how it is that joint activity proceeds in a coherent way (on those occasions when it does, of course). Coordination or *alignment* between individuals depends on mutual understanding of communicative intentions (as in conversation), as well as coordination of actions (such as collaborating in moving a piece of furniture or performing in a dance). Alignment between one or more individuals and a system in the environment includes operating a

machine (such as a car) or playing an instrument (such as a piano), or observing, appreciating, and understanding the behavior of an object or system (such as a forest or an episode of animal behavior).

Practices That Contribute to Alignment

Aspects of activity in subject-matter domains have been considered and analyzed extensively in cognitive science, and hypotheses about them have been represented in the form of symbolic structures: cognitive representations in individuals' memories. The situative approach explains alignment by examining the group's shared social practices and the ways in which individuals participate in an episode of activity. A group's shared social practices include conventions, such as patterns of turn taking in conversation, or appropriate ways to work together while accomplishing a task, or what kinds of products will provide evidence that the task has been accomplished. Conventions also include ways to use symbols and other representational practices in spoken communication, in written communication, and in interacting with information technologies and tools in the learning environment – books and computer software. Discourse conventions include guidelines for turn taking, and the participants' various positions of status in the social arrangement of the classroom. These patterns specify the ways that agency, competence, authority, accountability, and other aspects of participation are distributed among participants in an interaction.

Participating in a community includes understanding the conventions and practices that are significant in that community's discourse about its activities. Some of that discourse is about the explicit meaning of concepts; much successful practice, however, depends on a shared implicit understanding of concepts – even when people may not know the explicit representations that are used by other people to discuss the concepts' meanings (Greeno, 1995).

Alignment also depends on the participants' shared practices of constructing contributions to their activity. A general schema of interaction in tasks is shown in Figure 6.1, adapted from Clark and Schaefer's (1989) schema for contributions to discourse. Working on a task involves performing actions that contribute to achieving the task goals. The results of action can just be an addition of information to the common ground – information about properties of the task or situation, or about evaluations, intentions, or goals. Or the results of action can also be a change in the material situation of the task, by moving or constructing an object or by writing or drawing some kind of representation.

The schema sketched in Figure 6.1 provides a way of thinking about and representing participatory aspects of interaction at a turn-by-turn level. In addition, general patterns in the ways contributions are made in a group's or community's practices can be identified. For example, classroom practices differ in the extent to which they encourage problematizing of ideas and issues (e.g., Engle & Conant, 2002) and in the ways that differences are resolved (Ball & Bass, 2000; Greeno, 2003). In Figure 6.1, these correspond to frequent occurrence of the NEGOTIATE nodes, with discussion about alternative ideas, actions, and approaches to understanding and working on tasks. In relation to Figure 6.1, problematizing and reconciling correspond to encouraging responses to students' contributions that consider alternative ideas, actions, and approaches.

Participant Structures

Practices vary in the ways that agency is distributed between the participants. In interaction, different individuals are positioned differently regarding the competence, authority, and accountability that are attributed to them by others and by themselves. These differences in positioning mean that individuals are differentially entitled and expected to initiate proposals for action or interpretation, to question or challenge other participants' proposals, and to indicate that an issue has been settled (as in the Initiation-Response-Evaluation sequence discussed in Sawyer,

this volume, and in other patterns of classroom discourse interaction, such as revoicing, O'Connor & Michaels, 1996).

Positioning in relation to other participants involves entitlements and expectations of the individual for initiating topics or questions, making assertions and proposals for actions, questioning or challenging others' assertions and proposals, and so on. Positioning in relation to the subject-matter domain has been characterized by Pickering (1995) as a dance of agency, involving material agency, disciplinary agency, and conceptual agency. Conceptual agency is involved when an individual or group interacts with the subject-matter constructively – interpreting meanings, formulating questions, choosing and adapting a method, designing an apparatus, and so on. Material agency is involved when a system (such as an experimental apparatus) determines the outcome of an action. Disciplinary agency is involved when established methods such as algorithms or proof procedures determine the outcome of an action. School activities often position students with little conceptual agency, teaching them instead how to perform algorithms correctly (disciplinary agency) or to set up apparatus to obtain known empirical results (material agency). The emphasis by constructivist educators on knowledge construction in authentic practice is designed to grant students some conceptual agency.

Alignment among participants depends on how differences in ways that individuals participate are understood and incorporated into practice. Situative analyses include study of the participant structures of episodes of activity, particularly ways that individuals are positioned to take initiative or not, to question or challenge others' proposals and assertions or not, to engage in the group activity attentively or not, and so on.

In an individual's participation in a group or community over time, he or she generally has some ways of interacting that come to be characteristic and expected by her- or himself and others in the group. These characteristic patterns, which are coconstructed by the individual and others in the group, constitute that person's positional identity

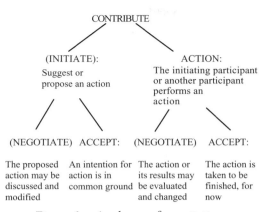

Figure 6.1. A schema of negotiation.

in that activity system. An individual's positioning can be understood both in regard to the other participants in the group – her or his characteristic positioning in participant structures – and in regard to the subject-matter of the group's activities – her or his characteristic positioning in relation to using and generating semiotic structures, for example, with or without conceptual agency. Individuals' identities in a classroom differ, such that some individuals are more likely than others to engage in working on tasks that are assigned, or to work collaboratively with others and try to reach mutual understanding, or to engage in social interaction not related to an assigned task (Gresalfi, 2004). Of course, an individual's participation is not always consistent with her or his general tendencies.

Situative researchers generally do not assume that our models of these conventions, practices, and identities necessarily correspond to cognitive representations inside participant's minds. Of course, people often do construct internal representations of these conventions and practices, and these constructions and interpretations are critical in activity and are an important topic for the learning sciences (e.g., Hall, 1996).

Community Practices

Communities and groups have practices that constrain (but do not determine) the subject-matter contents of their discourse and other activities in their subject-matter domains. These practices include

what counts as knowledge in the group's domain, including use and interpretation of its terminology, meanings of its concepts and principles, and applications of its methods. Communities of learners share standards about what characterizes worthwhile problems to engage in, and what constitutes an adequate or excellent solution of such a problem. Many of these standards are implicit: ways of formulating arguments and explanations, and ways of judging the relevance and significance of questions, information, evidence, and conclusions.

In the situative perspective, the institutional contexts of activity systems are important in understanding learning. Attitudes such as having a commitment to succeeding in schoolwork or not (Eckert, 1989, 1990), and having a positive or negative orientation toward activities of learning and knowledge construction, involve issues of affiliation and identity. In schools, students' affiliations in formally organized groups (band, chess club, gangs) as well as informal networks of friends are crucial in the development of their identities, and these groups sometimes shape student's identities in ways that oppose the school's preferred participation structures, as well as in ways that facilitate student engagement in academic pursuits that are valued by the institution. Students' motivation to learn depends on whether the learning activity supports the continual development of their personal identities. When learning environments do not support personal identity, learners will not be deeply engaged, even if they manage to maintain focus long enough to complete a classroom activity (Blumenfeld, Kemplar, & Krajcik, this volume).

Example: A Study of Learning a Classroom Practice

To illustrate how learning scientists can study the learning of practices using the situative perspective, I describe a case study: Hall and Rubin's (1998) analysis of how a representational practice became established in a classroom.[3] They documented how the practice originated in an individual's work, expanded through that student's small group, and then was broadcast to the class. Their analysis showed how learning to use and understand a representational form can be understood as an achievement of social interaction in activity.

The teacher, Magdalene Lampert, developed innovative practice-oriented teaching methods and examined the processes of her teaching for several years (e.g., 1990, 2001). Lampert often had her students work in groups of four or five students to discuss challenging problems. Each student kept a journal in which he or she recorded problem solutions and explanations. Hall and Rubin (1998) analyzed videotaped records of several segments of class activity involving the mathematics of distance, time, and speed of motion. They analyzed several incidents in the development and use of a kind of representational practice that they called a *journey line*, which represents two quantities – time and distance – by marking units along the line that are labeled with distances above the line, and corresponding times below the line. The sequence began with a student, Ellie, requesting help with a problem. Lampert recruited another student, Karim, to explain to Ellie why multiplication was the way to solve the problem, knowing that Karim had used the journey line in the explanation he had in his journal. Later, Lampert asked Karim to explain the representation to the class, characterizing the contribution as an example of students in a group working together. After Karim's presentation, Lampert had Ellie explain the representation to the class, affirming that it was a resource to be used generally in the class's practice. By attributing authorship of the explanation to Karim, making him the presenter of the explanation both to Ellie and to the class, and having Ellie present her concurring explanation, Lampert established the practice as an outcome of actions in which the students had significant conceptual agency.

Hall and Rubin (1998) distinguished between three levels of activity: private activity (writing in the journal), local activity (small group conversation) and public activity (presentations and discussions with the whole class). They identified several interactions in which the representational practice of the journey line played a key role – it functioned as a resource in the class's practices of problem solving and mutual sense-making. Learning sciences research often examines the role of representational forms as resources for collaborative sense-making and reasoning. It also examines ways that students develop their understanding in their joint activity (see Sawyer, this volume).

Example: A Study of a Learning Environment

To illustrate situative studies of learning environments, I describe a study by Nersessian and her colleagues (Nersessian et al., 2003; Nersessian, 2005), who recently extended this approach to focus more explicitly on learning – how laboratory groups develop over time toward increasing understanding.[4] These authors found it productive to consider activity in the scientific laboratory they studied as an evolving distributed cognitive systems. For example, Nersessian et al. (2003) gave a situative interpretation of several aspects of learning in a bioengineering lab that is trying to develop artificial blood vessels: the evolution of artifacts and methods, the evolution of relationships between individuals, and the evolution of relationships between individuals and artifacts.

Biomedical engineering is a new combination of disciplines in which new knowledge and practices are emerging continually, and the researchers are constantly learning during their problem solving activities. The laboratory team included undergraduates, doctoral students, and postdocs, and all of these participants learned over time and transformed their participation in the activity system. Much of the equipment used in the laboratory was designed and built by the team, and the members of the team often modified the technological artifacts during their practice – such that not only the people but also the tools underwent change over time.

Nersessian et al. (2003) found that to understand how problems were solved in this laboratory, they had to expand the traditional cognitive science notions of "problem space" and "mental representation" to consider these as being distributed across the people and the technology in the laboratory – a defining feature of situative research. The problem space comprised models and artifacts together with a repertoire of activities in which simulative model-based reasoning played a key role (cf. Lehrer & Schauble, this volume). The problem-solving processes of the lab were distributed throughout the cognitive system, which comprised both the researchers and the cognitive artifacts that they use (cf. Hutchins, 1995a).

Nersessian et al. (2003) used a mixed-method approach, combining cognitive analyses of the problems and models used by the biomedical researchers with an ethnographic analysis of the situative activities and tools and how they are used in the ongoing activity of the laboratory. Their close ethnographic analysis allowed them to document temporary and transient arrangements of the activity system – the laboratory routines, the organization of the workspace, the cultural artifacts being used, and the social organization of the team members. Their cognitive analysis allowed them to document how people and their relationships changed over time – as they evaluated and revised problem definitions (often working closely with technological artifacts), as they revised models of phenomena, and as their concepts changed over time.

Because it is impossible to test artificial blood vessels in a live human body, modeling practices were critical to the work. The researchers had to design working models to use for experimentation. Each iteration of a model represented the lab's collective understanding of the properties and behaviors of the human body. For example, the *flow loop* is a device that emulates the shear stresses experienced by cells within the blood vessels. The flow loop originated in the research of the senior scientist, and was passed down through generations of researchers, enabling each to build

on the research of others, as it was reengineered in the service of model-based reasoning. The flow loop is constructed so that the test fluid will create the same kinds of mechanical stresses as a real blood vessel. But because the model is a mechanical system, its design is subject to engineering constraints, and these often require simplification and idealization of the target biological systems being modeled. For example, in the body arterial wall motion is a response to the pulsating blood flow, but in the flow loop simulation, known as a *bioreactor*, the fluid doesn't actually flow, although it does model the pulsating changes in pressure experienced by the arterial wall.

In scientific laboratories, collaboration is often mediated by external representations such as these mechanical models, as well as diagrams and sketches. In this lab, devices were external representations of the collective knowledge of the group. Model-based reasoning is a distributed phenomenon, involving both the internal mental models that a researcher holds, as well as the shared external model manifested in devices and other models.

A situative analysis focuses on this distributed nature of cognition in the laboratory, treating it as a process involving multiple people and the technological artifacts that they create and modify together. In the situative view of an activity system, learning is conceived of as transformations over time in the nature of the interactions among people and between people and their constructed artifacts. For example, when newcomers to the lab were first introduced to a device like the bioreactor, they assumed that its design was fixed. As they began to interact with these devices, they quickly learned the many problems: tubes leak, sutures don't keep, reservoirs overflow, pumps malfunction. The newcomers soon realized that everyone else, including the most experienced old-timer, was always struggling to get things to work, always revising and modifying the devices. The newcomer's learning was a process of coming to understand the contingent and changing nature of these devices – the newcomers built relationships with the devices that Nersessian et al. (2003) called *cognitive partnerships*.

Conclusion

Analyses that use the situative perspective consider learning environments as activity systems in which learners interact with each other and with material, informational, and conceptual resources in their environment. The situative perspective is a synthesis of the two major scientific approaches to understanding human behavior: cognitive science and interactional studies. It combines the strengths of each of these approaches with the goal of better understanding how learning occurs and how to design learning environments.

Situativity is a general scientific perspective and as such does not say what educational practices should be adopted. Even so, it is well suited for analyzing processes of interaction and learning in the types of learning environments recommended by many progressive educators – a move away from a transmission-and-acquisition style of instruction, toward more collaborative, active, and inquiry-oriented classrooms.

By its focus on activity systems, the situative perspective emphasizes that the activities that take place in different learning environments are important, not only because of differences in how effectively they teach content knowledge but also because participation in practice is a central part of what students learn. If an aim in education is for students to learn practices of inquiry and sense-making, then learning environments must provide opportunities for them to participate in such practices. The situative perspective is reflected in a wide range of learning sciences projects, such as mathematics classrooms in which students participate in developing definitions, conjectures, representations, and arguments (e.g., Ball & Bass, 2000; Boaler, 2002; Fawcett, 1938; Lampert, 2001; Moses & Cobb, 2001; Schoenfeld, 1994; Schwartz, Yarushalmy, & Wilson, 1993). In science classrooms, students develop and evaluate hypotheses and arguments in science (Brown & Campione,

1994; Goldman, 1996; Hatano & Inagaki, 1991; Reiner, Pea, & Shulman, 1995) and in social studies (Collins, Hawkins, & Carver, 1991; Scardamalia, Bereiter, & Lamon, 1994).

This kind of practice was advocated by Dewey (e.g., 1910/1978) and is a major focus of learning sciences research and practice. The activities that contribute to these practices encourage students to participate in processes that include conceptual inquiry and the use of skills in solving meaningful problems as part of authentic projects (Krajcik & Blumenfeld, this volume). These learning environments include activities such as formulating and evaluating conjectures, conclusions, and arguments. In participation-oriented practices, class discussions are organized both to foster student learning of content and also to support their learning how to participate in the discourse practices that organize such discussions. Students learn about content and also learn how to participate in collaborative inquiry, and how to use the concepts and methods of a discipline to solve authentic problems. They learn representational systems, not only to express information in a domain but also to apply them in representational practices as they develop and share their understandings of questions, hypotheses, and arguments in the domain. A challenge for the learning sciences is to advance our theoretical understanding of learning to provide more coherent and definite explanations of learning in these environments, as well as more helpful guidance for the design of productive resources and practices. I have tried in this chapter to show that the situative perspective can be a valuable resource in this effort.

Acknowledgments

My research and writing are supported by a grant from the Spencer Foundation. This chapter benefited from energetic editing by Keith Sawyer. The conclusions in the chapter are mine, but there is significant material here that would not have been without Keith's contributions.

Footnotes

1. Contrasting participation structures with information structures, as I do here, is potentially misleading. Participation structures depend on information, which is produced and conveyed through gestures, timing, intonation, and other aspects of communicative action. Analyses of these aspects of discourse can be understood as analyses of information structures, in the sense that Gibson (1979) and more recent ecological psychologists have characterized their research as studies of information (e.g., Reed, 1996). The structures that I refer to with the term "information structures" are limited to information that participants construct that refers to objects and actions in their activities, and to properties and relations of those.

2. By "semiotic structures" I refer to patterns of information that are nearly (or perhaps completely) coextensive with information structures or symbolic structures in standard cognitive theory. A difference between the theories is that in a situative analysis, semiotic relations are between signs and their referents, including referents that are in the material situation or conceptual domain, rather than in a person's mental representation. These referents of terms in the information structures can be and often are specified, and cognitive processes are assumed to operate on objects in the environment as well as on symbols that represent them and their properties and relations.

3. There are many other studies that also illustrate this perspective, but space limitations prevent my reviewing them here. A few of them are Boaler (2002), Bowers, Cobb, and McClain (1999), Engle and Conant (2002), Rosebery, Warren, and Conant (1992), and Waterman (2004).

4. Again, there are several other examples that illustrate this approach to studying learning environments. Three such examples are Barab et al. (2002), Engeström (2001), and Hutchins (1993).

References

Ball, D., & Bass, H. (2000). Making believe: The collective construction of public mathematical knowledge in the elementary classroom. In D. C. Phillips (Ed.), Constructivism in education, opinions and second opinions on controversial issues, ninety-ninth yearbook of the National Society for the Study of Education (pp. 193–224). Chicago: University of Chicago Press.

Barab, S., Barnett, M., Yamagata-Lynch, L., Squire, K., & Keating, T. (2002). Using activity theory to understand the systemic tensions characterizing a technology-rich introductory astronomy course. Mind, Culture, and Activity, 9, 76–107.

Barron, B. (2003). When smart groups fail. Journal of the Learning Sciences, 12, 307–360.

Beach, K. (1995). Activity as a mediator of sociocultural change and individual development: The case of school-work transition in Nepal. Mind, Culture, and Activity, 2, 285–302.

Bellak, A. A., Kliebard, H., Hyman, R., & Smith, F. (1966). Language in the classroom. New York: Teachers College Press.

Boaler, J. (2002). Experiencing school mathematics: Traditional and reform approaches to teaching and their impact on student learning, revised and expanded edition. Mahwah, NJ: Lawrence Erlbaum Associates.

Bowers, J., Cobb, P., & McClain, K. (1999). The evolution of mathematical practices: A case study. Cognition and Instruction, 17, 25–64.

Brown, A. L., & Campione, J. C. (1994). Guided discovery in a community of learners. In K. McGilly (Ed.) Classroom lessons: Integrating cognitive theory and classroom practice(pp. 229–270). Cambridge, MA: MIT Press/Bradford.

Cazden, C. B. (1986). Classroom discourse. In M. C. Wittrock (Ed.). Handbook of research on teaching (pp. 432–463). New York: Macmillan.

Chi, M. T. H., Feltovich, P. J., & Glaser, R. (1981). Categorization and representation of physics problems by experts and novices. Cognitive Science, 5, 121–152.

Clark, H. H. (1996). Using language. Cambridge: Cambridge University Press.

Clark, H. H., & Schaefer, E. (1989). Contributions to discourse. Cognitive Science, 13, 19–41.

Clark, H. H., & Wilkes-Gibbs (1986). Referring as a collaborative process. Cognition, 22, 1–39.

Cole, M. (1996). Cultural psychology: A once and future discipline. Cambridge, MA: Harvard University Press.

Collins, A., Hawkins, J., & Carver, S. M. (1991). A cognitive apprenticeship for disadvantaged students. In B. Means, C. Chelemer & M. S. Knapp (Eds.), Teaching advanced skills to at-risk students. San Francisco: Jossey-Bass.

Dewey, J. (1896). The reflex arc concept in psychology. *Psychological Review, 3*, 357–370.

Dewey, J. (1978). How we think. In *How we think and selected essays, 1910–1911, The middle works of John Dewey, 1899–1924, volume 6* (Jo Ann Boydston, ed.) (pp. 177–356). Carbondale, IL: Southern Illinois University Press (originally published 1910).

Dewey, J. (1958). *Experience and nature.* New York: Dover (original work published 1929).

Dunbar, K. (1995). How scientists really reason: Scientific reasoning in real-world laboratories. In R. J. Sternberg & J. E. Davidson (Eds.), *The nature of insight* (pp. 365–395). Cambridge, MA: MIT Press/Bradford.

Eckert, P. (1989). *Jocks and burnouts.* New York: Teachers College Press.

Eckert, P. (1990). Adolescent social categories: Information and science learning. In M. Gardner, J. G. Greeno, F. Reif, A. H. Schoenfeld, A. diSessa, & E. Stage (Eds.), *Toward a scientific practice of science education* (pp. 203–218). Hillsdale, NJ: Lawrence Erlbaum Associates.

Engeström, Y. (1993). Developmental studies of work as a testbench of activity theory: The case of primary care medical practice. In S. Chaiklin & J. Lave (Eds.), *Understanding practice: Perspectives on activity and context* (pp. 64–103). Cambridge: Cambridge University Press.

Engeström, Y. (1999). Activity theory and individual and social transformation. In Y. Engestrtöm, R. Miettinen, & R.-L. Punamaki (Eds.), *Perspectives on activity theory* (pp. 19–38). Cambridge: Cambridge University Press.

Engeström, Y. (2001). Expansive learning at work: Toward an activity theoretical reconceptualization. *Journal of Education and Work, 14*, 133–156.

Engle, R. A., & Conant, F. R. (2002). Guiding principles for fostering productive disciplinary engagement: Explaining an emergent argument in a community of learners classroom. *Cognition and Instruction. 20*, 399–483.

Fawcett, H. P. (1938). *The nature of proof: A description and evaluation of certain procedures used in a senior high school to develop an understanding of the nature of proof, the thirteenth yearbook of the National Council of Teachers of Mathematics.* New York: Bureau of Publications, Teachers College, Columbia University.

Fujimura, J. H. (1996). *Crafting science: A sociohistory of the quest for the genetics of cancer.* Cambridge, MA: Harvard University Press.

Gibson, J. J. (1979). *An ecological approach to visual perception.* Boston: Houghton Mifflin.

Goldman, S. V. (1996). Mediating microworlds: Collaboration on high school science activities. In T. Koschmann (Ed.), *CSCL: Theory and practice of an emegting paradigm* (pp. 45–82). Mahwah, NJ: Lawrence Erlbaum Associates.

Goldman, S., & Moschkovich, J. (1995). Environments for collaborating mathematically: The middle-school mathematics through applications project. *CSCL '95 Proceedings.*

Goodwin, C. (1995). Seeing in depth. *Social Studies of Science, 25*, 237–274.

Goodwin, C. (1996). Transparent vision. In E. Ochs, E. A. Schegloff & S. A. Thompson (Eds.), *Interaction and grammar* (pp. 370–404). Cambridge: Cambridge University Press.

Greeno, J. G. (1995). Understanding concepts in activity. In C. A. Weaver III, S. Mannes, & C. R. Fletcher (Eds.), *Discourse comprehension: Essays in honor of Walter Kintsch* (pp. 65–96). Hillsdale, NJ: Lawrence Erlbaum Associates.

Greeno, J. G. (2003, November). A situative perspective on cognition and learning in interaction. Paper presented at a workshop, "Theorizing learning practice," University of Illinois.

Greeno, J. G., & Engle, R. A. (1995). Combining analyses of cognitive processes, meanings, and social participation: Understanding symbolic representation. *Proceedings of the Seventeenth Annual Conference of the Cognitive Science Society, Pittsburgh.*

Greeno, J. G., & the Middle-school Mathematics through Applications Project Group (1998). The situativity of knowing, learning, and research. *American Psychologist, 53*, 5–26.

Greeno, J. G., Smith, D. R., & Moore, J. L. (1993). Transfer of situated learning. In D. K. Detterman & R. K. Sternberg (Eds.), *Transfer on trial: Intelligence, cognition, and instruction* (pp. 99–167). Hillsdale, NJ: Lawrence Erlbaum Associates.

Gresalfi, M. S. (2004). *Taking up opportunities to learn: Examining the construction of mathematical identities in middle school classrooms.* Doctoral dissertation, Stanford University.

Hall, R. (1996). Representation as shared activity: Situated cognition and Dewey's cartography of experience. *Journal of the Learning Sciences, 5*, 209–238.

Hall, R., & Rubin, A. (1998). There's five little notches in here: Dilemmas in teaching and learning the conventional structure of rate.

In J. G. Greeno & S. V. Goldman (Eds), *Thinking practices in mathematics and science learning* (pp. 189–235). Mahwah NJ: Lawrence Erlbaum Associates.

Hatano, G., & Inagaki, K. (1991). Sharing cognition through collective comprehension activity. In L. B. Resnick, J. M. Levine, & S. D. Teasley (Eds.), *Perspectives on socially shared cognition* (pp. 31–348). Washington, DC: American Psychological Association.

Hutchins, E. (1993). Learning to navigate. In S. Chaiklin & J. Lave (Eds.), *Understanding practice: Perspectives on activity and context* (pp. 35–63). Cambridge: Cambridge University Press.

Hutchins, E. (1995a). *Cognition in the wild*. Cambridge, MA: MIT Press.

Hutchins, E. (1995b). How a cockpit remembers its speeds. *Cognitive Science, 19,* 265–288.

Jordan, G., & Henderson, A. (1995). Interaction analysis: Foundations and practice. *Journal of the Learning Sciences, 4,* 39–103.

Kintsch, W. (1998). *Comprehension: A paradigm for cognition*. Cambridge: Cambridge University Press.

Kitcher, P. (1993). *The advancement of science*. Oxford: Oxford University Press.

Kuhn, D. (1989). Children and adults as intuitive scientists. *Psychological Review, 96,* 674–689.

Lampert, M. (1990). When the problem is not the question and the solution is not the answer: Mathematical knowing and teaching. *American Educational Research Journal, 27,* 29–64.

Lampert, M. (2001). *Teaching problems and the problems of teaching*. New Haven, CT: University Press.

Latour, B., & Woolgar, S. (1986). *Laboratory life: The construction of scientific facts*. Princeton, NJ: Princeton University Press.

Lave, J. (1988). *Cognition in practice: Mind, mathematics, and culture in everyday life*. Cambridge: Cambridge University Press.

Lave, J., Murtaugh, M., & de la Rosa, O. (1984). The dialectic of arithmetic in grocery shopping. In B. Rogoff & J. Lave (Eds.), *Everyday cognition: Its development in social context* (pp. 67–94). Cambridge, MA: Harvard University Press.

Lave, J., & Wenger, E. (1991). *Situated cognition: Legitimate peripheral participation*. Cambridge: Cambridge University Press.

Levinson, S. (1983). *Pragmatics*. Cambridge: Cambridge University Press.

Lewin, K. (1935). *Dynamic theory of personality*. New York: Mcgraw-Hill.

Lewin, K. (1997). Behavior and development as a function of the total situation. In *Resolving social conflicts & Field theory in social science* (pp. 337–381). Washington, DC: American Psychological Association. (Originally published 1946).

Lynch, M. (1985). *Art and artifact in laboratory science: A study of shop work and shop talk in a research laboratory*. London: Routledge and Kegan Paul.

Mead, G. H. (1934). *Mind, self, and society*. Chicago: University of Chicago Press.

Mehan, H. (1979). *Learning lessons*. Cambridge, MA: Harvard University Press.

Moses, R. P., & Cobb, C. E., Jr. (2001). *Radical equations: Math literacy and civil rights*. Boston: Beacon Press.

Nersessian, N. (1984). *Faraday to Einstein: Constructing meaning in scientific theories*. Dordrecht: Martinus Nijhoff/Kluwer.

Nersessian, N. (2002). Maxwell and the "method of physical analogy": Model-based reasoning, generic abstraction, and conceptual change. In D. Malament (Ed.), *Reading natural philosophy: Essays in the history and philosophy of science and mathematics*. Lasalle, IL: Open Court.

Nersessian, N. J. (2005). Interpreting scientific and engineering practices: Integrating the cognitive, social and cultural dimensions. In M. Gorman, R. Tweney, D. Gooding, & A. Kincannon (Eds.), *Scientific and technological thinking* (pp. 17–56). Mahwah, NJ: Erlbaum.

Nersessian, N. J., Kurz-Milcke, E., Newstetter, W. C., & Davies, J. (2003). Research laboratories as evolving distributed cognitive systems. In R. Alterman & d. Kirsh (Eds.), *Proceedings of the Twenty-Fifth Annual Conference of the Cognitive Science Society* (pp. 857–862). Erlbaum.

Newell, A., & Simon, H. A. (1972). *Human problem solving*. Englewood Cliffs, NJ: Prentice Hall.

Nunes, T., Schliemann, A. D., & Carraher, D. W. (1993). *Street mathematics and school mathematics*. Cambridge: Cambridge University Press.

O'Connor, M. C., & Michaels, S. (1996). Shifting participant frameworks: Orchestrating thinking practices in group discussion. In D. Hicks (Ed.), *Discourse, learning, and schooling* (pp. 63–103). Cambridge: Cambridge University Press.

Okada, T., & Simon, H. A. (1997) Collaborative discovery ini a scientific domain. *Cognitive Science*, 21, 109–146.

Phillips, S. U. (1972). Participant structures and communicative competence: Warm Springs children in community and classroom. In C. B. Cazden, V. P. John, & D. Hymes (Eds.), *Functions of language in the classroom* (pp. 370–394). New York: Teachers College Press.

Pickering, A. (1995). *The mangle of practice.* Chicago: University of Chicago Press.

Reed, E. (1996). *Encountering the world: Toward an ecological psychology.* Oxford: Oxford University Press.

Reiner, M., Pea, R. D., & Shulman, D. J. (1995). Impact of simulator-based instruction on diagramming in geometrical optics by introductory physics students. *Journal of science education and technology*, 4, 199–226.

Rogoff, B. (1995). *Apprenticeship in thinking: Cognitive development in social context.* Oxford: Oxford University Press.

Rosebery, A. S., Warren, B., & Conant, F. R. (1992). Appropriating scientific discourse: Findings from language minority classrooms. *Journal of the Learning Sciences*, 2, 61–94.

Sawyer, K. (2003). *Group creativity: Music, theater, collaboration.* Mahwah, NJ: Lawrence Erlbaum Associates.

Sawyer, R. K. (2005). *Social emergence: Societies as complex systems.* New York: Cambridge.

Saxe, G. (1990). *Culture and cognitive development: Studies in mathematical understanding.* Hillsdale, NJ: Lawrence Erlbaum Associates.

Scardamalia, M., Bereiter, C., & Lamon, M, (1994). The CSILE project: Trying to bring the classroom into World 3. In K. McGilly (Ed.), *Classroom lessons: Integrating cognitive theory and classroom practice* (pp. 201–228). Cambridge, MA: MIT Press/Bradford.

Schegloff, E. A. (1991). Reflections on talk and social structure. In D. Boden & D. H. Zimmerman (Eds.), *Talk and social structure: Studies in ethnomethodology and conversation analysis* (pp. 44–70). Berkeley: University of California Press.

Schoenfeld, A. H. (1994). Reflections on doing and teaching mathematics. In A. H. Schoenfeld (Ed.), *Mathematical thinking and problem solving.* Hillsdale, NJ: Lawrence Erlbaum Associates.

Schwartz, D. L. (1995). The emergence of abstract representations in dyad problem solving. *Journal of the Learning Sciences*, 4, 321–354.

Schwartz, J. L., Yarushalmy, M., & Wilson, B. (1993). *The Geometric Supposer: What is it a case of?* Hillsdale, NJ: Lawrence Erlbaum Associates.

Scribner, S. (1984). Studying working intelligence. In B. Rogoff & J. Lave (Eds.), *Everyday cognition: Its development in social context* (pp. 9–40). Cambridge, MA: Harvard University Press.

Simon. H. A. (1969). *The sciences of the artificial.* Cambridge, MA: MIT Press.

Suchman, L. A. (1985). *Plans and situated action: The problem of human-machine communication.* Cambridge: Cambridge University Press.

Vygotsky, L. (1987). *The collected works of L. S. Vygotsky, volume 1: Problems of general psychology.* (R. W. Rieber & A. S. Carton, Eds.). New York: Plenum.

Waterman, M. W. (2004). *The joint achievement of group expertise and autonomy.* Doctoral dissertation, Stanford University.

CHAPTER 7

Knowledge Building

Theory, Pedagogy, and Technology

Marlene Scardamalia and Carl Bereiter

There are substantial similarities between deep learning and the processes by which knowledge advances in the disciplines. During the 1960s efforts to exploit these similarities gave rise to learning by discovery, guided discovery, inquiry learning, and *Science: A Process Approach* (American Association for the Advancement of Science, 1967). Since these initial reform efforts, scholars have learned a great deal about how knowledge advances. A mere listing of keywords suggests the significance and diversity of ideas that have come to prominence since the 1960s: Thomas Kuhn, Imre Lakatos, sociology of science, the "Science Wars," social constructivism, schema theory, mental models, situated cognition, explanatory coherence, the "rhetorical turn," communities of practice, memetics, connectionism, emergence, and self-organization. Educational approaches have changed in response to some of these developments; there is a greater emphasis on collaborative rather than individual inquiry, the tentative nature of empirical laws is more often noted, and argumentation has become an important part of some approaches. But the new "knowledge of knowledge" has much larger educational implications: Ours is a knowledge-creating civilization. A growing number of "knowledge societies" (Stehr, 1994), are joined in a deliberate effort to advance all the frontiers of knowledge. Sustained knowledge advancement is seen as essential for social progress of all kinds and for the solution of societal problems. From this standpoint the fundamental task of education is to enculturate youth into this knowledge-creating civilization and to help them find a place in it. In light of this challenge, traditional educational practice – with its emphasis on knowledge transmission – as well as the newer constructivist methods both appear to be limited in scope if not entirely missing the point.

Knowledge building, as elaborated in this chapter, represents an attempt to refashion education in a fundamental way, so that it becomes a coherent effort to initiate students into a knowledge creating culture. Accordingly, it involves students not only developing knowledge-building competencies but also coming to see themselves and their work as part of the civilization-wide effort to advance knowledge frontiers. In this context, the Internet becomes more than a desktop library and a rapid mail-delivery system. It becomes the first realistic means for students to connect with civilization-wide knowledge building and to make their classroom work a part of it.

The distinctiveness of a knowledge building approach was encapsulated for us by the comment of a fifth-grader on the work of a classmate: "Mendel worked on Karen's problem" (referring to Gregor Mendel, the great nineteenth-century biologist). Not "Karen rediscovered Mendel" or "Karen should read Mendel to find the answer to her problem." Rather, the remark treats Karen's work as continuous with that of Gregor Mendel, addressing the same basic problem. Furthermore, the Mendel reference is offered to help Karen and others advance their collective enterprise. In our experience, young students are delighted to see their inquiry connect with that of learned others, past or present. Rather than being overawed by authority, or dismissive, they see their own work as being legitimated by its connection to problems that have commanded the attention of respected scientists, scholars, and thinkers.

In this chapter, we elaborate six themes that underlie a shift from treating students as learners and inquirers to treating them as members of a knowledge building community. These themes are:

- Knowledge advancement as a community rather than individual achievement
- Knowledge advancement as idea improvement rather than as progress toward true or warranted belief
- Knowledge *of* in contrast to knowledge *about*
- Discourse as collaborative problem solving rather than as argumentation
- Constructive use of authoritative information
- Understanding as an emergent

One important advantage of knowledge building as an educational approach is that it provides a straightforward way to address the contemporary emphasis on knowledge creation and innovation. These lie outside the scope of most constructivist approaches whereas they are at the heart of knowledge building.

Community Knowledge Advancement

In every progressive discipline one finds periodic reviews of the state of knowledge or the "state of the art" in the field. Different reviewers will offer different descriptions of the state of knowledge; however, their disagreements are open to argument that may itself contribute to advancing the state of knowledge. The state of knowledge is not what everyone in the field or the average person in the field knows, but neither is it what the most knowledgeable people in the field know, except in some collective sense. Fundamentally, a description of the state of knowledge is not about what is in people's minds at all. If we look back at prehistoric times, using archaeological evidence, we can make statements about the state of knowledge in a certain civilization at a certain time, without knowing anything about any individuals and what they thought or knew.

An implicit assumption in state-of-the-art reviews is that the knowledge in a field does not merely accumulate but advances. There is the implicit image of a moving body, taking in new information and ideas at its leading edge and leaving behind solved or abandoned problems and disproved or outmoded ideas. Creative knowledge work may be defined as work that advances the state of knowledge within some community of practice, however broadly or narrowly that community may be defined.

Knowledge building pedagogy is based on the premise that authentic creative knowledge work can take place in school classrooms – knowledge work that does not merely emulate the work of mature scholars or designers but that substantively advances the state of knowledge in the classroom community and situates it within the larger societal knowledge building effort. This is a radically different vision from contemporary educational practice, which is so intensely focused on the individual student that the notion of a state of knowledge that is not a mental state or an aggregate of mental states seems to make no sense. Yet in knowledge creating organizations it makes obvious sense. People are not honored for what is in their minds but for the contributions they make to the organization's or the community's knowledge.

One component of knowledge building is the creation of "epistemic artifacts," tools that serve in the further advancement of knowledge (Sterelny, 2005). These may be purely conceptual artifacts (Bereiter, 2002), such as theories and abstract models, or "epistemic things" (Rheinberger, 1997), such as concrete models and experimental setups. Epistemic artifacts are especially important in education, where the main uses of knowledge are in the creation of further knowledge. When we speak of engaging students in "the deliberate creation and improvement of knowledge that has value for a community" (Scardamalia & Bereiter, 2003) the main value is this epistemic one – a feedforward effect, in which new knowledge gives rise to and speeds the development of yet newer knowledge. In this context, student-generated theories and models are to be judged not so much by their conformity to accepted knowledge as by their value as tools enabling further growth.

Idea Improvement

Engineers and designers do not think in terms of a final state of perfection (Petroski, 1996). Advances in a technology open up new problems to be solved and new possibilities for further advancement, so there is no end in sight. But many people still think of knowledge as advancing toward (though perhaps never reaching) a final state, which is truth: how the universe actually began, the true history of the invasion of Iraq, and so on. But advances in theoretical and historical knowledge always raise new problems and open new possibilities, just as do advances in

technology. Except in a few areas such as disease control, progress is measured by comparison to what has gone before, rather than by distance to a predetermined end-point.

As a criterion for evaluating individual performance, "improvement" is a familiar although by no means universally accepted notion in educational assessment. But improvement as a criterion for assessing knowledge itself is virtually unheard of. Here is an example of what this would mean in a learning context. Analysis of a grade 5/6 Knowledge Forum database showed that most of the students initially conceived of gravity as a substance residing within objects rather than as a relation between objects (as is typical: Chi, Slotta, & deLeeuw, 1994). By the end of a unit on gravity, most students still treated gravity as a substance. Thus, measured as distance from the goal – to teach students that gravity is a relationship between two masses – there had been little progress. However, comparing students' end-of-unit writings on gravity with their initial ones, changes could be detected. The students appeared less comfortable with the substance conception and more aware that there were other conceptions, even though they had not yet grasped them. There was also an awareness that gravity is everywhere and not just a property of large celestial bodies. One student wrote: "I need to understand. I know we are a mass our self but then why aren't little parts of dust and small objects attracted to us? . . . We are much bigger than a small ripped up pieces of paper, but yet you don't see the paper fly across the room or even a small distance to us. WHY?"

We noted similar patterns in another grade 5/6 class that had been studying evolution. Natural selection had not taken hold as the key explanatory concept, although there was a growing recognition that it had something to do with evolution. More tellingly, there was a growing recognition that *some* mechanism of evolution was required, that evolutionary adaptation could not merely be accepted as a primitive – the view that Ohlsson (1991) found characteristic of university undergraduates.

In knowledge building, idea improvement is an explicit principle, something that guides the efforts of students and teachers rather than something that remains implicit in inquiry and learning activities (Scardamalia, 2002). The direct pursuit of idea improvement brings schooling into much closer alignment with creative knowledge work as carried on at professional levels. Generating ideas appears to come naturally to people, especially children, but sustained effort to improve ideas does not. We believe that developing a disposition to work at idea improvement should be a major objective in the education of scholars, scientists, and designers, for without such a disposition the likelihood of a productive career is slight.

To propose idea improvement as an alternative to progress toward truth may suggest a relativist, antifoundationalist, or extreme social-constructivist theory of knowledge. The point we want to make here, however, is that you need not take a position on this issue in order to adopt a knowledge building pedagogy with idea improvement as a core principle. You can hold that there are preexisting truths and that, short of revelation, idea improvement is our only means of working toward them; or you can hold that what pass for truths are just conceptual artifacts that have undergone a successful process of development. All that is necessary is to adopt as a working premise that all ideas are improvable – or, at any rate, all interesting ideas.

An educational program committed to idea improvement has to allow time for iterations. Iterative idea improvement is in principle endless; in practice, the decision whether to continue a particular line of knowledge building or shift to another is a judgment call, taking into account the progress being made and measuring it against competing demands and opportunities. Ideally (although it is difficult in a graded school system), a student cohort should be able to pick up a thread of inquiry at a later time – even years later. For instance, elementary school students studying electric-ity often develop a good qualitative understanding of circuits, resistance, and conductance. They may be able to formulate and test interesting hypotheses about why some materials conduct electricity and others apparently do not. But they are unlikely to be able to grasp what electric current actually is. Instead of starting over in high school science, they could reconsider their earlier speculations in light of the more sophisticated concepts now available to them. Electronic media make such continuity technically feasible and could help to bring school knowledge building into closer alignment with the way knowledge advances in the disciplines.

One distinctive characteristic of students in knowledge building classrooms reflects epistemological awareness. When asked about the effects of learning, students in regular classrooms tend to say that the more they learn and understand, the less there remains to be learned and understood (a belief that accords well with the fixed curriculum that directs their work). Students in knowledge building classrooms, however, tend strongly toward the opposite view, as expressed by one fourth-grade student: "By researching it [a particular knowledge problem] you can find other things that you want to research about. And so you realize that there is more and more and more things that you don't know . . . so, first you know this much [gestures a small circle] and you know there is this much [gestures a large circle] that you don't know. Then you know this much [gestures a larger circle] but you know there is this much [gestures an even larger circle] that you don't know, and so on and so on."

Knowledge *of* in Contrast to Knowledge *About*

Since the 1970s, cognitive scientists largely focus on two broad types of knowledge, declarative and procedural (Anderson, 1980). This distinction now pervades the cognitive literature as well as educational psychology textbooks that take a cognitive slant. The declarative-procedural distinction has proven useful in rule-based computer modeling of cognitive processes, but its application to education and knowledge creation is questionable (Bereiter, 2002, Ch. 5). From a pragmatic standpoint, a more useful distinction is between knowledge *about* and knowledge *of* something. Knowledge *about* sky-diving, for instance, would consist of all the declarative knowledge you can retrieve when prompted to state what you know about sky-diving. Such knowledge could be conveniently and adequately represented in a concept net. Knowledge *of* sky-diving, however, implies an ability to do or to participate in the activity of sky-diving. It consists of both procedural knowledge (e.g., knowing how to open a parachute and guide its descent) and declarative knowledge that would be drawn on when engaged in the activity of sky-diving (e.g., knowledge of equipment characteristics and maintenance requirements, rules of particular events). It entails not only knowledge that can be explicitly stated or demonstrated but also implicit or intuitive knowledge that is not manifested directly but must be inferred (see Bransford et al., this volume). Knowledge *of* is activated when a need for it is encountered in action. Whereas knowledge *about* is approximately equivalent to declarative knowledge, knowledge *of* is a much richer concept than procedural knowledge.

Knowledge *about* dominates traditional educational practice. It is the stuff of textbooks, curriculum guidelines, subject-matter tests, and typical school "projects" and "research" papers. Knowledge *of*, by contrast, suffers massive neglect. There is instruction in skills (procedural knowledge), but it is not integrated with understanding in a way that would justify saying "Alexa has a deep knowledge *of* arithmetic" – or chemistry or the stock market or anything else. Knowledge about is not entirely useless, but its usefulness is limited to situations in which knowledge *about* something has value independently of skill and understanding. Such

situations are largely limited to social small talk, trivia games, quiz shows, and – the one biggy – test taking.

To be useful outside the limited areas in which knowledge *about* is sufficient, knowledge needs to be organized around problems rather than topics (Bereiter, 1992). Of course, topics and problems often go together, but in the most interesting cases they do not – for example, when the connection of knowledge to a problem is analogical, via deeper underlying mechanisms rather than surface resemblance. Such connections are vital to invention, theorizing, and the solving of ill-structured problems. For instance, it is useful for learners' knowledge of water skiing to be activated when they are studying flight, because it provides a nice experiential anchor for the otherwise rather abstract "angle of attack" explanation of lift. Ordinarily the teacher is responsible for making such connections, but in the out-of-school world people need to be able to do this themselves if they are to succeed as knowledge-builders. Making this connection promotes the realization that Bernoulli's principle is not the whole story in explaining what keeps airplanes aloft.

Across a broad spectrum of theoretical orientations, instructional designers agree that the best way to acquire what we are calling knowledge *of* is through problem solving – as in the *driving questions* of project-based learning (Krajcik & Blumenfeld, this volume) and in inquiry learning more generally (Edelson & Reiser, this volume). Research on transfer makes it clear, however, that solving problems does not automatically generate the deep structural knowledge on which analogical transfer is based (Catrambone & Holyoak, 1989). Problem-based learning environments fall somewhere on a continuum between context-limited to context-general work with knowledge (Bereiter & Scardamalia, 2003; in press). At the context-limited extreme, students' creative work is limited to problems of such a concrete and narrowly focused kind that they do not raise questions about general principles. Accordingly, the more basic knowledge (of scientific laws or causal mechanisms, for instance) that the curriculum calls for is often left to be conveyed by conventional instructional means. This raises concern that the deep knowledge that is most useful for transfer will not be connected with problems but will remain as knowledge *about* the relevant principles or laws. In knowledge building, students work with problems that result in deep structural knowledge *of.*

Knowledge-Building Discourse

In the view of science that flourished fifty years ago and that is still prominent in school science, discourse is primarily a way of sharing knowledge and subjecting ideas to criticism, as in formal publications and oral presentations, and question-and-answer sessions after these presentations. Lakatos (1976) challenged this idea, showing how discourse could play a creative role – actively improving on ideas, rather than only acting as a critical filter. Recent empirical studies of scientific discourse support Lakatos's view. For example, Dunbar (1997) showed that the discourse that goes on inside research laboratories is fundamentally different from the discourse that goes on in presentations and papers – it is more cooperative and concerned with shared understanding. Public discourse and collaborative discourse serve complementary functions, and practitioners of a discipline need to be proficient in both (Woodruff & Meyer, 1997). However, cooperative discourse oriented toward understanding is much more relevant to learning (Coleman, Brown, & Rivkin, 1997).

There are weak and strong versions of the claim that collaborative discourse plays a role in knowledge advancement. The weak version holds merely that *empirical findings and other products of inquiry only become contributions to community knowledge when they are brought into public discourse*. This version is compatible with the conventional view of discourse as knowledge sharing. The strong version asserts that *the state of public knowledge in a community only exists in the discourse of that community, and the progress of knowledge just is the progress of knowledge-building discourse*. If, as we argued earlier, the state of knowledge of a community is not something in the minds of individual members of the community, then there is no place else it can exist except in discourse. The weak version holds that the advance of knowledge is *reflected in* the discourse, whereas the strong version holds that there is no advance of community knowledge *apart from* the discourse. (Note that this is not a declaration about *what* knowledge is; it is only a self-evident statement about *where* public knowledge is.)

Both versions require that discourse be treated as having content, that it cannot be all form and process, and that this content can be described and evaluated outside the discourse in which it is constituted. Thus there has to be the possibility of a metadiscourse that takes the *content* of the first-order discourse as its subject. Knowledge building discourse, as we conceive of it, is discourse whose aim is progress in the state of knowledge: idea improvement. It involves a set of commitments that distinguish it from other types of discourse (Bereiter, 1994, 2002):

- a commitment to *progress*, something that does not characterize dinner party conversation or discussions devoted to sharing information and venting opinions
- a commitment to *seek common understanding* rather than merely agreement, which is not characteristic of political and policy discourse, for instance
- a commitment to *expand the base of accepted facts*, whereas, in court trials and debates, attacking the factual claims of opponents is common

By these criteria, argumentation and debate, as currently promoted in schools, falls short. Its emphasis on evidence and persuasion, while admirable in other respects, does not generate progress toward the solution of shared problems of understanding. Knowledge-building discourse in the classroom has a more constructive and progressive character (Bereiter et al., 1997).

Constructive Use of Authoritative Information

The use of authoritative information has presented problems for educators ever since the advent of student-centered and constructivist education. On the one hand, we do not want students to meekly accept authoritative pronouncements. "Because I say so" and "because the book says so" are no longer regarded as acceptable responses to students' skeptical queries. On the other hand, it is impossible to function in society without taking large amounts of information on authority. Even when it comes to challenging authoritative pronouncements, doing so effectively normally depends on bringing in other authoritative information as evidence.

A focus on knowledge building alleviates even if it does not solve the problems associated with authoritative information. Information of all kinds, whether derived from firsthand experience or from secondary sources, has value insofar as it contributes to knowledge-building discourse. Quality of information is always an issue, but its importance varies with the task. If the task is one where faulty design will put lives at risk (design of a new drug or of a suspension bridge, for instance), a much higher standard of information quality will be required than if less is at stake or if self-corrective measures can be built into the design. Judging the quality of information is not a separate problem from the knowledge-building task, it is part of the task. Judgment may involve argument, but it is argument in the service of the overall idea improvement mission.

Emergent Understanding

How are complex new concepts acquired? Indeed, how is it logically possible to learn "a conceptual system richer than the one that one already has" (Fodor, 1980, p. 149)?

The "learning paradox, "as it has come to be called (Bereiter, 1985; Pascual-Leone, 1980), poses a fundamental problem for constructivism: If learners construct their own knowledge, how is it possible for them to create a cognitive structure more complex than the one they already possess? Dozens of articles have appeared claiming to resolve the paradox but in fact failing to address the fundamental problem. The only creditable solutions are ones that posit some form of self-organization (Molenaar & van der Maas, 2000; Quartz, 1993). At the level of the neural substrate, self-organization is pervasive and characterizes learning of all kinds (Phillips & Singer, 1997). As Grossberg (1997, p. 689) remarked, "brains are self-organizing organs par excellence." Explaining conceptual development, however, entails self-organization at the level of ideas – explaining how more complex ideas can emerge from interactions of simpler ideas and percepts.

New conceptual structures, like crystals and ant colonies, emerge through the interaction of simpler elements that do not singly or in combination represent the new concept (Sawyer, 2003). This became evident with the rise of connectionism in the late 1980s (Bereiter, 1991). Connectionist models of learning and development characteristically generate progress from a conceptually impoverished to a conceptually richer system, sometimes by a process analogous to learning from experience and sometimes only by internal self-organization. Connectionist models are examples of the larger class of dynamic systems models, all of which attempt to deal in some rigorous way with emergent phenomena. The emergence of complexity from the interaction of simpler elements is found at all levels from the physicochemical to the sociocultural (Sawyer, 2005). If learning is paradoxical, so is practically everything else that goes on in the world.

The frequently stated constructivist principle, "Learners construct their own knowledge," can be restated in dynamic systems terms as "All understandings are inventions; inventions are emergents." Two obstacles stand in the way of making this more than just a restatement of the same vague principle. First, explanations in terms of dynamic systems are difficult to understand and do not yield the satisfying gestalts that attend narrative explanations. Second – and this is an obstacle much less commonly recognized – a dynamic systems explanation of conceptual growth posits (along with other kinds of interactions) ideas interacting with ideas to generate new ideas. This level of description is common in the philosophy of knowledge and in the history of ideas. The practical import of this discussion is that instructional designers need to think more seriously about ideas as real things that can interact with one another to produce new and more complex ideas. School-age students have shown themselves able to make sense of and profit from computer representations of self-organization at the idea level (Ranney & Schank, 1998).

From Computer-Supported Intentional Learning to Knowledge-Building Environments

Although the term "knowledge building" is now in wide use (in 125,000 Web documents, as of July, 2005) we were, as far as we can ascertain, the first to use the term in education, and certainly the first to have used it as something more than a synonym for active learning. Prying loose the concept of knowledge building from concepts of learning has been an evolutionary process, however, which continues. An intermediate concept is "intentional learning"(Bereiter & Scardamalia, 1989) – something more than "active" or "self-regulated" learning, more a matter of having life goals that include a personal learning agenda. This concept grew out of research revealing the opposite of intentional learning: students employing strategies that minimize learning while efficiently meeting the demands of school tasks (Brown, Day, & Jones, 1983; Scardamalia & Bereiter, 1987). Although students were responsive to a more "knowledge-transforming" approach (Scardamalia, Bereiter, & Steinbach, 1984), effects dissipated when they returned to ordinary classroom work. Many characteristics of classroom life conspire to discourage intentional learning (Scardamalia & Bereiter, 1996), but a key factor seems to be the structure of classroom communication, in which the teacher serves as the hub through which all information passes. Altering that information flow was one of our goals when we designed the software application we called CSILE – Computer Supported Intentional Learning Environments – first used in early prototype version in 1983 in a university course, more fully implemented in 1986 in an elementary school (Scardamalia, Bereiter, McLean, Swallow, and Woodruff, 1989).

Another motive guiding the design of CSILE was a belief that students themselves represented a resource that was largely wasted and that could be brought into play through network technology (Scardamalia & Bereiter, 1991). Classroom work with CSILE proved this to be true beyond anything we had imagined. The classroom, as a community, could indeed have a mental life that is not just the aggregate of individual mental lives but something that provides a rich context within which those individual mental lives take on new value. CSILE restructured the flow of information in the classroom, so that questions, ideas, criticisms, suggestions, and the like were contributed to a public space equally accessible to all, instead of it all passing through the teacher or (as in e-mail) passing as messages between individual students. By linking these contributions, students created an emergent hypertext that represented the collective rather than only the individual knowledge of the participants. We introduced epistemological markers ("My theory," "I need to understand," "New information," and so on), through "thinking types" that could be integrated into the text of notes to encourage metadiscourse as well as discourse focused on the substantive issues under investigation.

By the 1990s the idea of knowledge building as the collaborative creation of public knowledge had assumed ascendancy, with individual learning as an important and demonstrable by-product (Scardamalia, Bereiter, & Lamon, 1994). In this light, we undertook a major redesign of CSILE to boost it as an environment for objectifying ideas and their interrelationships and to support collaborative work aimed at improving ideas.

In scientific and scholarly research teams, knowledge building often proceeds with no special technology to support it. This is possible because knowledge building is woven into the social fabric of the group and in a sense all the technology used by the group supports it. This becomes evident if we consider successful research laboratories like those studied by Dunbar (1997) in light of the themes previously discussed:

- Knowledge advancement is the defining purpose of the research laboratory, and so it is not difficult to keep this purpose salient; schools, by contrast, have a multiplicity of purposes touching on many different aspects of student development.

- Although publications, speaking invitations, patents, and grants are markers of success in the research world, they all depend finally on idea improvement. You cannot get on the program at a scientific meeting or be awarded a patent by simply repeating last year's successful idea. In schools, by contrast, reproduction of existing ideas figures prominently in learning activities and assessment.

- Expertise in the research world presupposes deep knowledge *of* the problem domain; mere knowledge *about* gains little credit. In the school world, however, knowledge *about* is the basic indicator of academic achievement. A knowledge building technology, accordingly, ought to favor increasingly deep inquiry into questions of *how* and *why* rather than the shallower kinds of inquiry guided by questions of *what* and *when.*

- Discourse within a research group is geared to advancing the group's knowledge-building goals. Argumenta-

tion about knowledge claims takes place in public arenas. In the classroom, however, discourse can serve a wide range of purposes, from self-expression to knowledge recitation. Communication technology should help to move discourse along a knowledge-building path.

- Constructive use of authoritative information comes naturally to a research organization; original work is almost always built upon previous work, and theories are tested against data not only from local work but also from published research (Bazerman, 1985). In school, however, authoritative information is most commonly brought forward as *that which is to be learned.* Using it in knowledge building therefore requires a shift in focus, which may require external support. A knowledge-building technology should facilitate *using* information, as distinct from learning it. Obtaining, recording, and storing information would become subsidiary functions, designed to serve purposes of knowledge creation.

- Significant advances in knowledge by a research laboratory are obviously emergents; the knowledge didn't preexist in anyone's mind nor was it simply there to be read out of the "book of nature." But in schools a major concern is students' acquisition of knowledge that already exists as part of the culture. It needs to be recognized, however, that grasping this knowledge is also emergent, and so knowledge-building technology for schools needs to be essentially the same as what would support the work of knowledge-creating organizations.

The next generation of CSILE, called Knowledge Forum®, provides a knowledge building environment for communities (classrooms, service and health organizations, businesses, and so forth) to carry on the sociocognitive practices described earlier – practices that are constitutive of knowledge- and innovation-creating organizations. This is a continuing challenge; Knowledge Forum undergoes continual revision as theory advances and experience uncovers new problems and opportunities. It is an extensible environment supporting knowledge building at all educational levels, and also in a wide range of noneducational settings.

The distinctive characteristics of Knowledge Forum are perhaps most easily grasped by comparing it to the familiar technology of threaded discussion, which is to be found everywhere on the World Wide Web and also as a part of instructional management systems like Blackboard and WebCT. Threaded discussion is a one-to-many form of e-mail. Instead of sending a message privately to people the sender selects, the sender "posts" it to a discussion site, where all posted messages appear in chronological order, with one exception: a response to a message is shown indented under the original message, rather than in chronological order. Responses to that response are further indented, and so on, forming a "thread" that started with the very first posting. Like e-mail messages generally, a discussion forum message, once "posted," cannot be modified. "Threading" produces a downward-branching tree structure, which is the only structuring of information (besides chronological) that the technology allows. There is no way to create higher-level organizations of information, to comment simultaneously on a number of messages, or to make a connection between a message in one thread and a message in another. Thus the possibilities for knowledge-building discourse are extremely limited. In fact, our experience is that threaded discussion militates against deepening inquiry; instead, it is much more suited to rapid question-answer and assertion-response exchanges. Although communities based on shared interests do develop in some threaded discussion forums, this technology provides little means for a group to organize its efforts around a common goal. As the number of postings increases, what appears on the screen becomes an increasingly incoherent stream of messages, leading discussion monitors to impose arbitrary limits on thread length and to erase threads of a certain age. Thus a cumulative advance in the state of knowledge is hardly conceivable.

Knowledge Forum's technological roots are not in e-mail at all. Knowledge Forum is a multimedia database, designed so as to maximize the ability of a community of users to create and improve both its content and organization. Thus, the database itself is an emergent, representing at different stages in its development the advancing knowledge of the community. From the users' standpoint, the main constituents of a Knowledge Forum database are *notes* and *views*. A view is an organizing background for notes. It may be a concept map, a diagram, a scene – anything that visually adds structure and meaning to the notes whose icons appear in it. Notes are contributed to views and may be moved about to create organization within views. The same notes may appear in more than one view. Figure 7.1 shows several different views of the same notes produced by first graders in studying dinosaurs.

Wherever one is in a Knowledge Forum database, it is always possible to move downward, producing a lower-level note, comment, or subview; upward, producing a more inclusive note or a view of views; and sideways, linking views to views or linking notes in different views. Notes themselves may contain graphics, animations, movies, links to other applications and applets, and so on.

Knowledge Forum lends itself to a high level of what we call "epistemic agency" (Scardamalia, 2000). Although among philosophers this term denotes responsibility for one's beliefs (Reed, 2001), we use the term more broadly: epistemic agency refers to the amount of individual or collective control people have over the whole range of components of knowledge building – goals, strategies, resources, evaluation of results, and so on. Students can create their own views, as can authorized visitors (telementors) from outside the class. Groups of students may be given responsibility for different views, working to improve their usefulness to the class, to remove redundancies, and so on. Knowledge Forum provides

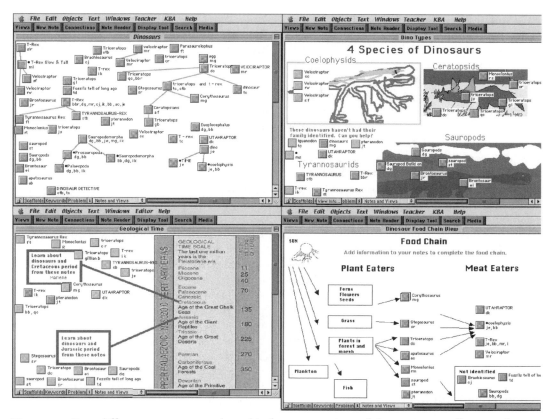

Figure 7.1. Four different user-generated graphical representations of the same notes illustrate the multiple perspectives, multiple literacies, and teamwork enabled by CSILE/Knowledge Forum.

"scaffolds" to help shape discourse to knowledge-building purposes – for instance, a set of theory-building scaffolds that include "My theory," "New information," "This theory explains," and "This theory cannot explain." Similar supports have been used in other collaborative learning software (see Andriessen, this volume; Edelson & Reiser, this volume; Linn, this volume; Stahl, Koschmann, & Suthers, this volume), but typically their use, and sometimes even the order in which they are used, is mandatory. In Knowledge Forum, use of the scaffolds is optional, and they may be modified as knowledge building progresses. One fourth-grade class decided that they were doing too much "knowledge telling" and so they introduced new scaffolds to focus attention on ideas.

We designed Knowledge Forum not simply as a tool, but as a knowledge-building *environment* – that is, as a virtual space within which the main work of a knowledge-building group would take place (Scardamalia, 2003). It has proven useful not only in formal educational settings but also in other circumstances where groups are striving to become knowledge-building organizations – service and professional organizations, teacher development networks, and businesses that are aiming to boost their innovation capabilities. Giving pragmatic support to the idea that the same process underlies both school learning and high-level knowledge creation, the same version of Knowledge Forum has been used without modification at levels ranging from kindergarten to graduate school and professional work.

Of course, students using Knowledge Forum do not spend all their time at the computer. They read books and magazines, have small-group and whole-class discussions, design and carry out experiments, build things, go on field trips, and do all the other things that make up a rich educational experience. But instead of the online work being an adjunct, as it typically is with instructional management systems, bulletin boards, and the like, Knowledge Forum is where the main work takes place. It is where the "state of knowledge" materializes, takes shape, and advances. It is where the results of the various offline activities contribute to the overall effort. If students run into a problem, they often recommend starting a space in Knowledge Forum to preserve and work out the ideas. At the end of grade 1, a child moving to a class without Knowledge Forum asked, "Where will my ideas go? Who will help me improve them?" The grade 2 teacher decided to use Knowledge Forum; the child's grade 1 ideas lived on, to be improved along with new ideas generated in grade 2.

Knowledge-Building Pedagogy

A knowledge-building pedagogy evolved along with the technology, with teachers' innovations and students' accomplishments instrumental in this evolution. Two different progressions in pedagogy over three-year periods are reported by Scardamalia, Bereiter, Hewitt, and Webb (1996) and Messina and Reeve (2004). The goal was not to evolve a set of activity structures, procedures, or rules, but rather a set of workable principles that could guide pedagogy in a variety of contexts. The six themes that have framed the discussion in this chapter reflect this emphasis, as does a more fully elaborated set of twelve knowledge building principles (Scardamalia, 2002). The problem has been that principles – whether framed as goals, rules, beliefs, design parameters, or diagnostic questions – are viewed by some as too abstract to be very helpful and by others as mere redescriptions of things they already do. Movies and examples from student and teacher work are effective in arousing interest in knowledge building and in showing

that something different from more familiar constructivist, discovery, and collaborative learning approaches is going on, but the result is a heightened demand for "how to do it" recommendations.

Adhering to a principled rather than a procedural approach has undoubtedly impeded the spread of knowledge building and Knowledge Forum, but the quality and innovativeness of the work carried on by teachers who have assimilated the principles appears to justify the approach. Numerous examples may be found in the posters presented at the annual Summer Institute on Knowledge Building (abstracts are available at http://ikit.org/summerinstitutes.html). An unanticipated benefit of a principle-based approach is that the students themselves may begin to use knowledge-building principles in conceptualizing their own work. We have already mentioned the students who diagnosed their work as "knowledge telling" – a term derived from a cognitive model of immature composing processes (Scardamalia, Bereiter, & Steinbach, 1984). Caswell and Bielaczyk (2001) report students' productive use of the principle of "improvable ideas." In another class, elementary school students in an inner city school – identified as one of the neediest in Toronto – have studied and begun to apply such concepts as epistemic agency, pervasive knowledge building, and community knowledge, and to describe their work at the Knowledge Building Summer Institute. These reports are themselves striking illustrations of the principle of turning higher levels of agency over to students. For decades educators have promoted constructivist ideas among themselves whereas their students have been expected to carry out constructivist activities without access to the constructivist ideas lying behind them. This is an internal contradiction that a principled approach to knowledge building should overcome.

Figures 7.1 through 7.6 illustrate elementary school knowledge building in Toronto and Hong Kong, as supported by Knowledge Forum. The notes in Figure 7.1 were produced by grade 1–3 students who were

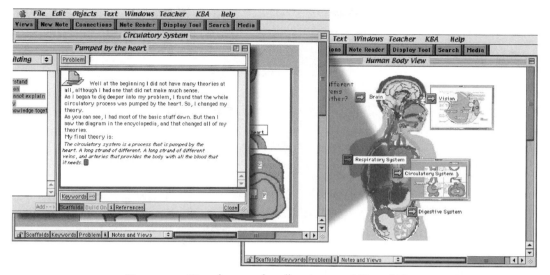

Figure 7.2. Rise-above and endless improvability of ideas.

contributing information and graphics concerning their favorite dinosaurs. The upper-left view shows what the discourse space looked like after the students had entered their early notes; these notes are not organized in any particular way. Soon after these initial postings were completed, the children discovered classmates who had the same favorite dinosaur (triceratops, brontosaurus, etc.). Several students had produced graphic rather than text notes, and others wanted to link their notes to these graphics. So students used these graphics to draw the background of a new view that organized the notes according to dinosaur type; this new view is shown in the upper-right corner of Figure 7.1.

At about the same time, students in a university course were provided with access rights to this grade 1–3 knowledge-building discourse. The university students noted, in reading these same notes, that they contained references to geological time, and they created a new "geological time" view and entered a geological-timeline graphic from the Internet as a background (see the lower left frame of Figure 7.1). They then searched the primary students' notes for periods of time (e.g., Jurassic), and the new collection was added at the appropriate point to the geological timeline. When

the primary students took a look at this new view, those who had not yet identified the time when their dinosaur roamed the earth quickly extended their research so their note would appear in this new view.

The last pane of Figure 7.1 (lower right frame) demonstrates yet another view of these same notes. A biologist was invited to join the knowledge-building collaborative efforts. She signed in from her office and created the "food chain" view that referenced students' dinosaurs as either plant or meat eaters.

Figure 7.2 is drawn from a Knowledge Forum database from a grade 5/6 class researching "systems of the body." The left side of Figure 7.2 shows what is called a "rise-above" note – in this case a student's summary of his knowledge advances made over a period of several months. The rise-above note subsumes a number of previous notes, which are now accessible only through this rise-above note. Rise-above notes are also used to synthesize ideas, create historical accounts and archives, reduce redundancy, and in other ways impose higher levels of organization on ideas.

The right side of Figure 7.2 illustrates the rise-above idea applied to views rather than notes. The smaller pictures are links to separate views created by groups of students

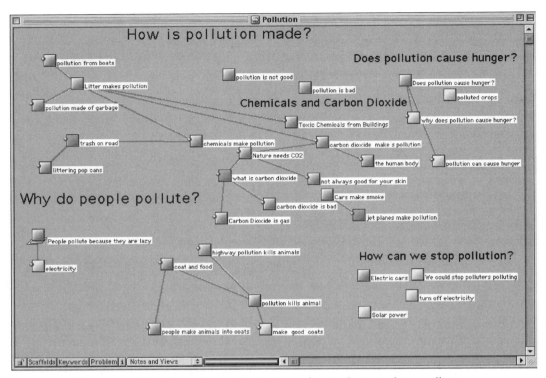

Figure 7.3. Rise-above view and note by grade 1 students studying pollution.

working on different body systems. Later, the higher-order "Human Body" view was created to integrate these separate views and to support a new discourse on how different parts of the body work together. As this figure suggests, notes and views operate as a form of "zoom in/zoom out," encouraging users to think in terms of relationships.

Endless improvability of ideas is further supported by the following:

- Ability to create increasingly high-order conceptual frameworks. It is always possible to reformulate problems at more complex levels, by creating a rise-above note that encompasses previous rise-above notes, or to create a more inclusive view-of-views.

- Review and Revision. Notes and views can be revised at any time, unlike most discussion environments that disallow changes after a note is posted.

- Published notes and views. Processes of peer review and new forms of publica-

tion engage students in group editorial processes. Published works appear in a different visual form and searches can be restricted to the published layer of a database.

Figures 7.3 through 7.6 show a progression across grade levels in the kinds of knowledge building achieved when the whole school is committed to it. These examples come from the Institute of Child Study at the University of Toronto, where knowledge building is so embedded in the work of the school that quite a few students have more experience than their teachers and are instrumental in introducing new teachers not only to Knowledge Forum technology but also to the knowledge-building culture of the school.

Figure 7.3 shows a view created by Grade 1 students. It represents an overview of their work on pollution. The teacher reports, "This year in grade one we studied ecology as an overarching theme throughout the year . . . we read newspaper

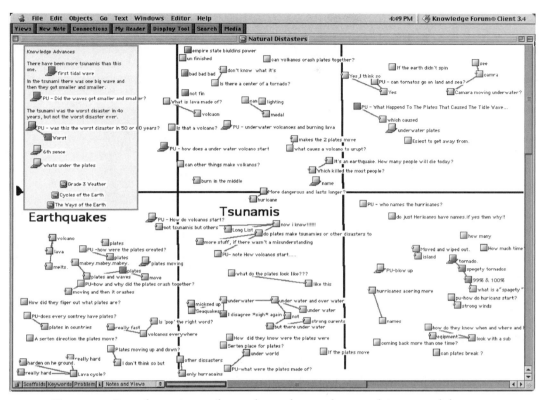

Figure 7.4. Rise-above view and notes by grade 3 students studying natural disasters.

articles, books, and World Wildlife Federation publications.... We frequently came across and discussed vocabulary such as pollution, oxygen, carbon dioxide, chemicals, pesticides, endangered, threatened, and so on." Several students generated the same theory – that pollution is caused by laziness – and the rise-above note in the lower

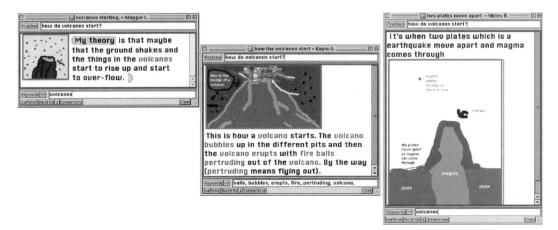

Figure 7.5. Idea improvement by grade 3 students studying volcanoes, as part of efforts to understand natural disasters.

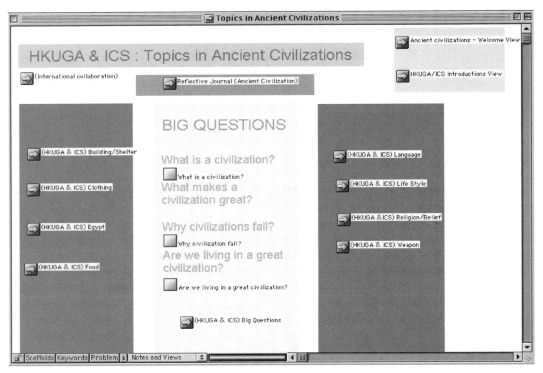

Figure 7.6. View-of-views by grade 5–6 students studying ancient civilizations.

left (basic note icon with leaves underneath) is used to assemble those theories into one note. By grade 3 – see Figure 7.4 – students are engaged in more complex rise-above activity, as indicated by rise-above notes throughout the view. The view itself represents an overview of the work of the class as a whole, with a section in the upper left titled "knowledge advances" providing an even higher-level summary, with links to related views. One of the related views is titled "volcanos." Figure 7.5 shows several notes in that view, and efforts to explain volcanoes, starting with surface features and later their "problem of understanding" shifts to trying to figure out what happens below the surface. In Figure 7.6 we see a view-of-views created by grade 5–6 Toronto students in collaboration with students in a Hong Kong public school affiliated with the Hong Kong University Graduates Association. They codesigned this view to identify their big questions and to organize their collaborative work.

Conclusion

In education, most of the twentieth century was occupied with efforts to shift from a didactic approach focused on the transmission of knowledge and skills to what is popularly called "active learning," where the focus is on students' interest-driven activities that are generative of knowledge and competence. We believe a shift of equal if not greater magnitude will come to dominate educational dialogue in the present century. The twentieth-century shift has been aptly characterized by Stone (1996) as a shift from "instructivism" to "developmentalism," for underlying the shift has been a strong belief in the natural disposition of children to do what is conducive to their personal development – in effect, to know better than the curriculum-makers what is best for them. Dispute over this proposition is by no means settled, but it is rendered moot by a societal shift that puts the emphasis on the ability of organizations and whole societies to create new knowledge and achieve new competencies. In this "knowledge age" context, it cannot be assumed that either the curriculum-makers or the individual students know what is best. The new challenge is initiating the young into a culture devoted to advancing the frontiers of knowledge on all sides, and helping them to find a constructive and personally satisfying role in that culture. The culture-transmission goals of liberal education and the more child-centered goals of developmentalism are not to be ignored, but they are to be realized within an educational environment that is itself an example of and at the same time a legitimate part of the emerging knowledge-creating culture (Smith, 2002). The driving force is not so much the individual interests of children as their desire to connect with what is most dynamic and meaningful in the surrounding society. That, fundamentally, is what knowledge-building pedagogy and knowledge-building technology aim to build on.

The proof of knowledge building is in the community knowledge that is publicly produced by the students – in other words, in visible idea improvement achieved through the students' collective efforts. Although ascertaining that knowledge building has taken place requires digging into the content of Knowledge Forum databases and recordings of class interactions, it is usually apparent when something is seriously wrong. Pedagogy that is far off the mark will often manifest itself in a Knowledge Forum database that is full of redundancy, that is merely a repository of facts, or that presents a deluge of questions, opinions, or conjectures with no follow-up.

When knowledge building fails, it is usually because of a failure to deal with problems that are authentic for students and that elicit real ideas from them. Instead of connecting to the larger world of knowledge creation, the tasks or problems are mere exercises and are perceived by the students as such. At the deepest level, knowledge building can only succeed if teachers believe students are capable of it. This requires more than a belief that students can carry out actions similar to those in knowledge-creating organizations and disciplines. It requires a belief that students can deliberately create knowledge that is useful to their community in further knowledge building and that is a legitimate part of the civilization-wide effort to advance knowledge frontiers.

Acknowledgments

The authors wish to acknowledge the generous support of the Social Sciences and Humanities Research Council of Canada. We are indebted to the students, teachers, and principals of the Institute of Child Study and Rose Avenue Public School in Toronto and the entire Institute for Knowledge Innovation and Technology team (http://www.ikit.org), without whose contributions the work reported here would not have been possible. We also are indebted to Keith Sawyer for thoughtful input and help beyond the call of editorial duty.

References

American Association for the Advancement of Science. (1967). *Science: A process approach.* Washington, DC: American Association for the Advancement of Science, Commission on Science Education. Distributed by Xerox Corporation.

Anderson, J. R. (1980). *Cognitive psychology and its implications.* San Francisco: W. M. Freeman.

Bazerman, C. (1985). Physicists reading physics: Schema-laden purposes and purpose-laden schema. *Written Communication, 2,* 3–23.

Bereiter, C. (1985). Toward a solution of the learning paradox. *Review of Educational Research, 55,* 201–226.

Bereiter, C. (1991). Implications of connectionism for thinking about rules. *Educational Researcher, 20,* 10–16.

Bereiter, C. (1992). Referent-centered and problem-centered knowledge: Elements of an educational epistemology. *Interchange, 23,* 337–362.

Bereiter, C. (1994). Implications of postmodernism for science, or, science as progressive discourse. *Educational Psychologist, 29*(1), 3–12.

Bereiter, C. (2002). *Education and mind in the knowledge age.* Mahwah, NJ: Lawrence Erlbaum Associates.

Bereiter, C., & Scardamalia, M. (1989). Intentional learning as a goal of instruction. In L. B. Resnick (Eds.), *Knowing, learning, and instruction: Essays in honor of Robert Glaser* (pp. 361–392). Hillsdale, NJ: Lawrence Erlbaum Associates.

Bereiter, C., & Scardamalia, M. (2003). Learning to work creatively with knowledge. In E. D. Corte, L. Verschaffel, N. Entwistle, & J. V. Merriënboer (Eds.), *Powerful learning environments: Unravelling basic components and dimensions* (pp. 73–78). Oxford: Elsevier Science.

Bereiter, C., & Scardamalia, M. (in press). Models of teaching and instruction in the knowledge age. In P. A. Alexander & P. H. Winne (Eds.), *Handbook of educational psychology* (2nd ed.). Mahwah, NJ: Lawrence Erlbaum Associates.

Bereiter, C., Scardamalia, M., Cassells, C., & Hewitt, J. (1997). Postmodernism, knowledge building, and elementary science. *Elementary School Journal, 97*, 329–340.

Brown, A. L., Day, J. D., & Jones, R. S. (1983). The development of plans for summarizing texts. *Child Development, 54*, 968–979.

Caswell, B., & Bielaczyk, K. (2001). Knowledge Forum: Altering the relationship between students and scientific knowledge. *Education, Communication & Information, 1*, 281–305.

Catrambone, R., & Holyoak, K. J. (1989). Overcoming contextual limitations on problem-solving transfer. *Journal of Experimental Psychology: Learning, Memory, and Cognition, 15*, 1147–1156.

Chi, M. T. H., Slotta, J. D., & deLeeuw, N. (1994). From things to processes: A theory of conceptual change for learning science concepts. *Learning and Instruction, 4*, 27–43.

Coleman, E. B., Brown, A. L., & Rivkin, I. D. (1997). The effect of instructional explanations on learning from scientific texts. *Journal of the Learning Sciences, 6*, 347–365.

Dunbar, K. (1997). How scientists think: Online creativity and conceptual change in science. In T. B. Ward, S. M. Smith, & S. Vaid (Eds.), *Conceptual structures and processes: Emergence, discovery and change* (pp. 461–493). Washington, DC: American Psychological Association.

Fodor, J. A. (1980). Fixation of belief and concept acquisition. In M. Piattelli-Palmerini (Eds.), *Language and learning: The debate between Jean Piaget and Noam Chomsky* (pp. 142–149). Cambridge, MA: Harvard University Press.

Grossberg, S. (1997). Principles of cortical synchronization. *Behavioral and Brain Sciences, 20*, 689–690.

Lakatos, I. (1976). *Proofs and refutations: The logic of mathematical discovery.* New York: Cambridge University Press.

Messina, R., & Reeve, R. (2004). Knowledge building in elementary science. In K. Leithwood, P. McAdie, N. Bascia, & A. Rodrigue (Eds.), *Teaching for deep understanding: Towards the Ontario curriculum we need* (pp. 94–99). Toronto: Elementary Teachers' Federation of Ontario.

Molenaar, P. C. M., & van der Maas, H. L. J. (2000). Neural constructivism or self-organization? *Behavioral and Brain Sciences, 23*, 783

Ohlsson, S. (1991). *Young adults' understanding of evolutionary explanations: Preliminary observations* (Tech. Rep. to OERI No. University of Pittsburgh, Learning Research and Development Laboratory.

Pascual-Leone, J. (1980). Constructive problems for constructive theories: The current relevance of Piaget's work and a critique of information-processing simulation psychology. In R. H. Kluwe & H. Spada (eds.), *Developmental models of thinking* (pp. 263–296). New York: Academic Press.

Petroski, H. (1996). *Invention by design.* Cambridge, MA: Harvard University Press.

Phillips, W. A., & Singer, W. (1997). In search of common foundations for cortical computation. *Behavioral and Brain Sciences, 20*, 657–722.

Quartz, S. R. (1993) Neural networks, nativism, and the plausibility of constructivism. *Cognition, 48*, 223–42.

Ranney, M., & Schank, P. (1998). Toward an integration of the social and the scientific: Observing, modeling, and promoting the explanatory coherence of reasoning. In S. Reed & L. Miller (Eds.), *Connectionist models of social reasoning and social behavior* (pp. 245–274). Mahwah, NJ: Lawrence Erlbaum Associates.

Reed, B. (2001). Epistemic agency and the intellectual virtues. *Southern Journal of Philosophy*, 39, 507–526.

Rheinberger, H.-J. (1997). *Toward history of epistemic things: Synthesizing proteins in the test tube*. Stanford, CA: Stanford University Press.

Sawyer, R. K. (2003). Emergence in creativity and development. In R. K. Sawyer, V. John-Steiner, S. Moran, R. Sternberg, D. H. Feldman, M. Csikszentmihalyi, & J. Nakamura, *Creativity and development* (pp. 12–60). New York: Oxford.

Sawyer, R. K. (2005). *Social emergence: Societies as complex systems*. New York: Cambridge.

Scardamalia, M. (2000). Can schools enter a Knowledge Society? In M. Selinger and J. Wynn (Eds.), *Educational technology and the impact on teaching and learning* (pp. 6–10). Abingdon: Research Machines.

Scardamalia, M. (2002). Collective cognitive responsibility for the advancement of knowledge. In B. Smith (Eds.), *Liberal education in a knowledge society* (pp. 76–98). Chicago: Open Court.

Scardamalia, M. (2003). Knowledge building environments: Extending the limits of the possible in education and knowledge work. In A. DiStefano, K. E. Rudestam, & R. Silverman (Eds.), *Encyclopedia of distributed learning* (pp. 269–272). Thousand Oaks, CA: Sage Publications.

Scardamalia, M, & Bereiter, C. (1987). Knowledge telling and knowledge transforming in written composition. In S. Rosenberg (Ed.), *Advances in applied psycholinguistics: Vol. 2. Reading, writing, and language learning* (pp. 142–175). Cambridge: Cambridge University Press.

Scardamalia, M., & Bereiter, C. (1991). Higher levels of agency for children in knowledge-building: A challenge for the design of new knowledge media. *The Journal of the Learning Sciences*, 1(1), 37–68.

Scardamalia, M., & Bereiter, C. (1996). Adaptation and understanding: A case for new cultures of schooling. In S. Vosniadou, E. DeCorte, R. Glaser, & H. Mandl (Eds.), *International perspectives on the design of technology-supported learning environments* (pp. 149–163). Mahwah, NJ: Erlbaum.

Scardamalia, M., & Bereiter, C. (2003). Knowledge building. In *Encyclopedia of education* (pp. 1370–1373). New York: Macmillan Reference.

Scardamalia, M., Bereiter, C., Hewitt, J., & Webb, J. (1996). Constructive learning from texts in biology. In K.M Fischer, & M. Kirby (Eds.), *Relations and biology learning: The acquisition and use of knowledge structures in biology* (pp. 44–64). Berlin: Springer-Verlag.

Scardamalia, M., Bereiter, C., & Lamon, M. (1994). The CSILE project: Trying to bring the classroom into World 3. In K. McGilley (Eds.), *Classroom lessons: Integrating cognitive theory and classroom practice* (pp. 201–228). Cambridge, MA: MIT Press.

Scardamalia, M., Bereiter, C., McLean, R. S., Swallow, J., & Woodruff, E. (1989). Computer supported intentional learning environments. *Journal of Educational Computing Research*, 5, 51–68.

Scardamalia, M., Bereiter, C., & Steinbach, R. (1984). Teachability of reflective processes in written composition. *Cognitive Science*, 8(2), 173–190.

Smith, B. (Ed.). (2002). *Liberal education in a knowledge society*. Chicago: Open Court.

Stehr, N. (1994). *Knowledge societies*. London: Sage Publications.

Sterelny, K. 2005. Externalism, epistemic artefacts and the extended mind. In (R. Schantz, ed) *The externalist challenge: New studies on cognition and intentionality*. Berlin: de Gruyter.

Stone, J. E. (1996). Developmentalism: An obscure but pervasive restriction on educational improvement. *Education Policy Analysis Archives*, 4(8). Retrieved from http://olam.edu. asu.edu/epaa/v4n8.html

Woodruff, E., & Meyer, K. (1997). Explanations from intra- and inter-group discourse: Students building knowledge in the science classroom. *Research in Science Education*, 27(1), 25–39.

Part II

METHODOLOGIES

CHAPTER 8

Learner-Centered Design

Reflections on the Past and Directions for the Future

Chris Quintana, Namsoo Shin, Cathleen Norris,
& Elliot Soloway

As new information technologies have emerged, whether radio, television, or computers, advocates of those technologies hoped that each would have a radically transformative effect on education. However, in many ways, the scope of the resulting educational transformation was less than many had hoped for. In the last two decades, a wide range of new information technologies, such as personal computers, handheld computers, wireless networking, and the Internet, have emerged that again have a potential to transform education. Cuban (1986) noted some reasons why previous technologies have been less than successful for supporting learning. First, there is a failure to understand how technologies must be shaped to support the needs of learners. Second, there is a failure to understand how technologies can be effectively integrated into educational contexts in ways that truly support learning activities and goals. Therefore, if computers are to positively impact learning, educational software must be designed around learners' goals, needs, activities, and educational contexts. This approach to designing software is called *learner-centered design (LCD)* (Soloway, Guzdial, & Hay, 1994).

Here we will provide an overview of learner-centered design and summarize how it is different from typical software design approaches. We will discuss both the critical role of scaffolding in learner-centered design and how software can serve a scaffolding function for learners. We will describe different design frameworks that can impact LCD by guiding designers and researchers in developing intellectual support in software. Finally, we conclude by briefly discussing some future research directions that the learning sciences community can pursue in terms of developing software to support learning.

Learner-Centered Design: Focusing on the Unique Needs of Learners

Software designers usually try to make their software easy for people to use: this approach is known as *user-centered design (UCD)* (Norman & Draper, 1986). The assumption with UCD is that software users

Table 8.1. *Differences Between Professional Users and Learners*

Professional Users	Learners
High expertise in the task domain	Low expertise in the task domain
Homogenous population	Diverse population
Higher motivation to engage in their tasks	Lower motivation to engage in their tasks
Little change in users	Learners develop and grow and they learn
Design of their tools should primarily address gulfs between user and tool (i.e., gulfs of execution and expertise)	Design of their tools should primarily address gulf between their knowledge and knowledge of an expert in the task domain

are knowledgeable about the underlying tasks they are using software to perform and simply need usable software to do those tasks. But when software is designed for learners, there are critical issues to consider beyond software usability, due to the novice nature of learners (Quintana, Soloway, & Krajcik, 2003; Soloway et al., 1994) (see Table 8.1).

Level of Expertise

User-centered design implicitly assumes that software users already have some measure of expertise in a given domain or in the practices and activities for which they are using the software. In contrast, learners do not possess an equal amount of expertise. Learners have an incomplete or naïve understanding of the activities, tools, and practices in a given domain of study. Whereas users simply need tools that will help them engage in their practices in an easy and efficient manner, learners need tools that address their lack of expertise and help them develop their understanding in the given domain.

Homogeneity

Since professional users understand the activities, tools, and practices in a given content area, they are often considered to be *homogenous* in many ways. Thus, user-centered software is typically designed to address the set of tasks being performed by an "ideal user" with less attention being paid to individual differences between users. In contrast, learners are more diverse since they do not necessarily share a given expertise or culture. Because the audience of learn-

ers may have a range of learning styles and characteristics, tools for learners must be designed to consider this diversity in background, development, gender, age, learning styles, and so on.

Motivation

Users are deeply involved in their activities, and they typically have both intrinsic and extrinsic motivation for those activities – intrinsic motivation, because they are performing authentic, deeply contextualized activities with a clear goal; and extrinsic motivation, such as salary increases, positive job evaluations, and respect from colleagues. So user-centered design does not consider supplying additional motivational factors; designers can assume that users have the necessary motivation to engage in their work. In contrast, learners are not always highly motivated to engage in new learning activities or to learn new content. Additionally, when learners have trouble understanding new concepts or activities, their motivation may further suffer (Hogan, Nastasi, & Pressley, 2000). Thus learner-centered design must address ways to initially and continually motivate learners as they work through difficult new material.

Growth in Skill

Because users start with a higher level of expertise, they will not necessarily display any significant growth in knowledge as they use their software. User-centered tools can be designed without considering how those tools may have to change in response to any growth in the users – if users largely

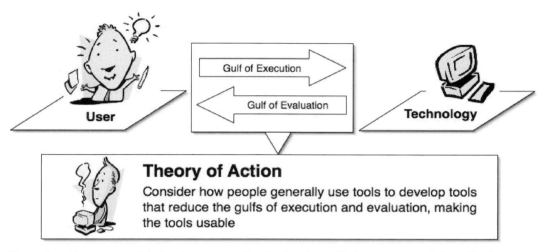

Figure 8.1. User-centered design is conceptualized using the gulf of execution and the gulf of evaluation. A theory of action can help inform how those gulfs can be reduced, resulting in usable technology.

stay the same, then their tools can also stay the same. However, developing new understanding is the central goal for learners. If learner-centered software is at all successful, a learner's understanding will grow and change significantly while using the software, and thus the software will have to change with them.

Scaffolding Learners Across the "Gulf of Expertise"

Norman (1986) described user-centered design in terms of addressing the *conceptual distance* between a computer user and the computer. When users use a tool to complete their work, they have specific goals in mind that they need to translate into actions they will execute on the tool. After executing some sequence of actions on the tool, users evaluate and interpret the resulting state of the tool with respect to their goals. Norman described these two conceptual distances between a computer user and the computer as "gulfs" between the goals of the user and the physical tool: a gulf of *execution* (the difference between the goals and intentions of the user and the permissible actions on the tool) and a gulf of *evaluation* (the amount of effort the user must exert to interpret the physical tool state) (Figure 8.1).

Designers can increase software usability by minimizing both gulfs to make execution and evaluation more straightforward. One way of reducing these usability gulfs is by understanding how people use tools. In order to inform usability design, Norman (1986) proposed a "theory of action" describing how people generally use tools to complete tasks via a series of execution steps (i.e., establishing a goal, an intention to achieve the goal, and a specific sequence of steps on the tool to meet the intention; and executing the specific action sequence) and evaluation steps (i.e., perceiving, interpreting, and evaluating the resulting state of the tool). Thus designers need to gain a deep understanding of how people perform their tasks and how people interpret information to design usable software that minimizes the gulfs of execution and evaluation.

In contrast, learner-centered tools need to address the conceptual distance – the *gulf of expertise* – that lies between the novice learner and the more developed understanding or expertise embodied by an expert in the domain (Figure 8.2; Quintana et al., 2003). The "size" of the gulf of expertise is proportional to the amount of conceptual change needed in the learner's domain model so that he or she can fully participate with domain experts (Quintana et al., 2003;

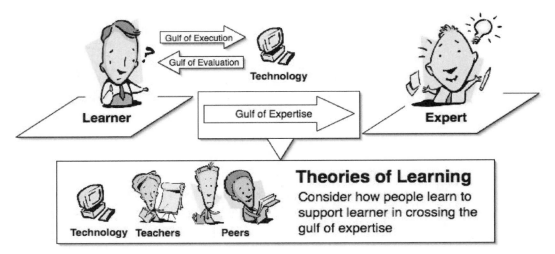

Figure 8.2. Learner-centered design is conceptualized using the gulf of expertise. Theories of learning can inform the development of technology (which can be situated in a broader context) that supports learners in crossing the gulf of expertise (while still considering usability issues in ways that do not interfere with learning).

also see diSessa, this volume). Thus designers need to understand how people learn in order to develop learner-centered software. Because the focus of learner-centered design is on learning rather than usability, learning sciences must be integrated into software design. For example, the gulf of expertise can be described in terms of the expertise held by a full participant in a community of practice. From this perspective, learning involves a learner's progress across the gulf of expertise as he or she moves from peripheral toward full participation in a community of practice (Lave & Wenger, 1991). Thus, we can say that learner-centered design involves developing software that can scaffold learners to facilitate mindful, intellectual work that can transition them across the gulf of expertise (Collins, this volume; Greeno, this volume). We can now show how learner-centered design greatly entails the design of effective scaffolding features, which requires designers to understand different aspects of the learning context, including the types of activities that are involved in the domain under study, the factual information used in the domain, and the tools and terminology that are part of the domain.

Scaffolding Learners Across the Gulf of Expertise

Piaget (1954) discussed the notion that learning is an active, constructive process, and learning sciences research has since continued in that direction (Brown, Collins, & Duguid, 1989; Papert, 1993). Learning is not a passive process of transferring information from expert to novice. Rather, learning is an active process, employing a "learning by mindful doing" approach where learners must cognitively manipulate the material they are learning to create cognitive links from the new material to their own prior knowledge.

Learning sciences research has also demonstrated the critical role played by social context – knowledge is contextualized and learners must build their knowledge within a community of peers and experts (Brown et al., 1989). Thus, gaining expertise involves participating in the context of the professional culture in order to understand the common practices, languages, tools, and values of that culture. For example, other work considers tenets of social constructivism in the design of learning materials (Singer et al., 2000):

- *Active construction*: Learners need to actively engage in mindful work (usually by being immersed in authentic practice) to develop a better understanding of that work.
- *Situated cognition*: Learners need to work in a context where they are surrounded by social and intellectual supports so they can see how knowledge is used in authentic practice (Greeno, this volume).
- *Discourse*: Learners need to engage in discourse with other members of the community (whether professionals or other learners) to discuss their ideas and further develop their understanding.
- *Community*: Learners need to be exposed to the community (or culture) of authentic practice. The community can serve as a means for learners to get social support, actively construct knowledge, and learn (and practice) professional discourse.

Thus learning sciences research considers different perspectives and theories on learning, and these all inform LCD. Much of the work that has emerged from LCD has focused on the development of software-based constructivist learning environments – comprehensive environments in which learners have access to tools, information resources, and collaboration support for pursuing learning goals and activities from a domain of authentic practice (Wilson, 1996). Such learning environments often immerse learners in particular contexts where they can participate in authentic activity from a given domain to begin developing an understanding of the domain. However, because of the complexity of such activity for novice learners, learners will need *scaffolding* to mindfully engage in the activity. With the support provided by scaffolding, learners can actively engage in authentic practice in productive ways to cross the gulf of expertise.

The concept of scaffolding comes from Vygotsky's (1978) notion of a more experienced adult or peer providing assistance to a novice. Wood, Bruner, and Ross (1975) expanded the notion of scaffolding as they described the nature of the support that an experienced adult tutor can provide a younger learner. The concept of scaffolding is now manifested in different contexts. For example, teachers can scaffold students by employing different scaffolding approaches, such as providing coaching, modeling a task, or giving advice, so that students can engage in authentic practice (Collins, this volume; Sawyer introduction, this volume). The challenge for LCD involves considering how software can incorporate different features that manifest scaffolding functions for the learners using the software. Since Guzdial (1994) first articulated the notion of "software-realized scaffolding," many challenges for incorporating scaffolding in software remain:

- *Traditional scaffolding vs. software-based scaffolding*. The notion of scaffolding has now been extended from teacher-student interaction to computer-student interaction, leading to new questions about scaffolding. Specifically, is the notion of scaffolding when applied to software broader than the traditional use of the term in the educational literature? With different examples of learner-centered software including features that are claimed to provide scaffolding, there is concern that the notion of scaffolding might be watered down to the point where it became a meaningless distinction.
- *New scaffolding approaches in software*. Computers have unique capabilities, so one challenge for designers is to develop new or different scaffolding approaches that are not possible in the teacher-student context.
- *The fading of scaffolding in software*. There are also challenges related to the fading of software-based scaffolding. The traditional view of scaffolding is that as learners develop more understanding, they need less and less scaffolding support – in other words, the scaffolding should fade as learners grow. The question for developers involves identifying the mechanisms by which software-based

scaffolding could fade and identifying when fading is appropriate. Additionally, there are questions about the difference between fading mechanisms for scaffolding provided by teachers versus scaffolding provided by software.

Thus, scaffolding in software can generally provide cognitive support for learners by situating them in a more authentic context of a practice (e.g., software features showing a science lab in the background), by making aspects of the authentic practice visible and explicit (particularly in disciplines such as science and mathematics that use software tools as part of their everyday practice), and by supporting students to engage in discourse with others.

We can summarize a LCD process with a brief example drawn from the design of Symphony, a scaffolded work environment for middle-school students that uses a range of different science tools, including air pollution databases and visualization tools, to explore air quality questions (Quintana, 2001). The goal of Symphony was to provide students with an overarching software environment that would also support them with the complexities they might face in authentic science inquiry practices. The development of Symphony served as a case study for outlining an explicit learner-centered design process that involved: (1) describing and characterizing the target learner audience, the practices they would engage in, and their learning goals; (2) identifying the areas where those learners would need support to engage in the specified practices; and (3) developing the scaffolding approaches that would be conceptualized and implemented in the software to address the support needs identified earlier (Quintana et al., 2003).

The analysis work for Symphony involved characterizing the inquiry work that students would be doing, and understanding the experience – and lack thereof – that ninth-grade students had with science inquiry. To describe the specific inquiry work that students would be doing, Quintana et al. (1999) developed a *process space approach* that included:

- The *activities* that students needed to perform, such as planning their investigation, looking for relevant information about air pollution, collecting air pollution data, graphing and visualizing that data, developing system models to consider air pollution scenarios, and synthesizing pollution information to answer their specific questions.

- The *tools* that students needed to perform these activities, such as planning tools, databases, graphing and modeling tools, and text editing facilities.

- The *artifacts* that students produced and later refered to throughout their investigation, such as the artifacts produced by their tools, including investigation plans, graphs, models, and so on.

- The *information objects* that students might need to refer to during their investigations, such as reference materials about air pollution, or information about scientific terminology (e.g., terms like "hypothesis").

- The analysis also helped articulate more general information about the nature of the investigation process itself. Specifically, the analysis showed that the investigation process was not linear and sequential, but rather that it was ill structured, iterative, and nonlinear.

After characterizing the type of investigations students would perform, the next step was to outline the difficulties or roadblocks ninth-grade students might encounter during an investigation due to their inexperience with such wide-ranging investigations. This involved looking at science education literature and having discussions with teachers. The results of this analysis included a set of learner support needs that revolved around the different aspects of the air pollution investigation process (Quintana et al., 1999). For example, students needed support to see what activities comprised an investigation, and needed information about the purposes of those activities. Students needed functional support to engage in planning or reflecting on the results of different activities. Students needed information about several aspects of their investigation, such as the meaning of scientific terms, or procedural information about how they should perform certain activities. Finally, given the number of artifacts that students would create and refer to, students also needed support to help manage those artifacts in ways that would help them focus on their work.

These specific areas where students would need support to engage in their work helped defined the types of scaffolding features needed for the software. The development of the scaffolding features involved developing a conceptual approach for supporting learners and then implementing that conceptual approach in the software. Each of these approaches was informed by different learning theories and other perspectives on supporting learners. (Many of these conceptual approaches and scaffolding examples contributed to the development of the Scaffolding Design Framework described in the next section.)

There were several different types of scaffolding features in Symphony. For example, planning is a more implicit activity since experts may plan in a more automatic fashion without explicitly thinking about the activity due to their experience. Because of their lack of experience, students may not realize that planning is an important part of the investigation process. Thus a conceptual approach for supporting learners is to provide reminders and guidance that facilitate productive planning (Quintana et al., 2004). Symphony implemented this conceptual scaffolding approach by including an explicit planning workspace that students had to use before they could continue with their work (Figure 8.3). Students constructed plans by dragging activities from the process map in the workspace to the planning grid below. Students also could modify their plans by moving activities to other positions in the grid, or by removing them altogether. The planning workspace also included other features aimed at supporting students. For example, as students may not know what activities comprise an investigation, the process map displayed the major investigation activities that students could perform; this implemented a conceptual approach of using an unordered task decomposition of the investigation process (Quintana et al., 2004). Furthermore, because learners may not know the purpose for different activities, the process map also contained activity guides that students could trigger by moving the mouse pointer over an activity in the map. The activity guides essentially embedded expert guidance about the rationales for different scientific activities, to help students make decisions for adding activities to their plan. Other scaffolding features in Symphony included support to help students to reflect on and articulate information about different aspects of their work, to see additional information about activity procedures or terminology, and to manage the artifacts they create in their investigations.

This research identified several key themes for LCD, including a thorough understanding of learners, their goals and intended practices, and the possible breakdowns that they face in doing those practices. This information can allow designers to determine the functionality and, more importantly, the scaffolding strategies and features that can help make the implicit knowledge that experts know and use more explicit for learners (Edelson & Reiser, this volume). Furthermore, with its focus on learning, LCD can not only result in tools that support learning but also in forms of design experiments to explore how learners learn and how technology may (or may not) support such learning (Barab, this volume; Confrey, this volume).

Design Frameworks That Inform the Learner-Centered Design Approach

Learner-centered design can leverage different design methods originally developed for user-centered design, such as traditional task analysis methods (e.g., Lesgold, 1986) and newer *contextual design* methods (Beyer & Holtzblatt, 2002) that help articulate

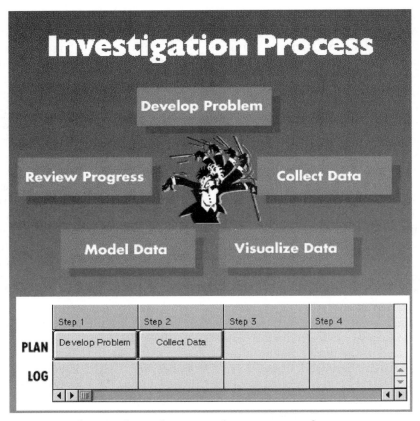

Figure 8.3. The Symphony planning workspace consists of a process map to display possible science inquiry activities to students along with a planning grid where students can set up and revise plans for their investigation.

different models of the context where the software will be used. These contextual models can help define how work is performed in a given context (e.g., a learning context like a classroom), the culture and policies involved in the context (e.g., the classroom culture established by a teacher), and the manner in which artifacts are produced and used in the domain (e.g., kinds of artifacts should students produce and use in the classroom). Other similar approaches include the *process space model* (Fitzpatrick & Welsh, 1995) and the corresponding process space analysis method (Quintana et al., 1999) mentioned earlier. The process space analysis method explicitly describes the different components that comprise the practice (e.g., science inquiry) that learners will engage in, such as the roles or responsibilities undertaken in the practice, the activities carried out by each role, the tools used to perform the activities, the artifacts produced in the activities or used to mediate the activities, and the information resources needed to perform the different activities.

Using these design approaches can make different components of authentic practice explicit, helping researchers and designers gain a wider understanding of the activity that learners will need to engage in. But understanding learners and their activities is only one aspect of the knowledge needed for LCD. Developers also need guidance to determine ways that the software they are developing can scaffold learners as they move across the gulf of expertise. In the following sections, we describe three design frameworks based in learning sciences research that can inform LCD from this perspective: the *Scaffolded Knowledge Integration Framework*, the *Scaffolding Design Framework*, and the *Learning for Use* approach.

Scaffolded Knowledge Integration Framework

The Scaffolded Knowledge Integration Framework (Linn, Bell, & Davis, 2004) consists of four basic metaprinciples that focus on supporting learners so they can integrate new science knowledge with their current understanding. The four metaprinciples that organize the framework include: (a) making science accessible, (b) making thinking visible, (c) helping students learn from others, and (d) promoting autonomy and lifelong learning. We can consider how these metaprinciples can be manifested in software by looking at the Knowledge Integration Environment (KIE), a software environment where learners gather and integrate different types of information to explore scientific questions (Bell, Davis, & Linn, 1995; also see Linn, this volume).

Each metaprinciple includes pragmatic pedagogical principles that together draw from learning sciences research and describe different ways to support learners. For example, the metaprinciple of making science accessible involves ways of capturing the interest and motivation of learners as they engage in learning activities. Different strategies can be used for this, many of which are derived from a situated cognition approach (Greeno, this volume). Different strategies can be used to provide students with problems that are personally meaningful, to motivate the learning activities and to help learners connect the material they are learning to familiar situations and their prior knowledge (Blumenfeld, Kempler, & Krajcik, this volume). For example, as students study different science questions and concepts (e.g., how light travels), KIE projects employ conceptual materials that help ground and make those concepts more accessible to those students (e.g., videoclips that show ways that

nighttime bicycle riders can reflect light). A similar approach can be found in the Jasper Woodbury series (Cognition and Technology Group, 1990), where students view videos of a young character – Jasper Woodbury – who describes the situation and the challenge that students will explore with him. The video provides a concrete situation and an arena for students to engage in problem solving in a more interesting and accessible context.

The second metaprinciple involves making thinking that is relatively implicit to experts visible and explicit to learners. Making expert thinking visible is also suggested by the cognitive apprenticeship perspective (Collins, this volume; also see Edelson & Reiser, this volume). Additionally, software can also be used to help learners make *their own* thinking visible so they better understand their thinking and make connections between the ideas they are developing (Linn, Davis, & Eylon, 2004). A wide range of learning sciences research has shown that students learn more when they reflect on their own thinking. Software can be used to help learners view and create different kinds of content-based and knowledge-based representations of their thinking, and make connections between the ideas in their representations. For example, SenseMaker, a component in KIE (Bell et al., 1995), made student thinking visible by allowing students to visually articulate and develop relationships between different pieces of information that students found during a science investigation. This way, students (and teachers) can analyze the current understanding that students construct and articulate new.

The third metaprinciple is to help students learn from others. Learning sciences research has shown the powerful role of social interaction in learning (Bereiter & Scardamalia, this volume; Greeno, this volume; A. L. Brown & Campione, 1994; Cohen, 1994). Learner-centered tools should facilitate social interactions between learners, their peers, teachers, and experts, and provide a forum where learners can post ideas, explanations, or other artifacts, and critique the artifacts posted by others (see

Stahl, Koschmann, & Suthers, this volume). For example, the SpeakEasy tool in KIE provided students with the means to share the work they produced, or other information they found useful, in group discussions with their classmates or a broader audience on the Web. Other projects that have provided similar social supports for learners include CoVis climate visualization tool (Gordin, Polman, & Pea, 1994) and online meeting places such as TappedIn (see Fishman & Davis, this volume).

The fourth metaprinciple is about promoting autonomy and lifelong learning. This involves creating a problem-solving context in which learners can engage in comprehensive activity that requires them to take ownership of their learning. Students should engage in complex projects where they actively set goals, engage in problem-solving activity, organize ideas, respond to feedback, and construct arguments. With scaffolding, learners can become more autonomous as they engage in authentic knowledge construction practices. Several comprehensive learning projects have addressed these kinds of issues. For example, one major goal for KIE is to convey the notion that there is no single "right" way to conduct a science investigation. Rather than describe investigations in rigid manner, KIE tries to support students with the software so they can learn problem-solving approaches and see how to actively integrate different pieces of science information. These problem-solving approaches not only help learners solve the science problem at hand, but hopefully students can see how they apply to other problems that they may encounter in everyday life. Other similar examples that aim to support more authentic open-ended activity include the Web-based Inquiry Science Environment (WISE) (Linn, this volume; Linn & Slotta, 2000), Symphony (Quintana et al., 1999), and the Biology Guided Inquiry Learning Environments project (Reiser et al., 2001).

Scaffolding Design Framework

The *scaffolding design framework* brings together a set of scaffolding guidelines and strategies within a structured framework (Quintana et al., 2004). The scaffolding design framework distills scaffolding guidelines and strategies that emerged from learning sciences studies of different situations in which learners face obstacles in science inquiry practices. As we saw in our LCD discussion, when learners are engaging in a new and unfamiliar activity such as science inquiry, they need support to make sense of the basic practices and types of representations involved in that activity. The guidelines and strategies in the scaffolding design framework are grouped according to three aspects of science inquiry that are complex for learners: (1) sensemaking, (2) process management, and (3) reflection and articulation. By grouping the different scaffolding guidelines and strategies into these three aspects, developers can look for guiding principles about the type of scaffolding they should consider, along with specific examples that describe how those scaffolding guidelines and principles were implemented in software.

For example, the first category, sensemaking, involves engaging in the basic practices in an activity – in this case, the basic practices of science inquiry. Sensemaking involves the different types of reasoning that are necessary to engage in a practice. For example, in a science inquiry context, sensemaking involves understanding and reasoning about data and other visual representations used by scientists (e.g., understanding important patterns in data visualizations; see Edelson & Reiser, this volume). Sensemaking also involves understanding disciplinary terminology (e.g., scientific language) and disciplinary strategies that are used throughout the practice (e.g., understanding the differences between different data analysis techniques). Learners need scaffolding for sensemaking because they will not understand the strategies experts use in science inquiry, nor will they be able to make connections between their prior knowledge and the disciplinary representations they are being introduced to. The scaffolding design framework describes three overarching scaffolding guidelines that can be implemented in software to support learners with sensemaking. First, designers can use representations and language that bridge learners' understandings, to help learners connect the representations to their understanding. Second, designers can organize tools and artifacts around the strategies and terminology of the discipline of study by making those aspects of the work explicit in the tools and artifacts they develop. Third, designers can provide learners with disciplinary representations (e.g., graphs) that they can inspect and manipulate in different ways so learners can try to understand the properties of those representations.

Designers also need to scaffold process management. Learners need support for engaging in, managing, and negotiating new disciplinary processes, especially when those processes are complex and open-ended. The scaffolding design framework describes three scaffolding guidelines for process management. First, designers should structure complex tasks by setting boundaries for learners, by using different kinds of task decompositions to describe complex tasks to learners (e.g., the process map in Figure 8.3 visually describes the tasks involved in science inquiry), and by using functional modes in software to constrain the space of available activities that learners can engage in at any given time. Second, designers should embed guidance about the practices that learners are engaging in by describing the characteristics and rationales for those practices. Third, designers should design scaffolding features that automatically handle the nonsalient and routine components of a task that would distract learners from the more important aspects of the work they are doing. This can include incorporating support to automate nonsalient aspects of a task, facilitating the organization of work products, and facilitating navigation among the tools they are using and the activities they are performing (compare to "reducing complexity" in Edelson & Reiser, this volume).

Finally, designers need to scaffold reflection and articulation for those many learners who tend to avoid or do not understand the importance of such reflective work. For example, designers can incorporate specific features in software to help learners plan and monitor their work. Many learning environments integrate specific tools to support planning and monitoring (e.g., the Symphony planning feature in Figure 8.3) so that learners can not only reflect on the work they will be doing, but also keep track of their progress so they can continue to work productively. Similarly, scaffolding features also can support learners in articulating different aspects of the work they are doing, which also can aid with developing new understanding. Common approaches for supporting articulation involve the use of textual prompts (e.g., Davis, 2003) and associated text areas that prompt learners to articulate a question to investigate and a hypothesis to that question, or to discuss what they learned after reading some text. Finally, scaffolding features can highlight the epistemic features of the practices that learners are engaging in and the products they are creating during their work (Collins & Ferguson, 1993). Epistemic forms are structures that show how knowledge is organized (e.g., a concept map, the periodic table of elements, argument outlines, etc.). Scaffolding features can make explicit the aspects and characteristics of epistemic forms to help learners work with, construct, and understand such knowledge structures. This in turn can help learners begin to understand the products and practices in the given domain of study (e.g., understanding different knowledge structures, such as arguments or plans in scientific inquiry). For example, the ExplanationConstructor includes question prompts and other features to help students organize information and construct explanations (Edelson & Reiser, this volume; Sandoval & Reiser, 2004). Animal Landlord is an ethnographic tool that includes features to help students describe and interpret animal behaviors that they are studying (Smith & Reiser, 1998). Both of these tools help students construct and understand specific kinds of epistemic forms used in scientific inquiry.

Learning-for-Use Framework

A third model called *Learning for Use* (LfU) emphasizes that software designers should focus on learning activities that intend to meet particular learning objectives (Edelson, 2001). The LfU model is based on the notion that learners construct their own knowledge through goal-directed behavior ideally initiated by the learners themselves (cf. Krajcik & Blumenfeld, this volume). Thus software should be designed to be part of an overall system of tools and activities that scaffolds three aspects of learning: motivation, knowledge construction, and knowledge refinement.

The LfU model calls for motivating learners by making explicit to them the limits of their current understanding. This approach can help learners see what knowledge they should acquire to meet their goal, and identify where they can integrate their new knowledge. In the knowledge construction phase, LfU states that learners can construct knowledge through direct experience, and through communication with others. Therefore, learners need to be exposed to different perspectives on and various experiences with the concepts they are trying to learn and internalize. Finally, in the knowledge refinement stage learners need to reflect on and apply knowledge in ways that allow them to retrieve and use that knowledge in the future. Because learning and knowledge acquisition is contextual, learners must be able to apply their knowledge in different situations in order to strengthen the generalizability and depth of that knowledge (Kolodner, this volume).

Edelson (2001) described the interplay between these three aspects of LfU in the design of the WorldWatcher system, a scientific visualization tool for students that supports data visualization and analysis via maps that students can build, customize, and interact with in different ways (Edelson & Reiser, this volume). A WorldWatcher project aims to motivate students by eliciting their curiosity as they build and explore different spatial data in the form of maps (e.g., maps of climate and environmental data). As learners engage in guided data analysis and visualization activities, they can begin to see different phenomena that ideally lead to more questions. Once learners have identified a question they wish to pursue, they can be supported in seeing the gaps and limits of their understanding, and supported in constructing the knowledge needed to answer their questions by actively finding, analyzing, and visualizing more data; these supports are provided by different features in WorldWatcher. Learners can also discuss their work with teachers or peers (e.g., describing the visualizations they created to other parties) to not only help learners build new knowledge but also to set the stage for knowledge refinement. Finally, learners can engage in reflective work, using WorldWatcher and other tools to record, organize, and explain observations they made from WorldWatcher maps and visualizations. Once students have considered their initial question, worked to construct knowledge through their visualization activities, and reflected on that work, they can apply that knowledge by using WorldWatcher to create new maps and data sets that can answer new climate questions and make climate predictions.

The Learning for Use model shows how software can be designed and situated in a broader context to help learners cross the gulf of expertise. WorldWatcher provides an example of how software can be developed to be part of an overall context of tools, activities, and social networks to support learners. Essentially, LfU can serve as an example of how learner-centered design needs to consider other aspects of the learning context (e.g., a classroom context with teachers, peers, and tools as seen in Figure 8.2). Designers need to describe the types of activity that learners need to engage in and develop software that support learners in performing those activities.

Assessing Learner-Centered Software

As with all design experiments (Barab, this volume; Confrey, this volume), an important element of learner-centered design is the assessment of the software, both to improve the software and to gain some understanding about the nature of learning and how to support learners. Traditional user-centered design focuses on evaluating factors such as software usability and ease-of-use (i.e., looking at whether the software has small gulfs of execution and evaluation). While these are important factors to understand, evaluating learner-centered software involves understanding how well the software supports learners in crossing the gulf of expertise. Salomon, Perkins, and Globerson (1991) described two important aspects of educational technologies that can be considered for assessment:

- The "effects with" technology: This involves the type of activity learners engage in and the changes in that activity as they use different software features. Here, assessment involves analyzing how learners interact with different individual scaffolding features in the software.
- The "effects of" technology: This involves the changes in the learner's understanding of some domain after learners have used the software. Here, assessment involves analyzing the effectiveness of the software with assessments of learning.

In other words, assessing learner-centered software involves understanding both the local effects of the software (i.e., how do novice learners do different activities with the software?) and the global effects of the software (i.e., what do learners learn as a result of using the software?). Assessing these different aspects of learner-centered software involves a range of methods. For example, many traditional methods can be used to assess the "effects of" the software, such as a pre/post test approach that would describe the learner's knowledge before and after using the software. Learners can be given a pretest about the target domain before using the software to measure their current domain knowledge. Learners can then be given a posttest to measure their domain knowledge after the software use (or at different intervals throughout the software use). The key is to determine the learning gains made while using the software.

Although assessing the "effects of" the software is important, developers also need to understand the "effects with" the software, or how the software was used and what individual features of the software were successful and unsuccessful. Assessing the "effects with" software typically requires a more observational approach: looking at learner actions and how the learner is interacting with different parts of the software to do the learning activities supported by the software. For example, one method for evaluating changes in practice involves using different benchmarks to judge both the usability of the scaffolding feature along with how well learners did the supported activity given the scaffolding support (Quintana, Krajcik, & Soloway, 2002). Such an evaluation involves observing every use of a scaffolding feature, and evaluating those uses according to different criteria such as whether the scaffolding features were accessible, used, and efficient to use; evaluating how efficiently and accurately learners performed the tasks supported by the scaffolding features; evaluating whether learners progressed from novice to expert ways of working; and evaluating how reflective learners were as they used scaffolding features to do a task (Quintana et al., 2002). The information resulting from this assessment can help developers see how learners use scaffolding features and whether those features are providing the intended support to help learners work in mindful, intellectually appropriate ways.

Concluding Remarks and Future Directions

Early computers were large, expensive, complex, and not capable of supporting sophisticated user interfaces. Beginning in the 1970s, the personal computer emerged and became mainstream, making computers available to a large nonspecialist audience. Thus, much software design work focused on developing usable computer systems that could be used by a wider audience. In this chapter, we have argued that designing software for learners holds its own set of unique challenges.

Learner-centered designers need to recognize that educational software is just one component of a complex learning context. The emphasis must be on designing software to support learning in such a context rather than a more narrow focus on the usability of the software in isolation.

We have described several examples of learner-centered software and summarized different design methods, assessment approaches, and examples of scaffolding features in software. We also have discussed design frameworks that incorporate different scaffolding guidelines, strategies, and approaches for supporting learners in developing and strengthening knowledge. Much of the current research focuses on making the notion of scaffolding more specific in software, and on the role of learner-centered software in different educational contexts. However, there are still many areas where research is needed and indeed, many of the original questions posed by Soloway, Guzdial, and Hay (1994) are still ripe for exploration. For example, there are questions surrounding the fading of scaffolding in software, including who makes the decision to fade the scaffolding (e.g., a teacher, the learner, or the software itself) and when is that decision made; how are scaffolding features in software designed to fade (e.g., do scaffolding features simply disappear from the software, do different versions of a scaffolding feature need to be designed to support different learners, etc.); and what is the mechanism by which scaffolding fades (e.g., are there scaffolding "preferences" in the software that can be used to fade certain scaffolding features, does the software automatically remove scaffolding features when it deems that they are no longer needed by learners, etc.) (Jackson, Krajcik, & Soloway, 1998). As new types of technology appear (e.g., handheld computers, wireless networking, etc.), we must explore how traditional scaffolding approaches can be implemented in these new technologies. And as new technologies emerge, we need to consider what new types of scaffolding approaches we can distill from them. We also can look to emerging areas of inter-est, such as design research (Confrey, this volume; Design-Based Research Collective, 2003; Edelson, 2002) to see how learner-centered software can be used in research contexts to better understand learning and cognition. Finally, researchers should continue to explore the notions of both traditional scaffolding and software-based scaffolding to continue our explorations on how different technologies can support learners. Although much has been accomplished, the challenge still remains to understand how technology can contribute to learning.

References

Bell, P., Davis, E. A., & Linn, M. C. (1995). The knowledge integration environment: Theory and design. In J. L. Schnase & E. L. Cunnius (Eds.), *Proceedings of the Computer Supported Collaborative Learning Conference '95*. Hillsdale, NJ: Lawrence Erlbaum Associates.

Beyer, H., & Holtzblatt, K. (2002). *Contextual design: A customer-centered approach to systems design*. San Francisco, CA: Morgan Kaufmann Publishers.

Brown, A. L., & Campione, J. C. (1994). Guided discovery in a community of learners. In K. McGilly (Ed.), *Classroom lessons: Integrating cognitive theory and classroom practice* (pp. 229–270). Cambridge, MA: MIT Press.

Brown, J. S., Collins, A., & Duguid, P. (1989). Situated cognition and the culture of learning. *Educational Researcher, 18*, 32–42.

Cognition and Technology Group. (1990). The Jasper series as an example of anchored instruction: Theory, program description, and assessment data. *Educational Psychologist, 27*, 291–315.

Cohen, E. G. (1994). Restructuring the classroom: Conditions for productive small groups. *Review of Educational Research, 64*, 1–35.

Collins, A., & Ferguson, W. (1993). Epistemic forms and epistemic games: Structures and strategies to guide inquiry. *Educational Psychologist, 28*(1), 25–42.

Cuban, L. (1986). *Teachers and machines: The classroom use of technology since 1920*. New York: Teachers College Press.

Davis, E. A. (2003). Prompting middle school science students for productive reflection:

Generic and directed prompts. *Journal of the Learning Sciences, 12* (1), 91–142.

Design-Based Research Collective. (2003). Design-based research: An emerging paradigm for educational inquiry. *Educational Researcher, 32* (1), 5–8.

Edelson, D. C. (2001). Learning-for-use: A framework for the design of technology-supported inquiry activities. *Journal of Research in Science Teaching, 38* (3), 355–385.

Edelson, D. C. (2002). Design research: What we learn when we engage in design. *The Journal of the Learning Sciences, 11*, 105–121.

Fitzpatrick, G., & Welsh, J. (1995). Process support: Inflexible imposition or chaotic composition. *Interacting with Computers, 7* (2), 167–180.

Gordin, D. N., Polman, J. L., & Pea, R. D. (1994). The Climate Visualizer: Sense-making through scientific visualization. *Journal of Science Education and Technology, 3*, 203–226.

Guzdial, M. (1994). Software-realized scaffolding to facilitate programming for science learning. *Interactive Learning Environments, 4* (1), 1–44.

Hogan, K., Nastasi, B. K., & Pressley, M. (2000). Discourse patterns and collaborative scientific reasoning in peer and teacher-guided discussions. *Cognition and Instruction, 17* (4), 379–432.

Jackson, S. L., Krajcik, J., & Soloway, E. (1998). The design of guided learning-adaptable scaffolding in interactive learning environments, *Human Factors in Computing Systems: CHI '98 Conference Proceedings* (pp. 187–194). Los Angeles: Addison-Wesley.

Lave, J., & Wenger, E. (1991). *Situated learning: Legitimate peripheral participation.* Cambridge: Cambridge University Press.

Lesgold, A. (1986). *Guide to cognitive task analysis.* Pittsburgh, PA: University of Pittsburgh Learning Research and Development Center.

Linn, M. C., Bell, P., & Davis, E. A. (2004). Specific design principles: Elaborating the scaffolded knowledge integration framework. In M. C. Linn, E. A. Davis & P. Bell (Eds.), *Internet environments for science education* (pp. 315–339). Mahwah, NJ: Lawrence Erlbaum Associates.

Linn, M. C., Davis, E. A., & Eylon, B.-S. (2004). The scaffolded knowledge integration framework for instruction. In M. C. Linn, E. A. Davis, & P. Bell (Eds.), *Internet environments for science education* (pp. 47–72). Mahwah, NJ: Lawrence Erlbaum Associates.

Linn, M. C., & Slotta, J. D. (2000). WISE science. *Educational Leadership, 58* (2), 29–32.

Norman, D. A. (1986). Cognitive engineering. In D. A. Norman & S. W. Draper (Eds.), *User centered system design.* Hillsdale, NJ: Lawrence Erlbaum Associates.

Norman, D. A., & Draper, S. W. (Eds.). (1986). *User-centered system design.* Hillsdale, NJ: Lawrence Erlbaum Associates.

Papert, S. (1993). *The children's machine: Rethinking school in the age of the computer.* New York: Basic Books.

Piaget, J. (1954). *The construction of reality in the child.* New York: Basic Books.

Quintana, C. (2001). *Symphony: A case study for exploring and describing design methods and guidelines for learner-centered design.* Unpublished Ph.D. Dissertation, University of Michigan, Ann Arbor.

Quintana, C., Eng, J., Carra, A., Wu, H., & Soloway, E. (1999). Symphony: A case study in extending learner-centered design through process-space analysis, *Human Factors in Computing Systems: CHI '99 Conference Proceedings* (pp. 473–480). Pittsburgh, PA: Addison-Wesley.

Quintana, C., Krajcik, J., & Soloway, E. (2002). A case study to distill structural scaffolding guidelines for scaffolded software environments, *Human Factors in Computing Systems: CHI 2002 Conference Proceedings.* Minneapolis, MN.

Quintana, C., Reiser, B. J., Davis, E. A., Krajcik, J., Fretz, E., Golan, R., et al. (2004). A scaffolding design framework for software to support science inquiry. *Journal of the Learning Sciences, 13* (3), 337–386.

Quintana, C., Soloway, E., & Krajcik, J. (2003). Issues and approaches for developing learner-centered technology. In M. Zelkowitz (Ed.), *Advances in computers* (Vol. 57, pp. 272–321). San Diego, CA: Academic Press.

Reiser, B. J., Tabak, I., Sandoval, W. A., Smith, B. K., Steinmuller, F., & Leone, A. J. (2001). BGuILE: Strategic and conceptual scaffolds for scientific inquiry in biology classrooms. In S. M. Carver & D. Klahr (Eds.), *Cognition and instruction: Twenty-five years of progress* (pp. 263–305). Mahwah, NJ: Lawrence Erlbaum Associates.

Salomon, G., Perkins, D. N., & Globerson, T. (1991). Partners in cognition: Extending human intelligence with intelligent technologies. *Educational Researcher*, 20(3), 2–9.

Sandoval, W. A., & Reiser, B. J. (2004). Explanation-driven inquiry: Integrating conceptual and epistemic supports for scientific inquiry. *Science Education*, 88(3), 345–372.

Singer, J., Marx, R., Krajcik, J., & Clay Chambers, J. (2000). Constructing extended inquiry projects: Curriculum materials for science education reform. *Educational Psychologist*, 35(3), 165–178.

Smith, B. K., & Reiser, B. J. (1998). National Geographic unplugged: Classroom-centered design of interactive nature films, *Human Factors in Computing Systems: CHI '98 Conference Proceedings*. Los Angeles: Addison-Wesley.

Soloway, E., Guzdial, M., & Hay, K. E. (1994). Learner-centered design: The challenge for HCI in the 21st century. *Interactions*, 1, 36–48.

Vygotsky, L. (1978). *Mind in society: The development of higher psychological processes*. Cambridge, MA: Harvard University Press.

Wilson, B. G. (1996). Introduction: What is a constructivist learning environment? In B. G. Wilson (Ed.), *Constructivist learning environments: Case studies in instructional design*. Englewood Cliffs, NJ: Educational Technology Publications.

Wood, D., Bruner, J. S., & Ross, G. (1975). The role of tutoring in problem-solving. *Journal of Child Psychology and Psychiatry*, 17, 89–100.

CHAPTER 9

The Evolution of Design Studies as Methodology

Jere Confrey

In the NRC report, *Scientific Research in Education* (Shavelson & Towne, 2002), three broad types of research were discussed: trends, causal effects, and mechanism. Mechanism was described as research that answers the question, "how or why is it happening"; the authors[1] described "design experiments" as an "analytic approach for examining mechanism that begins with theoretical ideas that are tested through the design, implementation, and systematic study of educational tools (curriculum, teaching methods, computer applets) that embody the initial conjectured mechanism" (p. 120). The Committee identified two products of such work as "theory-driven process of designing" and "data-driven process of refining [instructional strategies]" (p. 121). Both of these products can be viewed as related to a class of research known as design studies, the focus of this chapter.

Researchers across the country have recognized the need to strengthen the "instructional core" (Elmore, 1996) and to identify effective "instructional regimes" (Cohen, Raudenbush, & Ball 2003) as critical to the improvement of education. Likewise,

Lagemann (2002) focused on the need for more research that produces useable classroom guidance. This review synthesizes the current progress of the methodology and identifies areas for future development.

Design studies are defined as "entailing both 'engineering' particular forms of learning and systematically studying those forms of learning with the context defined by the means of supporting them. This designed context is subject to test and revision. Successive iterations that result play a role similar to systematic variation in experiment" (Cobb et al., 2003, p. 9).

A design study is an extended investigation of educational interactions provoked by use of a carefully sequenced and typically novel set of designed curricular tasks studying how some conceptual field, or set of proficiencies and interests, are learned through interactions among learners with guidance. The study seeks to document what resources and prior knowledge the students bring to the task, how students and teachers interact, how records and inscriptions are created, how conceptions emerge and change, what resources are used, and how teaching is accomplished over the course of instruction, by studying student work, video records, and classroom assessments.

Design researchers make, test, and refine conjectures about the learning trajectory based on evidence as they go, often collaborating with or acting as the teacher, and assembling extensive records on what students, teachers, and researchers learn from the process. They then conduct further analysis after the fact to produce research reports and/or iterations of the tasks, materials, and instrumentation. This class of research methods is also referred to as "design research," "design experiments," or "design-based research methods." I prefer to use the term "design studies" in recognition of the need for programmatic and iterative investigations over time. Design studies have been labeled an "emerging paradigm for the study of learning in context through the systematic study of instructional strategies and tools" (DBRC, 2003, p. 5). They are distinctive from curricular studies and evaluation (Confrey & Stohl, 2004), pure discourse analyses of classrooms (Gee, 1999) instructional design (Merrill, 2001; Reeves, 2000) and action research/lesson study (Fernandez & Yoshida, 2004). Design studies inherit many features from clinical interview studies and teaching experiments, and are clearly located within the larger field of the learning sciences; they seek both to provide systematic and warranted knowledge about learning, and to produce theories to guide instructional decision making toward improved student learning.

Design studies most often involve novel treatments of curricular areas, such as the introduction of new topics, new technologies, or novel forms of interaction. Examples of design studies include research on students' understanding of statistical ideas (Cobb, 2002; Lehrer & Pritchard, 2002), modeling (Lehrer & Schauble, 2004; Lesh, 1999), student and teacher reasoning about rational numbers (Confrey & Lachance, 2000; Simon, 2000), student representations (diSessa, 2004) and students' use of innovative technological tools (Collins, Joseph, & Bielaczyc, 2004; Greeno, 1997). This kind

of work rejects the view that one conducts pure research in laboratory or experimental settings and only later exports it to classrooms. Instead, one conducts the work in the complexity of the classroom (Brown, 1992; Greeno, 2003). Applied and pure research are merged.

Any developing field of research such as the learning sciences has roots in a variety of methods. Learning sciences emerged most extensively from cognitive science, developmental psychology, technological innovations, sociocultural theory, and mathematics and science education. Through these, one can also trace the developmental path of design studies. The first part of this chapter locates design studies in an evolution from clinical interviews, teaching experiments, and design experiments.

A methodology must be situated clearly within a set of goals and theories: philosophers of science have warned us repeatedly that method, in the absence of theory, becomes hollow and procedural (Elkana, 1974; Lakatos & Feyerabend, 1999). Hence, this chapter will also describe the class of theories related to the method, so as to promote a class of evidence-supported theories that can guide instructional decision making towards the goal of improving student learning (Cobb et al., 2003). The question of what kinds of theories can guide the development of instructional decision-making will be taken up in the second part of the article.

Finally, for design research to qualify as a methodology, it must have criteria for its conduct, a set of canons of evidence, and grounding for its warrant. In research, evidence of methodological rigor comes in three forms: (1) the experimentation/investigation has itself been adequately conducted and analyzed; (2) the claims are justified, robust, significant relative to the data and the theory, and are subjected to alternative interpretations; and (3) the relevance of the claims to the practices of education is explicit and feasible. A third section briefly discusses design research in relation to methods, evidence, praxis, and the basis for the warrant of its claims.

The Evolution of Design Experiments

Early Basis in Piaget, Vygotsky, Dewey, and Clinical Studies

Design studies are rooted in an abiding interest in understanding children's thinking. Piaget, Vygotsky, and Dewey all argued extensively that in the formation of student thought lay the genesis of the process that would be the key to characterizing learning. For Piaget, this basis was evident in his idea of "genetic epistemology." For Vygotsky, it lay in "genetic historic method." For Dewey, the sources of the formation of student thought were in the nature of inquiry and its connections to pragmatism. These scholars all recognized that understanding how thoughts are formed is key to understanding what counts as knowledge.

By contrast, more behavioristic traditions gauge learning primarily by measurable effects on performance on tests or other direct measures of student outcomes, emphasizing speed, efficiency, persistence, and, occasionally, the transfer of thought to new settings. In the learning sciences, these criteria are not sufficient, because they measure the outcomes of learning as fixed acquisitions only, and in the face of weakness or poor performance, cannot offer explanatory frameworks. In the learning sciences, key features of knowledge include why one believes something, how it came about, how it is related to other ideas, and what it permits one to do. Thus, methodologies in the learning sciences are obliged to include a broader set of outcome measures that capture the process of learning, as well as the final state of the learner.

Among Piaget's key assumptions was that a child is located in an environment and strives to make sense of that environment. Piaget contributed three primary insights that required new methodologies, including the "clinical method": (1) children's views are not congruent with adults' views; (2) the process by which children gain cognitive proficiency requires that their understandings are progressively refined through experience with a series of tasks that lead towards cognitive reconstructions, conceptual changes (including overcoming common "misconceptions," or considering alternative conceptions) involving a coordination of the processes of assimilation and accommodation; and (3) for ideas to become viable, children must assess ideas' feasibility, utility, and durability through a process of schema construction and reflective abstraction. Piaget's famous dictum, "one comes to know the world through knowing oneself" (cited in von Glasersfeld, 1982, p. 613), emphasizes his view that while knowledge involves descriptions of an external world, it also invariably involves an interaction between the knower and the known, and therefore knowledge is relational (Ackerman, 1995; Kegan, 2000).

Among Piaget's methodological contributions was the clinical method:

> The clinical examination is thus experimental in the sense that the practitioner sets himself a problem, makes hypotheses, adapts the conditions to them and finally controls each hypothesis by testing it against the reactions he stimulates in conversations. But the clinical examination is also dependent on direct observation, in the sense that the good practitioner lets himself be led, though always in control, and takes account of the whole of the mental context, instead of being the victim of "systematic error" as so often happens to the pure experimenter.
>
> The good experimenter must, in fact, unite two often incompatible qualities; he must know how to observe, that is to say, to let the child talk freely, without ever checking or side-tracking his utterance, and at the same time he must constantly be alert for something definitive, at every moment he must have some working hypothesis, some theory, true or false, which he is seeking to check. (Piaget, 1976, p. 9)

Piaget warned that "the greatest enemies of the clinical method are those who unduly simplify the results of an interrogatory, those who either accept every answer the child makes as gold or those on the other hand who class all as dross" (p. 9). For Piaget, the primary task of the clinical interview was to reveal children's' liberated convictions, which "implies previously formed schemas, tendencies of mind, intellectual habits, etc." (p. 13). "The hypothesis is that assertion that the child invents his explanations in such a way as to reveal something of the spontaneous tendencies of his mind" (p. 14). Awareness of such schemas is essential to the design of successful instruction.

Vygotsky's work has contributed powerfully to the evolution of these methodologies, emphasizing the individual's development within a sociocultural setting. For Vygotsky, cultural activities are the primary source of cognition, and they shape how one thinks in fundamental ways. This is summed up in his often-quoted statement, "Any function in the child's cultural development appears twice, or on two planes. First it appears on the social plane and then on the psychological plane. First it appears between people as an interpsychological category, and then within the child as an intrapsychological category" (Vygotsky, 1978, p. 57).

Vygotsky's work contributes to design studies through his attention to selecting the appropriate unit of analysis in experimentation. He used the term "unit of analysis" to connect thought and language and "contain in the most fundamental and elementary form those properties that belong to verbal thinking as a whole" (Vygotsky, 1986, p. 211). In any methodology, the key unit of analysis must be articulated.

A second methodological contribution derives from Vygotsky's examination of the relationship between scientific and spontaneous concepts, of which he wrote, "Systematic reasoning, being initially acquired in the sphere of scientific concepts later transfers its structure organization into spontaneous concepts, remodeling them from above" (Vygotsky, 1986, p. 172). Vygotsky saw scientific concepts essentially as cognitive tools, with "tool" referring to the indirect function of an object as a means of accomplishing activity. To capture the effects of tools on thought, he focused on the idea of signs and symbols as mediating cognitive tools. Vygotsky studied conceptual development

through interviews, but recognized that to understand the links between formal and informal ideas "an urgent methodological problem confronting us is to find ways of studying real concepts in depth" (Vygotsky, 1978, p. 91).

Vygotsky further recognized that to understand conceptual development, one needs to study teaching – the role of a "more knowledgeable other" in learning. His notion of the zone of proximal development suggested that "what the child can do in cooperation today, he can do alone tomorrow. Therefore, the only good kind of instruction is that which marches ahead of development and leads it. It must be aimed not so much at the ripe as at the ripening functions" (Vygotsky, 1986, pp. 188–189). This is an early impetus for learning sciences to investigate teaching within studies of development. Discourse, facilitated by inscriptions and representations, plays a key methodological role in studying developmental processes:

> We believe that child development is a complex dialectical process characterized by periodicity, unevenness in the development of different functions, metamorphosis or qualitative transformation of one form into another, intertwining of external and internal factors, and adaptive processes which overcome impediments that the child encounters. (Vygotsky, 1978, p. 73)

The third major source of influence on design studies methodology can be traced to Dewey's work, based in philosophy and epistemology as much as in psychology. Both James (pragmatism) and Darwin (evolution) fundamentally influenced his thinking.

> A theory corresponds to the facts when it leads us to the facts which are its consequences, by the intermediary of experience ... but they are always subject to being corrected by unforeseen future consequences or by observed facts that had been disregarded. Every proposition concerning truths is really in the last analysis hypothetical and provisional, although a large number of these propositions have been so frequently verified without failure that we are justified in using them as if they were

absolutely true. But logically, absolute truth is an ideal which cannot be realized, at least not until all the facts have been registered, or as James says, "bagged" and until it is no longer possible to make other observations and other experiences. (Dewey, 1981, pp. 49–50)

Pragmatism, as Dewey cast it, is a form of empiricism. But rather than suggest that experimentation produces facts whose links to hypotheses create truth, he recognized that consequences produced through action and experience are but one possible set of outcomes. It is only as they are realized through a variety of circumstances that they become stable and secure, even though always provisional. Pragmatism does not place theory on a shelf, useful only as a guide to pristine experimentalism, but rather places it squarely into the world of action and experience. It engages with complexity, rather than striving to artificially reduce it.

This theoretical perspective guides Dewey's emphasis on inquiry, defined as "the controlled or directed transformation of an indeterminate situation into one that is so determinate in its constituent distinctions and relations as to convert the elements of the original situation into a unified whole" (Dewey, 1981, p. 226). Dewey's emphasis on the transformation of a hypothesis in practice through the lens of inquiry provides us both praxis and a means to study it. He recognized that in the beginning, there is only the indeterminate, which undergoes transformation through a problematic to a hypothesis, which, by means of the activity of inquiry, is transformed to a determinate situation producing a set of knowledge claims. These claims will only reach the status of truth if they are borne out in other spheres of activity. That is, the claims must meet the pragmatic test that they prove useful in interpreting multiple situations over time.

The scholarship of Piaget, Vygotsky, and Dewey thus provides the theoretical rationale for selecting design studies as a methodology to produce theories about instructional guidance. Such studies support views

of the classroom not as deterministic, but as complex and conditional. In these settings, instructional guidance is based on affecting the likelihood of certain events and outcomes by adjusting the conditions of instruction. One can liken instructional guidance to the notion of different realizations of a simulation – one cannot predict an outcome precisely, because each realization is, in effect, unique, but the multiple realizations yield tendencies that can guide decision-making and parameter setting.

Based on these premises and rationales, one cannot prescribe practices, but one can guide practice by means of explanatory frameworks accompanied by data, evidence, and argument. An explanatory framework is: (1) at best a model of likely outcomes; (2) closely connected to its theories; (3) as robust as its links to evidence from multiple sources of interaction within ecologically authentic settings; (4) as rigorous as the documentation and analysis that underlies items 1, 2, and 3; and (5) as valid as it is useful to others who are familiar and experienced in similar contexts. The theory of design studies incorporates this epistemological view of classroom praxis.

From Constructivism and Sociocultural Theories to Teaching Experiments

During the 1970s and 1980s, mathematics and science education passed through a "structure of the disciplines" phase, in which content specialists encountered developmental theories (Duckworth, 1996; Hawkins, 2002). In the late seventies and eighties, the movement examined issues of problem solving, matured toward "constructivism" and comprised an orientation toward understanding student thinking and documenting the variety of ways of conceptualizing problems, heuristics, and strategies. In the late eighties, the clinical interview matured into the teaching experiment, imported from pedagogical research in the Soviet Union (Kantowski et al., 1978), as sociocultural approaches increasingly influenced math and science education. Investigators increasingly recognized the role of structured or guided apprenticeship in supporting changes over time.

The teaching experiment uncovered the process by which students learn subject matter. It included longitudinal study, intervention into student learning, an iterative process of data gathering and planning, and qualitative rather than quantitative data. Thompson (1979) argued that the teaching experiment could be adapted to the constructivist movement in the United States to yield "a constructivist teaching experiment" in which a researcher builds a model of a teacher interacting with a child. Steffe (1991) identified its characteristics. Researchers were to examine the mathematics of children (rather than traditional mathematics), viewed independently of their background and training, and locate it in negotiations of interactive communication (rather than import it from formal mathematics), to focus on the evolution of their activities rather than the products, in order to examine the modifications in their schemas, in relation to goal-directed activities.

> *Because the teaching experiment involves experimentation with the ways and means of influencing children's knowledge, it is more than a clinical interview. It is directed toward understanding the progress children make over extended periods of time, and one of the main goals is to formulate a model of learning the particular content involved. (Steffe, 1991, p. 178)*

Lesh and Kelly (2000) identified an essential recursiveness in design, originally recognized in Cobb and Steffe (1983). The student is expected to build knowledge of mathematics, the teacher builds knowledge of the student building knowledge of mathematics, and the researcher is building knowledge of both, as well as of the interactions between the two. Hence, they described the idea of a "multi-tiered teaching experiment." They identified bases for design including content quality, technology, school-to-career transitions, equity, teacher development, and instructional design. They argued for complex, multidimensional, and longitudinal studies of practice.

Simon (2000) suggested methods of analysis for teaching experiments. He identified key roles for emergent perspectives, conceptual framework, and framing of paradigmatic cases. In working on teacher development experiments, he framed his work in the context of joint teacher-researcher interactions and recognized a key role for "promoting the development of teachers." He wrote, "Teaching as a process of inquiry in which the teacher is engaged in an ongoing cycle of interaction and reflection has a great deal of potential" (p. 359).

Cobb (2000) discussed teaching experiments in relation to emergent perspectives, documenting their use in relation to investigating students' mathematical learning in alternative classroom contexts developed in collaboration with teachers. Teachers' learning is a second focus of his attention. Drawing on Gravemeijer (1995), Cobb also expressed interest in the "development of instructional sequences and the local, domain specific instructional theories that underpin them" (p. 313). He further elaborated the development and research cycle, first noted by Simon (1995). In evaluating the teaching experiment, Cobb discussed the role of generalizability, trustworthiness, and commensurability in retrospective analyses.

In the same volume, *Handbook of Research Design in Mathematics and Science Education*, Confrey and Lachance (2000) discussed their experience in a three-year teaching experiment. They coined the term "transformative teaching experiments" to indicate the need to study more speculative and innovative teaching practices. They argued that teaching experiments should study conjectures rather than hypotheses ("assertions waiting to be proved or disproved"). A conjecture is

> *...a means to reconceptualize the ways in which to approach both the content and pedagogy of a set of mathematics topics...a strong conjecture should shift one's perspective and bring new events,*

previously insignificant or perplexing, into relief. At points in its evolution, the conjecture should feel like a grand scheme beginning to emerge from many, previously disparate pieces, making them more cohesive. (Confrey & Lachance, 2000, p. 235)

Confrey and Lachance linked the conjecture to the work of Lakatos, who recognized that theory is established "through the incessant improvement of guesses by speculation and criticism" (Lakatos, 1976, p. 5). They identified two dimensions of the conjecture: one based in content, and the other in pedagogy, classroom organization, and tasks, activities, tools, and resources. Their research questions focused on how instruction would change if the conjecture were implemented in curriculum, classroom interactions, teaching, and assessment. They outlined how one could evaluate the quality of the experiment in terms of the face validity and peer review quality of the conjecture's development, the coherence of the rational reconstruction, and the quality of the student voice in terms of its extension, authenticity, and representativeness of students' comments. Externally, they evaluated the teaching experiment as to whether its range of products (reports, curricular products, professional development materials, and policy documents) were feasible, sustainable, compelling, adaptable, and generative.

For example, in 1988, I articulated the "splitting conjecture," positing that the cognitive roots of multiplication, division, and ratio are independent of the roots of counting, addition, and subtraction (Confrey, 1988). I linked splitting to partitioning, scaling, similarity, and related ideas in geometry. In 1992, I began a three-year teaching experiment with a group of third graders. For three years, I and my team taught the group of eighteen students. Each year, the team outlined a set of tasks that would strengthen students' understanding of the interrelationships among multiplication, division, and ratio. Each day of the experiment, we implemented the planned set of tasks, which included substantial opportunities to observe student work, and to listen to and record student discourse on the topics. We (1) conducted mini-interviews of students' work on tasks during seatwork periods, (2) captured sets of small groups' interactions around key tasks, and examined the participants' work and statements, and (3) engaged in interactive teaching, encouraging students to share their ideas and to respond to suggestions from others. Most of the instruction was accomplished through the introduction of carefully sequenced challenges selected to raise important topics for examination and instruction. The introduction and closing of class each day were critically important: the team presented summary statements of the day's progress and solicited comments from the students. Frequent performance-based assessments were used to document variations in student progress.

After each class, I met with the research team and we discussed what had occurred, and documented critical moments of activity in which the students' behaviors were surprising, needed strengthening, or played out what had been conjectured. Materials were revised in approximately two-week segments, in advance of instruction, in light of current classroom events, and again on a daily basis after examination of a single day's work. Team members presented alternative interpretations, being required to substantiate the claims with evidence linking these to a developing understanding of the conjecture. When disagreements arose, common assessments would often be developed to help determine which interpretation(s) was more likely, compelling, or viable. Observation and discussion notes were kept to highlight these instances. The team mapped the students' conceptual moves, documented alternative methods, created, transcribed, and studied video excerpts, and prepared research reports. At the end of the project, all students completed an interview on their experiences in the program (Confrey, Lachance, & Hotchkiss, 1996) and a posttest of common misconception items on ratio reasoning (Scarano & Confrey, 1996).

In shifting from the clinical interview to the teaching experiment these researchers retained, modified, and refined some aspects of the methodology while abandoning others, and adopted some new approaches. They maintained, and to some extent strengthened, their understanding of the importance of building a model of students' mathematical thinking, and maintained their commitment to children as active constructive agents – who if provided appropriate tasks, challenges, and opportunities to explain, could create interesting, creative, and often productive solutions. The researchers strengthened their own views on the importance of unleashing these aspects of active cognition to form viable models of their capabilities and proclivities. Furthermore, they strengthened their recognition of two bookends of the constructivist process – prior knowledge as influenced by the child's experience and beliefs, and the critical role of reflection in this activity of self-emergence – in bounding student conceptions in secure webs and structures.

A number of key elements have shaped the evolution of teaching experiments. This work was fostered in mathematics and science education communities; the influence of the Piagetian perspective of genetic epistemology has endured. The development of new computational and dynamic technologies has further propelled the work toward fresh considerations of the nature of mathematics and science. The choice to move to the complex setting of whole classrooms has accelerated the evolution of methodology by locating individuals' thinking in a web of sociocultural forces that shape the development of the ideas. Seeing knowledge as distributed and as mediated by the available tools has meant an increased need to consider how to adequately describe the events unfurling under teachers' guidance.

Early Development of Design Experiments

Most people trace the beginnings of the use of the term "design experiments" or "design research" to Allan Collins and Ann Brown in 1992. I would locate the movement toward engineering further back, to those who were involved in the earliest work on bringing new technologies into the classroom (Fisher, Dwyer, & Yoacam, 1996; Papert, 1980; Pea, 1987). These early pioneers recognized that by bringing technology into the classroom, one can shift learning in fundamental ways, both by improving student proficiency through stoking the fires of the individual mind, and by viewing learning as a distributed enterprise in which tools play key mediating roles and in which knowledge is built through collaborative activities.

In 1992, Allan Collins first used the term "design experiments," which he related to Herb Simon's classic book, *The Sciences of the Artificial* (Simon, 1969), which drew a distinction between the natural sciences and the sciences of the artificial or "design sciences." In his seminal paper, "Toward a Design Science of Education," Collins wrote,

> What is different today is that some of the best minds in the world are addressing themselves to education as experimentalists: their goal is to compare different designs to see what affects what. Technology provides us with powerful tools to try out different designs, so that instead of theories of education, may begin to develop a science of education. But it cannot be an analytic science like physics or psychology; rather it must be a design science more like aeronautics or artificial intelligence. . . . Similarly, a design science of education must determine how different designs of learning environments contribute to learning, cooperation, motivation, etc. (Collins, 1992, p. 16).

Collins listed eight decisions that permit exploration of a given design space: (1) involving teachers as co-investigators, (2) comparing innovations, (3) making objective appraisals, (4) selecting promising innovations, (5) involving multidisciplinary expertise, (6) incorporating systematic variation, (7) using frequent revisions, and (8) evaluating success using multiple criteria. Optimistically, he wrote, "This design theory will attempt to specify all the variables that affect the success or failure of different designs. Furthermore, it will attempt to specify what values on these variables maximize chances for success, and how different variables interact in creating successful designs" (Collins, 1992, p. 19).

Also in 1992, Ann Brown published "Design Experiments: Theoretical and Methodological Challenges in Creating Complex Interventions in Classroom Settings" (Brown, 1992). She specified that design experiments were working wholes, organized around a working environment for study, engineered to incorporate learning theory and dissemination and other forms of feasibility, and to possess input variables (classroom ethos, teachers, students as researchers, curriculum, technology), and outputs (assessments and accountability). She described her own professional journey, telling how her first grant application for design experiments was unkindly labeled, "Pseudo experimental work in quasi-naturalistic settings" (Brown, 1992, p. 152). She traced her new approach to a commitment to address the two diseases of learning: inert knowledge and passivity. A methodological hurdle was the need to make covert cognitive activity visible, first through interest in strategies, metacognition, and then in social contexts through guided instruction and reciprocal teaching. It was the transition from paired instructional strategies to a community of learners that led to the development of design research. Brown recognized the need to generate much richer data sources, including transcripts of group work, observations, student portfolios and other communications, and ethnographic studies of interactions. Her article also represented her first attempts to contrast methodologies: she compared her work on analogies in laboratory experiments and in design research. She wrote, "Although in the laboratory, this development from noticing to using, and from surface to deep, was thought to be age-dependent, the classroom work suggests that the shift is knowledge-based, occurring microgenetically within a year as readily as cross-sectionally across several years" (p. 153). She urged researchers to view both laboratories and classrooms as places where theoretical advances

can emerge, and not to treat one as temporally prior to the other. She discussed the choice of idiographic and nomothetic approaches, short and long time durations, and qualitative and quantitative analyses. She concluded with a preference for mixed methods, citing in particular evidence of changes in student thinking over time. However, she anticipated criticisms that, in using methods that produce copious quantities of information, it is possible to be critiqued on the basis of a selection bias that could lead to misrepresentation of data.

Recent Activity on Design Experiments and the Role of Theory

Collins et al. (2004) reviewed the history of design experiments, summarizing how the methodology had evolved into a means to create a design science, to study learning phenomena in the real world, to go beyond narrow measures, and to derive research from formative findings. In the first case, they commented that a design science must provide enough specificity to avoid "lethal mutations" during implementation (Brown & Campione, 1996), and yet recognized that:

> . . . *any implementation of a design requires many decisions that go beyond the design itself. This occurs because no design can specify all the details, and because the action of the participants in the implementation requires constant decisions about how to proceed at every level. Designs in education can be more or less specific, but can never be completely specified. Evaluation of designs can only be made in terms of particular implementations, and these can vary widely depending on the participant's needs, interest, abilities, interpretations, interactions and goals.* (Collins et al., 2004, p. 3)

They also developed the idea of "progressive refinement" in design, referring to the Japanese auto industry's strategy of frequent revisions for improved quality. Second, they referred to a design as an "integrated system" in which the elements must work together. As a result, they recognized that design experiments rely on multiple dependent variables and can only be understood by characterizing rather than controlling the variables. In terms of theory, they contrasted the testing of hypotheses with "developing a profile." They specified that design reports should include the goals and elements of the design, settings where it is implemented, descriptions of each phase, outcomes found, and lessons learned. In a final section, they identified the need to develop summative versions of design experiments that (1) include climate variables such as engagement, cooperation, risk taking, and student control; (2) learning variables such as content knowledge, skills, dispositions, metacognitive strategies; and (3) systemic variables such as sustainability, spread, scalability, ease of adoption, and costs.

What becomes evident in current work is a level of maturity absent from the previous decade. Limitations in the specification of variables are acknowledged. Strict interpretations of hypothesis-testing are replaced with other means of characterizing the use of and evolution of theory. The necessity for more complex outcome measures is noted, as well as the need to consider more cognitive and affective factors to capture the breadth of effects. Finally, the design study approach is linked to practice, with specific acknowledgment that when research is embedded in complex practices, it needs to consider adoption, adaptation, spread, feasibility, and sustainability (Collins et al., 2004; Confrey, Castro-Filho, & Wilhelm, 2000; Fishman et al., 2004).

In "Design Experiments in Educational Research," Cobb et al. (2003) argued that the purpose of design studies is to "develop a class of theories about both the process of learning and the means that are designed to support that learning, be it the learning of individual students, of a classroom community, of a professional teaching community, or of a school or school district viewed as an organization" (p. 10). Five crosscutting features of the methodology apply to all these diverse types of experiments.

They are all (1) design-based, (2) interventionist rather than naturalistic, (3) theory generative, (4) iterative, and (5) ecologically valid and practice-oriented.

The role of theory in design studies merits further elaboration. Like Lesh and Kelly's (2000) work on multitiered teaching experiments, and Confrey and Lachance's (2000) work on conjecture, Cobb et al. (2003) acknowledged a need for different kinds of theory at different stages of the inquiry. They stressed that design experiments tend to emphasize an intermediate theoretical scope that orients the theory to the particular circumstances of the experiment, and have the potential for rapid payoff. DiSessa and Cobb (2004) distinguished four uses of theoretical constructs in this methodology: (1) grand theories (e.g. Piaget's intellectual theories); (2) orienting frameworks to define social affiliations among scientists; (3) "domain specific instructional theories" which "entail the conceptual analysis of a significant disciplinary idea," which "are of heuristic value"; and (4) ontological innovations. The authors claimed that domain specific instructional theories, which "embody testable conjectures about both learning processes and the means of 'engineering' them," typically rely on "established theoretical constructs", limiting their ability to "scrutinize and reconceptualize aspects of competence in mathematics or to better handle the complexity and diversity of settings in which we conduct experiments" (p. 83). They proposed the idea of "ontological innovations," which entails finding and validating a new category of existence in the world – such as metarepresentational competence and socio-mathematical norms (diSessa & Cobb, 2004).

The strength of this treatment of theory is in directing the researcher to seek novel theoretical constructs that can emerge from instructional settings and novel tasks. Openness to discovery, and to rethinking the content, mediational means, and forms of praxis has been a hallmark of design studies, and reflects its speculative character. But it is not clear why such innovations are labelled "ontological" rather than "epistemological";

it seems unnecessary, and appears to compromise the pragmatist stance. What seems most important methodologically is to recognize that such theoretical constructs must provide explanatory power for a variety of classroom behaviors, utterances, and interactional patterns, should be shown to have systematic effects on learning as measured by a variety of outcome measures, must exhibit reasonably high levels of predictability, and must be examined for their stability, endurance, incubation period, and distribution across students.

At a broader grain size, I would argue that the primary contribution of design studies is the articulation of domain-specific guidance illuminating *conceptual corridors* for the learning of content. The aim of a design experiment is the articulation of two related concepts: a conceptual corridor and a conceptual trajectory. The *conceptual corridor* is a theoretical construct describing the possible space to be navigated successfully to learn conceptual content. During any particular set of episodes of teaching, that is, a design experiment, students will traverse a particular *conceptual trajectory* through the corridor. Experimental design requires capturing data that document the nature of one or more particular trajectories and their variants. Teachers need a sense of what possible fruitful pathways a student can negotiate, even though for any particular series of instructional episodes, only one trajectory (with variations among students) is traversed. The goal of the experiment, however, is broader: to model the conceptual corridor, a description of all possible conceptual trajectories.

From this theoretical perspective, effective instruction depends on how well one engineers the conceptual corridor, such that the likelihood of fruitful trajectories is increased. Design studies can be viewed as engineering and identifying multiple means for constructing that corridor. The design and sequence of tasks creates a set of constraints. Knowing and building from students' prior knowledge is a means of orienting the students' entry to the corridor. Creating the initial problematic challenge

or indeterminate situation is akin to issuing an invitation to entry. Anticipating students' responses and engaging in formative assessments create a set of landmarks that can help to guide them through. Successful navigation of the conceptual corridor should produce conceptual tools that then assist a student in moving into and through the next corridor. Instruction should strengthen students' understanding of navigational tools: the problem or interest in a project; sharing diverse methods; providing intermittent opportunities for closure and negotiated agreements; building representations, inscriptions, or common meanings for language; providing adequate practice; and developing explanation, argument, and discourse patterns. If teachers are familiar with these navigational tools, they can anticipate how to provide appropriate scaffolding for future instruction. Figure 9.1 represents the relationship between the trajectory and corridor.

A key point is that the conceptual corridor is never completely or rigidly specified, because other ways to approach an idea and to sequence and constrain it are possible, thus permitting the corridor to evolve. Nonetheless, teachers need guidance on documented ways to organize corridors, not as rigid curricular sequences, but rather as intellectual spaces through which students progress. These are the methodological tools for documenting findings on how to recognize the importance of genetic epistemology and how to instantiate the genetic historical method while recognizing a pragmatist's view of the complexity and uncertainty of practice.

Design studies are by their nature iterative, as researchers document the changes a particular group undergoes over time, and build a model of the trajectories and the corridor. As a study is iterated, the similarities and differences in evolution and path are compared.

Design studies should be complemented by other methods. A number of researchers have discussed how this is carried out in relation to clinical or lab-based studies (Barab & Squire, 2004; Brown, 1992), whereas

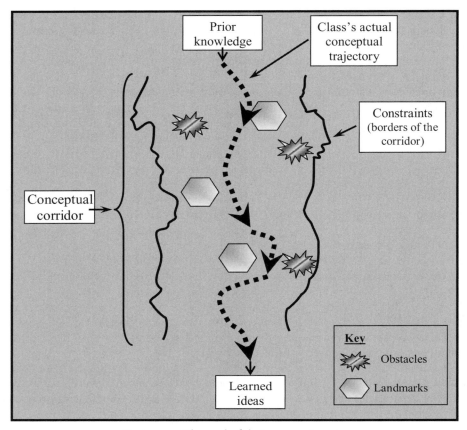

Figure 9.1. The goal of design experiments.

others have examined ways the results may be linked to curricular evaluation, larger-scale assessments, or perhaps ethnographies (Confrey et al., 2000; Fishman et al., 2004).

Design studies have the potential to promote easier dissemination of research into practice, due to the ecological validity of the study setting. A number of researchers have warned that such validity is limited, because classrooms typically have less support, are more rigidly linked into accountability systems, and lack the access to professional development typical in these experiments (Fishman et al., 2004). To strengthen transfer, researchers recommend that design studies anticipate these needs, and address issues of usefulness, trustworthiness, and sustainability from the outset of their work (Confrey & Lachance, 2000; Fishman et al., 2004).

Is Design Research Scientific? Discussion of Issues of Warrant

Design studies have come under considerable criticism, especially in light of recent federal policy initiatives that place a higher value on experimental research that aims to establish causal relationships as unequivocal as those strived for in some types of biological or physical science research. A statement such as the following: "Should we believe the results of design experiments?" (Shavelson et al., 2003), derived from interpretations of aspects of *Scientific Research in Education*, is actually nonsensical by the standards established in that same report. Any particular study must be judged as scientific or not, depending on how it is connected to the question under investigation. The majority of the principles for scientific studies (Shavelson & Towne, 2002) are easily met by design study methodology: important questions are being addressed and are linked to and generative of relevant theory, the literature on those questions is evolving in a systematic way, and the best of the studies demonstrate a coherent and explicit chain of reasoning. The question should really be: if design research is intended to produce knowledge claims about "a class of evidence-supported theories that can guide instructional decision-making towards the goal of improving student learning," then when should we believe the results, and how should we interpret them?

The most common critiques of design study methodology concern the representativeness of the work, the potential for replication, and questions about a design study's generalizability and possible warrants of cause or mechanism (Shavelson et al., 2003). These valid concerns are typically addressed by learning scientists in two ways. First, design studies are more akin to case studies and ethnographies, in that they seek to provide levels of detail and specificity about complex interactions over extended periods of time, rather than establishing broad and representative patterns. Second, design studies are not typically scaled up to widespread practice; instead, they often provide information that teachers find compelling as a means to make sense of their already rich experiences in practice. They are often the basis for a staged series of investigations which can be followed by curricular development and evaluation, or broader forms of instructional efficacy studies.

Representativeness and generalizability are at work in many design studies. Dede (2004) criticized design studies as "under-conceptualized and over methodological-ized," and proceeded to explain that the "freewheeling" and speculative part of design must be constrained by attention to principled variation. In addition, he suggested that the failure to use most of the data produced (approximately at 5 percent) meant that such work collects more than it can practically manage. These criticisms can be answered with reference to previously mentioned aspects of methodology. A clear specification of the initial conjectures

provides a sense of what must be varied. The focus on daily logs of activities, and discussions by research teams, to identify, interpret, and subsequently test alternative hypotheses provides such sources of principled variation. Formative assessments, designed to document representativeness across students, must be systematically used. In response to the concern for an overabundance of data, Dede was correct that at the stage of rational reconstruction, that is, a study's concluding analysis, the flexibility to test alternative conjectures and interpretations is more limited, but during this phase, the key is to search out both confirming and disconfirming events and to make explicit the case for the explanatory power of proposed constructs, over time, across circumstance, and across students.

Finally, the emphasis on inquiry and modeling, with its underpinnings of how learning best proceeds, is also a foundation for the warrant of the work. Design studies produce models of students' and teachers' learning in rich interactional settings with a variety of tasks and mediational means. In the complex settings of classrooms, understanding, explaining, and gaining predictability are not about finding universal, immutable laws but, rather, about creating models of likely means of scaffolding that lead to successful learning outcomes, by means of theories, materials, instructional approaches; and about providing instructional guidance on domain-specific topics.

Sloane and Gorard (2003) offered an interesting criticism of design study methodology from a framework of model building. Reiterating George Box's 1978 maxim that "All models are wrong, but some are useful" (cited in Sloane & Gorard, 2003), they identified three stages in model building: model formulation or specification, estimation or fit, and model validation. They outlined six objectives of model formulation: parsimonious description with adequate complexity, data set comparison, confirmation or refutation of theoretical relationships described a priori, understanding of the error component, provision of a yardstick, and empirical understanding of underlying processes. They suggested that design studies typically pay attention to the model formulation and local validation of the model, and tend to deemphasize fit of the data from the experiments to the model, and ignore broader validation. It could be argued that the fit of data to model is inherent in design studies, in the iterations of the experiment, and that broader validation of a model requires a study of efficacy under a different methodology. Future work might fruitfully examine and explore how to apply these ideas more completely to design studies.

So far there is very little discussion of how design studies might attend more adequately to issues of equity. I see this as a serious oversight that resides in the fact that those engaged in the work lack sufficient diversity of background. In addition, Flyvbjerg (2001) provided a question to be asked of all social science efforts, namely, "who gains and who loses in power relations?" which could also be asked of design studies. In addition, questions should be raised about how knowledge is distributed across members of a class and ways in which that knowledge is shared, partitioned, authorized, and accessed (Confrey & Makar, 2005).

Discussion and Conclusions

I began this chapter citing by *Scientific Research in Education* and acknowledging both the promise and the relative immaturity of design study methodologies. I close by reiterating that the fundamental role of this work lies in its potential to create instructional theories at the level that holds the best possibilities to provide solutions to common ills in education. In the recent publication by the National Research Council, *On Evaluating Curricular Effectiveness*,[2] the authors warn that an uncritical view of experimentalism may fail to recognize key elements of classroom instruction. They argue that experimentalism rests on ideal conditions and has a tendency to trade internal validity for external validity. In addition, they warn that feedback is a critical element that speaks to the adaptability of the process of learning, and raises questions as to whether cause-and-effect studies are the best way to improve classroom practice.

> *It is worth pointing out that the issues debated by members of this committee are not new, but have a long history in complex fields where the limitations of the scientific method have been recognized for a long time. Ecology, immunology, epidemiology, and neurobiology provide plenty of examples where the use of alternative approaches that include dynamical systems, game theory, large-scale simulations, and agent-based models have proved to be essential, even in the design of experiments. We do not live on a fixed landscape and, consequently, any intervention or perturbation of a system (e.g., the implementation of new curricula) can alter the landscape. The fact that researchers select a priori specific levels of aggregation (often dictated by convenience) and fail to test the validity of their results to such choices is not only common, but extremely limiting (validity). (Confrey & Stohl, 2004, p. 64)*

Design studies offer the field a methodology that seeks to recognize the complexity of classroom practices and to provide the kinds of insight needed to assist teachers in accomplishing their challenging task. Their success in doing so will depend in some measure on how well they can specify of what kinds of knowledge they seek to produce, and the warrants for the knowledge they do produce.

Acknowledgments

The author wishes to acknowledge the assistance in preparation and editing by Dr. Alan Maloney, Ms. Sibel Kazak, and Dr. Keith Sawyer.

Footnotes

1. The author of this chapter was a committee member. However, this chapter reflects the views of the author and not other members of the committee or the NRC.

2. Confrey was the chair of the committee; hence, there is less independence of the

comments here and the report than might appear at first glance. However, the use and interpretation of the report are the product of the author and should not be attributed to the committee, the NRC, or this report.

References

Ackerman, E. (1995). Construction and transference of meaning through form. In L. P. a. G. Steffe, J. (Ed.), *Constructivism in education* (pp. 341–354). Hillsdale, NJ: Lawrence Erlbaum Associates.

Barab, S., & Squire, K. (2004). Design-based research: Putting a stake in the ground. *The Journal of the Learning Sciences*, 13 (1), 1–14.

Brown, A. L. (1992). Design experiments: Theoretical and methodological challenges in creating complex interventions in classroom settings. *The Journal of the Learning Sciences*, 2 (2), 141–178.

Brown, A. L., & Campione, J. (1996). Psychological theory and the design of innovative learning environments: On procedures, principles, and systems. In L. Schauble & R. Glaser (Eds.), *Innovations in learning: New environments for education* (pp. 289–298). Mahwah, NJ: Lawrence Erlbaum Associates, Inc.

Cobb, P. (2000). Conducting teaching experiments in collaboration with teachers. In A. E. Kelly & L. R. A. (Eds.), *Handbook of research design in mathematics and science education* (pp. 307–333). Mahwah, NJ: Lawrence Erlbaum Associates.

Cobb, P. (2002). Modeling, symbolizing, and tool use in statistical data analysis. In K. P. E. Gravemeijer, R. Lehrer, B. v. Oers & L. Verschaffel (Eds.), *Symbolizing, modeling and tool use in mathematics education* (pp. 171–195). Dordrecht: Kluwer Academic Publishers.

Cobb, P., Confrey, J., diSessa, A., Lehrer, R., & Schauble, L. (2003). Design experiments in educational research. *Educational Researcher*, 32 (1), 9–13.

Cobb, P., & Steffe, L. P. (1983). The constructivist researcher as teacher and model builder. *Journal for Research in Mathematics Education*, 14 (2), 83–94.

Cohen, D. K., Raudenbush, S. W., & Ball, D. L. (2003). Resources, instruction, and research. *Educational Evaluation and Policy Analysis*, 25 (2), 119–142.

Collins, A. (1992). Toward a design science of education. In E. Scanlon & T. O'Shea (Eds.), *New directions in educational technology* (pp. 15–22). Berlin: Springer-Verlag.

Collins, A., Joseph, D., & Bielaczyc, K. (2004). Design research: Theoretical and methodological issues. *The Journal of the Learning Sciences*, 13 (1), 15–42.

Confrey, J. (1988, October). *Multiplication and splitting: Their role in understanding exponential functions.* Paper presented at the annual meeting of the North American Chapter of the International Group for the Psychology of Mathematics Education. DeKalb, IL.

Confrey, J., Castro-Filho, J., & Wilhelm, J. (2000). Implementation research as a means to link systemic reform and applied psychology in mathematics education. *Educational Psychologist*, 35 (3), 179–191.

Confrey, J., & Lachance, A. (2000). Transformative teaching experiments through conjecture-driven research design. In A. E. Kelly & R. A. Lesh (Eds.), *Handbook of research design in mathematics and science education* (pp. 231–265). Mahwah, NJ: Lawrence Erlbaum Associates.

Confrey, J. (Producer/Writer), Lachance, A. (Producer/Writer), & Hotchkiss, G. (Producer/Writer). (1996). *In the voices of children.* [Videotape]

Confrey, J., & Makar, K. M. (2005). Critiquing and improving the use of data from high-stakes tests with the aid of dynamic statistics software. In C. Dede, J. P. Honan, & L. C. Peteres (Eds.), *Scaling up success: Lessons learned from technology-based educational improvement* (pp. 198–226). San Francisco: Jossey-Bass.

Confrey, J., & Stohl, V. (Eds.). (2004). *On evaluating curricular effectiveness: Judging the quality of k-12 mathematics evaluations.* Washington, DC: National Academy Press.

DBRC. (2003). Design-based research: An emerging paradigm for educational inquiry. *Educational Researcher*, 32 (1), 5–8.

Dede, C. (2004). If design-based research is the answer, what is the question? Commentary on Collins, Joseph, and Bielaczyc; diSessa and Cobb; and Fishman, Marx, Blumenthal, Krajcik, and Soloway in the JLS special issue on design-based research. *Journal of the Learning Sciences*, 13 (1), 105–114.

Dewey, J. (1981). *The philosophy of John Dewey: Volume I – the structure of the experience,*

Volume II – the lived experience. Chicago: University of Chicago Press.

diSessa, A. A. (2004). Students' criteria for representational adequacy. In K. Gravemeijer, R. Lehrer, B. v. Oers, & L. Verschaffel (Eds.), *Symbolizing, modeling and tool use in mathematics education* (pp. 105–130). Dordrecht: Kluwer Academic Publishers.

diSessa, A. A., & Cobb, P. (2004). Ontological innovation and the role of theory in design experiments. *The Journal of the Learning Sciences, 13*(1), 77–103.

Duckworth, E. (1996). *The having of wonderful ideas*. New York: Teachers College Press.

Elkana, Y. (1974). *The discovery of the conservation of energy*. London: Hutchinson Educational, Ltd.

Elmore, R. F. (1996). Getting to scale with good educational practice. *Harvard Educational Review, 66*(1), 1–26.

Fernandez, C., & Yoshida, M. (2004). *Lesson study: A Japanese approach to improving mathematics teaching and learning*. Mahwah, NJ: Lawrence Erlbaum Associates.

Fisher, C., Dwyer, D., & Yoacam, K. (Eds.). (1996). *Education and technology: Reflections on computing in classrooms*. San Francisco: Jossey-Bass.

Fishman, B., Marx, R. W., Blumenfeld, P., Krajcik, J., & Soloway, E. (2004). Creating a framework for research on systemic technology innovations. *The Journal of the Learning Sciences, 13*(1), 43–76.

Flyvbjerg, B. (2001). *Making social science matter: Why social inquiry fails and how it can succeed again* (S. Sampson, Trans.). Cambridge: Cambridge University Press.

Gee, J. P. (1999). *An introduction to discourse analysis: Theory and method*. New York: Routledge.

Gravemeijer, K. P. E. (1995). *Developing realistic mathematics instruction*. Utrecht: Freudenthal Institute.

Greeno, J. G. (1997). Theories and practices of thinking and learning to think: Middle school mathematics through applications project. *American Journal of Education, 106*(1), 85–126.

Greeno, J. G. (2003, November). Positioning, problematizing, and reconciling: Aspects of productive cognition and learning in a situative perspective. Paper presented at a conference, "Theorizing learning practice," University of Illinois, Champagne-Urbana.

Hawkins, D. (2002). *The informed vision: Essays on learning and human nature*. New York: Algora Publishing.

Kantowski, M. G., Steffe, L. P., Lee, K. S., & Hatfield, L. H. (1978). *The soviet "teaching experiment": Its role and usage in American research*. Annual Meeting of the National Council of Teachers of Mathematics (NCTM). San Diego, CA.

Kegan, R. (2000). What "form" transforms? A constructive-developmental approach to transformative learning. In J. Mezirow & Associates (Eds.), *Learning as transformation: Critical perspectives on a theory in progress* (pp. 35–69). San Francisco: Jossey-Bass.

Lagemann, E. C. (2002). *An elusive science: The troubling history of education research*. Chicago: University of Chicago Press.

Lakatos, I. (1976). *Proofs and refutations: The logic of mathematical discovery*. Cambridge: Cambridge University Press.

Lakatos, I., & Feyerabend, P. (1999). *For and against method*. Chicago: University of Chicago Press.

Lehrer, R., & Pritchard, C. (2002). Symbolizing space into being. In K. Gravemeijer, R. Lehrer, B. v. Oers, & L. Verschaffel (Eds.), *Symbolizing, modeling and tool use in mathematics education* (pp. 59–86). Dordrecht: Kluwer Academic Publishers.

Lehrer, R., & Schauble, L. (2004). Modeling natural variation through distribution. *American Educational Research Journal, 41*(3), 635–679.

Lesh, R. (1999). The development of representational abilities in middle school mathematics: The development of student's representations during model eliciting activities. In I. E. Sigel (Ed.), *The development of mental representation* (pp. 323–349). Mahwah, NJ: Lawrence Erlbaum Associates.

Lesh, R. A., & Kelly, A. E. (2000). Multitiered teaching experiments. In A. E. Kelly & L. R. A. (Eds.), *Handbook of research design in mathematics and science education* (pp. 197–230). Mahwah, NJ: Lawrence Erlbaum Associates.

Merrill, D. M. (2001). Toward a theoretical tool for instructional design. *Instructional Science, 29*(4–5), 291–310.

Papert, S. (1980). *Mindstorms: Children, computers, and powerful ideas*. New York: Basic Books.

Pea, R. D. (1987). Cognitive technologies for mathematics education. In A. Schoenfeld (Ed.), *Cognitive science and mathematics education* (pp. 89–122). Hillsdale, NJ: Lawrence Erlbaum Assocates.

Piaget, J. (1976). *The child's conception of the world.* Totowa, NJ: Littlefield, Adams, & Co.

Reeves, T. C. (2000, April). *Enhancing the worth of instructional technology research through "design experiments" and other developmental research strategies.* Paper presented at the annual meeting of the American Educational Research Association. New Orleans, LA.

Scarano, G., & Confrey, J. (1996, April). *Results from a three-year longitudinal teaching experiment designed to investigate splitting, ratio and proportion.* Paper presented at the Annual Meeting of the American Educational Research Association, New York, NY.

Shavelson, R. J., Phillips, D. C., Towne, L., & Feuer, M. J. (2003). On the science of education design studies. *Educational Researcher,* 32(1), 25–28.

Shavelson, R. J., & Towne, L. (Eds.). (2002). *Scientific research in education.* Washington, DC: National Academy Press.

Simon, H. A. (1969). *The sciences of the artificial.* Cambridge, MA: MIT Press.

Simon, M. (1995). Reconstructing mathematics pedagogy from a constructivist perspective.

Journal for Research in Mathematics Education, 26(2), 114–145.

Simon, M. A. (2000). Research on the development of mathematics teachers: The teacher development experiment. In A. E. Kelly & L. R. A. (Eds.), *Handbook of research design in mathematics and science education* (pp. 335–359). Mahwah, NJ: Lawrence Erlbaum Associates.

Sloane, F. C., & Gorard, S. (2003). Exploring modeling aspects of design experiments. *Educational Researcher,* 32(1), 29–31.

Steffe, L. P. (1991). The constructivist teaching experiment: Illustrations and implications. In E. von Glasersfeld (Ed.), *Radical constructivism in mathematics education* (pp. 177–194). Boston: Kluwer Academic Publishers.

Thompson, P. W. (1979). *The constructivist teaching experiment in mathematics education research.* Paper presented at the Annual Meeting of the National Council of Teachers of Mathematics, Boston, MA.

von Glasersfeld, E. (1982). An interpretation of piaget's constructivism. *Revue Internationale de philosophie,* 36, 612–635.

Vygotsky, L. S. (1978). *Mind in society: The development of higher psychological processes.* Cambridge, MA: Harvard University Press.

Vygotsky, L. S. (1986). *Thought and language* (A. Kozulin, Trans.). Cambridge, MA: MIT Press.

CHAPTER 10

Design-Based Research

A Methodological Toolkit for the Learning Scientist

Sasha Barab

Design-based research (DBR) is used to study learning in environments which are designed and systematically changed by the researcher. The goal of DBR is to use the close study of a single learning environment, usually as it passes through multiple iterations and as it occurs in naturalistic contexts, to develop new theories, artifacts, and practices that can be generalized to other schools and classrooms. In describing design-based research, Cobb et al. (2003) state:

> Prototypically, design experiments entail both "engineering" particular forms of learning and systematically studying those forms of learning within the context defined by the means of supporting them. This designed context is subject to test and revision, and the successive iterations that result play a role similar to that of systematic variation in experiment. (p. 9)

This design process allows the researcher to move beyond simply understanding the world as it is, and involves working to change it in useful ways with the broader goal of examining how these systematic changes influence learning and practice (Barab & Squire, 2004). It is this innovative aspect of design-based research that makes it such a useful methodology for advancing new theory and practice.

One way of understanding the focus of design-based research is in terms of Pasteur's Quadrant (Stokes, 1997; see Figure 10.1). In this quadrant model for characterizing scientific research, the upper-left-hand cell consists of basic research for the sole purpose of understanding without an eye toward practical use. The lower-right-hand cell consists of research that focuses solely on applied goals without seeking a more general understanding of the phenomena. Last is the upper-right-hand cell, where design-based research is located, in which the focus is on advancing "the frontiers of understanding but is also inspired by considerations of use" (Stokes, 1997, p. 74). Barab and Squire (2004) argued that "such a system of inquiry might draw less from traditional positivist science or ethnographic traditions of inquiry, and more from pragmatic lines of inquiry where theories are judged not by their claims to truth, but by their ability to do work in the

		Consideration of Use	
		No	Yes
Seeks General Understanding	Yes	Pure basic research (Bohr)	Use-inspired basic research (Pasteur)
	No		Pure applied research (Edison)

Figure 10.1. Quadrant model of scientific research.

world (Dewey, 1938, p. 6). The design-based researcher must demonstrate local impact, at the same time making a case that this local impact can be accounted for in terms of the particular theory being advanced.

Design-based research involves more than simply reporting outcomes: DBR moves beyond descriptive accounts to offer insights about process, so that the work can be taken up by others. Such sharing involves methodological precision and rich accounts so that others can judge the value of the contribution, as well as make connections to their own contexts of innovation. Critics argue that any interpretation not generated using an experimental methodology can at best provide formative insights that must then be tested through more controlled experimentation. However, design-based research is not simply a precursor to later, more rigorous, experimental research; it is a form of research that is meaningful in its own right – as an end product. A well-presented and carefully conducted design narrative has the potential to support what Stake (1995) referred to as "petite generalizations," that is, work that provides others with insights into the challenges and opportunities that might emerge in their own work, as well as strategies for navigating these effectively.

According to many educational researchers and contrary to the arguments of those pushing for experimental designs as the gold standard, the messiness of real-world practice must be recognized, understood, and integrated as part of theoretical claims if the claims are to have real-world explanatory value. From this perspective, examining teaching and learning as isolated variables within laboratory or other artificial contexts will necessarily lead to understandings and theories that are incomplete. Experimental studies that simply indicate a variable is significant may be less useful than rich examples and case narratives are for informing how to implement a particular variable or theory within the context of real-world practice. Within learning environments, so-called confounding variables necessarily occur and must be taken into account (not controlled) if the findings are to be relevant to practitioners. Context is not simply a container within which the disembodied "regularities" under study occur, but is an integral part of the complex causal mechanisms that give rise to the phenomenon under study (Maxwell, 2004).

If researchers only study that which takes place in controlled conditions, they run the risk of developing artificial meanings and interactive dynamics that are so free of contextual realities that they may not be able to inform real-world practice. In contrast, the learning sciences are committed to producing change in real-world learning environments. Learning sciences research, rather than taking place in the laboratory or in the theorizing of the philosopher's mind, more often occurs in naturalistic contexts and involves confounding variables, political agendas, and multiple alternative hypotheses, and rarely includes randomized trials. Design-based research involves the creation of a theoretically-inspired innovation, usually a learning environment, to directly address a local problem. Although showing local gains is an important element of DBR, the focus is on simultaneously developing a design and generating new theory. Barab and Squire (2004, pp. 5–6) stated

> Although providing credible evidence for local gains as a result of a particular design may be necessary, it is not sufficient. Design-based research requires more than simply showing a particular design works but demands that the researcher (move beyond a particular design exemplar to) generate evidence-based claims about learning that address contemporary theoretical issues and further the theoretical knowledge of the field.

In other words, the design work, while addressing a local problem, should be in the service of theory generation with evidence of its effectiveness being a requisite to theory development.

To further complicate the picture, these learning environments are often developed by the researchers, the very people intending to study them and advance the theoretical claims. This is in part because an essential element of learning sciences research is that it moves beyond observing the world as it is, and actually involves systematically engineering the contexts of study in ways that allow for the generation and advancement of new theory (Barab & Squire, 2004). Such work requires a new methodological toolkit, design-based research. It is important to note that design-based research is less a method than it is a collection of approaches that involve a commitment to researching activity in naturalistic settings, many of which are designed and systematically changed by the researcher, with the goal of advancing theory and at the same time directly impacting practice. In this chapter, I focus

on the what, the how, and the why of such research.

Setting the Stage

Design-based research is frequently traced back to 1992 when Ann Brown (1992) and Allan Collins (1992) introduced a new methodological approach for conducting research and design work in the context of real-life settings. In complex learning environments, it is difficult to test the causal impact of particular variables with experimental designs. DBR deals with complexity by iteratively changing the learning environment over time – collecting evidence of the effect of these variations and feeding it recursively into future designs (Brown, 1992; Collins, 1992). As Confrey (this volume) points out, design-based research is especially useful for understanding the underlying reasons why something is happening, or the conditions under which a particular interaction or occurrence could happen (also see Shavelson & Towne, 2002). Because DBR takes place in naturalistic contexts, it also allows for the identification and examination of multiple interacting variables, thereby providing systems-level understandings.

A second motivation for DBR is the belief that the "factoring assumption" of experimental psychology is not valid in learning environments (Greeno, this volume). The factoring assumption is the assumption that we can analyze individual cognitive processes apart from any particular context. Instead, a core assumption of learning scientists is that the individual and the learning environment are inseparable, with the meaning of any content being mutually determined through local contextual particulars (Brown, Collins, & Duguid, 1989; Kirshner & Whitson, 1997; Salomon, 1993). Lave (1988), argued:

> There is a reason to suspect that what we call cognition is in fact a complex social phenomenon. The point is not so much that arrangements of knowledge in the head

correspond in a complicated way to the social world outside the head, but that they are socially organized in such a fashion as to be indivisible. "Cognition" observed in everyday practice is distributed – stretched over, not divided among – mind, body, activity and culturally organized settings which include other actors. (p. 1)

Cognition, rather than being a disembodied process occurring in the confines of the mind, is a distributed process spread out across the knower, the environment, and even the meaning of the activity (Salomon, 1993). From a situative perspective, studying a phenomenon such as motivation, meta-cognition, or even learning in a laboratory context might result in scientifically reliable but consequentially limited understandings that have little generalizable value (Greeno, this volume).

In addition to understanding learning in complex environments and engineering new learning environments, DBR accomplishes a third goal: it improves learning for those participants in the study. This is because a core commitment underlying DBR is that the work will have local impact. A challenge then becomes that of scaling up (Dede, this volume) – understanding the contextual dynamics that surround the implementation of a complex learning environment in such a way that the findings can inform implementation in other contexts. The goal is to advance theory-in-context. The phrase "theory-in-context" communicates the conviction that the theory is always situated in terms of local particulars. Drawing on Gibson's (1986) ecological psychology terminology, the phrase includes both a relatively invariant aspect, the theory, and a variant aspect, the context. Accounts of DBR should describe both the theory and the particulars in a way that allows others to understand how to recontextualize the theory-in-context with respect to their local particulars.

One way of understanding the relations among theory, design, and implementation is in terms of Dewey's (1915) notion of praxis, the act of translating theory into action. For Dewey, praxis was not a uni-directional

process, but a transactive one, involving inquiry and through which theory and practice mutually inform each other. Confrey (this volume), commenting on the process of praxis, states that Dewey "recognized that in the beginning, there is only the indeterminate, which undergoes transformation through a problematic to a hypothesis, which, by means of the activity of inquiry, is transformed to a determinate situation producing a set of knowledge claims" (p. 139). In this way, theory can come from action just as action can come from theory. Design-based research can be thought of as a form of praxis, with design/implementation being the practice. Dewey's notion of praxis as transactive further implies that in practice the theory (and design) will flex according to local particulars, possibly resulting in lethal design mutations even in the context of reasonable theory. Confrey (this volume), along similar lines, suggests that design-based research results in explanatory frameworks that "cannot predict an outcome precisely, because each realization is, in effect, unique, but the multiple realizations yield tendencies that can guide decision-making and parameter setting" (p. 139). As such, an essential part of advancing theory-in-context is to communicate the theory as well as the contextual particulars through which it is realized in practice – a process that design-based research is particularly effective in illuminating.

Defining Design-Based Research

Conducting DBR requires posing significant questions that can be investigated empirically; linking research to theory; providing a coherent and explicit chain of reasoning; disclosing research data and methods to enable and encourage professional scrutiny and critique; and employing methodological practices that are deemed credible and trustworthy, and that result in useful claims (Shavelson, Phillips, Towne, & Feuer, 2003). Because this work takes place in naturalistic contexts and involves the systematic tweaking of theoretically inspired

Table 10.1. Differences Between Design-based Research and Psychology Experiments

	DBR	Psychology Experiments
Location of research	Real-world learning environment	Laboratory
Complexity of variables	Multiple types of dependent variables	A few dependent variables
Treatment of variables	Not all variables of interest are known in advance; some emerge during the study	A few variables are selected in advance and remain constant during the study
Unfolding of procedures	Research procedures are flexible and evolve during the study	Fixed procedures are used
Social interaction	Complex social interactions with collaboration and sharing	Isolation of individuals
Reporting the findings	Describing design in practice	Report on whether hypotheses were supported
Role of participants	Experimenter and participants are active and influence the design of the research	Experimenter should not influence the subject; and subjects do not influence the design

aspects of the learning environment, this research can offer insights into *why* and *how* a particular intervention works. Such theoretical and methodological rigor is necessary if design-based research is going to evolve into an accepted methodology, advancing theoretical constructs (and even designs) that are of use to others. Collins, Joseph, and Bielaczyc (1999, 2004) posited seven major differences between traditional psychological methods and the design-experiment methodology (see Table 10.1).

Figure 10.2 characterizes the core elements (design, theory, problem, naturalistic context) of DBR, and communicates that each of these components transact with the other such that the design is predicated on

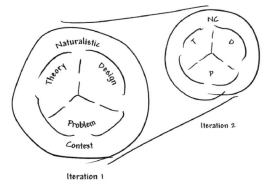

Figure 10.2. General characterization of design-based research.

theory and the strength of the theory is bound up with how the design addresses the problem. Additionally, it is not simply that the work happens *in* naturalistic settings but, rather, that the work *transacts* with these settings such that the design, the problem, and even the theory are fused with these settings in ways that are not easy to disentangle. Lastly, DBR usually involves multiple iterations or what Collins et al. (1999) referred to as progressive refinement, with each iteration providing a further refinement of the design in order to test the value of the innovation and, presumably, stimulate the evolution of theory.

Clearly, demonstrating the linkages between theory and design, between design and problem, between theory and problem, and between successive iterations of the design requires rigorous methods that make convincing arguments but almost never totally rule out alternative explanations. For the design-based researcher, the rigor comes from principled accounts that provide logical chains of reasoning and prove useful to others. Confrey (this volume) suggests that in research, evidence of methodological rigor comes from three sources:

1. the experimentation/investigation has itself been adequately conducted and analyzed,

2. the claims are justified, robust, and significant relative to the data and the theory and when subjected to alternative interpretations, and

3. the relevance of the claims to the practices of education is explicit and feasible.

Design-based researchers must employ rigorous methods if they wish others to believe (and benefit from) the theoretical claims they wish to advance.

A challenge is to describe the findings in a way that allows others to understand how to recontextualize them with respect to local particulars. A second challenge is that unlike experimental design, it becomes difficult to rule out alternative hypotheses. Given these complications, how is it that the design-based researcher convinces others about the credibility of the claims? More often than not, this requires a balance of qualitative and quantitative data but rarely does it allow for tightly controlled experimentation. Opening up the black box of theories-in-context reveals complex interactions that are not usefully disentangled so that one can conduct more rigorous examinations. Instead, it is necessary to communicate these theories in their full contextual splendor, illuminating insights about process while at the same time demonstrating local outcomes. Making convincing arguments when conducting DBR is challenging and involves developing complex narratives (Abbott, 1992; Mink et al., 1987) and building rich models of interaction (Lesh & Kelly, 2000) – not simply reporting outcomes or using the reports as precursors to more tightly controlled experiments.

Design-Based Research in Practice

Inquiry Learning Forum

An example of design-based research is the work my colleagues and I did during the three years we spent developing and researching an electronic knowledge network, the Inquiry Learning Forum (ILF) (Barab et al., 2001; Barab, MaKinster, & Scheckler, 2003). Our initial focus was on developing a Web site to support a virtual community of in-service and preservice mathematics and science teachers who were creating, sharing, and improving inquiry-based pedagogical practices. The project began in the late 1990s, during the Internet boom, when so-called "virtual communities" were springing up everywhere – from commercial vendors such as E-Bay to multiuser video games such as EverQuest to numerous chat rooms with a topical focus. The optimism at the time led us to a naïve "build it and they will come" belief. Initially, we thought the challenge would be primarily technical: to get a design online. We didn't think about whether teachers would want to participate in critical dialogue about their practice as part of an online community. But through a process of DBR, our design and theoretical conceptions with respect to facilitating virtual communities evolved (see Figure 10.3).

About five months after teachers started using the first iteration of the Web site, we began to question our initial design. Although there were discussion forums and other relevant resources, the essence of the Web site was videos of classrooms that provided examples of inquiry. Participation rates, as mined through the computer log files of member usage, were low, especially with respect to sustained viewing of the virtual classrooms. Interviews with a dozen teachers indicated that examining the videos of other teachers doing inquiry was overly time-consuming. Furthermore, the idea of being a part of a community was not as compelling to teachers as getting content that was directly useful to their practice of teaching. During focus groups with teachers, we heard a consistent message that to gain their participation, the project must meet their particular needs. In the words of one teacher,

You need a mission statement. The ILF needs to have a stronger, more obvious focus. It needs a theme and that theme needs to speak to teacher needs. You got to stand for something more than online learning community. For example, it could be sold as a resource for teachers who are

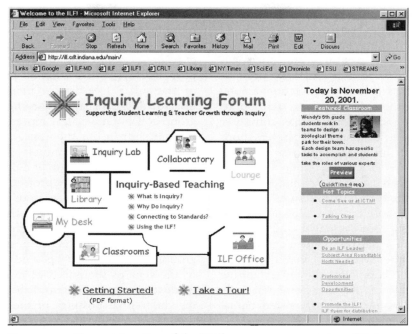

Figure 10.3. Current iteration of the ILF home screen, consisting of links to Classrooms, ILF Office, Collaboratory, Lounge, Library, Inquiry Lab., and My Desk.

trying to use inquiry teaching to meet state standards. A theme based on a problem that teachers have and know they have – this can be the subterfuge for pulling in customers.

As part of the DBR process with respect to this project, the research team met every week to debate observations, critique current conjectures, pose alternative explanations, and suggest design revisions.

Confronted with participation data and with the teacher interviews, we recognized that although we theoretically had a commitment to supporting online community, the focus had to be less about community in general, and more about something of immediate value to their teaching. This appreciation led to a number of design changes. For example, we changed the name of the project Web site. No longer the "*Internet* Learning Forum," the site and the project became known as the "*Inquiry* Learning Forum" (Barab et al., 2001). This change reflected an evolution in the perception of the ILF by those involved. Initially, the ILF was regarded as primarily an Internet-focused, professional-development project that sought to develop online community. In time, this vision grew to become a vision of the ILF as a project that is focused on supporting student and teacher inquiry, with participation on the Web site, in person, through workshops, and more. On a related note, this sentiment was integrated into our "tagline" on the opening page of the Web site. Our earlier tagline, "Building a community of Indiana math and science teachers," was changed to "Supporting student learning and teacher growth through inquiry."

This change did not simply take place in our design, but also represented an evolution in our theory about supporting online community. Specifically, there was an evolution from our initial rather abstract notion that the idea of community itself would be a strong draw to teachers, to an appreciation that community emerges only when individuals come together around shared goals and practices. Another change was from viewing the ILF project as the development of an electronic artifact (the Web site). Based on our discussions with teachers, our discussions at team meetings, and our reading of other related works, we began to view the ILF as including transactions among people, technology, resources, and populations – a move from human-computer interactions to human-human interactions as mediated through computers. This was revealed through a focus group with two teachers targeted toward helping us understand why the technical structures were not engendering more critical dialogue. We had two teachers come together and use the ILF to watch a classroom video and discuss with each other what they were observing. Although the comments they made during their face-to-face dialogue were relatively critical, the comments they posted online were fairly benign.

As we talked with the teachers, we gained a richer understanding of how the problem was not technical (e.g., usability issues), but social, and we began to understand that we needed to support teachers in becoming critical as colleagues more generally. We developed a richer appreciation for the importance of trust and for how challenging it was for teachers to post critical comments about their colleagues in public spaces where anyone could come and read them. Through a reading of the literature, it became clear to us that critique was not a big part of the face-to-face culture of these teachers and online critique was potentially more threatening in that the critique would be "out there" and could be read by anyone. Teachers told us that they were more comfortable working in small groups around more focused topics of direct interest to them. These statements were consistent with our field observations of how they engaged in professional development in their regular classrooms and with our reading of the literature around teacher professional development and online communities. Using this understanding, we developed ways for groups to collaborate in more intimate spaces not available to all community members.

These observations and our research discussions led us to conceive the members not as *one* community, but as a *collection of bounded groups*, and we developed support structures to partition off private areas of the e-ILF (see Figure 10.4). In addition to adding a virtual space for bounded-group collaborations, this represented a significant shift in our theoretical conception of what constitutes community. Instead of a four-thousand-plus group of individuals, we began to conceive of the project as supporting many communities, each of which used the e-ILF but had separate goals and interests. Our log file data revealed that members were much more willing to post in private groups of about twenty people: 80 percent of the tens of thousands of postings were made to these private areas. Through observing differential postings in these bounded groups, we also began to appreciate the role of a facilitator; the groups who had facilitators were posting significantly more critical comments than those with no facilitator. Facilitators became a necessary part of our theory of what it meant to support online community. On a related note, we focused less on issues of usability and more on issues of sociability, developing an appreciation of the challenges of establishing trust in online community. Furthermore, we spent more time at teachers' schools, saw the importance of local professional development, and began to think of the ILF as one component of a larger process that involved online and face-to-face interactions. In this way our theory shifted from being about online community to Web-supported community (Barab, Schatz, & Scheckler, 2004).

Reflecting back on the evolution of the ILF, we made these changes because the data indicated low levels of participation, and our interviews, focus groups, and observations suggested that we were not meeting the needs of the participants. We would implement a change and reexamine participation levels, and conduct interviews with members to understand their perspectives. Or sometimes, we would compare various structures to better understand the differential participation potentially elicited by

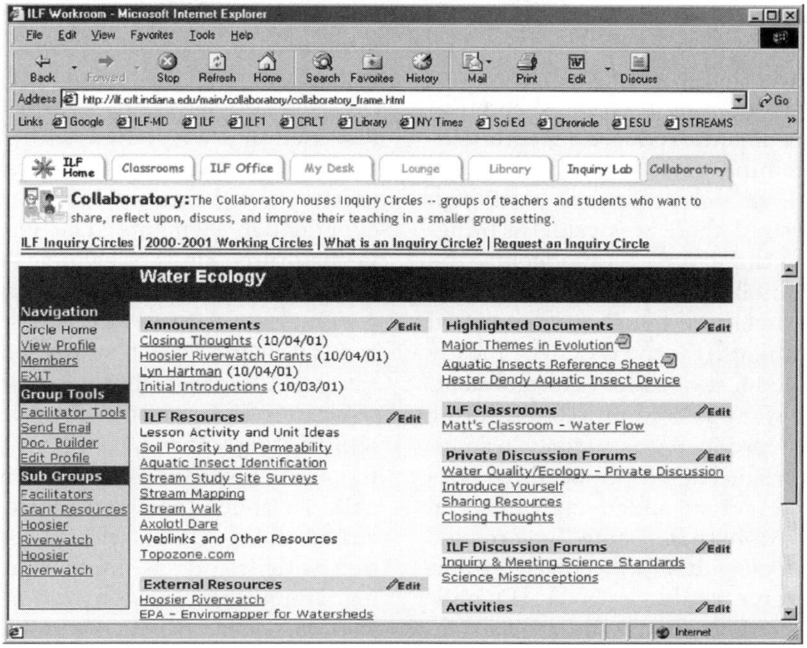

Figure 10.4. Current iteration of an ILF Inquiry Circle (Water Ecology). The sections within an Inquiry Circle include Announcements, Highlighted Documents, External Resources, ILF Resources, ILF Classrooms, ILF Discussion Forums, Private Discussion Forums, and Activities.

the design; for example, there were greater numbers of posts and participation in the bounded group areas (inquiry circles) of the Inquiry Learning Forum than in the other globally public areas. We even conducted some studies using more traditional experimental designs. For example, MaKinster et al. (in press) compared the reflections and carried out interviews with preservice teachers who were assigned conditions in which they either reflected on their student-teaching placements in a private journal, in a collaborative discussion forum involving other preservice teachers, or in a public discussion forum in the Lounge area. The Private Journal group wrote more complete initial reflections, but described the experience as just another assignment and attached little meaning or value to the exercise. Students in the Private Discussion Forum posted lower quality reflections, but several students expressed more perceived value in the experience. The students in the Lounge Discussion Forum posted even

lower quality reflections, but all of these students found significant value in the assignment, the interactions they had with their peers, the interactions with the larger community of in-service teachers, and the idea of reflecting on one's teaching as a means for personal and collaborative professional development.

This description of DBR demonstrates how researchers continually revise their design to optimize the learning environment. The evolution of the project was not simply in its design but also in our theoretical conceptions of community. Although some of these insights were project specific, we have learned that our findings have usefully informed others in terms of the struggles they are confronting in their community design projects. Overall, this design-based research project contributed to a much richer design, and a more informed theoretical perspective of the challenges and opportunities associated with Web-supported communities.

Quest Atlantis

My colleagues and I have been developing *learning engagement theory*: a theoretical perspective that unites education, entertainment, and commitment (Barab et al., 2005; Barab, Arici, & Jackson, 2005). Although we hypothesized there was value in bringing together these three components, the theory was initially relatively naïve, abstract, and shallow. In fact, although we mentioned life commitments, the project was mostly focused on education and entertainment, even though we were committed to ensuring the designed product was socially responsive in that it considered the needs of boys and girls and had an underlying pro-social component. More than testing some refined theory, the focus initially was on determining whether we could design a 3D multiuser environment that could be used in schools to immerse children, ages nine to twelve, in educational tasks. Over the last three years, this idea has grown into the globally distributed Quest Atlantis (QA) project (http://questatlantis.org).

Currently, we have about forty-five hundred children from five continents that use QA, and they have completed literally thousands of the educational activities – hundreds have been completed in their free time without explicit teacher prompting. Building on strategies from online role-playing games, QA combines strategies used in the commercial gaming environment with lessons from educational research on learning and motivation. It allows users to travel to virtual places to perform educational activities (known as Quests), to talk with other users and mentors, and to build virtual personae (see Figure 10.5). A Quest is an engaging curricular task designed to be entertaining yet educational. In its current instantiation, Quest Atlantis is also structured around seven Life Commitments (personal agency, environmental awareness, social responsibility, healthy communities, compassionate wisdom, creative expression, diversity affirmation) that frame all QA participation.

While the development of QA was informed by our conception of learning engagement theory, our development process has also served to inform the theory. For example, we started with a container metaphor that focused on education, entertainment, and commitment as design, not experiential, elements. The idea was that we had three kinds of elements in the container, some of which were educational, others entertaining, and still others about life commitments. Our first version had educational Quests, communication and play structures, and commitments, with all three representing somewhat distinct activities in the virtual space. When we interviewed children about their experience, most discussed doing Quests as one aspect, chatting with friends as another, and navigating around the 3D environment as still another aspect. Life commitments were rarely described. When we asked children about the core practices of being a Quester, rarely did they mention anything related to the seven life commitments. Even when explicitly prompted about the life commitments, their descriptions of the commitments were mostly inaccurate or trivial. Our examination of student work and participation in the online environment also showed that while children were excited by QA – in part because of its novelty – the depth of work and discussion, and the types of activities in which they engaged, were often fairly trivial.

Although there were individual learning gains with respect to academic content, we thought that perhaps similar gains could be achieved through didactic instruction; we were more concerned that children evidenced little change with respect to their knowledge, attitudes, and behaviors on the commitments. We also had observed, both through field visits and through an examination of our database, that some classrooms had students with higher quality work than other classrooms. When we interviewed children, we found that many of the classrooms that had the best academic Quests were the ones in which the

OTAK Interface

Toolbars
Menus and buttons to:
• Select avatar
• Control avatar expression
• Change between first and third person viewpoint
• Customize settings

OTAK Symbol
Click spinning object to open a Quest summary in the sidebar

QA Sidebar Pages
Functions such as:
• Info Page
• Quests
• Links
• E-mail

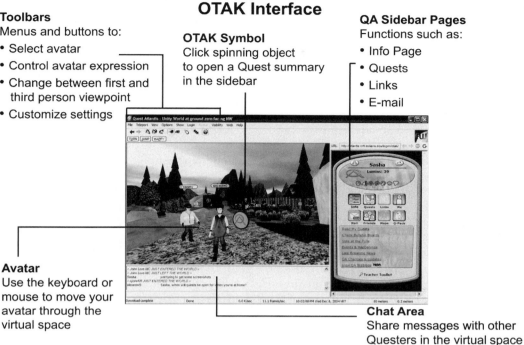

Avatar
Use the keyboard or mouse to move your avatar through the virtual space

Chat Area
Share messages with other Questers in the virtual space

Figure 10.5. Screenshot from QA showing a scene from a village on the left and the Quester homepage on the right.

backstory and the life commitments were emphasized. Although this might have been a result of exceptional teachers, we also hypothesized that connecting the experience to the life commitments might have educational benefits. These concerns were brought up in weekly meetings in which the life commitment data was introduced as a problem and it was suggested that we needed to better highlight all three aspects of the theory – especially the life commitment aspect of the experience. In this way, we debated the nuances of the theory, cycled through project data, and eventually posed new design trajectories. We altered the design so that the experience more directly focused on the life commitments (the underdeveloped element of the theory), so that each engendered experience would have an element of education, entertainment, and life commitment.

While the difference between the first and second design process might seem triv-

ial, it had profound implications both for the design and for the theory-in-action. At one level, rather than a theory about *design*, learning engagement theory became a theory about *experience* with an emphasis on *integration* of the elements at the phenomenological level. This latter shift is similar to the move from multidisciplinary to interdisciplinary or integrated curriculum in that the focus was on integrating all three as opposed to layering one on top of the other (Barab, 1999). Such an integrated perspective has been described in the curriculum literature as having a profound effect on curriculum design and as leading to user experience that is more meaningful than than that of layered curriculum, which leads to multiple compartmentalized experiences (Beane, 1996). In fact, in one study, Barab et al. (2004) compared the work of students completing the Quest tasks to another group of students who did identical tasks, but in the form of a worksheet.

Students completing the task framed as a Quest wrote more, had better quality work, and expressed deeper levels of empathy than children who completed the task as a worksheet – suggesting the educational worth of framing activities in the context of a socially responsive play space.

As part of our DBR process, we also described the different classroom experiences, and tried to develop schematics (e.g., activity theory triangles) for representing the challenges and opportunities that emerged when implementing QA. Specifically, the problem of balancing the tension between fantasy and reality as well as the tension between identification and negotiability continually emerged in different classrooms – the latter being a tension identified by Wenger (1998) that involves balancing the presence of existing structures with which participants can identify, while allowing for participants to have control over the meanings they create, and even over their ability to modify existing structures. With regard to the fantasy and reality tension, we identified many instances in which students and teachers suspended reality and engaged the underlying myth towards useful ends. In this way, they were able to connect the problems in the backstory of Atlantis with similar problems happening here on Earth. This tension allowed students and teachers to explore real-world issues in a playful context, an aspect of play that others have described as potentially transformational in terms of scaffolding individual development (Vygotsky, 1978).

To illustrate the theory more concretely, it is useful to look at one particular designed structure as an example of the design implications from this theoretical work. Figure 10.6 is a screenshot of two interrelated Quest Atlantis pages, the Shardflower page and the Life Commitment page. One of the key features of gaming is the process of leveling, that is, the evolution of one's character and game play over time. One's level indicates a certain level of expertise and creates new possibilities for interaction in the game space. Consistent with our underlying theory, we wanted to make leveling

not only entertaining but also educational, and we wanted it to provide a structure that tied more directly into the life commitments. Given our commitment to ensuring that each designed aspect had all three elements, our design team focused on developing a trajectory that necessarily encompassed each of these elements.

After examining various proposals in terms of their potential to engender an integrated experience, a storyline was developed into the underlying project narrative. Specifically, the story was that two of the mythical Council members had found broken shards on Atlantis that, when combined into a flower, would *luminate* according to the work the person holding it had completed. Each of the seven petals represented one of our life commitments, and we developed pages for each commitment through which students could better develop their own interpretation of the meaning of the commitment. Although multiple stories could have been developed, the important point is that they are theoretically consistent. Luminating, instead of leveling, was now based on students' academic work related to the project commitment. In this way, the designed structure had elements that resonated with learning engagement theory. Interviews with children suggested that their experience of luminating and the Shardflower had an educational component, an entertaining component, and directly related to the seven project commitments.

Additionally, and consistent with the identified tensions of our evolving theory, creating the designed structure involved balancing serious pursuits with fantasy play, and providing a structure that allowed students to have a concept with which to identify while allowing them to negotiate personal meanings – on luminating, children can vote on issues that affect the Council of Atlantis. Finally, and consistent with other findings in the project, classroom experience was very dependent on teacher implementation. Given this appreciation for the significance of the local adaptation, our efforts have involved creating

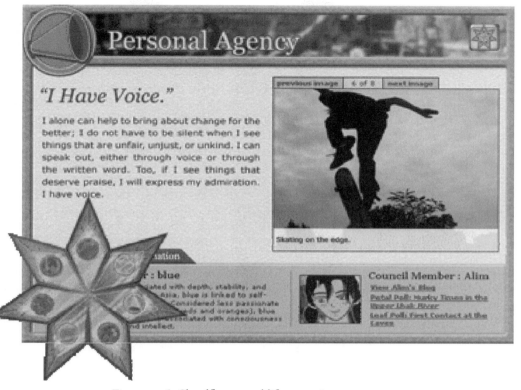

Figure 10.6. Shardflower and life commitment pages.

formal professional development workshops and working with teachers to situate the design in terms of their classroom context. Consistent with the motivations of DBR, as we spent time in classrooms and talking with teachers, we identified struggles and opportunities that were incorporated into our workshops and into our understanding of the challenges of instantiating learning engagement theory into a usable intervention.

As an example of the multiple forms of data used in DBR, we also administered questionnaires to better understand the extent to which our newly designed structure had all three elements. We also asked 153 Questers in fourth and fifth grade to rate a variety of activities in which they participated on a scale of 1 ("none") to 5 ("a whole lot") with respect to learning, playing, and helping. For example, students were asked, "How much is school about learning?"

and "How much is school about playing?" Some activities were rated as higher on one of the three, such as boys scoring videogames higher than school on playing. However, with respect to the composite score across the three dimensions, both genders rated QA (boys M = 3.68, girls M = 3.83) significantly higher than school (boys M = 3.39, girls M = 3.40), video games (boys M = 2.86, girls M = 2.37), and watching TV (boys M = 2.44, girls M = 2.07). These results indicate that children's perceptions of QA activities mirror our intended intersection of education, entertainment, and life commitment. We also conducted interviews with dozens of users to understand which aspects of QA were most engaging, leading to a rich account of the multiple motivations in games, including many motivations not mentioned in the older laboratory-based studies using single-player games.

Conclusions and Discussion

Educational researchers have been effectively using design-based methods to develop powerful technological tools, curricular interventions, and especially theory that can be used to improve the teaching and learning process (Bransford, Brown, & Cocking, 2000; Design-based Research Collective, 2003). Furthermore, in contrast to experimental manipulations, these types of "design experiments" have lent rich insight into the complex dynamics through which theories become contextualized. At the core of this design-based work is the conviction that because these innovations are informed by a particular theoretical perspective, the continual testing and refinement of what works can inform both theory and practice. However, and somewhat ironically, while Brown (1992) and Collins (1992) introduced design experiments as a method for understanding learning and developing theory within naturalistic contexts, the role of the learning scientist as a context manipulator may actually undermine the credibility of the claims being made. Therefore, in addition to the challenge of working in complex situations, learning scientists have the challenge of justifying their claims as usefully informing other contexts of participation even though at some level these researchers are responsible for producing the very claims on which they are reporting.

Critics of such research further argue that any interpretation not generated using an experimental methodology can at best provide formative insights that must then be tested through more controlled experimentation. As such, while learning scientists can present rich accounts of learning as it unfolds in complex contexts, we are going to have a difficult time if one of our goals is to convince policy makers, teachers, and other researchers of the theoretical and practical value of our work (Levin & O'Donnell, 1999). It is our responsibility as a field to address, not dismiss, the concerns of these various parties. If we are going to close the credibility gap between ourselves and policy makers (as well as colleagues arguing for the establishment of scientifically based research), we need to invest ourselves in both changing public opinion with respect to what counts as evidence, and become more sophisticated in our methodological prowess. We have the Herculean task of grounding our theory, supporting the development of an innovation, implementing this in a naturalistic context, collecting and analyzing data in rigorous ways, and reporting all of this in a way that will convince others of the value of our work with respect to local impact, and, at the same time, demonstrate its experience-distant value.

In this chapter, I presented two design-based research projects in order to highlight the notion of theory-in-action as a core focus of this type of work. In the first example, I described how we used our design work to illuminate the limitation in our thinking with respect to a theory about evolving online community. Through our design-based work, we moved from a rather naïve notion of "if we build it, they will come" to a focus on meeting local needs of bounded groups with community being an emergent result. Additionally, we developed other insights around issues of sociability, bounded groups, and trust. Using the second example, I illustrated how we used design-based research to evolve a theoretical framework called learning engagement theory. In the beginning we had a relatively naïve understanding of the theory and what it meant in terms of practice. Over time, as we used the design work to understand the interrelations of theory and context, we evolved our thinking – moving from a theory for design to a theory-in-context about experience.

Both studies involved complex interactions as part of naturalistic contexts that would be difficult, if not impossible, to compartmentalize and implement as part of a tightly controlled experiment. In both cases, this work persisted over multiple years with numerous design iterations and involved working with teachers and aspects of local context that were not directly part of the design. There are multiple avenues for conducting DBR, and it would be impossible to delineate a list of prescriptive steps that all researchers should use regardless of design, theory, or context. However, reflecting on these two projects, some steps that we took that may be of use to others include:

1. *Making assumptions and theoretical bases that underlie the work explicit.* At times, this has meant defining assumptions and theory before the design work and other times these have evolved out of the work. However, as theoretical claims became apparent, we discussed them as a group and wrote them down on paper – even if they were only naïve conjectures.

2. *Collecting multiple types of theoretically relevant data.* In our work this has involved field observations, log file data, interviews, questionnaires, and document analysis. These data were theoretically relevant, helping to inform our evolving theories.

3. *Conducting ongoing data analyses in relation to theory.* For us, this has meant weekly meetings among team members, again positioning the data to support or refute theoretical conjectures, and also determining how we could systematically change the design in theoretically informative ways.

4. *Inviting multiple voices to critique theory and design.* In our work this has involved inviting teachers, students, and even external consultants to critique the design and the resultant theoretical conjectures. We have found that these diverse groups provide different and much needed feedback.

5. *Having multiple accountability structures.* These structures include informal moments like when a student or teacher suggests they do not like a particular design aspect. At other times, this involved more formal meetings with local stakeholders to critique the project, and, at still others, this involved presenting our work at conferences or submitting articles and receiving feedback.

6. *Engaging in dialectic among theory, design, and extant literature.* In our work, we try to participate in conferences and attend related talks, as well as talk with colleagues and stay current on the academic literature as on related developments in commercial ventures.

Our commitment as a field to studying learning within its full contextual splendor is why our work both has the potential to truly change practice and, at the same time, to undermine the acceptance of our claims. It is our responsibility as an emerging community to ensure that we conduct our research, and that we prepare the upcoming generation of learning scientists to conduct their research, in a manner that is methodologically rigorous and that results in theoretically useful claims that others consider informative, convincing, and useful. This will not occur simply through offering richer accounts or employing the methodological toolkit of quantitative researchers, but instead requires that we as a community develop a common language for our own work. We need to convince policy makers and our colleagues that conducting good science involves more than employing experimental methods, but also involves demonstrating and evolving theory-in-context. Such a focus involves using theory to inform real-world practice (through design) at the same time this practice comes to inform theory – the essence of design-based research. Context, rather than being seen as something to be stripped away so as to produce some decontextualized yet ostensibly more generalizable theory, becomes interwoven with the theory in ways that allow others to see the relevance of the theory-in-context with respect to their local situation. Doing this in a manner that convinces others of the value of our work is a core challenge that design-based researchers must engage, especially if we want the learning sciences to be a consequential form of social science.

References

Abbott, A. (1992). What do cases do? Some notes on activity in sociological analysis. In C. C. Ragin & H. S. Becker (Eds.). *What is a case? Exploring the foundation of social inquiry* (pp. 53–82). Cambridge, MA: Cambridge University Press.

Barab, S. A. (1999). Ecologizing instruction through integrated Units. *Middle School Journal, 30,* 21–28.

Barab, S. A., Arici, A., & Jackson, C. (2005). Eat your vegetables and do your homework: A design-based investigation of enjoyment and meaning in learning. *Educational Technology 65*(1), 15–21.

Barab, S., MaKinster, J. G., Moore, J., Cunningham, D., & the ILF Design Team. (2001). Designing and building an online community: The struggle to support sociability in the Inquiry Learning Forum. *Educational Technology Research and Development, 49*(4), 71–96.

Barab, S. A., MaKinster, J., & Scheckler, R. (2003). Designing system dualities: Characterizing a web-supported teacher professional development community. *Information Society 19*(3), 237–256.

Barab, S. A., Schatz, S., & Scheckler, R. (2004). Using Activity Theory to conceptualize online community and using online community to conceptualize Activity Theory. *Mind, Culture, & Activity, 11*(1), 25–47.

Barab, S. A., & Squire, K. (2004). Design-based research: Putting a stake in the ground. *The Journal of the Learning Sciences, 13*(1), 1–14.

Barab, S. A., Thomas, M. Dodge, Carteaux, R., & Tuzun, H. (2005). Making learning fun: Quest Atlantis, a game without guns. *Educational Technology Research and Development 53*(1), 86–107.

Beane, J. (1996). On the shoulders of giants! The case for curriculum integration. *The Middle School Journal, 28,* 6–11.

Bransford, J. D., Brown, A. L., & Cocking, R. R. (Eds). (2000). *How people learn: Brain, mind, experience, and school.* Washington, DC: National Academy Press.

Brown, A. L. (1992). Design experiments: Theoretical and methodological challenges in creating complex interventions in classroom settings. *The Journal of the Learning Sciences, 2*(2), 141–178.

Brown, J. S., Collins, A., & Duguid, P. (1989). Situated cognition and the culture of learning. *Educational Researcher, 18*(1), 32–42.

Cobb, P., Confrey, J., diSessa, A., Lehrer, R., & Schauble, L. (2003). Design experiments in educational research. *Educational Researcher, 32*(1), 9–13.

Collins, A. (1992). Toward a design science of education. In E. Scanlon & T. O'Shea (Eds.), *New directions in educational technology* (pp. 15–22). New York: Springer-Verlag.

Collins, A., Joseph, D., & Bielaczyc, K. (1999). Design research: Theoretical and methodological issues. *The Journal of the Learning Sciences, 13*(1), 15–42.

Collins, A., Joseph, D., & Bielaczyc, K. (2004). Design research: Theoretical and methodological issues. *The Journal of the Learning Sciences, 13*(1), 15–42.

Design-Based Research Collective. (2003). Design-based research: An emerging paradigm for educational inquiry. *Educational Researcher, 32*(1), 5–8.

Dewey, J. (1915). *The school and society.* Chicago: University of Chicago Press.

Dewey, J. (1938). *Logic, the theory of inquiry.* New York: H. Holt and Co.

Gibson, J. J. (1986). *The ecological approach to visual perception.* Hillsdale, NJ: Lawrence Erlbaum Associates.

Kirshner, D., & Whitson, J. A. (Eds.). (1997). *Situated cognition: Social, semiotic, and psychological perspectives.* Mahwah, NJ: Erlbaum.

Lave, J. (1988). *Cognition in practice: Mind, mathematics, and culture in everyday life.* New York: Cambridge.

Lesh, R. A., & Kelly, E. A. (2000). Multitiered teaching experiments. In R. A. Lesh & E. A. Kelly (Eds.), *Handbook of research design in mathematics and science education* (pp. 197–230). Mahwah, NJ: Lawrence Erlbaum.

Levin, J. R., & O'Donnell, A. M. (1999). What to do about educational research's credibility gaps? *Issues in Education, 5*(2), 177–230.

MaKinster, J. G., Barab, S. A., Harwood, W., & Andersen, H. O. (in press). The effect of social context on the reflective practice of preservice science teachers: Incorporating a web-supported community of teachers. *Journal of Technology and Teacher Education.*

Maxwell, J. (2004). Causal explanation, qualitative research, and scientific inquiry in education. *Educational Researcher*, 33(2), 3–11.

Mink, L. O., Fay, B., Golob, E. O., & Vann, R. T. (1987). *Historical understanding*. Ithaca, New York: Cornell University Press.

Salomon, G. (Ed.) (1993). *Distributed cognitions: Psychological and educational considerations*. New York: Cambridge.

Shavelson, R. J., Phillips, D. C., Towne, L., & Feuer M. J. (2003). On the science of education design studies. *Educational Researcher*, 32(1), 25–28.

Shavelson, R. J., & Towne, L. (2002). *Scientific research in education*. Washington DC: National Academy Press.

Stake, R. (1995). *The art of case study research*. Thousand Oaks, CA: Sage.

Stokes, D. E. (1997). *Pasteur's quadrant: Basic science and technological innovation*. Washington, DC: Brookings Institution Press.

Vygotsky, L. (1978). Mind in society: The development of higher psychological processes. Cambridge, MA: Harvard University Press.

Wenger, E. (1998). *Communities of practice: Leaning, meaning, and identity*. Cambridge: Cambridge University Press.

CHAPTER 11

Guiding Inquiry-Based Math Learning

Paul Cobb and Kay McClain

In this chapter, we present a case study of a classroom approach whose development was inspired by learning sciences research. We conducted a sequence of classroom design experiments in urban seventh and eighth grade classrooms (see Barab, this volume, and Confrey, this volume, for discussions of design experiment methodology) focused on teaching and learning statistical data analysis. During this process, we formulated, tested, and revised specific conjectures about both the process of students' learning in the domain of statistics, and ways to scaffold that learning. The primary products of these design experiments were two sequences of instructional activities: one that focused on the analysis of univariate data and one on bivariate data, and three computer-based data analysis tools that were used in both. In this chapter, we restrict our focus to the first of the two classroom design experiments – the one focused on the analysis of univariate data.

We start by critically examining the traditional instructional goals of middle school math. Learning sciences research rejects a conception of knowledge as consisting of facts and procedures to be memorized; unfortunately, this traditional style of instruction still predominates in most mathematics classrooms. As part of this discussion, we briefly summarize recent developments in both the use of statistics in wider society and in statistics as a discipline. We then describe the initial assessments of students' statistical reasoning, and contrast them with the concluding assessments. Following this background, we discuss four aspects of the classroom learning environment that proved critical in supporting the students' learning. These were the instructional tasks, the organization of classroom activities, the tools that students used, and the nature of classroom discourse.

Critically Examining Curriculum

Statistics instruction at the middle school level typically emphasizes the memorization of procedures for calculating measures of the center of a distribution of values (i.e., mean average, mode, and median) together with conventions for drawing particular types of graphs (e.g., bar graphs, histograms, and box plots; examples of each are found in the figures that appear throughout this chapter). As is typical of research in the learning sciences, we did not simply accept the current practices of mathematics classrooms and attempt to devise methods for achieving the associated goals more effectively. Instead, we stepped back to examine a larger question: why should statistics be taught in school at all? Two common justifications are that (1) students need to learn how to work like statisticians, and (2) students need to know statistics because it is important in both everyday and work-related activities. However, we found a third justification to be the most compelling: the increasing use of computers in society has placed an increasing premium on quantitative reasoning in general and on statistical reasoning in particular. This development has significantly influenced how mathematics is used in public policy discourse, so that teaching statistics becomes an issue of democratic participation and power (Cobb & Moore, 1997). Policy decisions are increasingly justified with arguments based on the analysis of data. In many respects, mathematics has become part of the language of power in the public policy arena, with the consequence that inability to understand math results in de facto disenfranchisement. Cast in these terms, it is important for all citizens to be able to develop and critique data-based arguments. For these reasons, students should participate in classroom activities in which they present and critique arguments that they have developed, while analyzing data sets that they view as realistic, for reasons that they consider legitimate (cf. Delpit, 1988; Banks & Banks, 1995). Given these developments, the goal of statistics instruction is to enable participation in a democratic society; this goal gave our instructional design effort a general orientation.

In addition, we took account of developments that have occurred within the discipline of mathematics during the past twenty-five years, fueled primarily by the availability of desktop computers. Most graduate research methods classes continue to use a traditional approach that reduces statistics to statistical inference and teaches it as a set of computational methods. However, these traditional computational methods are increasingly being complemented by the newer methods of *exploratory data analysis (EDA)* that involve searching for patterns in data that give insight into the phenomenon under investigation by creating and manipulating graphical representations (cf. Edelson & Reiser, this volume). By analogy, EDA can be thought of as detective work in that it involves searching for evidence of possible patterns in specific batches of data (Biehler & Steinbring, 1991). Statistics provides tools that assess the viability of this evidence by asking whether similar patterns would be found if another batch of data were collected. In light of these developments with computers and EDA, we followed Cobb and Moore (1997) in concluding that statistics instruction should initially focus on the process of generating viable data and on EDA, and should involve the use of computer-based tools to create and manipulate graphical representations. Students' use of such tools contributes to mathematics learning because their development of increasingly sophisticated ways of reasoning about data is inextricably bound up with their development of increasingly sophisticated ways of representing and organizing data (Edelson & Reiser, this volume; Lehrer & Schauble, this volume; Biehler, 1993; Lehrer & Romberg, 1996).

The final issue that we addressed when preparing for our design experiment was that of identifying the central statistical ideas that should be the primary instructional focus, when students present and critique arguments by analyzing data. We sought to identify what Wiggins and McTighe (1998) term the "big ideas" that are at the heart of the discipline, that have enduring value beyond the classroom, and that offer potential for engaging students. This design principle is particularly important in the case of middle-school statistics instruction, because many textbooks reduce statistics to a collection of at best loosely related concepts (e.g., mean, mode, median) together with conventions for making various types of graphs, and do not teach students the big ideas that they can use to gain insight into consequential real-world phenomena by analyzing data. The most fundamental big idea is that of *distribution* (Cobb, 1999; Hancock, Kaput, & Goldsmith, 1992; Konold et al., 1997; McClain & Cobb, 2001; Wilensky, 1997). The following notions can be viewed as ways of characterizing how specific data sets are distributed (Bakker & Gravemeijer, 2004):

- The location of the center of the data as assessed by the median or mean
- The extent to which the data are spread out or bunched up
- The extent to which the data are skewed towards one end of the range
- The proportion or relative frequency of the data in a particular interval.

In this context, the types of statistical graphs that students are taught are then viewed as identifying relevant patterns that give insight into the phenomenon under investigation.

The resulting vision of classroom statistical activity contrasts sharply with typical instructional approaches. In many cases, learning sciences research finds that existing forms of classroom learning are not consistent with research. In such cases, the design experiment is a valuable methodology because it involves both engineering new learning environments and contributing to our knowledge about the process of students' learning.

Initial Assessments

Our design experiment was carried out in a seventh-grade classroom with twenty-nine twelve-year-old students and involved thirty-four lessons conducted over a ten-week period. Kay McClain served as the teacher throughout the experiment. In preparing for this experiment, we conducted interviews and whole-class performance assessments with a group of seventh graders from the same school in order to docu-ment the competencies that they had developed as a consequence of prior instruction in statistics. These findings documented the consequences of the students' prior instruction. The students had previously studied measures of center (i.e., mean, mode, and median) as well as several types of statistical graphs (e.g., bar graphs, histograms, and pie charts). Our analysis of students' reasoning as situated with respect to prior instruction is characteristic of research in the learning sciences.

These assessments indicated that most of these students thought that data analysis involved "doing something with the numbers" (McGatha, Cobb, & McClain, 2002). In other words, they did not view data as useful in understanding a real-world phenomenon or in making a decision. Rather than meaningfully analyzing data, the students were simply manipulating numbers in a procedural manner, without understanding the meaning or significance of what they were doing. Furthermore, when the students compared two data sets (e.g., the points scored by two basketball players in a series of games), they typically calculated the mean averages per game without considering whether this would enable them to address the question or issue at hand. For example, in the case of the points scored by the two basketball players, simply calculating the means would not necessarily be a good way to select a player for an important game because it ignores possible differences in the range and variability of the players' scores; the player with a slightly lower mean could be much more consistent, and a coach might value consistency over the otherwise mediocre player whose average is raised by a few great games.

These pretests gave us a starting point for our design experiment. For example, we concluded from the assessments that our immediate goal was not merely one of remediating certain competencies and skills. Instead, the challenge was to influence students' views about what it means to do statistics in school and in everyday life. In doing so, it would be essential that they begin to analyze real data with the goal of addressing a meaningful question rather than simply manipulate numbers and draw specific types of graphs as is the case in typical textbook tasks.

Concluding Assessments

The initial assessments contrasted sharply with the ways in which the students analyzed data at the end of the ten-week experiment. As an illustration, in one instructional activity, the students compared two treatment protocols for AIDS by analyzing patients' T-cell counts. Their task was to assess whether a new experimental protocol that forty-six people had enrolled in was more successful in raising T-cell counts than a standard protocol that 186 people had enrolled in. The assignment for the students was to write a report containing recommendations for a chief medical officer, and to prepare arguments to defend their recommendations. The data the students analyzed are shown in Figure 11.1 as they were displayed in the second of two computer-based tools that they used. All twenty-nine students in the class correctly concluded from their analyses that the experimental treatment protocol was more effective. Nonetheless, the subsequent whole-class discussion lasted for over an hour and focused on the adequacy of their reports.

For example, one group of students had partitioned the two data sets at T-cell counts of 525 by drawing a vertical line at 525 using one of the options on the computer tool as shown in Figure 11.1. In the course of the discussion, it became clear that they had observed that what they referred to as the "hill" – the rise in T-cells – in the experimental treatment data was above 525, whereas the "hill" in the standard treatment data was below 525. It was also apparent from the discussion that both they and the other students who contributed to the discussion reasoned about Figure 11.1 in terms of relative frequencies rather than absolute frequencies – they focused on the *proportion* of total patients

above 525, not the absolute number of the patients.

In contrast to peers in traditional mathematics classes, this group's analysis indicated that they had analyzed the data in order to gain insight into the situation under investigation, the relative effectiveness of the two AIDS treatments. Even so, this was one of the most elementary of all of the groups' presentations. A more advanced group of students had used an option on the computer tool that enabled them to hide the dots that represent the individual data values and had then used another option on the tool to partition the two data sets into four groups, each of which contained one-fourth of the data points (see Figure 11.2). In this option, 25 percent of the data in each data set is located in each of the four intervals bounded by the vertical bars (similar to a box plot). As one student explained, these graphs show that the experimental treatment is more effective because the T-cell counts of 75 percent of the patients in this treatment are above 550, whereas the T-cell counts of only 25 percent of the patients who had enrolled in the standard treatment are above 550. This student's argument showed that he was actually reasoning about data rather than attempting to recall procedures or manipulating numerical values, as students in traditional math classes do.

These classroom observations were corroborated by individual interviews that we conducted to document the students' reasoning at the end of the experiment. The analysis of these interviews indicates that a significant majority of the students could readily interpret graphs of two *unequal* data sets organized either into equal interval widths (an analog of histograms) or into four equal groups (an analog of box plots) in terms of patterns in how the data were distributed. Furthermore, when we began a follow-up design experiment with some of the same students nine months later, there was no regression in their statistical reasoning (Cobb, McClain, & Gravemeijer, 2003). In contrast, students in traditional mathematics classes frequently forget procedures that they have memorized for solving narrow

Experimental Treatment

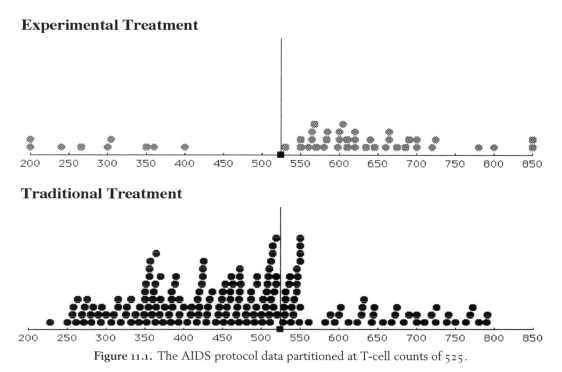

Traditional Treatment

Figure 11.1. The AIDS protocol data partitioned at T-cell counts of 525.

ranges of tasks. At the beginning of this follow-up experiment, *all* students could interpret univariate data sets organized into equal interval widths and into four equal groups in these relatively sophisticated ways within the first three or four class sessions.

This overview gives some indication of how the students' reasoning about data

Experimental Treatment

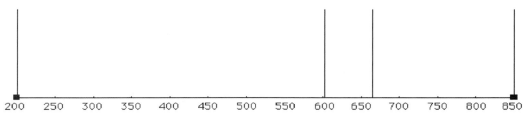

Traditional Treatment

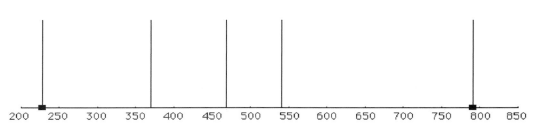

Figure 11.2. The AIDS protocol data organized into four equal groups with the individual data points hidden.

changed during the ten-week experiment. We now turn our attention to the process of that change, focusing in particular on four aspects of the classroom learning environment that proved critical in supporting the students' learning in the context of inquiry. These concern the instructional tasks, the organization of classroom activities, the tools that students used, and the nature of classroom discourse.

Instructional Tasks

In developing instructional tasks, one of our primary goals was to ensure that students' activity in the classroom involved the investigative spirit of the authentic practice of data analysis. In authentic statistical practice, data are always analyzed with particular audiences in mind, unlike traditional math classrooms (cf. Noss, Pozzi, & Hoyles, 1999). Most of the instructional activities that we developed involved comparing two data sets in order to make a decision, as in the AIDS treatment task. For example, students were required to write a report of their analyses for a chief medical officer. This requirement supported the students' engagement in authentic data analysis by orienting them to take account of a specific audience as they explored a phenomenon.

In addition to ensuring that the students' activity was imbued with the investigative spirit of authentic data analysis, we also had to make certain that students learned significant statistical ideas. The challenge for us was therefore to transcend what Dewey (1980) termed the dichotomy between process and content by supporting the emergence of key statistical ideas while simultaneously ensuring that the analyses the students conducted involved authentic practices. This is a critical issue for inquiry-based instructional approaches, because they are sometimes criticized for emphasizing the process of inquiry at the expense of substantive disciplinary ideas.

The data-based arguments that the students produced were used by the teacher to initiate and guide whole-class discussions that focused on significant statistical ideas. Taking the integration of process with content as a basic instructional design principle, our goal was to ensure that the students' reports could be used by the teacher in classroom discussions, enabling the teacher to guide whole-class discussions that taught content to the students. In the case of the AIDS instructional activity, for example, the issues that emerged as explicit topics of conversation during the whole-class discussion included the contrast between absolute and relative frequency, the interpretation of data organized into four equal groups (a precursor of box plots), and the use of percentages to quantify the proportion of the data located in particular intervals (Cobb, 1999; McClain, Cobb, & Gravemeijer, 2000). These issues are significant in statistics; a focus on the rate of occurrence (i.e., the proportion) of data within a range of values (e.g., above or below T-cell counts of 525) is at the heart of what Konold et al., (1997) term a *statistical perspective*. Based on our analyses of classroom discussions – which involved a concern for the proportion of data within various ranges of values – we concluded that students had developed a statistical perspective.

Because we wanted students' analyses to function as a resource for the teacher, we had to carefully plan the activities. We attempted to anticipate the many types of data-based arguments that the students might produce; minor modifications to an instructional activity could significantly influence the types of analyses the students produced. As a result, our discussions of seemingly inconsequential features of task scenarios and of the particular characteristics of data sets were quite lengthy.

For example, we purposely constructed data sets with a different number of total data points when we developed the AIDS task (46 vs. 186), so that the contrast between absolute and relative frequency would have to become explicit. This in turn required a task scenario in which the inequality in the size of the data sets would seem reasonable to the students. Although the AIDS task proved to be productive, on several occasions our conjectures about either the level of the students' engagement in an activity or the types of analyses they would produce turned out to be ill founded. In these situations, our immediate goal was to analyze the classroom session in order to understand why the instructional activity had proven to be inadequate, and then to revise our conjectures and develop a new version of the instructional task. This cyclic process of testing and revising conjectures about the seemingly minor features of instructional activities is the central defining feature of a design experiment. It is particularly critical if the goal is to develop relatively long-term instructional sequences. Such sequences allow knowledgeable teachers to transcend the false dichotomy between emphasizing disciplinary ideas or authentic inquiry practices.

The Organization of Classroom Activities

Our immediate challenge at the beginning of the design experiment was to ensure that the students would view data not merely as numbers, but as measures of a real-world situation that were relevant to a meaningful question. Toward this end, the teacher introduced each instructional activity by talking through the data generation process with the students. These conversations often involved protracted discussions during which the teacher and students together framed the particular phenomenon under investigation (e.g., AIDS), clarified its significance (e.g., the importance of developing more effective treatments), delineated relevant aspects of the situation that should be measured (e.g., T-cell counts), and considered how they might be measured (e.g., taking blood samples). After this contextual discussion, the teacher introduced the data the students were to analyze, and said they had been generated by this process. The resulting organization of classroom activities, which often spanned two or more class sessions, was (1) a whole-class discussion of

the data generation process, (2) an individual or small-group activity in which the students usually worked at computers to analyze data, and (3) a whole-class discussion of the students' analyses.

As a result of participating in discussions of the data generation process, students realized that data sets have a history, and that data are gathered to serve a purpose (cf. Latour, 1987; Lehrer & Romberg, 1996; Roth, 1996). For example, there were clear indications that within a week of the beginning of the design experiment, doing statistics actually meant "analyzing data" for the students (Cobb, 1999; McClain et al., 2000). In addition, as the design experiment progressed, the students increasingly raised concerns about sampling processes, as well as the control of extraneous variables (Cobb & Tzou, 2000). These concerns indicate that they had learned that the legitimacy of the conclusions drawn from data depends crucially on the data generation process. The teacher did not teach the students how to generate sound data directly, in a traditional transmission-and-acquisition approach; instead, she created a classroom culture in which students were encouraged to construct data-based arguments, and as they prepared arguments, they gradually became able to anticipate the implications of the data generation process for the conclusions that they would be able to draw from data.

Much of the literature on teaching statistics is about whether students should collect the data that they analyze. For pragmatic reasons, our students did not collect their own data, but we can readily envision situations in which it would be pedagogically sound for students to actually collect data – such as science projects that provide a context for statistical data analysis (Lehrer, Schauble, & Penner, 2000). However, in many cases a preoccupation with whether students should collect data misses the larger point that data collection is only one phase in the data generation process. The science education literature is filled with cases where students collected their own data but did not understand the fundamental reasons for doing so. Instead of acquiring deeper understanding, they were primarily concerned with following methodological procedures and getting "the right data." These outcomes result from instructional designs that fail to engage students in the phases of the data generation process that *precede* data collection. These preceding phases involve clarifying the significance of the phenomenon under investigation, delineating relevant aspects of the phenomenon that should be measured, and considering how they might be measured. Our findings indicate that it is critical to engage students in these phases whether or not they actually collect data; only then can students develop a sense of purpose that serves to orient their inquiries, and enables them to appreciate the influence of data generation on the legitimacy of the conclusions they can draw.

Tool Use

The use of computer-based tools to create and manipulate graphical representations of data is central to exploratory data analysis (EDA). In our design experiment, students used two computer tools that were designed to support the development of their statistical reasoning. The second of these tools is shown in Figure 11.1, which shows it being used to analyze AIDS treatment data. In the first tool, which was introduced before this one in the first week of the experiment, each data point is inscribed as a separate horizontal bar (see Figure 11.3). Figure 11.3 displays measures of the braking distances of ten cars of two different types that the students analyzed to determine which type was safer. This tool allowed students to sort data sets of up to forty values by size and by color, to isolate the data values in a selected interval, and to partition the data values at selected points by dragging a vertical bar along the horizontal axis.

A design principle that guided the development of both of these computer tools was that they should match students' reasoning at that point in the instructional sequence

(cf. Gravemeijer, 1994). It was apparent from our classroom observations that the tools did fit with the students' reasoning because the students were able to use them to investigate trends and patterns in data after minimal instruction. One of our goals was to teach students how to analyze authentic data rather than merely manipulate numbers. We therefore decided to inscribe each individual data value as a horizontal bar in the first tool, so that the students could visually grasp that the bars each represented stopping distance of a car. We selected data sets that had a sense of linearity and thus lent themselves to this type of inscription (e.g., the braking distances of cars, the life spans of batteries). The choice of this inscription, together with the approach of talking through the data generation process, allowed the teacher to initiate a shift in classroom discourse such that all the students actually began to reason about data as they completed the second instructional activity involving the first tool (Cobb, 1999; McClain et al., 2000).

As an illustration of this shift in classroom discourse, we focus on the discussion of students' analyses of the braking distance task. One group had calculated the mean of each make of car; a second group had compared the two makes in terms of their relative consistency in stopping distance. The teacher asked the first group and then the second group to explain their approaches. The teacher's intent in juxtaposing these two methods was to highlight the contrast between a purely calculational solution and one in which numerical values had been viewed as measures of braking distances (McClain & Cobb, 2001). The analysis that the second group presented called into question whether the mean average was in fact a useful way to compare the relative safety of the two types of cars. The second group had compared the data sets in terms of their relative consistency by using an option on the tool that enabled them to isolate the data points in selected intervals (the vertical bars in Figure 11.3). In doing so, they had concluded that the sedan was the safer type of car (because all of them stopped in under 68.9 feet, whereas three of the coupes took

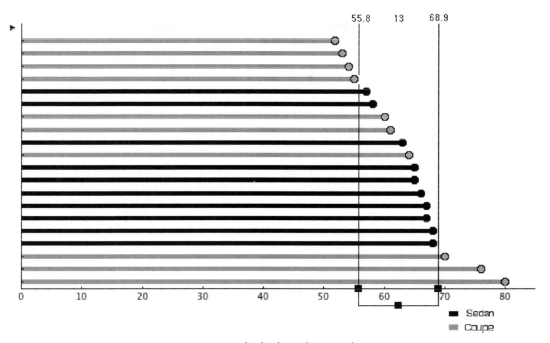

Figure 11.3. The braking distance data.

longer than that) whereas the group that had focused on the mean average had recommended the coupe.

Wes: I got something else. See, the [sedan] is more consistent on stopping. See, they got like right here a range (points to endpoints of range of sedan data), it's more consistent of stopping.
Teacher: That's a very good point.
Wes: But the [coupe], it stops on different ones.
Teacher: So, you are saying that the [sedan] is more consistent.
Wes: And then, but with the [coupe] if you bought the car and it happened and you're going and this happened to you, you couldn't rely on it to stop by a certain point but with the [sedan] it's pretty much within a range where it will stop.
Sharon: I don't get it.
Wes: Okay, if you bought the [sedan] car and had to stop all of a sudden, you could rely on it to stop between about 53 feet and 72 feet and that would be better. But with the [coupe], see, it has all these different places where it stopped so you don't know if it's

gonna stop short or you're gonna crash into whatever it is, so you wouldn't rely on the distance it takes to stop.
Dan: What is consistent?
Rob: It does the same thing every time or close to it.
Teacher: That's a really nice argument that Wes is making. He thinks it's kinda important if you own a car to know that if you have to stop it's gonna stop within this (points to range of sedan)...that the car, it's gonna stop within this range but this car (points to the coupe data) could stop anywhere.

The issue of whether the mean average is useful in this particular case became an explicit topic of conversation when several students then said that they had not previously considered comparing the data sets in terms of their relative spread, but now they found Wes's argument convincing. It was in the course of such exchanges that the teacher guided the renegotiation of what it meant to analyze data. After the discussion of this and a follow-up, there were no instances of a student completing a subsequent instructional task by reasoning about data merely as numerical values rather than measures of real-world phenomena.

A second design principle that guided the development of the two computer tools was that the students should come to reason about data in increasingly sophisticated ways as they used the tools and participated in the subsequent whole-class discussions of their analyses. We viewed the design of the tools as a primary means of supporting the reorganization of their statistical reasoning (cf. Dörfler, 1993; Kaput, 1994; Meira, 1998; Pea, 1993). In the case of the first tool, the inscription of data values as horizontal bars and the options for organizing data oriented the students toward comparing collections of data values in terms of how they are distributed. For example, the students dragged the vertical value bar along the axis to either partition data sets or find the value of specific data points. In addition, they used another option on the tool to isolate a particular interval and compare the number of data points of each data set that were in that interval (see Figure 11.3). It was as the students used the computer tool in these ways that they began to reason about (a) the maximum and minimum values and the range of data sets (b) the number of data points above or below a particular value or within a specified interval, and (c) the median and its relation to the mean. Against the background of these developments, the teacher introduced the second tool in which data points were inscribed as dots in an axis plot (see Figure 11.1).

Our intention in designing the second tool was to build on the ways of reasoning about data that the students had developed as they used the first tool. As can be seen by comparing Figures 11.1 and 11.3, the dots at the end of the bars in the first tool have, in effect, been collapsed down onto the horizontal axis in the second tool. The teacher in fact introduced this new way of inscribing data first by showing a data set inscribed as horizontal bars, and then by removing the bars to leave only the dots, and finally by sliding the dots down onto the horizontal axis. As we had conjectured, the students

were able to use the second tool to analyze data with little additional guidance, and it was apparent that the dot plot inscription signified a set of data values rather than merely a collection of dots scattered along a line. However, this development cannot be explained solely by the teacher's careful introduction of the new tool. Instead, we also have to take account of an aspect of the students' activity as they used the first tool in order to explain why the second tool fit with their new level of reasoning.

We can tease out this new aspect of the students' learning by focusing on their reasoning as they used the first tool to organize and compare data sets. As we have seen, one student explained that he had analyzed the braking distance data by isolating an interval in which the data for the ten sedans were located and argued that this type of car was safer because the braking distances were more consistent than those for the ten coupes. The crucial point to note is that in making an argument of this type, the students focused on the location of the dots at the end of the bars with respect to the horizontal axis. In other words, a subtle but important shift occurred as the students used the first tool. Originally, the individual data values were represented by the lengths of the bars. However, in the very process of using the tool, these values came to be signified by the endpoints of the bars – helping students to understand that dots on a graph actually represent measures of real-world phenomena.

As a result of this development, when they were presented with the second tool, they could readily understand the teacher's explanation of collapsing the dots at the end of the bars down onto the axis. Furthermore, the options in this new tool all involved partitioning sets of up to four hundred data values in various ways (e.g., dragging vertical bars along the axis in order to partition the data set into groups of points, partitioning the data into groups with a specified interval width, partitioning the data into four equal groups). As a consequence, the students could use the second tool immediately because they had routinely partitioned data sets when they used the first tool. As our

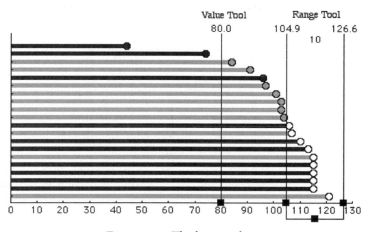

Figure 11.4. The battery data.

discussion of the AIDS treatment task illustrates, students came to view data sets as holistic distributions that have shape rather than as amorphous collections of individual data points, to reason about these shapes in terms of relative rather than absolute frequencies, and to structure data sets in increasingly sophisticated ways.

Software designers should consider how students' use of a proposed tool will change the nature of their activity, and the types of reasoning that they might develop, as they use it. In designing the two tools, we did not attempt to build the statistical ideas that we wanted students to learn into the two computer tools and then hope that they might come to see them in some mysterious and unexplained way. Instead, we focused squarely on how the students might actually use the tools and what they might learn as they did so. This approach to software design is quite general, but takes on particular importance with statistical data analysis because computer-based analysis is so central to authentic mathematical practice.

Classroom Discourse

Classroom discourse is an important activity for supporting students' learning. We have emphasized that whole-class discussions should focus on significant statistical ideas that advance the teachers' instruc-

tional agenda. In this section, we clarify the importance of the whole-class discussions by first considering the establishment of norms that are integral to productive classroom discourse, and then returning to our goal of ensuring that significant statistical ideas emerge as topics of conversation.

The establishment of productive classroom norms is as important in supporting students' learning as the use of appropriate tools, the careful planning of instructional activities, and the skills of the teacher in guiding whole-class discussions. One key classroom norm is what counts as an acceptable data-based argument. The students found Wes's argument about the braking distances of the two types of cars convincing because he explained how the relatively small range of the data for the ten sedan cars revealed an attribute of these cars that was relevant to deciding which type of car to buy, namely, that they were more consistent. In contrast, the students who had compared the two types of cars in terms of the means had not considered whether the mean actually helped them to assess the safety of the two types of cars. The importance of explaining why a particular pattern in the data gives insight into the issue under investigation became more explicit during the discussion of the next task, in which the students analyzed data on the life spans of ten batteries of two different brands (Figure 11.4).

The first student who explained her reasoning said that she had focused on the ten highest data values (i.e., those bounded as shown in Figure 11.4). She went on to note that seven of the ten longest lasting batteries were of one brand and concluded that this brand was better. However, during the ensuing discussion, it became apparent that her decision to focus on the ten rather than, say, the fourteen longest lasting batteries was relatively arbitrary. In contrast, the next student who presented an analysis explained that he had partitioned the data at eighty hours because he wanted a consistent battery that lasted at least eighty hours. In doing so, he clarified why his approach to organizing the data was relevant to the question at hand, that of deciding which of the two brands was superior. The obligation that the students should give a justification for their chosen method of analysis became increasingly explicit as classroom discussion continued. For example, a third student compared the two analyses by commenting that although seven of the ten longest lasting batteries were of one brand, the two lowest batteries were also of this brand, and "if you were using the batteries for something important, you could end up with one of those bad batteries."

In the course of exchanges like these, the teacher and students established relatively early in the design experiment that to be acceptable, an argument had to justify why the method of organizing the data was relevant to the question under investigation. The establishment of this norm of argumentation was critical in supporting the students' learning. On the one hand, it served to delegitimize analyses in which students simply produced a collection of statistics (e.g., mean, median, range) without considering whether they were relevant to the issue under investigation. On the other hand, it served as a means of inducting students into an important mathematical norm: that the appropriateness of the statistics used when conducting an analysis has to be justified with respect to the question being addressed.

It is challenging to ensure that classroom discussions focus on significant statistical ideas. To demonstrate these challenges, we summarize the approach the teacher took when planning for the whole-class discussions. In the latter part of the design experiment, we organized instructional activities so that the students conducted their analyses and wrote their reports in one class session, and then the teacher conducted the whole-class discussion with them in the following class session. The teacher found this arrangement productive because she could review the students' reports before the whole-class discussion to gain a sense of the various ways in which students had reasoned about the data. This in turn enabled her to develop conjectures about statistically important issues that might emerge as topics of conversation. Her intent in planning for discussions in this way was to capitalize on the students' reasoning by identifying data analyses that, when compared and contrasted, might give rise to substantive statistical conversations (McClain, 2002). In the case of the AIDS treatment data, for example, the teacher selected a sequence of four analyses for discussion, so that the issues of reasoning proportionally about data and of interpreting data organized into four equal groups would emerge from the discussion.

Our purpose in describing this planning process is to emphasize that although the design of instructional activities and tools is important, the expertise of a knowledgeable teacher in guiding productive discussions is also critical. Earlier in this chapter, we noted that the challenge of transcending the dichotomy between process and content is especially pressing in the case of statistical data analysis, given that an investigative orientation is integral to authentic practice in math. The importance that we attribute to the teacher contrasts sharply with approaches to design that attempt to make curricula teacher-proof. We in fact find it useful to view the teacher as a co-designer who is responsible for organizing substantive classroom discussions that can serve as primary means of supporting students' induction into the values, beliefs, and ways of knowing of the discipline. Consequently, when we develop instructional activities and tools, we always take account of the mediating role of the teacher. The approach we take to instructional design extends beyond the traditional focus on curriculum while simultaneously acknowledging the vital, mediating role of the teacher. The challenge is then to design tools that help the teacher organize productive learning experiences for students.

Discussion

In this chapter, we have presented a case study of inquiry-based math learning that is based on learning sciences theory and methodology. We discussed four aspects of the classroom learning environment that are highly interrelated in what we call a *classroom activity system*:

- The overall goal for doing statistics (i.e., to identify patterns in data that are relevant to the question or issue at hand).
- The structure of classroom activities (e.g., talking through the data generation process).
- The computer tools that the students used to conduct their analyses.
- The nature of the of the classroom discourse (e.g., engaging in discussion in which mathematically significant issues emerged as topics of conversation).

Our approach used the methodology of the design experiment (Barab, this volume; Confrey, this volume). More generally, our approach is based on the learning sciences approach summarized by Bransford, Brown, and Cocking (2000); they proposed a framework that consists of four overlapping lenses for examining learning environments.

The first of these lenses focuses on the extent to which learning environments are *knowledge centered* in the sense of being based on a careful analysis of what we want people to know and be able to do as a result of instruction. In this regard, we discussed the importance of organizing instruction around big statistical ideas like distribution; of ensuring that classroom discussions focus on significant statistical ideas; and of designing tools as a means of supporting the development of students' statistical reasoning.

The second lens is *learner centered* and examines the extent to which a learning environment builds on the strengths, interests, and preconceptions of learners. We illustrated this focus when we discussed the initial data generation discussions and the importance of cultivating students' interests in the issue under investigation; the approach of designing tools that fit with students' current statistical reasoning; and the process of planning whole-class discussions by building on students' analyses.

The third lens is *assessment centered* and examines the extent to which students' thinking is made visible, so that teachers can adjust instruction to their students' reasoning, and students have multiple opportunities to test and revise their ideas. This lens was evident when we discussed the value of whole-class discussions in which students shared their analyses and received feedback, and when we indicated how the reports the students wrote enabled the teacher to assess their statistical reasoning.

The final lens is *community centered* and examines the extent to which the classroom is an environment in which students not only feel safe asking questions but also can learn to work collaboratively. Our discussion of three instructional activities – AIDS, braking distance, and batteries – served to illustrate these general features of the classroom, and we also stressed the importance of the discipline specific norm of what counts as an acceptable data-based argument.

Thus, our approach to inquiry-based design is based on broad learning sciences themes. We believe that designers of learning environments should view classrooms as complex activity systems that are designed to support students' learning of significant mathematical ideas. The approach we have described is relatively broad in scope; approaches that consider only the design of instructional tasks or of the associated tools are overly narrow in comparison, and may fail because they do not address the entire classroom activity system.

Acknowledgments

The analysis presented in this paper was supported by the National Science Foundation under grant numbers REC 0231037. The opinions expressed in this paper do not necessarily reflect the position, policy, or endorsement of the Foundation.

References

Bakker, A., & Gravemeijer, K. (2004). Learning to reason about distribution. In D. Ben-Zvi & J. Garfield (Eds.), *The challenge of developing statistical literacy, reasoning, and thinking* (pp. 147–168). Dordrecht, Netherlands: Kluwer.

Banks, C., & Banks, J. (1995). Equity pedagogy: An essential component of multicultural education. *Theory into Practice, 34*, 152–158.

Biehler, R. (1993). Software tools and mathematics education: The case of statistics. In C. Keitel & K. Ruthven (Eds.), *Learning from computers: Mathematics education and technology* (pp. 68–100). Berlin: Springer.

Biehler, R., & Steinbring, H. (1991). Entdeckende statistik, stenget-und Blatter, Boxplots: Konzepte, Begrundungen and Enfahrungen eines Unterrichtsversuch es [Explorations in statistics, stem-and-leaf, boxplots: Concepts, justifications, and experience in a teaching experiment]. *Der Mathematikunterricht, 37*(6), 5–32.

Bransford, J. D., Brown, A. L., & Cocking, R. R. (Eds.). (2000). *How people learn: Brain, mind, experience, and school.* Washington, DC: National Academy Press.

Cobb, G. W., & Moore, D. S. (1997). Mathematics, statistics, and teaching. *American Mathematical Monthly, 104*, 801–823.

Cobb, P. (1999). Individual and collective mathematical learning: The case of statistical data analysis. *Mathematical Thinking and Learning, 1*, 5–44.

Cobb, P., McClain, K., & Gravemeijer, K. (2003). Learning about statistical covariation. *Cognition and Instruction, 21*, 1–78.

Cobb, P., & Tzou, C. (2000, April). *Learning about data creation.* Paper presented at the annual meeting of the American Educational Research Association, New Orleans.

Delpit, L. D. (1988). The silenced dialogue: Power and pedagogy in educating other people's children. *Harvard Educational Review, 58*, 280–298.

Dewey, J. (1980). Democracy and education. In J. A. Boydston (Ed.), *John Dewey: The middle works, 1899 –1924, Vol. 9* (pp. 1–370). Carbondale, IL: Southern Illinois University Press.

Dörfler, W. (1993). Computer use and views of the mind. In C. Keitel & K. Ruthven (Eds.), *Learning from computers: Mathematics education and technology* (pp. 159–186). Berlin: Springer-Verlag.

Gravemeijer, K. (1994). *Developing realistic mathematics education.* Utrecht, The Netherlands: CD-ß Press.

Hancock, C., Kaput, J. J., & Goldsmith, L. T. (1992). Authentic inquiry with data: Critical barriers to classroom implementation. *Educational Psychologist, 27*, 337–364.

Kaput, J. J. (1994). The representational roles of technology in connecting mathematics with authentic experience. In R. Biehler, R. V. Scholz, R. Strasser, & B. Winkelmann (Eds.), *Didactics of mathematics as a scientific discipline* (pp. 379–397). Dordrecht, Netherlands: Kluwer.

Konold, C., Pollatsek, A., Well, A., & Gagnon, A. (1997). Students' analyzing data: Research of critical barriers. In J. B. Garfield & G. Burrill (Eds.), *Research on the role of technology in teaching and learning statistics: Proceedings of the 1996 International Association for Statistics Education Roundtable Conference* (pp. 151–167). Voorburg, The Netherlands: International Statistics Institute.

Latour, B. (1987). *Science in action.* Cambridge, MA: Harvard University Press.

Lehrer, R., & Romberg, T. (1996). Exploring children's data modeling. *Cognition and Instruction, 14*, 69–108.

Lehrer, R., Schauble, L., & Penner, D. (2000). The inter-related development of inscriptions and conceptual understanding. In P. Cobb, E. Yackel, & K. McClain (Eds.), *Symbolizing, mathematizing, and communicating: Perspectives on discourse, tools, and instructional design* (pp. 325–360). Mahwah, NJ: Lawrence Erlbaum Associates.

McClain, K. (2002). Teacher's and students' understanding: The role of tool use in communication. *Journal of the Learning Sciences, 11*, 217–249.

McClain, K., & Cobb, P. (2001). Supporting students' ability to reason about data. *Educational Studies in Mathematics, 45*, 103–129.

McClain, K., Cobb, P., & Gravemeijer, K. (2000). Supporting students' ways of reasoning about data. In M. Burke (Ed.), *Learning mathematics for a new century (2001 Yearbook of the National Council of Teachers of Mathematics)* (pp. 174–187). Reston, VA: National Council of Teachers of Mathematics.

McGatha, M., Cobb, P., & McClain, K. (2002). An analysis of students' initial statistical understandings: Developing a conjectured learning trajectory. *Journal of Mathematical Behavior, 16*, 339–355.

Meira, L. (1998). Making sense of instructional devices: The emergence of transparency in mathematical activity. *Journal for Research in Mathematics Education, 29*, 121–142.

Noss, R., Pozzi, S., & Hoyles, C. (1999). Touching epistemologies: Statistics in practice. *Educational Studies in Mathematics, 40*, 25–51.

Pea, R. D. (1993). Practices of distributed intelligence and designs for education. In G. Salomon (Ed.), *Distributed cognitions* (pp. 47–87). New York: Cambridge University Press.

Roth, W. M. (1996). Where is the context in contextual word problems? Mathematical practices and products in grade 8 students' answers to story problems. *Cognition and Instruction, 14*, 487–527.

Wiggins, G., & McTighe, J. (1998). *Understanding by design*. Washington, DC: Association for Curriculum and Supervision.

Wilensky, U. (1997). What is normal anyway? Therapy for epistemological anxiety. *Educational Studies in Mathematics, 33*, 171–202.

CHAPTER 12

Analyzing Collaborative Discourse

R. Keith Sawyer

In traditional instruction, the teacher provides information to students, either through lectures or assigned readings. This information typically consists of single-sentence statements of fact, and step-by-step procedures for solving specific kinds of problems. Students are expected to memorize the information and then demonstrate that they've memorized it by doing well on a test – either by restating the facts correctly, or by applying the memorized procedure to solve a problem. This is known as a *transmission and acquisition* style of teaching and learning. In contrast, learning sciences research emphasizes a new style of learning – one in which the teacher works with students in a community of learners, providing appropriate scaffolds to student project groups as they build knowledge together. In a classroom based on the scientific principles emerging from the learning sciences, students often talk to each other as they construct knowledge together. The teacher is always present but is not dominating the discussion; the teacher often facilitates or channels the discussion, but if students are working together effectively an experienced

teacher may realize that the best thing to do is to stay silent.

In emphasizing peer collaboration, the learning sciences is drawing on over twenty years of educational research that has consistently demonstrated that collaboration helps students learn (e.g., Bossert, 1988–1989; Johnson & Johnson, 1992; Kumpulainen & Mutanen, 2000; Slavin, 1990, 1992; Webb & Palincsar, 1996). For example, peer teaching has been shown to provide enhanced learning to both the peer teacher and to the student (Bargh & Schul, 1980; Fuchs et al., 1997; Palincsar, Brown, & Campione, 1993), and cooperative classroom groups result in greater learning than competitive or individualistically structured learning environments (Johnson & Johnson, 1974, 1979, 1989). Collaboration in structured, in-class formats has been shown to increase student's knowledge in a wide range of subjects, including biology (Lazarowitz & Karsenty, 1990), mathematics (Fuchs et al., 1997; Webb, 1991), composing narratives (Daiute & Dalton, 1993), and computer programming (Webb, Ender, & Lewis, 1986). These accumulated research findings have had a significant influence on educational practice; practicing teachers believe that collaborating groups provide a uniquely effective learning environment (Antil, Jenkins, Wayne, & Vadasy, 1998), and both large-scale assessment programs and small-scale in-class assessments increasingly use collaborative group work (Webb, 1995; Webb et al., 1998). The National Research Council's *National Science Education Standards* (1996) and the National Council of Teachers of Mathematics' *Professional Standards for Teaching Mathematics* (1991) both advocate negotiation and collaboration in inquiry.

Greeno (this volume) argues that the learning sciences combine two traditions in the study of learning: the cognitive tradition and the interactional tradition. Researchers in the cognitive tradition typically use experimental methodologies, taking individual learners into laboratories so that all variables can be controlled except for the independent and dependent variables of interest. However, it is rarely possible to study interaction by using an experimental methodology, because when a group of learners is allowed to work together on a task, it becomes almost impossible to control for all of the many variables that are relevant to the interaction, even if the group is brought into a laboratory and given a carefully specified and limited task to talk about. And in any case, most interaction researchers believe that it's important to study interaction as it occurs in real-world settings: this is referred to as *naturally occurring conversation*. A group of students in a laboratory, working on an artificial task, may talk very differently than they would in a classroom.

As a result of these concerns, the interactional tradition has developed non-experimental methodologies to study conversation. These methodologies originated in the 1960s and have been continually refined since then. These methodologies, which I refer to collectively as *interaction analysis*, are designed to analyze naturally occurring conversation; in classrooms, naturally occurring conversation is the talk of students as they engage in their normal classroom activities. These methodologies have

been central in the learning sciences since the early 1990s; several articles describing methodologies to analyze learning interactions have been widely influential among learning scientists (including Chi, 1997; Jordan & Henderson, 1995; Lemke, 1998).

Many of the projects throughout this handbook describe learning environments that tap into the power of group collaboration. Learning scientists typically analyze real classrooms engaged in everyday learning activities, and in many studies they use interaction analysis. In this chapter, I describe the methodologies of interaction analysis that are used to closely examine how collaborative conversation contributes to learning.

Collaborative Conversation

The scientific study of conversation began in the 1960s, when researchers first gained access to film equipment. The first group of scholars to study everyday conversation became known as *conversation analysts*. Conversation analysts focused extremely closely on the microsecond dynamics of conversation that most people remain unaware of, and they created new methods of transcription to capture what words on the page cannot – pauses in speech, sighs, interruptions, and overlapping speech – as in this transcript of the beginning of a phone conversation, prepared by Emanual Schegloff:

Example 12.1. Initial dialogue of a phone conversation (from Schegloff, 1986, p. 114)[1]

1		(phone rings)
2	Nancy	H'llo:?
3	Hyla	Hi:,
4	Nancy	^Hi::.
5	Hyla	Hwaryuhh =
6	Nancy	= Fi:ne how'r you,
7	Hyla	Okay: [y
8	Nancy	[Goo:d,
9		(4 second pause)
10	Hyla	'mkhhh [hhh
11	Nancy	[What's doin,

We can all recognize this as an extremely ordinary conversation, but even though it's familiar, the transcript reveals many aspects that we all take for granted. For example, in line (3), Hyla does not introduce herself but simply says "Hi." The colon after the "i" indicates an elongated vowel – she draws out the "i" sound. Nancy's line (4) indicates that she recognizes Hyla's voice: she starts with a sharply higher pitch, indicated by the caret "^", her volume is louder, indicated by the underlining, and she elongates her "i" vowel even longer than Hyla did. In the remainder of the segment, the overlapping speech (indicated by the square brackets), the long pause, and the elongated vowels all symbolize a high degree of intimacy between these speakers. If we heard the tape of the conversation we would all "know" this at some subconscious level, but only with a detailed conversation analysis can we delve into the microsecond interactional features through which these understandings are possible.

When conversation analysts studied conversation in a wide range of contexts and cultures, they discovered that these implicit understandings don't apply everywhere. You can only understand the hidden meanings in this phone conversation if you share the middle-class European-American culture of the speakers. And these speakers, like all speakers, are quite capable of talking differently in other less intimate contexts; for example, on the phone with their boss or an IRS official. Part of what we share as "culture" is these implicit understandings of how relationships are constituted and maintained through distinctive interactional patterns. Through the 1960s and 1970s, the conversation analysts made major strides toward understanding everyday socially situated interaction.

Almost from the beginning of conversation analysis, researchers have applied these analytic methods to classrooms. The first study to tape and transcribe classroom discourse was reported in the 1966 book *The Language of the Classroom* (Bellack et al., 1966). They established a methodology that is still used today: they began by segmenting classroom discourse into interactional turns, or what they called "moves" by analogy with a board game. They then identified the speaker of each turn. And in the most important methodological step, they developed a system to categorize the interactional function of each move. After doing this, they looked for *teaching cycles*: routine sequences of moves that occurred frequently. They discovered that the most common teaching cycle, 48 percent of all cycles identified, was:

1. Soliciting move by teacher in the form of a question

2. Responding move by the student addressed

3. An optional evaluative reaction by teacher

Interaction analysts usually refer to this kind of repeating sequence as an *interactional routine*. Interactional routines have a loose structure that is understood by participants who share a culture, and they all know how to participate in the routine to bring it off smoothly. For example, the first few turns of a phone conversation (Example 12.1) are a routine. Interaction analysts have also discovered that almost all routines allow for variation; although they specify the basic flow of interaction, there are often branching possibilities and flexible spaces for improvisational action. There are many different ways that the beginning of a phone conversation could play out, depending on the relationship between the speakers and the goal of the phone call; these all represent variations on the same basic routine.

The methodology used by Bellack et al. in 1966 – segmenting conversation into turns, and then applying analytic codes to each turn – is subtly but importantly different from conversation analysis, because it does not involve detailed microsecond transcriptions, and overlapping speech is typically ignored. As a result of these differences, most scholars reserve the term "conversation analysis" for studies that use detailed transcription methods, and close qualitative analysis of single episodes of conversation (as in the Sawyer and Berson study described later). I use the term *interaction analysis* to refer broadly to all methodologies used to study verbal and nonverbal interaction, including the detailed methods of conversation analysis, the coding techniques of Bellack et al., and many others.

Interaction analytic methods were used in a series of important studies of classroom discourse in the 1970s. Sinclair and Coulthard (1975) studied the same routines as Bellack et al., but they extended the analysis by developing a more complex system of move types. Mehan (1979), who called this routine IRE – for Initiation, Response, Evaluation – analyzed the ways that teachers and students improvise variations on the basic format of the routine, and the ways that these routines connect together to form an overall one-hour lesson.

By the 1980s, conversation researchers had a good understanding of traditional classroom discourse. They had ample documentation of exactly how the transmission-and-acquisition style of teaching was realized in the classroom. Just at this time, the learning sciences were demonstrating that transmission-and-acquisition styles of teaching like the IRE routine were not the most effective for learning. For example, IRE was directly opposed to constructivism, because children were not given the opportunity to actively construct their own knowledge. IRE was nothing like the forms of discourse used by professionals and scientists as they engaged in inquiry and project research (Krajcik & Blumenfeld, this volume). IRE was nothing like the forms of situated discourse that occur in real-world apprenticeship settings (Collins, this volume). A classroom dominated by IRE is not a community of practice; it's a hierarchy dominated by the teacher.

As a result of findings emerging from the learning sciences, classrooms began to change their structure away from the transmission and acquisition model in which the teacher lectured or controlled the flow of discussion through IRE sequences. Studies of situativity and collaborative knowledge building convinced many teachers to have their students work together in groups, jointly engaged in a project, actively con-

structing their knowledge together (Greeno, this volume; Krajcik & Blumenfeld, this volume; Scardamalia & Bereiter, this volume). As a result, the types of conversation that occurred in these classrooms were very different from traditional discourse patterns like IRE. Much of the conversation occurred between classmates as they worked in collaborative groups. And even when teachers participated in the discussion, they did not dominate, but instead facilitated the students' own discussion.

In explaining how collaboration benefits learning, researchers from a wide range of theoretical perspectives have hypothesized that conversation mediates between the group and individual learning (Fisher, 1993; Johnson & Johnson, 1992; Kumpulainen & Mutanen, 2000; Mercer, 1996; Webb, 1991, 1995; Webb & Palincsar, 1996). Conversation is the place where group knowledge building translates into individual cognitive advancement. A key feature of the learning sciences is that it attempts to better understand how both cognitive development and interaction work together in learning environments (Greeno, this volume). To better understand how individual learning and group knowledge building work together in a learning sciences classroom, we need to apply the methods of interaction analysis to classroom discourse.

In the 1980s, education researchers began to use interaction analysis to study collaborative learning. Researchers that study collaborative learning have focused on three aspects of conversation that could contribute to learning. First, providing and receiving explanations are both thought to contribute to children's learning (Bargh & Schul, 1980; Fuchs et al., 1997; Swing & Peterson, 1982; Vedder, 1985; Webb, 1984, 1991, 1992). Second, researchers working within a sociocognitive framework have emphasized the mediating role played by conflict and controversy (Bearison, Magzamen, & Filardo, 1986; Doise & Mugny, 1984; Perret-Clermont, 1980; also see Andriessen, this volume). Third, researchers working within a Vygotskian or sociocultural framework have emphasized how participants build on each other's ideas to jointly construct a new understanding that none of the participants had prior to the encounter (Forman, 1992; Forman & Cazden, 1985; Palincsar, 1998).

Of these three, the sociocultural tradition has focused the most closely on conversation (Durán & Szymanski, 1995; Forman, 1992; Gee & Green, 1998; Hicks, 1995; Palincsar, 1998; Wells & Chang-Wells, 1992). Much of this research has combined Piaget's emphasis on cognitive conflict with Vygotsky's emphasis on social interaction, to develop a view that knowledge is co-constructed in social settings (Kelly, Crawford, & Green, 2001; Musatti, 1993; Tudge & Rogoff, 1989; Verba, 1994), and that meanings are socially constructed through discursive interaction (Wells & Chang-Wells, 1992). An emphasis on the processes of group interaction, rather than educational outcomes, has been a defining feature of the sociocultural tradition.

These three traditions have reached a consensus that conversational interaction is the mediating mechanism whereby collaboration contributes to learning. This is why learning scientists have increasingly studied the discourse processes of collaboration – the turn-by-turn interaction patterns that occur among students in a group. Drawing on sociocultural theory, many learning sciences researchers argue that knowledge is first collective and external – manifest in conversation – and then becomes internalized (Scardamalia & Bereiter, this volume).

Recent studies have examined the discourse processes of collaboration in science (van Boxtel, Linden, & Kanselaar, 2000; Finkel, 1996; Green & Kelly, 1997; Kelly & Crawford, 1997; Kelly, Crawford, & Green, 2001; Klaasen & Lijnse, 1996), math (Cobb, 1995; Cobb et al., 1997; Saxe & Bermudez, 1996; Sfard & Kieran, 2001; Sfard & McClain, 2002), and literacy education (Nystrand et al., 1997). Many education researchers have noted that collaborative discourse results in the emergence of new insights and representations, and that once these interactive social constructions have emerged, they both constrain and enable the ongoing collaboration (Cobb et al., 1997; Sawyer, 2001, 2003). In this "emergent perspective" (Cobb et al., 1997; Saxe & Bermudez, 1996), a complete understanding of educational collaboration requires a focus on both individual development and on social change over time (Saxe & Bermudez, 1996). In group discussion, both the overall group dynamic and each individual's learning collaboratively emerges from the group's conversation.

It is difficult to fully explain collaborative conversation by focusing on individual thought and action in isolation from the entire discursive context (Sawyer, 2003). This is why experimental methods are not used by interaction analysts. Many learning sciences researchers focus on discourse and communication as externally visible distributed emergent knowledge, in addition to what goes on in participants' heads (cf. Greeno, this volume; Kelly, Crawford, & Green, 2001, p. 268; Middleton & Edwards, 1990, p. 23; Sfard, 2002). Interaction analytic methods correspond to the learning sciences observation that knowledge and learning are often properties of groups, not only individuals (Hutchins, 1995; Rogoff, 1998).

Three Examples of Interaction Analysis

In the rest of this chapter, I provide detailed summaries of three different approaches to interaction analysis that have been taken by learning scientists. These three examples demonstrate two main points.

First, in all three examples, learning conversations are scaffolded by external representations. A wide range of learning sciences research has demonstrated that external representations can enhance the educational benefits of collaborative conversation (Lehrer & Schauble, this volume; Cobb, 1995, 2002; Kelly & Crawford, 1997; Kelly, Crawford, & Green, 2001; Saxe & Bermudez, 1996; Sfard & McClain, 2002). This research has suggested that representations are a publicly accessible version of the private thinking of individuals. External representation encourages deep learning by facilitating student *reflection*: the ability to reflect on what they are learning, and on the learning process itself.

Second, each example chooses a different level of detail for its analysis. The first two examples are taken from projects in which the researchers analyzed many hours of classroom discourse. When researchers gather a large amount of interactional data, they cannot analyze each episode in as much detail, simply due to time constraints – because interaction analysis is labor-intensive and time-consuming. The third example takes the smallest level of detail, using a conversation analytic methodology – with detailed microsecond transcription of interruptions, pauses, and overlapping speech. This example is taken from a study that analyzed only twelve minutes of conversation. I chose these examples to demonstrate the important methodological choice facing all interaction analysts: choosing an appropriate level of detail, one that corresponds to the research questions of the study.

Computer Scaffolding for Scientific Collaboration

The learning sciences have found that the best way for students to learn science is to have them engage with science content in the same ways that professional scientists do. Kelly and Crawford (1996) argued that for students to participate authentically in a scientific community, they need to learn to use the language of science. They designed a computer-based lab for twelfth grade science students that was designed to engage the students in conversations about physical phenomena – giving them a chance to learn how to talk scientifically.

They studied groups of three and four twelfth graders, and transcribed their conversation as they analyzed oscilliscope graphs that recorded the students' motion as they walked near a motion detector. The motion detector was attached to the floor, and when students walked by it or hopped up and down next to it, the oscilliscope would display a sine wave that represented the vibration of the floor. Kelly and Crawford analyzed each forty-five group session by (1) breaking down the episodes into turns of

Example 12.2. Transcript analyzed in Figure 12.1

Laura	That is really neat	looking at computer screen
Nancy	Do big circles Jump up and down	to Laura
Computer		representation appears
Nancy	So why does it go lower? Distance versus time so when you get closer, it goes further this way?	Nancy moves the mouse others look at the screen
Steve	[No, that's probably] just how far	Steve points to screen
Nancy	[No, that's time]	Nancy points with mouse.
Laura	That's time	
Steve	How far it is away	
Nancy	Time is that, and, and, distance is this when you're that close you go crazy Go crazy far away	Points with mouse Looks at Laura Shakes the mouse

dialogue; (2) identifying the ways that small episodes were put together to form larger participant structures; (3) using these larger units to identify patterns of interaction. Example 12.2 shows a sample transcript, and Figure 12.1 shows how the researchers represented these multiple levels of structure. The smallest level of structure was the *message unit*, a single turn of speech or a single computer action. Each message unit appears in a separate row in Figure 12.1. They then identified *action units*, which were composed of one or more message units and defined as having a semantic relationship with each other, and which represent a single intended action by a group member. Action units represent the thinking that students chose to display publicly. In Figure 12.1, action units appear as vertically elongated rectangles in the "Map" column. Third, they identified *interaction units* composed of one or more action units. Interaction units include an action and a response. In Figure 12.1, interaction units are separated by arrows between

line #	Nancy	Steve	Laura	computer	map	nonverbals	codes
232			that is really neat		r+	to computer screen	responding
233	do big circles				r+	to Laura	
234	jump up and down				r+	intiates an experimental run	
235				produces representation	r+	laughter (Nancy, Steve, Laura)	responding
236	so why does it go lower?				q+	Nancy moves mouse, others look to the	looking for clarification
237	distance versus time				r+	computer screen	demonstrating
238	so when you get closer				r+	"	claiming
239	it goes				r+	"	"
240	further this way?				q+	"	"
241	~no that's time~	~no that's probably~just how far			r+ r+	Nancy pointing with mouse. Steve points to screen	demonstrating (Nancy), claiming (Steve)
242			that's time		r+		
243		how far			r+		
244		it is away			r+		
245	time is that				r+	Nancy pointing with mouse while	claiming (Nancy)
246	and				r+	nodding her head	
247	and				r+	"	
248	distance is				r+	"	
249	this				r+		
250	when you're that close				r+	Nancy looks to Laura	
251	you go crazy				r+		
252	go crazy far away				r+	Nancy shakes the mouse	

Figure 12.1. A transcript of three students working together at a computer. From left to right, the columns represent the line numbers, the three speakers, the computer's actions, the discourse analysis map, the nonverbal actions, and the researcher-assigned codes.

action unit blocks in the "Map" column. The longest interaction unit starts with Nancy's question in line 236, and ends with Steve's response in line 244.

Kelly and Crawford focused on how the students' conversations made use of the computer display's representation of motion. At the level of the turn, the transcript reveals what information students choose to make public. At the level of the action unit, the transcript reveals how turns

are tied together to accomplish purposeful activity. The researchers used this level to understand the many different ways that the computer was used by students. In Figure 12.1, both verbal and nonverbal activity show how the computer is drawn into the conversation. Kelly and Crawford identified five ways that computer representations enter student conversations (see Figure 12.2). In these five types of interaction, the computer is treated as a member of the

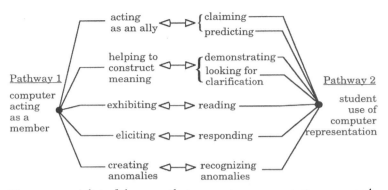

Figure 12.2. A list of the ways that computer representations are used in a conversation among three students. In Pathway 1, the computer functions as a fourth member in the conversation; in Pathway 2, the computer is used by a student in conversation. Each function in Pathway 1 is linked to its related function in Pathway 2.

group, participating almost as another entity in the conversation:

- The computer is used by a student to support his or her efforts to make a case.
- The computer helps the group to construct meaning, for example by clarifying conceptual differences in the group.
- The computer is an external representation of important data.
- The computer elicits student responses (an example is line 235 in Figure 12.1).
- The computer presents students with unexpected information that sometimes is difficult for them to explain within their existing conceptual framework.

On other occasions, the computer representations are used by each student participant; instead of treating the computer as another participant, they are treating it as a source of support for their own position (see Figure 12.2). As a result, the computer has a special dual status in the group that makes it uniquely effective at supporting learning.

Potential Pitfalls of Collaboration

Sfard and Kieran (2001) studied collaborative conversations in math classes, to evaluate the common claim that many school subjects are best learned through collabora-

tion. They collected two months of videotape data from a pair of thirteen-year-old boys learning algebra (Sfard & Kieran, 2001). After the two months of collaborative work, both boys' math scores had increased above the class average, seeming to demonstrate the value of collaboration. But the researchers believed that the collaboration had not been as effective as it could have been; for example, although both boys' scores increased, one of the boys increased much more than the other. They conducted an interaction analysis to better understand how this collaboration might have been more effective.

They analyzed two brief episodes extracted from their total of thirty hours of videotape. One of these was a discussion of how to understand a graph of the number of hours of daylight by the day of the year near the North Pole (showing 24 hours in the summer and 0 hours in the winter). They were asked to "Describe what happened to the number of hours of daylight over the year" and then given a series of five scaffolding questions such as "During which period of time did the number of hours of daylight increase most rapidly?" The transcript of one episode of this discussion appears in Figure 12.3.

Sfard and Kieran developed a new method of coding the transcript, one that resulted in an *interaction flowchart*

WHAT IS DONE	WHAT IS SAID
	- 19:14 -
	[1] A: During which period of time did the number of hours of daylight increase most rapidly? From day. to day
	[2] G: Woah.
	[3] A: Increase most rapidly?
[4] "day 60": G. points to (60.0) "to day": G. points to about (290,0)	[4] G: Yes (mumble). From day 60 to day ... 290.
	[5] A: From day 60 to
	[6] G: 290. Oh, no, no, no, no. (mumble)
	[7] A: From day 60 to a hundred.
	[8] (here, interruption from the teacher on some other matter)
[9] G. points along the x = 250 line	[9] G: So from day -
	[10] A: During which period of time did the number of hours of daylight increase most rapidly? From day
[11] G. points along the x = 100 line	[11] G: one hundred
	[12] A: 60 to 100. From day 60 to 100.
[13] "up here": G. points to (100,24) "to day -": G. goes along upper horizontal line, and down the vertical to arrive at about x=250.	[13] G: Cause, Oh no, no, no no no. Look, look. Up here. It's day 100 to day --- to day
	[14] A: What are you talking about?
	[15] G: 55.
	[16] A: Where?
	[17] G: Look, it changed most rapidly in between here and here. You see?
[17] "here and here": G. points back and forth several times to the extremes of the upper horizontal line, about (100,24) to (250,24)	[18] A: Oh? It's exactly the same.
	[19] G: No, because see, it moves up (mumble)
[19] G. traces the "descent" of the line from x=100 to 0	[20] A: It goes up most rapidly
	[21] G: So it's from day 100
	[22] A: To day 100
	[23] G: No, from day 100 to day ---
[23] G. is still pointing at about 250 on x axis.	[24] A: No, No, No.
	[25] G: 2 hundred and sixty,
	[26] A: That's not how you're supposed to do it.
	[27] G: two hundred and eighty. To day
	[28] A: See, during which time. The time, the period of time has to change rapidly.
	[29] G: Oh. No, it says from day to day what?
	[30] A: Read the question. During which period of <u>time</u> - time.
[30] A. underlines "time" on G's question sheet.	[31] G: Up here, time.
[31] G. traces horizontal line at 24 hours	[32] A: No, but that didn't change, it stayed still, which means it has to be right here,
[32] "that didn't change: here A. traces horizontal line at 24 hours. "right here": A. puts pencil mark along graph from y=20 to 24	[33] G: No
	[34] A: which is about 90
	[35] G: Right here
[35] G. traces ascent of graph from 0 to 100	[36] A: No, right here
	[37] G: You don't get it, do you? If it was like this
[37] G. traces a curve along graph from 0 to about 250.	[38] A: Fine, it's from 60 to a hundred, ok?
	[39] G: No.
	[40] A: Yes. I'm writing that.
	[41] G: Why?
	[42] A: We can have different answers.
	[43] G: Why? I don't care.
	[44] A: What was the maximum number of hours of sunlight in Alert?
[44] G. is still pointing around (250,0)	[45] G: To day 250.
	[46] A: 24
	[47] G: Just a sec, just a sec.
	[48] A: 24
	[49] G: 250. I'm telling you, change it. Anyway it doesn't matter.
	22:44 -

Figure 12.3. A transcript of two students analyzing a graph of the number of hours of daylight, throughout the year, at a point near the North Pole.

(Figure 12.4). Ari is shown in the left column, Gur in the center column, and their combined actions in the right column. Each circle represents a single utterance that corresponds to the transcript in Figure 12.3. A *reactive* arrow points vertically or diagonally backward or upward, expressing the fact that the utterance is a reaction to the pointed-to utterance; a *proactive* arrow points vertically or diagonally forward or downward, symbolizing the fact that the utterance invites a response, and that the following utterance is expected to be a reaction. Note that a proactive arrow is drawn even if the next utterance turns out not to actually be a response; this would happen in cases of miscommunication or ignoring. Vertical arrows relate utterances by the same speaker, and diagonal utterances relate the two speakers.

This visual coding method reveals several important facts that show why this discourse was not as effective as it could have been. First is that Ari's first column has almost no proactive arrows – meaning that Ari was not directing his comments to Gur – he made very few response-inviting utterances. And although he made some reactive utterances, these were not very responsive – they were more often than not simple statements of disagreement. In contrast, Gur made many proactive statements; he attempted to sustain contact and encourage response. The visual coding method shows that Gur was interested in true communication whereas Ari was not. Interpersonal interaction seemed to interfere with Ari's thinking. Sfard and Kieran concluded that Ari was focused on solving the math problem, even if alone, whereas Gur was focused on the interaction itself. And while both boys' scores increased above the class average, Ari's final score was much higher than Gur's. They concluded that collaborative problem solving involves a trade-off between the needs of managing interpersonal communication, and the need to engage in individual thinking (p. 64). As a result, many students may need explicit coaching in how to participate in effective collaboration (Azmitia, 1996).

Emergent Moments of Insight

In an analysis of the collaborative discourse of a university study group, Sawyer and Berson (2004) examined how students in a psychology class used their lecture notes to help structure their collaboration and their joint learning. During their study group discussion, the students mostly each looked down at their own notebooks while they were talking; but occasionally, they looked up at each other and engaged in conversation without looking at the notebooks. Conversation research has repeatedly demonstrated the importance of eye gaze in managing turn-taking and speaking rights (Goodwin, 1981; Kendon, 1990; Viechnicki, 1997).

We discovered that the conversation unfolded in very different ways, depending on whether or not the students were looking up at each other, or down at their notebooks. We identified three differences in conversational dynamics. First, when students were looking at their notebooks there was less *back channeling*. "Back channeling" refers to verbal and nonverbal communications made by the listener while the speaker continues talking. Second, when students were looking at their notebooks there was less overlapping speech, whereas overlapping speech frequently occurred while they were looking up. Third, while looking at the notebooks the participants left longer pauses between turns and within turns. To indicate when students were looking down at their notebooks, we transcribed their speech in italics. For example, in the first turn of the transcript, Mary reads from her notes, and during this utterance, no back channeling occurs. Contrast Beth's turn, of comparable length and content, in (4), when the group is looking up. Susan and Mary each nod twice during this turn and Mary back channels with the word "yeah" once:

(1) M: *And, so Healy comes up with the U-Unitization Hypotheses that says that eventually, complex patterns are processed as whole units. The stimulus doesn't require any ((4))*

(2) S: *So that's just a hypothesis, it's not necessarily. .?*

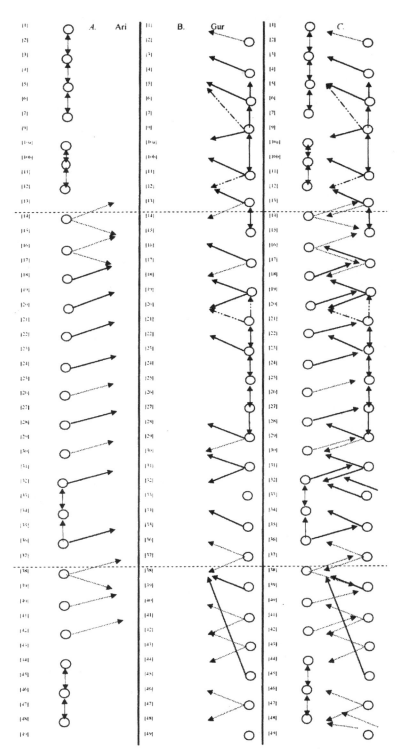

Figure 12.4. An interaction flowchart of the transcript in Figure 12.3.
Ari's actions appear in the left column, Gur's in the center column, and
a combination of both is shown in the right column. Up diagonal arrows
are responses to previous utterances; down diagonal arrows invite
responses from the other student.

(3) M: I- I guess it's just like a (2) conclusion almost, um ((4))

Sa: *(nods)*

(4) B: Probably because related to the thing above- umm- we probably see the words like "of" like, a lot, so then it's auto[matic,] so that's probably why. (3)

Sa, M:(nod)   M: [Yeah.] (nod)

Sa: (nod)

The use of the notebooks provided students with two different ways to engage in collaborative discourse. They could talk while each attending to an external representation, or they could talk directly to each other. The latter style had more of the characteristics of everyday conversation: verbal and nonverbal back channeling, overlapping speech, and shorter pauses.

LEARNING THROUGH COLLABORATIVE DISCOURSE

Discursive phenomena like overlaps and back channeling are fundamentally interactional and collaborative, and would be difficult to identify if one did not transcribe the discourse in detail, or if one coded only individual turns of speakers, in isolation from the unfolding stream of discourse. Those three contrasts were revealed by applying the detailed transcription notation of conversation analysis, and this has demonstrated the potential value of conversation analytic methods for studies of educational collaboration. However, it is not yet clear how these contrasts affect individual and group learning.

Occasionally a speaker shifted eye gaze within a turn; there were eight instances of shifts from looking up to down, and fifteen instances of shifts from looking down to up. These shifts served several distinct pedagogical functions. Perhaps the most interesting was that a shift from looking down to up allowed the speaker to revoice lecture material in their own words. When students read from their lecture notes, they are generally speaking in a scientific style of discourse, invoking the authoritative voice of the professor. The change in eye gaze corresponds to a change in voice – from the instructor's voice as encoded in the lecture material, to

the student's own voice commenting on that material. Turn (11) demonstrates this revoicing pattern. Beth summarizes the LaBerge and Samuels model, and at the point where she looks up, she begins to revoice what she has already said. She originally uses the technical term "recognize," and after looking up, changes her wording to the more colloquial "you're gonna pay more attention." Beth's mode shift occurs at the same time that she revoices her lecture notes.

(11) B: *So like the younger you are, the (1) more you're gonna recognize,* you're gonna pay more attention to each, each step.

These shifts in eye gaze serve an important educational function: they provide students with a technique to help them construct their own understanding. Within the sociocultural perspective, learning is a creative appropriation of material (Rogoff, 1998). Many researchers have focused on the differences between authoritative scientific discourse and everyday discourse, examining how teachers help students to appropriate scientific or mathematical forms of speech (Forman, 1992, 1996; O'Connor & Michaels, 1993). The use of the notebooks as mediating artifacts scaffolds students in the use of two discursive styles – a scientific style and an everyday style – and these are used as collective tools by students to help them appropriate the material. By revoicing the lecture material in their own words, the students appropriate it and thus enhance their own comprehension of the material. These analyses of students' shifts in eye gaze show how collaborative discourse with external representations helps participants to advance from simply memorizing lecture material to making it their own.

GROUP LEARNING THROUGH COLLABORATIVE DISCOURSE

A focus on discourse allows the researcher to examine patterns of group activity that emerge from the successive actions of speakers. Sawyer and Berson (2004) found that discussion of a topic began primarily with all students examining their notebooks; the group began their discussion of each topic by reading from their notebooks. Throughout the discussion, discourse gradually began to incorporate more and more face-to-face conversation, as the group members looked up and conversed about the topic, revoicing the lecture material and making connections to personal experience or to other lecture material. Finally, the topic unit concluded with all students looking up before moving to the next topic unit. This overall pattern is evidence of a collective group learning process. The pattern is not planned in advance, but emerges from the improvisational flow of the group's collaboration (cf. Cobb, 2002). The group's collective shift to a conversational style supports a learning process in which the group members gradually absorb the material and become less reliant on the notes. The external representations function as a scaffold for a collective appropriation of the material; as the group discussion proceeds, the scaffold is needed less and less – the typical pattern of guided participation emphasized by learning scientists.

Note that this emergent group pattern is parallel to the within-turn pattern identified above: individual speakers shift from looking down to looking up to revoice notebook material. The shift in eye gaze serves a similar function both at the individual level and at the group level; the external representations of the notebooks scaffold both individual learning and collective learning. This is one of the benefits of external representation that have been documented by studies of CSCL (Stahl et al., this volume; Scardamalia & Bereiter, this volume). The detailed transcription methods of conversation analysis resulted in the identification of an emergent group-level process of guided participation – where the external representation is gradually used less and less, as students increasingly revoice and appropriate the information.

Methodological Issues

Interaction analysis can be used to study several aspects of classroom interaction that are central to many of the chapters in this handbook: argumentation, communica-

tion, and critique; externalizing and articulating knowledge; how group patterns and communities of learners scaffold individuals in authentic practices. The examples I've presented focus on interaction rather than cognitive content; learning scientists are typically interested in both (Greeno, this volume). Identifying how individual knowledge emerges from collaborative discourse requires a combination of methodologies – interaction analysis to study the discourse patterns, and experimental and cognitive methodologies to study individual learning. This kind of study requires an extended analysis over a longer period of time, and results in a large amount of data. For example, one excellent example that combines interaction analysis and cognitive content required eighty published pages (Cobb et al., 1997), and that length is not unusual.

The transcripts in Sawyer and Berson (2004) contain a large amount of detailed, microsecond notation. Generating this type of transcript is incredibly time-consuming; if research goes into this much detail, it is only practical to study a rather small amount of discourse. Researchers who use the detailed transcription notation developed by the conversation analysts typically focus on only a few isolated cases at a time (see Table 12.1). The advantage of this method is that it can reveal implicit understandings and cognitive competencies that could not be discovered any other way. Transcribing a lot of detail, including overlapping speech, interruptions, and back channeling, can provide a lot of insights into the distributed, collaborative nature of group activities that are otherwise missed. Transcribing eye gaze, for example, can reveal a lot about how joint focus and intersubjectivity is established and maintained in groups. This is particularly important when two or more students are working together at a computer (or more generally, in the presence of shared external representations); without detailed transcriptions of where the students are looking, it will be difficult to fully explain the role of external representations in mediating collaborative learning.

The disadvantage of this method is that it can only focus on one small segment of

Table 12.1. Two Extremes of the Full Range of Interaction Analysis Methods

	Narrow	*Broad*
Transcription detail	Conversation analytic	Screenplay (words only)
Analytic method	Qualitative	Often combines qualitative and quantitative
Role of theory	No codes applied; meanings are expected to emerge from the data (grounded theory)	Coding scheme applied, based on researcher's theoretical framework
Generalizability	Low: Unable to claim how common the phenomenon is	High: Percentage of patterns can be identified across a large corpus of data
Strengths	Able to document the mechanisms whereby learning occurs	Able to generalize broader patterns, and to compare across settings

the complex flow of a classroom. A thirty-second segment of conversation can easily take ten hours to transcribe. Consequently, the studies by Sfard and Kieran and by Kelly and Crawford did not use this level of detail. Their transcriptions were more in the style of a screenplay: just the words spoken, leaving out volume and pitch marks, elongated vowels, and overlapping speech. The disadvantage of transcribing this way is that a lot of information is lost; and often, the importance and relevance of that detailed information doesn't become apparent until the transcript analysis stage. But the advantage is that it becomes feasible to study a much larger volume of discourse. An entire one-hour class can often be transcribed in ten hours.

Researchers who take a more narrow approach typically use the qualitative methods of conversation analysis. With this approach, it can take an entire journal article to identify exactly what is going on in a 30-second segment of discourse. The advantage is that this level of detail can often provide highly nuanced insights into what each participant must have known at each moment, and can identify the exact moment when a group of learners is constructing a new understanding. It is difficult to analyze emerging understandings in authentic, situated contexts any other way; stopping the interaction to administer a test of each student, for example, would destroy the situated nature of the activity.

Researchers who take a more broad approach typically categorize each of the turns of conversation using a *coding manual* that specifies what type of conversational turn qualifies as an example of each category. Because a large number of hours can be studied simultaneously, it becomes possible to apply quantitative and statistical methods to the database of turn codes. For example, classrooms at two different schools can be studied, and their broad conversational patterns can be contrasted statistically. And like the very first study of classroom discourse in 1966, descriptive statistics can indicate how often a given sequence of turns occurs, and what contexts are most likely to result in a particular sequence. Another advantage with the broad approach is that it becomes possible to group turns into higher-level organizing units, as Kelly and Crawford did.

Conclusion

Many learning sciences researchers study the role of collaboration in learning by analyzing collaborative discourse. This empirical method results in findings that extend our knowledge of learning in several ways.

First, interaction analysis provides the researcher with a method to study how peer groups learn without a teacher present. Several decades of research into cooperative groups has proven that peer groups contribute to learning. However, this tradition has not examined the conversational dynamics of these groups; studies of cooperative learning primarily focus on individual outcomes, task structures, and incentive structures (e.g. Slavin 1990). By contrast, interaction studies of classroom discourse have tended to focus on teacher-student conversation. As a result, there have been few studies of the discourse processes of collaborative peer groups, and few studies that have attempted to identify which features of conversation are associated with the most effective collaboration. The studies I've reviewed here demonstrate how interaction analysis can allow us to look inside the "black box" of collaboration (Bossert, 1988–1989) to identify specific discourse processes that make collaboration a uniquely effective learning environment.

Second, interaction analysis can reveal the interactional mechanics whereby external representations affect discourse processes and learning. Learning scientists have explored the important educational role played by articulation and externalization. Interaction analyses can extend this work by examining how the discourse processes of the group are mediated by these representations. As in the three examples given here, external representations act as scaffolds that guide the group's activity, and this guided participation seems to allow a group to attain a higher level of shared focus and intersubjectivity.

The learning sciences have increasingly examined the conversational dynamics of educational classroom talk. Many of these studies have focused on short, isolated episodes of discourse. Interaction analysis can also be used to examine the longer-term emergent patterning of educational talk (Cobb & McClain, this volume; Cobb et al., 1997). For example, Sawyer and Berson (2004) found that students always engaged in a period of talk on a given topic by looking down at their notebooks, and only later did they begin to engage in face-to-face conversation on that same topic. This pattern collaboratively emerged from the group's conversation, and it became an important element contributing to the educational value of collaboration.

Interaction analysis has the potential to reveal how these emergent patterns can contribute to individual learning. Very few studies have examined how collective group phenomena emerge from extended sequences of discourse, and how these unintended emergent effects might then contribute to learning; rather, most studies of classroom discourse have examined the knowledge that students are meant to learn, often by focusing on individual students in the classroom. For example, Sawyer and Berson (2004) found that a speaker sometimes begins talking while reading from the notebook, invoking the instructor's voice, and then looks up to revoice the material in his or her own words. This shift served as an interactional technique that scaffolded students in their appropriation of the lecture material. The fact that this sequential pattern is reproduced on both the individual and the group level suggests that external representations guide not only individual learning but also group learning. These analyses suggest that learning is both an individual and a group process, and that a full explanation of learning requires a simultaneous examination of both individual and social processes.

Footnote

1. Transcript conventions can be found in (Atkinson & Heritage, 1999), and are summarized as follows.

[]	overlapping speech
((x))	unintelligible speech of x seconds
(x)	a pause of x seconds
=	indicates two turns were spoken together without any pause, or "latched"
:	elongated vowel, each colon indicates one second of elongation
_	(underlining) emphasis
ˆ	Pitch rise
,	a comma indicates a pause of less than one second
-	an en-dash at the end of an utterance indicates flat pitch

References

Antil, L. R., Jenkins, J. R., Wayne, S. K., & Vadasy, P. F. (1998). Cooperative learning: Prevalence, conceptualizations, and the relation between research and practice. *American Educational Research Journal*, 35(3), 419–454.

Atkinson, J. M., & Heritage, J. (1999). Jefferson's transcript notation. In A. Jaworski & N. Coupland (Eds.), *The discourse reader* (pp. 158–166). New York: Routledge.

Azmitia, M. (1996). Peer interactive minds: Developmental, theoretical, and methodological issues. In P. B. Baltes & U. M. Staudinger (Eds.), *Interactive minds: Life-span perspectives on the social foundation of cognition* (pp. 133–162). New York: Cambridge.

Bargh, J. A., & Schul, Y. (1980). On the cognitive benefits of teaching. *Journal of Educational Psychology*, 72(5), 593–604.

Bearison, D. J., Magzamen, S., & Filardo, E. K. (1986). Socio-cognitive conflict and cognitive growth in young children. *Merrill-Palmer Quarterly*, 32(1), 51–72.

Bellack, A. A., Kliebard, H. M., Hyman, R. T., & Frank L. Smith, J. (1966). *The language of the classroom*. New York: Teacher's College Press.

Bossert, S. T. (1988–1989). Cooperative activities in the classroom. *Review of Research in Education*, 15, 225–252.

Chi, M. T. H. (1997). Quantifying qualitative analyses of verbal data: A practical guide. *Journal of the Learning Sciences*, 6(3), 271–315.

Cobb, P. (1995). Mathematical learning and small-group interaction: Four case studies. In P. Cobb & H. Bauersfeld (Eds.), *The emergence of mathematical meaning: Interaction in classroom cultures* (pp. 25–129). Hillsdale, NJ: Erlbaum.

Cobb, P. (2002). Reasoning with tools and inscriptions. *Journal of the Learning Sciences*, 11(2–3), 187–215.

Cobb, P., Gravemeijer, K., Yackel, E., McClain, K., & Whitenack, J. (1997). Mathematizing and symbolizing: The emergence of chains of signification in one first-grade classroom. In D. Kirshner & J. A. Whitson (Eds.), *Situated cognition: Social, semiotic, and psychological perspectives* (pp. 151–233). Mahwah, NJ: Erlbaum.

Daiute, C., & Dalton, B. (1993). Collaboration between children learning to write: Can novices be masters? *Cognitive and Instruction*, 10, 281–333.

Doise, W., & Mugny, G. (1984). *The social development of the intellect*. New York: Pergamon Press.

Durán, R. P., & Szymanski, M. H. (1995). Cooperative learning interaction and construction of activity. *Discourse Processes*, 19, 149–164.

Finkel, E. A. (1996). Making sense of genetics: Students' knowledge use during problem solving in a high school genetics class. *Journal of Research in Science Teaching*, 33(4), 345–368.

Fisher, E. (1993). Distinctive features of pupil-pupil classroom talk and their relationship to learning: How discursive exploration might be encouraged. *Language and Education*, 7(4), 239–257.

Forman, E. A. (1992). Discourse, intersubjectivity, and the development of peer collaboration: A Vygotskian approach. In L. T. Winegar & J. Valsiner (Eds.), *Children's development within social context, Volume 1: Metatheory and theory* (pp. 143–159). Mahwah, NJ: Erlbaum.

Forman, E. A. (1996). Learning mathematics as participation in classroom practice: Implications of sociocultural theory for educational reform. In L. P. Steffe, P. Nesher, P. Cobb, G. A. Goldin, & B. Greer (Eds.), *Theories of mathematical learning* (pp. 115–130). Mahwah, NJ: Erlbaum.

Forman, E. A., & Cazden, C. B. (1985). Exploring Vygotskian perspectives in education: The cognitive value of peer interaction. In J. V. Wertsch (Ed.), *Culture, communication, and cognition: Vygotskian perspectives* (pp. 323–347). New York: Cambridge University Press.

Fuchs, L. S., Fuchs, D., Hamlett, C. L., Phillips, N. B., Karns, K., & Dutka, S. (1997). Enhancing students' helping behavior during peer-mediated instruction with conceptual mathematical explanations. *The Elementary School Journal*, 97(3), 223–249.

Gee, J. P., & Green, J. L. (1998). Discourse analysis, learning, and social practice: A methodological study. *Review of Educational Research*, 23, 119–169.

Goodwin, C. (1981). *Conversational organization: Interaction between speakers and hearers*. New York: Academic Press.

Green, J., & Kelly, G. (Eds.). (1997). *Special issue of Journal of Classroom Interaction on "discourse in science classrooms," Volume 32, Issue 2*. Houston, TX: University of Houston.

Hicks, D. (1995). Discourse, learning, and teaching. *Review of Research in Education*, 21, 49–95.

Hutchins, E. (1995). *Cognition in the wild.* Cambridge, MA: MIT Press.

Johnson, D. W., & Johnson, R. T. (1974). Instructional goal structure: Cooperative, competitive, or individualistic. *Review of Educational Research, 44*(2), 213–240.

Johnson, D. W., & Johnson, R. T. (1979). Conflict in the classroom: Controversy and learning. *Review of Educational Research, 49*(1), 51–70.

Johnson, D. W., & Johnson, R. T. (1989). *Cooperation and competition: Theory and research.* Edina, MN: Interaction Book Company.

Johnson, D. W., & Johnson, R. T. (1992). Positive interdependence: Key to effective cooperation. In R. Hertz-Lazarowitz & N. Miller (Eds.), *Interaction in cooperative groups: The theoretical anatomy of group learning* (pp. 174–199). New York: Cambridge University Press.

Jordan, B., & Henderson, A. (1995). Interaction analysis: Foundations and practice. *Journal of the Learning Sciences, 4*(1), 39–103.

Kelly, G. J., & Crawford, T. (1996). Students' interaction with computer representations: Analysis of discourse in laboratory groups. *Journal of Research in Science Teaching, 33*(7), 693–707.

Kelly, G. J., & Crawford, T. (1997). An ethnographic investigation of the discourse processes of school science. *Science Education, 81*, 533–559.

Kelly, G., Crawford, T., & Green, J. (2001). Common task and uncommon knowledge: Dissenting voices in the discursive construction of physics across small laboratory groups. *Linguistics & Education, 12*(2), 135–174.

Kendon, A. (1990). *Conducting interaction: Patterns of behavior in focused encounters.* New York: Cambridge.

Klaasen, C. W. J. M., & Lijnse, P. L. (1996). Interpreting students' and teachers' discourse in science classes: An underestimated problem? *Journal of Research in Science Teaching, 33*(2), 115–134.

Kumpulainen, K., & Mutanen, M. (2000). Mapping the dynamics of peer group interaction: A method of analysis of socially shared learning processes. In H. Cowie & G. v. d. Aalsvoort (Eds.), *Social interaction in learning and instruction: The meaning of discourse for the construction of knowledge* (pp. 144–160). New York: Elsevier Science.

Lazarowitz, R., & Karsenty, G. (1990). Cooperative learning and students' academic achievement, process skills, learning environment, and self-esteem in tenth-grade biology classrooms. In S. Sharan (Ed.), *Cooperative learning: Theory and research* (pp. 123–149). New York: Praeger.

Lemke, J. L. (1998). Analyzing verbal data: Principles, methods, and problems. In B. J. Fraser & K. G. Tobin (Eds.), *International handbook of science education, Part Two* (pp. 1175–1189). Dordrecht: Kluwer Academic Publishers.

Mehan, H. (1979). *Learning lessons.* Cambridge, MA: Harvard University Press.

Mercer, N. (1996). The quality of talk in children's collaborative activity in the classroom. *Learning and Instruction, 6*, 359–377.

Middleton, D., & Edwards, D. (1990). Collective remembering. In D. Middleton & D. Edwards (Eds.), *Collective remembering* (pp. 23–45). Newbury Park, CA: Sage.

Musatti, T. (1993). Meaning between peers: The meaning of the peer. *Cognition and Instruction, 11*(3/4), 241–250.

National Council of Teachers of Mathematics. (1991). *Professional standards for teaching mathematics.* Reston, VA: Author.

National Research Council. (1996). *National science education standards.* Washington, DC: National Academy Press.

Nystrand, M., Gamoran, A., Kachur, R., & Prendergast, C. (1997). *Opening dialogue: Understanding the dynamics of language and learning in the English classroom.* New York: Teacher's College Press.

O'Connor, M. C., & Michaels, S. (1993). Aligning academic task and participation status through revoicing: Analysis of a classroom discourse strategy. *Anthropology and Education Quarterly, 24*(4), 318–335.

Palincsar, A. S. (1998). Social constructivist perspectives on teaching and learning. In J. T. Spence, J. M. Darley, & D. J. Foss (Eds.), *Annual Review of Psychology* (Vol. 49, pp. 345–375). Palo Alto, CA: Annual Reviews.

Palincsar, A. S., Brown, A. L., & Campione, J. C. (1993). First-grade dialogues for knowledge acquisition and use. In E. A. Forman, N. Minick, & C. A. Stone (Eds.), *Contexts for learning: Sociocultural dynamics in children's development* (pp. 43–57). New York: Oxford.

Perret-Clermont, A. N. (1980). *Social interaction and cognitive development in children.* New York: Academic Press.

Rogoff, B. (1998). Cognition as a collaborative process. In D. Kuhn & R. S. Siegler (Eds.),

Handbook of child psychology, 5th edition, Volume 2: Cognition, perception, and language (pp. 679–744). New York: Wiley.

Sawyer, R. K. (2001). Creating conversations: Improvisation in everyday discourse. Cresskill, NJ: Hampton Press.

Sawyer, R. K. (2003). Group creativity: Music, theater, collaboration. Mahwah, NJ: Erlbaum.

Sawyer, R. K., & Berson, S. (2004). Study group discourse: How external representations affect collaborative conversation. Linguistics and Education, 15, 387–412.

Saxe, G. B., & Bermudez, T. (1996). Emergent mathematical environments in children's games. In L. P. Steffe, P. Nesher, P. Cobb, G. A. Goldin, & B. Greer (Eds.), Theories of mathematical learning (pp. 51–68). Mahwah, NJ: Erlbaum.

Schegloff, E. A. (1986). The routine as achievement. Human Studies, 9, 111–151.

Sfard, A. (2002). The interplay of intimations and implementations: Generating new discourse with new symbolic tools. Journal of the Learning Sciences, 11 (2–3), 319–357.

Sfard, A., & Kieran, C. (2001). Cognition as communication: Rethinking learning-by-talking through multi-faceted analysis of students' mathematical interactions. Mind, Culture, and Activity, 8(1), 42–76.

Sfard, A., & McClain, K. (Eds.). (2002). Analyzing tools: Perspectives on the role of designed artifacts in mathematics learning (Special issue of The Journal of the Learning Sciences, Volume 11, Numbers 2 and 3). Mahwah, NJ: Erlbaum.

Sinclair, J. M., & Coulthard, R. M. (1975). Towards an analysis of discourse: The English used by teachers and pupils. London: Oxford University Press.

Slavin, R. E. (1990). Cooperative learning: Theory, research, and practice. Boston: Allyn & Bacon.

Slavin, R. E. (1992). When and why does cooperative learning increase achievement? Theoretical and empirical perspectives. In R. Hertz-Lazarowitz & N. Miller (Eds.), Interaction in cooperative groups: The theoretical anatomy of group learning (pp. 145–173). New York: Cambridge University Press.

Swing, S. R., & Peterson, P. L. (1982). The relationship of student ability and small-group interaction to student achievement. American Educational Research Journal, 19(2), 259–274.

Tudge, J., & Rogoff, B. (1989). Peer influences on cognitive development: Piagetian and Vygotskian perspectives. In M. Bornstein & J.

Bruner (Eds.), Interaction in cognitive development (pp. 17–40). Hillsdale, NJ: Erlbaum.

van Boxtel, C., van der Linden, J., & Kanselaar, G. (2000). Deep processing in a collaborative learning environment. In H. Cowie & G. van der Aalsvoort (Eds.), Social interaction in learning and instruction: The meaning of discourse for the construction of knowledge (pp. 161–178). New York: Elsevier Science.

Vedder, P. (1985). Cooperative learning: A study on processes and effects of cooperation between primary school children. Groningen, Netherlands: Rijksuniversiteit Groningen.

Verba, M. (1994). The beginnings of collaboration in peer interaction. Human Development, 37, 125–139.

Viechnicki, G. B. (1997). An empirical analysis of participant intentions: Discourse in a graduate seminar. Language & Communication, 17(2), 103–131.

Webb, N. M. (1984). Stability of small group interaction and achievement over time. Journal of Educational Psychology, 76(2), 211–224.

Webb, N. M. (1991). Task-related verbal interaction and mathematics learning in small groups. Journal for Research in Mathematics Education, 22(5), 366–389.

Webb, N. M. (1992). Testing a theoretical model of student interaction and learning in small groups. In R. Hertz-Lazarowitz & N. Miller (Eds.), Interaction in cooperative groups: The theoretical anatomy of group learning (pp. 102–119). New York: Cambridge University Press.

Webb, N. M. (1995). Group collaboration in assessment: Multiple objectives, processes, and outcomes. Educational Evaluation and Policy Analysis, 17(2), 239–261.

Webb, N. M., Ender, P., & Lewis, S. (1986). Problem-solving strategies and group processes in small groups learning computer programming. American Educational Research Journal, 23(2), 243–261.

Webb, N. M., Nemer, K. M., Chizhik, A. W., & Sugrue, B. (1998). Equity issues in collaborative group assessment: Group composition and performance. American Educational Research Journal, 35(4), 607–651.

Webb, N. M., & Palincsar, A. S. (1996). Group processes in the classroom. In D. C. Berliner & R. C. Calfee (Eds.), Handbook of educational psychology (pp. 841–873). New York: Simon & Schuster Macmillan.

Wells, G., & Chang-Wells, G. L. (1992). Constructing knowledge together: Classrooms as centers of inquiry and literacy. Portsmouth, NH: Heinemann.

CHAPTER 13

Assessing for Deep Understanding

Sharon M. Carver

Imagine that at the end of this chapter I have written some well-crafted comprehension questions related to the chapter's key content and that you are highly motivated to answer them to the best of your ability. Will your answers provide a good assessment of your understanding of the topic? How well will I understand what you have learned from reading, based on reviewing your answers? What might you, and I, be missing?

In part, the answers to these questions depend on the goals I have for your learning and for my assessment of your progress. To the extent that my goal is only for you to be able to restate my key points soon after reading the chapter, then the assessment may fit, assuming that you understand the questions and have the communication skills to formulate answers. By contrast, since my goal is really for you to be able to use the assessment principles that you glean from these pages to strengthen your own research designs and, thereby, gain a deeper understanding of the learning you are studying, then your answers to the comprehension questions likely have little to do with your ability to apply the

principles effectively (although perhaps the comprehension is a prerequisite).

This reflection begins to highlight the challenge of assessment in the learning sciences where the goal is for students to acquire deep understanding, the kind of knowledge experts use to accomplish meaningful tasks. Such understanding goes well beyond basic recall of facts and procedures to include the organization of concepts and strategies into a hierarchical framework that is useful for determining how and when to apply knowledge for understanding new material and solving related problems. Traditional classroom tests and standards-based assessments focus almost exclusively on the recognition and recall of superficial course content and are, therefore, not appropriate for assessing the thinking and problem solving that deep understanding supports (Means, this volume).

Fortunately, learning sciences researchers have access to valuable cognitive science strategies for developing clear models of deep understanding in particular domains, diverse methodologies for instruction and assessment geared to deep understanding, and a tiered research approach for studying the teaching/learning process. The key is to explicitly focus on assessing aspects of students' learning that are directly related to the specified deep understanding, together with critical features of the teaching/learning process, in order to maximize the usefulness of the assessment within the constraints of time and resources (Barab & Squire, 2004; Fishman et al., 2004).

My goal in this chapter is to help learning sciences researchers incorporate effective assessments into their investigations. It is organized according to my three central recommendations.

1. Prepare cognitive foundations for research by clearly defining deep understanding and by specifying the instructional methods and assessments designed to promote and document such learning.
2. Focus assessment design decisions on the hypothesized core of the teaching/learning process, strategically following the guidelines for valid experimental research as appropriate for the context.
3. Use a tiered research approach to iteratively refine the definition of deep understanding, the instructional and assessment methods, and the research designs to yield progressively deeper explanations of effective teaching/learning processes.

Table 13.1 foreshadows my key principles in the form of questions. By considering each issue relative to a particular learning sciences investigation, researchers can strengthen their assessment designs and, thereby, gain a deeper understanding of the students' learning.

Cognitive Foundations for Assessment in the Context of Complexity

The fact that learning sciences researchers study real-world settings in which communities of learners are actively engaged in dynamic processes for building deep understanding heightens the importance of explic-itly focusing the investigation on a thorough specification of the learning goals, or "learning target," and then precisely aligning both instruction and assessment with that target. If the goal is to teach for deep understanding, then the learning target will be the cognitive structures educators want their students to internalize in order to perform proficiently. Well-specified learning goals must serve as the basis for principled instructional design, focused intervention monitoring, and thorough assessments that cover the full range of the targeted knowledge and skills.

Cognitive Modeling of Goals

Cognitive task analysis methods and studies of expertise can be combined to develop a detailed definition of deep understanding, or a cognitive model, for a particular learning sciences investigation. Task analyses are "careful examinations of problems, intended to identify the processes needed to solve them" (Siegler, 1998, p. 249). Studies of novice and expert performance on such problems reveal the particular approaches typical of individuals with varying levels of experience in the discipline. By combining these ideal and actual approaches, the learning sciences researcher can develop a detailed cognitive model of what it takes to perform proficiently at the level expected for the students within the learning situation being studied.

To be complete, the cognitive model should include specification of the knowledge representation and organization (from individual facts to conceptual networks), processing skills (procedures and strategies for performance), and developmental trajectories for any learning that researchers want to investigate (National Research Council, 2001). To emphasize deep understanding, such specifications must include the full range of competence from knowledge and comprehension to application, analysis, synthesis, and evaluation (Bloom, 1956). Researchers should also consider including metacognitive knowledge and skills for planning, monitoring, and controlling learning, as well as the attitudes and motivation

Table 13.1. Key Considerations for Assessment in the Learning Sciences

---

Cognitive Foundations

Models of Deep Understanding
> Are the learning goals clear?
> - Are the critical features of proficiency well-specified?
> - Are knowledge, skill, metacognition, attitudes, and motivation included?
>
> Is the learning process clear?
> - Has the developmental / novice → expert path been outlined?
> - Is the rationale for specific instructional interventions explicit?

Alignment of Instruction and Assessment with Goals for Deep Understanding
> Is every aspect of the learning goals & process included in the intervention?
> How will the actual implementation be documented?
> Is the full set of learning goals covered by the proposed set of assessments?
> Is there sufficient triangulation to transparently interpret the assessments?

Assessment Design Decisions

General Standards
> What steps can be taken to enhance internal, external, & empirical validity?
> How can the design be made sensitive to diverse learner characteristics?
> How can consistency and reliability be enhanced?

Tasks and Recording Techniques
> What range of tasks might be combined to accurately assess learning?
> Which recording techniques best fit the goals and constraints?
> Has the alignment with learning goals been double-checked?

Experimental Designs
> Could core manipulations be tested using split-class or now-and-later designs?
> Is stratified random assignment applicable?
> Are assessments counterbalanced?
> Are inter-rater reliability tests planned?

Tiered Research Approach

Which of the current assessments are primary vs. secondary vs. tertiary?
Which analyses are primary vs. secondary vs. tertiary?
Which research questions are planned for subsequent studies with a narrower focus?

---

necessary for learning. Detailed explanations of the modeling process can be found in numerous resources (Anderson, 1987; Anderson, 2000; Simon, 1979). From my own research, extended examples of elementary children's learning of debugging skills and middle school students' research and communication skills are available (Carver, 1988; Carver, 1995; Carver et al., 1992; Klahr and Carver, 1988).

Instructional Design in Theory and Practice

When planning any type of instructional intervention, learning sciences researchers must (1) explicitly target each aspect of deep understanding via instruction designed according to accepted cognitive principles, and (2) plan to carefully document the actual intervention. One practical strategy for assuring the alignment of instruction with goals is to create a table listing each of the learning objectives related to deep understanding, the specific curriculum emphasis for each objective, the theoretical rationale for each activity, and the plans for documenting the actual implementation.

The cognitive models derived from task analyses and studies of expert-novice differences make knowledge, strategies, and communicative practices visible so that both teachers and students can focus on them purposefully (National Research Council,

2001). Cognitive science theory is also helpful for considering general principles that apply to any instructional approach. For example, Carver (2001) discussed the top five "metaprinciples" used for designing the laboratory school program for young children, teachers, parents, and undergraduates at Carnegie Mellon's Children's School. They include building on prior knowledge, making thinking explicit, emphasizing links, providing practice opportunities, and expecting individual variability.

Learning sciences researchers are already well aware, however, that theory is often far from practice (Collins, Joseph, & Bielaczyc, 2004). A strength of design-based approaches (Barab, this volume) is the emphasis on how designs actually function in authentic settings. The Design-Based Research Collective (2003) offers three intervention case studies (the Jasper Series, BGuILE, and the Passion School) to demonstrate ways of linking teaching/learning processes with their outcomes to identify contextual factors and learning mechanisms central to the intervention. The key to developing cognitive foundations for instruction in the learning sciences is to use principled design to both plan an intervention and to monitor its implementation, because the assessment results can only be interpreted in the context of understanding the teaching/learning processes that actually occurred (i.e., in contrast to the idealized design).

The Assessment Triangle

The National Research Council publication, *Knowing What Students Know* (2001), elucidates the assessment dilemma and the importance of cognitive theory and methodology for advancing educational research. Because cognitive models of deep understanding highlight critical features of proficiency, assessment tasks and feedback can focus on them explicitly (Fishman et al., 2004). Researchers can then systematically experiment with aspects of the intervention "to test and generate theory in naturalistic contexts" (Barab & Squire, 2004,

p. 3). Assessment of differential outcomes involves a process of reasoning from evidence, which requires careful alignment of the researchers' *cognitive models, observation techniques,* and *interpretation methods* of drawing inferences from performance (NRC, 2001, Box 8.1). This "assessment triangle" requires (1) an explicit model of both deep understanding and the process of acquiring it, (2) tasks carefully designed to assess the targeted knowledge, together with reliable scoring methods based on the original model, and (3) a valid process for drawing inferences from performance, typically involving triangulation across diverse tasks.

Cognitive science can enhance each of the three elements of the assessment triangle. Using detailed cognitive models as the foundation for planning observations of learning and inferences from performance facilitates explicitness and transparency. The goals are to encourage educators to teach directly to the theory of deep understanding and learning that underlies an assessment (Frederiksen & Collins, 1989) and to encourage students to appropriate the same goals for learning, both of which are necessary for a "comprehensive, coherent, and continuous assessment system" (NRC, 2001, p. 2) that is fair and equitable.

As with instructional design, cognitive science can recommend specific classroom assessment techniques that can be matched to particular aspects of deep understanding, as well as methods and technologies for data collection appropriate in rich task environments that require analysis of action sequences, problem solving, participation, and so on (NRC, 2001). Because Confrey (this volume) and Quintana et al. (this volume) focus on design experiments and learner-centered design, respectively, I focus on ways to incorporate experimental approaches within learning sciences studies when such approaches are theoretically important and practically possible. Also, because many other chapters describe specific types of assessment, I offer general principles that learning sciences researchers should consider during the process of planning assessments, and I suggest strategies for narrowing the assessment focus within complex investigations so that the data collected can maximally address the research questions within the practical constraints of the research context. Although my examples represent classroom assessments, the principles would be the same for large-scale assessments.

Strategic Assessment Design

After preparing the foundations for assessment by clearly defining deep understanding, designing instruction to teach each of its components, and planning to document the actual progress of the intervention, the learning sciences researcher must design the set of assessments that will together provide data to answer the research questions. Critiques of design-based approaches to the learning sciences highlight the unprincipled nature of the assessments. For example, Dede (2004) stated that "only the first five percent or so of the data collected were needed to induce the findings" (p. 107). Given finite time and resources within complex educational contexts, learning sciences researchers need to systematically focus their assessment designs by objectively determining which data to collect under what conditions, as well as which data *not* to collect (diSessa & Cobb, 2004; Kelly, 2004).

In this section, I suggest ways to focus assessment design decisions according to the specifications of deep understanding. Furthermore, I endorse increased consideration of experimental research, as appropriate to the context. To this end, I begin with an overview of standards and options for assessments. I then provide brief descriptions of several recent projects that highlight key principles for designing specific assessments, with an emphasis on outlining experimental approaches that could strengthen assessments in the learning sciences.

Standards for Effective Assessments

In order to be effective, each assessment must be *sound, sensitive, and systematic* (McAfee, Leong, & Bodrova, 2004). To design *sound* assessments, researchers must consider issues of validity. Traditionally, experimentalists strive for internal validity, which enables clear causal conclusions, discrimination of constructs, and predictions regarding future performance. Learning sciences researchers instead often emphasize an aspect of external validity: ecological validity (i.e., the assessment's alignment with realistic contexts of learning). Recently, developmental scientists Hirsh-Pasek, Kochanoff, Newcombe, and deVilliers (2005) introduced the concept of empirical validity to stress that assessments should be based on solid research foundations.

The challenge for learning sciences researchers is to creatively balance internal, external, and empirical validity to enhance the rigor of their assessments. Cognitive science offers principles for enhancing empirical validity, particularly for defining deep understanding and the processes of learning relevant to the desired outcomes. The recommendations made earlier for aligning assessments with the learning target can enhance construct validity, which can also be strengthened by triangulating multiple sources and kinds of data (DBRC, 2003, p. 7). Finally, validity can be enhanced in learning sciences investigations by involving diverse partners whose emphases on different aspects of validity will impact successive designs to "result in increasing alignment of theory, design, practice, and measurement over time" (DBRC, 2003, p. 7).

Sensitive assessments are suited to the developmental characteristics of learners. For example, assessments designed for young children must be sensitive to their context dependence by aligning assessment and learning contexts, to their limited interest in being assessed by designing inviting and engaging tasks, to their limited language skills by carefully wording instructions and providing visual cues, and to their uneven development by offering multiple opportunities to demonstrate competence across tasks and over a period of time (McAfee et al., 2004). In addition, sensitivity to individual differences, including culture and gender effects, can enhance both the internal validity of the assessment and its generalizability.

A *systematic* assessment is consistently administered according to an explicit protocol so that data collected from each individual is uniform, with consistent scores that are clearly interpretable. The assessment need not be standardized; in other words, each subject may progress through the protocol in different ways depending on particular responses. In such a dynamic assessment, subjects can be given help in prescribed ways, but the amount and level of assistance is consistently recorded and factored into the analysis. Thus, assessment reliability can be achieved without sacrificing the researchers' emphasis on diverse learning processes. Collins et al. (2004) also stressed the importance of objective scoring by multiple raters to enhance the reliability of each measure.

Assessment Options Targeting Deep Understanding

There are numerous assessment types for documenting deep understanding in ways that meet the standards for effective assessment described above and that are feasible within learning sciences investigations. McAfee et al. (2004) suggested considering five basic methods for assessment, including systematic observation, studying learners' work products, eliciting responses from learners (whether selected responses or constructed responses), noting how learners respond to assistance during instruction (dynamic assessment, scaffolding analysis), and using questionnaires or interviews. Additional possibilities include cognitive and social process measures of classroom discourse, body posture and gesture, tasks and activity structures, patterns of participation and social interaction, strategies and conditions, errors and responses to feedback,

inscriptions and notations, and responses to assessment.

"Design-based research combines inductive qualitative approaches with quantitative and quasi-experimental approaches, varying the method to suit research questions" (Fishman et al., 2004, p. 47). Collins et al. (2004) offered a thorough outline of variables to consider, methods to use, and ways to report findings in learning sciences studies. They encouraged a clear focus on critical design elements, and recommended considering such independent variables as setting, learners, technology and financial support, professional development, and implementation path, together with the impact of these variables on dependent variables like climate, learning, and system factors. Basic quantitative and qualitative recording techniques, suggested by McAfee et al. (2004), included descriptions (narratives, jottings, photos, concept maps, video and audio recordings), counts or tallies (checklists, participation charts, frequency counts), ratings or rankings (scales, rubrics, etc.), and work products with associated learner and teacher comments. Cognitive scientists extend this basic list to include rich observations of think-aloud protocols, classroom discourse, human-computer interaction logs, and so on, and researchers continue to develop data mining and analysis tools to help manage the unwieldy volume of data collected via these methods (Cobb et al., 2003). Here again, the challenge is to align the choice of assessment with the targeted deep understanding so that each of the specified components in the cognitive model can be clearly discriminated in the analysis, while at the same time working within the resource constraints.

Cobb et al. (2003) suggested that assessments should focus *both* on testing conjectures about significant shifts in student reasoning and on conjectures about the specific methods for facilitating those advances. For example, Chi, Siler, and Jeong's (2004) research on how accurately undergraduate tutors monitor eight grade students' understanding of the human circulatory system demonstrated the importance of documenting the intervention process, together with both the students' understanding and the teachers' understanding of the students. The researchers' coding of tutoring protocols was streamlined to focus on the assessment and diagnosis of particular conceptual structures and was supplemented by pre-post test definitions, questions, and diagramming for tutees, as well as intermittent diagramming for both tutees and tutors. The analyses contrasted the tutors' strength in assessing whether the student explanations match the normative model of the correct concept with their limited ability to diagnose the students' alternative conceptions of the system.

In addition to such focused exploration of deep understanding and the instructional processes that support change, the learning ecology developed in a design experiment involves a system of interactions including discourse, learning activities, norms of participation, diverse tools, materials, and teaching strategies, etc., which "precludes complete specification of everything that happens" (Cobb et al., 2003, p. 10). For this reason, some of the assessment resources should be dedicated to documenting the design experiment history as it unfolds, both to facilitate retrospective analysis and to suggest additional measures that might be incorporated either immediately or during the next iteration of the design.

Experimental Design Options

For those teaching/learning processes that are hypothesized to be central in promoting deeper understanding, learning sciences researchers should consider including specific experimental manipulations within design experiments or running concurrent experiments to establish clear causal explanations that can then serve as foundations for other design decisions. Numerous critiques of design-based investigations advocate including more experimental methods and using both design and analysis strategies to minimize researcher bias (Dede, 2004; Kelly, 2004). Two experimental designs that

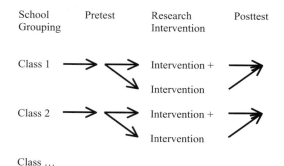

Figure 13.1. Split-class design.

I have found useful from a researcher's standpoint and acceptable from a practitioner's point of view are the **split-class design** and **the now-and-later design**. In this section, I describe the general designs, their benefits, and some practical tips for negotiating their objective use.

SPLIT-CLASS DESIGN

The split-class design enables the researcher to limit the impact of many variables within the learning ecology by keeping a class together for all aspects of the intervention except for one manipulation, using random, or stratified random, assignment to determine which students get the treatment ("intervention+"). Figure 13.1 visually represents the basic design. By having each class split, rather than assigning one class to treatment and one to control, or one to treatment A and the other to treatment B, the researcher limits the potential confounds, such as different teachers, different class compositions, and so on, such that any pretest → posttest changes can be causally linked to the treatment.

From a practical standpoint, students involved in the treatment condition can be physically separated from the other students (e.g., working in the library, etc.). If multiple classes are involved, then students from multiple classes can be recombined to receive the treatment. In other words, treatment groups from classes A and B can meet in classroom A, while the other students from both classes meet in classroom B.

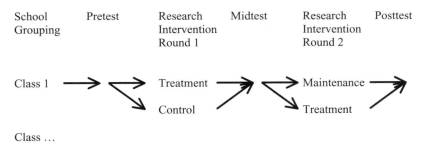

Figure 13.2. Now-and-later design.

NOW-AND-LATER DESIGN

When the intervention must be tested as a whole, then a split-class design can be extended as follows (see Figure 13.2). Each class is split, as described above, and then one group participates in the intervention for a period of time, while the other group serves as the control. After testing the effects of the intervention compared to the control, the control group then participates in the intervention. With this design, all students are eventually part of the treatment group, thereby maximizing the number of subjects without sacrificing the control group. In addition, researchers can test the stability of learning over time by noting whether any gains by the original treatment group are maintained during the period with no further treatment. From a practical standpoint, educators and parents favor this design because all students have the potential to benefit from the full intervention, and the control group actually gets the benefit of participating during the second, presumably smoother, iteration.

Kaufman and Carver (2000) used this design to test the effects of piano instruction on kindergartners' visual-motor integration, based on Kaufman's model of the shared skills required by a standardized Visual Motor Inventory (VMI) and the beginning piano curriculum used in the Carnegie Mellon music school. Kaufman split the VMI into three equivalent shorter versions for counterbalancing with the three test times and then split the class using stratified random assignment by gender, prior school experience, and music lesson experi-

ence. During the regularly scheduled learning center time, students received two brief, small-group sessions per week for eight weeks in the undergraduate piano lab with a piano instructor, either during the first or second semester of the year. Though there was no difference between the two groups at pretest, on the mid-year VMI the first semester piano students showed a significantly greater gain than the control group. That gain was maintained throughout the second semester, though it was surpassed by the gain the second semester piano students made between the midtest and posttest. Kaufman also developed an assessment of piano learning focusing on aspects that related most directly to visual-motor integration according to his model. Using this assessment, he found additional evidence for the hypothesized effect of the piano instruction in the fact that the students who scored the highest on the piano assessment were also the ones whose VMI scores improved the most. Details of the learning target, instruction, assessments, and scores can be found in Kaufman and Carver (2000).

The validity of both split-class and now-and-later designs depends on the stratified random assignment and counterbalanced assessments exemplified in Kaufman and Carver (2000). One practical point that encourages educators to permit random assignment is "veto power." We offer participating teachers the option of refusing any particular assignment so that potentially explosive student combinations can be avoided, but we require that an equivalent student (re: the stratification) be substituted. As always, statistical tests are used to determine the equivalence of groups at pretest, as well as to test whether there are any differences associated with the stratifying variables or among the counterbalanced test forms. In addition to these precautionary analyses, reliability of assessments can be tested by inter-rater comparisons (with .9 being high reliability and .8 moderate), preferably with one or both raters being blind to condition.

Focusing Assessment Design on Teaching/Learning Processes

While in my laboratory school administrator role, I collaborate with a talented and experienced staff to design our preschool and kindergarten program to meet our stated developmental objectives using a multifaceted design supported by a wide range of psychology-based principles (Carver, 2001). In other words, we are conducting a full-time design experiment. In this context, our observations of the teaching/learning process yield intuitions about what works and why, some of which can be translated into testable research questions. In some cases, particular methods can be tested in fairly controlled, but ecologically valid, conditions, but in others the complex mix must be preserved, either because the components are not clearly understood or because they are inseparable. The following examples are offered to give researchers the opportunity to reflect on design decisions related to assessment in such complex contexts. In each case, I emphasize the targeted deep understanding and processes used to facilitate learning, the researchers' choices regarding what could and could not be controlled, the type of assessments involved, which data were and were not collected, and the basic findings.

ORDERING DIRECT INSTRUCTION AND GUIDED
DISCOVERY TEACHING METHODS

Educators often contrast direct instruction methods with guided discovery, typically claiming that the latter is the most develop-mentally appropriate method for young children. Teachers' intuitions suggest, however, that well-timed direct teaching can be a catalyst for enhanced learning from more open-ended experiences. To test the effectiveness of utilizing these two methods in a complementary fashion, Brosnahan (2001) designed an intervention study for using water table activities to teach children how to accurately predict whether an object would sink or float.

The cognitive foundations for Brosnahan's study included defining deep understanding at the early childhood level with a precise decision tree model of sink/float judgments, beginning with weight estimates and consideration of the object's shape, and including the fact that some objects may float for a time and then sink. She then constructed multiple equivalent collections of objects to highlight contrasting characteristics and worked with an experienced teacher to develop one group lesson script for directly teaching the decision tree steps, and one designed to help students discover the key properties via guided experimentation. Finally, she constructed an interactive assessment during which an individual student could demonstrate deep understanding by predicting, explaining, testing, and re-explaining sink/float judgments for a set of objects.

Both the lessons and the assessments were designed as part of the regular school program, but issues like crowd control, noise level, and teacher availability led us to conduct them in a separate room. This choice allowed us to have one experienced teacher conduct all of the lessons for the study, as well as to reduce the number of distractions and interruptions.

Fifteen four-year-old and twenty five-year-old children were randomly assigned to small groups, each of which received four hands-on lessons involving prescribed sets of six objects and a water table to learn about making sink/float judgments. Using a split-class design, half of the groups at each age level were randomly assigned to receive the first two lessons via direct instruction and the latter two via guided discovery. The other groups received the two types of lessons in the opposite order.

Children were individually tested prior to the lesson series, after the first two lessons, and after the full set of four lessons, using one of three sets of eleven assessment objects in counterbalanced order. In addition, Brosnahan videotaped the actual implementation of the lessons, and she interviewed the teacher after the study to explore her perceptions of the lesson plans and implementation.

With respect to subject variables, Brosnahan found no gender differences but that kindergartners outperformed preschoolers on the every measure at all three test times. From the experimental manipulation of the lesson approaches, she found that preschoolers improved their predictions more than kindergartners from the direct instruction → guided discovery sequence, but that learning was equal to the other lesson order.

Brosnahan described additional observational findings that were derived from the videotapes and confirmed via the interview with the educator who conducted the lessons. Students seemed less interested in the direct instruction lessons, particularly when they followed the guided discovery. This effect was strongest for preschoolers, who had less experience with direct instruction. Observation also revealed that it was impossible to control for the differential time needed to conduct the two types of lessons; guided discovery simply takes longer.

Details of the decision model, lesson and assessment scripts, object sets, scoring systems and results can be found in Brosnahan (2001). The study's results are limited by ceiling effects, but its strategic assessment design is nonetheless instructive. Brosnahan was able to focus her research question on one factor that could be experimentally manipulated between randomly assigned comparison groups, while still enabling all of the children to participate in the sink/float intervention in a manner that had high ecological validity. She focused her primary data collection and analysis on the children's use of the specific decision tree that she modeled for sink/float predictions, but also included more open-ended approaches to capture the nature of the actual instructional process and demonstrate which aspects could and could not be controlled.

METHODS OF FOSTERING KNOWLEDGE BUILDING IN A THEMATIC UNIT

To demonstrate a more complex set of decisions regarding assessment focus, experimental manipulation versus documentation of process, and streamlining data collection and analysis, I will briefly describe a study designed to test the impact of the school's use of thematic explorations as a way to build children's knowledge. During each thematic unit, teachers incorporate theme-based books, songs, demonstrations, and games in their circle time discussions; plan specific theme-focused experiments; and create a theme-oriented dramatic play area. Both parents and teachers shared anecdotal evidence of the children's amazing knowledge gains, so we wanted to systematically assess the depth and breadth of concept acquisition to test our intuitions and to determine which aspects of our units were most effective for teaching thematic content. The staff agreed to participate in the study during our one-month summer program, for which they had chosen the theme Ocean, and an undergraduate secured a research grant to conduct the project as her honors thesis (Ciesielski, 2001).

As with all of our units, we examined literature about children's understanding of the topic, and then developed the unit's conceptual organization to match the deep understanding we wanted to foster. The targeted knowledge for the ocean theme included properties of land and water, plant and animal life adapted to the habitat, means of transportation available, and different recreation opportunities, so we gathered developmentally appropriate learning materials for each part of the conceptual focus. Immediately, the complexity of the design and documentation of the unit became clear; the theme would be emphasized during most of each four-hour program day for twenty days.

To focus the assessment design, Ciesielski interviewed the teachers about which instructional strategies had the most impact on children's knowledge gain. The teachers unanimously identified nonfiction books and theme-rich songs as the predicted source of significant conceptual learning. Ciesielski then focused her experimental manipulation and primary data collection on the content-rich books and songs, while planning to document other aspects of the unit for potential analysis if interesting observations emerged.

Ciesielski randomly assigned one teacher to teach with content-rich, nonfiction books and fiction songs, while the other teacher used content-rich, nonfiction songs and fiction books. To allow flexibility, she gave each teacher sets of books and songs from which to choose, but one got the primary content from books and one from songs. Typically, books have more content information but are read infrequently; whereas songs have less content that gets sung repeatedly. Predictions regarding which would be superior for promoting content learning could go in either direction, depending on the relative benefit of total content vs. repetitions.

To test these effects, Ciesielski used a split-class design, with thirty three- to five-year-old children randomly assigned to one of two groups, stratified by age, gender, and experience with the ocean (based on a parent survey). All children participated in the same activities during the ocean unit, but their circle time experiences had a different primary content source (books vs. songs) and a different leader. To document the experience of each group, Ciesielski audiotaped these daily twenty- to thirty-minute sessions and transcribed them to determine which books and songs were read/sung how many times, what content was emphasized by the teacher or students, and so on. Also, to document the children's participation in other aspects of the unit, Ciesielski prepared checklists and had educators record involvement (simple yes/no judgment).

Prior to the beginning and during the last week of the unit, Ciesielski used an individual dynamic assessment to assess each child's content knowledge about the ocean. The assessment involved progressively more specific prompts to probe deeper into the child's knowledge base, together with several prompts that approached the topic from different angles. The first general prompt asked the child to "Tell me about the ocean." Next came a series of sensory prompts of the form, "What can you see (hear, feel, smell) at the ocean?" The next series related specifically to the four subtopics of the unit (ocean water & land, plants & animals, etc.). The session finished with time spent completing an ocean puzzle to determine whether the visual cue would enable the child to reveal additional knowledge. Ciesielski also asked about the difference between the ocean and a pond (previous unit) to see if the contrast might yield a different type of knowledge.

To visualize and quantify children's deepening knowledge, Ciesielski transcribed the assessment audiotapes onto concept maps and scored each piece of knowledge both for its depth (detail and conceptual connections) and salience (i.e., high salience requires only general prompts). Figures 13.3 and 13.4 include sample pretest and posttest maps for one child to highlight the richness of the data; details of the scoring system and additional concept maps can be found in Ciesielski (2001).

Knowledge scores increased from an average of 41.4 on the pretest to an average of 66.6 (p < .001) on the posttest, with four- and five-year-olds gaining significantly more than three-year-olds. There were no gender or experience differences. The children in the content-rich books group gained more knowledge than those in the content-rich songs group, with the significant gain being for the animals and plants subtopic. Sixty percent of the children gained between ten and forty points from pretest to posttest, so the unit impact was widespread. Of the six children whose scores increased less than ten points, five were from the content-rich songs group, whereas four of the six children who gained more than forty points were in the content-rich books group. Transcripts of the circle time tapes revealed that both groups sang an equal number of songs

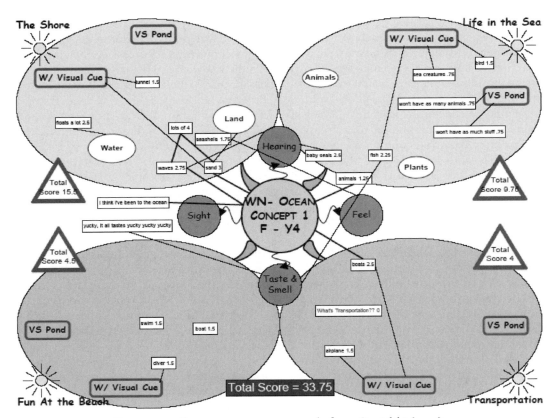

Figure 13.3. Pretest concept map sample from Ciesielski (2001).

and read almost the same number of books. More important, the transcripts revealed that the teacher in the content-rich songs group compensated for the fact that she had only fiction books by introducing ocean photographs and artifacts. These strategies mimic the content in nonfiction books and may, in fact, have decreased the book/song experimental contrast. The most interesting finding from the activity participation logs was that there appear to be individual differences in children's dispositions to seek content knowledge, with some actively choosing the higher content activities (e.g., playing an ocean bingo game vs. playing in the sandbox). These children also tend to have both higher initial scores and higher gain scores on the dynamic assessment. See Ciesielski (2001) for additional detail on the results.

Ciesielski's study demonstrates the value of having researchers and educators collaborate to identify which of the many

complex design aspects were the hypothesized core of the instructional process, so that experimental manipulation, assessments, and related data collection and analysis could focus on that core. Streamlining in this way enabled the researcher to allocate some additional resources for collecting secondary data to document the broader teaching/learning process. Both developmental and cognitive science contributed to the initial specification of the thematic content to be targeted in the unit, as well as to planning developmentally appropriate activities to facilitate knowledge acquisition and to map the children's growing knowledge networks. Because the concept maps are so detailed, and the process documentation includes both circle time discussion transcripts and activity choices for individual children, further analyses could locate the specific experiences associated with particular gains. Assessment and analysis for additional studies could then focus

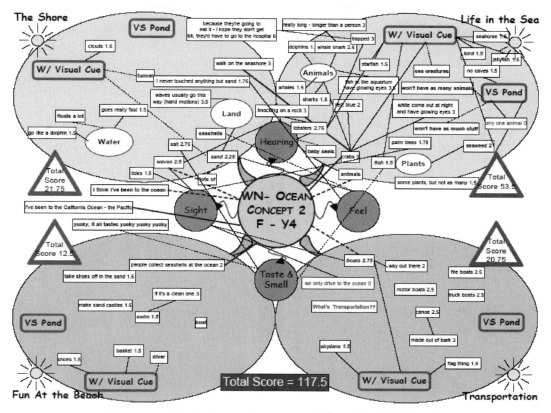

Figure 13.4. Posttest concept map sample from Ciesielski (2001).

on contrasting experience types, exploring individual differences, and so on, to gradually refine the researchers' and educators' understanding of young children's thematic content learning.

Assessment within a Tiered Research Approach

As several of the studies highlighted above demonstrate, focused assessment design based on cognitive foundations can help researchers avoid the trap of designing one massive study to explore the impact of multiple interacting factors. In this section, I advocate a research approach with multiple tiers for handling different aspects of one study, different phases of analysis, or different stages of a research program. In this way, the learning sciences can effectively incorporate design science and cognitive science approaches to study the complexities

of real-world learning using methodologies that meet high scientific standards and yield valid data for causal conclusions. Basically, the more you narrow your focus to the heart of the matter, the clearer you will be about where to invest the time and energy to do the deepest investigation and analysis (see Figure 13.5). Initial studies and analyses

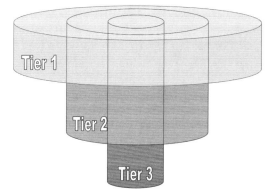

Figure 13.5. Tiered research approach.

should be centered on the area hypothe-sized as the key but usually also should cover secondary and tertiary possibilities (Tier 1). Subsequent analyses and studies can then be targeted according to the clearer focus yielded by the first round, and so on (Tiers 2 and 3).

Clark and Linn (2003) exemplified this approach when investigating the impact of instructional time with the Computer as Learning Partner (CLP) curriculum on eighth graders' deep understanding of thermodynamics, which they defined as students' addition of "new ideas and sorting through connections to develop a cohesive account of scientific phenomena" (p. 451). Regarding the cognitive foundations for their assessment, Clark and Linn highlighted the alignment between their instructional goals, curricular activities, and assessments, listed their pragmatic instructional design principles, and described the iterative design studies they conducted to refine the intervention.

Clark and Linn's research program involved sustained study at multiple lev-els using assessments that were carefully designed to reveal deep understanding untapped by standard assessments. Clark and Linn's scoring system involved a con-cise way of representing the range of ther-modynamics ideas. They used a straightfor-ward scoring system with a 4-point scale from nonnormative, to transitional, to nor-mative, to nuanced and normative under-standing. Their results showed that norma-tive understanding was sufficient for many multiple-choice questions but answering inquiry questions required nuanced knowl-edge integration.

Their broadest coverage involved study-ing three thousand students taught by the same teacher over twenty semesters using four increasingly streamlined versions of the CLP curriculum. They documented pre-post improvements on multiple-choice assessments and inquiry extensions requiring examples, reasons, and evidence. Students' answers on inquiry questions reflected the *decreasing depth of learning* associated with the *more streamlined curriculum versions*;

whereas the answers on the multiple-choice items remained at relatively high levels (80–90 percent) across CLP versions. At the second tier, they randomly selected fifty students from three hundred using the curriculum in one year and followed them longitudinally during eighth grade via inter-view, with specific probes for contradictions, connections, differentiations, and reasoning patterns. Finally, the third tier involved fol-lowing one representative student through high school via interview to better under-stand the knowledge integration process and determine why it takes so long to truly learn the core science concept (most notably because the student's response to conceptual conflicts was to discount instructed concepts in favor of preexisting concepts and idiosyn-cratic explanations, and because the student needed to revisit ideas in multiple contexts, explore pivotal cases, and receive scaffolding to develop mature concepts).

By using multiple methods with differ-ing sensitivity to deep understanding, plus a tiered approach ranging from a broad sam-ple over a period of years to a single case study, Clark and Linn were able to iden-tify the specific role of instructional time in the learning process. In addition, they were careful to identify and address possi-ble research confounds. For example, col-laborating with the same teacher yielded consistency over the years and, if anything, the teacher's increasing experience teach-ing thermodynamics might favor students in later years of the project. Similarly, the most streamlined versions of the CLP curriculum benefited from the most refinements, which should be biased in favor of deeper under-standing among later participants. The find-ings showed, however, that students using the later, more streamlined versions of the curriculum actually demonstrated less depth of learning on inquiry questions.

Multiple tiers for assessment research are especially crucial for assessing deep under-standing in the learning sciences because of the extensive intervention and multiple iter-ations necessary for creating a culture of pro-moting deep understanding. Kolodner et al., (2003) contrasted the deep understanding of specific science content that might be achieved by using their Learning by Design approach during one course, with the understanding of learning sciences practices that required multiple course experiences, and with the understanding necessary for a culture of inquiry that would require system-wide change (also see Kolodner, this volume). Assessment of understanding across these levels of depth would require a tiered research approach applied to studying the learning of students, instructors, researchers, and other stakeholders in the educational process.

In fact, all of the preceding discussions about a specific model of deep understanding serving as the foundation for instruction and assessment related to students' understanding also apply to learning sciences investigations of the educators' understanding, which is known to have a significant impact on teaching/learning processes and student outcomes. Similarly, the researchers' understanding of the learning goals, instructional design, and assessment evolves throughout the investigation and could be the subject of study. Finally, the same process of effectively connecting cognitive theory and methodology with educational assessment practice to promote deep understanding could be applied to policy-makers and the public (NRC, 2001, Figure 8.1). The assessment principles discussed in this chapter could equally well be applied to studies of deep understanding at any of these levels. In fact, Cobb et al. (2003) advocated multiple levels of analysis within design experiments to handle the processes and learning of students, the classroom community, the professional teaching community, and the school and/or district.

Deep Understanding of Assessment

Envision the range of learning sciences researchers, yourself included, who may peruse, skim, or read this chapter as part of a course assignment, while preparing a dissertation proposal, or when designing a specific assessment. Would their answers to any set of comprehension questions I could have written be able to reveal whatever deep understanding of assessment they may have gained from my instruction? The answer is clearly no, in part because the learners' prior knowledge, levels of expertise, and goals for reading vary so widely that each undoubtedly uses quite different processes for learning that would yield highly individualized knowledge acquisition. The same problem exists, of course, for all of the studies I mentioned, as well as for those described throughout this volume. Diverse learners and facilitators interact with a wide range of tools using multiple teaching and learning processes with varied levels of interest and motivation in the context of a complex system of interactions developed over the course of unique learning histories.

On the one hand, learning sciences researchers face the challenge of studying hopelessly complex situations with severe constraints of time and resources. On the other hand, the complexity and constraints are precisely the reasons that researchers can benefit greatly from applying cognitive theory and methodology to specifying their models of deep understanding, the key components of their instructional designs, and the streamlined documentation of interventions and assessment of learning that I outlined earlier and summarized in Table 13.1. By focusing individual investigations on the specified deep understanding, with clearly aligned manipulations, measures, and scoring systems, researchers can systematically explore aspects of complex learning environments in manageable ways, gaining understanding both of general patterns and individual processes. By progressively refining their models, designs, and assessments, researchers can continually deepen their understanding of the teaching/learning process that yields deep understanding in different ways among diverse learners.

The other reason to answer my question with a resounding no is that a deep understanding of assessment is unlikely to be gained even by the most careful study of these pages. Since my goal was to improve the way learning sciences researchers plan assessments to maximize their yield within severe resource constraints, the impact of my efforts could only be measured after learners have multiple opportunities to apply the ideas to thinking about their own and others' research contexts and assessment designs. Even then, I would need to go beyond comprehension questions to expose the thinking process, perhaps by triangulating protocol analysis, observation of research meetings, and interview methods. In fact, if I were to design a study to test the impact of learning from this chapter, I too would have to consider all of the issues raised herein to effectively assess deep understanding.

References

Anderson, J. R. (1987). Methodologies for studying human knowledge. *Behavioral and Brain Sciences, 10,* 467–505.

Anderson, J. R. (2000). *Cognitive psychology and its implications: Fifth edition.* Worth: New York.

Barab, S. and Squire, K. (2004). Design-based research: Putting a stake in the ground. *The Journal of the Learning Sciences, 13*(1), 1–14.

Bloom, B. S. (Ed.) (1956). *Taxonomy of educational objectives: The classification of educational goals: Handbook I, cognitive domain.* New York: Longmans, Green.

Brosnahan, H. (2001). *Effectiveness of direct instruction and guided discovery teaching methods for facilitating young children's concepts.* Unpublished senior honors thesis, Carnegie Mellon University, Pittsburgh, PA.

Carver, S. M. (1988). Learning and transfer of debugging skills: Applying task analysis to curriculum design and assessment. In R. E. Mayer (Ed.), *Teaching and learning computer programming: Multiple research perspectives* (pp. 259–297). Hillsdale, NJ: Lawrence Erlbaum Associates.

Carver, S. M. (1995). Cognitive apprenticeships: Putting theory into practice on a large scale. In C. N. Hedley (Ed.) *Thinking and literacy: The mind at work* (pp. 203–228). Hillsdale, NJ: Lawrence Erlbaum Associates.

Carver, S. M. (2001). Cognition and instruction: Enriching the laboratory school experience of children, teachers, parents, and undergraduates. In *Cognition and instruction: Twenty-five years of progress* (pp. 385–426). Carver, S. M. and Klahr, D. (Eds.). Mahwah, NJ: Lawrence Erlbaum Associates.

Carver, S. M., Lehrer, R., Connell, T. and Erickson, J. (1992). Learning by hypermedia design: Issues of assessment and implementation. *Educational Psychologist, 27*(3), 385–404.

Chi, M. T. H., Siler, S. A., and Jeong, H. (2004). Can tutors monitor students' understanding accurately? *Cognition and Instruction, 22*(3), 363–387.

Ciesielski, C. (2001). *Preschool theme teaching: What works and what doesn't?* Unpublished senior honors thesis, Carnegie Mellon University, Pittsburgh, PA.

Clark, D. and Linn, M. C. (2003). Designing for knowledge integration: The impact of instructional time. *The Journal of the Learning Sciences, 12*(4), 451–493.

Cobb, P. Confrey, J., diSessa, A., Lehrer, R., and Schauble, L. (2003). Research as design. *Educational Researcher, 32*(1), 9–13.

Collins, A., Joseph, D., and Bielaczyc, K. (2004). Design research: Theoretical and methodological issues. *The Journal of the Learning Sciences, 13*(1), 15–42.

Dede, C. (2004). If design-based research is the answer, what is the question? *The Journal of the Learning Sciences, 13*(1), 105–114.

Design-Based Research Collective. (2003). Design-based research: An emerging paradigm for educational inquiry. *Educational Researcher, 32*(1), 5–8.

diSessa, A. and Cobb, P. (2004). Ontological innovation and the role of theory in design experiments. *The Journal of the Learning Sciences, 13*(1), 77–103.

Fishman, B., Marx, R. W., Blumenfeld, P., Krajcik, J., and Soloway, E. (2004). Creating a framework for research on systemic technology innovations. *The Journal of the Learning Sciences, 13*(1), 43–76.

Frederiksen and Collins (1989). A systems approach to educational testing. *Educational Researcher, 18*(9), 27–32.

Hirsh-Pasek, K., Kochanoff, A., Newcombe, N. S., and deVilliers, J. (2005). *Using scientific knowledge to inform preschool assessment: Making the case for "empirical validity."* SRCD Social Policy Report, 19(1).

Kaufman, G. F. and Carver, S. M. (2000). The effects of piano instruction on the visual-motor development of kindergartners. *National Association of Laboratory Schools Journal*, 24(2), 9–17.

Kelly, A. E. (2004). Design research in education: Yes, but is it methodological? *The Journal of the Learning Sciences*, 13(1), 115–128.

Klahr, D. and Carver, S. M. (1988). Cognitive objectives in a LOGO debugging curriculum: Instruction, learning, and transfer. *Cognitive Psychology*, 20, 362–404.

Kolodner, J. L., Camp, P. J., Crismond, B. F., Gray, J., Holbrook, J., Puntambekar, S., and Ryan, M. (2003). Problem-based learning meets case-based reasoning in the middle-school science classroom: Putting Learning by Design™ into practice. *The Journal of the Learning Sciences*, 12(4), 495–547.

McAfee, O., Leong, D. J., and Bodrova, E. (2004). *Basics of assessment: A primer for early childhood educators*. Washington, DC: National Association for the Education of Young Children.

National Research Council (2001). *Knowing what students know: The science and design of educational assessment*. Washington, DC: National Academy Press.

Siegler, R. S. (1998). *Children's thinking: Third edition*. Upper Saddle River, NJ :Prentice Hall.

Simon, H. A. (1979). *Models of thought*. New Haven, CT: Yale University Press.

Part III

THE NATURE OF KNOWLEDGE

CHAPTER 14

Case-Based Reasoning

Janet L. Kolodner

In this chapter, I tell the story of case-based reasoning's contributions to the learning sciences. It is a story that begins in Artificial Intelligence and Cognitive Science in the 1970s. Roger Schank and his students were investigating ways for the computer to understand the everyday language we speak, and they were basing their work on observations about the way people seem to understand everyday language (Schank & Abelson, 1977). As part of those investigations, they were identifying schema-like knowledge structures that might organize different types of knowledge, and at the same time, identifying processes that could make inferences from those knowledge structures. Case-based reasoning (CBR) was born from this research in the 1980s as an attempt to make intelligent systems behave more like experts. As these researchers learned more about the processes that allow a reasoner to reason based on previous experiences, it became clear that case-based reasoning had much to offer education. Researchers began to use the principles of case-based reasoning to design learning environments, including adult education,

museums, K–12 classrooms, and undergraduate education. Sometimes the computer has been integrated into those learning environments – as a tool that can provide the kinds of information and advice case-based reasoning says is useful for promoting successful project work and goal achievement, as a tool for eliciting the kinds of reflection that case-based reasoning says are important for learning productively from experience, or as an organizer of the learning sequence. Sometimes the computer has played little or no role. Instead, case-based reasoning's cognitive model has been used as a framework for designing systems of classroom activities, classroom scripts, and roles for teachers and peers to promote learning from project and problem-solving experiences.

A Short History of Case-Based Reasoning

In the late 1970s, researchers in Schank's group at Yale had proposed representational frameworks for everyday knowledge, and processes for using those representations to understand English-language stories about everyday kinds of experiences. For example, Schank and Abelson (1977) proposed that common event sequences are stored in generalized "scripts" that people use to get through the day. A script, they proposed, is a knowledge structure in memory, representing the common scenes, sequence of events, characters, and props common to a particular kind of experience. The "restaurant script," for example, was proposed as a knowledge structure an individual would form after several restaurant visits. Such a knowledge structure is general enough to be applied any time you repeat a kind of event, for example, going to a restaurant – to anticipate what will be happening next and what your behavior and that of others should be. These representations and processes were implemented on the computer, and a program called SAM (Schank & Abelson, 1977) could apply the script for "going to a restaurant" to infer, for example, that if John ordered steak in the restaurant, then he probably ate it and paid the bill and left a tip before he left.

By the late 1970s, Schank's research group was discovering that at least some understanding requires access not only to these generalized scripts but also to the events they were created from. Consider, for example, going to an anniversary dinner at a restaurant. Your restaurant script can help you predict that you'll sit down and be served by a waiter, and if you have been to several parties, you will have a party script that can predict that there will be a cake and singing and presents. But only if you had been to an earlier fancy celebration dinner at a restaurant would you be able to just as easily predict how the pomp and ceremony of the anniversary celebration would be interleaved with the restaurant meal.

Research in Schank's lab began to address the issue of how scripts develop and the relationship between individual memories and scripts. CYRUS (Kolodner, 1983a, 1983b), for example, stored events in the life of Cyrus Vance when he was Secretary of State of the United States, and it could answer questions about his everyday experiences, finding experiences in memory (e.g., the last trip he took to the USSR) and imagining or "reconstructing" probable experiences based on those memory structures when the specific event could not be remembered (e.g., a state dinner where Vance's wife might have been in attendance).

The theory of mind that developed from these endeavors became known as case-based reasoning (CBR; Schank, 1982; 1999; Kolodner, 1993). CBR claims that our minds are filled with thousands of "cases" – some the stories of specific events and some more generalized, scriptlike stories about common sequences of everyday events – and that intelligent behavior is based on a person's ability to identify the important features of a new situation and retrieve the best-matching case from this large repertoire. Almost like a movie script, a case includes a setting, the actors and their goals, a sequence of events, the expected results, what actually happened (if it is known), and explanations linking outcomes to goals and means.

CBR explains how people apply their previous experiences to solve problems in new situations. Continuing with the fancy dinner example, according to CBR, the next time you went to a fancy anniversary dinner you would remember the anniversary dinner referred to above and use its specifics to anticipate that same pomp and ceremony and celebration. Although your restaurant and party scripts are also applicable, the individual memory is more specifically applicable than either script. Other special experiences at restaurants would similarly be available to guide reasoning when appropriate – for example, the time the clumsy waitress spilled soup on you might be remembered the next time a waitress seems clumsy, and you might consider not ordering soup or being careful to move away when the waitress brings soup; the time you had excellent Chinese food in a vegetarian restaurant may be remembered next time you are in that same restaurant or another vegetarian restaurant, and you might use that memory to decide to order a Chinese dish. In the general case of going to a restaurant without any novel characteristics, the restaurant script itself would allow you to navigate your way through the situation.

From Case-Based Reasoning to a Case-Based Approach to Learning

CBR programs (see the list in Kolodner, 1993) seemed to be more flexible than other ways of modeling expertise, and because they could learn from experience, these programs got smarter over time. Early CBR systems included MEDIATOR (Kolodner & Simpson, 1989), which mediated simple disputes (e.g., two sisters want the same orange); CHEF (Hammond, 1989), which created new recipes from old ones; and JULIA (Kolodner, 1993), which planned meals. Making these computer systems work taught us about *the indexing problem*, the problem of identifying which case in memory best matches a new situation; *knowledge application*, the processes involved in applying that best-matching case to the new situation in order to interpret it or make inferences about what to do next; the role of *expectation failure* in learning – that it helps focus a learner on what to pay attention to in the future and on what else the reasoner needs to learn; and *adaptation*, processes for fixing plans and interpretations based on such expectation failures. We learned that the better a program was at remembering a case – its details, the connections between its pieces, and what could be learned from it – the more accessible and usable the case would be later. The better a program interpreted a new situation, the better chance it had of recalling a useful similar case to help with reasoning.

We later used case-based reasoning programs to try to model the reasoning in novice learners – to learn how a reasoner might go from having very little knowledge about a task or domain to becoming expert in its vocabulary and practices. CELIA (Redmond, 1992), for example, used cases to model the troubleshooting and learning of an apprentice mechanic. From CELIA we learned about the powerful role a novice's prior experiences can play during learning, how important it is for a learner to have a variety of similar experiences so as to be able to extract the subtleties and nuances of the lessons being learned and when each lesson applies (Kolodner, 1993).

These studies helped us articulate a case-based theory of learning (Schank, 1982, 1999; Kolodner, 1993, 1997):

1. Learning will happen best in contexts of trying to achieve goals of interest.
2. To learn well from their experiences, learners need to interpret their experiences so as to make them into well-articulated cases in their memories. The better learners connect their goals to their reasoning about achieving the goals, the more useful the case will be for later reasoning. The better learners are at pulling out lessons learned and anticipating when those lessons might be useful, the more accessible the case will be. The better learners do at explaining failures and expectation failures, the more useful and accessible the case will be.
3. Experience applying cases from memory allows further learning. Failures at application and failures of expectations tell the learner that more needs to be learned, and provide an opportunity to reinterpret an old experience. Figuring out how to apply a case and how to adapt its lessons for use in a new situation results in new and more specialized cases. The more opportunities learners have to apply their cases, the better they are able to debug their interpretations and add to their knowledge and capabilities.
4. Learners can learn from the cases of others as well as from their own.
5. Learners can best learn from their mistakes and expectation failures if they get immediate feedback so that they have a way to recognize their errors and expectation failures, and if they can explain why the errors and expectation failures happened and what they should have done differently.

Using CBR to Improve Education

With these principles in mind, the first attempts to apply CBR to education were in the form of Schank's Goal-Based Scenarios (GBS; Schank et al., 1994; Schank &

Cleary, 1994). In a goal-based scenario, a learner is asked to complete a mission – a substantial challenge placed within a context of realistic complexity that puts the learner in an authentic role that has goals associated with it. If the learner is engaged enough with the mission goals, the reasoning went, she will attempt to achieve those goals and in the process learn targeted reasoning skills and content. For example, to help high-schoolers learn modern history and learn to write so as to address their audience well, learners were given the mission of writing text for and anchoring a television news show (using the Broadcast News program). To promote learning about selling advertisements (using the Yello program), adult learners were asked to play the role of a sales person in a simulated environment and make appropriate sales. Placing learners in these roles gave them an incentive to learn the targeted reasoning skills well enough for success; practice in the roles allowed them to succeed and fail in their reasoning and learn from those experiences; and computer software was available as they were playing their roles to help them identify errors and expectation failures, to explain what might have gone wrong, and to draw out from each experience what could be learned from it.

Attempts to introduce CBR's principles into educational environments have taken three directions.

1. New pedagogical approaches have been designed based on CBR's entire set of principles.
2. Based on CBR's claim that learners can learn from the experiences of others, case libraries have been designed as resources for learners and integrated into a variety of learning activities.
3. Based on what CBR suggests about the kinds of interpretations of experience that lead to productive learning, case authoring tools have been designed to help learners reflect on and articulate the highlights of their problem-solving and project experiences and what they've learned from them.

In the remainder of this chapter, I summarize what's been done in each of these areas and provide detail on one or more projects in each category. I make these presentations with three purposes in mind: (1) to show the variety of contributions CBR, as a cognitive theory, can make to improving education, (2) to present CBR's most influential and well-known models for promoting learning, and (3) to show the work required in moving from principles of a cognitive theory to principles of practice that can be implemented in an educational environment.

New Pedagogy for Promoting Learning: Learning by Design

While the GBS approach focuses on designing computer programs that help a learner achieve an exciting mission, an approach designed in my lab called Learning by Design (LBD; Kolodner, 1997, Kolodner, Crismond, et al., 2003; Kolodner, Gray, & Fasse, 2003), uses case-based reasoning's theory of learning to orchestrate an entire classroom environment. LBD's focus has been on designing pedagogy based on CBR that it is doable within the constraints of school – fortyfive-minute class periods, one subject at a time, one teacher for twenty to thirty-five students, and only very part-time access to computers. LBD's pedagogy includes a system of activity structures for the classroom (classroom scripts) and guidelines about teacher roles; roles peers should play in helping each other learn from experience; sequencing of individual, small-group, and whole-class activities; and physical and text resources that are needed. We designed this pedagogical approach to give students the kinds of experiences that afford deep learning and to support students in interpreting their experiences in ways that will result in productive learning.

LBD is a project-based inquiry approach (Blumenfeld et al., 1991; Krajcik & Blumenfeld, this volume); students learn by attempting to achieve design challenges. For example, students have designed miniature vehicles and their propulsion systems to

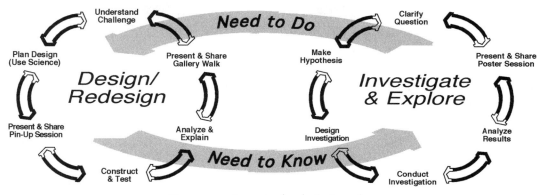

Figure 14.1. Learning by design's cycles.

learn about forces, motion, and Newton's laws, and they have designed ways to manage the erosion on barrier islands to learn about erosion, water currents, and the relationship between people and the environment. CBR suggests that the best learning experiences are those that afford clear feedback in a timely way; designing, building, and testing working devices provides that kind of feedback. Constructing working physical objects gives students the motivation to learn, the opportunity to discover what they need to learn, the opportunity to use science and to reason scientifically, and the opportunity to test their conceptions and discover the gaps in their knowledge and capabilities. Design challenges provide opportunities for students to engage in and learn complex cognitive, social, and communication skills. The LBD units we've designed are aimed at middle school students (grades 6–8; ages twelve to fourteen).

LBD's Activities and Sequences

Design challenges afford the kinds of experiences that will lead to deep learning; LBD's cycles and activity structures promote the kinds of reflection on experience needed to learn productively from those experiences. Figure 14.1 shows how LBD's activities are sequenced. Activities in the design/redesign cycle (on the left) are those needed to successfully achieve a design challenge. Because successful achievement of a challenge often requires investigation, an investigative cycle

(on the right) is a natural part of LBD. Activity begins at the top of the design/redesign cycle, and when students discover a need to learn something new, they engage in investigation. Results of investigations, in turn, provide content for application to the design in progress. Individual activities in each cycle are designed to move learners toward successful achievement of a challenge, and they integrate a variety of science, design, collaboration, and communication practices.

Enactment of LBD's cycles of activities involves participation in a variety of carefully scripted activity structures and sequences (Table 14.1). These classroom scripts are designed so that they allow success at carrying out the tasks in the cycles in Figure 14.1 at the same time that they provide practice at scientific reasoning and use of newly learned science concepts.

There are two types of classroom scripts represented in the cycles: action and discourse. *Action activities*, such as "designing an experiment," are associated with the skills and practices of science and design, and they promote methodological habit and rigor. Students carry out action activities in small groups, dividing up responsibilities for investigations across teams. *Discourse activities* suggest the modes and content of presentations and the focus of discussions that follow. Each discourse activity is inserted into LBD's sequencing at a time when listening to others might help in achieving the project challenge. Discourse activities

Table 14.1. A Selection of LBD's Scripted Activity Structures (Classroom Scripts)

Function(s) in Cycle	LBD Scripted Activity Structure (Classroom Script)	Type and Venue	Description
Design an investigation	**Design an experiment**	Action: small group	Given a question to investigate (in the form of discovering the effect of a variable), design an experiment where variables are controlled well, with appropriate number of trails, etc.
Analyze results; analyze and explain, present and share	**Creating and refining design rules of thumb**	Action, discourse: small group	Identify trends in data and behaviors of devices; connect scientific explanations so as to know when the trends apply (small groups suggest new rules of thumb and the need for changes in existing ones)
Present and share (investigate cycle)	**Poster session**	Discourse: present & share: whole class	Present procedures, results, and analysis of investigations for peer review, followed by rules of thumb
Plan design	**Plan design**	Action: small group	Choose and integrate design components to achieve the design challenge, basing choices on evidence
Present and share (design/redesign)	**Pin-up session**	Discourse: present & share: whole class	Present design ideas and design decisions and their justifications for peer review, followed by plan design or by construction and test of design
Construct and test	**Test design**	Action: small group	Run trials of constructed device, gather data about behavior, attempt to explain; followed by gallery walk
Present and share (design/redesign)	**Gallery walk**	Discourse: present & share: whole class	Present design experiences and explain design's behavior for peer review and advice; followed by whiteboarding and rules of thumb

encourage students to reflect on and interpret important aspects of their experiences during action activities – what they are doing, how successful they have been, what science content they are using, what they know about that science content, how the science connects to their project goals, and how their reasoning connects to their project goals.

LBD's Relationship to Case-Based Reasoning

The ultimate purpose of LBD sequencing is to scaffold the kinds of deliberation that result in students recognizing and revising their understanding, skills, and practices. Usually, small groups perform actions and make a first pass at reflecting, while whole-class activities provide a venue for presentations from small groups, sharing advice and concerns, struggling together to understand some phenomena, pulling out abstractions and generalizations across what small groups have presented, and discussing how to do the next action. The whole-class activities provide a way for students to learn from the experiences of their peers, extending the set of cases they might remember and be able to use at another time. Together, this entire system of activities enacts the set of learning principles that come from case-based reasoning:

Learning will happen best in contexts of trying to achieve goals of interest. LBD's design challenges are designed based on what we know about what middle-school children are interested in, and early activities in each unit help children become excited about the design challenge.

To learn well from their experiences, learners need to interpret their experiences so as to make them into well-articulated cases in their memories. LBD's whole-class discourse activities are inserted into the LBD cycle at times when students have had experiences they can learn science from, and requirements of the presentations they make are designed to encourage them to interpret their experiences such that they connect together their goals and what they did, identify and try to explain their mistakes and failures, and pull out lessons that will be useful at later times.

Experience applying cases from memory allows further learning. In LBD, students often repeat activities, using what they've just learned during discussions and discovering whether they understand those concepts and skills fully. They also have multiple opportunities to reuse the content and skills they've been learning.

Learners can learn from the cases of others as well as from their own. Presentation sessions are designed so that students not only hear about the experiences of their peers but also process their peers' experiences in order to be able to glean new ideas or provide advice. Teachers put posters students make for their presentations on the walls so that it

is easy to refer back to them, and in classes where case-authoring software is used to help with reflection (using SMILE: Nagle & Kolodner, 1999; Kolodner, Owensby, & Guzdial, 2004), students write their experiences into the computer as cases, creating an online case library for others to use. In addition, for some challenges, libraries of expert cases are available as resources (Owensby & Kolodner, 2004).

Learners can best learn from their mistakes and expectation failures if they get immediate feedback so that they have a way to recognize their errors and expectation failures, and if they can explain why the errors and expectation failures happened and what they should have done differently. In LBD, learners are asked to obtain real results or get something to work. If a device doesn't work as expected, students know there is a gap in their knowledge or capabilities. The whole-class discourse activities they engage in after each experience encourage explanation of what happened, recognition that they have gaps in their knowledge if they can't explain, and the opportunity to get help from their peers in putting explanations together.

An LBD Scenario

UNDERSTANDING THE CHALLENGE

In the Balloon Car Challenge, the second module in the *Vehicles in Motion* unit, students are challenged to design and build a propulsion system from balloons and straws that can propel a coaster car as far as possible. They begin by working in small groups to identify what might affect a balloon engine's behavior. Then they work as a class to identify investigations they might do to learn more about those effects. During this public session, they volunteer what they've observed (e.g., "It seems like a wider straw makes the car go farther,"), argue about what they saw and how to interpret it, (e.g., "I don't think we can compare across those cars because they didn't go exactly the same distance off the ramp. We'll need to run fair tests to really know."), try to explain what they observed (e.g., "I think the wider

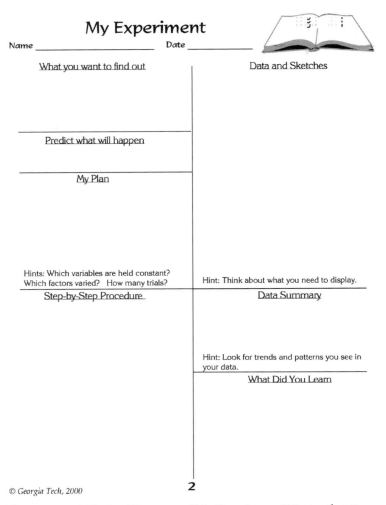

Figure 14.2. A Design Diary page: "My Experiment." Notice that it prompts learners for some of the important issues they need to discuss and/or plan for (See Puntambekar & Kolodner, 2004, for more detail).

straw makes it go farther because more air comes out of it, and that must mean more force."), and identify variables whose effects they want to know about conclusively (e.g., length of straw, extra engines, amount of air in the balloon). The teacher helps them turn their initial questions into questions that can be answered through well-controlled experiments (e.g., what effect does the size of a balloon have on the distance the car will travel?), each group is assigned one question to investigate, and the teacher reminds them about the ins and outs of good experimentation.

INVESTIGATE AND EXPLORE

Each group of students takes responsibility for investigating a question, and designs and runs an experiment to find an answer. Students use a "Design Diary" page (Figure 14.2) or SMILE's Designing an Experiment Tool (Figure 14.3) to prompt them on what to pay attention to as they design and run an experiment and collect data.

Students spend a day or two designing and running their experiments and collecting and analyzing their data, and at the beginning of the following day, each group

Procedure
Include step-by-step instructions so another team could run the same procedure. Be sure to include steps for measuring and recording data in your procedure.

Plan
Describe your plans for investigating your problem.

Plan Summary

What variable will you change?	Length of whirly gig wing
What values will you give it?	Original (template) Original + 1 inch Original + 2 inches
What conditions (variables) will you control?	Length of stem; Number of paperclips
How many trials will you run?	5
What will you measure and how?	The time the whirly gig is in the air

Step-by-step Procedure

Procedure step description	Thing(s) to be careful about	How you will be careful
Create 3 whirly gigs with different wing lengths	Keep the wing width and stem length constant	Use the template and only change the wing length
Have one person stand on a chair and drop a whirly gig.	Drop each whirly gig from the same height each time.	The same person should drop the whirly gig each time.
Have another person use a stopwatch to time how long the whirly gig is in the air.	Make sure the time is accurate.	Start the stopwatch as soon as the dropper lets go; stop the watch as soon as the whirly gig hits the ground.
For each whirly gig, repeat steps 1-2 five times.		
Find the average of the 5 trials for each whirly gig to see which one was the slowest.	Getting the average	Use a calculator

Figure 14.3. Additional prompting for "My Plan" and "Step-by-Step Procedure" in the software templates for "My Experiment" found in SMILE (See Kolodner et al., 2004, for more detail); details on an experiment are filled in.

prepares a poster to present to the class. Posters show their experimental design, data, and data interpretations, and – if the group can do it – a piece of advice for the class in the form of a rule of thumb. Each group presents to the class in a "poster session." Because students need to learn about each other's investigative results to be more successful balloon car designers, they listen intently and query each other about procedures and gathering and interpretation of data (much as in a poster session of a professional conference). This provides an opportunity to discuss the ins and outs of designing and running experiments. When some groups' results are not trustworthy yet, the class decides they should redo their experiments, and the cycle of activities just described is repeated.

When the class agrees that the results of most groups are believable, the teacher helps students abstract over the full set of experiments and experimental results to notice commonalities and extract out "design rules of thumb," for example, "By using double-

walled balloon engines, the car goes farther because a larger force is acting on the car." To learn the explanations behind these phenomena, students read about the science content involved, and the teacher might perform demonstrations of the science concept. Students also generate examples of the science concept from everyday life experiences. They then revisit the rule of thumb, producing a more informed and complete statement, for example, "By using double walled balloon engines, the car goes farther because a larger force is acting on the air inside, so then an equally large force from the air acts on the car."

BACK TO THE DESIGN CHALLENGE:
DESIGN PLANNING

With investigation complete, activity returns to the design/redesign cycle, and each group uses the results of the class's investigations to plan its balloon car design. They use a Design Diary page to record and justify design decisions, or the Pin-Up tool in SMILE to help with design planning (Figure 14.5).

Each group prepares another poster – this time presenting their design ideas along with the evidence that justifies each decision and their predictions about how it will perform. They present and justify their design decisions in a "pin-up session," using evidence from investigations, and they make predictions. After groups present to their peers and entertain their peers' questions and suggestions, the class discusses the ideas everyone has presented, followed by discussion of the practices and skills students have just engaged in – justifying, identifying, and using good evidence, and making predictions.

CONSTRUCT AND TEST; ANALYZE AND EXPLAIN; GALLERY WALK

Students modify their designs based on what they've discussed in class, and then they construct and test their first balloon-powered engine. They use another design diary page or SMILE tool here, this time with prompts helping them to keep track of their predictions, the data they are collecting as they test, whether their predictions are met, and if not, explanations why.

None of their balloon cars work exactly as predicted, sometimes because of construction problems and sometimes because of incomplete understanding of scientific principles. After working in small groups to try to explain their results, the class engages in a "gallery walk," with each group's presentation focused on what happened when their design was constructed and tested, why it worked the way it did, and what to do next so that it will perform better. Some students can explain quite well, but some students have not understood the science well and need help explaining. The teacher helps students state their explanations scientifically and calls on others in the class to help. Gallery walks are followed by classroom discussion summarizing the set of experiences presented, and design rules of thumb are revisited and revised, with a focus on better explaining why each one works. Discussion also focuses on the explanations students made and what good explaining entails.

REDESIGN: ITERATION AND FINISHING UP

In traditional classrooms, after solutions have been generated and discussed, the class moves on to its next topic or project. But in LBD, as CBR suggests, learners are given the opportunity to try again, often several times. Students revise their designs based on explanations their peers have helped them develop and on new things they've learned. They construct and test their new designs and present results to the class for discussion, iterating toward better solutions and better science understanding.

The entire balloon car module takes ten to twelve 45-minute class periods. At the end, the class holds a final gallery walk and a competition, and they compare and contrast across designs to better understand the scientific principles they are learning, going back to the rules of thumb yet again to revise and explain them better. They finish up, as well, by discussing their collaboration experience, their design process, their use of evidence, and so on. Following all of this group work, each student writes up and hands in a project report – including a summary of the reasoning behind their group's final design and what they've learned about collaboration, design, use of evidence, and so on.

Assessing the Success of Learning By Design

We've carried out field tests in over a dozen classrooms and compared knowledge and capabilities of students participating in LBD environments to students in matched comparison classes (with matched teachers). Our assessments are in two areas: (1) assessing content learning by comparing change from pre- to post-curriculum on written, mostly multiple-choice exams, and (2) assessing students' use of science practices as they occur during data-gathering and analysis activities and during experimental design activities. Our results show that LBD students consistently learn science content as well or better than comparison students. The data we are most proud of, however, comes from our analysis of student performance capabilities. This data shows large, consistent differences between all LBD classes and their comparisons. While they are engaging in science activities, LBD students recall more of what they've learned than do comparison students, and they greatly outperform comparison students in their abilities to design experiments, plan for data gathering, and collaborate. Indeed, some mixed-achievement LBD classes outperform comparison honors students on these measures (Gray et al., 2001; Kolodner, Gray, & Fasse, 2003).

Case Libraries as Resources: Archie-2 and Case Application Suite (CAS)

One of CBR's claims is that we can learn from the experiences of others. That's the reason LBD has students present to each other several times during a project – so that they can learn from their peers. As an alternative, cases can be made available in databases; we call such resources "case libraries." Cases available from the literature can be compiled into a case library; experts can be interviewed to collect their experiences, students can record their experiences online for other students to use, and so forth. Case libraries can offer a variety of different kinds of information of value to learners:

- *Advice in the form of stories*: Cases are like stories, and the stories experts and peers tell can be useful. Valuable stories are those that help a student understand a situation, the solution that was derived and why it was derived that way, and what happened as a result, as well as the explanations that tie those pieces together. For example, in Yello, video stories told by experts were made available to help learners explain their sales mistakes.

- *Vicarious experience using a concept or skill*: We know that it takes several encounters with a concept or skill to learn it well (Redmond, 1992) – encounters that cover the range of applicability of the concept or skill allow the learner to see its varied uses, the other concepts or skills it is related to, and to debug its applicability and refine its definition. But there isn't time in school for students

to actively experience the full range of applicability of a concept. Sharing experiences with other students and looking at the ways experts have applied concepts and skills can fill those gaps. For example, LBD's "tunneling" unit challenges students to plan the underground route of a transportation tunnel, taking into account the geology of the region. They read cases about tunnels and mines that help them understand the geological issues they need to consider in making their recommendations. Case libraries have also been integrated into university engineering and architecture classes, usually for the purpose of giving students easy access to the experiences of experts. Archie-2, a case library that recorded experiences of experts in designing public libraries, was used in several architecture classes at Georgia Tech (Domeshek & Kolodner, 1993; Zimring et al., 1995), whereas engineering classes at UC Berkeley used case libraries to teach mechanical design (e.g., Agogino & Hsi, 1994). Computer science classes at Georgia Tech used Stable (Guzdial & Kehoe, 1998) to get ideas about designing complex algorithms.

- *The lay of the domain and guidance on what to focus on*: A case library's indexing system, if it is available for examination, can serve as an advanced organizer for the student or even can scaffold how the student thinks about his or her own cases (Spiro et al., 1991). For example, the system of indexes in Archie-2 helped students develop an understanding of the issues that need to be addressed in designing public libraries, the kinds of spaces libraries have, and the perspectives different kinds of library users might take on how well it functions. The case library's indexing system provides a view of the domain's major concepts and their relationships and guidance on what to focus on when designing or solving problems, while the cases themselves provide advice about how to address each of those issues.

- *Strategies and procedures*: For novices in a domain, the biggest problem is sometimes how to start. In many theories of design, defining the problem properly is the most challenging task (Schon, 1982). Cases that describe somebody's problem-solving or design process can show how others have defined problems and proceeded through to a solution. Guzdial's Stable program (Guzdial & Kehoe, 1998) provides a good example of this functionality.

- *How to use cases*: Learning about others' experiences in such a way that learners can reuse the lessons learned in novel situations is a complex metacognitive activity (Silver, Branca, & Adams, 1980). Cases that are about applying someone else's case can help students understand how experts reuse cases. Case libraries that prompt for the kind of analysis that is necessary in deciding whether a case is relevant and how to adapt it for re-use can help learners develop case-based reasoning skills. A tool called the Case Application Suite, or CAS (Figure 14.4; Owensby & Kolodner, 2004; Kolodner et al., 2004), used in some LBD classes when students are reading tunneling cases, provides such help.

Case libraries can have beautiful interfaces or less fancy ones. Archie-2 shows its stories using a combination of text, photos, and schematics, the kinds of representations architects work with. Stable, on the other hand, was designed for computer scientists and shows its cases fully as text – programs with annotations attached. Broadcast News' and Yello's cases are presented as videos.

The case library tool used with LBD's tunneling unit is in the form of text plus illustrations, and because its users are not sophisticated reasoners, it also provides guidance in interpreting and applying those cases to the learners' design challenge. Figure 14.4 shows a screen from CAS used by students in LBD earth science classes. On the far left is the case students are reading; in the middle are questions to help learners organize what they are reading in the case, and on the

right is more detail on how to answer those questions.

It is important in designing case libraries that cases be presented in a format that typical users of the system will be able to understand and make sense of, that they have the content that learners need for whatever purpose the case library is designed for, that learners have a way of knowing the range of cases in the case library, and that learners have a way of finding appropriate cases. For learners who might not be able to interpret and use cases well, a case library tool also should provide guidance for understanding and using cases.

Case Authoring Tools in Support of Reflection: The Reflective Learner and SMILE

Research has shown that using case libraries helps students learn (e.g., Zimring et al., 1995). We've discovered that having students build case libraries can be even more valuable educationally. Students building a case library have to deal explicitly with issues of interpreting experiences, expressing their contents in ways that will allow others to understand and use them, and identifying appropriate ways of indexing or labeling them for easy access. The activity of building a case library also can motivate students to want to interpret their own or somebody else's experience because they are creating a public artifact whose purpose is to help future students (cf. Papert, 1991; Scardamalia & Bereiter, this volume; Kafai, this volume).

Authoring a case requires reflecting on a situation, sorting out its complexities, making connections between its parts, and organizing what one has to say into coherent and memorable chunks – exactly the kinds of interpretations of experience that CBR tells us are important to productive learning from experience. CBR suggests that the more attention is put to each of these interpretation tasks, the more productive learning will be. The need to write up one's experiences for others to read requires reflection

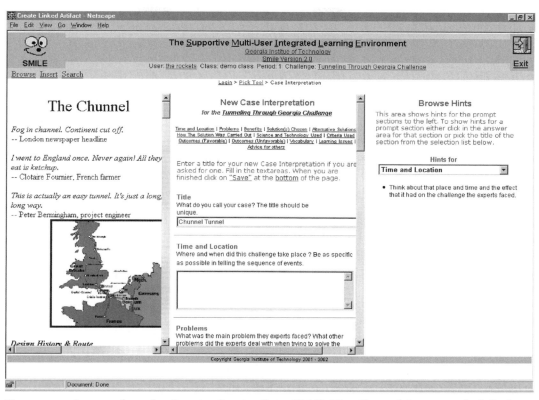

Figure 14.4. A screen from the Case Application Suite (CAS); The Chunnel Case is on the left; the center and right columns provide guidance to help learners know what they should extract from the case when reading it.

on one's experience, or at least sufficient review of the experience to be able to summarize its most salient parts.

CBR-inspired case authoring provides support for reflection by encouraging learners to think about (1) the kinds of problems they've faced in solving a problem or developing a skill or achieving a design challenge; (2) the kinds of solutions they constructed; (3) what happened as a result of those solutions, and if the solution didn't work as well as expected, why not; (4) lessons that can be learned from the situation; and (5) the future situations in which those lessons might be used in the future. Case authoring can be integrated into a learning environment in a way that seems fitting to students if cases they author will be placed into a case library and will be valuable to someone at a later time.

Turns' Reflective Learner program (Turns et al., 1997) was the first of these case-

authoring tools. It helps undergraduate students in project-based design courses write "learning essays" about their design experiences, providing them with a way to keep a personal portfolio of what they have learned. Turns discovered that these engineering students often didn't know what they were supposed to be learning, why they were engaging in the activities they were being asked to engage in, or how to reflect upon their activities in order to learn from them.

The Reflective Learner responds to these learner needs and provides prompts directly informed by CBR's suggestions about the reflection needed to be able to learn from and reuse one's experiences. It asks students:

- To identify and describe a problem that they had encountered when undertaking the current phase of their design project;
- To describe their solution to the problem;

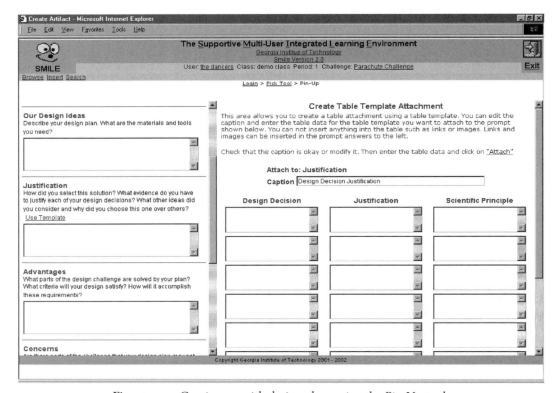

Figure 14.5. Coming up with design plans using the Pin-Up tool.

- To say what they had learned from the experience; and
- To anticipate the kinds of situations in which a similar solution might be useful.

Reflective Learner prompts students to articulate their goals, how they went about achieving them, what was difficult, and what could be learned from their experience. Despite the simplicity of its prompts, analysis showed that students who used Reflective Learner wrote longer, more structured essays and received significantly higher grades than those that did not (Turns, 1997).

Whereas those using Reflective Learner write up their experiences for their own benefit, in LBD classrooms that use software, students write up their experiences for others in the school to learn from. LBD's optional case authoring software tool, called SMILE (Kolodner et al., 2004; Nagel & Kolodner, 1999), provides prompts and other scaffolding to help students reflect on their experiences in ways that CBR suggests are

effective for learning, as they are authoring cases for others to use. SMILE is designed as a suite of tools, each providing prompting for a specific kind of experience students have during project-based inquiry activities. Two tools prompt students to write up their experiences designing and running an experiment, another prompts students to write up their experiences designing a solution to the project challenge, another prompts students to write up their experiences trying out a solution in progress, and so on. Though each has different prompts, each tool asks students to reflect on their goals, solutions, how well those solutions worked, what they learned, and when what they learned might be useful.

Figures 14.5 and 14.6 show two of those tools. The left-hand sides of the screens provide structure for writing up whatever kind of experience students are having or have just had, while the right side holds hints, examples, and templates to help with completing the task. Each prompts learners

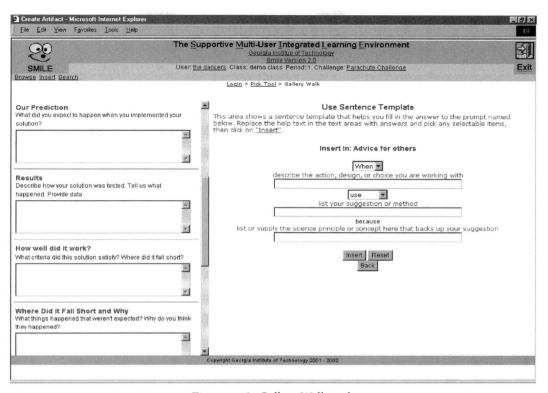

Figure 14.6. Gallery Walk tool.

to write down what they did in the task they are reporting on, because case-based reasoning suggests that interpreting what one has experienced so as to connect the pieces to each other and identify what's been learned will promote good learning.

The Pin-Up tool (Figure 14.5), for example, helps students use the results of investigations to come up with their best solution to their project challenge. Students formulate design decisions and justify them with evidence – from experiments just performed, rules of thumb extracted, and science principles read about. SMILE provides a template to help them line up their design decisions with their justifications. They use the Pin-Up tool as they are working to list their design decisions, justify why they have made each decision, and provide a scientific principle that supports each.

The Gallery Walk tool (Figure 14.6) scaffolds students as they reflect on their experiences with their solutions-in-progress

and plan presentations for their peers. It is used after they've constructed and tested a solution to their challenge. The first time students construct a solution, they construct it based on design decisions reported in their Pin-Up presentation. But those solutions rarely work exactly as they had thought. After trying out their ideas, this tool helps them look back on the decisions they had made and articulate what happened differently than they had imagined and explain why it happened. The Gallery Walk tool is linked to the Pin-Up tool so that students can see their decisions and justifications as they are analyzing their results. If students use the Gallery Walk tool after each of their iterations, then at the end of their design challenge, they have full documentation of their experience that chronicles the decisions that were made for each iteration and why each decision was made. This set can serve later to help them reflect over the whole design experience, and also as a case to be used by other students as they are engaging in the same challenge in future years.

After a team publishes its investigations, design ideas, or design experiences, their published artifacts are available to other teams. Looking at another team's case provides peers with ideas and helps them with explanations, but they don't always understand or agree with what's written in cases. Thus, each time a student opens a case in the case library in SMILE, the case appears on the left with a window on the right for comments. As in Knowledge Forum (Scardamalia & Bereiter, this volume), this part of the system provides scaffolds that (1) help students differentiate between continuing an old discussion and beginning a new one, (2) suggest to students what kinds of comments they might want to make – "praises," "wonders," and "suggests" for new threads; "replies," "wonders," and "suggests" for continuing threads.

Concluding Thoughts

Research on case-based reasoning provides powerful suggestions about how to make hands-on learning more effective: (1) make sure students have the opportunity to iteratively apply what they are learning – getting real feedback about what they've done so far, being helped to explain what happened if it was not what was expected, and having an opportunity to try again and again until they are successful and come to a full understanding of what they are learning; and (2) make sure to involve students in discussions and activities that ask them to reflect on their experiences, extract what they are doing and learning, and articulate it for themselves or others. CBR suggests *resources* that might be useful during learning – well-indexed libraries of expert cases and well-indexed libraries that hold the ideas and lessons learned by their peers – and *activities* that can enhance learning in any setting – writing cases to share with others, reading the cases of experts and preparing them for other students to learn from.

We have had considerable success in applying this cognitive theory to classroom learning. But it's a long way from cognitive theory to classroom implementation. For example, case-based reasoning says nothing about collaboration; it focuses on individual minds only. But sharing experiences across groups in a classroom is a substantial piece of what makes LBD successful. When we turn to the task of better defining CBR's theory of learning, our observations of this process reveal the need to integrate social construction of knowledge (see Scardamalia & Bereiter, this volume; Greeno, this volume) into CBR's framework to make it more complete (Kolodner, Crismond et al., 2003).

Identifying a good foundational theory of learning was a prerequisite to achieving the working designs for learning environments and educational software presented in this chapter. But my experience suggests that identifying a good foundational theory is only the first necessary step in that long process. One can't simply "apply" a theory to the classroom, because one can't identify beforehand the full range of affordances and constraints that will be present in the learning environment. Nor are any of our theories of learning complete enough to be fully predictive. Rather, we need to use our theoretical foundations as a first step in carefully designing learning environments or educational software, keeping track of why we made each of our design decisions, and then we need to test our designs iteratively in the kinds of environments in which we want them to be used, using design-based research methodologies (Barab, this volume). This approach was essential to the design of each of the computer systems and pedagogical approaches presented in this chapter. I look forward to hearing how others use the ideas about CBR presented in this chapter in their design research, and to learning about new tools and ways of managing learning that are created through such work. I also look forward to contributions by others to CBR's theory of learning, and to the possibility that guidelines put forth in this chapter might serve to improve learning in our schools.

References

Agogino, A., & Hsi, S (1994). The impact and instructional benefit of using multimedia case studies to teach engineering Design, *Journal of Educational Hypermedia and Multimedia*, 3(3/4), 351–376.

Blumenfeld, P. C., Soloway, E., Marx, R. W., Krajcik, J. S., Guzdial, M., & Palincsar, A. (1991). Motivating project-based learning: Sustaining the doing, supporting the learning. *Educational Psychologist*, 26(3 & 4), 369–398.

Domeshek, E., and Kolodner, J. L. (1993). Using the points of large cases. *Artificial Intelligence for Engineering Design, Analysis and Manufacturing (AIEDAM)*, 7(2), 87–96.

Gray, J., Camp, P., Holbrook, J., Fasse, B., & Kolodner, J. L. (2001). Science talk as a way to assess student transfer and learning: Implications for formative assessment. http://www.cc.gatech.edu/projects/lbd/pubtopic.html.

Guzdial, M., & Kehoe, C. (1998). Apprenticeship-based learning environments: A principled approach to providing software-realized scaffolding through hypermedia. *Journal of Interactive Learning Research*, 9(3/4), 289–336.

Hammond, K. J. (1989) *Case-based planning: Viewing planning as a memory task*. Boston: Academic Press.

Kolodner, J. L. (1983a). Maintaining organization in a dynamic long-term memory. *Cognitive Science*, 7(4), 243–280.

Kolodner, J. L. (1983b). Reconstructive memory: A computer model. *Cognitive Science*, 7(4), 281–328.

Kolodner, J. (1993). *Case Based Reasoning*. San Mateo, CA: Morgan Kaufmann Publishers.

Kolodner, Janet L. (1997). Educational implications of analogy: A view from Case-Based Reasoning. *American Psychologist*, 52(1), 57–66.

Kolodner, J. L., Crismond, D., Fasse, B., Gray, J., Holbrook, J., Puntembakar, S. (2003). Problem-based learning meets Case-Based Reasoning in the middle-school science classroom: Putting Learning-by-Design™ into practice. *Journal of the Learning Sciences*, 12(4).

Kolodner, J. L., Gray, J., & Fasse, B. B. (2003). Promoting transfer through Case-Based Reasoning: Rituals and practices in Learning by Design™ Classrooms. *Cognitive Science Quarterly*, 3, 183–232.

Kolodner, J. L., Owensby, J. N., & Guzdial, M. (2004). Case-based learning aids. In Jonassen, D. H. (Ed.) *Handbook of research for educational communications and technology* (2nd Ed.). Mahwah, NJ: Lawrence Erlbaum Associates, pp. 829–861.

Kolodner, J. L., & Simpson, R. L. (1989). The MEDIATOR: Analysis of an early case-based problem solver. *Cognitive Science* 13(4), 507–549.

Nagel, K., & Kolodner, J. L. (1999). SMILE: Supportive Multi-User Interactive Learning Environment http://www.cc.gatech.edu/projects/lbd/pubtopic.html.#software.

Owensby, J. N., & Kolodner, J. L. (2004). Case interpretation and application in support of scientific reasoning. In K. D. Forbus, D. Genter and T. Regier (Eds.), *Proceedings of the 26th annual conference of the cognitive science society* (pp. 1065–1070). Mahwah, NJ: Lawrence Erlbaum Associates.

Papert, S. (1991). Situating constructionism. In I. Harel & S. Papert (Eds.), *Constructionism* (pp. 1–11). Norwood, NJ: Ablex Publishing Company.

Puntambekar, S., & Kolodner, J. L. (2004). Toward implementing distributed scaffolding: Helping students learn science from design. *Journal of Research on Science Teaching*, 42(2), 185–217.

Redmond, M. (1992). *Learning by Observing and Understanding Expert Problem Solving*. Unpublished Ph.D. dissertation, College of Computing, Georgia Institute of Technology.

Schank, R. C. (1982). *Dynamic memory*. New York: Cambridge University Press.

Schank, R. C. (1999). *Dynamic memory revisited*. New York: Cambridge University Press.

Schank, R. C., & Abelson, R. L. (1977). *Scripts, plans, goals, and understanding*. Hillsdale, NJ: Lawrence Erlbaum Associates.

Schank, R. C., & Cleary, C. (1994). *Engines for education*. Lawrence Erlbaum Associates. http://www.ils.nwu.edu/~e_for_e.

Schank, R. C., Fano, A., Bell, B., & Jona, M. (1994). The design of goal-based scenarios. *Journal of the Learning Sciences*, 3(4), 305–346.

Schon, D. A. (1982). *The reflective practitioner: How professionals think in action*. New York: Basic Books.

Silver, E. A., Branca, N. A., & Adams, V. M. (1980). Metacognition: The missing link in problem solving? In R. Karplus (Ed.), *Proceedings of the Fourth International Conference for the Psychology of Mathematics Education* (pp. 213–222). Berkeley: University of California.

Spiro, R. J., Feltovich, P. J., Jacobson, M. J., & Coulson, R. L. (1991). Cognitive flexibility, constructivism, and hypertext: Random access instruction for advanced knowledge acquisition in ill-structured domains. *Educational Technology, 31*(5), 24–33.

Turns, J. (1997). *Learning Essays and the Reflective Learner: Supporting Assessment in Engineering Design Education.* Unpublished Ph.D. dissertation. School of Industrial and Systems Engineering. Georgia Institute of Technology.

Turns, J. A., Newstetter, W., Allen, J. K., & Mistree, F. (1997, June). The reflective learner: Supporting the writing of learning essays that support the learning of engineering design through experience, *Proceedings of the 1997 American Society of Engineering Educators Conference.* Milwaukee, WI.

Zimring, C. M., Do, E, Domeshek, E. and Kolodner, J. (1995) Supporting case-study use in design education: A computational case-based design aid for architecture. In J. P. Mohsen, ed., *Computing in engineering: Proceedings of the second congress* (pp. 1635–1642). New York: American Society of Civil Engineers.

CHAPTER 15

The Knowledge Integration Perspective on Learning and Instruction

Marcia C. Linn

The knowledge integration perspective emerged from studies of the conceptions of scientific phenomena that students bring to science class, from design studies refining science instruction, and from longitudinal studies of students' learning over weeks, months, and years. These studies stress that learners grapple with multiple, conflicting, and often confusing, ideas about scientific phenomena. They characterize learners as developing a repertoire of ideas, adding new ideas from instruction, experience, or social interactions, sorting out these ideas in varied contexts, making connections among ideas at multiple levels of analysis, developing more and more nuanced criteria for evaluating ideas, and formulating an increasingly linked set of views about any phenomenon.

The knowledge integration perspective capitalizes on the varied ideas held by students both individually and collectively to stimulate science learning. The knowledge integration perspective synthesizes recent investigations of science learning and instruction, culminating in a set of design patterns that promote coherent and cohesive

understanding, and design principles that guide customization of patterns. This chapter describes the process of knowledge integration and how knowledge integration resonates with current research programs. It offers guidance to researchers and curriculum designers wishing to promote lifelong science learning.

Learning and Knowledge Integration

My colleagues and I conducted over forty case studies of middle school students who were studying thermodynamics (Clark & Linn, 2003; Linn & Hsi, 2000). These studies illustrate the typical process of knowledge integration. We found that students generate a repertoire of ideas about each concept they are learning and about the links between concepts. The term *idea* refers to each view held by the learner. For example, students report multiple views of heat (Clark & Linn, 2003; Linn & Hsi, 2000). They report ideas based on experiences (metal feels colder than wood at room temperature), colloquial uses of language (heat and temperature are used interchangeably), analogies (heat as a substance that can be absorbed), connections to ideas about air (as a medium for transporting heat or as a barrier that prevents heat flow), contexts of learning (only heat flows in the classroom but heat, cold, and even temperature flow at home), or causality (heat causes objects to have the same temperature).

The case studies show that students form a personal repertoire of ideas and encounter similar and new ideas held by classmates, introduced in curriculum materials, and described by teachers. Students form fleeting and enduring ideas, hold consistent and seemingly contradictory ideas, and report causal, observational, visual, analogical, mathematical, abstract, and experiential ideas. The repertoire includes ideas at many levels of analysis, ideas that many students hold, and unique ideas often tied to a specific context. The case studies and other research suggest that students generate ideas about the science topic, methods of investigation, the nature of science and scientists, and their own science learning (see Table 15.1).

Observations of classroom science discourse show how students use evidence to sort out, compare, analyze, and critique the varied ideas they hold and encounter. For example, many students argue that metals are colder than wood because they feel colder at room temperature (Linn & Hsi, 2000). When asked for justification, students generate mechanisms saying, for example, that metals have the property of imparting cold. Evidence from a thermometer showing that metal and wood have the same temperature motivates students to generate new explanations for the way objects feel. They may attribute the measurements to the role of air or justify their view that objects have separate temperatures by arguing that humans, rabbits, and turtles have unique body temperatures. Some students point out that stoves, refrigerators, and tables also have different temperatures, demoting the evidence from the thermometer. Others note small differences in the thermometer read-

ings as supportive of their view about the difference in temperature of the objects. Some students try to make sense of the normative view that objects reach the same temperature by considering the temperature of their hand. Students often argue that heating and cooling are governed by separate processes, wonder how thermoses know when to cool and when to heat, and think some materials serve as barriers. Even expert scientists generate nonnormative ideas when asked whether it is better to wrap ice cream in a wool sweater or aluminum foil to keep it cold for a picnic (Lewis & Linn, 1994).

Students express various forms of uncertainty about which ideas apply in each situation, signaling that they are grappling with the repertoire. They change their responses when questioned about slightly different contexts or situations. They respond to countersuggestions with new ideas. They answer "I don't know" not only when they have no clue but also when they cannot reconcile alternatives.

Knowledge Integration Trajectories

Hsi and I (Linn & Hsi 2000) summarized the trajectories students follow as they formulate and refine their repertoire of ideas. In a five year longitudinal study, we highlighted how students' ideas about scientific phenomena, scientific investigations, the nature of science and scientists, as well as their own learning contribute to the way they integrate ideas. We identified four typical trajectories that offer guidance to those designing instruction.

For a given topic, some students follow a trajectory described as *conceptualizing*. They start with a broad range of ideas about a phenomenon but quickly promote normative ideas and adopt abstract ideas such as heat flow. These students sometimes use evidence to explain why their nonnormative ideas appeared compelling, but often they neglect everyday examples that were the source of their original views. Consistent with most textbook accounts of science, these students quickly embrace general principles. When these students dominate class

Table 15.1. *Varieties of student ideas. These four varieties of student ideas have emerged in research on student learning. Students hold multiple ideas of each variety relevant to most science topics. They link these ideas both within and across varieties. The boundaries between varieties may blur within a specific context.*

Variety of Idea	Sources and Examples	Evidence
Ideas about disciplinary phenomena	Students form multiple views of concepts like force, atoms, heat, temperature, or DNA. They rely on colloquial use of terms such as model, evolution, reproduction, catalyst, and bond. They distinguish meanings from experience in specific contexts, arguing, for example, that objects remain in motion in science class but come to rest on the playground. They add views advocated by peers, family, and even persuasive messages such as advertisements.	Pfundt & Duit (1991) have compiled an extensive bibliography of studies of intuitive ideas about science organized by discipline. Numerous studies of topics like heat and temperature (Linn & Hsi, 2000), buoyancy (Howe, et al., 2000), and force (diSessa et al., 2004) describe the varied ideas by the same individual.
Ideas about scientific investigation	Students build conceptions about science investigations – how to research a topic, distinguish evidence and hypotheses, form an argument, communicate to an audience, interpret findings, and identify a research question – in formal and informal settings. They may control variables for cars on a ramp and confound experiments concerning ingredients for cakes. Students may overgeneralize the power of controlled experiments and conclude that scientists cannot explore the causes of dinosaur extinction because you "cannot vary the conditions."	Students' ideas about investigations often vary by disciplinary topic (diSessa, 2000; Metz, 2000). Most students design fair footraces but confound experiments with unfamiliar variables (Linn & Hsi, 2000). An emphasis on recipe-like scientific methods can deter students from careers in science (AAUW, 2000) and from appreciating the nature of science (Millar & Driver, 1987; Osborne & Young, 1998).
Ideas about the nature of science and scientists	Students develop ideas about how science progresses, how scientists establish valid results, how scientists select topics for study, and how laboratories work. Students often have quite impoverished views of the nature of science – assuming that science unfolds, that scientists disagree most of the time, that all disputes are resolved by empirical experiments, or that all results from investigations are accurate.	Ideas about the nature of science interact with science learning (Bell & Linn, 2002; diSessa, Elby, & Hammer; 2002). When students endorse the idea that science unfolds, they may inhibit their own efforts to make sense of science – preferring to memorize the right answers (Songer & Linn, 1992).
Ideas about the nature of science learning	Students develop ideas about how to monitor progress, the value of memorizing, who is welcome in science, and how to deploy personal resources. They often act like cognitive economists, allocating the minimum amount of effort to learning. Students who report that memorizing is better than understanding and that everything in the science textbook is true are less successful in inquiry science courses than students who report making sense of science (Linn & Hsi, 2000).	Students' ability to monitor their progress and allocate their efforts judiciously contributes to success in science (Bjork, 1999; Chi, 1996). Students' beliefs about who can learn science impact decisions about participation and persistence in science (AAUW, 2000; Crouch & Mazur, 2001) and performance on high-stakes tests (Steele, 1999).

discussions, they may lull instructors into thinking that all students are following this path.

Students who follow a trajectory described as *experimenting* start with numerous ideas, seek new ideas, test their ideas in multiple contexts, and regularly reprioritize their ideas. These students add both normative and nonnormative ideas, frequently generalizing ideas from one context to explain an observation in another context. They often develop unique and insightful accounts of everyday scientific phenomena. For example, Linn and Hsi (2000) reported on an experimenter who began by making an analogy between the size of holes in sweaters, blankets, or shawls and the ability of the material to insulate. Initially, the student described the hole as like a door, arguing that a hole would let heat flow out. Later, this student added a new analogy between a hole and a bubble, and described the bubble as consisting of still air. The bubble analogy enabled the student to connect to normative ideas while also continuing to make sense of everyday experiences.

Students who follow the *strategizing* trajectory rigorously separate the school context from other contexts and seek to succeed with minimal effort. These students argue against connecting school and out-of-school ideas and view science as a collection of facts that come from authorities. Strategizers often report that science involves figuring out ways to answer the questions likely to be on the test. For example, Linn and Hsi (2000) described a student who relied on memorizing in middle school and reported that this approach works. In high school, looking back, the student realized some benefits of understanding. The student, however, continued to avoid efforts at understanding, arguing that depictions of heat in chemistry do not connect to problems encountered in middle school physical science.

Students who *contextualize* isolate ideas in specific contexts rather than seeking connections. Students following this trajectory often say they do not know the answer in interviews because they lack criteria for selecting among alternatives. They regularly explain potential conundrums by distinguishing situations, arguing, for example, that heating and cooling are different or that objects reach their own temperature in an oven.

These trajectories illustrate the processes students use to grapple with diverse ideas. In each trajectory, students limit their focus to a subset of ideas. Conceptualizers focus on abstract, normative ideas, experimenters pay attention to intriguing contexts, strategizers learn the textbook ideas, and contextualizers view each context as unique. The longitudinal studies reveal leverage points for strengthening instruction so students learn to reconcile their ideas (Linn, Davis, & Bell, 2004).

Roots and Support of the Repertoire of Ideas

The emphasis on the repertoire of ideas has its roots in my experience working with Piaget in Geneva. I was fascinated by Piaget's description of structuralism and perplexed by his depiction of an age-related transition from concrete to formal reasoning (Piaget, 1970). As I sat at the table in Geneva listening to Piaget interpret the experimental findings reported in the seminar each week, I began to wonder about the boundaries between stages. I visited schools with Alina Szeminska and listened to the students struggling to explore complex problems such as predicting the path of a marble on a curved track. Students were surprised when the marble escaped from the track, and Szeminska was masterful at eliciting a variety of explanations for the phenomena. These experiences drew my attention to the richness of student ideas.

When I returned from Geneva, I investigated adolescent reasoning in multiple contexts (Linn, Clement, & Pulos, 1983). I interviewed students about traditional physics tasks, such as the balance beam, pendulum, and bending rods, and about everyday tasks that require similar logic, such as comparing advertised specials, determining which factors influence plant growth, or designing fair foot races. Scoring student responses to these interviews echoed my experience in Geneva: students gave multiple answers to the same question. Students often used sophisticated logic to reach multiple, nonnormative conclusions. They used unsophisticated logic to reach normative conclusions. They combined concrete ideas with abstract arguments. Familiarity with the variables in everyday tasks led students to give more complete explanations than they gave for the often unfamiliar physics tasks.

Recent research strengthens the knowledge integration emphasis on the repertoire of ideas. Howe et al. (2000) interviewed precollege students about scientific phenomena such as buoyancy, heat transfer, motion, and force. They reported, for example, that for buoyancy, the group generated over two hundred distinct ideas and each individual held between five and fifteen ideas. Even when several students have the same idea they often justify their view quite differently. Metz (2000) studied upper elementary students' investigations of the behavior of organisms. Metz identified more than twenty variables mentioned by students such as imprecise measurement, artificial lab conditions, order effects, range of conditions, or idiosyncratic behavior. She found that student ideas are similar across age groups and reflect understanding of the context. diSessa (diSessa, Elby, & Hammer, 2002) analyzed seven interviews with a college physics student to show that scientific knowledge is fragile and fragmented. Siegler (1996) analyzed research from mathematics, biology, reading, memory, and physics to show that students report multiple ideas in the same interview.

These research programs suggest that students develop a repertoire that includes ideas that are sound, contradictory, confused, idiosyncratic, arbitrary, and based on flimsy evidence. The way students justify and organize their ideas reveals their epistemology of science, beliefs about learning, and views of scientists. Many students combine evidence from authoritative statements about phenomena, experiments they conduct themselves, and persuasive messages,

suggesting that they hold multiple criteria for scientific claims. Most students lack criteria for distinguishing ideas or evaluating the cohesion of their ideas. Research on instruction and knowledge integration seeks to take advantage of the variation in ideas while at the same time encouraging students to sort out their ideas and develop criteria, so they can build coherent accounts of scientific phenomena that include links among all the varieties of ideas they hold.

Instruction and Knowledge Integration

Initial investigations of knowledge integration instruction sought to increase the success of students underrepresented in science and engineering by enabling them to develop more coherent accounts of the discipline (Linn, 1995). Classroom observations and interviews revealed that students struggling in introductory college courses often believe they should be able to solve problems without encountering dead ends or wrong paths. Clancy and I (Linn & Clancy, 1992) created case studies to be used as a component in university computer science courses. Instruction using the case studies emphasized selecting among several alternative solutions to a complex problem to illustrate the process of program design. Our observations of the use of these case studies yielded four tenets that describe how this pedagogical approach promotes knowledge integration. First, the case studies *make computer science accessible* by requiring students to compare multiple solutions to personally relevant complex problems like cataloguing record collections or developing reservation systems for railroads. Second, the case studies help *make the thinking of the program designer visible*, illustrating wrong paths, and erroneous forms of reasoning, as well as methods for comparing alternative designs for complex problems. Third, the use of case studies *enables students to learn from others*, because they were required to negotiate among the repertoire of ideas in the classroom. When students negotiate,

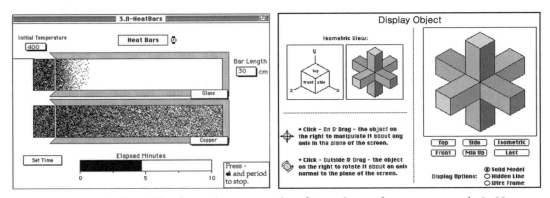

Figure 15.1. Pivotal Cases. This figure shows examples of pivotal cases from past research. In Heat Bars (http://clp.berkeley.edu/CLP/pages/S_hbdemo.htm), students use an interactive animation to explore the rate of heat flow in different materials. In Display Object (http://best.me.berkeley.edu/~aagogino/fie95/FIE95.4a2.1.agogino.html), students use an interactive construction animation to explore the various views of a three-dimensional object.

they respond to alternative designs advocated by their peers, develop personal criteria for their decisions, and make their solutions comprehensible to others. Fourth, the use of case studies *promotes lifelong learning* by engaging students in reflecting on alternative solutions, monitoring their own progress, and developing personal practices that involve sorting out ideas. Students who critique alternatives, develop criteria for distinguishing solutions, and reflect on progress, develop more coherent understanding of computer science. This coherent understanding shows itself in knowledge integration assessments that tap ability to contrast solutions, test potential connections, and solve novel, complex problems.

Clancy (Clancy et al., 2003; Linn & Clancy, 1992) compared partial and full case study instruction to evaluate the effectiveness of elements of the case studies. The full case study was more effective than exploring the code without narrative, or exploring the narrative without reflection notes. Clancy found that revising programming courses to include case studies improved the performance of all students and had the additional effect of reducing the gap between the performance of male and female students. Case studies became a part of many university courses and are required of all students taking Advanced Placement computer science courses and examinations.

Researchers seeking to improve an undergraduate graphical communication course built on the findings of the above study by using the four tenets as guidelines to design the course (Linn, 1995). For example, to make graphical design accessible, the course added a 3-D visualization tool that helps students interpret three dimensional problems using two dimensional representations (see Figure 15.1). The revised course improved the ability of all students to create and interpret graphically presented information and also closed the gap between performance of males and females (Linn, 1995).

The Computer as Learning Partner research program tested and refined the four tenets in a middle school thermodynamics course using an iterative process of design, analysis, and revision. The tenets guided eight revisions of the curriculum, each taught to a new cohort of about three hundred students. The revisions resulted in a 400 percent improvement in coherent understanding (Linn & Hsi, 2000). To make science accessible, the revisions included emphasizing everyday problems such as designing a container to keep picnic food cold. An animation called heat bars that illustrates the relative rate of heat flow in different materials helped students link seemingly disparate ideas about thermal equilibrium and insulation (see Figure 15.1). Adding predictions to experimental investigations

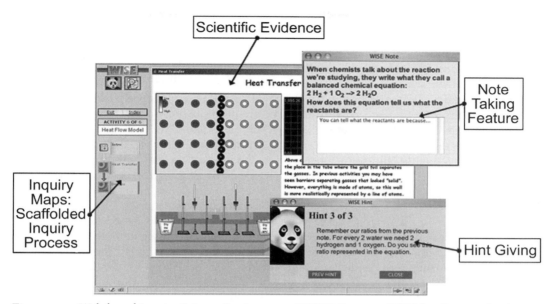

Figure 15.2. Web-based Inquiry Science Environment (WISE) Features. WISE has features (such as reflection notes, argument construction tools, concept maps, group discoveries, and opportunities to make predictions and get feedback) to support authors, teachers, and researchers wishing to improve knowledge integration (see http://WISE.berkeley.edu). This screen comes from a Chemical Reactions project.

helped students reflect on their ideas. The research on thermodynamics instruction strengthened the definitions of the four main tenets of knowledge integration and yielded evidence for fourteen specific principles that elaborated on the tenets (Linn & Hsi, 2000).

Technology-Enhanced Learning Environments and Knowledge Integration

A partnership of researchers, classroom teachers, and technologists designed the Web-based Inquiry Science Environment (WISE) to test the knowledge integration tenets with more topics, teachers, and learning contexts (Linn, Davis, & Bell, 2004). The WISE technology-enhanced learning environment (see Figure 15.2) enables collaborators to rapidly author new activities, document student learning with embedded assessments, and design powerful comparison studies that vary elements of instruction such as prompts for reflection even within the same classroom (Linn, Clark, & Slotta, 2003). WISE guides students using

an inquiry map that captures the sequence of activities students follow and enables teachers to devote more attention to resolving the challenges and difficulties faced by individuals. Researchers have designed and tested over twenty-five WISE projects that are available without cost to teachers everywhere (see http://WISE.Berkeley.edu).

Research with WISE takes advantage of design study methodologies (Barab, this volume; Design-Based Research Collective, 2003; Linn, Davis, & Bell, 2004). Iterative refinement studies and comparison studies capture design knowledge that can then be synthesized in design principles and patterns. These studies use knowledge integration assessments that enable students to display their repertoire of ideas and show how those ideas are connected; traditional multiple-choice items such as those found on high-stakes tests often lack sensitivity to instruction that promotes knowledge integration (Clark & Linn, 2003). Reflection questions, embedded in instruction, document progress in knowledge integration at regular intervals and help partnerships identify strong and weak aspects of their designs. Short essay questions that require students to use evidence and formulate arguments offer opportunities to display progress in knowledge integration.

Design studies using WISE projects and assessments have refined understanding of the tenets of knowledge integration. Research on making science accessible shows that students who see science as personally relevant – when studying topics such as genetically modified foods – learn more than when they study traditional abstract versions of the science (Linn & Hsi, 2000). Studies reveal the characteristics of ideas that, when added to the mix held by students, promote integrated understanding. For students who do not understand the particulate nature of matter, adding inaccessible ideas such as the molecular model of heat can interfere with learning (see Figure 15.1).

Research on making thinking visible has resulted in argumentation tools such as SenseMaker and projects that introduce students to contemporary scientific controversies (Andriessen, this volume; Linn, Davis, & Bell, 2004). Research on argumentation shows that students benefit from preparing arguments for both sides of a debate, exploring their whole repertoire rather than only preparing one perspective. Developing arguments for controversial topics like the causes of the declining amphibian population in the United States give students a window on science in the making and help students interpret scientific evidence.

Research on learning from others offers guidance about the many decisions involved in designing a productive discussion, including determining sources of evidence, collaborative structures, and negotiation goals (Linn & Slotta, 2006). Inspired by work on reciprocal teaching (Brown & Campione, 1994), CSILE (Scardamalia & Bereiter, 1991, this volume), and Kids as Global Scientists (Songer, 1996), WISE designers have demonstrated how students can learn from discussion alone and identified productive patterns involving discussion (Linn, Davis, & Bell, 2004).

Research on lifelong learning stresses the importance of critique of experiments and evidence, a topic often neglected in the curriculum. Research on helping students monitor their learning demonstrates both successful and unsuccessful ways to incorporate prompts into science projects. Prompts for predictions, to elicit explanations, and for alternative ideas all promote knowledge integration. Prompts that ask students to evaluate their progress have had mixed success (Davis & Linn, 2000; White & Frederiksen, 1998).

Researchers have tested and elaborated the knowledge integration perspective for diverse contexts such as chemistry education (Kali et al., 2003), modeling (Linn & Eylon, in press), and informal learning environments such as aquariums (Zimmerman, 2005). They have applied the perspective to preservice (Davis, 2003) and in-service professional development (Sisk-Hilton, 2002; Williams et al., 2004). Cognitive scientists have used the perspective to test ideas from laboratory studies in classrooms (Richland et al., 2005). Together these studies suggest design patterns and principles that can guide future designers.

Design Patterns and Principles

To synthesize research on knowledge integration, researchers have sought to systematically capture *design patterns* (Linn & Eylon, in press; see Table 15.2) from multiple research programs. A design pattern is a sequence of activities followed by teachers and students in a classroom.

The WISE inquiry map delineates the activities that students perform. Activities such as discussion, evidence gathering, prompts for reflection, hands-on experiments, or diagnosis of ideas can occur in productive and unproductive patterns. Design patterns to promote knowledge integration contrast with the traditional instructional pattern that might be described as *motivate, inform, and assess*. In the traditional pattern, demonstrations or unusual events motivate interest, lectures plus textbooks provide information about science,

Table 15.2. Design patterns. Design patterns emphasize the four processes of knowledge integration: Eliciting ideas, adding normative ideas, developing criteria, and sorting out ideas. They describe activity structures used in science classrooms to promote knowledge integration

Pattern	Description	Relevant Research
Orient, diagnose, and guide	The *orient, diagnose, and guide* pattern recursively defines the scope of a topic, connects the topic to personally relevant problems, links the new topic to prior instruction, identifies students' entering ideas, and adds ideas to stimulate knowledge integration.	Instructors often find student ideas surprising (Linn & Hsi, 2000). Benchmark lessons (diSessa & Minstrell, 1998), bridging analogies (Clement, 1993), didactic objects (Thompson, 2002) and pivotal cases (Linn, 2005), when added to the mix of student ideas, can help promote knowledge integration. Designing instruction to respond to student ideas can improve learning (Crouch & Mazur, 2001).
Predict, observe, explain	The *predict, observe, explain* pattern involves recursively eliciting student ideas about a topic, demonstrating the phenomenon, and asking students to reconcile contradictions (Songer, 1996; White & Gunstone, 1992).	Using this pattern improves student learning compared to demonstration alone (Sokoloff & Thornton, 2004; Linn & Hsi, 2000). Predictions enable students to test their ideas and evaluate the results (Linn, Songer, & Eylon, 1996).
Illustrate ideas	The *illustrate ideas* pattern models authentic reasoning about a topic, making visible strategies for grappling with complex questions. Students try out the strategies and reflect on their views.	Case studies and historical notebooks illustrate how scientists framed and explored problems to improve student outcomes (Clancy et al., 2003; Palinscar et al., 2001).
Experiment	The *experiment* pattern involves a recursive process of framing a question, generating methods for investigating the question, carrying out an investigation, evaluating the results, and using the findings to sort out the repertoire of ideas.	This pattern enables students to make decisions about what is a good experiment and what can be learned from an experiment. Teachers need experience to use the pattern successfully to improve knowledge integration (Linn, et al., 2004; Polman, 2000).
Explore a simulation	The *explore a simulation* pattern involves a recursive process of framing a challenge, contest, or question, testing conjectures with a simulation, applying criteria supplied by the simulation, and revising ideas.	This pattern requires well-designed environments to succeed (Pallant & Tinker, 2004). Simulations of the layers of the earth improve student understanding (Kali, Orion, & Eylon, 2003) when supported by prompts to evaluate outcomes.
Create an artifact	The *create an artifact* pattern involves a recursive process of framing a question, selecting or creating a draft artifact, evaluating the results, improving the artifact, and connecting the results to views of the topic.	Learners gain deeper understanding of complex systems such as behavior of ants, planetary motion, electricity, genetics, heat flow, or oxygenation of blood using this pattern (diSessa, 2000; Pallant & Tinker, 2004; Redish, 2003).

(continued)

Table 15.2 (*continued*)

Pattern	Description	Relevant Research
Construct an argument	The *construct an argument* pattern involves selecting a question, generating ideas, identifying evidence, articulating a viewpoint, and revising the viewpoint based on feedback or new evidence.	Debates where students emulate the techniques used by practicing scientists to defend competing hypotheses about topics like dinosaur extinction improve understanding of science (Linn et al., 2004).
Critique	The *critique* pattern asks learners to recursively evaluate ideas about scientific phenomena, apply criteria, warrant assertions with evidence, and revise their criteria.	Critique, although neglected in science courses, is often easier than creating a solution and can help students begin to formulate criteria (Linn & Hsi, 2000; diSessa et al., 2002).
Collaborate	In the *collaborate* pattern, students generate their own ideas, respond to group ideas, support their views, and reach consensus. Negotiating meaning is central to student knowledge integration.	Consistent with Vygotsky's (1978) notion of the zone of proximal development, the *collaborate* pattern succeeds when groups respect the ideas of each participant (Brown & Campione, 1994; Cohen, 1994) and negotiate understanding (Linn & Slotta, in press).
Reflect	The *reflect* pattern encourages learners to analyze the connections they make between their ideas and to monitor their understanding. Varying prompts reveals which approaches succeed (Linn, Davis, & Bell, 2004).	Reflection stimulates metacognition, encouraging learners to identify gaps in their ideas and seek ways to fill the gaps (Bjork, 1999; Chi, 1996; Krajcik et al., 1999).

and tests plus homework assess whether students have understood the material.

Research on instruction suggests four interrelated processes that jointly lead to integrated understanding: eliciting current ideas, adding new ideas, evaluating ideas, and sorting out ideas. These processes characterize design patterns that promote knowledge integration (see Table 15.2).

ELICIT CURRENT IDEAS

Instruction that *elicits current ideas* from the many contexts students encounter including home, museum, recreation, and school provides the variety that improves knowledge integration. Students benefit from considering all their ideas, as they form links and connections, rather than isolating ideas in one context or another (Linn & Hsi, 2000). Considering the variety of ideas held

by their community often spurs students to recall more of their own ideas and to make new connections among ideas (Clark & Linn, 2003).

ADD NEW, NORMATIVE IDEAS

Instruction that *adds new, normative ideas* can provoke knowledge integration. Because students prefer adding ideas over distinguishing and comparing ideas, designers need to find ideas that stimulate reconsideration of existing views. When students isolate normative ideas rather than connecting them to existing ideas, the new ideas are quickly forgotten. When analogies or examples distract learners or reinforce unproductive ideas, they can interfere with knowledge integration. Research suggests that the image of electricity as water flowing might mislead students (Eylon &

Linn, 1988). Holyoak (Pedone, Hummel, & Holyoak, 2001) showed benefits of animated analogies but not of regular analogies. Eylon (Linn, Songer, and Eylon, 1996) showed how models of single particles can convince students that individual atoms or molecules have the properties of the collection such as color or viscosity. Ideas that stimulate knowledge integration have been called *prototypes* (Songer & Linn, 1992), *bridging analogies* (Clement, 1993), *didactic objects* (Thompson, 2002), *benchmark lessons* (diSessa, 2000), and *pivotal cases* (Linn, 2005). Songer and Linn (1992) defined prototypes as examples where students can accurately predict the outcome of an experiment but do not necessarily understand the mechanism. For example, students can predict that wooden spoons are better than metal spoons for stirring boiling water because the wooden spoon will be cooler to the touch, but they cannot explain that metal conducts heat better than wood.

The knowledge integration perspective combines these research findings to define *pivotal cases* as new ideas that, when added to the repertoire, lead to more cohesive and normative understanding (see Figure 15.1). Research suggests that successful pivotal cases (a) make a compelling, scientifically valid comparison between two situations; (b) draw on accessible, culturally relevant contexts, such as everyday experiences; (c) provide feedback that supports students' efforts to develop criteria and monitor their progress; and (d) encourage students to create narrative accounts of their ideas using precise vocabulary so they can discuss them with others. For example, to help explain why objects that feel differently can have the same temperature, teachers encourage students to distinguish the feel of wood and metal at home on a cool day with the feel of these materials at the beach on a hot day. This example fits the criteria for a pivotal case because it offers a rigorous comparison between hot and cool days, describes familiar situations, provides feedback that helps students evaluate ideas, and offers students an example they can discuss with others.

DEVELOP CRITERIA

Instruction that helps students *develop criteria* to evaluate ideas promotes cohesive understanding. Students get ideas from the textbook, the Internet, advertisements, experiments, personal experience, teachers, and peers. Students often report that everything in the science text is true. They accept bogus results – available on the Internet or in popular publications – because they are cloaked in scientific jargon. Science courses neglect the controversies that led to scientific advance, rarely discuss limits of research methods, and often uncritically accept ideas attributed to scientists. Students successfully evaluate ideas and develop criteria when they combine knowledge of methods for investigation, understanding of techniques for studying the disparate kinds of phenomena that they might encounter (such as earthquakes, cloning, design of new drugs, and environmental conservation), and insight into the work of scientists. Students need criteria that help them to integrate all their ideas (see Table 15.1) to build coherent understanding.

SORT OUT IDEAS

Instruction that helps students sort out their ideas and build strong connections among ideas provides a basis for future learning. Students need to use their criteria to distinguish levels of analysis, resolve contradictions, identify overlaps and gaps in their knowledge, and seek connections (Bransford, Brown, & Cocking, 2000). When students reflect, they can use their criteria to promote some ideas and demote others. To succeed, students need to allocate their limited energy to the most central conundrums and to monitor their progress. Many students instead respond to the barrage of information in science courses by memorizing information they expect to be on the test and later forgetting what they memorized.

These four processes (elicit ideas, add ideas, form criteria, sort out ideas) play out in ten design patterns that combine activities from curriculum materials, instructors, and peers (see Table 15.2). To achieve goals such as inquiry or autonomy, and to take advantage of varied learning contexts such as computer labs, lecture halls, or after school programs, effective curriculum materials generally use a combination of the design patterns. For example, in inquiry learning, students may benefit from multiple opportunities to add ideas such as experiments, models, and demonstrations. Combination patterns may vary learning activities to appeal to diverse students, or to activate verbal, visual, and social modes of learning.

The design patterns leave unanswered questions about which disciplinary issues to emphasize. To achieve an instructional goal, designers need to combine patterns, select pivotal cases, and determine the scope of instruction for the scientific topic.

The knowledge integration perspective stresses the importance of iterative refinement in the design of instruction. Even the most well thought-out instruction informed by the design patterns benefits from refinement in the contexts of use. The repertoire of ideas represented among students varies from one setting to another. Ideally, instruction designers should develop activities that are readily customized, while retaining all four of the processes that promote knowledge integration. Such activities enable teachers to find ways to customize instruction for all learners and to meet the needs of students at risk of failure in science. To guide customization and to capture promising features of learning environments, Kali (Kali et al., 2002; see Figure 15.3) created a design principles database and motivated researchers to add features that have proven successful in classroom studies. Design principles help designers find the right feature to add to an activity. Customizers can use the database to locate alternatives when one approach fails.

Integrating Views of Science Learning and Instruction

The knowledge integration perspective builds on the broad range of research in science education – offering a way to link and connect research from multiple paradigms. Just as encouraging student ideas to bump up against each other improves science understanding, the field can also benefit when the varied ideas developed in research programs collide. People have argued that educational theories are like toothbrushes – valuable to their owners, but never shared. The knowledge integration perspective values variety in accounts of learning and instruction. Knowledge integration encourages researchers to analyze their diverse views – identifying similarities as well as disparities – and to increase the coherence in the field. The design patterns and principles illustrate forms of research synthesis to support this process.

Research from the developmental, sociocultural, cognitive, and constructivist research programs helps clarify how students generate ideas and make sense of them. Piaget's developmental theory stimulated the early research on adolescent reasoning that motivated the focus on knowledge integration. The sociocultural research program showcases the broad range of sources for ideas students encounter. Cognitive research helps explain how ideas are learned, remembered, and forgotten; and the constructivist research program strengthens understanding of the importance of the intentions of the learner.

Developmental

Piaget described an equilibrium in student reasoning at concrete operations for much of the early school years, and then a rapid transition to a new equilibrium at formal operations in adolescence. Piaget argued that only at formal operations do students become capable of questioning their ideas, making conjectures, appreciating the methods of natural science, identifying contradictions, and reasoning abstractly.

Many research programs cast doubt on Piaget's postulated transition from concrete to formal reasoning. Case (1985) conducted research showing that young children could control variables with appropriate supports. Recent research suggests

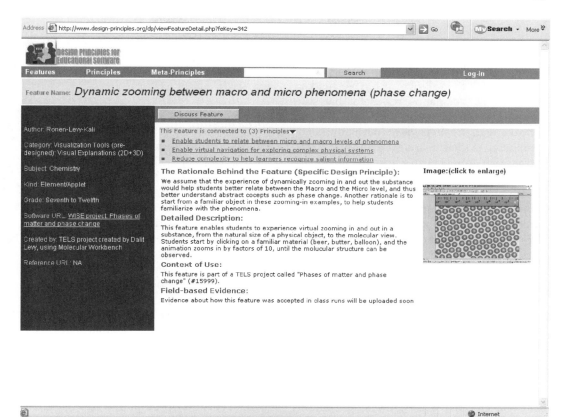

Figure 15.3. Design Principles Database. The design principles database captures findings from research on learning at multiple levels (Kali et al., 2002; see http://www.telscenter.org/research/research%20update/research_dpdatabase.html).

that students have the competence to conduct convincing experiments early in their schooling but may also conduct investigations that others consider inconclusive. Masnick and Klahr (2003) studied how students design and interpret experiments where they can manipulate variables to test factors influencing the rate a car descends an inclined plane or factors determining the trajectory of an airplane. They found that young students conduct fair as well as biased experiments. Masnick and Klahr also described the rich but unsystematic and poorly integrated conceptions of experimental error that these students have in their repertoire of ideas. This research provides evidence for the value of variation in ideas. It suggests how students might learn about experimentation in science by negotiating understanding with their peers, as emphasized in the *experiment* pattern (see Table 15.2).

Research on more varied problems than those studied in Geneva also draws attention to the context of the problem. Students lack knowledge of the important variables in experiments about topics like global warming, and they have difficulty generalizing knowledge of experimental methods to investigations of topics like dinosaur extinction that involve analysis of historical records. Students might use logical strategies in familiar contexts (Linn et al., 1983), but neglect normative variables (Linn & Hsi, 2000; Polman, 2000). These research studies reinforce the value of the *make science accessible* tenet of knowledge integration, because personally relevant problems stimulate students to compare their everyday ideas to ideas in science texts.

Recent developmental research programs have renewed attention to transitions in reasoning. Researchers following the *theory-theory* view link Piaget's notion of a transition to Kuhn's notion of scientific revolutions (diSessa, this volume; Carey, 1992; Gopnik & Wellman, 1994; Vosniadou et al., 2001). Vosniadou reported that students who view the earth as round like a pancake warrant their views with coherent, convincing evidence, and protect their ideas in ways that are similar to those used by practicing scientists. diSessa (diSessa, Gillespie, & Esterly, 2004) reanalyzed some of Vosniadou's results and disputed the coherence of student ideas, arguing that student knowledge is more fragmented (also see diSessa, this volume). The knowledge integration research program draws attention to situations where students have coherent but nonnormative ideas, and underscores the need for powerful pivotal cases to deal with these views.

Chi (1996) described the importance of ontological categories in designing science instruction. She argued that most learners categorize emergent phenomena like heat and electricity as material substances, rather than constraint-based processes. She showed that students defend their material substance views instead of entertaining more normative views in traditional courses. Resnick (1994), studying emergent phenomena like traffic jams or behavior in ant colonies, viewed student intuitions as stemming from a centralized mindset and demonstrated that simulation environments can offer an alternative, emergent view.

In summary, Piaget postulated age-related transitions in reasoning that influence images of the learner and design of science instruction. Current research favors more varied developmental pathways, consistent with the four trajectories identified by Linn and Hsi (2000). Researchers from the theory-theory and ontological category perspectives look for revolutions leading to the establishment of new ideas. This research alerts instructional designers to consider cases where students generate coherent nonnormative ideas and to seek convincing pivotal cases to add to the mix, including ideas that help students distinguish among substance- and process-based categories. The *orient, diagnose, and guide* pattern as well as the *predict, observe, explain* pattern implement this approach.

Sociocultural

The sociocultural perspective, informed by the work of Vygotsky (1978), draws attention to the impact of culturally derived norms, uses of language, and social interactions (Greeno, Collins, & Resnick, 1996), and stresses that variation in student ideas is moderated by the learning context.

Vygotsky (1978) described the *zone of proximal development* to explain why teachers or more able peers collaborating with a student can elicit additional and more sophisticated ideas from the learner than the learner would produce alone. My dissertation research explored Vygotsky's (1978) zone of proximal development and helped me understand how teachers and peers contribute to knowledge integration (Linn, 1970). Peers may prompt and scaffold learners even when they lack sophisticated views themselves. The Computer as Learning Partner project revealed the perplexing use of language in the discussions of heat and temperature, as well as the opportunities these uses offer students seeking to understand scientific phenomena (Linn & Hsi, 2000). Peer interaction research illustrates both ameliorating and troubling aspects of learning from others. When the learning context elicits stereotypes about who can succeed in science, designers need to consider how learners respond.

In summary, the sociocultural perspective emphasizes the role of norms, beliefs, language, and cultural practices in shaping science understanding, providing insight into the sources of ideas in the repertoire. Ideas in the repertoire emanating from social and cultural experiences can be inspected and reconsidered by the community using patterns such as *collaborate* or *critique* (see Table 15.2). These patterns take advantage of the zone of proximal development. They illustrate how communities can devise

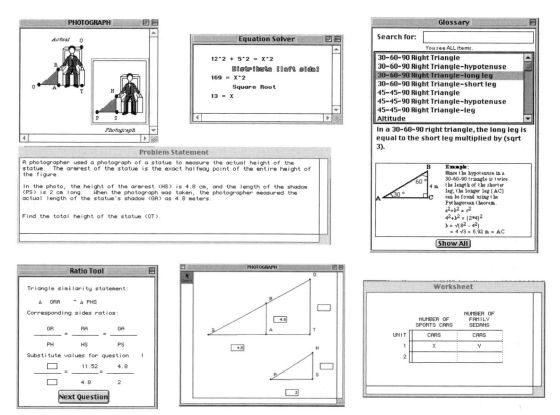

Figure 15.4. Cognitive Tutors. The Geometry Tutor allows students to use several visual and interactive tools and provides hints specific to the step they are working on in the problem. Students can use the tools in virtually any order and each tool is available on-screen for all applicable problems (see Aleven & Koedinger, 2002; http://act.psy.cmu.edu/awpt/Geometry/GeometryInterface.html).

prosocial norms, neutralize stereotypes, and emphasize the strengths of peer interactions.

Cognitive

The cognitive perspective captures a long history of research on how college students remember and forget facts and word meanings (Bjork, 1999). Inspired by the work of Thorndike, this work reinforces the traditional design pattern that was described above as *motivate, inform,* and *assess* (Lagemann, 2000). To extend this research to more complex tasks, cognitive researchers take advantage of technology enhanced learning environments, and study a broader range of learners. Informed by basic research on human memory and problem solving, cognitive tutors keep students engaged and improve ability to solve algebra, geometry, or programming problems (Aleven & Koedinger, 2002; Koedinger & Corbett, this volume). To create effective tutors, researchers have designed new representations for topics like geometry (see Figure 15.4). Building on research that examined learning of simple material, cognitive scientists have designed tutors to quickly intervene when students select unproductive solution paths. This immediate feedback keeps students engaged, but also makes some students incorrectly conclude that the tutor only accepts a subset of the total correct paths (Schofield, 1995).

Work in cognitive neuroscience underscores the importance of activating varied pathways in the brain, including pathways associated with figural and animated material (e.g., Shonkoff & Phillips, 2000). These findings resonate with studies showing the benefit of animated analogies over static analogies (Pedone et al., 2001) and contribute to understanding of pivotal cases (Linn, 2005).

Research on desirable difficulties helps clarify why the repertoire of ideas fluctuates, and explains why students fail to understand ideas introduced in science classes (Bjork 1999). Understandably, instructors and students often assume that when activities enhance performance *during* instruction they also will lead to durable understanding. That assumption, however, is sometimes dramatically wrong: activities that speed the rate of acquisition during instruction can fail to support long-term retention and transfer. Activities that appear to introduce difficulties for the learner can enhance postinstruction performance. Desirable difficulties include spacing rather than massing study of individual topics; interleaving rather than blocking practice on separate topics; varying the representations used for instructional materials; reducing feedback; and using embedded assessments as learning opportunities. Studies of desirable difficulties typically use unfamiliar tasks like learning Swahili words, and use retention intervals of less than a day. Research extending these findings to complex material and longer retention intervals offers insight for the knowledge integration perspective. Results from studies of jumbled text (Kintsch, 1998) and complex science material (Richland et al., 2005) consistently show the value of requiring students to generate connections among ideas rather than only reading or recognizing ideas. Knowledge integration research raises issues for cognitive researchers as well, by illustrating that complex learning tasks generally require students to interleave ideas from multiple contexts, and by showing that students sometimes fail at generation tasks because they are unable to make the required connections (e.g., Linn, Davis, & Bell, 2004).

Research from the cognitive perspective underscores the benefit of interleaving school and out-of-school contexts and points to the value of enabling students to revisit social and natural world experiments by designing activities that prompt spaced practice (Bjork, 1999). Patterns such as *critique* and *reflect* prompt learners to connect ideas across contexts and to develop scientific perspectives that apply to multiple contexts.

Constructivist

The constructivist research program emphasizes harnessing the learner's efforts to guide and monitor their own activities. Research on self-monitoring and metacognition resonates with evidence that learners link and connect ideas. A series of research projects have sought to harness this intellectual effort by emphasizing conceptual change (Strike & Posner, 1985), knowledge in pieces (diSessa, 1988, this volume), intentional learning (Scardamalia & Bereiter, 1991), fostering communities of learners (Brown & Campione, 1994), and cognitive apprenticeship (Collins, this volume).

Constructivist researchers disagree about how knowledge integration occurs. Those motivated by Piaget's focus on transitions often endorse cognitive conflict (Inhelder & Piaget, 1958/1972). Strike and Posner (1985) articulated a conceptual change pattern that calls for providing evidence to refute existing ideas and supplying normative ideas. This approach, while potentially valuable, frequently fails. The experimenter and strategizer trajectories described above show how students can sidestep contradictions by narrowing their focus or contextualizing the contradiction. Thus, when shown, for example, that the weight of the bob does not influence the frequency of the pendulum, students could decide to accept this idea. Or, they could invent explanations that support their initial idea such as saying that the frequency changed slightly.

diSessa offered an alternative to conceptual change for explaining how constructivism works. diSessa synthesized studies of the ideas held by many students to describe learners as having knowledge in pieces. diSessa (1988) defined phenomenological primitives ("p-prims" for short) as descriptive accounts of the natural world that often lead to reasonable predictions. diSessa has shown that these ideas are contextually grounded and loosely connected to other ideas. Some p-prims have similar characteristics, such as that light "dies out" and that sound "dies out." Frequently, p-prims reflect specific experiences. Students may conclude that light dies out because they cannot see it as they go farther from the source. diSessa advocated building on these ideas and those of other students.

Recently, a variety of research programs have detailed ways to design instruction informed by the constructivist perspective. The cognitive apprenticeship approach to constructivism (Collins, this volume) draws on successful instructional programs to explain why students benefit from working on complex, authentic problems, succeed when they are scaffolded in performing complex tasks until they can perform the whole task on their own, profit from investigating meaning in collaboration with others, and sustain their understanding when they develop metacognitive abilities. In the intentional learning perspective, Scardamalia and Bereiter (1991) emphasize the importance of self monitoring. Using the Knowledge Forum, a collaborative tool, students draw attention to gaps in community knowledge and consult peers or experts to fill those gaps (Scardamalia & Bereiter, this volume). They help each other monitor understanding and learn how to recognize inconsistencies. Brown and Campione (1994), in their work on fostering communities of learners, show how science courses can promote learning and take advantage of the zone of proximal development. They encourage learners to specialize in specific aspects of a topic, such as individual species in the rain forest, and then create activities that require the community to develop expertise. They show how students gain insight into the nature of science and negotiate the meaning of scientific language by interacting with their peers.

The constructivist research program emphasizes the unique trajectories of learners. Even when reaching similar conclusions, students often draw on distinct evidence. Patterns such as *experiment, construct an artifact, explore a simulation,* or *construct an argument* take advantage of the constructivist perspective and could scaffold learners to gain coherent understanding (see Table 15.2).

Taken together, these research programs reinforce the idea that learners benefit from the variety of ideas in their repertoire and in the collective repertoire. They suggest that students use a range of methods to make sense of science consistent with the conceptualizer, experimenter, strategizer, and consumer trajectories described above. Piagetian and conceptual change researchers pay attention to those moments when new ideas replace less normative ideas. The sociocultural perspective emphasizes the wide range of sources for ideas and explains why ideas are often idiosyncratic. The cognitive perspective helps explain how students develop durable ideas. The constructivist perspective emphasizes how instruction can support the continuous effort of the learner to seek more coherent understanding.

Conclusions

The knowledge integration perspective integrates research findings from a broad range of traditions. It emphasizes the varied and unique ideas that each student formulates, and encourages students to take responsibility for building their repertoire and monitoring its success. The knowledge integration perspective benefits from emerging research methods such as case studies and design studies. It offers the community design patterns and principles to encourage grounded deliberation and generative research synthesis.

The knowledge integration perspective draws on extensive evidence to show that variety is the spice of learning and that adding pivotal cases often amplifies the flavor. Careful examination of the trajectories of student learning emphasizes the unique approaches students take to dealing with science instruction. Instruction typically adds ideas that students isolate rather than integrate. Students can passively read ideas or listen to lectures. They can actively experiment or design artifacts. These instructional activities can fail unless students also hold these new ideas up to their existing ideas, develop criteria for distinguishing ideas, and sort out their varied views. Students succeed when they make this process a lifelong habit. By continuously researching their repertoire and seeking criteria to guide the process, students gain a more and more internally consistent and cohesive view of science.

The tenets of knowledge integration, as translated into activities in the design patterns, suggest ways to meet the needs of students following all four of the trajectories. Conceptualizers do a good job of finding cohesive ideas, but often neglect connections to practical problems. These students benefit when instruction makes science accessible and forces them to consider practical problems. They are likely to learn especially well from the *collaborate* and *construct an artifact* patterns because they need to respond to ideas of others, as well as design a solution to a problem that is relevant to society (see Table 15.2).

Experimenters do a good job of articulating new, intriguing ideas, but often neglect cohesion. These students benefit from instruction that makes thinking visible and models the process of developing cohesive ideas. They are likely to learn especially well from the *construct an argument* pattern because they need to connect ideas and convince others (see Table 15.2).

Strategizers succeed in school, often without any noticeable impact on their ability to reason about science. These students benefit from instruction that promotes lifelong learning and insists that they reflect on

and monitor their progress. They learn especially well from the *predict, observe, explain* and *explore a simulation* patterns because they need to contrast ideas and develop criteria for distinguishing among ideas.

Contextualizers present the greatest challenge to the knowledge integration perspective because they avoid making links or connections. They benefit most from instruction that emphasizes learning from others since peers may provide examples of connections they understand. Contextualizers benefit even from examples of nonnormative links among ideas because they need examples they can appreciate. The *elicit, diagnose, and guide* pattern seems likely to help contextualizers by focusing their attention on a manageable set of alternatives.

In summary, the knowledge integration perspective emerged from analyses of case studies of varied learners and offers guidance to designers seeking to have an impact on the full range of students. The perspective continues to emerge and to benefit from the rich, varied research traditions in science education.

Acknowledgments

This material is based on work supported by the National Science Foundation under grants numbers 9873180, 9805420, 0087832, 9720384, and 0334199. Any opinions, findings, and conclusions or recommendations expressed in this material are those of the author and do not necessarily reflect the views of the National Science Foundation.

The author gratefully acknowledges helpful discussions of these ideas with members of the Web-based Inquiry Science Environment group and members of the memory group at the Center for Advanced Study in the Behavioral Sciences. Special thanks go to Philip Bell, Robert Bjork, Douglas Clark, Allen Collins, Elizabeth Davis, Andy diSessa, Rick Duschl, Bat-Sheva Eylon, Sherry Hsi, and Jim Slotta for stimulating discussions and comments on earlier drafts.

The author appreciates help in production of this manuscript from David Crowell and Jonathan Breitbart.

© Regents of the University of California

References

AAUW. (2000). *Tech-savvy: Educating girls in the new computer age*. Washington, DC: AAUW.

Aleven, V. A., & Koedinger, K. R. (2002). An effective metacognitive strategy: Learning by doing and explaining with a computer-based cognitive tutor. *Cognitive Science, 26*, 147–179.

Bell, P., & Linn, M. C. (2002). Beliefs about science: How does science instruction contribute? In B. K. Hofer & P. R. Pintrich (Eds.), *Personal epistemology: The psychology of beliefs about knowledge and knowing* (pp. 321–346). Mahwah, NJ: Lawrence Erlbaum Associates.

Bjork, R. A. (1999). Assessing our own competence: Heuristics and illusions. In D. Gopher & A. Koriat (Eds.), *Attention and performance XVII. Cognitive regulation of performance: Interaction of theory and application* (pp. 435–459). Cambridge, MA: MIT Press.

Bransford, J. D., Brown, A. L., & Cocking, R. R. (Eds.). (2000). *How people learn: Brain, mind, experience, and school*. Washington, DC: National Research Council.

Brown, A. L., & Campione, J. C. (1994). Guided discovery in a community of learners. In K. McGilly (Ed.), *Classroom lessons: Integrating cognitive theory and classroom practice* (pp. 229–270). Cambridge, MA: MIT Press/Bradford Books.

Carey, S. (1992). The origin and evolution of everyday concepts. In R. N. Giere (Ed.), *Cognitive models of science* (Vol. XV, pp. 89–128). Minneapolis: University of Minnesota Press.

Case, R. (1985). *Intellectual development: Birth to adulthood*. Orlando, FL: Academic Press.

Chi, M. T. H. (1996). Constructing self-explanations and scaffolded explanations in tutoring. *Applied Cognitive Psychology, 10*, S33–S49.

Clancy, M., Titterton, N., Ryan, C., Slotta, J., & Linn, M. C. (2003). New roles for students, instructors, and computers in a lab-based introductory programming course. *ACM SIGCSE Bulletin, 35*(1), 132–136.

Clark, D. B., & Linn, M. C. (2003). Scaffolding knowledge integration through curricular depth. *Journal of Learning Sciences, 12*(4), 451–494.

Clement, J. (1993). Using bridging analogies and anchoring intuitions to deal with students' preconceptions in physics. *Journal of Research in Science Teaching, 30*(10), 1241–1257.

Cohen, E. G. (1994). Restructuring the classroom: Conditions for productive small groups. *Review of Educational Research, 64*(1), 1–35.

Collins, A., Brown, J. S., & Holum, A. (1988). The computer as a tool for learning through reflection. In H. Mandl & A. M. Lesgold (Eds.), *Learning issues for intelligent tutoring systems* (pp. 1–18). Chicago: Springer-Verlag.

Crouch, C. H., & Mazur, E. (2001). Peer instruction: Ten years of experience and results. *American Journal of Physics, 69*, 970–977.

Davis, E. (2003). Knowledge integration in science teaching: Analysing teachers' knowledge development. *Research in Science Education, 34*(1), 21–53.

Davis, E. A., & Linn, M. C. (2000). Scaffolding students' knowledge integration: Prompts for reflection in KIE. *International Journal of Science Education, 22*(8), 819–837.

Design-Based Research Collective. (2003). Design-based research: An emerging paradigm for educational inquiry. *Educational Researcher, 32*(1), 5–8.

diSessa, A. (1988). Knowledge in pieces. In G. Forman & P. Pufall (Eds.), *Constructivism in the computer age* (pp. 49–70). Hillsdale, NJ: Lawrence Erlbaum Associates.

diSessa, A. A. (2000). *Changing minds: Computers, learning and literacy*. Cambridge, MA: MIT Press.

diSessa, A., Elby, A., & Hammer, D. (2002). J's epistemological stance and strategies. In G. M. Sinatra & P. R. Pintrich (Eds.), *Intentional Conceptual Change* (pp. 237–290). Mahwah, NJ: Lawrence Erlbaum Associates.

diSessa, A. A., Gillespie, N. M., & Esterly, J. B. (2004). Coherence versus fragmentation in the development of the concept of force. *Cognitive Science, 28*, 843–900.

diSessa, A. A., & Minstrell, J. (1998). Cultivating conceptual change with benchmark lessons. In J. G. Greeno & S. Goldman (Eds.), *Thinking practices* (pp. 155–187). Mahwah, NJ: Lawrence Erlbaum Associates.

Eylon, B. S., & Linn, M. C. (1988). Learning and instruction: An examination of four research perspectives in science education. *Review of Educational Research, 58*(3), 251–301.

Gopnik, A., & Wellman, H. M. (1994). The theory theory. In L. A. Hirschfeld & S. A. Gelman (Eds.), *Mapping the mind: Domain specificity in cognition and culture* (pp. 257–293). New York: Cambridge University Press.

Greeno, J., Collins, A, and Resnick, L. (1996). Cognition and learning. In D. B. a. R. Calfee (Ed.), *Handbook of educational psychology* (pp. 15–46). New York: Macmillan.

Howe, C., Tolmie, A., Duchak-Tanner, V., & Rattray, C. (2000). Hypothesis testing in science: Group consensus and the acquisition of conceptual and procedural knowledge. *Learning and Instruction, 10*, 361–391.

Inhelder, B., & Piaget, J. (1958/1972). *The growth of logical thinking from childhood to adolescence; An essay on the construction of formal operational structures.* New York: Basic Books.

Kali, Y., Bos, N., Linn, M. C., Underwood, J., & Hewitt, J. (2002). Design principles for educational software. In G. Stahl (Ed.), *Computer support for collaborative learning: Foundations for a CSCL community (Proceedings of CSCL 2002)* (pp. 679–680). Mahwah, NJ: Lawrence Erlbaum Associates.

Kali, Y., Orion, N., & Eylon, B. (2003). The effect of knowledge integration activities on students' perception of the earth's crust as a cyclic system. *Journal of Research in Science Teaching, 40*(6), 415–442.

Kintsch, W. (1998). *Comprehension: a paradigm for cognition.* Cambridge, MA: MIT Press.

Krajcik, J. S., Blumenfeld, P. C., Marx, R. W., & Soloway, E. (1999). Instructional, curricular, and technological supports for inquiry in science classrooms. In J. Minstrell & E. V. Zee (Eds.), *Inquiry into inquiry: Science learning and teaching.* (pp. 283–315). Washington, DC: AAAS Press.

Lagemann, E. C. (2000). *An elusive science: The troubling history of education research.* Chicago: University of Chicago Press.

Lewis, E. L., & Linn, M. C. (1994). Heat energy and temperature concepts of adolescents, adults, and experts: Implications for curricular improvements. *Journal of Research in Science Teaching, 31*(6), 657–677.

Linn, M. C. (1970). *Effects of a training procedure on matrix performance and on transfer tasks.* Unpublished doctoral dissertation, Stanford University, Stanford, CA.

Linn, M. C. (1995). Designing computer learning environments for engineering and computer science: The Scaffolded Knowledge Integration framework. *Journal of Science Education and Technology, 4*(2), 103–126.

Linn, M. C. (2005). WISE design for lifelong learning-pivotal cases. In P. Gärdenfors & P. Johannsson (Eds.), *Cognition, education and communication technology* (pp. 223–256). Mahwah, NJ: Lawrence Erlbaum Associates.

Linn, M. C., & Clancy, M. J. (1992). The case for case studies of programming problems. *Communications of the ACM, 35*(3), 121–132.

Linn, M. C., Clark, D., & Slotta, J. D. (2003). WISE design for knowledge integration. *Science Education, 87*, 517–538.

Linn, M. C., Clement, C., & Pulos, S. (1983). Is it formal if it's not physics? *Journal of Research in Science Teaching, 20*(8), 755–770.

Linn, M. C., Davis, E. A., & Bell, P. (Eds.). (2004). *Internet environments for science education.* Mahwah, NJ: Lawrence Erlbaum Associates.

Linn, M. C., & Eylon, B.-S. (in press). Science education: Integrating views of learning and instruction. In P. A. Alexander & P. H. Winne (Eds.), *Handbook of educational psychology* (2nd ed.). Mahwah, NJ: Lawrence Erlbaum Associates.

Linn, M. C., & Hsi, S. (2000). *Computers, teachers, peers: Science learning partners.* Mahwah, NJ: Lawrence Erlbaum Associates.

Linn, M. C., & Slotta, J. D. (2006). Enabling participants in on-line forums to learn from each other. In A. M. O'Donnell, C. E. Hmelo-Silver, & G. Erkens (Eds.), *Collaborative learning, reasoning, and technology.* Mahwah, New Jersey: Lawrence Erlbaum Associates.

Linn, M. C., Songer, N. B., & Eylon, B. S. (1996). Shifts and convergences in science learning and instruction. In R. Calfee & D. Berliner (Eds.), *Handbook of educational psychology* (pp. 438–490). Riverside, NJ: Macmillan.

Masnick, A. M., & Klahr, D. (2003). Error matters: An initial exploration of elementary school children's understanding of experimental error. *Journal of Cognition and Development, 4*, 67–98.

Metz, K. (2000). Young children's inquiry in biology. Building the knowledge bases to empower independent inquiry. In J. Minstrell & E. Van Zee (Eds.), *Inquiring into inquiry learning and teaching in science* (pp. 3–13). Washington, DC: American Association for the Advancement of Science.

Millar, R., & Driver, R. (1987). Beyond processes. *Studies in Science Education, 14*(9), 33–62.

Osborne, J. F., & Young, A. R. (1998). The biological effects of ultra-violet radiation: A model for contemporary science education. *Journal of Biological Education, 33*(1), 10–15.

Palinscar, A. S., Magnusson, S., & Cutter, J. (2001). Making science accessible to all: Results of a design experiment in inclusive classrooms. *Learning Disability Quarterly, 24,* 15–32.

Pallant, A., & Tinker, R. (2004). Reasoning with atomic-scale molecular dynamic models. *Journal of Science Education and Technology, 13*(1), 51–66.

Pedone, R., Hummel, J. E., & Holyoak, K. J. (2001). The use of diagrams in analogical problem solving. *Memory and Cognition, 29,* 214–221.

Pfundt, H., & Duit, R. (1991). *Students' alternative frameworks (3rd ed.)*. Federal Republic of Germany: Institute for Science Education at the University of Kiel/Institut für die Pädagogik der Naturwissenschaften.

Piaget, J. (1970). *Structuralism*. New York: Basic Books.

Polman, J. L. (2000). *Designing project-based science: Connecting learners through guided inquiry*. New York: Teachers College Press.

Redish, E. F. (2003). *Teaching physics with the physics suite*. New York: John Wiley and Sons, Inc.

Resnick, M. (1994). *Turtles, termites, and traffic jams: Explorations in massively parallel microworlds*. Cambridge, MA: MIT Press.

Richland, L. E., Bjork, R. A., Finley, J. R., & Linn, M. C. (2005). Linking cognitive science to education: Generation and interleaving effects. In B. G. Bara, L. Barsalou & M. Bucciarelli (Eds.), *Proceedings of the twenty-seventh annual conference of the Cognitive Science Society*. Mahwah, NJ: Lawrence Erlbaum Associates.

Scardamalia, M., & Bereiter, C. (1991). Higher levels of agency for children in knowledge-building: A challenge for the design of new knowledge media. *Journal of the Learning Sciences, 1,* 37–68.

Schofield, J. W. (1995). *Computers and classroom culture*. New York: Cambridge University Press.

Shonkoff, J. P., & Phillips, D. A. (Eds.). (2000). *From neurons to neighborhoods: The science of early childhood development*. Washington, DC: National Academy Press.

Siegler, R. S. (1996). *Emerging minds: The process of change in children's thinking*. New York: Oxford University Press.

Sisk-Hilton, S. (2002). We'll take the parts that make sense: The evolution of an inquiry-oriented professional development model. In P. Bell, R. Stevens & T. Satwicz (Eds.), *Keeping learning complex: Proceedings of the fifth international conference of the learning sciences (ICLS)*. Mahwah, NJ: Lawrence Erlbaum Associates.

Sokoloff, D. R., & Thornton, R. K. (2004). *Interactive lecture demonstrations in introductory physics*. New York: John Wiley and Sons.

Songer, N. (1996). Exploring learning opportunities in coordinated network-enhanced classrooms – A case of kids as global scientists. *Journal of the Learning Sciences, 5*(4), 297–327.

Songer, N. B., & Linn, M. C. (1992). How do students' views of science influence knowledge integration? In M. K. Pearsall (Ed.), *Scope, sequence and coordination of secondary school science, Volume I: Relevant research* (pp. 197–219). Washington, DC: The National Science Teachers Association.

Steele, C. M. (1999). Thin ice: "Stereotype threat" and black college students. *Atlantic Monthly,* 44–54.

Strike, K. A., & Posner, G. J. (1985). A conceptual change view of learning and understanding. In L. H. West & A. L. Pines (Eds.), *Cognitive structure and conceptual change* (pp. 211–231). Orlando, FL: Academic Press.

Thompson, P. W. (2002). Didactic objects and didactic models in radical constructivism. In K. Gravemeijer, R. Lehrer, B. v. Oers & L. Verschaffel (Eds.), *Symbolizing and modeling in mathematics education* (pp. 191–212). Dordrecht, The Netherlands: Kluwer.

Vosniadou, S., Ioannides, C., Dimitrakopoulou, A., & Papademetriou, E. (2001). Designing learning environments to promote conceptual change in science. *Learning and Instruction, 11*(4–5), 381–419.

Vygotsky, L. S. (1978). *Mind in society: The development of higher psychological processes.* Cambridge, MA: Harvard University Press.

White, B. Y., & Frederiksen, J. R. (1998). Inquiry, modeling, and metacognition: Making science accessible to all students. *Cognition and Instruction, 16*(1), 3–118.

White, R., & Gunstone, R. (1992). *Probing understanding.* New York: Falmer Press.

Williams, M., Linn, M., Ammon, P., & Gearhart, M. (2004). Learning to teach inquiry science in a technology-based environment: A case study. *Journal of Science Education and Technology, 13*(2), 189–206.

Zimmerman, T. (2005). *Promoting knowledge integration of scientific principles and environmental stewardship: Assessing an issue-based approach to teaching evolution and marine conservation.* Unpublished Doctoral Dissertation, University of California, Berkeley.

CHAPTER 16

A History of Conceptual Change Research

Threads and Fault Lines

Andrea A. diSessa

Characterizing Conceptual Change

Within the learning sciences, conceptual change is probably best defined by its relevance to instruction. In the broad educational experience, some topics seem systematically to be extremely difficult for students. Learning and teaching in these areas are problematic and present persistent failures of conventional methods of instruction. Many areas in the sciences, from elementary school through university level, have this characteristic, including, in physics, concepts of matter and density, Newtonian mechanics, electricity, and relativity; in biology, evolution and genetics.[1] To learn such topics, students must go through a conceptual change. Conceptual change contrasts with less problematic learning such as skill acquisition and acquisition of facts, where difficulty may be evident, but for more apparent reasons such as sheer mass of learning, or the necessity of practice to produce quick, error free, highly refined performance.

The name "conceptual change" embodies a first approximation of what constitutes the primary difficulty: students must build new ideas in the context of old ones; hence, the emphasis on "change" rather than on simple acquisition. Strong evidence exists that prior ideas constrain learning in many areas. The "conceptual" part of the conceptual change label must be treated less literally. Various theories locate the difficulty in such entities as "beliefs," "theories," or "ontologies," in addition to "concepts."

Conceptual change is among the most central areas in the learning sciences for several reasons. First, many of the most important ideas in science seem to be affected by the challenges of problematic learning. Conceptual change also engages some of the deepest, most persistent theoretical issues concerning learning. What is knowledge in its various forms? When and why is it difficult to acquire? What is deep understanding; how can it be fostered? Conceptual change is important not only to education but also to developmental psychology, epistemology, and the history and philosophy of science. In the history of science, consider: What accounts for the challenges posed by scientific revolutions, such as those engendered by Newton, Copernicus, and Darwin?

Conceptual change research is difficult to review. Problems (what changes; why is change difficult; how does it happen?) have led only slowly to solutions, and solutions have been tentative and partial. In addition, the involvement of multiple disciplines has produced a plethora of orientations and theories. There are, in fact, no widely accepted, well-articulated, and tested theories of conceptual change. Instead, the field consists of multiple perspectives that combine many commonsense and theoretical ideas in kaleidoscopic fashion. My review aims to highlight critical *threads* and *fault lines* – the former through a historical orientation, and the latter by noting a few important changes in perspective and differences of opinion. The review ends with a set of recommendations for future work.

Preview

This section uses one example to demonstrate several of the most important issues in conceptual change research. These issues can serve as landmarks with respect to which other important, but more subtle issues, can be located.

The concept of force in physics provides an excellent example of conceptual change. Figure 16.1 shows the correct scientific account of the simple event of tossing a ball into the air. Physicists would say that there is only one force, gravity, on the ball after it has left the hand. Gravity acts on the speed of the ball, diminishing it until the object reaches zero speed at the peak of the toss. Then, gravity continues acting, "pulling" the speed of the ball downward, and so the ball accelerates downward until it is caught.

Before conceptual change research began, instructors who noticed student difficulties with problems like the toss might have attributed their difficulties to the abstractness of physics, or to its complexity. Instructional interventions might include simplifying exposition or repeating basic

instruction. These reactions to student difficulties assume a simple acquisition model of learning. In contrast, listening closely to student explanations yielded a stunning discovery. Students do not exhibit lack of descriptive or explanatory capability, but they have radically different things to say than experts. Figure 16.2 illustrates a typical novice explanation: Your hand imparts a force that drives the ball upward against gravity. The upward force gradually dies away until it balances gravity at the peak. Then, gravity takes over and pulls the ball downward. Students seem to have a prior concept of force, but it is different from experts'. Instruction must deal with these ideas and change them: enter the era of conceptual change.

How should one deal with students' "misconceptions"? Early in conceptual change research, most people assumed that student ideas were coherent and integrated. Under such an assumption, one has little choice but to argue students out of their prior ideas, and convince them to accept the ideas of physicists. But a very different view has gradually grown in influence. Rather than a coherent whole, students' ideas may consist of many quasi-independent elements. Instead of rejecting student conceptions, one can pick and choose the most productive student ideas, and refine them to create normative concepts. For example, students see balancing at the peak of the toss. And, balancing is a rough version of an incredibly important principle in physics, conservation (e.g., of energy or momentum). Similarly, students see speed as proportional to net force. A subtle change can turn this into correct physics. Force does not act *directly* to change position; instead, it acts directly on an intermediary, velocity, and velocity does the work of changing position.[2] Finally, the upward "force" in the incorrect explanation is not absent, but it is what physicists call momentum.

The opposing views of students' naïve ideas as either (1) coherent and strongly integrated, or (2) fragmented so as to allow disassembling, refining, and reassembling into correct physics, constitute a watershed

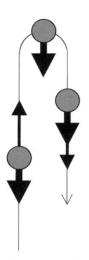

Figure 16.1. Expert explanation of a toss includes only one force (a) Gravity (thick arrow) drives the ball's velocity (thin arrow) downward, (b) bringing it to zero at the peak, (c) then gravity extends velocity downward in the fall.

fault line whose history and current status will occupy a prominent place in this chapter.

I now turn to a chronology of conceptual change research.

Premonitions in the Work of Piaget

Jean Piaget and his colleagues contributed an immense body of work on children's developing understanding (see Gruber & Voneche, 1977, for a compendium), which had a strong influence on conceptual change studies. The philosophical study of knowledge – epistemology – had traditionally concentrated almost exclusively on issues of certainty: "Knowledge is justified, true, belief." Piaget introduced the idea of *genetic epistemology*, that ideas and thinking grow gradually, and that the *evolution* of knowledge and understanding is a more productive study than certainty and timelessness. His empirical work produced an incredibly rich corpus on how children's ideas develop in many domains. His group studied biology (e.g., the notion of being alive), physics (e.g., the concept of force), conceptions of space and time (e.g., perspective and simultaneity), representation (drawing), catego-

rization, logic, and other topics. His work in biology has been particularly influential on conceptual change studies.

Some of Piaget's theoretical apparatus penetrated into conceptual change research. For example, Piaget viewed *equilibration* as a key mechanism: new experiences disequilibrated prior knowledge, and re-equilibration drives learners toward better, more advanced thinking. For the most part, however, Piaget's belief in equilibration is a fault line separating his ideas from modern conceptual change work. It remained too vague to provide satisfying explanations.

A more definitive fault line separating Piaget from most conceptual change work is that Piaget tried to develop an encompassing, domain independent theory of intelligence, where changes in conceptualization in multiple domains all reflected common, core differences in thinking. Conceptual change approaches to learning are domain specific, although the mainstream view is that the mechanisms are similar across domains. Researchers now generally regard Piaget's stage theory of intelligence

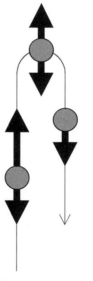

Figure 16.2. Novice explanation of a toss includes two forces (a) An upward force overcomes gravity, (b) but the force gradually dies away and comes into balance with gravity at the peak, (c) then it gives way to gravity on the fall.

as perhaps his most famous, but least interesting, contribution.

Piaget established the continuing, central thread of *constructivism* – the notion that new ideas and ways of thinking emerge from old ones. This foundational dynamic helped seed conceptual change work proper. Piaget also undermined older one-sided views, including both the *empiricist* view that knowledge originates either in purely empirical observations (as claimed by British philosophers such as David Hume), as well as the *rationalist* view that knowledge is inherently the product of rigorous thought, independent of experience (as epitomized by Descartes). Constructivism and the astounding revelation that children systematically think in very different ways than adults constitute the most important threads from Piagetian studies into conceptual change.

The Influence of the Philosophy and History of Science

Akin to Piaget, prior study in the history and philosophy of science exerted great influence, starting from the earliest theorizers of conceptual change in the learning sciences. I review here the ideas of Thomas Kuhn. To many, Kuhn defines the enduring relevance of the history of science to studies of conceptual change broadly. By contrast, Kuhn had strong opposition within the history of science, and there was probably never a time when his work represented the consensus view in that field. To represent Kuhn's opponents, I discuss Stephen Toulmin, who anticipated important threads in current opposition to Kuhn's ideas. The enduring fault line between coherence and fragmentation, which I introduced in the Preview section, can be traced back to Kuhn (coherence) versus Toulmin (fragmentation).

Kuhn's Scientific Revolutions

In his landmark work, *The Structure of Scientific Revolutions* (1970), Kuhn laid out a different view of progress in science, compared to most of his predecessors. Kuhn rejected the idea that science progresses incrementally. Instead, he claimed that ordinary "puzzle-solving" periods of science, called "Normal Science," are punctuated by revolutions, periods of radical change that work completely differently than Normal Science. In particular, the entire *disciplinary matrix* (referred to ambiguously but famously as a "paradigm" in the earliest edition) gets shifted in a revolution. What counts as a sensible problem, how proposed solutions are judged, what methods are reliable, which symbolic generalizations apply, and so on, all change at once in a revolution. Kuhn famously compared scientific revolutions to gestalt switches, where practitioners of the "old paradigm" and those of the "new paradigm" simply do not see the same things in the world. Gestalt switches happen when the coherence of ideas forces many things to change at once.

Kuhn articulated his belief in discontinuity in terms of *incommensurability*. Concepts simply come to refer to different things. Incommensurability means that claims of the new theory cannot be stated in the old terms, and vice versa. Incommensurability constitutes both a definitional property of conceptual revolutions and also a cause for their problematic nature. As such, Kuhn's incommensurability established an enduring thread in conceptual change work. In contrast, the more sociological aspects of Kuhn's views, such as the importance of the disciplinary matrix, were not imported into conceptual change work. This is ironic since, to Kuhn, sociology is absolutely central. Kuhn's own defense and elaboration of *Scientific Revolutions* ended:

> Scientific knowledge, like language, is intrinsically the common property of a group, or else nothing at all. To understand it we shall need to know the special characteristics of the groups that create and use it. (p. 208)

Few conceptual change researchers comment on this core precept when adapting Kuhn to individual learning. Those who do (e.g., Karmiloff-Smith, 1988) treat it as something one can take or leave.[3]

Toulmin's Rejection of Strong Coherence

In addition to selectively incorporating Kuhn's ideas, conceptual change research ignored competing perspectives in the history of science. Stephen Toulmin's *Human Understanding* (1972) provides a good example, particularly since it appeared only a few years after *Scientific Revolutions* and since this work perspicuously introduces the other side of the coherence versus fragmentation fault line.

Human Understanding begins with an extensive review and rejection of assumptions about the level and kind of systematicity (a synonym Toulmin used for "coherence") that philosophers assumed in scientific thought. Toulmin traced the "cult of systematicity" back to the model of logicomathematical coherence abstracted from certain mathematical forms, such as Euclidean geometry viewed as an axiomatic system.[4]

Presumptions of systematicity were, for Toulmin, pernicious. Not only is there no global fixed framework for all science (as, for example, the philosopher Kant claimed), but the assumption that local frameworks (particular theories) are strongly systematic fails as well. Toulmin singled out Kuhn for criticism. Presumptions of incommensurability are an artifact of mistaken assumptions. Assuming strong systematicity, in addition to being factually inaccurate, guarantees the appearance of incommensurability and also guarantees that change will always appear mysterious (Kuhn's "gestalt switch"). There can be no account of how a complex, rigid framework "jumps" to a new one.

> Rather than treating the content of a natural science as a tight and coherent logical system, we shall therefore have to consider it as a conceptual aggregate, or "population", with which there are – at most – localized pockets of logical systematicity. (p. 128)

In the context of his attack on strong systematicity, Toulmin made two important methodological observations. First, he maintained that the dominant "before and after" view of conceptual change had to be abandoned.

> This change of approach [away from strong systematicity] obliges us to abandon all those static, "snapshot" analyses.... Instead, we must give a more historical, "moving picture" account . . . (p. 85)

Toulmin also complained about the adequacy of treatment of central ideas in conceptual change.

> The term concept is one that everybody uses and nobody explains – still less defines. (p. 8)

Misconceptions

> Even the brightest students in the class [have] false ideas based on enduring misconceptions that traditional instructional methods cannot overcome. (Promo materials for A Private Universe: Harvard-Smithsonian Center for Astrophysics (1987), http://www.learner.org/onesheet/series28.html)

Students Have False, Persistent Beliefs

Starting in the mid to late 1970s, a huge social movement, which we dub "misconceptions," began modern conceptual change studies in educational research and in neighboring disciplines, including experimental psychology and developmental psychology. The movement exploded to prominence in the early 1980s, spawned a huge literature, and tailed off somewhat in the early 1990s, although its presence and influence is still strong. The power of the movement can be gauged by the fact that an early bibliography collected literally hundreds of studies (Pfundt & Duit, 1988). Confrey (1990) provided an excellent review of misconceptions in physics, biology, and mathematics.

Physics was the locus of much early work. Three European scholars were important contributors. R. Driver, L. Viennot, and A. Tiberghien did foundational studies, often involving reformulated instructional interventions, of such topics as elementary school students' conceptions of matter, high school students' conceptions of force and motion, and middle school students' conceptions of heat and temperature (Driver, 1989; Tiberghien, 1980; Viennot, 1979). These and other researchers discovered, documented, and theoretically considered "false beliefs" such as "small bits of matter – say, a speck of dust – don't weigh anything," "forces cause movement at a speed proportional to their strength" (as opposed to the Newtonian: *acceleration* is proportional to force), and "heat and cold are different things."

In the United States, some important early misconceptions researchers were D. Hawkins (1978), J. Clement (1982), J. Minstrell (1982), and M. McCloskey (1983a & b). David Hawkins formulated a succinct, early view of the presence and influence of false ideas that systematically block science learning; he called them "critical barriers." Terminology for student ideas has been diverse, including alternative conceptions, alternative frameworks, intuitive or naïve theories, and naïve beliefs. However, the term "misconceptions" caught the broadest public.

One of the great positive influences of misconceptions studies was bringing the importance of educational research into practical instructional circles. Educators saw vivid examples of students responding to apparently simple, core conceptual questions in nonnormative ways. Poor performance in response to such basic questions, often years into the instructional process, could not be dismissed. One did not need refined theories to understand the apparent cause: entrenched, "deeply held," but false prior ideas. The obvious solution was very often phrased, as in the quotation heading this section, in terms of "overcoming," or in terms of convincing students to abandon prior conceptions.

This simple story – entrenched but false prior beliefs interfere with learning and need to be overcome – drove much of the misconceptions movement. Many of the leading researchers developed more refined views,

some elements of which we review in the next section. However, public impact and the broadest swath of research remained largely at the primitive level of documenting misconceptions: "entrenched false beliefs that need to be overcome."

Three Early Threads

THE ANALOGY WITH THE HISTORY OF SCIENCE

Three important and related threads in conceptual change research came to prominence nearly simultaneously early in the misconceptions movement. The richest and arguably the most generally influential was the analogy of the development of students' ideas with the history of science. Susan Carey (1991, 1999) was one of the earliest and most consistent in citing Kuhn's ideas in the context of children's conceptual change. She has systematically used the idea of incommensurability between conceptual systems as a primary index of conceptual change ("deep restructuring"). Incommensurability distinguishes conceptual change from "enrichment" (adding new ideas or beliefs) or even mere change of beliefs. Carey's main work was in biology, where she argued that children undergo a spontaneous and important conceptual change (Carey, 1985). The concepts "living," "real," "intentional" (as in having wishes and desires), and "animate," for example, are merged and confused before children sort out a true biology, where "alive" participates cleanly in a theory of "the body as a machine that sustains life," distinct from psychology and other domains. Carey began with observations by Piaget but argued that domain-independent theories of intelligence cannot explain changes in childhood biology. The extensive empirical and theoretical argumentation in Carey's work constituted an influential landmark, especially among developmental psychologists.

Carey also worked with Marianne Wiser in the domain of heat and temperature, where a prominent subthread of the analogy with the history of science appeared. Not only are the structures, critical attributes, and processes (concepts, theories, incommensurabilities, radical restructuring) similar or the same in children compared to the history of science, but content shows remarkable commonalities as well. Wiser and Carey (1983) built the case that naïve conceptions of heat and temperature parallel the ideas of an early group of scientists.

The analogy with history of science has been used in multiple ways. Karmiloff-Smith (1988) denied or downplayed content parallelism between child development and the history of science, but she highlighted process-of-change parallelisms. Similarly, Nersessian (1992) advocated the use of "cognitive-historical analysis" to determine empirically the processes involved in scientists' change of theories. Those processes include bootstrapping using analogical and imagistic models, thought experiments, and extreme cases. Nersessian projected that the same processes could be used to help students' conceptual change in school (p. 40).

THE THEORY THEORY

The second thread that emerged in early misconceptions research is closely related to the analogy with the history of science. *The theory theory* is the claim that children or beginning students have theories in very much the same sense that scientists have them. While this may have been inspired by the broader analogy with the history of science, it has often been invoked independent of content or process similarity. Carey consistently advocated a version of the theory theory. With respect to another domain, theories of mind, Allison Gopnik (Gopnik & Wellman, 1994) strongly advocated the theory theory. Gopnik was fairly extreme in the parallelism she claimed (while still admitting some differences between scientists and children, such as metacognitive awareness); others are more conservative in allowing such differences as limits in systematicity and breadth of application (Vosniadou, 2002). By and large, theory theorists align themselves strongly with the coherence side of the coherence/fragmentation fault line.

Michael McCloskey (1983a, 1983b) did a series of studies that became perhaps the most famous of all misconceptions studies. He claimed that students entered physics with a remarkably coherent and articulate theory that competed directly with Newtonian physics in instruction. The naïve theory, in fact, was very nearly the novice explanation of the toss (Figure 16.2). Within McCloskey's theory theory, he also proposed a strong content connection to medieval scientists' ideas, such as those of John Buridan and early claims of Galileo. In contrast to others, however, he made little of process-of-change similarities and, for example, did not refer in any depth to Kuhn or the philosophy of science. His attitude seemed to be that the content connection to the history of science was empirically evident rather than theoretically motivated.

McCloskey's work was incredibly influential. Despite counter arguments and empirical claims by others, McCloskey has often been cited authoritatively as showing that naïve ideas in physics are strongly coherent, and, indeed, theoretical (e.g., Wellman & Gelman, 1992, p. 347).

A RATIONAL VIEW OF CONCEPTUAL CHANGE

Another early landmark was the introduction of rational models of conceptual change. Rational models hold that students, like scientists, maintain current ideas unless there are good (rational) reasons to abandon them. Rationality is a highly contested idea, often fraught with cultural overtones of the superiority of Western scientific thinking as opposed to "primitive" irrational or mystical thinking (Goody, 1977). However, the rational view has proved persistent.

Posner, Strike, Hewson, and Gertzog (1982) established the first and possibly most important standard in rational models. They argued that students and scientists change their conceptual systems only when several conditions are met: (1) they became *dissatisfied* with their prior conceptions (experiencing a "sea of anomalies," in Kuhn's terms); (2) the new conception is *intelligible*; (3) the new conception should be more than intelligible, it should be *plausible*; (4) the new conception should appear *fruitful* for future pursuits (in Lakatos's [1970] terms: should contribute to a *progressing paradigm*).

The relationship of Posner et al.'s framework to studies in the history of science is complex. The framework drew from both Kuhn and Lakatos, even while the latter strongly criticized the former for abandoning rationality for "mob rule," and despite the implausibility that Kuhn's inherently sociological framework might transfer easily to individual students. Posner et al. drew equally from Kuhn's opponent, Toulmin, appropriating the idea of "conceptual ecology" (as opposed to "logical system").

A later version of this rational model of conceptual change (Strike & Posner, 1990) stepped back from a purely rational framework, admitting the importance of motivation and other such factors, while also admitting less articulate and less propositional forms of encoding (e.g., imagistic or enactive forms).

Despite continuing protests by Posner et al. that their framework was epistemological and did not reflect direct psychological reality – and, further, that it was far from a scheme for instruction (e.g., establishing these conditions as prerequisites to conceptual change) – many science educators were inspired to organize instruction around the framework (e.g., Smith et al., 1997). Some educators went so far as introduce students explicitly to Posner et al.'s framework (Hewson & Hennessey, 1992).

Assessing the Misconceptions Movement

POSITIVE CONTRIBUTIONS:

1. Misconceptions highlighted the importance of qualitative understanding and explanation against a historical background of emphasis purely on ability to solve quantitative problems.

2. Misconceptions established a broad prominence for contructivist thinking in instruction in contrast to prior, "blank slate" acquisition models of learning.

3. Misconceptions provided a focus for instructional problems, and new measures of attainment. It diminished attention to domain-general student difficulties (e.g., Piagetian stages), and emphasized the domain specific.

NEGATIVE CONTRIBUTIONS:

1. Recognizing important exceptions, most misconceptions studies were relatively devoid of theory development or testing. The "depth" of misconceptions was often uncalibrated, and an essential question was unasked: whether a wrong answer given by a significant number of students could always, on the face of it, count as a "conception."

2. Misconceptions work strongly emphasized negative contributions of prior knowledge. There were exceedingly few claims that prior concepts provided productive resources.

3. Following item 2, how learning is actually possible was minimally discussed.

4. Misconceptions studies led to a preemptive dominance for theory theory points of view and "conflict" models of instruction (e.g., item 1 of Posner et al.'s framework; also see McCloskey, 1983a, or Hewson & Hewson, 1983).

See Smith, diSessa, and Roschelle (1993) for an extended analysis of the misconceptions movement.

Beyond Misconceptions

I review work that transcended the misconceptions perspective in three categories: elaborated content analysis of conceptual change in particular domains; "knowledge in pieces"; and theory development.

Conceptual Change in Particular Domains

What, in detail, do students or children know about any particular domain at any particular age? Some lines of research that began in the heyday of misconceptions continued to ask and answer this question, with much greater precision and empirical support than previously.

Two domains stand out in developmental studies: naive psychology and naive biology.[5] Especially naïve biology has advanced in part in virtue of a substantial interacting community of researchers (Carey, Keil, Hatano, Inagaki, Atran, and others) who shared innovative methods, and critiqued and built on each other's ideas.

What, then, do children know about biology? Is learning the accretion of ideas, or enrichment, or, in contrast, does it involve "radical restructuring," which is true conceptual change? Carey (1985, 1986) argued that a conceptual change quite specific to biology occurs in childhood. Carey maintained that the concept of "animal" was embedded in a childhood theory of psychology; for example, that animals are distinct from inanimate objects in their perception- and goal-directed activities. She argued that, because of a near total ignorance of bodily mechanisms, a childhood biology is established only by about age ten, and it represents a true conceptual change from prior, psychological, ideas.

The burgeoning field of developmental studies of biological knowledge revised and refined Carey's ideas, and it provides at present a wonderfully enriched view of the emergence of biological knowledge. Two prime innovators were Frank Keil and Giyoo Hatano (with his collaborator, Kayoko Inagaki). These researchers pushed the emergence of distinctive biological thinking back at least six years. Keil developed an extensive program that isolated children's sensitivity to biological phenomena in multiple strands, including the biological essence of animals, inheritance, biological contagion, and the distinctive properties of the "insides" of living things. In the latter category, Keil (1994) showed that children age four or even earlier systematically expect the insides of rocks to be random while plants' and animals' insides are more organized. In one of his studies, Keil showed that very young children believe it is easy to paint or in other ways physically change a skunk into a raccoon, whereas older children, still before the age of six, feel such operations cannot essentially change the creature. He also showed that parents and offspring become much more important in establishing the essence of animals, compared to visible form or behavior.

Inagaki and Hatano (2002) brought a new degree of order to early biology by describing a core theory, which they called a *vitalist* biology. In this theory, the ingestion and use of some vague vital force accounts for animals' (and, later, plants') activity, health, and growth. Their experiments established a vitalist biology by age six, if not earlier. Hatano, Inagaki, and Keil argued and produced data to dispute Carey's earlier claim that biology emerged from psychology, transforming previously psychological concepts "animal" and "alive." Inagaki and Hatano also claimed that a subsequent shift – from a vitalist biology to a mechanistic one – constituted a true conceptual change during childhood.

Knowledge in Pieces

The theory theory thread dominates studies of naïve biology (and naïve psychology). It represents the "coherence" side of the coherence/fragmentation fault line. This section introduces a historical line, which I call "knowledge in pieces," that takes the "fragmented" side of the issue. Both Minstrell and I were early advocates of knowledge in pieces. Thus, we advanced Toulmin's critique of strong coherence.

From an instructional perspective, Minstrell (1982, 1989) viewed intuitive ideas as resources much more than blocks to conceptual change in physics, in contrast with the predominant misconceptions point of view. He described intuitive ideas as threads that, rather than rejecting, need reweaving into a different, stronger, and more normative conceptual fabric. Recent work has charted hundreds of "facets" – which are elemental and instructionally relevant ideas students have upon entering instruction – in many topics in physics instruction (Hunt & Minstrell, 1994). Coherent naïve theories are nowhere to be seen in this view.

In the same book in which McCloskey provided perhaps his definitive statement of "naïve theories," I (1983) introduced the idea that intuitive physics consisted largely of hundreds or thousands of elements, called p-prims, at roughly the size-scale of Minstrell's facets. P-prims are explanatorily primitive, provide people with their sense of which events are natural, which are surprising, and why. P-prims are many, loosely organized and sometimes highly contextual, so that the word "theory" is highly inappropriate. P-prims are hypothesized to play many productive roles in learning physics. For example, "Ohm's p-prim" prescribes that more effort begets more result, and a greater resistance to that effort begets less result. Ohm's p-prim applies to a very broad set of circumstances, including moving everyday objects (where size might be a "resistance" variable) and personal psychology (the reason for "greater effort" in the face of failure), and it accounts for the relative learnability of Ohm's law in electrical circuit theory. Several of the productive elements of novice students' toss explanation (Figure 16.2) – such as balance are p-prims.

The idea of knowledge in pieces has been all but ignored in developmental psychology. Even in early educational studies, syntheses of conceptual change research emphasized theory theory perspectives, and reported the ideas of researchers supporting fragmentation as minority opinions (see, for example, Driver, 1989, and Smith et al., 1997). A more extensive review of the history of theory theory versus knowledge in pieces appears in (diSessa, Gillespie, & Esterly 2004).

However, the knowledge in pieces perspective has picked up steam, at least in educational circles. Marcia Linn, for example, has elaborated "scaffolded knowledge integration" as an instructional framework (see Linn, this volume). In this view, the multiplicity of intuitive ideas is explicitly recognized, and integration (increasing systematicity) is virtually the definition of conceptual advancement.

Fragments of Theory

I referred earlier to conceptual change research as kaleidoscopic in the sense that many threads are combined in diverse ways into many different theoretical perspectives. This section follows that observation by sketching the theoretical landscape of conceptual change in terms of glosses on a number of theoretical threads. The alternative would be to select a few leading theorists and to present their perspectives in more detail. But this would produce a less broad and less illuminating view of the theoretical landscape of conceptual change.

I discuss two groups of theoretical issues. First, what are the mental entities involved in conceptual change, and how are they organized? Second, why is conceptual change difficult, and how does it happen when it does?

ENTITIES AND SYSTEMS IN CONCEPTUAL CHANGE

The obvious answer to the question of what changes in conceptual change is "concepts." However, this scarcely does justice to the diverse assumptions pursued by the field.

A perspective advocated early on by Carey makes an excellent entry point. Carey (1986) distinguished beliefs from concepts. Beliefs are relational entities. For example, "people are animals" relates two important concepts, people and animals; Newton's laws (summarized by $F = ma$) relate the concepts force, mass, and acceleration. Carey believed that belief change is relatively easy, and that the difficulty is change in the very concepts in which beliefs are expressed. When children eventually come to believe that people are animals, a very different concept of animal is implicated, compared to their earlier beliefs.

Carey is, as mentioned, an adherent of the theory theory perspective. Concepts and beliefs are constituents of larger-scaled systems, intuitive theories, which strongly constrain concepts and, hence, beliefs. Generalizing, most theories of conceptual change are *nested* in the sense that at least two levels (entities and systems) are implicated, and the relational constraints involved in the higher level are critical; those relations constrain individual concepts and beliefs so that incremental change is difficult or impossible. Of course, this brings us directly to the core of the coherence vs. fragmentation fault line. If relational constraints are too tight, then the difficulty of change is insuperable. So, a great deal rests precisely on the relations at the system level, which is a theory in Carey's case.

I mention three other nested theories. Vosniadou has proposed two versions. In her work concerning children's models of the earth's shape, she implicated vague but strongly persistent *framework theories*. When children are asked questions about the shape of the earth, their framework theories constrain a generation of specific models to a few possibilities. So, in this case, *models* are nested in, and constrained by, (framework) theories. Models can change relatively easily, but the framework theories take a long time. In more recent work, Vosniadou extended her theory to deal with force and motion. In Ioannides and Vosniadou (2002), framework theories constrain meanings (not models) such as "force," and the higher, relational level (theories) is still the real locus of difficulty in change.[6]

Keil (1994) introduced the idea of *modes of construal* as a weaker version of theories at the system level. Modes of construal weaken the presumed relational structure and simultaneously appear to address the issue that some ways of thinking cross core domain boundaries. For example, the natural home of teleological (purpose-oriented) thinking is in psychology. Yet, thinking in terms of purposes is important in naïve biology: "Fingers are for picking things up; hearts are for pumping blood."

A third nested view of conceptual change involves concepts as entities, but the higher level is not theories, but ontologies. Micheline Chi (1992) posited that concepts are strongly constrained by their presumed ontological nature. In her early work on this view, intuitive physics was claimed to be largely bound up in the ontology of matter, but Newtonian physics lies predominantly in an ontology very different from matter, "constraint-based processes." Shifting ontologies, like shifting theories,

is very difficult. Often, the new ontology has to be developed first, and then new concepts or radically revised concepts can grow more naturally within the new ontology.

Contrasting with theory-theory perspectives, adherents to knowledge in pieces tend to rely less on terms provided by the history and philosophy of science (concepts, theories, ontologies). In my own work, I have used a series of constructs, each with its own definition and model: following a rough spectrum from low to higher level, "p-prims," "nominal facts," "narratives," "mental models," and "coordination classes" (diSessa, 1996; diSessa & Wagner, 2005). A coordination class is an explicit model of a certain kind of concept. Coordination classes are complex systems that include many coordinated parts, including p-prims. A distinctive characteristic of this view of conceptual change is multilevel nesting of multiple cognitive types: p-prims are nested in coordination classes (concepts), and coordination classes – along with mental models and other entities – constitute the "conceptual ecology" of students.[7] Constraints arising from nesting exist in this view also, but they are diverse (according to particular entities and levels in the system) and weak (compared to "logically consistent"). See diSessa and Wagner (2005) for a review of studies that use the coordination class model.

MODELS OF CONSTRAINT AND CHANGE

Following Kuhn, incommensurability has been a proposed locus of difficulty in change. In view of incommensurability, how is conceptual change at all possible? Inspired by the history of science, various researchers have proposed such mechanisms as analogy and use of imagistic models. A common assumption is that differentiation of diffuse initial concepts (heat and temperature become distinct), and coalescence of old categories (plants and animals become joined in the category of living things) are generic processes that must take place in overcoming incommensurability (Carey, 1986 and 1999; Smith et al., 1997).

Knowledge in pieces leads to a broader set of hypotheses about difficulties of change and feasible pathways. Any particular version of a nested model provides specific kinds of difficulties and specific pathways. However, a more generic type of difficulty is the mere collection and coordination of a large set of elements into a newly organized system. For example, the coordination class model proposes that the use of one concept might involve distinct knowledge in different circumstances. Not only is it necessary to collect a large amount of situation-specific knowledge for use in different situations, but ensuring that the concept works in functionally the same way in different contexts is problematic and takes time. A distinctive characteristic of the knowledge in pieces perspective is that the reasons for difficulty of change may be the same in cases where a conceptual structure evolves from scratch, compared to cases where one conceptual system emerges from a different one (theory change).[8] Collecting and coordinating elements is difficult whether or not a prior competitor system exists. Indeed, one of the key difficulties might be creating an entirely new level of breadth and coherence, compared to naïve ideas.

Rational models continue to be surprisingly well regarded, despite sparse evidence for their adequacy in dealing with conceptual change. Gopnik and Wellman (1994) mentioned most of the same elements as Posner et al., including the accumulation of counter evidence, and a version of the requirement that an intelligible and plausible replacement exists. In terms of blockage or resistance, they mentioned quasi-rational processes resonant with professional science, such as denial of the need for change, and the formation of auxiliary hypotheses to fend off deep change.

Although, as I mentioned, Piaget's equilibration has diminished in popularity, some new versions have appeared. Inagaki and Hatano (2002, pp. 173–175), for example, provided two models of conceptual change where new ideas disturb the coherence of prior ideas, and reestablishing coherence drives conceptual change. See also Ioannides and Vosniadou (2002, p. 58).

Instruction and Intuitive Epistemology

This section mentions issues that cannot be treated in detail here. Of principal importance for conceptual change research is improving instruction. Theory theory views and knowledge in pieces prescribe some strong differences in strategy and process (e.g., rational decision making vs. a long period of multicontext accumulation and coordination). However, evaluating interventions has been indecisive for the following sorts of reasons.

1. Instruction is a complex mixture of design and theory, and good intuitive design can override the power of theory to prescribe or explain successful methods. Almost all reported innovative interventions work; almost none of them lead to improvements that distinguish them categorically from other good instruction.

2. The very general constructivist heuristic of paying attention to naïve ideas seems powerful, independent of the details of conceptual change theory. Interventions that merely teach teachers about naïve ideas have been surprisingly successful.

3. Researchers of different theoretical persuasions often advocate similar instructional strategies, if for different reasons. Both adherents of knowledge in pieces and of theory theories advocate student discussion, whether to draw out and reweave elements of naïve knowledge, or to make students aware of their prior theories in preparation for judgment in comparison to instructed ideas. The use of instructional analogies, metaphors, and visual models is widespread and not theory-distinctive.

4. Many or most interventions rely primarily on pre/post evaluations, which do little to evaluate specific processes of conceptual change.

"Intuitive epistemologies" concern how children and students view the nature of knowledge. Posner et al. mentioned student epistemological attitudes, particularly concerning rationality. Since then, a substantial literature has proposed different versions of "student ideas about knowledge," and it seems clear that these exert powerful influence (consult, for example, Sinatra & Pintrich, 2002, and Hofer & Pintrich, 2002).

Finally, conceptual change has its own distinctive set of sociocultural issues, such as the contribution of culture to intuitive theories. I note here simply that sociocultural views of conceptual development must at least be compatible with the cognitive/individual ones described here, and vice versa.

Mapping the Frontier

I close with suggestions about what seem to be the best near-future pursuits in studying conceptual change. I focus on the persistent fault line of coherence versus fragmentation, and on a set of more general recommendations concerning near-future pursuits.

Coherence: A Central Fault line

Historically, I introduced the issue of coherence vs. fragmentation in terms of the debate between Kuhn, who has been immensely influential in conceptual change research, and Toulmin, who has been less influential. Toulmin emphasized problems of overestimating systematicity and proposed that we need to rethink it. Kuhn motivated the idea of theory change in studies of conceptual change, in which the coherence of different theories provides for an essential incommensurability across them, and hence the necessity of holistic change. Coherence is a byword of theory theorists; it is recognized as the defining attribute that distinguishes naïve theories from other forms of knowledge (e.g., Wellman & Gelman, 1992); and it is among the most common adjectives describing naïve conceptions in the broad-

est range of conceptual change research. Yet few explicit models of coherence exist,[9] and still less empirical work has been done to test them.

This fault line has not been well articulated in the history of conceptual change research. Theory theorists with a strong commitment to coherence have held sway, particularly in developmental psychology. Many influential researchers completely ignore the issue, while others briefly mention fragmentation views as "minority opinions." Others, such as Chi (1992, p. 161), dismiss the issue as unimportant.

However, the tide seems to be turning, both in terms of facing the issue and in terms of the center of gravity in the debate. Recent studies have explicitly provided empirical or theoretical argument and counter-argument concerning coherence in naïve ideas (Ioannides & Vosniadou, 2002; diSessa et al., 2004). In educational studies the ascendancy of views favoring fragmentation seems vivid; both Linn's instructional framework, and Minstrell's facet analysis of learning physics, have been extensively developed and brought to widespread instructional practice, whereas no views based on the idea of intuitive theories have passed beyond research prototypes. No "naïve theories" have become influential, for example, in extensive, empirically based curriculum development in physics (e.g., McDermott et al., 2002). Finally, the trend in intuitive epistemologies seems distinctly toward knowledge in pieces views, and away from "intuitive theories of knowledge" (Hammer & Elby, 2002).

The modern view of the content of intuitive biology, despite the commitment to the idea of naïve theories by many researchers, has trends that undermine strong systematicity. In particular, the multiple lines in biological knowledge developed by Keil and others beg the question of how much they cohere with each other. Vitalism, as described by Inagaki and Hatano, is only a part of naïve biology, not a full, pervasive theory. And the "theory" that defines the mechanistic phase of intuitive biology is not succinctly characterized, nor is its coherence empirically measured. Inagaki and Hatano show that more primitive ways of reasoning about biology than naïve theories (based, for example, on similarity rather than biological categories) persist into adulthood. Adults also use vitalism long past the supposed transition to mechanistic biology. How is this consistent with strongly coherent theories and gestalt switch transitions?

Settling the coherence/fragmentation dispute requires theory development. We need better cognitive models and more precise coordination between models and evidence. The metaphor of theory drawn from the history of science ambiguously covers both strongly and weakly systematic knowledge systems, as exemplified by Kuhn and Toulmin's debate (even if theory theorists emphasize coherence). Specifications such as "theories have domains, are abstract, define distinctive explanatory ontologies, and are coherent" are immensely ambiguous as cognitive models. The field must do better.

The debate over coherence versus fragmentation is subtle. No one thinks children are completely unsystematic in their thinking about domains such as physics or biology. Furthermore, all existing views of scientific competence, when actually achieved by students, entail substantial systematicity (see diSessa, 1993, concerning the emergence of systematicity from the knowledge in pieces point of view). The central issue, rather, is *specification of the nature and extent of systematicity*. A proper resolution involves more precise models and better empirical determination of their parameters.[10]

Foci for Near-Future Work

The purpose of this review has been to prepare readers (a) to understand the history and state of conceptual change, and (b) to help orient researchers to productive avenues of future pursuit. Here is a list of suggestions.

1. *Pursue detailed specification of the content development of conceptual domains.* For example, the rich empirical work in naïve biology provides a protean resource for developing and testing theories of conceptual change. In addition, educational application will likely depend as much on content details as on general theoretical schemes.

2. *Assume domain variation, and empirically validate commonalities (or intractable differences).* Almost all conceptual change research homogenizes domains theoretically. But, consider the nature of conceptual competence in three regimes.
   a. Babies may be surprised by certain events (the core methodology of studies of infant conceptualization), but the extent of instrumental use of the schemas involved is highly uncertain. Data show a long, gradual emergence of, for example, adult common sense about gravity, and it cannot be taken for granted that the nature of "concept" involved has much in common from babies to adult common sense.
   b. Pre- and early-elementary school students integrate a large number of observations and ideas into their naïve biology, almost certainly under far less innate guidance than baby causality. Are the principles of conceptual growth and even the meaning of "concept" at all comparable at these two levels of development?
   c. Learning the concept of force in physics almost certainly builds on one of the richest and most directly useful (in everyday actions) naïve domains. Can such a difference in context *not* be consequential in development, compared to other domains? The context of use of the instructed concept of force is "high stress," where an extended series of problems require precise, reductive, and quantitative analysis. Could that fact be irrelevant to the nature of conceptual development, compared to the low-stress use of naïve biology to make rough and ready sense of the biological world?

3. *Develop explicit models of constructs like "concept" and "theory," and test them*

against data; models need to highlight relational structure (coherence). Researchers need to commit themselves to particular constructs, with specified meanings. What is an "entrenched belief"? We have not progressed enough since Toulmin complained that no one ever says what a concept is. I also highlighted the critical importance of understanding the nature and level of coherence in naïve and instructed competences.

4. *Accept the challenge of process validation of models of entities and change.* Again, Toulmin presciently argued for abandoning both snapshot models of conceptual change and snapshot validation of theories of change. Everyone agrees change is slow; but few models exist to track the slow progress.

5. *Make contextuality a central concern.* The body of research on intuitive physics often reveals sensitive dependence on problem context, on framing of questions, on modality (viewing, drawing, enacting), and so on (diSessa et al., 2004). In naïve biology, subjects reveal early vitalist sensitivities only when explicitly prompted. Can this be inconsequential to the nature of the child's "theory"? To offer a comparable example from physics, articulate, "high-stress" use of the schooled concept of force, where a claim such as "students think of using $F = ma$ only when prompted" would be unacceptable. More generally, developmental studies consistently report intrusion of one way of thinking into others (e.g., psychology intrudes on biology; or weight intrudes on density). When? Why? What are the general implications?

Footnotes

1. The conceptual change paradigm is systematically less often applied in mathematics.

2. That force acts directly on velocity is the essence of the expert explanation in Figure 16.1.

3. Kuhn carefully guarded the coverage of his theory. Fields that (1) do not have the Normal Science phases of puzzle solving, that (2) have multiple, persistent schools of thought, or in which (3) rights of judgment are not strictly confined to specialists, simply are not candidates for his model. It seems unlikely that Kuhn would have sanctioned use of his ideas for conceptual development outside of professional research communities of a very restrictive sort.

4. Toulmin did not restrict his critique to strictly logical forms of sytematicity. For example, he also rejected Collingwood's model of "systematicity in hierarchical presumptions."

5. Naïve physics is a third important developmental domain. However, coverage was spotty compared to psychology and biology. Studies of baby cognition of physics revealed stunning early competence and development (Spelke, Philips, & Woodword, 1995; Baillargeon, 1986). But middle years received less attention, and late development was mainly left to misconceptions researchers.

6. Vosniadou often emphasized the nature of framework theories as "background assumptions," similar to Collingwood's view, which Toulmin criticized for lack of rendering such assumptions explicit and testable.

7. In contrast, Carey has concepts embedded in theories, but concepts are not described as decomposable objects.

8. Incommensurability does not make obvious sense when no prior competitive system exists.

9. Thagard (2000) is a notable exception.

10. Few if any researchers believe that intuitive ideas are deductively coherent. Yet explicit alternative forms of coherence are rarely presented and also generally vague. Wellman and Gelman (1992) mention two meanings for coherence: lack of contradiction (which, as they point out, could apply to a set of beliefs that have nothing to do with one another), and the idea that concepts refer to each other (where "reference" is undefined).

References

Baillargeon, R. (1986). Representing the existence and the location of hidden objects: Object permanence in 6- and 8-month infants. *Cognition, 23*, 21–41.

Carey, S. (1985). *Conceptual change in childhood*. Cambridge, MA: MIT Press/Bradford Books.

Carey, S. (1986). Reorganization of knowledge in the course of acquisition. In S. Strauss (Ed.) *Ontogeny and phylogeny of human development*. Norwood, NJ: Ablex.

Carey, S. (1991). Knowledge acquisition: Enrichment or conceptual change? In S. Carey & R. Gelman (Eds.), *The epigenesis of mind* (pp. 257–291). Hillsdale, NJ: Lawrence Erlbaum Associates.

Carey, S. (1999). Sources of conceptual change. In E. Scholnick, K. Nelson, S. Gelman, & P. Miller (Eds.), *Conceptual development: Piaget's legacy* (pp. 293–326). Mahwah, NJ: Lawrence Erlbaum Associates.

Chi, M. T. H. (1992). Conceptual change across ontological categories: Examples from learning and discovery in science. In F. Giere (Ed.), *Cognitive models of science: Minnesota studies in the philosophy of science* (pp. 129–160). Minneapolis: University of Minnesota Press.

Clement, J. (1982). Students' preconceptions in introductory mechanics. *American Journal of Physics*, 50(1), 66–71.

Confrey, J. (1990). A review of the research on student conceptions in mathematics, science, and programming. In C. Cazden (Ed.), *Review of Research in Education*, 16 (pp. 3–56). Washington, DC: American Educational Research Association.

diSessa, A. A. (1983). Phenomenology and the evolution of intuition. In D. Gentner and A. Stevens (Eds.), *Mental models* (pp. 15–33). Hillsdale, NJ: Lawrence Erlbaum Associates.

diSessa, A. A. (1993). Toward an epistemology of physics. *Cognition and instruction*, 10 (2–3), 105–225; Responses to commentary, 261–280. (*Cognition and Instruction*, Monograph No. 1.)

diSessa, A. A. (1996). What do "just plain folk" know about physics? In D. R. Olson and N. Torrance (Eds.), *The handbook of education and human development: New models of learning, teaching, and schooling*. Oxford: Blackwell, 709–730.

diSessa, A. A., Gillespie, N., & Esterly, J. (2004). Coherence vs. fragmentation in the development of the concept of force. *Cognitive Science*, 28, 843–900.

diSessa, A. A., & Wagner, J. F. (2005). What coordination has to say about transfer. In J. Mestre (Ed.), *Transfer of learning from a modern multi-disciplinary perspective* (pp. 121–154). Greenwich, CT: Information Age Publishing.

Driver, R. (1989). Students' conceptions and the learning of science. *International Journal of Science Education*, 11, 481–490.

Goody, J. (1977) *The domestication of the savage mind*. Cambridge: Cambridge University Press.

Gopnik, A., & H. M. Wellman (1994). The theory theory. In L. A. Hirschfeld & S. A. Gelman (Eds.), *Mapping the mind: Domain specificity in cognition and culture* (pp. 257–293). New York: Cambridge University Press.

Gruber, H., & Voneche, J. (1977). *The essential Piaget*. New York: Basic Books.

Hammer, D., & Elby, A. (2002). On the form of a personal epistemology. In B. Hofer, & P. Pintrich (Eds.), *Personal epistemology* (pp. 169–190). Mahwah, NJ: Lawrence Erlbaum Associates.

Harvard-Smithsonian Center for Astrophysics (1987). *A private universe*. Video. Annenberg/CPB: http://www.learner.org.

Hawkins, D. (1978) Critical barriers to science learning, *Outlook*, 29, 3–23.

Hewson, P., & Hennessey, M. G. (1992). Making status explicit: A case study of conceptual change. In R. Duit, F. Goldberg, & H. Niedderer (Eds.), *Research in physics learning: Theoretical and empirical studies* (pp. 176–187). Kiel, Germany: IPN.

Hewson, W. H., & Hewson, M. G. A. (1983). The role of conceptual conflict in conceptual change and the design of science instruction. *Instructional Science*, 13, 1–13.

Hofer, B., & Pintrich, P. (2002). *Personal epistemology*. Mahwah, NJ: Lawrence Erlbaum Associates.

Hunt, E., & Minstrell, J. (1994). A cognitive approach to the teaching of physics. In K. McGilly (Ed.), *Classroom lessons: Integrating cognitive theory and classroom practice* (pp. 51–74). Cambridge, MA: MIT Press.

Inagaki, K., & Hatano, G. (2002). *Young children's naive thinking about the biological world*. New York: Psychology Press.

Ioannides, C., &Vosniadou, C. (2002). The changing meanings of force. *Cognitive Science Quarterly*, 2, 5–61.

Karmiloff-Smith, A. (1988). The child as a theoretician, not an inductivist. *Mind and Language* 3(3), 183–195.

Keil, F. (1994). The birth and nurturance of concepts by domains: The origins of concepts of living things. In L. Hirschfield & S. Gelman (Eds.), *Mapping the mind: Domain specificity in cognition and culture* (pp. 234–254). Cambridge: Cambridge University Press.

Kuhn, T. S. (1970). *The structure of scientific revolutions* (2nd ed.). Chicago: University of Chicago Press.

Lakatos, I. (1970). Falsification and the methodology of scientific research programmes. In I. Lakatos & A. Musgrave (Eds.), *Criticism and the growth of knowledge* (pp. 91–196). London: Cambridge University Press.

McCloskey, M. (1983a). Naive theories of motion. In D. Gentner and A. Stevens (Eds.) *Mental Models* (pp. 299–323). Hillsdale, NJ: Lawrence Erlbaum Associates.

McCloskey, M. (1983b, April). Intuitive physics. *Scientific American*, 122–130.

McDermott, L., Shaffer, P., et al., (2002). *Tutorials in introductory physics*. Upper Saddle River, NJ: Prentice Hall.

Minstrell, J. (1982). Explaining the "at rest" condition of an object. *The Physics Teacher*, 20, 10–14.

Minstrell, J. (1989). Teaching science for understanding. In L. Resnick, & L. Klopfer (Eds.), *Toward the thinking curriculum* (pp. 129–149). Alexandria, VA: Association for Supervision and Curriculum Development.

Nersessian, N. (1992). How do scientists think? In F. Giere (Ed.), *Cognitive models of science: Minnesota studies in the philosophy of science* (pp. 3–44). Minneapolis: University of Minnesota Press.

Pfundt, H., & Duit, R. (1988). *Bibliography: Students' alternative frameworks and science education.* (2nd ed.). Kiel, Germany: IPN.

Posner, G. J., Strike, K. A., Hewson, P. W., & Gertzog, W. A. (1982). Accommodation of a scientific conception: Toward a theory of conceptual change. *Science Education*, 66(2), 211–227.

Sinatra, G., & Pintrich, P. (2002). *Intentional conceptual change*. Mahwah, NJ: Lawrence Erlbaum Associates.

Smith, C. Maclin, D., Grosslight, L., & Davis, H. (1997). Teaching for understanding: A study of students' preinstruction theories of matter and a comparison of the effectiveness of two approaches to teaching about matter and density. *Cognition and Instruction*, 15, 317–393.

Smith, J. P., diSessa, A. A., & Roschelle, J. (1993). Misconceptions reconceived: A constructivist analysis of knowledge in transition. *Journal of the Learning Sciences*, 3(2), 115–163.

Spelke, E. S., Phillips, A., & Woodword, A. (1995). Infants' knowledge of object motion and human action. In D. Sperber, D. Premack, & A Premack (Eds.), *Causal cognition: A multidisciplinary debate* (pp. 44–78). Oxford: Clarendon Press.

Strike, K. A., & Posner, G. J. (1990). A revisionist theory of conceptual change. In R. Duschl & R. Hamilton (Eds.), *Philosophy of science, cognitive science, and educational theory and practice* (pp. 147–176). Albany: SUNY Press.

Thagard, P. (2000). *Coherence in thought and action.* Cambridge, MA: MIT Press.

Tiberghien, A. (1980). Modes and conditions of learning: The learning of some aspects of the concept of heat. In W. Archenhold, R. Driver, A. Orton, & C. Wood-Robinson (Eds.), *Cognitive development research in science and mathematics: Proceedings of an international symposium* (pp. 288–309). Leeds: University of Leeds.

Toulmin, S. (1972). *Human understanding.* Vol. 1. Oxford: Clarendon Press.

Viennot, L. (1979). Spontaneous reasoning in elementary dynamics. *European Journal of Science Education*, 1, 205–221.

Vosniadou, S. (2002). On the nature of naïve physics. In M. Limón & L. Mason (Eds.), *Reconsidering conceptual change: Issues in theory and practice* (pp. 61–76). Dordrecht: Kluwer Academic Publishers.

Wellman, H., & Gelman, S. (1992). Cognitive development: Foundational theories of core domains. *Annual Review of Psychology*, 43, 337–375.

Wiser, M., & Carey, S. (1983). When heat and temperature were one. In D. Gentner & A. Stevens (Eds.), *Mental models* (pp. 267–298). Hillsdale, NJ: Lawrence Erlbaum Associates.

CHAPTER 17

Spatial Representations and Imagery in Learning

Daniel L. Schwartz and Julie Heiser

Spatial representations, when used well, support learning in reading, mathematics, and science. They also enable mental simulations and visualizations that prompt innovation and scientific discovery. Spatial representations, both external drawings and internal images, exploit people's sophisticated perceptual-motor system. The embodiment of thought in perceptual processes has promising implications for learning. In this chapter, we emphasize spatial representations that people construct and transform in their mind's eye. The process of working with these mental spatial representations is called *imagery*.

Spatial representation is different from other forms of cognitive representation studied by learning scientists – linguistic, conceptual, logical – because spatial representations partake of perceptual processes and experiences. Neurological evidence, for example, indicates that perceptual regions of the brain activate when people imagine movement (Kosslyn, 1994). Yet, spatial representations are not mere echoes of perception. They can integrate nonperceptual knowledge that allows people to imagine things they have

not seen. Spatial representations have four key properties that determine their unique value for education. We begin with a brief review of early psychological research on spatial memory, and then describe the four key properties. We show how these properties can be used to help people learn about the world through mental models and simulations. Afterward, we discuss ways to help people leverage imagery to innovate new ideas and scientific insight.

Spatial Representations Become Special

Much of the inspiration for examining spatial representations for learning began with studies of pictorial memory. People have expansive memories for pictures. In a heroic study, Standing (1973) showed people ten thousand pictures over five days. (This is the equivalent of one picture every fifteen seconds for eight straight hours on five consecutive days!) Afterwards, people saw a combination of new pictures and original pictures.

People correctly recognized the original pictures at a rate of 83 percent. Vivid pictures were recognized even more frequently. Standing extrapolated that if people saw a million vivid images, they would retain 986,300 in the near term, and would recognize 731,400 after a year. This estimate is well beyond memory for words and sentences (Shepard, 1967). The implication is that visuals can be an excellent way to help students remember.

One explanation for this impressive memory is Paivio's (1986) "dual coding" hypothesis. When people see a visual scene, they also explain its content to themselves. Pictures yield a perceptual code and a verbal code in memory, which doubles the chances of retrieval. Additionally, the perceptual and verbal representations can commingle. For example, the ancient Greeks invented the Method of Loci: orators memorized long speeches by associating elements of their speech with objects along a standard path through a cathedral, and retracing the objects on the path cued their memory for the speech. More recently, Bower, Karlin, and Dueck (1975) gave people nonsensical drawings, which they called "droodles," with or without descriptive captions (e.g., "a midget playing a trombone in a telephone booth"). Participants who received the descriptive captions better recalled and reproduced the droodles. The dual coding hypothesis implies that mental spatial representations are not simply pictures in the head. Instead, they can be changed by other mental processes. For example, Stevens and Coupe (1978) found that people who lived in San Diego judged that Reno was to their east. This is wrong, and people made the error because they had schematized San Diego as a coastal city and Reno as an inland city. On the positive side, the ability to integrate perceptual and verbal information is extremely valuable for learning – for example, when reading an evocative story.

The last thirty years of research have revealed several distinct features of spatial representations in relation to learning, starting with huge memory effects and their permeability to verbal information. More recent research has found that spatial representations and imagery also support understanding (we describe this research later in this chapter). Four distinct qualities of perception make spatial representations special for thinking and learning.

Unique Features of Spatial Representation

Representations of spatial information, whether internal or external, capitalize on the perceptual system. The perceptual system has a structure that enforces and enables specific spatial computations. Imagery is a representation of perceptual experience; therefore, it inherits the structure of perception to complete computations that are difficult to perform linguistically. Knowing which computations imagery handles particularly well can help one decide when to use spatial materials and processes in education. The four properties of perception with special relevance to education are effortless structure, determinism, perception-action coupling, and pre-interpretation.

These four properties of perception are ubiquitous, and they should be distinguished from perceptual experiences that need to be learned. For example, all people experience a world in depth, but not all people have learned exactly what the face of a penny looks like. Nickerson and Adams (1979) found that only 42 percent of their subjects could select the correctly drawn penny from a set of fourteen variants. These Americans had handled thousands of pennies, but they had never learned to see them well.

One of the most beguiling aspects of perception is that people easily see what they have learned, yet they can completely overlook what they have not. Consequently, people often believe they perceive all there is to be seen in a situation. This is highly relevant to issues of learning; educators often provide explanations of phenomena that students have not learned to perceive, and therefore, students do not realize they are missing something. Bransford, Franks, Vye, and Sherwood (1989) described clinical psychology students who learned to diagnose symptoms from print materials. When the students began their internships, they were unable to perceive the symptoms in patients and had difficulty making diagnoses.

In a seminal paper, Gibson and Gibson (1955) argued that perceptual learning involves the increased discernment or pickup of information; for example, the ability to distinguish an edible and a poisonous mushroom. So rather than describing learning as a constructive process of creating more abstract mental representations, they argued that learning gets people closer to the world by improving their abilities to perceive information that has always been there. Gibson and Gibson suggested the use of contrasting cases, much like tasting wines side-by-side. By juxtaposing cases that are similar in many ways, people can begin to notice what makes the cases distinctive. For example, Howard Gardner (1982) described an art exhibit that juxtaposed original paintings and forgeries. At first people could not tell the difference, but over time, they began to perceive the features that differentiated the originals from the copies (cf. Eisner, 1972; Goodwin, 1994). It is an important lesson for educators that what they perceive may not be the same thing that their students perceive (Nathan & Koedinger, 2000), and it takes special strategies, like contrasting cases, to help students see what is important.

Four Qualities of Perception That Make Imagery Special

When students can see what is important, they can use the special qualities of the perceptual system for thinking with imagery. We now describe four features of perception used by imagery.

EFFORTLESS STRUCTURE

The function of perception is to provide a cohesive, stable experience that permits action. Perception differs from sensation. Sensation provides spatial information through modalities like sound, sight, and touch. It is perception's task to integrate and structure the information provided by sensation. When people handle a piece of typing paper, for example, they perceive a white rectangle. However, their fingers sense edges and corners, not a complete object. Their retinas sense a trapezoid due to foreshortening. Moreover, the shape of the trapezoid changes as the paper gets moved around. Nevertheless, perception delivers the unitary experience of a constant rectangle.

Perception packages sensation with little discernible effort, because evolution has conferred specialized abilities that are well matched to recurrent structures in the spatial world, including shape, motion, and color. The early perceptual research by the Gestalt psychologists attempted to catalog environmental structures that make "good form" for perception (Wertheimer, 1938). One indicator that perception includes specialized abilities is that different types of visual information – color, motion, brightness, shape, and location – are processed in separate brain regions. A benefit of these evolved specializations is that cognition gets structural output from perception "for free" – without requiring cognitive processing or conscious attention. This is relevant to imagery and learning because it suggests that spatial representations can be useful when they provide structures that do not require intensive cognitive effort to manage. For example, students may more easily grasp the structure of a factorial experiment when they can see the factors crossed in a matrix.

DETERMINISM

Perceptual structure is deterministic – at any given moment, people only see one set of structures. In Figure 17.1, there are two ways to perceive the orientation of the cube, but perception limits people to one version at a time, and they cannot see mutually inconsistent consequences.

The determinism of spatial perception can be contrasted with language. People can say "the tree is next to the bush" but this

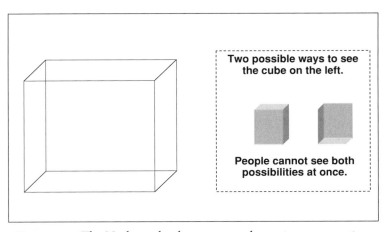

Figure 17.1. The Necker cube demonstrates determinate perception.

statement is vague about exactly where the tree is. In contrast, vision is not vague; the tree is perceived as being in front, behind, left, or right of the bush. The spatial relations are perceived by the visual system and cannot be easily omitted, as they can in language. This is relevant to imagery, because it implies that people will represent specific situations in their imagination. Mani and Johnson-Laird (1982), for example, provided people sentences like "the cross is above the square, and the triangle is next to the square" – a sentence that is ambiguous, because the triangle could be either to the right or to the left of the square. People then saw pictures and were asked if they matched the sentence. Some people rejected pictures that showed the triangle to the left of the square, and other people rejected pictures that showed the triangle to the right of the square. They had taken the indeterminate sentence and made it spatially determinate when they constructed their image. Determinism can be valuable for learning, because it prevents people from being vague.

PERCEPTION-ACTION COUPLING

The third relevant property of perception involves the motor system. Visual perception is much more than watching; perception is tightly coupled with people's abilities to take action, and perception guides motor action. Also, motor actions guide

perception; people move their heads to get a better look at something, and active touch (Gibson, 1962) helps people figure out the shape of an object. People are constantly learning perceptual-motor couplings so that their perceptions and actions are coordinated. For example, people quickly learn to adjust their swing when they change tennis rackets. This recalibration is handled by the perceptual-motor system and involves minimal cognitive effort.

The coupling between perception and action is relevant to imagery, because people need to imagine the consequences of an action. For example, a person might imagine what happens if they try to jump across a wide chasm. To conduct this imagery, people need to animate their image, creating a mental simulation of the jump. The animations that people can complete are related to the types of actions they can take, including changing perspective, moving an object, using a tool, walking down a path, and so forth. The relevance of the coupling between action and perception for imagery is exemplified in a study by Parsons (1987). Participants sat at a computer keyboard that showed a hand on the monitor. They had to determine whether it was a left or right hand. The time people took to make the decision was related to how much time it would take to move their own hand from the keyboard into that position, even though people did not actually move their hands.

One implication for education is that it is fruitless to ask people to imagine spatial changes or movements that humans could never possibly do in reality, such as rotating four-dimensional structures.

PRE-INTERPRETATION

The final quality is that perception is largely bottom-up. Perception often occurs prior to one's beliefs or knowledge about a situation, and one's beliefs cannot easily override a perception. Some aspects of perception are learned, particular those aspects that vary across many environments (e.g., the flavor of wine), and those things that are learned are more prone to interpretation than those things built into the system. Many researchers have argued about the line between those aspects of perception that can and cannot be influenced by experience. For example, one hypothesis proposed that people who live in environments without buildings cannot see straight lines, because "straightness" is a learned property of a "carpentered world" (Gregory, 1966).

There will always be arguments about which aspects of perception can be influenced by beliefs and culture. Regardless, perception can occur independently of beliefs, and optical illusions are a good example; sometimes the world violates the expectations programmed into the human brain by evolution, and the automatic processes of perception get fooled. Figure 17.2 displays an illusion where the two line segments look like they have different lengths. Even after people convince themselves that the lines are the same length, by using a ruler or some other measuring device, they still cannot see them as the same length (though they can nonetheless assert that they are).

When perception operates independently of beliefs, it is preinterpretive. Pre-interpretation is an important quality for imagery. People can do imagery work before they get "locked" into a particular interpretation. With language, people need to interpret words, and this shapes the kinds of conclusions they will reach. Pre-interpretive images, on the other hand, allow people

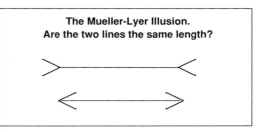

Figure 17.2. Knowing that the lines are the same length does not block the illusion.

to manipulate images to see what forms emerge. In the next section, we discuss the relevance to learning of pre-interpretation and the other three properties.

Imagery for Getting Closer to the World: Mental Models and Simulations

People can create images from visual input. For example, people slowly build a mental map while navigating a city. People can also create images from touch. Shelton and McNamara (2001) asked people to arrange a number of objects without looking at them. This improved people's abilities to recognize the layout of the objects when viewed from novel orientations. People can form images based on sound and language; for example, when hearing a book read to them. Sometimes, when people need to construct an image that conflicts with concurrent visual input (e.g., words on a page), it interferes with their imagery (Brooks, 1968). People can also create images in the absence of any immediate input – for example, when anticipating an encounter.

Determining whether people are using imagery is difficult. The fact that someone is working with spatial information does not imply the use of imagery. For example, Schwartz and Black (1996) found that people initially solve gear problems by imagining their movement, but over time they learn to use a quick verbal rule even though the problem is spatial (e.g., adjacent gears turn opposite directions). For most learning scientists, it is more important to design tasks that harness imagery than to prove its existence. Therefore, we emphasize the four perceptual properties of spatial representations that educators can use to improve thinking and learning.

In this section, we emphasize research where imagery helps people anticipate or learn how a possible world might appear. We begin with examples of people constructing mental models to understand a situation, and we emphasize the relevance of effortless structure and determinism. We then present examples of people using simulations to draw inferences, and we emphasize action-coupling and pre-interpretation. To help highlight the four perceptual properties in imagery, we emphasize them separately, but all four are at play in each example.

Constructing Mental Models

One role for imagery in education is to help people make sense of things they have not experienced firsthand and can only hear or read about. Zwaan (2004) describes language comprehension as "guided experience." Guided experience, of course, is not as vivid as direct experience, but it engages common mechanisms. These common mechanisms permit people to construct spatial mental models and draw inferences, almost as though they were there. Mental models are internal representations where changes within the model correspond to changes in the world (as opposed, for example, to manipulating an algebraic formula – a manipulation that does not correspond directly to a change in the physical world). For example, Morrow, Greenspan, and Bower (1987) demonstrated that, when reading, people track the spatial location of the story's characters in a mental model; people can quickly answer questions about a spatial location if the character recently moved to that location, which is what would occur if people were actually walking about the space themselves (see Zwaan & Radvansky, 1998, for a review). Mental models can greatly enhance people's abilities to learn from what they read. To help early readers, it is important to provide information that

supports the effortless structure of imagery, and to help students learn to construct determinate mental models.

EFFORTLESS STRUCTURE

Good readers often rely on imagery when trying to comprehend discourse. People, for instance, can generate metric structures in imagery. Metric structures include the intervals between positions and object boundaries. For example, a metric image that portrays the distance between New York and Los Angeles would include the space in between (scaled, of course). This is different from stating that New York and Los Angeles are three thousand miles apart, because in that statement there is no representation of the space in between the two cities. The effortlessness of creating spatial structures often yields cases where people spontaneously create metric structures that extrapolate beyond the information in the text. Morrow and Clark (1988), for example, asked participants to read "The tractor is approaching the fence," or "The mouse is approaching the fence." Afterwards, when asked to estimate the distance between the fence and the mouse or the tractor, they estimated a larger distance between the tractor and the fence, even though the sentences said nothing about how far either was from the fence. More generally, one benefit of the effortless structure of imagery is that it permits people to generate images easily so they can scan them for interesting relations.

However, if the available information does not provide structural cues, people can have difficulty recruiting the effortless structure of imagery. Rock and Di Vita (1987), for example, showed people wire figures that looked something like a twisted coat hanger. People could not recognize identical wire figures when they were shown at a different orientation. People were quite bad at this task, because there was so little structural information in the figures. Farah, Rochlin, and Klein (1994) replicated the study, but they molded clay into the wire so the stimuli now looked like complicated potato chips. In this case, people were quite good at the task, because the clay provided more cues to the

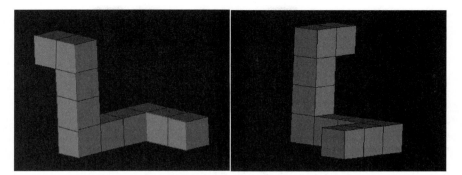

Figure 17.3. People imagine rotating the objects to solve the problem.

overall structure of each object. Imagery can only be as good as the structural information people have to begin with, and designers of information displays and texts need to keep this in mind.

DETERMINISM

Good readers spontaneously construct deterministic structures of what they are reading. For example, consider these two sentences: "A turtle is on a log" and "A fish swims under the log." Most people easily infer that the fish swam under the turtle. People construct an image that determines this relation, and they can see it in their image. Given a brief delay, people are even likely to think they read the sentence, "The fish swam under the turtle" (Bransford, Barclay, & Franks, 1972). Early readers, however, do not always construct determinate models of what they read, and therefore, they may leave ideas vague. Schoenfeld (1992) described examples of students blindly solving math word problems where the situation was impossible, but the students never realized the problem was impossible to solve because they did not try to model it. Although imagery can provide determinate structures, people need to learn that they should construct images. Imagery does not always arise spontaneously.

It is particularly important to encourage early readers to imagine narratives so they can better understand. Compared to adults, young children have difficulties with imagery; therefore, they need special support (Reiser, Garing, & Young, 1994).

Glenberg et al. (2004) described an experiment where young children read a passage and manipulated figurines so they portrayed the actions in the passage (e.g., the farmer walked in the barn). After some practice, children were asked to simply imagine manipulating the figurines. As a posttest, the children read a final passage without any prompting. Children who completed this sequence were better at remembering and drawing inferences about the new passage compared to children who received no training, to children who were only instructed to imagine the passage, and most importantly, to children who manipulated the figurines without the intermediate instructions to imagine manipulating. Encouraging imagery through the initial use of physical modeling helped the children learn a strategy to make more determinate relations in their understanding of a text, and this improved their comprehension.

Running Mental Simulations

A second application of imagery is to help people imagine changes through a mental simulation. Shepard and colleagues (see Shepard & Cooper, 1986) performed ground-breaking studies that proved people can simulate the movement of objects. They called it *analog imagery* to emphasize that people were imagining *continuous* movements through metric space. Participants saw two objects at different angles. Figure 17.3 provides an example where the angular disparity between the objects is

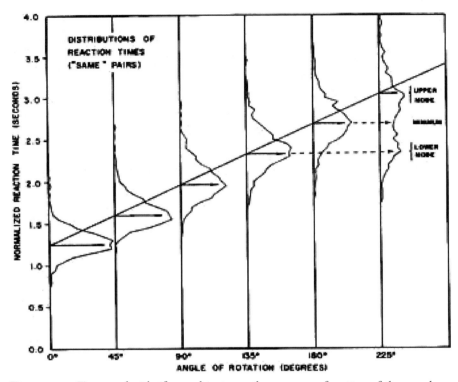

Figure 17.4. Time to decide if two objects are the same as a function of the angular disparity between the objects. At each angle of disparity, the graph also shows the distributions of response times. From Shepard and Cooper (1986, p. 58).

about 90°. People had to decide if the objects were the same shape. Shepard varied the angular disparity between the objects (15°, 45°, etc.) and measured how long it took people to decide if they matched. Shepard reasoned that people would take longer to complete the task when the two objects had a greater angular disparity, because people would have to mentally rotate one of the objects farther so they could see if it matched.

Figure 17.4 shows one set of results. People exhibited a strong linear relationship between the angular disparities of the objects and how long it took them to solve the problems. If one looks closely at the data for 225°, there are two clusters of times to solve the problem; this is because some people rotated the object the shorter direction (135°), so it took them less time than participants who rotated the object 225°. Simulations like these can greatly help students

draw inferences; and as with mental models, students need to learn to conduct these simulations. This requires learning both how to set up simulations so they match different possible actions, and checking their answers lest they rely on faulty pre-interpretations.

PERCEPTION-ACTION COUPLING

Simulations anticipate the consequences of possible motor actions (e.g., turning a block, drawing a line). Simulations are possible because of perception-action coupling. Relevant evidence comes from studies where people accomplish imagery tasks more quickly and accurately when they are allowed to move as they engage in the task. Simons and Wang (1998), for example, showed that people more easily imagine looking at a set of objects from a new perspective when they are allowed to walk to that perspective, even if they keep their

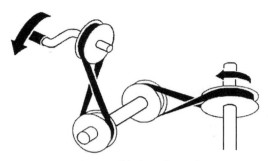

Figure 17.5. Gear and belt task used to examine complex imagery. From Hegarty (2000).

eyes closed. Wohlschläger and Wohlshläger (1988) and Wexler and Klam (2001) showed that people imagine object rotations more quickly when they can physically rotate an object with their hands, even if they are not directly touching the object (e.g., Schwartz & Holton, 2000 had people pull a string that turned a table on which an object rested, but did not allow them to directly touch the object). People often think of simulations as guiding possible actions. However, in these cases, actions guided imagery.

The coupling of imagery to the motor system is relevant to reading. Klatzky et al. (1989), for example, told people to form their hand into an open grip or a flat palm. They were then asked, "Is it possible to squeeze a tomato?" People were faster to say "yes" when they had made the open grip. So, not only does embodying words through imagery and action improve comprehension (as described earlier), it also improves access to relevant possible actions and their likely consequences.

The coupling of imagery with the motor system enables people to anticipate possible changes, and this can help students solve problems – for example, when rotating molecular models to see if they can bond with each other. At the same time, imagery is often limited to the complexity of action available to the body. People can only image so much in a single simulation. Hegarty (1992, 2000) examined people's abilities to "mentally animate" complex pulley systems as shown in Figure 17.5. Hegarty found that good problem-solvers simulated one interaction at a time and in the right order. For

example, they imagined how the belt would rotate if they turned the crank. They would then propagate the result by imagining how the moving belt would turn the next pulley in the series. Spatial representations interact with other forms of knowledge – in this case problem decomposition – and therefore, it is important to help students to develop the skills necessary to decompose a problem into a form that is amenable to imagery.

PRE-INTERPRETATION

Pre-interpretation is relevant to simulations of interacting objects. When people simulate interacting objects, they need to coordinate their relative rates of movement. For example, imagine a large gear driving a small gear. The speed of the small gear will depend on the large gear, and it will be faster than the large gear. To simulate this scenario, people need to coordinate their relative rates. The same is true of most simulations involving multiple components – for example, scissors with long blades but short handles. Pre-interpretive expertise helps people coordinate movements in complex simulations.

The role of pre-interpretive expertise in imagery was demonstrated by Schwartz and Black (1999). Participants received the problem in Figure 17.6. A wide and narrow glass of the same heights are filled to identical levels of water. Will the two glasses start spilling water at the same angle of tilt? Very few people gave the right answer when they could only look at the glasses. In a second condition, participants were handed one glass at

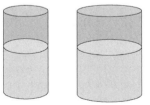

Does one glass start pouring water at a lesser angle of tilt?

Figure 17.6. A problem in which pre-interpretive knowledge helps solve a problem that people typically cannot solve verbally. Adapted from Schwartz and Black (1999).

a time. There was no water in the glass, just a black strip indicating the "pretend" water level. People closed their eyes and tilted the glass until they thought the water would just start to spill out. They repeated the process with the second glass. In this case, every individual correctly tilted the narrow glass farther than the wider glass. Thus, people had pre-interpretive, action-dependent expertise that enabled them to simulate the water-glass movement interactions.

Scientists often use simulations to tap their intuitions (Clement, 1994), and asking learners to imagine "what would happen if" can help them ground explicit understanding with their own pre-interpretive expertise. At the same time, educators need to watch for student misconceptions that are borne of pre-interpretive expertise. Pre-interpretive expertise is for pragmatic action, and therefore, it does not always match scientific truths and can interfere with science learning (e.g., naïve physics, McCloskey, 1983; also see diSessa, this volume).

Pre-interpretive expertise often appears in tasks that involve motor activity, especially with young children. Krist, Fieberg, and Wilkening (1993) asked children to push a ball off a ledge so it would land on a target on the floor. The researchers varied the height of the ledge, and children accurately modified their pushing force. However, when asked explicitly how hard they needed to push the ball, the children assumed a higher ledge called for a great push because the ball was further away from the target. Of particular relevance to educators, Alibali and Goldin-Meadow (1993) found that children who are in transition between developmental stages demonstrate competence through the motor system before they achieve explicit understanding. For example, when pouring two identical amounts of water into a narrow and a wide glass, six-year-old children often say that the narrower glass has more water, because the water is reaches a higher level. But when the children are close to realizing that the amounts are identical in spite of the difference in height, they often tacitly indi-cate the width of the class with their hands, even though they are discussing the water's height. Alibali and colleagues have shown that teachers who attend to these types of speech-gesture mismatches (which also appear in mathematics) can better deliver just-in-time instruction that guides children toward explicit understanding. It is an interesting question whether training teachers to look at gestures is a tractable method to increase their abilities to tailor instruction.

Imagery for Going Beyond the World: Emergence and Covariance

Here, we consider imagery that goes beyond experience and creates innovations in thought. Human imagination may never be as creative as nature; for example, who could imagine a rainbow had they never seen or heard of one? Still, human imagination is an impressive affair, and spatial representations are implicated. The history of science is filled with eminent scientists who claim imagery helped them infer structures hidden from perception.

Thus far, we have described how people use imagery to help anticipate what they might be likely to perceive. Imagery helps people be more efficient in connecting them to the empirical world of experience, when measures of performance use speed and accuracy. When imagery is used for innovation and going beyond experience, the measures of success are found in the novelty and appropriateness of the structures that people create. Innovation is critical to learning, because the goal of education is not only to make people more proficient at what they already know; it is also to help them develop new structures for thinking (Schwartz, Bransford, & Sears, 2005). In this section, we describe two uses of imagery for innovation: emergence and covariant representations.

Emergence

The effortless structure and simulations of spatial representations are important contributors to innovation and discovery. People imagine changes to see whether new patterns emerge. First consider visible action. Martin and Schwartz (in press) asked nine-year-olds to solve equivalent fraction problems – for example, "What is one-fourth of eight?" Children received eight small plastic tiles and had to indicate their answers. When children could only look at the pieces without touching, they tended to indicate one or four pieces as the answer. They mapped the pieces in one-to-one fashion to the numerals "1" and "4" in the fraction $\frac{1}{4}$. However, when children could push the pieces around, they were nearly four times more successful. By moving the pieces, the children began to notice grouping structures. They discovered it is possible to make 4 groups, with each group containing two pieces.

Imagery, like visible action, supports innovation because it helps people to move shapes into new configurations relatively effortlessly. Finke (1990), for example, asked people to imagine the letter 'C' and the letter 'J'. He asked people to imagine rotating the 'C' so it was on top of the 'J'. He asked people what they saw, and they often said an umbrella. Though people had not started with the idea of an umbrella, it emerged from the reconfiguration of the shapes in their imagination. In another set of studies, people were not told what geometric pattern to construct, but they still exhibited emergence. People saw a number of abstract shapes (e.g., square, circle, line). Finke asked the participants to close their eyes and imagine, for example, how the shapes could create a piece of equipment for cleaning gutters. They produced many creative solutions.

Asking students to imagine may also help them innovate emergent solutions to important problems, but simply telling them to close their eyes and be creative is probably insufficient. A major challenge of innovation is that explicit interpretations can interfere with developing new ones. For example, Chambers and Reisberg (1985) asked people to look at Figure 17.7, which can be interpreted as a duck or a rabbit. Once people had an interpretation, they

Figure 17.7. Duck/rabbit image used in many experiments (e.g., Chambers & Reisberg, 1985).

closed their eyes. Chambers and Reisberg asked if they could come up with a second interpretation; could they overcome their original interpretation (e.g., duck) and see a second interpretation (e.g., rabbit)? Not a single participant over several studies could do the re-interpretation. Explicit interpretations interfered with people's abilities to see an alternative.

More generally, the great challenge of innovation is "breaking set." Once reasoning begins with an interpretation, it is hard to shake free. In Finke's studies, where new interpretations did emerge, people did not begin with a pre-interpretation. They simply encoded a set of geometric shapes. Because imagery can transform shapes without interpretation, people could move the shapes in their imagination and continue to make determinate structures until they saw an interesting pattern and develop an interpretation of it.

To help students use their imaginations to innovate new (for them) ideas, it is important to remember that innovation favors the prepared mind. Kekulé, who famously imagined the circular structure of the benzene molecule, knew that he needed a structure that could join multiple atoms, and he was prepared to recognize the significance of what he imagined. To recognize an emergent structure, students need a strong understanding of the constraints and problems the structure must handle, and this is something that appropriate instruction can do. Yet, at the same time, students must avoid interpretations that prefigure their solutions, because this will interfere with their ability to develop new interpretations. Thus, innovation through imagery requires a delicate balance. Compared to the massive efficiency literature on how to make people faster and more accurate, the learning sciences could use more research on techniques for fostering innovation (Sawyer, 2004; Schwartz, Bransford, & Sears, 2005).

Covariant Representations

Perhaps the most impressive instances of spatial innovation involve covariant representations. Covariant spatial representations do not resemble their referents. For example, a speedometer does not look like a speeding car and a clock does not look like time. However, changes in speed or time map neatly onto the changes displayed in the dials. Among their strengths, covariant representations make it possible to represent nonspatial phenomena in spatial form. Venn diagrams, for example, can represent a space of personality traits. There are a many visual representations that people have invented to support reasoning about both spatial and nonspatial matters.

Creating a covariant spatial representation is an impressive feat of creativity. Galileo has been credited with inventing the first covariant representation to make an argument (Cummins, 1989). He used area to represent distance. Students can learn to invent covariant representations, given appropriate educational support. Schwartz (1993) found that very few adolescents spontaneously construct visualizations to solve problems. However, once they were encouraged to invent their own representations, and they experienced the exceptional benefits for problem solving, the students spontaneously started to invent their own forms several weeks later on novel problems. Bamberger (1991) described how children, given prompting, invented increasingly precise visual representations of musical form that included pitch and duration. There have been promising educational efforts that capitalize on children's facility with covariant representations. diSessa et al. (1991) described children's "meta-representational expertise" as they are encouraged to progressively create more refined visual representations of motion.

One of the benefits of covariant representations is that they distill the most critical aspects of a situation into a form that enables people to bring to bear their spatial abilities for working with structure. Larkin and Simon (1987), for example, investigated why "a picture is worth 10,000 words." They found that the structure of spatial representations makes them very easy to search. A matrix that uses rows for trip locations and columns for costs permits a person to index their search by cost or location. Covariant representations also create gestalts that guide the perception of important forms. Descartes' invention of the X, Y coordinate system permits the easy detection of linear and curvilinear patterns. When experts externalize and communicate covariant representations, they can help learners see how they structure their thoughts.

One scaffold for helping students build covariant representations comes from work on Teachable Agents (Schwartz et al., in press). Students teach a computer agent by using predefined forms to build important covariant representations. In turn, the agent can show how it reasons based on the structure the student creates. Figure 17.8 shows Betty, whom students teach by creating a directed graph that uses links like "increases" and "decreases." Betty can then animate her reasoning by tracing through the links to answer questions. Students learn to structure their thought visually and trace relations in their own thoughts. For example, students who teach Betty are more likely to reason about multiple causal pathways (Biswas et al., 2001).

Conclusions

A search of the learning-sciences relevant databases indicates that human spatial competence has received well below half the attention given to either language or social behavior. This is surprising, given human

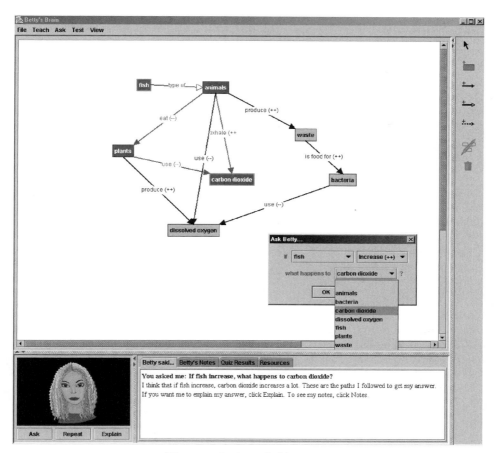

Figure 17.8. A teachable agent.

abilities to wield space to create art, visualizations, and multipart tools. Hopefully, this imbalance will change as new technologies permit more spatial methods of interacting with information. Because much of the research that does exist is about subtle individual differences in spatial abilities, people overlook how capable all humans are with spatial representations. In some cases, it leads to the belief that "spatial" students should receive special instruction that emphasizes imagery, but that nonspatial students should receive some other form of instruction. It may be a mistake to assume that only people with high imagery abilities should be presented with visual information. For example, they may find visual tasks too easy, and therefore, they may not elaborate as deeply. Additionally, there is evidence that spatial visualization ability develops with experience (Baenninger & Newcombe, 1989), suggesting that denying low-spatial individuals the chance to work with visual information may limit their development. Finally, although subtle differences in spatial ability appear when spatial information is presented in difficult ways, they usually disappear when effective visual representations are designed to scaffold spatial reasoning (Heiser, 2004). Assembly diagrams that are step-by-step and present consistent structural cues erase the differences between low and high spatial individuals on assembly tasks. The learning sciences should focus on learning rather than assumptions about ability, and it should examine how to design visual environments that will benefit all learners.

Our review of imagery has been unorthodox. Most work on imagery has emphasized its introspective vividness or its geometric properties (e.g., does it use a viewpoint or object-centered coordinate system?). In contrast, we argued that it is important to understand the relation of imagery to other sources of knowledge, and therefore, we identified four properties that can supplement nonspatial forms of reasoning: effortless structure, determinism, perception-action coupling, and pre-interpretation. When people learn calculus, they need to combine linguistic, mathematical, and spatial processes, and therefore, it is important to investigate the strengths and weaknesses that imagery can bring to a larger learning endeavor.

We also made a distinction between uses of imagery that mimic perceptual experience and uses of imagery that go beyond experience. This is an important distinction, because the ways that we assess the educational benefits of imagery will be quite different for each (e.g., speed and accuracy versus novel structure). We have primarily discussed internal spatial representations, but this distinction cuts across both internal and external spatial representations. External spatial representations, such as maps and diagrams, can serve to bring you closer to the world but also farther from the world. For example, when architects use their sketches as abstractions to help them innovate new forms, they omit details that would have to be determinate and therefore would constrain their thinking. Further along in the design process, these sketches are used to represent details and make all structures determinate (Suwa & Tversky, 1997). Similarly, people can use imagery to work with abstract shapes to see what structures emerge, and they can use imagery to construct specific models and run simulations to comprehend and predict in more detail. The fundamental challenge for the learning sciences is not to determine whether people use imagery or whether imagery is educationally valuable in some vague, universal way. Rather the challenge is more precise – when and how can people use which function of imagery to support learning, creativity, and reasoning?

Acknowledgment

This material is based upon work supported by the National Science Foundation under Grant Nos. BCS-0214548 and REC-0231946. Any opinions, findings, and conclusions or recommendations expressed in this material are those of the authors and do not necessarily reflect the views of the National Science Foundation.

References

Alibali, M. W., & Goldin-Meadow, S. (1993). Gesture-speech mismatch and mechanisms of learning: What the hands reveal about a child's state of mind. *Cognitive Psychology, 25*, 468–523.

Baenninger, M., & Newcombe, N. (1989). The role of experience in spatial test performance: A meta-analysis. *Sex Roles, 20*, 327–344.

Bamberger, J. (1991). *The mind behind the musical ear: How children develop musical intelligence.* Cambridge, MA: Harvard University Press.

Biswas, G., Schwartz, D. L., Bransford, J. D., & TAG-V. (2001). Technology support for complex problem solving: From SAD environments to AI. In K. Forbus & P. Feltovich (Eds.), *Smart machines in education* (pp. 71–98). Menlo Park, CA: AAAI/MIT Press.

Bower, G. H., Karlin, M. B., & Dueck, A. (1975). Comprehension and memory for pictures. *Memory & Cognition, 3*, 216–220.

Bransford, J. D., Barclay, J. R., & Franks, J. J. (1972). Sentence memory: A constructive versus interpretive approach. *Cognitive Psychology, 3*, 193–209.

Bransford, J. D., Franks, J. J., Vye, N. J., & Sherwood, R. D. (1989). New approaches to instruction: Because wisdom can't be told. In S. Vosniadou & A. Ortony (Eds.), *Similarity and analogical reasoning* (pp. 470–497). New York: Cambridge University Press.

Brooks, L. R. (1968). Spatial and verbal components of the act of recall. *Canadian Journal of Psychology, 22*, 349–368.

Chambers, D., & Reisberg, D. (1985). Can mental images be ambiguous? *Journal of Experimental Psychology: Human Perception and Performance, 11*, 317–28.

Clement, J. (1994). Use of physical intuition and imagistic simulation in expert problem solving. In D. Tirosh (Eds.), *Implicit and explicit knowledge*. Norwood, NJ: Ablex.

Cummins, R. (1989). *Meaning and mental representation*. Cambridge, MA: MIT Press.

diSessa, A., Hammer, D., Sherin, B., & Kolpakowski, T. (1991). Inventing graphing: Metarepresentational expertise in children. *Journal of Mathematical Behavior, 10*, 117–16.

Eisner, E. W. (1972). *Educating artistic vision*. New York: Macmillan Company.

Farah, M., Rochlin, R., Klein, K. (1994). Orientation invariance and geometric primitives in shape recognition. *Cognitive Science, 18*, 325–344.

Finke, R. (1990). *Creative imagery: Discoveries and inventions in visualization*. Hillsdale, NJ: Erlbaum.

Gardner, H. (1982). *Art, mind and brain*. New York: Basic Books.

Gibson, J. J. (1962). Observations on active touch. *Psychological Review, 69*, 477–491.

Gibson, J. J., & Gibson, E. J. (1955). Perceptual learning: Differentiation or enrichment. *Psychological Review, 62*, 32–41.

Glenberg, A. M., Gutierrez, T., Levin, J. R., Japuntich, S., & Kaschak, M. P. (2004). Activity and imagined activity can enhance young children's reading comprehension. *Journal of Educational Psychology, 96*, 424–436.

Goodwin, Charles (1994). Professional vision. *American Anthropologist, 96*, 606–633.

Gregory, R. L. (1966). *Eye and brain*. London: Weidenfeld and Nicholson.

Hegarty, M. (1992). Mental animation: Inferring motion from static diagrams of mechanical systems. *Journal of Experimental Psychology: Learning, Memory and Cognition, 18*, 1084–1102.

Hegarty, M. (2000). Capacity limits in diagrammatic reasoning. In M. Anderson, P. Cheng, & V. Haarslev (Eds.). *Theory and application of diagrams*. Berlin: Springer.

Heiser, J. (2004). *External Representations as Insights to Cognition: Production and Comprehension of Text and Diagrams in Instructions*. Unpublished Doctoral Dissertation, Stanford University.

Klatzky, R. L., Pellegrino, J. W., McCloskey, B. P., & Doherty, S. (1989). Can you squeeze a tomato? The role of motor representations in semantic sensibility judgments. *Journal of Memory & Language, 28*, 56–77.

Kosslyn, S. M. (1994). *Image and brain: The resolution of the imagery debate*. Cambridge, MA: MIT Press.

Krist, H., Fieberg, E., & Wilkening, F. (1993). Intuitive physics in action and judgment: The development of knowledge about projectile motion. *Journal of Experimental Psychology: Learning, Memory, and Cognition, 19*, 952–966.

Larkin, J., & Simon, H. (1987). Why a diagram is (sometimes) worth ten thousand words. *Cognitive Science, 11*, 65–99.

Mani, K., & Johnson-Laird, P. N. (1982). The mental representation of spatial descriptions. *Memory & Cognition 10*, 181–187.

Martin, T., & Schwartz, D. L. (in press). Physically distributed learning: Adapting and reinterpreting physical environments in the development of fraction concepts. *Cognitive Science*.

McCloskey, M. (1983) Naive theories of motion. In D. Gentner and A. Stevens (Eds.), *Mental models*, (pp. 229–324). Hillsdale, NJ: Erlbaum.

Morrow, D. G., & Clark, H. H. (1988). Interpreting words in spatial descriptions. *Language and Cognitive Processes, 3*, 275–292.

Morrow, D. G., Greenspan, S. L., & Bower, G. H. (1987). Accessibility and situation models in narrative comprehension. *Journal of Memory and Language, 26*, 165–187.

Nathan, M. J., & Koedinger, K. R. (2000). An investigation of teachers' beliefs of students' algebra development. *Cognition and Instruction, 18*, 209–237.

Nickerson, R. S., & Adams, J. J. (1979). Long-term memory for a common object. *Cognitive Psychology, 11*, 287–307.

Paivio, A. (1986). *Mental representations: A dual coding approach*. Oxford: Oxford University Press.

Parsons L. M. (1987). Imagined spatial transformations of one's hands and feet. *Cognitive Psychology 19*, 178–24.

Reiser, J. J., Garing, A. E., & Young, M. E. (1994). Imagery, action, and young children's spatial orientation. It's not being there that counts, it's what one has in mind. *Child Development, 65*, 1262–1278.

Rock, I., & Di Vita, J. (1987). A case of viewer-centered object perception. *Cognitive Psychology*, 19, 280–293.

Sawyer, R. K. (2004). Creative teaching: Collaborative discussion as disciplined improvisation. *Educational Researcher*, 33(2), 12–20.

Schoenfeld, A. (1992) Learning to think mathematically: Problem solving, metacognition and sense making in mathematics. In D. Grouws (Ed.), *Handbook of research on mathematics thinking and learning* (pp. 334–370). New York: Macmillan.

Schwartz, D. L. (1993). The construction and analogical transfer of symbolic visualizations. *Journal of Research in Science Teaching*, 30, 1309–1325.

Schwartz, D. L., & Black, J. B. (1996). Shuttling between depictive models and abstract rules: Induction and fallback. *Cognitive Science*, 20, 457–497.

Schwartz, D. L., & Black, T. (1999). Inferences through imagined actions: knowing by simulated doing. *Journal of Experimental Psychology: Learning, Memory, and Cognition*, 25, 116–136.

Schwartz, D. L., Blair, K. P., Biswas, G., Leelawong, K., & Davis, J. (in press). Animations of thought: Interactivity in the teachable agent paradigm. To appear in R. Lowe & W. Schnotz (Eds.), *Learning with animation: Research and implications for design*. Cambridge: Cambridge University Press.

Schwartz, D. L., Bransford, J. D., & Sears, D. L. (2005). Efficiency and innovation in transfer. (in press). In J. Mestre (Ed.), *Transfer of learning from a modern multidisciplinary persepctive*. Greenwich, CT: Information Age Publishing.

Schwartz, D. L., & Holton, D. (2000). Tool use and the effect of action on the imagination. *Journal of Experimental Psychology: Learning, Cognition, and Memory*, 26, 1655–1665.

Shelton, A. L., & McNamara, T. P. (2001). Visual memories from non-visual experiences. *Psychological Science*, 12, 343–347.

Shepard, R. N. (1967). Recognition memory for words, sentences and pictures. *Journal of Verbal Learning and Verbal Behavior*, 6, 156–163.

Shepard, R. N., & Cooper, L. A. (1986). *Mental images and their transformation*. Cambridge, MA: MIT Press.

Simons, D. J., & Wang, R. F. (1998). Perceiving real-world viewpoint changes. *Psychological Science*, 9, 315–320.

Standing, L. (1973). Learning 10,000 pictures. *Quarterly Journal of Experimental Psychology*, 25, 207–222.

Stevens, A., & Coupe, P. (1978). Distortions in judged spatial relations. *Cognitive Psychology*, 10, 422–437.

Suwa, M., & Tversky, B. (1997). What do architects and students perceive in their design sketches? A protocol analysis. *Design Studies*, 18, 385–403.

Wertheimer, M. (1938). Laws of organization in perceptual forms. In W. B. Ellis (Ed.), *A sourcebook of gestalt psychology*, (pp. 71–88). New York: Harcourt, Brace and Company.

Wexler, M., & Klam, F. (2001). Movement prediction and movement production. *Journal of Experimental Psychology: Human Perception and Performance*, 27, 48–64.

Wohlschläger, A., & Wolshläger, A. (1998). Mental and manual rotation. *Journal of Experimental Psychology: Human Perception and Performance*, 24, 397–412.

Zwaan, R. A. (2004). The immersed experiencer: toward an embodied theory of language comprehension. In B. H. Ross (Ed.), *The psychology of learning and motivation*, Vol. 43 (pp. 35–62). New York: Academic Press.

Zwaan R. A., & Radvansky G. A. (1998). Situation models in language comprehension and memory. *Psychological Bulletin*, 123, 162–185.

CHAPTER 18

Literacy and the Learning Sciences

Annemarie Sullivan Palincsar and Barbara G. Ladewski

At the time this chapter is being written, two billion Instant Messages are being sent daily, 92 percent of public school classrooms in the United States have access to the Internet, the College Board is introducing a test of technological literacy, novelists are publishing their works on-line, prize-winning journalists are setting up Web logs and assuming new identities, public spaces are "war chalked" indicating to passers-by that they are at a location where they can piggyback on a high-speed network supported by a business or resident, Wikipedia – a free-content encyclopedia – is available in 57 languages, and the University of Michigan has negotiated with Google to digitize its seven million volume collection to be accessed by anyone the world over. In short, one needn't look far to find examples of the continual reshaping of literacy by virtue of technologies. In fact, the evolution of literacy is a series of sociotechnical changes; from papyrus, to paper, to printing press, to electronic spaces, technologies have influenced how we use and make meaning with text.

To set the stage for this chapter, consider for a moment the multiple forms of literacy that are required to interpret and learn from a typical Web site. On first entering, one must immediately interpret navigational cues and chart a path that will support knowledge building with the site. Frequently, the user can select from among several media links; simultaneously listening to and reading information, and activating simulations, which also must be interpreted. The user must decode meaning-bearing icons. Mouse-overs may cause an image to pop up; that image may, in turn, expand to provide additional information. Graphs and diagrams may be called up and manipulated to address specific questions. All of this information must be coordinated, integrated, and evaluated for its credibility and relevance to the questions guiding the user. Color cues – signaling glossary terms and links – must be decoded. In addition, the user may have the option of participating in a forum discussion or forwarding the site to a fellow learner. The user is at once both reader and author, both consumer and generator of knowledge, engaging in both an individual and collective enterprise.

Circumscribing the Problem Space

There are many parallels and points of intersection between the learning sciences and literacy communities:

1. The learning sciences encompass educational technology (Hoadley, 2004), while representatives of the literacy community have advanced the notion that "literacy and technology are no longer mutually exclusive but have merged in a combined vocabulary" (Reinking et al., 1998).

2. For both the learning sciences (Kolodner, 1991) and literacy communities, modeling learning – and not instruction – is the core focus. Learning scientists are curious about learning in real-world situations (Duffy, 2004) and literacy scholars have a long tradition – that continues today – of studying literacy in real-world situations (Scribner & Cole, 1981).

3. Cognitive and sociocultural perspectives on constructivism are alive in both the learning science and literacy communities with threaded discussions, interactive chats, and collaborative databases providing more opportunities for each community to study the social processes in the construction of knowledge. Leander (2003) similarly recognized the need for grounding a theory of media in the cognitive and social processes by which knowledge is constructed, and proposed that cultural historical activity theory (CHAT), with its focus on "the analysis of mediation, material technologies, language, culture, and the relations between individual and systemic change" (p. 395) be used to describe online contexts.

4. Although both communities engage in experimental and naturalistic inquiry, there is more emphasis on the nature of design in the learning sciences, while design experiments are rarely used in the literacy community.

5. Literacy is a vast topic; as Lemke has noted, "Literacies are legion. Each one consists of a set of interdependent social practices that link people, media objects, and strategies for meaning making" (Lemke, 1998, p. 283). Definitions of literacy are legion as well. We chose to adopt a sociocultural perspective in the preparation of this chapter which defines literacy as a repertoire of practices for communicating and accomplishing goals in particular social and cultural contexts (Nixon, 2003). This definition is compatible with the focus in the learning sciences on authentic and situated practices.

These points of comparison suggest that cross-fertilization between the literacy and learning sciences communities could benefit both fields. However, it often seems that literacy is invisible in the learning sciences; there are few literacy scholars who contribute to the learning sciences literatures and there are few scholars identified with the learning sciences community who deal with literacy in an explicit way. Furthermore, the literacy community has marginalized new technologies and literacy (Bruce, 1997; Lankshear & Knobel, 2003b), as one can see by scanning the four leading journals in literacy (i.e., *Reading Research Quarterly, Journal of Literacy Research, Written Communication, Research on the Teaching of English*). Between the years 1990 and 1995, the combined percentage of articles on technology was only 2.7 percent (Kamil & Lane, 1998). A similar examination of the years 1995–2004 indicated that the percentage increased to a still meager 5.2 percent (Palincsar & Dalton, 2004).

In this chapter we focus on *the teaching and use of literacy to advance the acquisition and development of knowledge about oneself and the world.* We did not include in our review studies that principally focused on the acquisition of reading, writing, and oral language, although these are active and productive areas of inquiry by members of the literacy community; nor did we review studies that principally focused on the acquisition of computer, Internet, or media skills.

Instead, we focus on the role of literacy in learning more broadly.

To prepare this chapter, we began with a close survey of the four primary literacy journals (*Journal of Literacy Research, Reading Research Quarterly, Written Communication,* and *Research on the Teaching of English*) for the past decade. We also surveyed *Cognition and Instruction* and the *Journal of the Learning Sciences* for the past five years. When we searched by topic, we surveyed: hypermedia, assistive technology, multimedia, and adaptive hypermedia systems. These topics took us to journals in computer science and information and computer technology. In addition, we consulted a number of recent handbooks.

We begin by tracing the development of the term *literacy* and review research related to three dimensions of literacy that are of particular interest to the learning sciences: operational literacy, cultural literacy, and critical literacy. We conclude the chapter with discussions of future directions for research, and of methodological and theoretical issues at the intersection of literacy and the learning sciences.

Literacy: A Historical Look

The term *literacy*, which now figures so prominently in discussions of the means, purposes, and assessments of education, is actually a newcomer on the scene, while *reading* has a much longer history. Nila Blanton Smith (1965) demonstrated how this history has been shaped in the United States: "The story of reading is a fascinating one to pursue. It is a story which reflects the changing religious, economic, and political institutions of a growing country" (p. 2). To support her claim, Smith described the influences shaping different periods of reading instruction in this country, including: religion (1607–1776), nation building and morality (1776–1840), the education of an intelligent citizenry (1840–1880), the view of reading as a cultural asset (1880–1910), the scientific investigation of reading (1910–

1935), international conflict (1935–1950), culminating in today's expanding knowledge and technological revolution (1950-present) (Leu et al., 2004, p. 4).

As we prepared this chapter, we were mindful of a burgeoning perspective called *new literacies*: "The new literacies of the Internet and other ICTs [information and communication technologies] include the skills, strategies, and dispositions necessary to successfully use and adapt to the rapidly changing information and communication technologies and contexts that continuously emerge in our world and influence all areas of our personal and professional lives. These new literacies allow us to use the Internet and other ICTs to identify important questions, locate information, critically evaluate the usefulness of that information, synthesize information to answer these questions, and then communicate the answers to others" (Leu et al., 2004, p. 2).

There has been active discussion in the literacy community about the need for expanded definitions of literacy and new theories that place Information and Communication Technologies (ICT) at their center. Leu et al. (2004) argued that for the past five hundred years, literacy has emerged from a variety of social contexts but has primarily been shaped by the book and printing press. But today, both the social context and technologies are rapidly changing, with ICTs and the Internet becoming the central technologies of literacy. They have identified a set of ten principles that would guide a theory of new literacies:

1. New literacies and ICTs are central technologies for literacy within a global community in an information age.
2. The Internet and other ICTs require new literacies to fully access their potential.
3. New literacies are deictic.[1]
4. The relationship between literacy and technology is transactional.
5. New literacies are multiple in nature.

6. Critical literacies are central to the new literacies.

7. New forms of strategic knowledge are central to the new literacies.

8. Speed counts in important ways within the new literacies.

9. Learning often is socially constructed within new literacies.

10. Teachers become more important, although their role changes, within new literacy classrooms (Leu et al., 2004, p. 15).

To study literacy in today's technological age, one has to consider many "media objects" other than the traditional book. *Traditional multimedia* refer to a mixture of media, such as photographs, audio recordings, video, and three-dimensional objects presented in combination – but in a nondigitized form. *Digitized multimedia* refer to digitized mixed media (e.g., video, sound, graphics, text, photographs) that are presented in a linear structure. *Hypertext* and *hypermedia* refer to those documents that are constructed in parallel or hyperbased structures. Hypertexts consist exclusively of alphanumeric text and graphics, while hypermedia are documents that consist of sound, video, animation, or virtual reality environments (Hailey & Hailey, 1998).

There have been many attempts to capture the differences between traditional (print) text, multimedia, and electronic media and the implications of these differences for defining and studying literacy. Typically, although print literacy is described as linear, ordered, sequential, hierarchical, and logical, hypertext is characterized as fluid, spatial, decentered, bottom up, and playful (Burbulus, 2001; Ryan, 1999). A book is "linear" because the words follow one another in sequence, and readers are constrained to read from beginning to end; Web sites are fluid and decentered because different readers can take different paths through the information. Linear media are often referred to as *author driven* (Bernhardt, 1993; Hailey & Hailey, 1998) because readers of such documents are limited to reading forward (and

sometimes backward to the previous page), whereas hypermedia are thought of as *reader driven* to the extent that readers choose the paths they take as they navigate or browse through such an environment.

An important characteristic of the new literacies is that they are constantly changing, a feature that prompted Leu (2000) to suggest that they have a "deictic" character. This feature, in turn, leads to discussions of whether it is appropriate to think of the goal of literacy instruction as *being literate, becoming literate*, or learning *adaptive literacy*:

> *What I've been trying to wrestle with is the notion of adaptive literacy modeled somewhat on the notion of adaptive expertise . . . as new technologies evolve, things that we might not even be able to conceptualize at the present make the notion of . . . adaptive literacy very interesting. We adapt the abilities and skills and literate knowledge that we have to a particular task. So, if we are reading a text, we might sample and use certain things we know; if we are reading on the screen, we might sample other things we know and apply that knowledge. But adaptive literacy also implies that we will have to adapt our literacy practices in terms of learning new practice. (Kinzer, cited in Palincsar & Dalton, 2005)*

From a sociocultural perspective (Bruce, 1997; Green, 1988), there are three dimensions of literacy that we wish to propose are relevant to the learning sciences community: *operational literacy*, which includes competence with the tools, procedures, and techniques involved in handling written language proficiently; *cultural literacy*, which is defined as competence with the meaning system of a practice; and *critical literacy*, or competence in attending to how texts represent the self and others.

Operational Literacy

There are three categories of research that we sample in this section. One category draws our attention to the new vistas open to researchers by virtue of new technologies. A second category consists largely of research examining aspects of learning from media and texts that have implications for the design and mediation of learning from new technologies. A third category addresses the deployment of new technologies for enhancing learners' abilities to handle language proficiently; for example, the design of software to improve text comprehension.

Before proceeding, we start with a brief tutorial regarding reading comprehension theory – because although there are indeed new skills, strategies, and dispositions that are called for by new literacies, most of them build on and do not replace foundational literacies such as word recognition, vocabulary knowledge, and the ability to draw inferences, interpret, evaluate, and apply information from text. Most research into text comprehension has been conducted with traditional printed text. We then examine each of the three categories identified above, in turn, providing an overview and then sampling one or two studies in more detail.

The predominant theory informing contemporary researchers' understanding of text comprehension is *schema theory*, which suggests that reading comprehension is the process of interpreting new information and assimilating and accommodating this information into memory structures, or *schemata* (Anderson & Pearson, 1984). From this perspective, reading is defined as "the process of constructing meaning through the dynamic interaction among the reader's existing knowledge, the information suggested by the written language, and the context of the reading situation" (Wixson & Peters, 1984, p. 5). In this process, the reader attends to both the content and the structure of the text to construct meaning. Kintsch (1998; van Dijk & Kintsch, 1983), via his *situation model*, called attention to the role that the organization of the text plays in the construction of mental representations of the ideas in the text. The *microstructure* of the text refers to the local structure, or sentence-by-sentence information in the text, while the *macrostructure* refers to the hierarchically ordered set of propositions that represent the global structure of the text and are derived from the microstructure. Hence, the reader draws upon the rhetorical structure of the text, as well as the semantic content of the text, to make sense of the text. Readers know that particular text types are organized in particular ways (e.g., narrative, procedural description, compare/contrast), and they typically use this knowledge in the construction of meaning.

New Technologies: An Arena for Redefining and Studying Operational Literacy

The literacy community rejects the notion that any texts, no matter what their structure, ever have predetermined meaning, because the reader is always making connections: reading in and reading between the lines (Purves, 1998). Given that hypertexts are even more reader-driven, they make more salient the role of the reader in co-authoring the text, since the reader determines the paths taken and ignored, and can reorder, change, augment, and delete paths that may have initially been forged by the creator of the hypertext. Hence, the reader must rely more on broader domain knowledge than upon rhetorical knowledge of the specific text structure initially created by the author to aid in constructing meaning.

The most well-examined area of study regarding hypertext is in the area of navigation. Researchers have identified three common navigational styles: (1) *knowledge seekers* who are guided in their search by the information they seek and are drawn toward screens that enhance their understanding of the topic(s) specific to their search, (2) *feature explorers*, who display more interest in understanding how the hypertext works and what kinds of screens it contains than they do locating and integrating information, and (3) *apathetic hypertext users* whose navigation is marked by its brevity and by the linear paths taken in the search (Barab, Bowdish, & Lawless, 1997; Dillon, 1991; Lawless & Brown, 1997).

There have been very few studies of hypertext comprehension that take into consideration the multiple features of hypertext and the multiple user characteristics that might well influence interaction with hypertext. One such exemplary study was conducted by Lawless, Brown, Mills, and Mayall (2003). The purpose of their research was to investigate: (1) the nature of the relationships among domain knowledge, individual interest, and situational interest within a hypertext environment, and (2) the impact of these characteristics on the recall of information presented in a hypertext environment. The participants were undergraduate students studying the topic of Lyme disease. The instructional program was implemented as a sixty-card Hypercard text in which six topics were presented in a Web-like fashion. In addition, there was supplementary information presented via sound, animation, and digitized video. Log file data were collected, as were measures of recall. The findings indicated that while domain knowledge was correlated with individual interest and then with situational interest, only domain knowledge was a significant predictor of both structured and unstructured recall, while neither the individual nor situational interest measures significantly predicted recall.

Further exploration of the data revealed that high knowledge readers appeared to use navigational strategies that mirror the kinds of strategies competent readers use when interacting with traditional text. For example, they compared and contrasted information on the screens (alternating between screens) and separated relevant from irrelevant information (not recalling screens that presented information that did not enhance understanding). In contrast, participants with low-domain knowledge appeared to engage in random search and selection of resources, and allocated more time to viewing special features (movies and sound effects).

In sum, while high-knowledge users engaged in a mean of 8.4 strategies, low-knowledge users engaged in 2.1 strategies (Lawless & Brown, 2003). The researchers wisely caution that studies of this kind require replication, particularly because domains vary in their degree of structure

(Spiro & Jehng, 1990). Furthermore, the experimental hypertext was contrived for this study, and users may respond differently to naturally occurring hypertext. Finally, young learners, who are just being introduced to domains of study, may respond differently than college-age learners.

Another study addressing these issues was conducted by Wallace, Kupperman, Krajcik, and Soloway (2000). Working with sixth grade participants, these researchers investigated the question: What use do students make of the Web as an information resource and what issues does their use raise for the design of tools and structures useful to creating digital information environments? This research was conducted in the context of inquiry-based science instruction (Krajcik & Blumenfeld, this volume); students were assigned a structured "scavenger hunt" within a unit on ecology. They were instructed on the use of hyperlinks and keyword searching. The students worked in pairs to locate information related to three specific questions they were given, and the students' research was used to develop a culminating presentation.

Case studies were conducted with four dyads of students who were selected to represent mixed gender and race, as well as a range of achievement. The findings revealed that with regard to their interpretation and enactment of the task, students reduced the task to finding the "perfect source," which they regarded as a single site with the answer; this goal appeared to supercede the issue of coming to a deep understanding of the content. The findings also revealed the challenges students experienced with the information gathering itself; they had trouble engaging in a style of productive exploration that would ultimately yield useful questions to guide one's ongoing search. With regard to the use of technological tools, the researchers found that while the students had sufficient basic skills to use a Web browser and a search engine, they made relatively simplistic use of these tools in their navigation and search activity. They infrequently used hyperlinks, failed to modify keywords when provided feedback, and often engaged in apparently random search behavior.

Studies like these two suggest that there is considerable work to be done, not only in further specifying how different learners (with various literacy, knowledge, and interest profiles) interact with various new technologies, but also to design both activities and tools that will support users to productively engage in the use of these technologies to develop a deeper understanding of the content.

Bootstrapping from Psychological Research

There is a tantalizing spectrum of choices that authors might make relative to the design of hypermedia presentations, but few empirically validated guidelines for choosing among these capabilities (Hegarty, Narayanan, & Freitas, 2002). One might, for example, ask: Are diagrammatic representations better than sentential? Are three-dimensional representations better than two-dimensional? Are animated representations better than static? Are interactive better than noninteractive? In this section, we present a summary of the research conducted by Hegarty and her colleagues. We present their work as much to highlight their model of inquiry as their findings. We then summarize design principles derived from a complementary program of research conducted by Mayer, and conclude with a critique of this research from a learning sciences perspective.

Hegarty and her colleagues (Hansen et al., 1998; Hegarty, Narayanan, & Freitas, 2002; Kozhevnikov, Hegarty, & Mayer, 2002) argued that because new media are studied in learning environments that use novel methods of instruction (e.g., discovery, collaborative learning, inquiry) and then are compared to traditional media being used in a transmission-and-acquisition fashion, the effects of media and learning environment are confounded. The overarching question guiding their program of research has been whether multimedia presentations (including animations, commen-

taries, hyperlinks) lead to different learning outcomes when compared to traditional printed media, when both contain the same information.

In a typical study conducted by this research group, the content to be learned is an understanding of a complex system, such as the mechanical system of a flushing cistern. Their participants are typically undergraduate students. They begin their research by studying the potential sources of comprehension problems learners might encounter with this content. They then design curriculum materials to ameliorate these difficulties, and present it using different formats. Learning is assessed with an array of measures including: *mental animation questions* (i.e., asking students to predict how the motion of one component of a system will influence another), *function questions* (e.g., "what is the function of the float and float arm?"), *fault-behavior questions* asking how the system would behave were there to be a breakdown in one part of the system, and *trouble-shooting questions*, which ask the learner to diagnose all possible problems with the system, given a set of symptoms.

In one experiment (Hegarty et al., 1999), the researchers compared the learning of students assigned to one of three conditions: a hypermedia manual (complete with hyperlinks and animations), and two linear text conditions. They found no learning differences among the three groups, even though participants in the hypermedia group spent more time interacting with the content than did the groups in the text conditions. The researchers proposed that the additional information presented via the hypertext was possibly superfluous given the fact that a toilet tank is a common household item with which the participants were already sufficiently familiar.

In a second experiment, they compared the effects of constraining the learner's use of the hypermedia manual with a condition in which the learner could navigate freely. While participants who viewed the navigation-restricted version spent more time in the system than did those in the free-navigation condition, the type of presentation did not affect performance on any of the four types of comprehension assessments. The authors caution that this was a limited test of navigational freedom because the total number of sections to be navigated was relatively small (seven).

In a third set of experiments, the authors queried the effects of: (a) viewing a static diagram, (b) engaging in a mental animation (in which the learners studied the static diagram but then attempted to explain to the experimenter how it worked), (c) viewing a static version and then an animation of the system, accompanied by a verbal commentary, or (d) a condition that combined (b) and (c). The results indicated that viewing the animation and hearing the commentary (condition c) significantly enhanced performance on the outcome measures. Furthermore, attempting to mentally animate the machine before viewing the animation (condition d) enhanced the ability to describe how a machine works (also see Schwartz & Heiser, this volume). These studies suggest that merely translating information from a traditional print medium to a hypermedia system does not affect comprehension and learning if the content is held constant.

A second program of research addressing multimedia learning has been conducted by Richard Mayer and his colleagues and is summarized in Mayer (2001). A caveat relative to this research is that multimedia are construed very narrowly in this research to mean "the presentation of material using both words and pictures" (p. 2) and do not study information technologies specifically. Furthermore, the preponderance of his research has been conducted with young adults. Nevertheless, we include his work because: (a) it is informed by and contributes to a theory of multimedia learning, drawing upon Paivio's (1986) dual coding theory, Baddeley's (1992) working memory theory, and Mayer's (1996) theory of meaningful learning; (b) it attends to the issue of individual differences; and (c) it may productively inform the work of learning scientists studying new literacies.

This program of research has yielded seven principles regarding the effective integration of words and pictures:

1. *Multimedia principle* – Students learn better from words and pictures than from words alone,
2. *Spatial contiguity principles* – Students learn better when corresponding words and pictures are presented near rather than far from each other on the page or screen,
3. *Temporal contiguity principle* – Students learn better when corresponding words and pictures are presented simultaneously rather than successively,
4. *Coherence principle* – Students learn better when extraneous material is excluded rather than included,
5. *Modality principle* – Students learn better when an animation is accompanied by spoken text, rather than printed text,
6. *Redundancy principle* – Students learn better from an animation accompanied with spoken text rather than an animation accompanied with spoken text and printed text, and
7. *Individual differences principle* – Design effects positively correlate with users' domain knowledge and spatial ability.

Learning scientists should study whether these principles still hold in the contexts they find most compelling: real-life settings in which learning is taking place through interaction with others and with technological artifacts.

The Use of Technology to Enhance Operational Literacy

It has been estimated that in the United States, there are 8.7 million students in grades 4 through 12 who have difficulty doing anything more than reading text at the most basic level (Kamil, 2003). They cannot build knowledge from text, use text to solve novel problems, or take a stance toward the ideas in the text. A significant percentage of these students is poor, has special needs, and includes English language learners. This finding does not augur well for these students' success with the literacy demands associated with the information and communication technologies prominent in today's global economy and associated with contemporary modes of knowledge production and dissemination.

Several researchers study the role that scaffolded hypertexts and other computer supports might play in enhancing the comprehension of struggling readers (Strangman & Dalton, 2005; MacArthur et al., 2001; McKenna et al., 1999; and Woodward & Rieth, 1997). Among the issues these authors have examined is the question of whether using digital text to have words or phrases read aloud helps readers to learn more from these texts. Variations in the technologies, as well as the research designs, make it difficult to summarize the findings. Nevertheless, these authors concluded that the instructional effects of speech feedback varied as a function of the reader's age and initial literacy levels, with older (i.e., grades 4 through 6) students benefiting more from the use of text-to-speech supports, perhaps because they encounter more complex text, or perhaps because these students are more strategic in their use of these supports. However, as Strangman and Dalton (2005) noted, if the text is too challenging as measured by unfamiliar vocabulary, density of concepts, complexity of syntax, or demands on prior knowledge, simply having access to text-to-speech will not suffice to enhance text comprehension.

Another line of research investigates the use of digital and hypertext environments to scaffold students' learning from text. Much of this research has been conducted with children with special needs (including learning disabilities and sensory impairments), and the number of participants in each study is typically quite small. Examples include adding descriptions of main ideas and definitions to a text passage (Feldman & Fish, 1991), which *did not* improve the passage comprehension of high school students; and adding online glossaries, links between questions and text, highlighted main ideas, and supplementary explanations (MacArthur &

Haynes, 1995), which *did* result in greater learning for 9 out of 10 high school students with learning disabilities. Once again, the findings are ambiguous, with differences across studies suggesting several factors that could affect the outcomes: the type and quality of the enhancements, the characteristics of the students, the demands of the text and learning task, and the extent to which students actually use the enhancements.

We now take an in-depth look at one example of a program designed to support students in gaining access to and learning specific content: *The Thinking Reader* (Dalton et al., 2002). This program provides multiple levels of support, including a multimedia glossary, background knowledge links, and embedded strategy instruction (modeled after Reciprocal Teaching: Palincsar & Brown, 1984). As students interact with the text, they are periodically prompted to "stop and think," using one of five reading strategies to which they have been introduced: predicting, questioning, summarizing, clarifying, and visualizing. Prior research indicated that students experience a high degree of challenge using the targeted strategies, so *The Thinking Reader* varies its level of support, with the most demanding strategy (summarizing) heavily supported when students begin to use the program, while the least demanding strategy (predicting) is minimally supported throughout the program. They are also encouraged to build a personal connection with the text and to self-reflect on their progress as a reader. Avatars – animated on-screen characters – serve as coaches – offering hints, modeling responses, and engaging in think-alouds. Students' responses (oral or written) to the text are captured and used to provide assessment information to teachers and students as well.

Initial research on *The Thinking Reader* was conducted by comparing the reading achievement gains of two groups of middle school students, half of whom experienced Reciprocal Teaching with *The Thinking Reader* and half of whom experienced Reciprocal Teaching with print versions of the same reading materials (three age-appropriate and appealing novels). Controlling for initial reading levels, students in *The Thinking Reader* group made significantly greater gains than did the students who did not have access to this environment. As the researchers acknowledge, from these data it is not possible to identify how the specific affordances of the software (e.g., digitized text, leveled supports, and multimedia) contributed to the success of its users.

Cultural Literacy

The research that we examined above focused almost exclusively on school tasks. In the following, we broaden the context to consider literacy in and out of school. From a cultural literacy perspective, literacy is not a unitary construct but rather is embedded in and develops out of the social practices of a culture (Gee, 1991, 1996). This perspective throws open the study of literacy in multiple ways. In this chapter, we have the space to provide but a mere glimpse at how a cultural literacy perspective shapes the nature of the questions researchers ask, the kinds of inquiry in which they engage, and the ways in which they relate their research to the lives of students and teachers.

Why is a cultural literacy perspective useful? To consider this question is to consider the ways in which computers and new media are increasingly central to the lives of today's children and youth; global popular media culture, including online culture, have become integrally bound up with children's and youth's affiliations, identities, and pleasures (Hull, 2003; Lankshear & Knobel, 2003a; Leander, 2003). Gitlin (2001) has reported that the average child in the United States lives in a household with 2.9 televisions, 1.8 VCRs, 3.1 radios, 2.6 tape players, 2.1 CD players, 1.4 video game players, and 1 computer. Our youth's participation in global media culture shapes the way they communicate and the kinds of social identities they assume. This kind of social participation is integral to the ways in which symbolic meanings are constructed

and negotiated, and therefore of central import to both literacy researchers and learning scientists.

There are a number of literacy researchers who are attending to the significance of images, television, games, and other forms of media in the literate lives of children and youth (Alvermann et al., 1998; Dyson, 1991; Flood & Lapp, 1998; Gee, 2003). For example, Chandler-Olcott and Mahar (2003) study *fanfiction*, or the raiding of mass culture by fans who use media texts, such as anime (Japanese animation), as starting points for their own writing. Lankshear and Knobel (2003a) describe *Digitarts*, an online multimedia project space that was originally constructed by and for young women in Australia, and now invites the participation of socially and culturally disadvantaged youth across genders. *Digitarts* provides courses on Web-page development and a venue for showcasing multimedia works, and for gaining access to the knowledge and tools necessary to the development of art and cultural practice with new technologies.

Hull (2003) conducted an ethnography in a university-community collaborative called *DUSTY* – Digital Underground Storytelling for Youth. Similar to *Digitarts*, this project is aimed at closing the digital divide, and provides youth with access to new technologies and a context in which they can create, envision and revise, represent themselves and their ideas, and learn the power of communication. Hull documented the distinctive affordances associated with different forms of representation, and urged educators to provide alternative learning spaces centered on youth culture, new media, and new literacies, both in and outside of school.

We conclude this section by presenting a program of research that is exemplary in bridging the worlds of home and school, and that illustrates the power of bringing a cultural literacy perspective to the study of education. Moje and her research group (Moje et al., 2004) engage in scholarship for the purpose of advancing the strategic integration of the kinds of knowledge and uses of language that youth experience in out-of-school contexts for the purpose of enhancing in-school content area literacy. Drawing upon the writings of Bhabha (1994), Gutiérrez and her colleagues (1999), and Soja (1996), this group refers to this integration as the construction of "third space." From this theoretical perspective, individuals can be thought of as occupying several "spaces," each of which offers unique opportunities to acquire knowledge and engage in particular conventions regarding the uses of reading, writing, and oral language. "First space" refers to people's home, community, and peer networks, whereas "second space" refers to the contexts experienced in work, school, or church; in other words, contexts in which there are more formalized uses of language and literacy (Moje et al., 2004, p. 41).

The goal of their research is to document the *funds of knowledge*, that is, the intellectual and social knowledge existing in families and communities (Moll, Veléz-Ibanéz, & Greenberg, 1989; also see Nasir et al., this volume) and ways of using language and print literacy (Gee, 1996) that shape students' interactions with texts in and out of school. This ethnographic research is being conducted in a predominantly Latino/a community and public school in Detroit. Using participant observation, interviews, and collections of artifacts, the researchers documented the community, peer, and popular culture funds of knowledge that students had access to and engaged in both in and out of school. Their findings revealed how seldom the students brought out-of-school funds of knowledge to bear in the (science) classroom context even though these funds were sufficiently rich with possibilities to not only build bridges between in- and out-of-school contexts, but also to expand and deepen understanding of the target content knowledge. Their scholarship culminated in a compelling argument regarding why and how teachers should actively develop third space by engaging students in experiments, discussions, and reading and writing activities that focus on, or at least

include, texts and experiences of different communities.

Critical Literacy

It has been argued that the information age calls for new *critical literacies* that enable children and youth to evaluate information in terms of the stance of the person authoring the message, as well as the motive behind the message (Muspratt, Luke, & Freebody, 1998). Bolter (1991) noted that becoming literate in a hypermedia environment challenges the notion that any single text represents an author's complete, separate, or unique expression. As Alvermann (2004) suggested: "central to much of the discussion surrounding new media and Information and Communication Technologies use is the perceived need to develop young people's critical awareness of how all authored texts (print, visual, oral) situate them as readers, writers, and viewers within particular cultural and historical contexts. At the same time, developing youth's critical awareness suggests teaching students that all texts, including their textbooks, routinely promote or silence particular views" (p. 78). For example, because there is no editorial or peer review process that attends the posting of a Web site, students need to learn to question and evaluate the credibility of information posted on the Internet.

There have been relatively few studies of critical literacy within school contexts. Alvermann, Moon, and Hagood (1999) have studied critical media literacy practices in secondary language arts classes. Beach and Myers (2001; Myers & Beach, 2001) presented several examples from language arts classrooms illustrating how critical awareness and engagement are called for in the new literacies and are fostered by immersion in new forms of representation. For example, students can be taught to think about the ways in which issues of gender, race, socioeconomic class, and interpersonal relationships are treated in advertisements, video, and literature.

Alvermann and Xu (2003), in their discussion of the uses that teachers and children make of *popular culture* or everyday culture in classroom settings, noted that there are essentially four approaches educators can take. The first is denigrating that culture and the second is encouraging a critical stance to the culture. Neither of these has been observed to make enduring impressions or changes. A third approach is to emphasize the pleasures students take in various forms of media-produced text; the problem with this approach is that students' thinking is not challenged, and they do not develop tools for exploring their likes and dislikes. A fourth approach is to develop students' ability to be self-reflective in their uses of popular culture. From this perspective, teachers provide opportunities for students to explore "how media and mass-produced icons of popular culture situate us in relations of power by shaping our emotional, political, social, and material lives" (Alvermann, 2004, p. 81). Alvermann (2004) provided a sampling of the kinds of questions with which teachers might invite students to critical literacy:

- Are hypertext readings privileged in ways that traditional (linear) readings are not? For example, do hypertexts allow readers to make multiple interpretations of what they read with greater ease than do traditional texts? If so, what might be the consequences of this privileging? What kind of reader would stand to benefit? Who might fail to benefit?

- How does hypertext create opportunities for readers to manipulate information in ways that are unavailable to them in print-based media? What are the trade-offs in working within such an environment?

Future Directions

As we have illustrated in the previous two sections, the field needs research that explores how children and youth transfer literacy skills across media. Toward this end, Lankshear and Knobel (2003a, 2003b) proposed a scheme for research that is consistent with two contemporary themes in learning sciences research: how technology affects learners and learning environments and how collaboration and social context relate to learning. They suggested that research can be conceived in four quadrants. Quadrant 1 has investigations of stand-alone machines used to teach encoding and decoding skills requisite to working with either print or multimodal texts and for one or more social purposes. Quadrant 2 has research using stand-alone machines to enhance discursive prowess. Quadrant 3 features networked machines to enhance encoding/decoding competence. Quadrant 4 attends to investigations using networked machines to enhance discursive prowess within communities of practice. An example of research in Quadrant 4 is Scardamalia and Bereiter's research on knowledge building (this volume; Scardamalia, 2004; Scardamalia, Bereiter, & Lamon, 1994). In this research, student ideas are the focus of classroom discourse; technological advances enable increasingly ambitious instructional agendas; textual, graphical, and computer literacy are integral to advancing learning and are both the grist for and outcome of curriculum and instruction.

The field is ripe for border crossing and even more cross-disciplinary collaborations. Scholars who are well-versed in literacy learning and teaching might be called on to identify and plan for the literacy demands and learning opportunities in those new learning environments being designed and investigated by learning scientists. Scholars traditionally identified with studies of *assistive technology* (e.g., Horney & Anderson-Inman, 1999), for example, could be called on to identify ways that more diverse learners might be the beneficiaries of ambitious instructional contexts. Learning scientists and psychologists could collaborate to study how the mostly decontextualized study of learning from hypertext and hypermedia might be complemented by studies of authentic situated learning. As a final suggestion, the rich findings of literacy researchers engaged in naturalistic studies of children and youth engaged in multiple literacies could be applied to the design of intervention and instructional research.

Issues Facing Literacy Research

The time seems ripe for applying methods that allow us to examine patterns of relationships among individuals, technologies, and learning environments. As Lemke (1999) has argued, we need to shift from a fixation upon technological tools to mapping the ecosocial systems of their use. These methods include multidimensional scaling and small space analysis.

Literacy researchers might work together with learning scientists to use design experiments (Barab, this volume; Brown, 1992; Collins, 1992; Confrey, this volume; Design-Based Research Collective, 2003). Design experiments would be fruitfully complemented by the conduct of intensive case studies of classrooms to understand the complex interaction among learners, teachers, information and communication technologies, and the context of individual classrooms in the service of learning.

Conclusion

In this chapter, we have conceived of literacy as a repertoire of practices for communicating to advance a broad range of goals. The array of tools now available to support literacy learning and engagement provide rich and diverse contexts in which to study these practices. It is a propitious time to be: (a) working across school and out-of-school contexts, (b) employing diverse theoretical lenses that can illuminate issues specific to literacy learning and use, (c) employing mixed methods to document and explore literacy, and (d) working at the intersection of literacy and the learning sciences.

Footnote

1. Linguists use the term *deixis* to reflect the unique characteristic of words like "there," "now," "soon"; words whose meanings are dependent on the time or space in which they are uttered (Leu, 2000).

References

Alvermann, D. E. (2004). Media, information communication technologies, and youth literacies: A cultural perspective. *American Behavioral Scientist, 48*(1): 78–83.

Alvermann, D. E., Hinchman, K. A., Moore, D. W., Phelps, S. F., & Waff, D. R. (Eds.). (1998). *Reconceptualizing the literacies in adolescents' lives.* Mahwah, NJ: Lawrence Erlbaum.

Alvermann, D. E., Moon, J. E., & Hagood, M. C. (1999). *Popular culture in the classroom: Teaching and researching critical media literacy.* Newark, DE: International Reading Association and National Reading Conference.

Alvermann, D. E., & Xu, S. H. (2003). Children's everyday literacies: Intersections of popular culture and language arts instruction. *Language Arts, 81*(2): 145–154.

Anderson, R. C., & Pearson, P. D. (1984). A schema-theoretic view of basic processes in reading comprehension. In P. D. Pearson (Ed.). *Handbook of reading research* (255–292). New York: Longman.

Baddeley, A. (1992). Is working meory working? The Fifteenth Bartlett Lecture. *Quarterly Journal of Educational Psychology, 44A*(1), 1–31.

Barab, S. A., Bowdish, B. E., & Lawless, K. A. (1997). Hypermedia navigation: Profiles of hypermedia users. *Educational Technology Research and Development, 45*(3), 23–42.

Beach, R., & Myers, J. (2001). *Inquiry-based English instruction: Engaging students in life and literature.* New York: Teachers College Press.

Bernhardt, S. (1993). The shape of things to come. *College Composition and Communication, 44*(2), 151–175.

Bhabha, H. K. (1994). *The location of culture.* London and New York: Routledge Press.

Bolter, J. D. (1991). *Writing space: The computer, hypertext and the history of writing.* Hillsdale, NJ: Lawrence Erlbaum. [Also published in hypertext form.]

Brown, A. L. (1992). Design experiments: Theoretical and methodological challenges in creating complex interventions in classroom settings. *Journal of Learning Sciences, 2*(2), 141–178.

Bruce, B. C. (1997). Literacy technologies: What stance should we take? *Journal of Literacy Research*, 29(2): 289–309.

Burbulus, N. (2001). Paradoxes of the Web: The ethical dimensions of credibility. *Library Trends*, 49(3), 441–453.

Chandler-Olcott, K., & Mahar, D. (2003). Adolescents' *anime*-inspired "fanfictions": An exploration of multiliteracies. *Journal of Adolescent & Adult Literacy*, 46(7): 556–566.

Collins, A. (1992). Toward a design science of education. In E. Scanlon & T. O'Shea (Eds.), *New directions in educational technology*. New York: Springer-Verlag.

Dalton, B., Pisha, B., Eagleton, M., Coyne, P., & Deysher, S. (2002). *Engaging the text: Strategy instruction in a computer-supported reading environment for struggling readers* (Executive Summary). Wakefield, MA: CAST.

Design-Based Research Collective. (2003). Design-based research: An emerging paradigm for educational inquiry. *Educational Researcher*, 32(1), 5–8.

Dillon, A. (1991). Requirements analysis for hypertext applications: The why, what and how approach. *Applied Ergonomics*, 22(4), 458–462.

Duffy, T. M. (2004). Theory and the design of learning environments: Reflections on differences in disciplinary focus. *Educational Technology*, 44(3), 13–15.

Dyson, A. H. (1991). Toward a reconceptualization of written language development. *Linguistics and Education*, 3, 139–162.

Feldman, S. C., & Fish, M. C. (1991). The use of computer-mediated reading supports to enhance reading comprehension. *Journal of Educational Computing research*, 7(1), 25–36.

Flood, J., & Lapp, D. (1998). Broadening conceptualizations of literacy: The visual and communicative arts (Visual Literacy). *Reading Teacher*, 51(4), 342–344.

Gee, J. P. (1991). What is literacy? In C. Mitchell & K. Weiler (Eds.), *Rewriting literacy: Culture and the discourse of the other*. New York: Bergiin & Garvey.

Gee, J. P. (1996). *Social linguistics and literacies: Ideology in discourses* (2nd ed.). Bristol, PA: Taylor and Francis.

Gee, J. P. (2003). *What video games have to teach us about leaning and literacy*. New York: Palgrave/Macmillan.

Gitlin, T. (2001). *Media unlimited*. New York: Metropolitan Books.

Green, B. (1988). Subject-specific literacy and school learning: A focus on writing. *Australian Journal of Education*. 32(2), 156–179.

Gutiérrez, K., Baquedano-Lopez, P., & Tejeda, C. (1999). Rethinking diversity: Hybridity and hybrid language practices in the third space. *Mind, Culture, & Activity: An International Journal*, 6(4), 286–303.

Hailey, D. E., Jr., & Hailey, C. (1998). Hypermedia, multimedia, and reader cognition: An empirical study. *Technical Communication*, 45(3): 330–342.

Hansen, S., Schrimpsher, D., Narayanan, N. H., & Hegarty, M. (1998). Empirical studies of animation-embedded hypermedia algorithm visualizations. (Technical Report No. CSE98–06). Auburn, AL: Dept. of Computer Science & Software Engineering, Auburn University.

Hegarty, M., Narayanan, N. H., & Freitas, P. (2002). Understanding machines from hypermedia and hypermedia presentations. In J. Otero, J. A. Leon, & A. C. Graesser (Eds.), *The psychology of science text comprehension* (pp. 357–384). Mahwah, NJ: Lawrence Erlbaum Associates.

Hegarty, M., Quilici, J., Narayanan, N. H., Holmquist, S., & Moreno, R. (1999). Multimedia instruction: Lessons from evaluation of a theory-based design. *Journal of Educational Multimeda and Hypermedia*, 8(2), 119–150.

Hoadley, C. M. (2004). Learning and design: Why the learning sciences and instructional systems need each other. *Educational Technology*, 44(3), 6–12.

Horney, M. A., & Anderson-Inman, L. (1999). Supported text in electronic reading environments. *Reading and Writing Quarterly*, 15(2), 127–168.

Hull, G. A. (2003). Youth culture and digital media: New literacies for new times. *Research in the Teaching of English*, 38(2), 229–233.

Kamil, M. L. (2003). *Adolescents and literacy: Reading for the 21st century*. Washington, DC: Alliance for Excellent Education.

Kamil, M. L., & Lane, D. M. (1998). Researching the relationship between technology and literacy: An agenda for the 21st Century. In D. Reinking, M. C. McKenna, L. D. Labbo, & R. D. Kieffer (Eds.), *Handbook of literacy and technology: Transformations in a post-typographic world* (pp. 323–341). Mahwah, NJ: Lawrence Erlbaum Associates.

Kintsch, W. (1998). *Comprehension: A paradigm for cognition*. New York: Cambridge University Press.

Kolodner, J. L. (1991). Improving human decision-making through case-based decision aiding. *AI Magazine, 12*(2), 52–68.

Kozhevnikof, M., Hegarty, M., & Mayer, R. E. (2002). Revising the visualizer-verbalizer dimension: Evidence for two types of visualizers. *Cognition and Instruction, 20*(1), 47–77.

Lankshear, C., & Knobel, M. (2003a). *New literacies: Changing knowledge and classroom learning*. Buckingham, UK: Open University Press.

Lankshear, C., & Knobel, M. (2003b). New technologies in early childhood literacy research: A review of research. *Journal of Early Childhood Literacy, 3*(1), 59–82.

Lawless, K. A., & Brown, S. W. (1997). Multimedia learning environments: Issues of learner control and navigation. *Instructional Science, 25*, 117–131.

Lawless, K. A., & Brown, S. W. (2003). Introduction: From digital dirt road to educational expressway: Innovations in web-based pedagogy. *Instructional Science, 31*(4–5), 227–230(4).

Lawless, K. A., Brown, S. W., Mills, R., & Mayall, H. J. (2003). Knowledge, interest, recall, and navigation: A look at hypertext processing. *Journal of Literacy Research, 35*(3), 911–934.

Leander, K. M. (2003). Writing travelers' tales on new literacy scapes. *Reading Research Quarterly, 38*(3), 392–397.

Lemke, J. L. (1998). Metamedia literacy: Transforming meanings and media. In D. Reinking, M. C. McKenna, L. D. Labbo, & R. D. Kieffer (Eds.), *Handbook of literacy and technology: Transformations in a post-typographic world* (pp. 283–301). Mahwah, NJ: Lawrence Erlbaum Associates.

Lemke, J. L. (1999). Typological and topological meaning in diagnostic discourse. *Discourse Processes 27*(2), 173–185.

Leu, D. J., Jr. (2000). Literacy and technology: Deictic consequences for literacy education in an information age. In M. L. Kamil, P. Mosenthal, P. D. Pearson, & R. Barr (Eds.), *Handbook of reading research* (Vol. III, pp. 743–770). Mahway, NJ: Erlbaum.

Leu, D. J., Jr., Kinzer, C. K., Coiro, J. L., & Cammack, D. W. (2004). Toward a theory of new literacies emerging from the internet and other information and communication technologies. In R. B. Ruddell and N. Unrau (Eds.), *Theoretical models and processes of reading* (5th Ed.). Newark, DE: International Reading Association.

MacArthur, C. A., Ferretti, R. P., Okolo, C. M., & Cavalier, A. R. (2001). Technology applications for students with literacy problems: A critical review. *The Elementary School Journal, 101*(3), 273–301.

MacArthur, C. A., & Haynes, J. B. (1995). The Student Assistant for Learning from Text (SALT): A hypermedia reading aide. *Journal of Learning Disabilities, 3*, 150–159.

Mayer, R. E. (1996). Learning strategies for making sense out of expository text: The SOI model for guiding three cognitive processes in knowledge construction. *Educational Psychology Review, 8*, 357–371.

Mayer, R. E. (2001). *Multimedia learning*. New York: Cambridge University Press.

McKenna, M. C., Reinking, D., Labbo, L. D., & Kieffer, R. D. (1999). The electronic transformation of literacy and its implications for the struggling reader. *Reading & Writing Quarterly, 15*, 111–126.

Moje, E. B., Ciechanowski, K. M., Kramer, K. Ellis, L., Carrillo, R., & Collazo, T. (2004). working toward third space in content area literacy: An examination of everyday funds of knowledge and discourse. *Reading Research Quarterly, 39*(1), 38–70.

Moll, L. C., Veléz-Ibanéz, C., & Greenberg, J. (1989). *Year one progress report: Community knowledge and classroom practice: Combining resources for literacy instruction.* (IARP Subcontract L-10, Development Associates). Tucson: University of Arizona.

Muspratt, A., Luke, A., & Freebody, P. (Eds.). (1998). *Constructing critical literacies: Teaching and learning textual practice.* Cresskill, NJ: Hampton.

Myers, J., & Beach, R. (2001). Hypermedia authoring as critical literacy. *Journal of Adolescent & Adult Literacy, 44*(6), 538–546.

Nixon, H. (2003). New research literacies for contemporary research into literacy and new media? *Reading Research Quarterly, 38*(3), 407–413.

Paivio, A. (1986). *Mental representations*. New York: Oxford University Press.

Palincsar, A. S., & Brown, A. L. (1984). Reciprocal teaching of comprehension fostering and comprehension monitoring. *Cognition and Instruction, 1*(2), 117–175.

Palincsar, A. S., & Dalton, B. (2004). Speaking literacy and learning to technology; Speaking technology to literacy and learning. *2004 National Reading Conference (NRC) Research Address*.

Palincsar, A. S., & Dalton, B. (2005). Literacy and learning speak to technology: Technology speaks to literacy and learning. *The fifty-fourth yearbook of the National Reading Conference, 54*, 83–102.

Purves, A. (1998). *The web of text and the web of God: An essay on the third information transformation*. New York: Guilford Press.

Reinking, D., McKenna, M. C., Labbo, L. D., & Kieffer, R. D. (1998). *Handbook of literacy and technology: Transformations in a post-typographic world*. Mahwah, NJ: Lawrence Erlbaum Associates.

Ryan, M. (1999). Cyberspace, virtuality, and the text. In M. Ryan (Ed.), *Cyberspace textuality: Computer technology and literary theory* (pp. 78–107). Bloomington: Indiana University Press.

Scardamalia, M. (2004). CSILE/Knowledge Forum. In A. Kovalchick & K. Dawson (Eds.), *Education and technology: An encyclopedia* (pp. 183–192). Santa Barbara: ABC-CLIO.

Scardamalia, M., Bereiter, C., & Lamon, M. (1994). The CSILE project: Trying to bring the classroom into World 3. In K. McGilley (Eds.), *Classroom lessons: Integrating cognitive theory and classroom practice* (pp. 201–228). Cambridge: MA: MIT Press.

Scribner, S., & Cole, M. (1981). *The psychology of literacy*. Cambridge, MA: Harvard University Press.

Smith, N. B. (1965). *American reading instruction*. Newark, NE: International Reading Association.

Soja, E. W. (1996). *Thirdspace: Journeys to Los Angeles and other real-and-imagined places*. Oxford: Blackwell.

Spiro, R. J., & Jehng, J. (1990). Cognitive flexibility and hypertext: Theory and technology for the non-linear and multidimensional traversal of complex subject matter. D. Nix & R. Spiro (eds.), *Cognition, education, and multimedia*. Hillsdale, NJ: Lawrence Erlbaum Associates.

Strangman, N., & Dalton, B. (2005). Technology for struggling readers: A review of the research. In D. Edyburn (Ed.), *The handbook of special education technology research and practice* (pp. 545–569). Whitefish Bay, WI: Knowledge by Design.

van Dijk, T. A., & Kintsch, W. (1983). *Strategies of discourse comprehension*. New York: Academic Press.

Wallace, R. M., Kupperman, J., Krajcik, J., & Soloway, E. (2000). Science on the web: Students online in a sixth-grade classroom. *The Journal of the Learning Sciences, 9*(1), 75–104.

Wixson, K. K., & Peters, C. W. (1984). Reading redefined: A Michigan Reading Association position paper. *Michigan Reading Journal, 17*, 4–7 (see p. 5).

Woodward, J., & Rieth, H. (1997). A historical review of technology research in special education. *Review of Educational Research, 67*(4), 503–536.

Part IV

MAKING KNOWLEDGE VISIBLE

CHAPTER 19

Project-Based Learning

Joseph S. Krajcik and Phyllis C. Blumenfeld

Any teacher or parent can tell you that many students are bored in school. But many of them tend to assume that boredom is not a problem with the best students, and that if students tried harder or learned better they wouldn't be bored. In the 1980s and 1990s, education researchers increasingly realized that when students are bored and unengaged, they are less likely to learn (Blumenfeld et al., 1991). Studies of student experience found that almost all students are bored in school, even the ones who score well on standardized tests (Csikszentmihalyi, Rathunde, & Whalen, 1993). By about 1990, it became obvious to education researchers that the problem wasn't the fault of the students; there was something wrong with the structure of schooling. If we could find a way to engage students in their learning, to restructure the classroom so that students would be motivated to learn, that would be a dramatic change.

Also by about 1990, new assessments of college students had shown that the knowledge they acquired in high school remained at a superficial level. Even the best-scoring students, those at the top colleges, often had not acquired a deeper conceptual understanding of material – whether in science, literature, or math (Gardner, 1991). Educators still face these critical problems today.

Learning sciences research provides a potential solution to these problems. Drawing on the cognitive sciences and other disciplines, learning scientists are uncovering the cognitive structure of deeper conceptual understanding, discovering principles that govern learning, and showing in detail that schools teach superficial knowledge rather than deeper knowledge. Drawing on this research, many learning scientists are developing new types of curricula, with the goal of increasing student engagement and helping them develop deeper understanding of important ideas. Our own contribution is articulating the features of *project-based learning* (Blumenfeld et al., 2000; Krajcik et al., 1994). Project-based learning allows students to learn by doing and applying ideas. Students engage in real-world activities that are similar to the activities that adult professionals engage in.

Project-based learning is a form of situated learning (Greeno, this volume) and it is based on the constructivist finding that students gain a deeper understanding of material when they actively construct their understand by working with and using ideas. In project-based learning, students engage in real, meaningful problems that are important to them and that are similar to what scientists, mathematicians, writers, and historians do. A project-based classroom allows students to investigate questions, propose hypotheses and explanations, discuss their ideas, challenge the ideas of others, and try out new ideas. Research has demonstrated that students in project-based learning classrooms get higher scores than students in traditional classrooms (Marx et al., 2004; Rivet & Krajcik, 2004; William & Linn, 2003).

Project-based learning is an overall approach to the design of learning environments. Learning environments that are project-based have five key features (Blumenfeld et al., 1991; Krajcik, et al., 1994; Krajcik, Czerniak, & Berger, 2002):

1. They start with a driving question, a problem to be solved.

2. Students explore the driving question by participating in authentic, situated inquiry – processes of problem solving that are central to expert performance in the discipline. As students explore the driving question, they learn and apply important ideas in the discipline.

3. Students, teachers, and community members engage in collaborative activities to find solutions to the driving question. This mirrors the complex social situation of expert problem solving.

4. While engaged in the inquiry process, students are scaffolded with learning technologies that help them participate in activities normally beyond their ability.

5. Students create a set of tangible products that address the driving question. These are shared artifacts, publicly accessible external representations of the class's learning.

In the next section, we summarize the learning sciences theory behind project-based learning. Our own efforts have emphasized applying project-based methods to science classrooms, so in the section after that, we show how our work builds on project-based learning principles. Based on over ten years working in science classrooms, we have learned several important lessons about how to apply project-based learning in schools, and in the bulk of the chapter, we group our lessons around the five key features of project-based learning. We close by discussing issues that we encountered in scaling up our curriculum.

Theoretical Background of Project-Based Learning

The roots of project-based learning extend back over a hundred years, to the work of educator and philosopher John Dewey (1959), whose Laboratory School at the University of Chicago was based on the process of inquiry. Dewey argued that students will develop personal investment in the material if they engage in real, meaningful tasks and problems that emulate what experts do in real-world situations. In the last two decades, learning sciences researchers have refined and elaborated Dewey's original insight that active inquiry results in deeper understanding. New discoveries in the learning sciences have led to new ways of understanding how children learn (Bransford, Brown, & Cocking, 1999). We build on four major learning sciences ideas: (1) active construction, (2) situated learning, (3) social interactions, and (4) cognitive tools.

Active Construction

Learning sciences research has found that deep understanding occurs when a learner actively constructs meaning based on his or her experiences and interaction in the world, and that only superficial learning occurs when learners passively take in information transmitted from a teacher, a computer, or a book (Sawyer introduction, this volume). The development of understanding is a continuous process that requires students to construct and reconstruct what they know from new experiences and ideas, and prior knowledge and experiences. Teachers and materials do not reveal knowledge to learners; rather, learners actively build knowledge as they explore the surrounding world, observe and interact with phenomena, take in new ideas, make connections between new and old ideas, and discuss and interact with others. In project-based learning, students actively construct their knowledge by participating in real-world activities similar to those that experts engage in, to solve problems and develop artifacts.

Situated Learning

Learning sciences research has shown that the most effective learning occurs when the learning is situated in an authentic, real-world context. In some scientific disciplines, scientists conduct experiments in laboratories; in others, they systematically observe the natural world and draw conclusions from their observations. Situated learning in science would involve students in experiencing phenomena as they take part in various scientific practices such as designing investigations, making explanations, modeling, and presenting their ideas to others. One of the benefits of situated learning is that students can more easily see the value and meaning of the tasks and activities they perform. When students do a science experiment by following detailed steps in the textbook, that's hardly any better than passively listening to a lecture. Either way, it's hard for them to see the meaning in what they're doing. But when they create their own investigation design to answer a question that is important to them and their community, they can see how science can be applied to solve important problems.

A second benefit of situated learning is that it seems to generalize better to a wider range of situations (Kolodner, this volume). When learners acquire information through memorization of discrete facts that are not connected to important and meaningful situations, the superficial understanding that results is difficult for students to generalize to new situations. When students participate in step-by-step science experiments

from the textbook, they don't learn how and where to apply these same procedures outside of the classroom. However, when students acquire information in a meaningful context (Blumenfeld et al., 1991) and relate it to their prior knowledge and experiences, they can form connections between the new information and the prior knowledge to develop better, larger, and more linked conceptual understanding.

Social Interaction

One of the most solid findings to emerge from learning sciences research is the important role of social interaction in learning (Collins, this volume; Greeno, this volume; Sawyer, this volume). The best learning results from a particular kind of social interaction: when teachers, students, and community members work together in a situated activity to construct shared understanding. Learners develop understandings of principles and ideas through sharing, using, and debating ideas with others (Blumenfeld et al., 1996). This back-and-forth sharing, using, and debating of ideas helps to create a community of learners.

Cognitive Tools

Learning sciences research has demonstrated the important role of tools in learning (Salomon, Perkins, & Globerson, 1991). Cognitive tools can amplify and expand what students can learn. A graph is an example of a cognitive tool that helps learners see patterns in data. Various forms of computer software can be considered cognitive tools because they allow learners to carry out tasks not possible without the software's assistance and support. For instance, new forms of computer software allow learners to visualize complex data sets (Edelson & Reiser, this volume). In such situations, we refer to the computer software as a learning technology.

Learning technologies can support students (1) in accessing and collecting a range of scientific data and information; (2) by providing visualization and data analysis tools similar to those used by scientists;

(3) by allowing for collaboration and sharing of information across sites; (4) by planning, building, and testing models; and (5) by developing multimedia documents that illustrate student understanding (Novak & Krajcik, 2004). These features expand the range of questions that students can investigate and the multitude and type of phenomena students can experience. Although learners can use a variety of cognitive tools in project-based learning, we place a special focus on the use of learning technologies.

Project-Based Science

In the early 1990s, educators increasingly realized that most students were not motivated to learn science, and that even the best students acquired only a superficial understanding of science. Researchers began to discover that these superficial understandings were caused by a combination of ineffective textbook design and instructional style. Science textbooks covered many topics at a superficial level, focused on technical vocabulary, failed to consider students' prior knowledge, lacked coherent explanations of real-world phenomena, and didn't give students an opportunity to develop their own explanations of phenomena (Kesidou & Roseman, 2002). And although most science teachers have their classes do experiments, most teachers specify the exact sequence of steps that students are supposed to perform – what scientists often refer to as "cookbook" procedures. Following a cookbook recipe doesn't require a deeper understanding of the material, and at best it results in only superficial learning.

In response to these findings, several researchers began to work collaboratively with middle school and high school science teachers to develop project-based instruction in science (Blumenfeld et al., 2000; Krajcik et al., 1994; Krajcik et al., 1998; O'Neill & Polman, 2004; Polman, 1999; Ruopp et al., 1992; Tinker, 1997; William & Linn, 2003). In project-based science (PBS), students engage in real, meaningful problems that are important to them and that are similar to what scientists do. A project-based science classroom allows students to explore phenomena, investigate questions, discuss their ideas, challenge the ideas of others and try out new ideas. Research shows that PBS has the potential to help all students – regardless of culture, race, or gender – engage in and learn science (Atwater, 1994; Haberman, 1991).

PBS responds to science education recommendations made by national organizations. The National Science Education Standards (National Research Council, 1996) highlight the importance of students doing inquiry to promote personal decision making, participation in societal and cultural affairs, and economic productivity. The AAAS report *Science for all Americans* (AAAS, 1989) calls for students to develop habits of mind such as being aware that there may be more than one good way to interpret a given set of findings, keeping honest and thorough records, and deciding what degree of precision is adequate.

During the 1990s, our group at the University of Michigan, the Center for Highly Interactive Computers in Education (hi-ce) developed strategies for fostering learning in a PBS environment, and designed and developed curriculum materials using the principles of PBS (Blumenfeld et al., 1991; Krajcik et al., 1998; Marx et al., 2004). We worked with high school teachers to develop PBS environments so that different science disciplines (biology, chemistry, and earth science) were integrated into a three-year program (Heubel-Drake et al., 1995). hi-ce also has worked with middle school teachers to transform their teaching (Fishman & Davis, this volume; Novak & Gleason, 2001; Scott, 1994). More recently, we developed curriculum materials as one approach to bring about systemic change in the Detroit Urban Systemic Initiative funded by NSF (Blumenfeld et al., 2000; Marx et al., 2004).

Lessons for Project-Based Learning Environments

Over the last seven years, through our involvement in the Center for Learning

Technologies in Urban Schools (LeTUS) (Blumenfeld et al., 2000; Marx et al., 2004) and the Investigating and Questioning our World through Science and Technology (IQWST) project (Reiser et al., 2003), we worked closely with teachers to design, develop, and test PBS curriculum materials. LeTUS was a collaborative effort among Detroit Public Schools, Chicago Public Schools, Northwestern University, and the University of Michigan to improve middle school science teaching and learning. The collaborative work in LeTUS took as its core challenge the use of inquiry and the infusion of learning technologies to support learning in urban classrooms. IQWST is a joint venture between the University of Michigan and Northwestern University to develop the next generation of middle school curriculum materials. To date, LeTUS materials developed at the University of Michigan have resulted in five different PBS-based curriculum units that teachers can use at the sixth, seventh, or eighth grade levels.[1]

While engaged in this work, we have learned many lessons that are relevant to all project-based learning (Blumenfeld et al., 1994; Krajcik et al., 1998; Marx et al., 1997; Tinker & Krajcik, 2001). We've grouped these lessons around the five key features of project-based learning: driving questions, situated inquiry, collaboration, learning technologies, and artifacts.

Feature 1: Driving Questions

The hallmark of project-based learning is a driving question that guides instruction and that learners find meaningful and important (Blumenfeld et al., 1991; Krajcik et al., 2002). A driving question encompasses worthwhile content that is meaningful and anchored in a real-world situation. The driving question serves to organize and drive activities of the project, provides a context in which students can use and explore learning goals and scientific practices, and provides continuity and coherence to the full range of project activities. As students pursue solutions to the driving question, they develop meaningful understandings of key scientific concepts, principles and practices. A good driving question elicits a desire to learn in students (Edelson, 2001), and it makes students realize that there is an important problem that genuinely needs to be solved (Reiser, 2004). Throughout the project, the teacher calls attention to the driving question to link together the various ideas students explore during the project.

Good driving questions have several features. Driving questions should be (1) *feasible* in that students can design and perform investigations to answer the question; (2) *worthwhile* in that they contain rich science content that aligns with national or district standards and relates to what scientists really do; (3) *contextualized* in that they are real world, nontrivial, and important; (4) *meaningful* in that they are interesting and exciting to learners; (5) *ethical* in that they do no harm to individuals, organisms or the environment (Krajcik et al., 2002).

In PBS, the teacher or curriculum designer select the driving question, or sometimes the students work together with the teacher to select the question (Krajcik et al., 2002; Scardamalia & Bereiter, this volume). Some project-based methods start the process by having students develop their own driving question. This has the advantage that it results in a question that is meaningful to students. However, it is extremely difficult for students to develop driving questions that have all the properties of a good driving question. Our approach has been to design curriculum around a driving question that we select in collaboration with teachers but that allow students either to explore solutions to their own related questions or to engage in a design project to ask related questions in the unit. One of our units is based on the driving question *How Do Machines Help Me Build Big Things? (Big Things)* (Rivet & Krajcik, 2004). In *Big Things* students learn about balanced and unbalanced forces and their effect on motion, simple machines and how they work together in complex machines, and the concept of mechanical advantage, and use this understanding to design and explain a complex machine of their own choosing.

Lesson 1a: Helping Students See the Value of Driving Questions

Often students do not see the value of a driving question. One of the major challenges facing teachers and designers of curriculum materials is to find ways to help students realize the value of the driving questions. One way in which we met this challenge was through the use of *anchoring experiences* (Cognition and Technology Group at Vanderbilt, 1992). Anchoring experiences provide students with common experiences which help them relate to the new ideas explored in the project (Rivet & Krajcik, 2002; Sherwood et al., 1987). Anchoring experiences also present meaningful contexts for the science ideas explored in the project. We use anchoring experiences at the beginning of and throughout a project to show the value of the project's driving question (Cognition and Technology Group at Vanderbilt, 1992; Marx et al., 1997; Rivet & Krajcik, 2004).

In *Can Good Friends Make Me Sick?* (Hug & Krajcik, 2002), an eight-week unit that addresses national standards related to cells, systems, microbiology, and disease, teachers introduce students to the driving question by reading and discussing a story about a young South African boy who contracted aids and became an AIDS activist. This story is an anchoring experience that provides a context for discussing how disease relates to them and other middle school children. In a second anchoring experience, students participate in an activity that simulates how an infectious disease might spread through a community. First, they each mix a solution in a test tube. Then, students walk around the class, and when they meet another student, they mix the contents of their test tubes. Some test tubes contain an indicator that reacts with a substance in other test tubes. As students share the content of their test tubes, more and more test tubes change color – simulating the transfer of a communicable disease. This activity provides a common experience to discuss and relate back to throughout the project (Hug & Krajcik, 2002).

Lesson 1b: Standards Versus In-Depth Examining of Content

A second lesson that we have learned is that many driving questions do not meet important learning goals aligned to national or district standards. In LeTUS, we began by designing curriculum materials using contexts that would engage students and be of interest and value to the community. We selected issues like "What is the quality of air in my community?" and "What is the water like in my river?" Although students find these projects motivating and they met some important learning goals that aligned to national and local standards, starting with these questions did not allow us to systematically meet standards.

In a new materials development effort, *Investigating and Questioning our World through Science and Technology* (IQWST) (Reiser et al., 2003), the IQWST team plans to design, develop, and test the next generation of curriculum materials that teachers and students can use throughout the nation. If these materials are to scale up so that numerous teachers and students use them (Dede, this volume), then one criterion that the materials need to meet is they must help students achieve major learning goals that align with national and district standards. To ensure PBS curriculum aligns with these standards, we plan a three-step process. We start by selecting the national standards students should achieve (Wiggins & McTighe, 1998). For instance, a standard from the National Science Education Standards (NRC, 1996) states that students should know the following:

> *A substance has characteristic properties, such as density, a boiling point, and solubility, all of which are independent of the amount of the sample. (Content Standard B 5–8: 1A)*

But what is it that we expect students to do with this knowledge? To specify what reasoning we expect students to be able to do with this knowledge, we rewrite the standard in terms of *learning performance* (Perkins et al., 1995). Learning performances restate standards in terms of the cognitive tasks students should perform (Reiser et al., 2003; McNeill & Krajcik, in press). Learning performances reflect the cognitive tasks that we want students to be able to do using scientific knowledge: describe phenomena, use models to explain patterns in data, construct scientific explanations, and test hypotheses (Reiser et al., 2003).

After determining learning performances, we use them as guides for designing the driving question, tasks, and assessments. We believe that this new process will ensure that PBS methods align better with standards. However, we are concerned that when we start with the standards rather than the driving question, it may be hard to find questions that students find meaningful and interesting. In the development of one of the first IQWST units, we started with standardized learning goals related to understanding the nature of chemical reactions and the conservations of mass (McNeill & Krajcik, in press). We had several meetings with teachers to discuss possible driving questions. Some seemed too trivial and did not lead to opportunities for students to explore phenomena. We finally settled on "How do I make new stuff from old stuff?," and we created an anchoring experience of making soap as an example of making new stuff from old stuff.

Feature 2: Situated Inquiry

Throughout the history of science education, national organizations and prominent scientists have argued that science instruction should mirror the scientific process (Hurd, 1970; National Research Council, 1996; Rutherford, 1964; Scardamalia & Bereiter, this volume). Of course, science classrooms are not scientific laboratories. But science classrooms need to be consistent with science. The goal of science is to explain and predict various phenomena – events such as erosion, diseases, rusting,

plant growth, and objects falling to the ground. To answer their questions, scientists take part in scientific inquiry. In scientific inquiry, scientists frame hypotheses that build from theories and previous research; design investigations that allow them to use tools and technologies to gather, analyze, and interpret data; and create explanations of the phenomena. These are *scientific practices*: the multiple ways of knowing and doing that scientists use to study the natural world (National Research Council, 1996). Although scientists do not follow a fixed set of steps that leads them to new scientific understandings, all scientists rely on the use of evidence and theories to explain and predict phenomena that occur in the world.

In PBS classrooms, students explore the driving question using new ideas that they're learning, and they investigate the driving question over a sustained period of time. This is different from traditional science classrooms, which engage in short-term activities and provide cookbook procedures that are not situated in an inquiry process. In the project "*What is the quality of water in our river?*" (Singer et al., 2000) students conduct different water quality tests, such as pH, turbidity, temperature, and dissolved oxygen to infer water quality. In the project, "*Can Good Friends Make Me Sick?*" students design and conduct investigations to explore various questions regarding the growth of bacteria. By exploring these questions, learners take part in various scientific practices.

Lessons 2 a: Helping Students Design an Investigation

Middle school students find it difficult to engage in the inquiry process, particularly if they've had no previous experiences in science (Edelson & Reiser, this volume; Krajcik et al., 1998). To support teachers, our curriculum materials present very thorough details about how to perform a basic investigation related to the driving question. The teacher first models the investigation while asking students to provide suggestions. Next, the students use these techniques to perform their own investigations while the teacher guides and provides feedback on the process. Hug and Krajcik (2002) explored this strategy in the Communicable Diseases project, in which students explore the growth of bacteria. The teacher begins by asking: "Do I have bacteria on my hands?" and discusses why this makes a good question. The teacher then models how to explore this question by cultivating bacteria, using appropriate experimental techniques such as noncontaminated plate as a control. The next day, after bacteria have grown, the teacher shows students how to count the bacteria colonies and how to use the data to write an evidence-based explanation.

After the teacher models the process, students ask related questions and conduct their own investigations by modifying the procedure modeled by the teacher. Working in teams, students ask questions such as "Does washing my hands make a difference?," "Do different types of soap make a difference?," and "Is there bacteria on the lunch tables after they are cleaned?" The class discusses why these make reasonable and useful questions, encouraging reflection. Next, students design investigations to find solutions to their questions by modifying the procedure the teacher modeled. For instance, if students in a team ask the question, "Does washing my hands make a difference in the amount of bacteria I have on them?," the students need to modify the procedure by designing conditions in which they contaminate the agar plates using nonwashed and washed hands. During the process, teachers give feedback or allow peer feedback to determine if a team's question and a modified procedure is feasible and appropriate. Our curriculum materials support teachers with detailed commentary that provides a rationale for what is occurring as well as how to do it (Davis & Krajcik, 2005).

Lesson 2 b: Writing Conclusions and Explanations

After completing investigation procedures and gathering data, the next step is to scaf-

fold students as they develop their own explanations of the findings. Unfortunately, many studies have found that students have a hard time developing scientific explanations (McNeill & Krajcik, in press; Palincsar, Anderson, & David, 1993). Prior research suggests that it is hard for students to use their explanations to articulate and defend their claims (Sadler, 2004), to understand what counts as evidence, to use appropriate evidence (Sandoval & Reiser, 2004), and to not rely on their personal views (Hogan & Maglienti, 2001). Drawing and justifying conclusions using primary evidence requires sophisticated thinking and much experience, and this type of reasoning has not been required of most students. In fact, even many teachers have trouble engaging in this type of reasoning. Although middle school teachers have experience working with data from highly structured cookbook experiments, they are less likely to have experience using and inferring from real data. As a result, teachers need support in helping students to create explanations and conclusions (Krajcik et al., 1998).

To overcome this challenge, we have become very explicit in the process and reasons behind how to scaffold students as they write explanations (McNeill & Krajcik, in press; Moje et al., 2004). Our scaffolding strategies include making the rationale behind explanations explicit, modeling how to construct explanations, providing students with opportunities to engage in explanation construction, and writing scaffolding comments on students' investigation sheets. We have students use an explanation framework that includes three components: a claim, evidence, and reasoning. The *claim* makes an assertion that addresses the phenomena students are exploring. The *evidence* supports the claim using scientific data that can come from several sources – observations, reading material, archived data, or an investigation that students complete. The *reasoning* provides a justification that links the claim and evidence together, showing why the data count as evidence to support the claim by using the appropriate scientific ideas (McNeill & Krajcik, in press).

Feature 3: Collaborations

Project-based learning provides opportunities for students, teachers, and members of society to collaborate with one another to investigate questions and ideas. The classroom becomes a community of learners (Brown & Campione, 1994). Students collaborate with others in their classroom and with their teacher to ask questions, write explanations, form conclusions, make sense of information, discuss data, and present findings. For example, we ask students to critique and provide feedback to each others' explanations. Collaboration helps students build shared understandings of scientific ideas and of the nature of the discipline as they engage in discourse with their classmates and adults outside the classroom.

Lessons 3a: Creating a Discourse Community

Students do not naturally collaborate with other students in the classroom (Azmitia, 1996). Teachers need to help students develop skills in collaborating, including turn-taking, listening, and respect for others' opinions (Krajcik et al., 2002). Because students lack skills in collaborating and have had little experience in collaborating, teachers need to build collaborations over the entire school year. Teachers can use a technique in which they first asking students to write down their ideas and then work with a partner to compare their ideas. Written prompts like "My ideas are similar to my partners' ideas in these ways" and "My ideas are different from my partners' ideas in these ways" help students learn to listen to others and compare their ideas to others (Krajcik et al., 2002; compare Andriessen, this volume; Scardamalia & Bereiter, this volume).

Another challenge that teachers face is changing the culture of the classroom from the transmission-and-acquisition style that students expect. Because most students are used to classrooms in which the teacher tells the students the correct answer, they don't take collaborative inquiry seriously at first.

They are conditioned to sit and wait for the teacher to give them the answer, so they don't expend much energy trying to find the answer on their own. Often, teachers too easily fall into this trap and just tell the students the answer, because after all, they will be evaluated on whether or not the students learn the material. To break students out of the habits that they've learned from a lifetime of transmission-and-acquisition instruction, teachers need to work throughout the entire year to get students used to a collaborative way of learning.

Another challenge that we have observed is that teachers will often cut short the time for students to collaborate. Perhaps one reason behind this challenge is that teachers lack appropriate strategies to support students in collaboration. However, another reason might be that teachers don't see collaboration as essential to the meaning making process. This challenge, unfortunately, is much harder to overcome, because it lies at teachers' belief about what fosters understanding.

Feature 4: Using Technology Tools to Support Learning

Technology tools can help transform the classroom into an environment in which learners actively construct knowledge (Linn, 1997; Tinker, 1997; White & Fredrickson, 2000). Edelson (2001) gives three reasons to use technology tools in schools: (1) they align with the practice of science, (2) they can present information in dynamic and interactive formats, and (3) they provide unprecedented opportunities to move teaching away from a transmission-and-acquisition model of instruction.

Students can use learning technologies to access real data on the World Wide Web, to collaborate with others via networks (Stahl et al., this volume; Novak & Krajcik, 2004; Scardamalia & Bereiter, this volume; Schofield, this volume), to gather data, to graph and analyze data (Edelson & Reiser, this volume; Schwartz & Heiser, this volume), to create models (Lehrer &

Schauble, this volume), and to produce multimedia artifacts. Learning technologies allow students to extend what they can do in the classroom, and serve as powerful cognitive tools that help teachers foster inquiry and student learning (Krajcik et al., 2002; Novak & Krajcik, 2004; Linn, 1997; Metcalf-Jackson, Krajcik, & Soloway, 2000).

In the Water Quality project, students use various sensors to gather data about the pH, temperature and turbidity of the river. The students take handheld computers with them to the river, and the data are displayed immediately in a graph. Other sensor devices allow students to collect the data and then view them on computer graphs back in the classrooms. Students use the new ideas they have learned to develop a computer-based model that shows how various factors influence water quality. These technologies help students build connections among the science ideas, forming a deeper and richer understanding.

Lesson 4a: Lack of Computer Access

The *"Can Good Friends Makes Me Sick?"* project utilizes a five-day online activity with *Artemis*[2] – a digital resource designed for student use (Hoffman et al., 2003). Students used Artemis to explore the sources, causes, symptoms and treatments of various communicable diseases. Teachers and researchers agreed that this was a valuable activity because it allowed students to search and synthesize information.

However, teachers seldom used Artemis because of challenges in gaining access to the computer lab or because the computers were not configured to access the World Wide Web. Limited access is a major obstacle to the use of learning technologies (Fishman et al., 2004; Schofield, this volume). Because most middle school teachers do not have computers in their rooms, they need to use the school technology laboratory. Unfortunately, computer laboratories are not assigned exclusively to the science class. Teachers would plan to use the computer room only to find it occupied by another class for the desired day or not available for other reasons. Occasionally, the computer teacher would tell the science teacher that some science technology tools, such as sensors, were not appropriate for the school's computer lab. At other times, the room would not be configured in a way that was conducive to the use of various software and hardware applications. Still other times, the teacher would prepare the computers for his or her class in advance, only to find that the computers had been changed.

The lesson is that before computers can be fully integrated into classroom instruction, networked computers must be available in every classroom, not only in a dedicated computer lab (Blumenfeld et al., 2000; Fishman et al., 2004; Schofield, 1995, this volume).

Lesson 4b: Time Demand of Using Technology Tools

Because the Artemis search task took five days, teachers were hesitant to use it. They recognized its value, but they could not justify the time commitment when faced with other curriculum goals. This lesson corresponds to one of the fundamental tensions facing all constructivist methods – it takes more time to complete a task where students are constructing their own knowledge in meaningful, situated activities.

Lesson 4c: Integrating Learning Technologies into Curriculum Materials

It is important to introduce new learning technologies within the context of an existing curriculum unit. Initially, we did not use PBS ideas to develop curriculum materials for teachers and students, but rather worked with teachers to help them develop understanding for the features of project-based science and modify their curriculum to a project-based format (Krajcik et al., 1994). Teachers and administrators clearly told us that if we wanted teachers with different experiences, skills, and comfort levels in teaching science to use learning technology and do inquiry, we needed to provide materials that guided teachers in the process. To support teachers with this diversity, we began to develop curriculum materials based on the premises of PBS that incorporated learning technologies (Marx et al., 2004, McNeill & Krajcik, in press; Rivet & Krajcik, 2004).

For example, our *Model-It* software comes packaged with curriculum materials. Students use Model-It to build, test, and evaluate qualitative, dynamic models of complex systems such as the human body (Metcalf-Jackson, Krajcik, & Soloway, 2000). The process of model building helps students to understand more deeply the interrelationships among the variables involved within any complex system (Lehrer & Schauble, this volume; Spitulnik et al., 1997; Stratford, Krajcik, & Soloway, 1998).

Software tools like Model-It need to be used throughout a project and across several projects, so that students develop deeper understandings of the processes involved in using the tool and of the tool's potential. When students use Model-It several times in one project, students come to better understand how to build and test models as well as the importance of model building (Fretz et al., 2002).

Feature 5: Creation of Artifacts

Learning sciences research shows that students learn more effectively when they develop artifacts – external representations of their constructed knowledge. In PBS, these artifacts result from students' investigations into the driving question (Blumenfeld et al., 1991). Students develop physical models and computer models, reports, videotapes, drawings, games, plays, Web sites, and computer programs. To be effective, artifacts need to address the driving question, show the emerging understanding of students, and support students in developing understanding associated with the learning goals of the project.

PBS focuses on artifact development for several reasons. First, through the development of artifacts, students construct and reconstruct their understanding. As students build and reflect on their artifacts, they actively manipulate science ideas. For instance, when developing explanations, students tie together science principles and concepts to support claims they make about phenomena. Such thinking helps form connections between ideas. This manipulation of ideas generates deeper levels of understanding.

Second, because learning does not occur in linear, discrete steps, assessments should not be constructed around small, discrete bits of information (Pellegrino, Chudowsky, & Glaser, 2001). Learning difficult ideas takes time and often these ideas come together as students work on a task that forces them to synthesize ideas. When students build artifacts throughout a project, they display their learning in a fashion consistent with real-life learning – it unfolds as a continuous process (Krajcik et al., 2002; Scardamalia & Bereiter, this volume). Teachers can use artifacts to see how student understandings develop throughout and across various projects. Artifact development allows teachers to assess for higher level cognitive outcomes such as asking questions, designing investigations, gathering and interpreting data, and creating scientific explanations (Carver, this volume; Atkin & Coffey, 2003; Marx et al., 1997). Third, when students publish what they create, it enhances their understanding. The artifacts that students develop make their understandings visible to others. Because artifacts are concrete and explicit, they allow students to share and have their artifacts reviewed by others – teachers, students, parents, and members of the community (Scardamalia & Bereiter, this volume). Critiquing supports the development of student understanding by providing feedback about what the student knows and doesn't know, permitting learners to reflect on and revise their work.

Lesson 5 a: Giving Feedback

Learning sciences research shows that providing feedback on the artifacts that students develop is critical to the learning process (Koedinger & Corbett, this volume; Kolodner, this volume). But unfortunately, teachers rarely give extensive feedback to students. Teachers with large classes and numerous sections do not have enough time in a day or week to give high quality and individual feedback to students. In addition, many middle school science teachers lack knowledge of how to give quality feedback to students.

To help teachers give valuable feedback to students, we provide them with written descriptions of different levels of quality for student performance, to be used for scoring and giving feedback. By providing a common and consistent set of rubrics for PBS tasks such as developing driving questions and providing explanations, teachers learn how to give feedback and students learn how to further their understanding. Teachers have also developed some worthwhile techniques. Many teachers who have large numbers of students per classroom, or who teach the same course to multiple sections, give group feedback. Although not as effective as individual feedback, group feedback does support learning.

Scaling Up

One of the core goals of the Center for Learning Technologies in Urban Schools (LeTUS) (Blumenfeld et al., 2000; Marx et al., 2004) was to work with teachers and administrators to scale the use of project-based science throughout the middle schools in the Detroit Public School System (see Dede, this volume). Throughout the existence of LeTUS, Detroit public schools increasingly adopted the units. In the 1998–1999 school year, our first year of using the projects beyond initial pilot sites, thirteen teachers across ten schools used at least one of the curriculum units. In 2003–2004, sixty-three teachers in twenty-six schools used and completed the enactment of at least one of the units.

Student performance on curriculum-based posttests, compared to their pretest performance, showed statistically significantly gains across all projects in Detroit (Marx et al., 2004). For example, in both the 1998/1999 and the 2000/2001 school year, students using the Air Quality unit showed statistically significant learning gains.[3] Three reasons help explain these gains: (1) each year we revised the materials based on analysis of the test scores and observations of classroom enactments, (2) our professional development efforts became more focused (Fishman et al., 2003), and (3) teachers gained experience in using the materials.

In addition to showing learning gains on curriculum-based pre- and posttests, we also have examined student performance on Michigan's state standardized examination – the Michigan Educational Assessment Program. The findings show that students in Detroit who used at least one LeTUS unit did statistically and substantially better on the required state science test than a matched group of students who did not use the LeTUS materials (Geier et al., in press). Moreover, students who used more than one LeTUS unit did significantly better on the state examination than students who used only one LeTUS unit. Our studies of student motivation show that students' attitudes in science remain positive (Blumenfeld et al., this volume; Blumenfeld et al., 2005). This is an important finding, considering that the literature reports that students' attitudes toward science typically decrease substantially during the middle school years (Yager & Penick, 1986).

Findings from other studies that examined student learning in project-based environments also corroborate the findings from our work in LeTUS (Tinker & Krajcik, 2001; Williams & Linn, 2003; Schneider et al., 2001). Taken as a whole, these findings demonstrate that carefully designed, developed and enacted projects result in substantial learning gains.

In order to scale up, we found that we needed to develop what Ball and Cohen (1996) call highly *specified* and *developed* materials. *Specification* refers to the explicitness of curriculum materials. Our materials clearly specify the design principles, intended teaching practices, and desired learning goals, and describe why these are important in enacting PBS. *Development* refers to the provision of resources required to enact the various units, including materials for students and teachers, professional development, and examples of teaching practice.

The drawback to becoming more developed is that the materials are somewhat closed compared to our original vision of PBS. We originally hoped it would be possible for teachers to create projects tailored to their students and community. Although a few teachers can do this, most teachers do not have the time to develop projects; however, highly developed and specified does not mean a return to cookbook experiments or to teacher proof curriculum. Instead, we provide teachers with models of how to enact project-based science and strategies to help learners engage in scientific practices.

Conclusion

Since beginning our efforts in the early 1990s, we have learned how to better design project-based environments. We learned the importance of selecting driving questions that can help students meet important learning goals and the importance of helping students see the value of the driving question. We learned the challenges of using technology and explored various techniques to integrate technology throughout the curriculum. We also learned the importance of supporting teachers in complex instruction by providing them with explicit strategies.

We have learned about how to help teachers do project based science by developing highly developed and highly specified materials. The materials focus instruction on a driving question that students find meaningful and important, and around which students can develop an understanding of central learning goals. Using these materials, teachers can engage students in scientific investigations, make use of cognitive tools, promote collaboration, and teach them the deeper conceptual understanding that traditional methods of instruction cannot.

Although our research has focused on project-based science, the lessons that we learned apply to any subject area. Projects are widely used in social studies, arts, and English classes. In these subjects, project ideas tend to be passed down by word of mouth, or are developed from scratch by teachers themselves. For the most part these projects are not based in learning sciences research, and researchers have not examined the most effective ways to design these projects. The lessons that we've learned from our research can improve the educational effectiveness of projects in all subjects, because our research is based on core learning sciences principles, and our designs have become progressively better through a process of iterative design experiments (Barab, this volume; Confrey, this volume). As such, they can provide a model for applying project-based methods to classrooms across the curriculum.

Acknowledgments

This research is partially funded by the Center for Curriculum Materials in Science through a grant from the Center for Learning and Teaching, grant number #0227557, from the National Science Foundation. However, any opinions, findings, and conclusions or recommendations expressed in this publication are those of the authors.

We are grateful for the thorough and thoughtful feedback provided by Professor Keith Sawyer and students in his 2005 Central Topics in Learning Sciences Research course.

Professor Krajcik completed work on this manuscript while at the Weizmann Institute of Science in Israel as the Weston Visiting Professor of Science Education.

Footnotes

1. You can learn more about and view the materials online at http://www.hice.org/know.
2. You can learn more about the technology tools at www.goknow.com/Products/Artemis.
3. Readers can learn more about our assessment procedures in the following manuscripts: Marx et al. (2004), Rivet and Krajcik (2004), and McNeill and Krajcik (in press).

References

American Association for the Advancement of Science. (1989). *Science for all Americans*. New York: Oxford Press.

Atkin, J. M., & Coffey, J. E. (2003). *Everyday assessment in the science classroom (science educators' essay collection)*. Arlington, VA: National Science Teachers Associations.

Atwater, M. (1994). Research on cultural diversity in the classroom. In D. L. Gabel (Ed.), *Handbook of research on science teaching and learning* (pp. 558–576). New York: Macmillan.

Azmitia, M. (1996). Peer interactive minds: Developmental, theoretical, and methodological issues. In P. B. Baltes & U. M. Staudinger (Eds.), *Interactive minds: Life-span perspectives on the social foundation of cognition* (pp. 133–162). New York: Cambridge.

Ball, D. L., & Cohen, D. K. (1996). Reform by the book: What is – or might be – the role of curriculum materials in teacher learning and instructional reform? *Educational Researcher, 25*(9), 6–8.

Blumenfeld, P., Fishman, B. J., Krajcik, J., Marx, R. W., & Soloway, E. (2000). Creating usable innovations in systemic reform: Scaling-up technology-embedded project-based science in urban schools. *Educational Psychologist, 35*, 149–164.

Blumenfeld, P. C., Krajcik, J. S., Kam, R., Kempler, T. M., & Geier, R. (2005, April). *Opportunity to learn in PBL for middle school science: Predicting urban student achievement and motivation*. Paper presented at the Annual Meeting of the American Association for Research in Education, Montreal, Canada.

Blumenfeld, P. C., Krajcik, J, Marx, R. W., & Soloway, E. (1994) Lessons learned: A collaborative model for helping teachers learn project-based instruction. *Elementary School Journal, 94*(5), 539–551.

Blumenfeld, P. C., Marx, R. W., Krajcik, J. S., & Soloway, E. (1996). Learning with peers: From small group cooperation to collaborative communities. *Educational Researcher, 25*(8), 37–40.

Blumenfeld, P., Soloway, E., Marx, R. W., Krajcik, J. S., Guzdial, M., & Palincsar, A. (1991). Motivating project-based learning: Sustaining the doing, supporting the learning. *Educational Psychologist, 26*, 369–398.

Bransford, J., Brown, A. L., & Cocking, R. R. (1999). *How people learn: Brain, mind, experience, and school*. Washington, DC: National Academy Press.

Brown, A. L., & Campione, J. C. (1994). Guided discovery in a community of learners. In K. McGilly (Ed.), *Classroom lessons: Integrating cognitive theory and classroom practice* (pp. 229–270). Cambridge, MA: MIT Press.

Cognition and Technology Group at Vanderbilt. (1992). The Jasper series as an example of anchored instruction: Theory, program description, and assessment data. *Educational Psychologist, 27*, 291–315.

Csikszentmihalyi, M., Rathunde, K., & Whalen, S. (1993). *Talented teenagers: The roots of success and failure*. New York: Cambridge University Press.

Davis, E. A., & Krajcik, J. S. (2005). Designing educative curriculum materials to promote teacher learning. *Educational Researcher, 34*(3), 3–14.

Dewey, J. (1959). *Dewey on education*. New York: Teachers College Press.

Edelson, D. C. (2001). Learning-for-use: A framework for integrating content and process learning in the design of inquiry activities. *Journal of Research in Science Teaching, 38*, 355–385.

Fishman, B., Marx, R., Best, S., & Tal, R. (2003). Linking teacher and student learning to improve professional development in systemic reform. *Teaching and Teacher Education, 19*(6), 643–658.

Fishman, B., Marx, R., Blumenfeld, P., Krajcik, J. S., & Soloway, E. (2004). Creating a framework for research on systemic technology innovations. *Journal of the Learning Sciences,* 13(1), 43–76.

Fretz, E. B., Wu, H.-K., Zhang, B., Krajcik, J. S., Davis, E. A., & Soloway, E. (2002). An Investigation of software scaffolds as they support modeling practices, *Research in Science Education,* 32(4), 567–589.

Gardner, H. (1991). *The unschooled mind: How children think and how schools should teach.* New York: Basic Books.

Geier, R., Blumenfeld, P., Marx, R., Krajcik, J., Fishman, B., & Soloway, E. (in press). Standardized test outcomes of urban students participating in standards and project based science curricula. *Journal of Research in Science Teaching.*

Haberman, M. (1991). The pedagogy of poverty versus good teaching. *Phi Delta Kappan,* 73(4), 290–294.

Heubel-Drake, M., Finkel, L., Stern, E., & Mouradian, M. (1995). Planning a course for success. *The Science Teacher,* 62, 18–21.

Hoffman, J., Wu, H-K, Krajcik, J. S., & Soloway, E. (2003). The nature of middle school learners' science content understandings with the use of on-line resources. *Journal of Research in Science Teaching,* 40(3), 323–346.

Hogan, K., & Maglienti, M. (2001). Comparing the epistemological underpinnings of students' and scientists' reasoning about conclusions. *Journal of Research in Science Teaching,* 38(6), 663–687.

Hug, B., & Krajcik, J. (2002). Students, scientific practices using a scaffolded inquiry sequence. In P. Bell, R. Stevens, & T. Satwicz (Eds.), *Keeping learning complex: The proceedings of the Fifth International Conference for the Learning Sciences (ICLS).* Mahwah, NJ: Earlbaum.

Hurd, P. D. (1970). *New directions in teaching secondary school science.* Chicago: Rand McNally.

Kesidou, S., & Roseman, J. E. (2002). How well do middle school science programs measure up? Findings from Project 2061's curriculum review. *Journal of Research in Science Teaching,* 39(6), 522–549.

Krajcik, J., Blumenfeld, P. C., Marx, R. W., Bass, K. M., Fredricks, J., & Soloway, E. (1998). Inquiry in project-based science classrooms: Initial attempts by middle school students. *Journal of the Learning Sciences,* 7, 313–350.

Krajcik, J. S., Blumenfeld, P. C., Marx, R. W., & Soloway, E. (1994). A collaborative model for helping middle grade teachers learn project-based instruction. *The Elementary School Journal,* 94(5), 483–497.

Krajcik, J. S., Czerniak, C. M., & Berger, C. F. (2002). *Teaching science in elementary and middle school classrooms: A project-based approach (2nd ed.).* New York: McGraw Hill.

Linn, M. C. (1997). Learning and instruction in science education: Taking advantage of technology. In D. Tobin & B. J. Fraser (Eds.), *International handbook of science education* (pp. 265–294). The Netherlands: Kluwer.

Marx, R. W., Blumenfeld, P. C., Krajcik, J. S., Fishman, B., Soloway, E., Geier, R., & Revital, T. T. (2004). Inquiry-based science in the middle grades: Assessment of learning in urban systemic reform. *Journal of Research in Science Teaching,* 41(10), 1063–1080.

Marx, R. W., Blumenfeld, P., Krajcik, J., & Soloway, E. (1997). Enacting project-based science. *Elementary School Journal,* 97(4), 341–358.

McNeill, K. L., & Krajcik, J. S. (in press). Middle school students' use of evidence and reasoning in writing scientific explanations. In M. Lovet & P. Shah (Eds.), *Thinking with data: The proceedings of the 33rd Carnegie symposium on cognition.*

Metcalf-Jackson, S., J. S. Krajcik, & E. Soloway. (2000). Model-It: A design retrospective. In M. Jacobson & R. B. Kozma, (Eds.), *Innovations in science and mathematics education: Advanced designs for technologies and learning.* Mahwah, NJ: Lawrence Erlbaum Associates, pp. 77–116.

Moje, E. B., Peek-Brown, D., Sutherland, L. M., Marx, R. W., Blumenfeld, P., & Krajcik, J. (2004). Explaining explanations: Developing scientific literacy in middle-school project-based science reforms. In D. Strickland & D. E. Alvermann, (Eds.), *Bridging the gap: Improving literacy learning for preadolescent and adolescent learners in grades 4–12* (pp. 227–251). New York: Teachers College Press.

National Research Council. (1996). *National science education standards.* Washington, DC: National Research Council.

Novak, A., & Gleason, C. (2001). Incorporating portable technology to enhance an inquiry, project-based middle school science classroom. In R. Tinker & J. S. Krajcik (Eds.), *Portable technologies: science learning in context* (pp. 29–62). The Netherlands: Kluwer.

Novak, A., & Krajcik, J. S. (2004). Using learning technologies to support inquiry in middle school science. In L. Flick & N. Lederman (Eds.), *Scientific inquiry and nature of science: Implications for teaching, learning, and teacher education* (pp. 75–102). The Netherlands: Kluwer Publishers.

O'Neill, K., & Polman, J. L. (2004). Why educate "little scientists"? Examining the potential of practice-based scientific literacy. *Journal of Research in Science Teaching, 41*(3), 234–266.

Palincsar, A., Anderson, C. S., & David, Y. M. (1993). Pursuing scientific literacy in the middle grades through collaborative problem solving. *The Elementary School Journal, 93*, 643–658.

Pellegrino, J. W., Chudowsky, N., & Glaser, R. (2001). *Knowing what students know: The science and design of educational assessment.* Washington, DC: National Academy Press.

Perkins, D., D. Crismond, Simmons, R., & Unger, C. (1995). Inside understanding. In D. Perkins, J. Schwartz, M. West, & M. Wiske (Eds.), *Software goes to school: Teaching for understanding with new technologies* (pp. 70 –88). New York: Oxford University Press.

Polman, J. (1999). *Designing project-based science: Connecting learners through guided inquiry.* New York: Teachers College Press.

Reiser, B. J. (2004). Scaffolding complex learning: The mechanisms of structuring and problematizing student work. *Journal of the Learning Sciences, 13*(3), 273–304.

Reiser, B. J., Krajcik, J., Moje, E. B., & Marx, R. (2003, March). *Design strategies for developing science instructional materials.* Paper presented at the Annual Meeting of the National Association of Research in Science Teaching, Philadelphia, PA.

Rivet, A., & Krajcik, J. (2002). Contextualizing instruction: Leveraging students' prior knowledge and experiences to foster understanding of middle school science. In P. Bell, R. Stevens, & T. Satwicz (Eds.), *Keeping learning complex: The proceedings of the fifth international conference for the learning sciences (ICLS).* Mahwah, NJ: Earlbaum.

Rivet, A., & Krajcik, J. (2004). Achieving standards in urban systemic reform: An example of a sixth grade project-based science curriculum. *Journal of Research in Science Teaching 41*(7), 669–692.

Ruopp, R. R., Gal, S., Drayton, B., & Pfister, M. (Eds.). (1992). *LabNet: Toward a community of practice.* Hillsdale, NJ: Lawrence Erlbaum Associates.

Rutherford, J. F. (1964). The role of inquiry in science teaching." *Journal of Research in Science Teaching, 2*(2), 80–84.

Sadler, T. D. (2004). Informal reasoning regarding socioscientific issues: A critical review of research. *Journal of Research in Science Teaching, 41*(5), 513–536.

Salomon, G., D. N. Perkins, & Globerson, T. (1991). Partners in cognition: Extending human intelligence with intelligent technologies. *Educational Researcher, 20,* 2–9.

Sandoval, W. A., & Reiser, B. J. (2004). Explanation-driven inquiry: Integrating conceptual and epistemic scaffolds for scientific inquiry. *Science Education, 88*(3), 345–372.

Schneider, R. M., Krajcik, J., Marx, R., & Soloway, E. (2001). Performance of student in project-based science classrooms on a national measure of science achievement. *Journal of Research in Science Teaching, 38*(7), 821–842.

Schofield, J. W. (1995). *Computers and classroom culture.* Cambridge: Cambridge University Press.

Scott, C. (1994). Project-based science: Reflections of a middle school teacher. *The Elementary School Journal, 95*(1), 75–94.

Sherwood, R., Kinzer, C. K., Bransford, J. D., & Franks, J. J. (1987). Some benefits of creating macro-contexts for science instruction: Initial findings. *Journal of Research in Science Teaching, 24*(5), 417–435.

Singer, J., Marx, R. W., Krajcik, J., & Chambers, J. C. (2000). Constructing extended inquiry projects: Curriculum materials for science education reform. *Educational Psychologist, 35,* 165–178.

Spitulnik, M. W., Stratford, S., Krajcik, J., & Soloway, E. (1997). Using technology to support student's artifact construction in science. In B. J. Fraser & K. Tobin (Eds.), *International handbook of science education* (pp. 363–382). Netherlands: Kluwer Publishers.

Stratford, S. J., Krajcik, J., & Soloway, E. (1998). Secondary students' dynamic modeling processes: Analyzing, reasoning about, synthesizing, and testing models of stream ecosystems. *Journal of Science Education and Technology,* 7(3), 215–234.

Tinker, R. (1997). *Thinking about science.* http://www.concord.org/library/papers.html. Cambridge, MA: Concord Consortium.

Tinker, R., & Krajcik, J. S. (Eds.) (2001). *Portable technologies: Science learning in context. Innovations in science education and technology.* New York, Kluwer Academic/Plenum Publishers.

Wiggins, G., & McTighe, J. (1998). *Understanding by design.* Alexandria, VA: Association for Supervision and Curriculum Development.

Williams, M., & Linn, M. (2003). WISE Inquiry in fifth grade biology. *Research in Science Education,* 32(4), 415–436.

Yager, R. E., & J. E. Penick (1986). Perceptions of four age groups toward science classes, teachers, and the value of science. *Science Education,* 70(4), 355–363.

CHAPTER 20

Making Authentic Practices Accessible to Learners

Design Challenges and Strategies

Daniel C. Edelson and Brian J. Reiser

In recent years, it has become increasingly common for researchers and educators to advocate engaging learners in authentic practices as part of their learning experiences.[1] In the United States, authentic practices are central to many educational standards documents. For example, the *National Geographic Standards* argue that "students should be given the opportunity to ask geographic questions, acquire geographic information, organize geographic information, analyze geographic information, and answer geographic questions" (Geography Education Standards Project, 1994, p. 47). These are the same tasks that geographers and others who use geographic knowledge perform in the course of their professional practice. Similarly, the *National Science Education Standards* state, "Students at all grade levels and in every domain of science should have the opportunity to use scientific inquiry and develop the ability to think and act in ways associated with inquiry..." (National Research Council, 1996, p. 10).

The arguments for engaging learners in authentic practices tend to focus on three

benefits. First, learning to participate in a particular practice may be valuable to a population of students because they will engage in that practice outside of the learning environment. Second, engaging learners in authentic practices can provide a meaningful context that may increase their motivation to learn and may improve their learning of content by focusing their attention in ways that will enhance their ability to apply what they have learned in the future (Edelson, 2001; Kolodner et al., 2003; Rivet, 2003). Third, engaging learners in authentic practices can assist them in understanding the structure of knowledge, or the *epistemology*, of the domain under study. Researchers are increasingly recognizing the importance of epistemology as an element of subject matter understanding and as an organizing feature of that understanding (Smith et al., 2000; Elby & Hammer, 2001). Often, the practices of a discipline are the most obvious representation of its epistemology.

Engaging students in authentic practices raises a number of challenges for designers of learning experiences. Although any specific authentic practice presents its own challenges, there are some challenges that are common across a wide range of practices. Two critical pedagogical challenges are:

1. helping students deal with the complexity of authentic practices, and
2. helping them to understand the rationale for the elements of these practices.

Two practical challenges also arise in the implementation of authentic practices. First, teachers may have never incorporated such practices into their instruction in the past or even engaged in the practices themselves. Second, teachers have limited time and resources to support the implementation of learning activities that engage students in authentic practices.

To respond to these four challenges, it is necessary to take a systemic perspective in design. It is not sufficient to alter one of the components of the learning environment – such as the tools learners use – without changing the tasks that structure the learning or the ways that learners interact with one another and with teachers (Blumenfeld et al., 2000; Tabak, 2004; Edelson, Gordin, & Pea, 1999). In this chapter, we focus on three critical elements that any design must address:

- the activities in which learners are engaged, that is, the curriculum;
- the tools and resources in the learning environment;
- the social structures that learners participate in, including facilitation and instruction by the teacher.

For illustrative purposes, we describe four design strategies in this chapter that we have used to address these challenges:

- *Situate authentic practices in meaningful contexts.* To provide students with a sense of purpose and to help them understand the rationale for authentic practices, the practices must be integrated into a curriculum that is motivated by goals that are meaningful to learners.

- *Reduce the complexity of authentic practices.* The practices used by highly trained professionals are typically complicated and unfamiliar to nonexperts. To reduce the cognitive load required to master authentic practices, learning environments should scaffold students by reducing the complexity of the practices, while retaining their key elements.

- *Make implicit elements of authentic practices explicit.* During years of training, professionals internalize elements of practice and are able to execute those elements efficiently and rapidly. But if these elements remain implicit, students can never gain access to them. Learning environments should make the implicit elements of authentic practice explicit, so that they can be examined, discussed, and mastered.

- *Sequence learning activities according to a developmental progression.* To allow students to develop the skills and knowledge to successfully engage in authentic practices, learning environments should sequence activities so that they bridge from students' prior knowledge, abilities, and experiences to the authentic practices.

In this chapter, we focus on a particular example of an authentic practice that has been a primary focus of the research of both authors, the analysis of archival data in science to reach and justify conclusions in an investigation. We organize this discussion around three components of this authentic practice that we have focused on in our research: *analysis and interpretation of data, construction and justification of a conclusion for an audience,* and *reflection.* All three are heavily intertwined. The first two are distinguished by their relative emphasis on sense-making and communication. The third, reflection, is a metacognitive practice that supports the other two.

Although the stages of inquiry are typically cyclical and difficult to distinguish in practice, we find it helpful to draw a distinction between the stage of inquiry in which an investigator is primarily attempting to make sense of the data to reach a conclusion, and the stage in which he or she is attempting to construct an argument that uses the data to support the conclusion. We characterize the earlier sense-making stage as the practice of *data analysis and interpretation*. We characterize the later process of constructing the argument as both *construction* and *justification* because the justification captures the importance of constructing an explanation or argument that can be defended. Analysis and interpretation is an explanatory sense–making process, whereas construction and justification of a conclusion emphasize the rhetorical goals of communication and persuasion, organized around the scientific practices of argumentation (Bell & Linn, 2000; Kyza, 2004; Sandoval, 2003; Sandoval & Reiser, 2004).

The third practice that we focus on in this chapter is reflection. The goal of reflection is to be aware of the progress one is making toward the goals of interpretation and justification, in order to make good decisions about how to proceed. When an individual is being reflective, he or she has a plan in mind, monitors his or her progress, modifies the plan when appropriate, and makes informed judgments about when he or she is done (Chi et al., 1989; Palincsar & Brown, 1984; Schoenfeld, 1987).

We discuss the challenges of making these authentic inquiry activities accessible to learners in the context of two cases of middle school curriculum units: one on physical geography and climate, entitled Planetary Forecaster (Edelson et al., 2004) and one on adaptation and natural selection entitled The Struggle for Survival (Reiser et al., 2000). In Planetary Forecaster, students use a visualization and analysis environment for geographic data called WorldWatcher (Edelson et al., 1997), and in Struggle for Survival, students use a visualization and analysis environment for population biology data called The Galapagos Finches (Tabak et al., 2000). WorldWatcher enables students to visualize global geographic data in the form of color maps (Figure 20.1) and analyze it using simple arithmetic and statistical operations.

Galapagos Finches enables students to construct a variety of types of graphs to make comparisons across different subsets of the population or periods of time (Figure 20.2).

In the following sections, we describe the challenges learners face with each component of data analysis, and how we have used the four design strategies described above to address those challenges.

Analyzing and Interpreting Data

The first authentic practice we discuss is the use of computational tools to analyze and interpret archival data. This is one aspect of the larger practice that Quintana et al. (2004) call *sense-making*. In the context of the cases we consider here, this practice includes:

- selecting a subset of available data to work with,
- inspecting individual data items or subsets,
- selecting and performing analytical operations on the data,
- constructing visual representations (visualizations) of the data,
- finding patterns in representations of data, including coordinating among multiple representations,
- constructing and articulating interpretations of the data, and
- comparing and negotiating interpretations with others.

Each of these component practices is complex in and of itself. To engage in these practices effectively, students need to understand the goals of the practices, the mechanics of conducting them, and the results or products. The cognitive load involved in engaging in the combination of these components is substantial for a novice. However, separating the components from each other during the learning process would decontextualize them, and in any case would not reduce the overall cognitive load, because

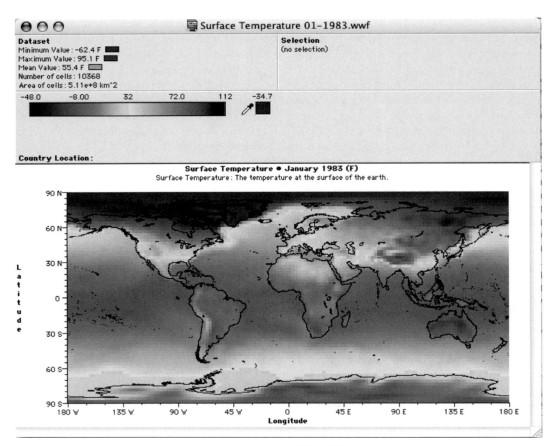

Figure 20.1. A color map visualization from WorldWatcher (Edelson et al., 1997).

students would then have to learn to combine them.

Supporting Analysis and Interpretation Through Curriculum Design

The overall structure provided by both Planetary Forecaster and Struggle for Survival helps make authentic practices accessible by situating the practices in a meaningful context, and by sequencing learning activities according to a developmental progression.

Both Planetary Forecaster and Struggle for Survival use a project-based science approach (Krajcik & Blumenfeld, this volume) to situate authentic practices in a meaningful context. A project-based science unit contextualizes learning through a driving goal or question. In the case of Plane-

tary Forecaster, the goal is to model temperatures on a fictitious planet in order to identify areas that are appropriate for colonization. In the case of Struggle for Survival, the students' goal is to determine what caused many finches on the Galapagos island Daphne Major to die over a relatively short period of time during the 1970s and what enabled some to survive, a scientific puzzle drawn from the research literature. In both of these cases, the students are offered access to data sets and analysis tools to pursue these goals. Middle school students in classroom trials have found these project scenarios to be motivating (Pitts & Edelson, 2004).

Both curriculum units sequence activities according to a developmental progression, using a sequencing strategy we call *expression*

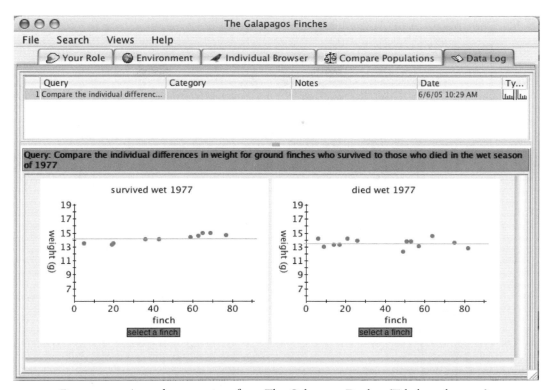

Figure 20.2. A graph comparison from The Galapagos Finches (Tabak et al., 2000).

before interpretation. In this sequence, students use the representation to express their existing understanding before using the representation to understand an unfamiliar phenomenon. This technique provides a bridge from students' current understandings to more advanced understandings, including the ability to manipulate and revise representations (cf. Lehrer & Schauble, this volume). For example, in Planetary Forecaster, students' first use of the color map representation – which uses different colors for different numerical values, like the weather maps of temperature seen on the evening news or in the newspaper – is through an activity in which they draw temperature maps with crayons on paper that represent their understanding of global temperature patterns at the beginning of the unit. As the unit proceeds, they use a paint tool in WorldWatcher to input their handdrawn maps into the computer, and finally they use the data interpretation and analysis tools within World-Watcher to compare their maps to actual data. In Struggle for Survival, students construct graphs of the sort used in Galapagos Finches on paper with crayons or markers before moving on to the activities where they interpret those representations in the software.

In this progression, their first use of the representation is for expression; they are using it to represent their own ideas. The representation is also created using the familiar medium of crayons and paper, which allows them to focus on expressing their ideas before having to focus on the unfamiliar medium of the software. The progression helps them to bridge to the computer-based representations described in the next section by allowing them to move their representation to the computer and start to interact with archival data and analysis tools within the context of the familiar representation of their own understanding.

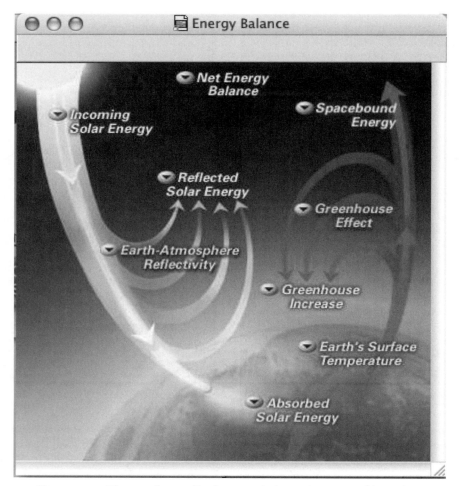

Figure 20.3. The interface to Earth energy balance data in WorldWatcher.

Tools to Support Analysis and Interpretation

The software tools used in Planetary Forecaster and Struggle for Survival reduce complexity by scaffolding three different authentic practices: selecting data to investigate, constructing data representations, and interpreting data representations.

SUPPORT FOR SELECTING DATA

Selecting the appropriate data to investigate for a particular question was a challenge for students, because they are not well versed in the concepts and vocabulary of the scientific domain. The typical interface for selecting data in an experts' software tool has users select data by choosing from a list of variable names using scientific terms that are unfamiliar to students – for example, insolation and albedo.

In the case of WorldWatcher, the designers chose to address this challenge by providing an interface to the data that is structured around a graphical, conceptual representation of the phenomena under study. For the data used in Planetary Forecaster, WorldWatcher displays a diagram of energy transfer in the Earth/atmosphere system (Figure 20.3). To select data to visualize and analyze, students select the corresponding element in the diagram (e.g., incoming solar energy). This diagram is less challenging than traditional interfaces

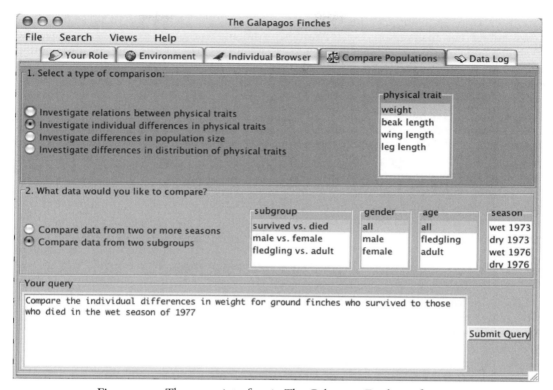

Figure 20.4. The query interface in The Galapagos Finches software.

because it provides students with a conceptual representation of the domain and it uses more familiar terminology, such as "incoming solar energy" instead of "insolation."

The Galapagos Finches software helps students to select data by using a different type of representation of the domain. In this case, the interface is organized according to discipline-specific strategies for analyzing data, such as longitudinal (i.e., "seasons") or cross-sectional (i.e., "subgroups") comparisons. Galapagos Finches contains a conceptually organized template that students use to specify analyses to perform (Figure 20.4). This interface requires students to communicate their desired queries in terms of disciplinary strategies. As with WorldWatcher, they are able to construct their queries using familiar vocabulary. To select an analysis, students identify what they want to compare in terms of strategic distinctions; for example, examining how a variable is distributed

or how a variable is related to another variable. Because students are forced to formulate their queries using authentic disciplinary strategies, while using familiar vocabulary, authentic expert strategies are made visible.

SUPPORT FOR CONSTRUCTING DATA
REPRESENTATIONS

In both WorldWatcher and The Galapagos Finches, data and the results of operations are displayed using visual representations. In the case of WorldWatcher, numerical values are represented as colored sections of a map, and in Galapagos Finches, numerical values are represented on a variety of 2D graphs. In both cases, we felt that the difficulty of constructing the representations – for example, specifying the ranges on axes – did not have enough educational benefit to merit the time and effort that it would require for students to do it themselves, particularly because these actions would take attention away from interpreting the representations. For that reason, both World-Watcher and Galapagos Finches automate nonsalient portions of tasks to reduce cognitive demands (Quintana et al., 2004): the software automatically sets display parameters for the representations without requiring any action on the part of the student. For example, in WorldWatcher, the software displays data with an appropriate color scheme and scale from minimum to maximum for the variable. Similarly, Galapagos Finches selects the most appropriate graph type and range for the data values that the user has chosen to display.

SUPPORT FOR INTERPRETING DATA
REPRESENTATIONS

Interpreting visual data representations is the central element of data analysis in the Planetary Forecaster and Struggle for Survival units. In both cases, we took advantage of two supports for interpreting visual representations that computers make possible. First, we developed interactive representations that allow users to sample one datum at a time. For example, in WorldWatcher, as the user moves the cursor over a map, a dynamic readout displays the data value and the latitude and longitude at the location of the cursor. Second, we developed multiple linked representations (Kaput, 1989; Kozma et al., 1996). For example, in Galapagos Finches, the user can click on any point in a graph representing a value from an individual finch and the software will display an image of that individual, with all of the data in that individual's record in the database. Both of these features scaffold complex practices by providing additional information or simplifying potentially complex operations.

Using Social Structures to Support Interpretation

As with most designs for project-based science, both Planetary Forecaster and Struggle for Survival engage students in collaborative work in small groups. Group work helps to make authentic practices accessible by reducing the complexity of those practices: students working in groups can manage the cognitive load of the task by distributing responsibility, assigning different elements of the practice to different members of the group.

For example, when students are conducting data analyses using WorldWatcher or Galapagos Finches, we frequently observed a division of cognitive labor in which one student takes responsibility for manipulating the software and one or more other students take responsibility for directing that student and monitoring his or her activities, or for recording important results in their lab notebooks. It was common for one student to unknowingly make a small error in execution and have it be caught by a partner. To take advantage of this type of distributed cognition (Hollan et al., 2000), the activities in both Planetary Forecaster and Struggle for Survival are conducted by students in pairs or small groups.

Another social structure that helps to make authentic practices accessible is to have multiple groups work independently on the same task. For example, in Struggle for Survival, different project groups use the Galapagos Finches software to conduct simultaneous investigations of the causes of differential finch survival. Throughout the investigation, student groups are encouraged to share their interpretations and findings, pointing each other toward useful data in the system. This allows students to see how other students approach the same problem and interpret the data. As they reflect on the other groups' practices, those practices become more explicit to students. In this way, the community of learners contributes to individual learning.

Constructing and Justifying an Explanation

The second component of data analysis that we discuss in this chapter is the practice of constructing an explanation, expressing it in the form of an argument, and communicating it to an audience. These practices are hard for students; constructing an explanation and arguing with real data are complex tasks (Andriessen, this volume). Without support, students often fail to cite sufficient supporting evidence, and frequently do not articulate the reasoning that communicates to the audience why the particular data they have chosen help make the point they are trying to make. For example, students often display a graph but with no guidance for the audience about what to look for in the graph or why the graph is supposed to support a particular claim. Of course, students' explanations may be incomplete because their understanding is incomplete. However, in many cases, students' explanations do not do justice to the level of understanding they have reached within their research team, because they have not mastered the practice of constructing an explanation. In this section, we consider strategies for helping students construct and communicate explanations.

Curriculum Design to Support Explanation

The first challenge is to give students a reason to construct an explanation. Both Planetary Forecaster and Struggle for Survival address this challenge by providing students with an audience (real or pretend) for their explanations. For example, in Planetary Forecaster, students are asked to create a climate model and justify it for a fictitious space agency. In Struggle for Survival, students present their explanations and justifications to each other in a forum modeled on a scientific poster session.

Tools to Support Explanation

Tools can play a powerful role in helping students learn to engage in the construction and communication of explanations based on data. Andriessen (this volume) describes a wide range of software tools that scaffold the practice of argumentation. In our work, we have pursued strategies for supporting students by using both software tools and more traditional instructional materials such as worksheets. The structure provided by these tools makes the elements of explanatory practice explicit, so that students are aware both of what is expected and why the practice takes the form that it does. This explicit task structuring also reduces the complexity of practices by providing students with reminders of what they need to do, a default sequence for performing components of the task, and guidance for how to do them.

For example, as part of the Struggle for Survival unit, students are scaffolded in explanation construction with software called the ExplanationConstructor (Reiser et al., 2001; Sandoval, 2003; Sandoval & Reiser, 2004). The ExplanationConstructor is a computer-based notebook for constructing scientific arguments. It is designed to help make explicit the task of constructing an explanation and justifying it to an audience. Practicing scientists share many implicit understandings about explanation and argumentation: Questions can be investigated by comparing competing explanations; explanations should tell a causal story that resolves the research question; the central claims in the causal account must be backed up by empirical evidence; explanations that were pursued and then rejected because of disconfirming evidence should be included to make the final explanation stronger. ExplanationConstructor makes these implicit elements of scientific practice explicit.

As students begin to make sense of their findings in the Galapagos Finches, they start synthesizing an argument to support their conclusions in ExplanationConstructor. Using a simple outlining tool (Figure 20.5), students identify candidate explanations in response to each research question. The outline view of students' work reveals whether they have only pursued one explanation in response to a question, or have considered alternative explanations.

When students construct an explanation, they can link evidence to the explanation in order to support the empirically based

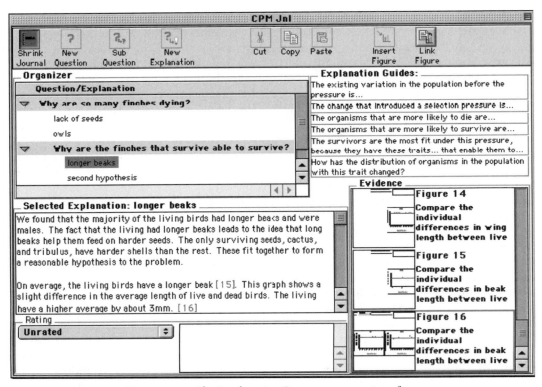

Figure 20.5. The ExplanationConstructor user interface.

claims in their account. These evidence links make explicit an important characteristic of scientific arguments – claims must be justified with evidence (Andriessen, this volume).

ExplanationConstructor also helps to make authentic practices accessible by reducing the complexity of constructing an explanation. The system contains *explanation guides* that articulate central constituents of particular explanatory frameworks – for example, natural selection. These guides help focus students on the critical constituent questions to address, and can help them organize their work into a coherent argument. For example, the explanation guides for natural selection ask students to identify an environmental stress, a variation in a population, and the survival advantage that some members of the population possess.

The approach taken in more recent work relies on more traditional support materials

to achieve some of these same goals. The What Will Survive unit is part of a middle grades series now under development called IQWST, Investigating and Questioning our World Through Sciences and Technology (Krajcik & Reiser, 2004). A central design principle in IQWST units is the scaffolding of scientific practices such as explanation, argumentation, and modeling (Andriessen, this volume; Kuhn & Reiser, 2005; McNeill & Krajcik, in press). In IQWST units, evidence-based explanations are structured into three important components: a *claim*, which states a position or answer to a question; *evidence* for the claim; and *reasoning*, which articulates how the evidence supports the claim, and includes how general scientific principles can be applied to the claim. This three-part framework is used to organize the worksheets that students use to report and justify their findings. The framework reminds students of the components they need to address, and provides a structure to organize their written explanations. This argument support system makes elements of authentic practice explicit by directing students' attention to important elements, and reduces complexity by providing a structure that students can use to map out and better communicate these elements.

Social Structures to Support Construction and Justification of Explanations

The practice of constructing an explanation and preparing an argument is a fundamentally social practice, because arguments are designed to be communicated to other members of the community. Researchers in the learning sciences have reported that engaging learners in authentic practices requires not only changing the cognitive aspects of the task but also the way learners interact with one another (Barron et al., 1998; Brown & Campione, 1994; Kolodner et al., 2003). This is particularly true for the practice of constructing an explanation. Learning environments should require students to prepare explanations, but also should prepare students to act as a critical audience and provide feedback to their peer's explanations.

One common learning sciences approach is to scaffold the classroom interaction by specifying different social roles for students. For example, in reciprocal teaching (Palincsar & Brown, 1984), different students are assigned different roles that together comprise the task of reading: questioning, summarizing, and predicting the future flow of the text. In a second example, Herrenkohl and colleagues (Herrenkohl & Guerra, 1998; Herrenkohl et al., 1999) assigned roles that corresponded to different aspects of the thinking practices that students were meant to learn. Some students played the role of questioning theories and predictions, while others focused on questioning results or making connections between results and theories.

The Struggle for Survival unit has a midpoint peer review activity when each group shares their in-progress explanations with another group. The audience is asked to provide constructive feedback, attending to whether the presenters have articulated their claims clearly, cited evidence, and explained the reasoning that makes clear why the evidence indeed supports the claim. Although this activity is challenging for learners, it creates opportunities for students to receive feedback early enough to act on it to improve their work, and can suggest alternative paths to pursue or flaws in their arguments that can be addressed. It also teaches them how to be a critical audience and teaches them that constructive feedback is an important element of scientific practice.

At the end of each unit, students participate in a *culminating task*: each research team presents their findings to the class, and audience members are charged with asking critical but constructive questions about the plausibility and support for the interpretations (Brown & Campione, 1994; Engle & Conant, 2002; Linn et al., 2004). Making the role of the audience explicit in this way is designed to teach students that the process of review and critique are important elements of authentic practices. The culminating task teaches students the authentic practice of constructing and communicating explanations. The ultimate purpose of scientific research is to communicate what has been learned, and to attempt to convince others in the community of the strength of the findings and interpretations.

Reflecting on Practice

Reflection is an important part of making authentic practices accessible, particularly with project-and-inquiry based teaching methods that require advance planning, ongoing monitoring and evaluation to track progress, and dynamic re-planning in response to the outcome of activities.

Supporting Reflection Through Curriculum Design

The first challenge to supporting students' engagement in reflection is helping them to understand the need for reflection. When students' experience is limited to assignments that they can complete within a class period or that are structured for them, they do not have the opportunity to engage in metacognitive monitoring and planning. For that reason, the principal characteristic of curriculum units that are intended to help students develop reflective practices is that they extend over a substantial period and give students responsibility for structuring their own activities. Because students may fail to recognize the need for reflective monitoring in their first experiences with long-term open-ended activities, it is likely that they will need multiple experiences with such activities to learn to recognize the need for reflection.

In a scientific investigation, both the investigator's understanding and the inquiry process itself can be objects for reflection. To elicit reflection about *understanding*, the activities we have designed require that students articulate hypotheses that represent their current understandings, examine and test their hypotheses, and revise them. In the case of the Planetary Forecaster curriculum, students formulate hypotheses about the geographic factors that affect Earth surface temperature, which they examine and test through discussions, hands-on laboratory activities, and investigation of archival temperature data. In the case of the Struggle for Survival curriculum, students formulate hypotheses about the reasons that some of the finches died and why others survived. They examine and revise these hypotheses through explorations of qualitative and quantitative data about the finches and their environments.

To elicit reflection about *the inquiry process*, these activities require students to plan and monitor their own investigations. In Struggle for Survival, students spend as many as eight class periods in an open-ended investigation of the data using the Galapagos Finches software. During that time, students are asked to investigate two questions: "What caused the unusually large number of deaths in one year?" and "Why did some sur-

vive while others did not?" Within that loose structure, students are given the responsibility for managing their own investigations with the data, and this requires that they plan and monitor their own activities.

Tools to Support Reflection

In our curricula, software tools provide a way for students to store ideas and artifacts so that they can become objects of reflection, and they provide explicit prompts for reflection. Many learning sciences projects support reflection with software tools that structure the steps in an investigation, making the implicit elements of expert practice explicit (Krajcik & Blumenfeld, this volume). This is the approach taken by WISE (Linn & Slotta, 2000), Symphony (Quintana et al., 2002), Knowledge Forum (Scardamalia & Bereiter, this volume), the Collaboratory Notebook (Edelson et al., 1996), and Project INQUIRE (Brunner, 1990). These tools provide students with a plan to follow and make it easy for them to monitor their progress.

To investigate the possibility for technology to support students in engaging in reflective practices, we developed an inquiry-support environment called the Progress Portfolio (Loh et al., 1997; Loh et al., 2001). The Progress Portfolio is a stand-alone computer application that provides a way for students to store text, graphics, and sound files. It allows students to capture images from other software applications (e.g., graphs from Galapagos Finches or visualizations from WorldWatcher), and place them in pages in the Progress Portfolio along with text or audio annotations. The Progress Portfolio scaffolds reflection by giving students the opportunity to record their current understandings and any products of their investigations.

The Progress Portfolio also has a mechanism for prompting students to reflect: Teachers and curriculum developers can create page templates that contain text prompts asking students to record specific text or graphics and asking them to reflect upon

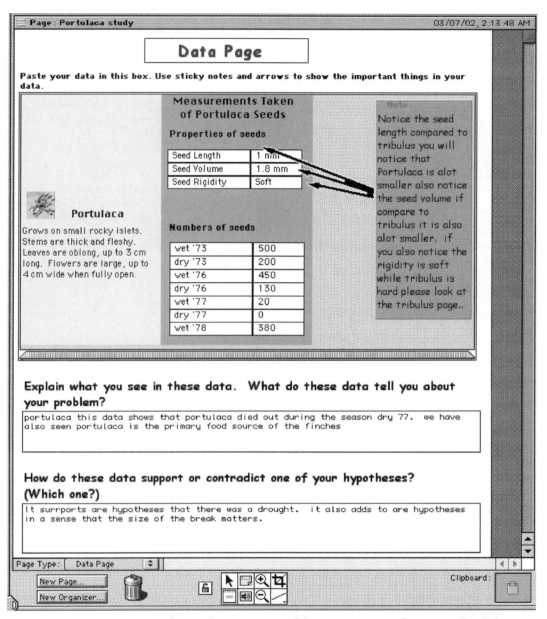

Figure 20.6. A Data Page template in the Progress Portfolio to encourage reflection in The Galapagos Finches investigation (Kyza, 2004).

them. For example, Figure 20.6 displays a "data page" template that was used for the Galapagos Finches investigation in a study by Kyza (2004). This template provides a box for students to paste a graph into with two reflective prompts underneath: "Explain what you see in these data? What do these data tell you about your problem?" and "How do these data support or contradict one of your hypotheses?" These prompts make explicit two elements of reflective inquiry. Kyza's case study provided compelling evidence that the Progress Portfolio encouraged reflective practices.

Table 20.1. Examples of Situating Practices in Meaningful Contexts

Practice	System Component	Challenge	Strategy
Analyzing and interpreting data	Curriculum	Motivating students to engage in interpretation	Project-based units in Planetary Forecaster and Struggle for Survival motivate investigations of data.
Justifying and communicating conclusions	Curriculum	Motivating students to support their arguments	What Will Survive and Looking at the Environment place students in the role of scientist who must develop and argue for a solution to an environmental problem.
Reflection	Curriculum	Helping students to understand the need for reflection.	Engage students in investigations that are sufficiently complex to require metacognitive planning and monitoring.

Supporting Reflection Through Social Structures

Our experiences indicate that working in cooperative dyads or triads enables students to engage in reflective inquiry practices by distributing cognitive and metacognitive tasks across the group. For example, in the case studies of pairs conducted by Kyza, we observed pairs of students working in a pattern where one student (typically the student at the keyboard) would be focused on the investigative activities while the other would be more reflective – monitoring progress, suggesting next steps, and composing responses to reflective prompts (Kyza, 2004). It would appear that the cognitive load of open-ended inquiry is such that, for students who are still learning to engage in these complex practices, distributing the load across a small number of students enables them to successfully integrate both cognitive and metacognitive practices in a way that they are not prepared to do individually. As with the practice of data analysis we described earlier, this distributed cognition scaffolds complex practices by reducing the individual cognitive load and increasing the diversity of abilities and knowledge available to engage in the practices.

Strategies for Making Authentic Practices Accessible

We chose these two case studies to demonstrate both the possibility of engaging students in complex, authentic practices, and the need for multifaceted design solutions to make these practices accessible – solutions that included curriculum, tools, and classroom social structures. In our discussion, we focused on four ways that these two learning environments make authentic practices accessible: situating practices in meaningful contexts, reducing complexity, making implicit elements of the practice explicit, and sequencing learning activities.

The first strategy, situating practices in meaningful contexts (see Table 20.1), addresses the need to motivate students to engage in particular authentic practices (Blumenfeld, Kempler, & Krajcik, this volume). Designers of learning environments can motivate students by creating a

Table 20.2. Examples of Reducing Complexity

Practice	System Component	Challenge	Strategy
Analyzing and interpreting data	Curriculum	Number of options to investigate in Struggle for Survival	Struggle for Survival separates interpretation process into discrete steps.
Analyzing and interpreting data	Tools	Lack of familiarity of students with available data to investigate	WorldWatcher offers support for selecting data to investigate through a diagrammatic interface to the data that reflects relationships among variables.
Analyzing and interpreting data	Tools	Setting up data representations takes time away from analysis and interpretation.	WorldWatcher and Galapagos Finches automatically set appropriate defaults for display of data representations.
Analyzing and interpreting data	Tools	Difficulty of interpreting complex data representation	Both WorldWatcher and Galapagos Finches offer interactive data sampling and multiple-linked representations.
Analyzing and interpreting data	Social structures	Cognitive load of demanding task	In both Struggle for Survival and Planetary Forecaster, students work in groups that distribute cognition across two or three students.
Justifying and communicating conclusions	Tools	Assembling the elements of an argument supported by evidence is challenging for students.	Both the ExplanationConstructor software used in Struggle for Survival and the worksheets used in What Will Survive provide students with templates to complete to justify conclusions.
Reflection	Tools	Capturing objects for reflection can be difficult.	The Progress Portfolio makes it easy for students to capture the intermediate products of investigations and store them as objects for reflection.
Reflection	Social structures	Balancing the demands of inquiry and reflection is challenging.	Distributing the cognitive load over members of a group makes reflective inquiry more tractable.

curricular context that provides meaning for the practices, either by situating them in the context of the real world settings in which those practices are conducted or by situating them in a context that taps into students' interests and concerns.

The second strategy, reducing complexity, responds to the challenge for learners of managing the multiple interacting elements of complex practices (see Table 20.2). The implementation of the strategy consists of reducing the cognitive load of the practice

Table 20.3. Examples of Making Elements of Authentic Practices Explicit

Practice	System Component	Challenge	Strategy
Analyzing and interpreting data	Tools	Helping students to understand discipline specific strategies for analysis (e.g., longitudinal vs. cross-sectional comparisons)	Galapagos Finches organizes its interface around these different strategies, making the differences and their results explicit.
Analyzing and interpreting data	Social structures	Understanding value of community knowledge-building in scientific inquiry.	Sharing findings across groups throughout an investigation is an explicit part of the Struggle for Survival social structure.
Justifying and communicating conclusions	Tools	Students do not appreciate the importance of supporting conclusions with evidence	Both the ExplanationConstructor software used in Struggle for Survival and the worksheets used in What Will Survive represent the elements of a well-supported argument explicitly.
Justifying and communicating conclusions	Social Structures	Students do not construct explanations or arguments with an audience in mind.	Create an explicit audience for intermediate and final work made up of the other members of the class, who provide feedback.
Reflection	Tools	Students do not know what the practices that comprise reflection are.	The Progress Portfolio provides prompts for specific elements of reflection, e.g., planning and evaluating progress.

by simplifying it in a variety of ways, such as separating it into discrete elements or automating portions of tasks for learners.

The third strategy, making elements of authentic practices explicit, addresses the challenge of helping students to understand what an unfamiliar practice actually consists of and what the rationale is for its elements (see Table 20.3). Designers implement this strategy by creating explicit representations of the elements of a practice that may not be apparent to an observer or novice practitioner.

The fourth strategy, sequencing learning activities according to a developmental progression, addresses the challenge of practices that are either conceptually difficult for learners or overwhelming in their complexity (see Table 20.4). In the developmental progression known as scaffolding and fading, sequencing is designed to reduce complexity (Collins, this volume). However, in the examples described in the previous section and summarized in Table 20.4, the primary challenge is conceptual difficulty, not overwhelming complexity. In the case of conceptual challenges, the learning activities are sequenced by providing learners with conceptual bridges to practices and knowledge that they already possess. Fading is not as important as is building conceptual bridges to existing knowledge.

Table 20.4. Example of Sequencing Learning Activities According to a Developmental Progression

Practice	System Component	Challenge	Strategy
Analyzing and interpreting data	Curriculum	Challenge of learning new data representations.	In Planetary Forecaster, students draw color maps of their prior conceptions of global temperature patterns on paper with crayons, before interpreting visualizations of data on the computer.
Analyzing and interpreting data	Tools	Challenge of learning new data representations	WorldWatcher has a tool to allow students to draw their own visualizations on the computer as a bridge between the familiar medium of crayons on paper and the computer medium.
Analyzing and interpreting data	Curriculum	Challenge of learning new data representations	In Struggle for Survival students construct graphs of different types on paper to plot familiar data before working with the unfamiliar data in The Galapagos Finches software.

Conclusion

If educators are to achieve the benefits of engaging students in authentic activities, they must address the significant challenges of introducing and supporting complex activities. The lesson of the research described here is that systemic design that attends to the challenges of authentic activities through a research-driven, iterative process can produce designs that enable teachers to engage students in authentic practices. This design process depends critically on insights from the design research methodologies used by learning scientists (Barab, this volume; Confrey, this volume). The starting point must be an understanding of authentic practices based on theory and prior research. The next stage is a process of principled, systemic design that is based on theory, prior research on design challenges, and existing system designs. This design process continues through an iterative process of design and formative evaluation that identifies unanticipated challenges and evaluates strategies to address them. As a community of researchers, the learning sciences have a great deal to contribute to this process and also to learn from it.

Acknowledgments

The work presented here represents several different collaborations extending over more than a decade among numerous educational researchers, developers, and practitioners – too many to name individually. Contributors to this work include members of the CoVis, SSciVEE, BGuILE, WorldWatcher, SIBLE, and IQWST Projects, as well as the Center for Learning Technologies in Urban Schools and the Center for Curriculum Materials in Science. This chapter is based on work supported in part by the National Science Foundation under grants numbers 9253462, 9454729, 9453715, 9720377, 9720383, 0227557 and by the McDonnell Foundation. Any opinions, findings, and conclusions or recommendations expressed in this material are those of the authors and do not necessarily reflect the views of the National Science Foundation.

Footnote

1. The term *authentic practice* can have many different meanings. In this chapter, we use the term to describe the activities through which experts in a domain apply their understanding to achieve valued goals. When we talk about engaging students in authentic practices, we are talking about developmentally appropriate versions of the authentic practices of experts.

References

Barron, B. J. S., Schwartz, D. L., Vye, N. J., Moore, A., Petrosino, A., Zech, L., et al. (1998). Doing with understanding: Lessons from research on problem- and project-based learning. *Journal of the Learning Sciences, 7*(3–4), 271–311.

Bell, P., & Linn, M. C. (2000). Scientific arguments as learning artifacts: Designing for learning from the web with KIE. *International Journal of Science Education, 22*, 797–817.

Blumenfeld, P. C., Fishman, B. J., Krajcik, J., Marx, R. W., & Soloway, E. (2000). Creating usable innovations in systemic reform: Scaling-up technology-embedded project-based science in urban schools. *Educational Psychologist, 35*, 149–164.

Brown, A. L., & Campione, J. C. (1994). Guided discovery in a community of learners. In K. McGilly (Ed.), *Classroom lessons: Integrating cognitive theory and classroom practice* (pp. 229–272). Cambridge, MA: MIT Press.

Brunner, C. (1990). *Designing INQUIRE* (Technical Report No. 50): Center for Children and Technology.

Chi, M. T. H., Bassok, M., Lewis, M. W., Reimann, P., & Glaser, R. (1989). Self-explanations: How students study and use examples in learning to solve problems. *Cognitive Science, 13*, 145–182.

Edelson, D. C. (2001). Learning-for-use: A framework for the design of technology-supported inquiry activities. *Journal of Research in Science Teaching, 38*(3), 355–385.

Edelson, D. C., Gordin, D. N., Clark, B. A., Brown, M., & Griffin, D. (1997). *Worldwatcher [Computer Software]*. Evanston, IL: Northwestern University.

Edelson, D. C., Gordin, D. N., & Pea, R. D. (1999). Addressing the challenges of inquiry-based learning through technology and curriculum design. *Journal of the Learning Sciences, 8*(3&4), 391–450.

Edelson, D. C., Pea, R. D., & Gomez, L. M. (1996, April 1996). The collaboratory notebook: Support for collaborative inquiry. *Communications of the ACM, 39*, 32–33.

Edelson, D. C., Slusher, D., Owns, L., Pitts, V., Matese, G., & Marshall, S. (2004). *Planetary forecaster*. Evanston, IL: Northwestern University.

Elby, A., & Hammer, D. (2001). On the substance of a sophisticated epistemology. *Science Education, 85*, 554–567.

Engle, R. A., & Conant, F. R. (2002). Guiding principles for fostering productive disciplinary engagement: Explaining an emergent argument in a community of learners classroom. *Cognition and Instruction, 20*(4), 399–483.

Geography Education Standards Project. (1994). *Geography for life: National geography standards 1994*. Washington, DC: National Geographic.

Herrenkohl, L. R., & Guerra, M. R. (1998). Participant structures, scientific discourse, and student engagement in fourth grade. *Cognition and Instruction, 16*(4), 431–473.

Herrenkohl, L. R., Palincsar, A. S., DeWater, L. S., & Kawasaki, K. (1999). Developing scientific communities in classrooms: A sociocognitive approach. *Journal of the Learning Sciences, 8*(3–4), 451–493.

Hollan, J. D., Hutchins, E., & Kirsh, D. (2000). Distributed cognition: Toward a new foundation for human-computer interaction research. *ACM Transactions on Computer-Human Interaction, 7*, 174–196.

Kaput, J. J. (1989). Linking representations in the symbol systems of algebra. In S. Wagner & C. Kieran (Eds.), *Research issues in the learning and teaching of algebra*. Hillsdale, NJ: Erlbaum.

Kolodner, J. L., Camp, P. J., Crismond, D., Fasse, B., Gray, J., Holbrook, J., et al. (2003). Problem-based learning meets case-based reasoning in the middle-school science classroom: Putting learning by design into practice. *The Journal of the Learning Sciences, 12*(4), 495–547.

Kozma, R. B., Russell, J., Jones, T., Marx, N., & Davis, J. (1996). The use of multiple, linked representations to facilitate science understanding. In S. Vosniadou, R. Glase, E. DeCorte, & H. Mandel (Eds.), *International perspective on the psychological foundations of technology-based learning environments* (pp. 41–60). Mahwah, NJ: Lawrence Erlbaum Associates.

Krajcik, J., & Reiser, B. J. (Eds.). (2004). *IQWST: Investigating and questioning our world through science and technology*. Ann Arbor, MI: University of Michigan.

Kuhn, L., & Reiser, B. J. (2005, April). Students constructing and defending evidence-based scientific explanations. Paper to be presented at the Annual Meeting of the National Association of Research in Science Teaching, Dallas, TX.

Kyza, E. (2004). *Understanding reflection-in-action: An investigation into middle-school students' reflective inquiry practices in science and the role that software scaffolding can play*. Unpublished Ph.D. Dissertation, Northwestern University, Evanston, IL.

Linn, M. C., Bell, B., & Davis, E. A. (2004). *Internet environments for science education*. Mahwah, NJ: Erlbaum.

Linn, M. C., & Slotta, J. D. (2000, October). Wise science. *Educational Leadership, 29–32*.

Loh, B., Radinsky, J., Reiser, B. J., Gomez, L. M., Edelson, D. C., & Russell, E. (1997). The progress portfolio: Promoting reflective inquiry in complex investigation environments. In R. Hall, N. Miyake, & N. Enyedy (Eds.), *Proceedings of CSCL 97: Computer support for collaborative learning, Toronto, Canada, December 10–14, 1997* (pp. 169–178). Mahwah, NJ: Lawrence Erlbaum Associates.

Loh, B., Reiser, B. J., Radinsky, J., Edelson, D. C., Gomez, L. M., & Marshall, S. (2001). Developing reflective inquiry practices: A case study of software, the teacher, and students. In K. Crowley, C. D. Schunn, & T. Okada (Eds.), *Designing for science: Implications from everyday, classroom, and professional settings* (pp. 279–323). Mahwah, NJ: Erlbaum.

McNeill, K. L., & Krajcik, J. (in press). Middle school students' use of appropriate and inappropriate evidence in writing scientific explanations. In M. C. Lovett & P. Shah (Eds.), *Thinking with data: The proceedings of the 33rd carnegie symposium on cognition*. Mahwah, NJ: Erlbaum.

National Research Council (NRC). (1996). *National science education standards*. Washington, DC: National Academy Press.

Palincsar, A. S., & Brown, A. L. (1984). Reciprocal teaching of comprehension-fostering and comprehension-monitoring activities. *Cognition and Instruction, 1, 117–175*.

Pitts, V. M., & Edelson, D. C. (2004). Role, goal, and activity: A framework for characterizing participation and engagementin project-based learning environments. In Y. B. Kafai, W. A. Sandoval, N. Enyedy, A. S. Nixon, & F. Herrera (Eds.), *Proceedings of the sixth international conference of the learning sciences, Santa Monica, CA, June 23–26, 2004* (pp. 420–426). Mahwah, NJ: Lawrence Erlbaum Associates.

Quintana, C., Reiser, B., Davis, E. A., Krajcik, J., Golan, R., Kyza, E., et al. (2002). Evolving a scaffolding design framework for designing educational software. In P. Bell, R. Stevens, & T. Satwicz (Eds.), *Keeping learning complex: The proceedings of the fifth international conference of the learning sciences (icls)*. Mahwah, NJ: Lawrence Erlbaum Associates.

Quintana, C., Reiser, B. J., Davis, E. A., Krajcik, J., Fretz, E., Duncan, R. G., et al. (2004). A scaffolding design framework for software to support science inquiry. *Journal of the Learning Sciences, 13*(3), 387–421.

Reiser, B. J., Carney, K., Holum, A., Laczina, E., Rodriguez, C., & Steinmuller, F. (2000). *The struggle for survival*. Evanston, IL: The Center for Learning Technologies in Urban Schools, Northwestern University.

Reiser, B. J., Tabak, I., Sandoval, W. A., Smith, B. K., Steinmuller, F., & Leone, A. J. (2001). BGuILE: Strategic and conceptual scaffolds for scientific inquiry in biology classrooms. In S. M. Carver & D. Klahr (Eds.), *Cognition and instruction: Twenty-five years of progress* (pp. 263–305). Mahwah, NJ: Erlbaum.

Rivet, A. E. (2003). Contextualizing instruction and student learning in middle school project-based science classrooms. University of Michigan, Ann Arbor, MI.

Sandoval, W. A. (2003). Conceptual and epistemic aspects of students' scientific explanations. *Journal of the Learning Sciences, 12*(1), 5–51.

Sandoval, W. A., & Reiser, B. J. (2004). Explanation-driven inquiry: Integrating conceptual and epistemic scaffolds for scientific inquiry. *Science Education, 88*(3), 345–372.

Schoenfeld, A. H. (1987). What's all the fuss about metacognition? In A. H. Schoenfeld (Ed.), *Cognitive science and mathematics education* (pp. 189–215). Hillsdale, NJ: Lawrence Erlbaum Associates.

Smith, C. L., Maclin, D., Houghton, C., & Hennessey, M. G. (2000). Sixth-grade students' epistemologies of science: The impact of school science experiences on epistemological development. *Cognition and Instruction, 18,* 349–422.

Tabak, I. (2004). Synergy: A complement to emerging patterns of distributed scaffolding. *The Journal of the Learning Sciences,* 13(3), 305–335.

Tabak, I., Sandoval, W. A., Reiser, B. J., & Steinmuller, F. (2000). *The Galapagos finches,* in J. Jungck & V. Vaughan (Eds.), The BIOQUEST library volume vi [Computer Software]. San Diego, CA: Academic Press.

CHAPTER 21

BioKIDS

An Animated Conversation on the Development of Curricular Activity Structures for Inquiry Science

Nancy Butler Songer

The art of developing and utilizing curriculum materials to foster understanding involves, as Bruner puts it, an active conversation between learners and materials:

> All one can do for a learner en route to her forming a view of her own is to aid and abet her on her own voyage. The means for aiding and abetting a learner is sometimes called a "curriculum," and what we have learned is that there is no such thing as the curriculum. For in effect, a curriculum is like an animated conversation on a topic that can never be fully defined, although one can set limits upon it. (Bruner, 1996, pp. 115–116)

For decades, scientists and science educators have struggled to develop curriculum materials that support frequently changing definitions of scientific literacy. Today, definitions of scientific literacy include understanding specific concepts in science, and also being able to engage in several kinds of complex reasoning including distinguishing salient from irrelevant information, explaining and predicting scientific events, reading with understanding, and evaluating and applying evidence and arguments appropriately (National Research Council, 1996).

Curricular reforms in science often represent one-shot interventions intended to develop an understanding of scientific facts or complex reasoning skills in as little as a few days or weeks, despite the suggestion from theories of learning (e.g., Bransford, Brown, & Cocking, 2000) that the development of conceptual knowledge in science takes years and multiple exposures. Although many science programs outside the United States support sequential building of concepts and reasoning (e.g. Japan; see Linn, Lewis, Tsuchida, & Songer, 2000), American precollege science curricula rarely take into account the organized, longitudinal development of science concepts or reasoning skills. What is needed is a systematic progression of science units that take into account how to work with early, middle and advanced levels of reasoning and that sequentially build complex understandings of important concepts.

In this chapter, I describe a year-long curricular program designed to systematically foster and evaluate science content development and complex reasoning in science. I describe how one research project has addressed the challenge of supporting learners' journeys toward understanding fundamental ideas about science, by articulating both *what* scientific knowledge should be emphasized and *how* it should be presented to learners. In particular, this study exemplifies my efforts to develop curricular activity structures and accompanying technological tools that emphasize the development of complex reasoning skills. My research team has developed three consecutive eight-week curricular units that comprise students' science during their sixth-grade year.

What Do We Mean by Complex Reasoning in Science?

Scientists and science educators believe that being a scientifically literate citizen requires more than just an understanding of scientific facts or concepts in the earth, life, or physical sciences. Science literacy also includes several types of complex reasoning abilities such as explaining, predicting, posing scientific arguments based on evidence, and applying conclusions to new contexts (National Research Council, 1996, 2000). The learning sciences similarly emphasize the necessity of both a strong foundation of scientific facts or concepts and an understanding of the interdependence of facts and concepts with scientific reasoning skills such as explaining arguments based on evidence (e.g., Bransford et al., 2000). The scientific knowledge that represents both concepts and reasoning skills and is often developed within authentic scientific contexts is called *science inquiry* (National Research Council, 2000; Minstrell & van Zee, 2000). Science inquiry represents modes of thinking and the processes of knowledge-building commonly associated with practicing scientists. These can be difficult to translate into classroom-based activities for students.

Many science educators and scientists view the development of science inquiry as an essential focus of precollege science education (e.g. National Research Council, 2000; Minstrell & van Zee, 2000). Although

national science standards and policy documents also value students' inquiry reasoning (e.g., National Research Council, 1996; 2000), schools are often caught between fostering inquiry, on the one hand, and intense pressure to perform well on high-stakes tests, on the other. Too often, this tension is resolved in favor of test preparation activities at the expense of inquiry. One recent survey of middle school teachers found that 40 percent of the science year was devoted to test-related activities (Songer, 2005).

Another enduring challenge for inquiry-focused researchers has been to define tangible and measurable reasoning skills of science inquiry. Working from definitions of science inquiry in the National Science Standards (National Research Council, 1996; 2000), my research team selected three specific and measurable areas of inquiry to emphasize within our curricular programs. These are:

1. The formulation of scientific explanations from evidence;
2. The analysis of various types of scientific data (charts, graphs, maps);
3. The building of hypotheses and predictions (based on relevant evidence).

Targeting specific inquiry reasoning skills for emphasis in curricular activities was the first step of our systematic approach to providing guidance of inquiry throughout an entire year of middle school science. After the selection of these three areas of inquiry reasoning, we began the development of curricular activity structures that would provide repeated guidance for students' development of these areas of inquiry reasoning. The following sections provide a brief history of work by others in the development of curricular activity structures that are designed to promote students' reasoning skills, followed by a discussion of our work in this area.

Curricular Activity Structures to Promote Scientific Literacy

The design of curricular programs to promote scientific reasoning has been an enduring challenge for science educators. In the early 1960s, Robert Karplus presented a curricular framework for the learning of science called The Learning Cycle that specified which science knowledge should be learned and how it should be presented. Karplus claimed that "autonomous recognition of relationships by the pupils" would "produce understanding rather than rote verbalization" (Atkin & Karplus, 1962, p. 45).

Rooted in the learning theories of Piaget, The Learning Cycle was one of the first systematic attempts to outline a sequence of how and when certain ideas in science should be introduced to students in order to promote deep conceptual understanding of scientific ideas (Karplus, 1977). The Learning Cycle articulated three sequential instructional phases to address the *how* and *when* of concept development: *exploration*, *concept introduction/invention*, and *concept application*. In *exploration*, students work in authentic contexts with scientific materials to ask questions and gather data. In *concept introduction/invention* a central scientific concept is defined relative to the experiences and questions raised in the *exploration* phase. In *concept application*, students apply the new definition or principle to a similar context or situation to extend the understanding of the general principle beyond a single problem context or situation. After one cycle is completed, the three phases are repeated with new material, to revisit and encourage deep conceptual understandings of scientific phenomena.

Since Karplus's groundbreaking work, several others have outlined visions for curricular sequences that would promote deep conceptual understandings of science content. Bruner (1996) expanded Learning Cycle ideas into a "spiral curriculum" that builds from intuitive to a more structured understanding of concepts through repeated revisiting of the concept with increasing complexity. John Bransford and colleagues (Bransford et al., 2000) articulated a vision of subject-matter competence that emphasized fluid use of facts and conceptual frameworks that would lead towards a mastery of concepts.

The revisiting of concepts is an approach rooted in constructivism (e.g., Inhelder & Piaget, 1958) and supported by many constructivist-oriented researchers (e.g., Bransford et al., 2000). This approach draws from an understanding that the development of complex understandings of science takes time, guidance, and repeated exposures. Many believe that learners require assistance, in the form of *catalysts* and *mediation* (Bransford et al., 2000), and that deep understandings of content develop as a result of organized *recyclings*, for example, activities that embrace rich conceptual ideas through repeated interactions at increasingly abstract levels. This view of curriculum and learning also takes into account an organized developmental progression of activities that includes higher-order thinking even at younger ages (Metz, 1995, 2000).

A central component of the repeated interaction strategy is the idea of organized, learner-focused guidance, often in the form of cognitive scaffolds (Quintana et al., 2004; Lee & Songer, 2003; Palincsar, 1998). Although a growing body of strong research investigating cognitive scaffolds is emerging (e.g. Davis & Miyake, 2004), the challenge of the systematic development and implementation of cognitive supports within classrooms of heterogeneous learners remains substantial. Even with the current interest in scaffolding, much classroom-based research investigating cognitive scaffolds fails to embrace a longer-term study of cognitive supports such as research on when and how scaffolds should fade with time (Lee & Songer, submitted). One exception is a study by Clark and Linn (2003) that provided empirical evidence that longer interventions were essential for deeper conceptual understandings of physical science concepts. Although some research projects are able to provide convincing evidence of inquiry reasoning (see, for example, White & Fredricksen, 1998), many projects cannot demonstrate such evidence, no doubt in part because the duration of intervention and study is often only a few weeks rather than several months or years. As a result, much of the current research falls short of providing a complete view of the best means to support a progression of conceptual ideas as they develop over many weeks, months, or years.

Research Context: A Year of Sixth Grade Science

Contemporary learning theories and many policy documents emphasize the importance of extended time to develop deep conceptual understandings of concepts. Learning theories such as constructivism also provide a foundation for the kinds of knowledge and beliefs learners bring to the learning context (e.g., Inhelder & Piaget, 1958; Von Glaserfeld, 1998); however, they fall short in articulating a sequence of activities to guide students in the development of these target understandings in science. In other words, learning theories are often more successful at articulating the activity of learners (for example, describing how learners interact in certain ways with information and with each other: Piaget & Inhelder, 1969; Vygotsky, 1978) than they are at articulating the processes by which learning might be mediated or fostered.

Recognizing the need to articulate the process by which learning might be fostered over time, my research team developed The Kids' Inquiry of Diverse Species (BioKIDS) research project to support the idea of *inquiry readiness* through three sequential, inquiry-fostering curricular units that comprise an entire sixth grade science year. We use the term "inquiry readiness" to describe how students' first in-depth development of inquiry science serves as a foundation for subsequent explorations in science at later ages. As Bruner (1996) articulated, complex knowledge development can be fostered in younger children – assuming that appropriate work is done to translate the complex reasoning into appropriate levels of abstractness. In Bruner's words, "readiness is not only born but made" (1996, p. 119). As I discuss in more detail later, our work to translate complex reasoning activities into appropriate levels of abstractness for our target

audience included both the development of written curricular scaffolds and the redesign of computer resources into age-appropriate cognitive tools.

We chose a target population of sixth graders because research shows that late elementary and early middle school students are a pivotal population for the development of complex reasoning in science. Comparative international standardized test results in mathematics and science often show American students performing in the top half in fourth grade but dropping considerably by the eighth grade and beyond (Schmidt, McKnight, & Raizen, 1996; Linn et al., 2000). In addition, science education and learning technologies research suggests that children and early adolescents are capable of guided reasoning about complex scientific phenomena (e.g., Metz, 1995, 2000; Pea, 2004), although many late elementary and early middle school science curricula do not promote complex thinking.

Our first curricular unit of the sixth grade year is an eight-week unit focusing on animal interactions and biodiversity. Although we initially selected this topic to conform to state and national science standards requirements, the topic turned out to be an excellent focus for the development of inquiry readiness for several reasons. Research on students' development of complex reasoning in biology suggests that fostering complex thinking about living things and animal interactions is not easy. Previous research has shown that children often lack critical thinking skills related to the complexities of animals' lives and their interaction with surrounding environments (Carey, 1985). Furthermore, research has shown that children often hold many alternative conceptions related to food and energy, predator/prey relationships, and population size (Leach et al., 1992). Many current biology activities for late elementary students oversimplify concepts, and investigations are limited to observation or classification of animals based on physical characteristics (Barrett & Willard, 1998) rather than science inquiry. Activities seldom go beyond simple animal facts, to address relationships between animals and habitats and environments, or to develop understandings of advanced concepts like adaptation and conservation.

On balance, learning sciences research suggests that fifth and sixth grade students are capable and ready for complex thinking about animal relationships and adaptation. Science education researchers provide evidence that with appropriate guidance, young children can reason about complex animal interactions, and these understandings can serve as a foundation for additional reasoning in biology (e.g., Metz, 2000). But they are rarely provided with the challenge and supports needed to pursue this kind of inquiry.

Our premise was that a year-long program that could guide the development of specific areas of science inquiry reasoning (e.g., formulation of explanations, analysis of data, and building hypotheses) within each of three consecutive eight-week science units (unit 1, life science: biodiversity; unit 2, earth science: weather; and unit 3, physical science: simple machines) could serve as a mechanism for jump starting the science inquiry abilities of learners, leading to a productive content and reasoning foundation for more advanced reasoning in subsequent units and years. Each eight-week curricular unit was organized around a similar curricular activity structure. The following section articulates the development of the major components of our curricular activity structure, using examples from the first unit – the biodiversity unit – to illustrate key points.

The Development of BioKIDS Curricular Activity Structures

Building on prior work by other researchers, we chose to design curricular sequences that would emphasize content development within each eight week unit, but that would also build the development of scientific reasoning skills both within each content

area and sequentially in consecutive content areas. In other words, whereas we focused on the development of science inquiry in the first unit – including the development of scientific explanations around biodiversity content – we also wished to guide students to build productively on what they had learned about the development of scientific explanations while studying biodiversity as they later developed scientific explanations around weather and simple machines in units 2 and 3. As mentioned, our larger goal was the development of three parallel curricular activity structures that would work productively in concert, and that the three units would cycle through scientific reasoning in each subsequent unit, leading toward mastery of deep conceptual thinking and reasoning around science concepts.

One of our first goals in the development and coordination of the units was to identify what content to teach in each of the three sixth grade units. Our early examinations of content and learning goals began with an examination of science standards at three levels: national (National Research Council, 1996), state (Michigan Curriculum Framework Science Benchmarks, 2000), and district (DPS Science Core Curriculum Outcomes, 2000). For the first unit on biodiversity, we examined standards relative to the physical characteristics of animals, habitat, adaptation, food web, animal classification, human interaction, and conservation. Although the target audience was late-elementary students, we examined standards at various levels to gain a better understanding of the scope and the sequence of related concepts. We also examined textbooks, published materials, and Internet resources (Barrett & Willard, 1998; Fletcher, Lawson, & Rawitscher-Kunkel, 1970).

For all three units, we selected science content that represented both essential scientific facts as well as authentic reasoning in the content area (e.g., science inquiry) as determined by scientist specialists in each discipline. Content and reasoning choices often led to lengthy discussions between science educators, teachers, and scientists, as they weighed the consequences of focusing on topics that would engage children in authentic reasoning, as experienced by practicing scientists, while also taking into account time, testing, and logistical constraints. We chose the following science content for emphasis in the biodiversity unit:

- Students will learn about the concepts of abundance, richness, and biodiversity.
- Students will identify and describe various habitats in the schoolyard.
- Students will understand the role of microhabitat in supporting different species.
- Students will be able to use their observations and data to describe the abundance and richness of different species in their schoolyard.
- Students will examine the concept of biodiversity in the schoolyard using the data they have collected.

After the topics were selected, we began the difficult process of developing and organizing activities into a guided sequence that would support the development of complex reasoning in science, as suggested by Learning Cycle and other activity structures of Karplus (1977), Bybee (Bybee et al., 1989), Bruner (1996) and others. Many factors needed to be considered in these deliberations, including both *when* each concept was introduced relative to others, and *how* students were engaging with each of the concepts that would lead to sequential content and reasoning development. In addition to the actions students were performing in each activity, we also designed all three units around an overall sequence of four curricular phases: *engage, explore, explain,* and *synthesize.* Following the work of Karplus and others, these phases supported deep conceptual development of science inquiry (engage, explore, and explain) as well as the integration and application of concepts to new contexts (synthesize). Table 21.1 illustrates the curricular phases and sequence developed for the eight-week biodiversity unit.

The Development of Curricular Scaffolds to Guide Science Inquiry

While essential, the selection of the science content to be emphasized and the development of curricular activity structures were not sufficient in the development of our three sequential curricular units. As implied in Bruner's comment about readiness being "not only born but made," research on children's knowledge development suggests not only that the development of complex reasoning requires assistance (e.g., Bransford et al., 2000), but that more or different kinds of assistance may be necessary at different stages of development or in different contexts, such as real-world settings (e.g., Lee & Songer, 2003; Palincsar & Brown, 1984). Our previous research on students' learning in atmospheric science suggested that the development of complex reasoning skills through activities grounded in real-world contexts can be particularly difficult for novice students, especially when students are expected to draw from discipline-based knowledge to distinguish salient from irrelevant variables. As suggested by Lee and Songer (2003), activity structures are an important technique for structuring student experiences, but additional support is needed to assist students in managing problem complexity, determining relevant evidence, and providing appropriate guidance for both productive and unproductive learning attempts.

Therefore, a major challenge of the development of the biodiversity, weather, and simple machines curricular units was to determine the right character and level of guidance, hints, and prompts, that would support students in the management of problem complexity and in determining relevant evidence, as they worked to develop explanations or analyze data focused around topics in biodiversity, weather, or simple machines.

First drawing from design-based research methodology (Barab, this volume; Confrey, this volume), and subsequently in quasi-experimental design (e.g., Cook &

Table 21.1. Biodiversity Activity Structure

Curricular Phase	Activity	Inquiry Goal	Selected Examples of Content Goal	Role of Technology
Engage	Students observe schoolyard as a place for animals (habitats). Students collect habitat data and map the schoolyard.	Students *engage in a question* provided by the teacher, materials, or other source)	Students identify and describe various habitats in the schoolyard	None
Explore	Students explore tools of a field researcher and animal groupings. Students collect animal species and habitat data on one schoolyard zone.	Students *directed to collect certain data*	Students view, describe, and identify organisms on the basis of observable physical characteristics and structure	Introduction and use of CyberTracker on PDAs for accurate and efficient data collection and organization
Explain	Students examine class data to determine the zone with the highest biodiversity (richness and abundance).	Students guided in *formulating explanations from evidence*	Students use observations and data to describe the abundance and richness of animals in their schoolyard	Students use class data for observation of patterns and analysis. Students graph and analyze PDA-collected data.
Synthesize	Students use knowledge about specific animals towards activities on food webs and animal interactions.	Students guided in *formulating explanations from evidence*	Students explain how physical and behavioral characteristics help a species survive in its environment	Students use Critter Catalog to collect animal data. Students transform PDA-collected data into other formats such as tables, graphs or maps

Question 1	
Version B	**Version C**
As a team, decide which one photo you think shows the highest animal biodiversity: Photo_____ Give two reasons why you chose that photo:	Which photo (A, B, or C) shows the highest biodiversity? Claim: We think photo _____ shows the highest biodiversity because... [Data or Evidence • **Which photo has the highest abundance?** • **Which photo has the highest richness?** • **Which photo has both high abundance AND high richness?]**
Sample student answers	
Partial: "Diversity is like richness and there is more kinds of animals in photo A." **Complete:** "It has richness and abundance, the others have just one of the two."	
Question 2	
Version B	**Version C**
Looking at these two bar graphs, discuss as a class which zone has the highest biodiversity. Zone _____has the highest biodiversity. Describe what data lead you to this answer.	Looking at the two results you obtained from the data analysis, discuss as a class which zone in your schoolyard has the highest biodiversity. Which schoolyard zone has the highest biodiversity? Claim: I think zone _____ has the highest biodiversity. because... [Data or Evidence • **How many animals and different kinds of animals were found in this zone compared to other zones?** • **Where were animals found in this zone?** • **How does this zone support both high abundance and high richness of animals?]**
Sample student answers	
Partial: "They have the most of animals" **Complete:** "I chose, because zone C has a high richness and a high abundance"	

Figure 21.1. Sample curricular questions with content hints and student answers.

Campbell, 1979), we conducted research to examine the character and quality of student explanations, data analysis, and hypotheses/predictions in each of the three content units and across the academic year. Figure 21.1 illustrates two questions in the biodiversity unit as manifested in two curricular versions and sample responses for each question. Versions B and C asked the same analysis and explanation questions; however, Version B provided no content hints to guide in determining salient evidence, whereas Version C contained several content hints associated with each of ten activities. Version C content hints are illustrated in bold text.

For each cohort of students and each curricular unit, mixed-methods data were collected in the form of pre- and posttest comparisons, written responses, and think-aloud interviews of students' explanation-building. As illustrated in Figure 21.2 – which shows comparison results on these two questions from curricular versions B and C – our results consistently demonstrate significant improvements in students' ability to generate scientific claims and valid scientific explanations when provided with appropriate content hints and prompts that support the development of explanations. Additional results from quasi-experimental studies demonstrate not only experimental

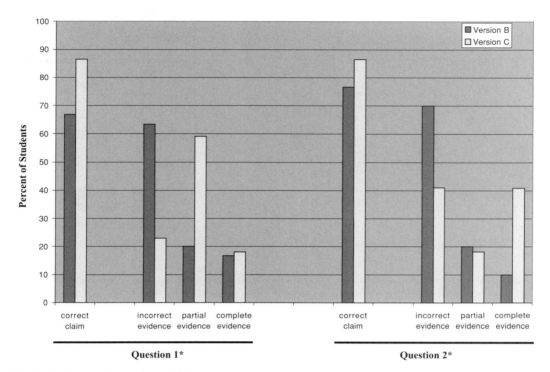

*Statistically significant (p > 0.05)

Figure 21.2. Student responses on scientific claim/evidence. $N = 30, 22$.

students' significant improvement relative to control students on simple inquiry reasoning, but also more dramatic improvements relative to control students as the inquiry reasoning tasks become more advanced, such as explanation-building without the guidance built in with the biodiversity, weather and simple machine units. (For more information, see Songer & Gotwals, 2005).

From Digital Resource to Cognitive Tool

Our animated conversation of what constitutes a curriculum to foster science inquiry among sixth graders continues with reflection on what constitutes scientific literacy. As defined in the national science standards, a central component of today's scientific literacy is the appropriate use of

technology to support learning goals (Bransford et al., 2000; National Research Council, 1996). Most American schools now have many computers and other technology, but some research has documented the underutilization of digital resources by teachers and students (e.g., Cuban, 2001). In particular, digital resources are not often used to support the development of complex reasoning such as that required to conduct science inquiry.

Learning sciences research suggests several ways that technologies can be used to foster complex reasoning in science: scaffolds to enhance learning, more opportunities for feedback and revision, building local and global communities (Bransford et al., 2000). This continues to be a cutting edge research topic. Scientists utilize technology to support higher-order thinking, including advanced analysis, modeling, and data representation (Edelson & Reiser, this volume; Lehrer & Schauble, this volume). Of course,

Figure 21.3. CyberTracker icon-based entry for recording field-based data.

children's use of technology for science learning is not identical to that of scientists, even if some selected features are the same. This is why learning sciences researchers are transforming scientists' tools into appropriate versions for children (e.g., Edelson & Reiser, this volume) even through this translation process is far from simplistic and is not yet well understood (Songer, 2004).

Recognizing the need to translate the rich digital resources used by scientists into cognitive tools for learning, we began by searching for rich digital resources that had the potential to become cognitive tools to foster inquiry reasoning. The process of searching for tools and ways to translate them is ongoing for each of the three curricular units. I focus on the search and translation of tools associated with the first curricular unit, the biodiversity unit.

Early on, our search revealed two digital resources with rich potential: CyberTracker [http://www.cybertracker.co.za] and the Animal Diversity Web [http://animaldiversity.ummz.umich.edu]. Whereas we recognized that each of these tools were resource wealthy, neither tool was initially useful for learning science inquiry about biodiversity by fifth and sixth graders.

CyberTracker is an icon-based interface that runs on a Palm OS handheld computer (Figure 21.3). It was developed by professional African animal trackers to quickly record animal sightings and identification in the field. While the original CyberTracker software was designed to track and record African animals, we recognized CyberTracker's potential as a cognitive tool for Michigan-based student data collection of animal data relative to determining the biodiversity of schoolyard zones.

The second tool, the Animal Diversity Web (ADW), is a database containing information on the natural history, distribution, classification, and conservation biology of animals all over the world (Figure 21.4). ADW had rich potential as a cognitive tool; it contained a large database of species including the animals students were observing and studying in their schoolyard zones.

Once we had selected these technologies for transformation into learning tools, we began to design the learning environment. We found the icon-based, data entry format of CyberTracker to be a good fit for our audience of young and language diverse fifth and sixth graders. Therefore, our redesign of CyberTracker involved little vocabulary adjustment. In contrast, whereas ADW contained a great deal of rich scientific information on animal species, the reading level was far too complex for our target audience. In order for fifth and sixth graders to use species information in ADW, we needed to find a means of translating scientific text into language and presentation formats well

Figure 21.4. The Animal Diversity Web.

suited to middle school children. The result of our redesign of ADW is the Critter Catalog (Figure 21.5), a Web-based database containing natural history, distribution, classification, and conservation biology information for Michigan-based animals written at a middle-school reading level.

After these redesigns, CyberTracker and the Critter Catalog could be used by our target audience. But they still were not yet ready to be used effectively towards science inquiry. In the next step, we examined the cognitive benefits of the learning tool relative to our desired learning goals. We began with a review of the learning goals emphasized in each of our curricular units, and an examination of how each tool might be utilized towards these goals. As mentioned earlier, our curricular units are focused around three dimensions of inquiry

reasoning: building explanations from evidence, analyzing data, and making hypotheses and predictions. For each of these goals, the collection and organization of scientific data is essential (cf. Edelson & Reiser, this volume). Therefore, we began the process of redesigning CyberTracker to focus on children's accurate collection of animal data in their Michigan schoolyards. This transformation involved both a reworking of the manner in which animal data entries were organized in animal groups, as well as a streamlined sequence focusing on a small number of types of data (habitats, animal group, animal, number and zone). Figure 21.6 displays a sample Habitat Summary Sheet of student-gathered data on Michigan-based animals.

Similarly, making the Critter Catalog ready for inquiry support required an

Figure 21.5. The Critter Catalog.

examination of how this tool could foster the learning goals of explanation-building and data analyses. The transformation of the ADW text into a database suitable for use by late elementary students involved many challenges, including:

a. translating concepts in a way that reduced text without content dilution,

b. simplifying organization of species accounts,

c. enhancing visual information, and

d. substituting familiar species names for scientific names.

For more information on the redesign and user-interface evaluation of CyberTracker and the Critter Catalog, see Parr, Jones, & Songer (2004).

The redesign of digital resources into learning tools involves a series of examinations focused around the target audience, the cognitive benefits of the tool, and the learning goals. With many science technologies, these examinations are not conducted, and this neglect could contribute to the under-utilization of many computer resources in schools, particularly relative to challenging learning goals such as inquiry reasoning in science.

Habitat	Animal Group	Animal	How Many?	Location (Zone)
Short grass	6 LEGS Insects	Unknown beetle	13	A
Short grass	6 LEGS Insects	Bee	2	F
Bare ground	Mammals	Norway rat	1	D
Bare ground	Mammals	Rox squirrel	1	F
In the soil	10+ LEGS Myriapods and Crustaceans	Centipede	2	E
Under rock or log	0 LEGS Annelids and Mollusks	Earthworm	1	D
In the air	6 LEGS Insects	Bee	1	A
Single tree	Birds	American robin	1	F

Figure 21.6. Sample habitat summary table for Michigan CyberTracker data.

Conclusions

Taken together, constructivist learning theory and learning cycle–style activity structures suggest that learning environments should be designed to support the systematic development of inquiry science through cycles of guidance and revisitation in various contexts. Although this general approach is clear, learning theories and research studies have not yet told us how to sequence, organize, prompt, and fade of guidance, and have not yet provided us with resources that support learning complex thinking such as that required to conduct science inquiry. Learners need assistance and scaffolding to develop the ability to build an accurate scientific explanation, or to distinguish salient from irrelevant data; but the details of what type of assistance and support are productive for different learning environments and target audiences are not well known. Cycles of iterative design-based and quasi-experimental research studies are needed to build from theory-supported approximations to more specific and productive sequences and types of prompts and guidance.

In our studies, we work with three sequential eight-week curricular units focusing on biodiversity, weather, and simple machines. The biodiversity unit was the first of the three sequential curricular units designed to foster science inquiry among cohorts of sixth grade students, and was the example that I described in detail in this chapter. Although it was not possible to discuss each curricular unit in depth, the ideas behind inquiry readiness and curricular activity structures guided the systematic redesign of digital resources into cognitive tools and the development of activity sequences, structures, and hints to foster complex reasoning skills in each of the three science units. Associated with each unit, mixed-methods research guided the iterative refinement of resources, sequences, and learning goals.

In summary, I agree with Cohen, Raudenbush, and Ball (2000) and with Bruner (1996): learning is affected not necessarily by a given written curriculum, but by the way these resources are used by a particular target audience and toward particular learning goals. The more we continue to examine this animated conversation – including the careful examination of, the *what* and *hows* to foster the development of scientific explanations, data analysis, and hypotheses generation – the more our ideals can be realized.

References

Atkin, J. M., & Karplus, R. (1962). Discovery or invention? *Science Teacher* 25, 45.

Barrett, K., & Willard, C. (1998). *Schoolyard ecology: Teacher's guide*. Berkeley, CA: Lawrence Hall of Science.

Bransford, J., Brown, A. L., & Cocking, R. R. (2000). *How people learn: Brain, mind, experience and school*. Washington, DC: National Academy Press.

Bruner, J. (1996). *The culture of education*. Cambridge, MA: Harvard University Press.

Bybee, R., Buchwald, C., Crissman, S., Heil, D., Kuebis, P, Matsumoto, C., & McInerney, J. (1989). *Science and technology education for the elementary years: Frameworks for curriculum and instruction*. Washington, The National Center for Improving Science Education.

Carey, S. (1985). *Conceptual change in childhood*. MIT Press, Cambridge Massachusetts.

Clark, D., & Linn, M. C. (2003). Designing for knowledge integration: The impact of instructional time. *The Journal of the Learning Sciences*, 12(4), 451–493.

Cohen, D., Raudenbush, S., & Ball, D. L. (2000) Resources, instruction and research. *Center for the Study of Teaching and Policy Working Paper W-00-2*. The University of Washington.

Cook, T. D., & Campbell, D. T. (1979) *Quasi-experimentation: Design and analysis issues for field settings*. Boston, MA: Houghton Mifflin.

Cuban, L. (2001). *Oversold and overused: Computers in the classroom*. Cambridge, MA: Harvard University Press.

Davis, E. A., & Miyake, N. (Eds.). (2004). *The journal of the learning sciences: Special issue on scaffolding*. Volume 13, Number 3. Mahwah, NJ: Erlbaum.

DPS Science Core Curriculum Outcomes. (2000). http://www.detroit.k12.mi.us/index.shtml.

Fletcher, S., Lawson, C. A., & Rawitscher-Kunkel, E. (1970). Organisms, teacher's guide. *Science Curriculum Improvement Study*. Rand McNally & Co.

Inhelder, B., & Piaget, J. (1958). *The growth of logical thinking from childhood to adolescence*. Basic Books, Inc.

Karplus, R. (1977). Science teaching and the development of reasoning. *Journal of Research in Science Education* 14(2), 169–175.

Leach, J., Driver, R., Scott, P., & Wood-Robinson, C. (1992). *Progression in understanding of ecological concepts by pupils ages 5 to 16*. Leeds: University of Leeds.

Lee, H. S., & Songer. N. B. (2003) Making authentic science accessible to students. *International Journal of Science Education*. 25(1), 1–26.

Lee, H. S., & Songer, N. B. (submitted) Expanding an understanding of scaffolding theory using an inquiry-fostering science program. *The Journal of the Learning Sciences*. October, 2004.

Linn, M. C., Lewis, C., Tsuchida, I., & Songer, N. B. (2000) Beyond fourth grade science: Why do US and Japanese students diverge? *Educational Researcher* 29 (3), 4–14.

Metz, K. (1995). Reassessment of developmental constraints on children's science instruction. *Review of Educational Research* 65(1): 93–127.

Metz, K. (2000). Young children's inquiry in biology: Building the knowledge bases to empower independent inquiry. In J. Minstrell and E. van Zee (Eds.) *Inquiring into inquiry learning and teaching in science* (pp. 371–404). Washington, DC: AAAS.

Michigan Curriculum Framework Science Benchmarks. (2000). http://www.michigan.gov/mde/0,1607,7-140-28753_28760–,00.html.

Minstrell, J., & van Zee, E. H. (2000). *Inquiring into inquiry learning and teaching in science*.

Washington, DC: American Association for Advancement of Science.

National Research Council (1996). *National science education standards*. Washington, DC: National Academy Press.

National Research Council. (2000). *Inquiry and the national science education standards: A guide for teaching and learning*. Washington, DC: National Academy Press.

Palincsar, A. S. (1998). Social constructivist perspectives on teaching and learning. *Annual Review of Psychology 49*, 345–375.

Palincsar, A. S., & Brown, A. L. (1984). Reciprocal teaching of comprehension-fostering and comprehension-monitoring activities. *Cognition and Instruction 1*(2), 117–175.

Parr, C., Jones, T., & Songer, N. B. (2004). Evaluation of a handheld data collection interface for science. *Journal of Science Education and Technology. 13*(2), 233–242

Pea, R. D. (2004). The social and technological dimensions of scaffolding and related theoretical concepts for learning, education, and human activity. *The Journal of the Learning Sciences, 13*(3), 423–451.

Piaget, J., & Inhelder, B. (1969). *The psychology of the child*. New York: Basic.

Quintana, C., Reiser, B., Davis, E., Krajcik, J., Fretz, E., Duncan, R. G., Kyza, E., Edelson, D., & Soloway, E. (2004). A scaffolding design framework for software to support science inquiry. *The Journal of the Learning Sciences, 13*(3), 337–386.

Schmidt, W. H., McKnight, D. C., & Raizen, S. A. (1996). *Splintered Vision: An investigation of U.S. and mathematics education*. U.S. National Research Center for the Third International Mathematics and Science Study (TIMSS), Michigan State University.

Songer, N. B. (2004). *Evidence of complex reasoning in technology and science: Notes from inner city Detroit, Michigan, USA*. IPSI-2004 Pescara Conference, Italy.

Songer, N. B. (2005). *Congressional testimony: Challenges to American competitiveness in math and science, Committee on Education and the Workforce, Subcommittee on 21st Century Competitiveness*. United States House of Representatives. http://edworkforce.house.gov/hearings/109th/21st/mathscience051905/wl051905.htm.

Songer, N. B., & Gotwals, A. (2005). *Persistence of inquiry: Evidence of complex reasoning among inner city middle school students*. Paper presented at the American Educational Research Association (AERA) annual meeting.

Von Glaserfeld, E. (1998). Cognition, construction of knowledge, and teaching. In M. R. Matthews (Ed.), *Constructivism in science education* (11–30). Dordrecht, The Netherlands: Kluwer.

Vygotsky, L. S. (1978). *Mind in society*. Cambridge, MA: Harvard University Press.

White, B. Y., & Frederiksen, J. R. (1998). Inquiry, modeling, and metacognition: Making science accessible to all students, *Cognition and Instruction, 16*(1), 3–118.

CHAPTER 22

Cultivating Model-Based Reasoning in Science Education

Richard Lehrer and Leona Schauble

Social studies of scientific practice reveal considerable diversity in the methods and material means of production across scientific disciplines (e.g., Galison & Stump, 1995). Yet, in spite of this diversity and regardless of their domain, scientists' work involves building and refining models of the world (Giere, 1988; Hestenes, 1992; Stewart & Golubitsky, 1992). Scientific ideas derive their power from the models that instantiate them, and theories change as a result of efforts to invent, revise, and stage competitions among models. These efforts are mobilized to support socially grounded arguments about the nature of physical reality, so model-based reasoning is embedded within a wider world that includes networks of participants and institutions (Latour, 1999); specialized ways of talking and writing (Bazerman, 1988); development of representations that render phenomena accessible, visualizable, and transportable (Gooding, 1989; Latour, 1990); and efforts to manage material contingency, because no model specifies instrumentation and measurement in sufficient detail to prescribe practice (Pickering, 1995).

Studies of modeling practices and model-based reasoning encompass a wide spectrum of approaches and disciplines. Some investigators rely on laboratory tasks that are intended to identify important aspects of model-based reasoning (e.g., Craig, Nersessian, & Catrambone, 2002; Gentner & Gentner, 1983). For example, Gentner and Gentner (1983) investigated how different analogical models of electricity influenced participants' reasoning about circuits. Participants who employed an analogy that emphasized the similarities of electricity flow to fluid flow made predictions about the consequences of different arrangements of batteries in a circuit that were more accurate than their predictions about the effects of resistors. The converse held for people using a particle analogy; they made more accurate predictions about configurations of resistors than about configurations of batteries. The fluid analogy helped reasoners distinguish between flow rate and pressure, a distinction that mapped onto an analogous distinction between current (the number of electrons passing a given point per second) and voltage (the pressure difference through which the current moves). Novices in electricity often fail to understand this difference and instead merge both into a generalized notion of "strength." The particle analogy, in contrast, helped individuals understand that current is defined as the number of electrons passing a point per each unit of time, which in turn, supported thinking of a resistor as analogous to a barrier containing a narrow gate.

Other investigators focus on historical studies of prominent scientists. For example, Gooding (1989) examined how Faraday harnessed curves, originally used to depict patterns of iron filings, to represent motions of matter in a field. Gooding (1990) further explained how these representations influenced emerging conceptions of magnetism, so that new forms of representation and the construction of new models evolved together. Systems of representation and modeling practices evolve together in science: this relationship has been documented across a wide range of historical investigations (Nersessian, 2002). Indeed, Nersessian (2002) argued that these representational and modeling practices, not the forms of logic or reasoning that are more frequently focused on by psychological investigators, are the defining features of scientific thinking.

A third approach, ethnographic study, examines scientific practices using direct observation of practicing scientists (Dunbar, 1993, 1998). For example, Latour's (1999) study of soil scientists traced the flow of representations of soil from the edge of a forest in the Amazon to a laboratory in Paris, and back again. The round trip was sustained by successive transformations of dirt to data, a process that involved rendering phenomena into forms that took the place of the original situation. These forms or "inscriptions" (Latour, 1990) selected some features of the phenomena and omitted others, and they made stable and visible features of the world that were changeable or difficult to see, so that the Amazon could be transported to Paris.

Each of these methodological traditions – laboratory, historical, and ethnographic – has contributed to a wider understanding of model-based reasoning. For the most part, however, this chapter focuses on a fourth approach, the one we use – a form of investigation rooted in pedagogical design. The central question that organizes our approach is, "How can modeling practices be cultivated in ways that honor children's emerging capabilities, so that they can come to participate in science by inventing and revising models of the natural world?" There are several legitimate ways to pursue this question. Our approach is to work with teachers to craft classroom ecologies that cultivate model-based reasoning across grades and years of schooling, and then study the practices and outcomes that result (Lehrer & Schauble, 2005). Consistent with design studies (Confrey, this volume), our studies of the development of model-based reasoning have the practical goal of identifying effective ways to cultivate it in students.

Because we focus on modeling in school students, rather than in professional scientists, we devote considerable effort to understanding the development of model-based reasoning and to forms of practice that support this form of reasoning. When thinking about the developmental roots for modeling, we find it useful to recall that at its most basic level, a model is an analogy (Hesse, 1965). Hence, one informational resource for pedagogical design is research that considers how analogical reasoning develops.

Gentner and Toupin (1986) suggested that there is a continuum of complexity in analogies, captured by the nature of the mapping between base and target domains. These mappings range from literal similarity to pure relational structure. The most accessible mappings are based in literal similarity: A stands in for B because it resembles B in some way. For example, when we asked first graders to use springs, dowels, Styrofoam^{TM}, and other materials to build a model that "works like your elbow," the children's initial constructions were guided almost exclusively by a concern for copying perceptually salient features. This confusion between "represents" and "resembles" has also been found in other research with children (Grosslight et al., 1991). The first graders insisted on using round foam balls to simulate the "bumps" in their elbow joints, and insisted on using Popsicle sticks to simulate fingers (Penner et al., 1997), even though neither of these features captured anything about the way the elbow functions.

This initial concern with "looks like" may, however, serve an important developmental function. In particular, it appeared to assist these young children with understanding the very idea of representation – that is, that a bunch of sticks, springs, and other hardware junk can somehow be made into something that represents a body part. But for the children, working from an active, personal intention that their model should represent an elbow seemed to be insufficient. They were equally concerned with communicating that intent to others and justifying the representational status of their model – they wanted to persuade other students that their model was a good one. "Fingers" and an "elbow bump" enhanced the persuasive quality of the model – it could more readily be accepted by other students, who did not have a hand in constructing it, to serve as legitimate "stand-in" for the elbow. However, having resolved this communication challenge to their satisfaction, children next began to turn their attention to function – that is, to mappings that encompassed relations, as well as objects. These concerns surfaced in the next round of revisions to their models. As they experienced range of motion and constraints on motion in their own elbows, many students began to experiment with materials and designs to restrict the range of motion of the dowels as a stand-in for the restriction of range imposed by the design of the elbow joint.

This shift from literal similarity to mapping relations is a hallmark of analogical reasoning (Gentner & Gentner, 1983). More powerful analogies are based not on surface similarity, but on interconnections and constraints among relations and systems of relations. Mathematical models are emblematic of higher-order relational mappings: The mathematical system expresses the structure of the natural system in important ways (Gentner & Gentner, 1983; Kline, 1980). For example, in our studies, third-grade children went on to explore relationships between the position of a load and the point of attachment of the tendon in a more complex elbow model (Penner, Lehrer, & Schauble, 1998). The model treated the arm as a third-class lever, with the elbow acting as the fulcrum. Students expressed the torque of the system as product of effort (supplied by the biceps) and distance (from elbow to point of attachment of biceps on the forearm). This mathematical description instigated explorations of the trade-offs between the range of motion and effort in different elbow designs.

A Typology of Models Based on Analogical Mapping

Considering models as forms of analogy suggests prospective developmental pathways based on types of mappings between model and natural system. We regarded this developmental pathway as a conjecture about the optimal sequence for introducing progressively more complex forms of modeling into instruction. We have found it useful to consider four types of mappings, and in this section, we consider some of the research support for these distinctions. We do not intend this classification to be interpreted as "stages" or levels of developmental progression; certainly all are used in professional practice, and moreover, science often includes hybrids of the forms that we consider. Furthermore, mappings are determined by the intentions and purposes of modelers, not solely by the qualities of the models. Models, like all symbols and representations, have external features and qualities, but their status as models relies on interpretation, rendering any typology of models approximate. For example, one might suggest that a pendulum is a model system for periodic motion. Yet, for most, the pendulum simply swings back and forth and does not stand in for anything other than itself.

Physical Microcosms

Mechanical models of the solar system, planetarium models of the cosmos, and terrarium models of ecosystems are miniatures of the systems they are intended to represent. Other physical models, such as a plastic model of a cell, may be larger than the target phenomenon. Although these models differ in scale, they rely on physical resemblance and direct correspondence for their power. For example, the orbits of the planets around the sun in the mechanical model are elliptical, like those in the solar system, and the rates of revolution around the sun are directly proportional to those in the solar system. Model airplanes resemble real planes, and their wings function in a wind tunnel in a manner that is analogous (it is hoped) to that of a real plane moving in air. Architects and city planners often build scale models of communities that preserve the look and feel, as well as the relationships among, the buildings that are planned for a particular location.

These perceptual correspondences facilitate mappings between physical microcosms and natural systems. As we noted earlier, children's initial efforts in modeling are particularly likely to be guided by literal similarity (Penner et al., 1997), so physical models are often effective entry points to modeling practices. For example, we observed a group of first-graders who watched with interest as their Halloween pumpkins decayed. Their engagement in this process blossomed into a full-blown study of "rot." Their investigation, initially conducted in the playground, came to a standstill when winter descended and rot was replaced by freeze. The children then designed compost columns so that they could continue their study indoors (Lehrer, Carpenter, Schauble, & Putz, 2000). Children's choices of materials to include in the columns were motivated by resemblance to the outdoor system, so moldy tomatoes, dirt, leaves, gum wrappers, and foam were all incorporated. Water was added, too, as a stand-in for rain, and children observed changes in the compost column over time. Many of the observed changes stimulated new questions, including whether or not compost columns really needed to include wrappers and foam. As children considered which elements were essential to the process of rot and which had no significance, they

engaged in analysis of the relations between model and the world. Over time, their modeling activities were guided less by resemblance and more by systems of relation, but resemblance was critical in surmounting the initial hurdle of ensuring that the compost columns were accepted by all as legitimate models of the process occurring on the playground.

Hence, physical microcosms afford early entrée to modeling via literal similarity, but they also can be used to raise questions about relational structure as students consider what to include in a model system and why, and how to modify the model to account for new observations and data. For example, Stewart and his colleagues (Stewart et al., 2005) engaged ninth-grade students in building physical models of the Earth-Moon-Sun system. During the course of instruction, students modified their models to account for an increasing range of data (e.g., direction of sunrise, time of moonrise), resulting in models that featured a greater number of relations among the celestial objects. These increases in relational structure had explanatory payoff; in post-instructional assessments, students offered coherent explanations of a wide range of events, ranging from eclipses to seasonal variation (Cartier, Barton, & Mesmer, 2001).

Although we have emphasized that microcosms are effective starting points for modeling in school, they also play an important role in many forms of professional practice and in the conduct of disciplined inquiry. For example, Nersessian et al. (2003) characterized research in a biomedical engineering laboratory as a distributed system that involves partnerships between technological artifacts and people (see also Latour, 1999; Shapin & Schaffer, 1985). Some of these artifacts were physical devices that employed biological substrates (e.g., cell cultures). These devices were mechanical models of vascular systems. The devices were not replicas, but rather idealizations that mimicked key aspects of vascular function. Although far removed from the problem experienced by the first-graders thinking about qualities of compost columns, the microcosms developed in this laboratory were continually transformed as researchers' understandings of the natural system changed. Re-engineered artifacts, in turn, set the stage for developing new understandings of the biological system. Nersessian et al. (2003) noted that the partnership between artifacts and people ultimately transforms both the artifact and the investigator's understanding of the natural system. Indeed, Latour (1993) suggested that "irruptions" of objects into researchers' investigations has been essential to the pursuit of "modern" science.

Partnership between artifacts and person is not mere curiosity, but rather, has pedagogical implication. Consider, for example, sixth graders who conducted field studies of aquatic systems and then attempted to design a sustainable system in a one-gallon jar (Lehrer & Schauble, 2004). Students initially regarded this task as unproblematic, to be solved by merely copying the elements (substrate, plants, animals) found in a nearby pond. To their surprise, the jar microcosms proved difficult to design and to harness to inquiry. Unexpected events, such as algal blooms, laid low many a design (and contributed to unpleasant aromas in the classroom). These resistances from the material world (cf. Pickering, 1995) transformed students' understandings of the functioning of aquatic systems, and spurred new lines of inquiry.

Representational Systems

Models are typically expressed as systems of representation. For example, a map models the world. Latour (1990) suggested that systems of scientific representation (Latour called them *inscriptions*) share properties that make them especially well–suited for mobilizing cognitive and social resources in the service of scientific argument. His candidates for these vital properties include: (a) the literal mobility and immutability of inscriptions, which tend to obliterate barriers of space and time and thus fix change so that it can be an object of reflection (e.g.,

maps are transported and the earth's surface is not); (b) the scalability and reproducibility of inscriptions, which guarantee their economy but preserve the configuration of relations among elements of the represented phenomenon; (c) the potential for recombining and superimposing inscriptions, operations that generate structures and patterns that might not otherwise be visible or even conceivable; and (d) the control of reference, because inscriptions circulate throughout a program of study, taking the place of phenomena, yet maintaining an index to the original events that inspired their creation (Latour, 1999, p. 72). Lynch (1990) added that inscriptions not only preserve change, they also edit it. Inscriptions both reduce *and* enhance information.

The pedagogical challenge, then, is to support children's use and understanding of these roles of representation. The developmental psychology literature illustrates that there are myriad ways in which even preschool children come to regard one thing as representing another. For example, long before they arrive at school, children have some appreciation of the representational qualities of pictures, scale models, and video representations (DeLoache, 2004; DeLoache, Pierroutsakos, & Uttal, 2003; Troseth, 2003; Troseth & DeLoache, 1998; Troseth, Pierroutsakos, & DeLoache, 2004). During pretend play, children treat objects as stand-ins for others (a block stands in for a teacup; a banana for a telephone), yet still understand that the object has not really changed its original identity, character, or function (Leslie, 1987).

In parallel with these early representational capacities, children are also developing a repertoire of ways of inscribing or notating the world. By the age of four, they typically have constructed a wide range of inscriptional techniques (Karmiloff-Smith, 1992; Lehrer & Lesh, 2003), including drawing. For example, Karmiloff-Smith (1979) asked 7- to 12-year-olds to create an inscriptional system that could be used to provide driving directions to guide a driver through a route marked on a large, scrolling landscape with branching roads. Because the landscape was unrolled as the driver proceeded, the children could not provide directions that referred to the overall spatial array, and instead had to signal maintenance or change in direction at a series of local decision-points. In response to this challenge, children invented a wide variety of marks, including maps, letter codes (like "L" for a left turn), arrows, and lines with different thicknesses. Many children changed their strategies in the middle of the task. All of these changes served to make implicit information more explicit – that is, they served to enhance the communicative effectiveness of the inscriptional system. This was the case even when the implicit information was more economical (for example, nonredundant), and even when the more economical representation seemed sufficient (for example, adding an extra mark to indicate an unacceptable turn, which was technically unnecessary because there was already a mark indicating the correct turn). Karmiloff-Smith suggested that these inscriptional changes reflected a change in children's internal representations of the task.

Emerging symbolic capacities like these are the foundation for engaging children in the invention and revision of systems of inscription – ways of representing – the natural world. In instruction, we attempt to place students in a position to invent inscriptions – to visually denote their commitments and conjectures about how a system functions – and to compare and contrast the affordances and constraints of different systems of inscription. For example, children mapping their school's playground invented competing ways of representing distance, direction, origin, and scale (Lehrer & Pritchard, 2002). Contrasting their tentative maps provided children with a venue to reconsider the meanings of place and space, and to re-create the playground symbolically, as a mathematical (polar coordinate) system. diSessa (2004) refered to instructional goals like these as the development of metarepresentational competence. Systems of representation do not simply communicate thought; they also shape it (Olson, 1994). Acquiring a vocabulary of inscriptions

and notations and a critical understanding of their qualities is essential for modeling.

We sequence classroom activity so that children's drawings and related resources for representing a natural system are gradually stretched into forms that are increasingly mathematical and systematic. For example, in a series of investigations in which third-graders invented a variety of means for describing plant growth, we and the teacher supported a "cascade" of inscriptions, in which initial inscriptional forms were incorporated as inputs into later-developing systems (Latour, 1990). In this case, children initially created drawings from different perspectives and created pressed plant silhouettes (see Figure 22.1) that relied on perceptual resemblance. These early representations mediated the development of inscriptions that were further removed from phenomena. For example, the plant silhouettes served as records of plant height/width at different days of growth, enabling students to index their measurements over a period of time to create other descriptions of change, such as graphs depicting changing ratios (e.g., change in height to change in time). The silhouettes thus participated in a pattern of what Latour (1999) calls "circulating reference" (p. 72) in which scientists establish a chain of reference from the world to sets of inscriptions, and back again. These early representational forms also spurred new attention to related attributes of the plant, including number of leaves, seed-pods, number of seeds, and plant width (Lehrer, Schauble, Carpenter, & Penner, 2000).

Collectively, this ensemble of inscriptions changed the ways in which students conceived of growth. The natural world became increasingly de-natured but also more accessible and transportable. Inscriptional development transformed the conceptual terrain, so that students began to pose new questions about the plants. For example, do plant roots grow like shoots? To explore this new question, students relied on technologies of display that were novel for them (Cartesian systems) and new forms of representation (piece-wise linear segments) to craft

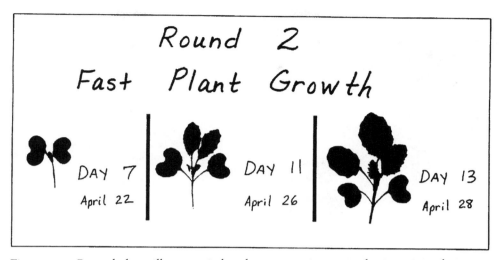

Figure 22.1. Pressed plant silhouettes index change over time, contributing to circulating reference.

arguments for and against the claim that roots grow like shoots. Students noticed that during any given interval, the rates of growth differed. However, "S" curves, showing slow initial growth, a rapid spurt, and then a slowing, characterized both roots and shoots. Noticing this similarity in form, students began to wonder about the significance of the similar S-curves. They wondered, why might the growth of different parts of the plant have the same form? When was growth the fastest, and what might be the significance of these periods of rapid growth? All of these questions were inspired by interaction with inscriptional forms and indicated fundamentally new ways of viewing biological growth.

Other researchers also pursue the claim that there are tight couplings between systems of representation and conceptual change. For example, Stenning et al. (2002) credited a shift in representational modalities (from equations to graphs) as the critical factor in transforming middle school students' conceptions of growth in populations. As students who were employing a linear model to describe growth prepared a graphical display, they came to see multiplication differently – as a series of additions – and they also more readily mapped from mathematics to the biological situation. The shift

in representation instigated a shift in mathematical description, toward ways of accounting for changes in ratio. A developmental change in systems of reference often keys conceptual development.

Syntactic Models

The previous section pointed out that representational systems often have their start in fundamental symbolic capacities of pretense or imitation, and in basic inscriptional capacities such as drawing. Representational systems like maps and globes are half-in and half-removed from the world. They exhibit elements of resemblance (e.g., globes are spheres, lines on maps correspond to roads) but also rely on conventions that more clearly separate them from their intended referents. For example, on the map, stars may represent major cities, while dots are used to depict smaller cities or towns.

In contrast to physical models and maps and globes, syntactic models summarize the essential functioning of a system and typically bear little resemblance to the system being modeled. For example, to find the height of a tree or a building, one could use right isosceles triangles as a model. Similarly, a computer program that does not resemble a conch shell in any way can be

Figure 22.2. The World View representation of Model-It.

used to model the shell, if its action captures essential aspects of the growth of the organism (Abelson & diSessa, 1980). Animal behaviors, such as food preference, can be investigated via a repeated process of flipping a coin to answer questions like: Are choices intentional, or simply a matter of chance?

Syntactic models derive their power from relational mappings. Many programs of research that bring modeling to the classroom are consistent with this orientation, although some of them employ resemblance as a bridge to syntactical structure. For example, Figure 22.2 depicts the World View, one of the main representations provided by Model-It (Metcalf, Krajcik, & Soloway, 2000). Model-It provides an environment for model building and testing, and in this instance, students aim to develop models of the functioning of stream ecology. The World View relies on physical resemblance to situate inquiry; but note, too, the magnified and idealized views of organisms that may be living in the stream.

To create a model, students describe qualities of the system and their prospective relations. For example, students might construct the stream as an object, define as its factors "phosphate" and "quality," and then define the relationship between them, as depicted in Figure 22.3. The graph on the right-hand side of the screen is linked to the text expression, and the graph changes whenever the student changes the relationships.

Model-It uses differential equations to implement the relationships that the students describe qualitatively. The Relationship Editor shown in Figure 22.3 hides this complexity from the student. The philosophy, in keeping with much of the research in science education, is to foreground qualitative description, in anticipation that these experiences will later guide quantitative reasoning.

Other modeling approaches are more quantitatively oriented. The genetics construction kit (Jungck & Calley, 1985) allows students to perform a wide range of genetic crosses and to match simulated frequencies

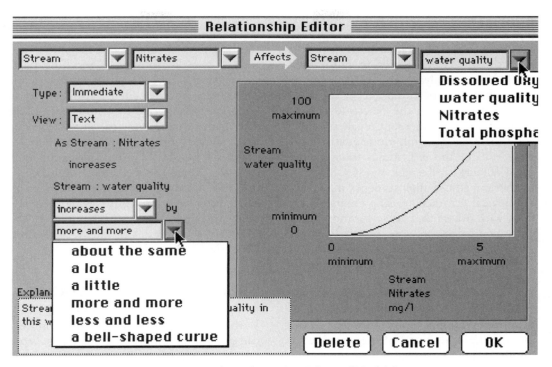

Figure 22.3. The Relationship Editor of Model-It.

of offspring with observed populations in the field. When coupled with classroom instruction that emphasizes cycles of models, especially opportunities to revise models, students typically can generate models that explain complex patterns of inheritance (Stewart et al., 1992; 2005).

Emergent Models

Emergent models impose a further restriction on mapping between model and world: Relations between objects produce emergent behaviors that are not apparent in the description of either the object or the relation. For example, the behavior of a gas can be modeled as billiard balls colliding; increasing the speed of these collisions increases the force with which the billiard ball hits the side of the container (or pool table). The implication of this model is that faster molecules will exert more pressure – a testable prediction of the model. We see examples of emergence in systems every day. The "V" shape of a bird flock is emergent; there is no leading

bird that the other birds follow. Instead, the "V" shape emerges from simple interaction rules that each bird follows relative only to its immediate neighbors – the birds know nothing about the shape of their flock, and are unaware that there is a "leader" bird in the front. The price of a stock on the market is emergent; no central government authority sets the value of a company's stock. Instead, it emerges from the independent decisions of thousands or millions of investors.

Resnick and Wilensky (Resnick, 1994, 1996; Resnick & Wilensky, 1998; Wilensky & Resnick, 1999) suggested that people often find emergent models implausible or even contradictory because they believe that complex systems must be orchestrated centrally. A common example is found in arguments contrasting evolutionary theory to intelligent design. It is difficult for people to believe that the watchmaker is blind (Dawkins, 1996). Penner's (2000) investigation of middle school students' understanding of emergent phenomena concluded that there are three challenges for developing an appreciation of this form of modeling: (a) recognition that there may not be a single cause (e.g., a central authority); (b) distinguishing between aggregate and individual levels of analysis; and (c) tracing the consequences of perturbations at the micro level to behavior at the macro level. Students often treat emergent levels as if they were hierarchies of inheritance, attributing properties of the individuals to the aggregate (Wilensky & Resnick, 1999). Chi (2005) further suggested that students may make ontological errors, confusing emergent systems with others that allow for more direct correspondences between model behaviors and world behaviors.

Although these investigations may be right about some of the sources of difficulty in this form of modeling, recall that social studies of science emphasize the importance of representational tools and infrastructure in grasping and investigating novel ideas. Similarly, new representational tools could conceivably render these challenging notions about emergence quite accessible. Recently, new systems of modeling tools have been developed that may well afford more access to emergent modeling. What was once the province of differential equations can now be described by programming languages that allow models to be constructed as ensembles of independent agents acting in parallel, according to a comparatively simple set of relations (Resnick, 1996; Wilensky, 1996, 2003; Wilensky & Resnick, 1999). The resulting behavior of the system relies on the interactions of the agents, which cannot be foreseen from the rules being followed by any of the actors. Moreover, it is not necessary that emergence models be locked inside the computer. For example, Wilensky and Stroup (1999) and Colella (2000) described a series of participatory simulations in which high school students carried calculators or wore computers and thus participated in an enactment of the spread of a viral disease. Each student-agent contributed to an emerging and collective description of the disease process.

Very simple tools employed in new ways may also provide intuitions about emergent modeling. For example, a class of fourth-grade children who independently measured the height of their school's flagpole experienced the distribution of resulting measures as an emergent phenomenon. Children easily interpreted the distribution as being the result of most students getting approximately the same measure of height, while some students measured a little under the actual height and others measured a little over. Thus, the collection or distribution of measures was not generated by any single agent-measurer but was nevertheless easily interpretable by thinking about the likely collective result of individual actions (Petrosino, Lehrer, & Schauble, 2003).

Supporting Modeling in Instruction

We have argued that analogical development can serve as an important guide for incorporating modeling into instruction. Informed decisions about how and when to introduce increasingly challenging forms of models are critical if one's goal is to support the development of a kind of thinking, like model-based reasoning, that emerges over the long term. Yet as we noted previously, considering only the qualities of models is not sufficient for establishing modeling practices in school. Scientific models are generated within institutional settings and are deployed as means of argument in these settings (e.g., Latour, 1999). They represent particular, even peculiar, epistemic commitments: The search for and evaluation of rival models when considering alternative hypotheses is a form of argument that does not emerge spontaneously (Driver et al., 1996; Grosslight et al., 1991).

Since it is impossible (and, moreover, undesirable) to immerse students in professional practice, decisions must be made about the aspects of practice that should be adapted in schools to support model-based reasoning and to develop a modeling epistemology. By "practice," we refer to a system of activity that emerges from the joint participation of its members. This collective emphasis contrasts to skill development, for which a focus on individuals may be the appropriate scale of analysis. Of course, individual and collective development are always intertwined (Mead, 1910), but from the perspective of designing a learning environment, it is useful to consider explicitly the forms of collective activity that are likely to support the growth and development of individuals. Three that have been widely found to be essential are (a) finding ways to help students understand and appropriate the process of scientific inquiry (Edelson & Reiser, this volume); (b) emphasizing the development and use of varying forms of representations and inscriptions; and (c) capitalizing on the cyclical nature of modeling.

Supporting Inquiry

Modeling approaches to science take hold only within contexts in which inquiry is shaped, valued, and supported. As in professional scientific communities, the material and social contexts strongly influence the kinds of questions considered worth asking, the appropriate methods for pursuing questions, the forms of evidence deemed persuasive, and the means of communicating results that are most authoritative. In instructional communities, these norms must be established and maintained at the classroom level. Indeed, acquiring a nuanced form of reasoning like modeling relies on a long-term effort, so ideally, these norms are consistently employed and progressively deepened across grades of schooling.

For example, explaining their approach to modeling in genetics instruction, Stewart et al. (1992) stated, "Science is as much about conceptual invention and developing shared meaning within a community as it is about empirical discoveries" (p. 318). Consistent with this position, the research team worked with the collaborating teacher to mirror in the classroom aspects of a scientific research community that they considered most important. Accordingly, students worked together in small research groups, learned to pose their own questions, investigated those questions by using or adapt-

ing models to explain observed phenomena (in this case, patterns of inheritance observed in simulated populations of organisms generated by the Genetics Construction Kit, a computer-based laboratory), and attempted to persuade members of their own and other research groups that their own model best accounted for the observed data. Indeed, each of the candidate models was publicly posted, and the authoring research group presented its model to classmates and defended it against any criticisms that were offered, whether the criticisms were aimed directly at the models themselves or at the underlying strategies for investigation. The critiques, in turn, instigated model revision, as students attempted to generate revised models that adequately explained the findings produced by all the groups and to predict the outcomes they thought would occur under novel conditions. The teacher in this class was regarded by all not as a dispenser of knowledge, but as a senior research scientist who mentored students, encouraged new ideas, and participated in and monitored the critiquing process. For their part, the researchers focused on how the research groups made sense of the data they generated, how they persuaded classmates about the utility of their models, and how they came eventually to converge on consensually accepted procedures for deciding what counted as a good explanation and a definitive solution to a problem.

Similarly, in research conducted by White and colleagues (White & Frederiksen, 1998; Schwartz & White, 2005) on computer-assisted modeling of force and motion, there was a strong instructional emphasis that extended beyond the conceptual tasks and computer tools to an explicit concern with the design of a classroom environment that would lend meaning and context to modeling. In their ThinkerTools curriculum, White and colleagues encouraged students to generate and test their own causal conceptual models of scientific phenomena. In addition, there was an equal emphasis on leading the classroom members to monitor and reflect on their own progress in achieving this goal. The general intent was to scaffold for students a shift from the more typical role of following a prescribed sequence of activities dictated by the curriculum and teacher to one in which students became increasingly capable of developing their own experimental and observational plans for testing the adequacy of their current theory, comparing their theory and findings to those generated by others, and then revising the model to improve its generality and predictive power.

Although their instructional designs for achieving this goal were different, the Stewart and White research teams shared a conviction about the importance of lending explicit instructional attention to fashioning a classroom community in which the norms of engagement, activity, talk, and evaluation are supportive of the modeling epistemology they sought to generate.

Meta-representational Competence

Modeling is much more likely to take root and flourish in students who are building on a history of pressing toward meta-representational competence (diSessa, 2004). Developing, revising, and manipulating representations and inscriptions to figure things out, explain, or persuade others are key to modeling but are not typically nurtured in schooling. Instead, students are often taught conventional representational devices as stand-alone topics at a prescribed point in the curriculum, and may be given little or no sense of the kind of problems that these conventions were invented to address. For example, students might be taught in a formulaic manner how to construct pie graphs, but with no problem or question at hand to motivate the utility of that design over any other, students are unlikely to consider the communicational or persuasive trade-offs of that or any alternative representational form. Moreover, in school, there is nearly a monoculture of representational forms, but as we have noted, environments that allow students greater latitude, and that support the expression of their ideas, result in a profusion and proliferation of forms.

When students are routinely asked to invent, use, and critique their own representations developed in the service of solving problems, communicating, or persuading others, they learn a variety of useful lessons that are typically left unspoken or are never learned in traditional classrooms (Greeno & Hall, 1997). These points include, for example, that representations are intended to serve a communicative function, that they are meant for audiences who may need to read the author's intention from the inscription alone, that there are alternative solutions to most representational problems, that those solutions have advantages and disadvantages that may vary as one's goals vary, and that representational choices highlight some aspects of the represented world and hide others.

Cycles of Modeling

Student learning is enhanced when students have multiple opportunities to invent and revise models and then to compare the explanatory adequacy of different models. Entertaining variability in models engenders better learning about the domain being modeled and also appears to prompt students' epistemic understanding of modeling (Hestenes, 1992; Lehrer & Schauble, 2000; Metz, 2004; Stewart et al., 1992). These cycles of producing various models and then evaluating, revising, and applying them can occur in different time scales. Some cycles stretch over prolonged periods of time (e.g., a student's understanding of particulate models of matter typically undergoes revision across years of study), whereas others may occur within the span of a single lesson or sequence of lessons. For example, Lesh and his colleagues designed instruction that features cycles of modeling intended for completion within one or two class periods. The modeling cycle begins with the presentation to students of a *model-eliciting problem* (Lesh et al., 2000). These problems are often adapted from professional practice, especially from engineering, business, and the social sciences. They typically require students to integrate multiple forms of mathematics, rather than to simply apply a single solution procedure (see Lesh & Doerr, 2003). For example, students may be shown a table of data representing the outcomes achieved by eight different children on each of ten different sports events. The outcomes for each event are in different numerical form. That is, for "100-yard dash" the outcome recorded may be the time it took each person to run that event. For "high dive," on the other hand, the outcome is a numerical rating from 1 (poor) to 5 (excellent). "Broad jump" may be operationalized as "longest distance jumped on three trials." The task posed to students is to consider the scores for the eight children across all ten events and to use the data to develop a model that will identify the three best performing children to serve on the camp sports team. Students are asked to publicly explain and justify their model.

Students work in small groups to invent an initial model to use in solving the problem. As one might expect, the groups propose a variety of models; typically, each model has characteristic weaknesses. Teachers lead the class in a discussion about the strengths and weaknesses of each model and encourage the groups to make revisions that respond to the issues raised in discussion. Thus, student modeling evolves through a series of develop-test-revise cycles. Revisions, of course, often entail changing one's solution steps, but they are equally likely to entail the incorporation of different ways of interpreting the assumptions or goals of the problem. As students refine their models to achieve more consistency and coherence, they often notice unexpected implications of a particular representational choice or an additional feature of the world that their model fails to account for.

These cycles of modeling always involve developing and evaluating multiple and interacting systems of inscription. During the early phases of modeling, there are usually diverse and uncoordinated ideas in the air, and students engage in model-based dialogue as they create and revise inscriptions, so that they can reconcile and choose among these ideas (e.g., Lehrer & Lesh, 2003). In this way, inscriptions and models develop together. Students tend to begin by developing a model that fits a specific local problem or situation and only later extend the model to account for more general structures (e.g., Doerr & English, 2003).

Of course, these three features of classroom environments – supporting inquiry, inscription, and cycles of invent-test-revise – are closely interrelated. Each of the features enhances the others, so that together, they form a web of self-reinforcing classroom norms and practices.

Discussion

Taking a commitment to modeling seriously entails related changes in ideas about what constitutes a science education. From a modeling perspective, one important outcome of a student's school career over the long term should be a growing repertoire of models that are extensible, general, and mathematically powerful. This does not mean that science content should not be valued. To the contrary, one of the advantages of organizing instruction around modeling is that it permits educators to sidestep the recurring and useless debates about the relative virtues of emphasizing "science process" or "science content." One cannot engage in the activity of modeling without modeling *something*, and the something (the content and domain) is critical with respect to the questions raised, the inquiry pursued, and the conclusions reached. At the same time, modeling is a practice, not a predigested heap of facts. It is *because* content is so important that perhaps it should be selected with an eye toward its potential for constructing and extending students' model repertoire. Beyond its value for students, modeling also holds strong advantages for teachers. Because models are inscribed (often, mathematically), and because they are publicly defended and debated, an emphasis on models tends to render student thinking highly visible to teachers. This visibility greatly facilitates the kind of ongoing informal assessment that should guide instruction (Means, this volume).

An emphasis on modeling entails changes in students' epistemic goals. Rather than working to find answers to questions posed by curriculum designers or teachers, students learn to pose, evaluate, and pursue worthwhile questions of their own. Indeed, in one sixth grade class, students worked over the course of the school year to develop, revise, and apply their own criteria for what counts as a "good" scientific question (and also for associated criteria for what counts as credible evidence) (Lucas et al., 2005). In classrooms like this, students also learn that the point of scientific inquiry is not to find the "correct" answer (the one known already by the teacher). Instead, they come to see that answers inevitably lead to additional questions, and that deeper study of a phenomenon leads to deeper understanding, not mere repetition (as in, "We already covered that").

Last, but far from least in importance, modeling promotes students' opportunities to craft their identities as inventors of models, not simply as appliers of models from the textbook. They come to believe in their capability to make contributions that are novel, rather than merely to replicate contributions made earlier by others. Finally, students come to understand a little more about the nature of science – in particular, how those conventionally accepted scientific models were built in the first place: via a process much like the one they engaged in.

References

Abelson, H., & diSessa, A. (1980). *Turtle geometry: The computer as a medium for exploring mathematics*. Cambridge, MA: MIT Press.

Bazerman, C. (1988). *Shaping written knowledge: The genre and activity of the experimental article in science*. Madison: University of Wisconsin Press.

Cartier, J. L., Barton, A. M., & Mesmer, K. (2001, March). *Inquiry as a context for meaningful learning in a 9th-grade science unit*. Paper presented at the annual meeting of the National Association for Research on Science Teaching, St. Louis, MO.

Chi, M. T. H. (2005). Commonsense conceptions of emergent processes: Why some misconceptions are robust. *The Journal of the Learning Sciences, 14*, 161–199.

Collela, V. (2000). Participatory simulations: Building collaborative understanding through dynamic modeling. *The Journal of the Learning Sciences, 9*, 471–500.

Craig, D. L., Nersessian, N. J., & Catrambone, R. (2002). Perceptual simulation in analogical problem solving. In L. Magnani & N. J. Nersessian (Eds.), *Model-based reasoning. Science, technology, values*. (pp. 167–189). Dordrecht, Netherlands: Kluwer Academic Press.

Dawkins, R. (1996). *Climbing mount improbable*. New York: W. W. Norton.

DeLoache, J. S. (2004). Becoming symbol-minded. *Trends in Cognitive Sciences, 8*(2), 66–70.

DeLoache, J. S., Pierroutsakos, S. L., & Uttal, D. H. (2003). The origins of pictoral competence. *Current Directions in Psychological Science, 12*(4), 114–118.

diSessa, A. A. (2004). Metarepresentation: Native competence and targets for instruction. *Cognition and Instruction, 22*, 293–331.

Doerr, H. M., & English, L. (2003). A modeling perspective on students' mathematical reasoning about data. *Journal for Research in Mathematics Education, 34*(2), 110–136.

Driver, R., Leach, J., Millar, R., & Scott, P. (1996). *Young people's images of science*. Buckingham, England: Open University Press.

Dunbar, K. (1993). Scientific reasoning strategies for concept discovery in a complex domain. *Cognitive Science, 17*(3), 397–434.

Dunbar, K. (1998). How scientists really reason: Scientific reasoning in real-world laboratories. In R. J. Sternberg & J. F. Davidson (Eds.), *The nature of insight* (pp. 265–395). Cambridge, MA: MIT Press.

Galison, P., & Stump, D. (1995). *The disunity of science. Boundaries, context, and power*. Stanford, CA: Stanford University Press.

Gentner, D., & Gentner, D. R. (1983). Flowing waters or teeming crowds: Mental models of electricity. In D., Gentner & A. L. Stevens (Eds.), *Mental models* (pp 99–129). Hillsdale, NJ: Lawrence Erlbaum Associates.

Gentner, D., & Toupin, C. (1986). Systematicity and surface similarity in the development of analogy. *Cognitive Science, 10*, 277–300.

Giere, R. N. (1988). *Explaining science: A cognitive approach*. Chicago: University of Chicago Press.

Gooding, D. (1989). "Magnetic curves" and the magnetic field: Experimentation and representation in the history of a theory. In D. Gooding, T. Pinch, & S. Schaffer (Eds.), *The uses of experiment. Studies on the natural sciences.* (pp. 183–223). Cambridge: Cambridge University Press.

Gooding, D. (1990). *Experiment and the making of meaning.* London: Kluwer Academic Publishers.

Greeno, J. G., & Hall, R. (1997). Practicing representation: Learning with and about representational forms. *Phi Delta Kappan* (January), 361–367.

Grosslight, L., Unger, C., Jay, E., & Smith, C. (1991). Understanding models and their use in science: Conceptions of middle and high school students and experts. *Journal of Research in Science Teaching, 28,* 799–822.

Hesse, M. B. (1965). *Forces and fields.* Totowa, NJ: Littlefield, Adams & Co.

Hestenes, D. (1992). Modeling games in the Newtonian world. American *Journal of Physics,* 60(8), 732–748.

Jungck, J. R., & Calley, J. (1985). Strategic simulations and post-Socratic pedagogy: Constructing computer software to develop long-term inference through experimental inquiry. *American Biology Teacher, 47,* 11–15.

Karmiloff-Smith, A. (1979). Micro- and macro-developmental changes in language acquisition and other representational systems. *Cognitive Science, 3,* 91–118.

Karmiloff-Smith, A. (1992). *Beyond modularity: A developmental perspective on cognitive science.* Cambridge, MA: MIT Press.

Kline, M. (1980). *Mathematics: The loss of certainty.* Oxford: Oxford University Press.

Latour, B. (1990). Drawing things together. In M. Lynch & S. Woolgar (Eds.), *Representation in scientific practice* (pp. 19–68). Cambridge, MA: MIT Press.

Latour, B. (1993). *We have never been modern.* Cambridge, MA: Harvard University Press.

Latour, B. (1999). *Pandora's hope: Essays on the reality of science studies.* London: Cambridge University Press.

Lehrer, R., Carpenter, S., Schauble, L., & Putz, A. (2000). Designing classrooms that support inquiry. In J. Minstrell & E. V. Zee (Eds.), *Inquiring into inquiry learning and teaching in science* (pp. 80–99). Washington, DC: American Association for the Advancement of Science.

Lehrer, R., & Lesh, R. (2003). Mathematical learning. In W. Reynolds & G. Miller (Eds.), *Handbook of psychology: Vol. 7, Educational psychology* (pp. 357–391). New York: John Wiley.

Lehrer, R., & Pritchard, C. (2002). Symbolizing space into being. In K. Gravemeijer, R. Lehrer, B. van Oers, & L. Verschaffel (Eds.), *Symbolization, modeling and tool use in mathematics education.* (pp. 59–86). Dordrecht, Netherlands: Kluwer Academic Press.

Lehrer, R., & Schauble, L. (2000). Modeling in mathematics and science. In R. Glaser (Ed.), *Advances in instructional psychology: Educational design and cognitive science. Vol. 5* (pp. 101–159). Mahwah, NJ: Lawrence Erlbaum Associates.

Lehrer, R., & Schauble, L. (2004, April). *Modeling aquatic systems: Contexts and practices for supporting inquiry, agency and epistemology.* Paper presented at the annual meeting of the American Educational Research Association, San Diego, CA.

Lehrer, R., & Schauble, L. (2005). Developing modeling and argument in the elementary grades. In T. Romberg & T. P. Carpenter (Eds.), *Understanding mathematics and science matters.* (pp. 29–53). Mahwah, NJ: Lawrence Erlbaum Associates.

Lehrer, R., Schauble, L., Carpenter, S., & Penner, D. E. (2000). The inter-related development of inscriptions and conceptual understanding. In P. Cobb, E. Yackel, & K. McClain (Eds.), *Symbolizing and communicating in mathematics classrooms: Perspectives on discourse, tools, and instructional design* (pp. 325–360). Mahwah, NJ: Lawrence Erlbaum Associates.

Lesh, R., & Doerr, H. (2003). Foundations of a models and modeling perspective on mathematics teaching, learning, and problem solving. In R. Lesh & H. Doerr (Eds.), *Beyond constructivism: Models and modeling perspectives on mathematics problem solving, learning, and teaching.* (pp. 3–33). Mahwah, NJ: Lawrence Erlbaum Associates.

Lesh, R., Hoover, M., Hole, B., Kelly, A., & Post, T. (2000). Principles for developing thought revealing activities for students and teachers. In A. Kelly & R. Lesh (Eds.). *The handbook of research design in mathematics and science education.* (pp. 591–646). Mahwah, NJ: Lawrence Erlbaum Associates.

Leslie, A. M. (1987). Pretense and representation: The origins of "theory of mind." *Psychological Review,* 94(4), 412–426.

Lucas, D., Broderick, N., Lehrer, R., & Bohanan, R. (2005, November). Making the grounds of scientific inquiry visible in the classroom. *Science Scope*. Available at http://www.nsta.org/middleschool, accessed November 23, 2005.

Lynch, M. (1990). The externalized retina: Selection and mathematization in the visual documentation of objects in the life sciences. In M. Lynch & S. Woolgar (Eds.), *Representation in scientific practice* (pp. 153–186). Cambridge, MA: The MIT Press.

Mead, G. H. (1910). Social consciousness and the consciousness of meaning. *Psychological Bulletin*, 7, 397–405.

Metcalf, S. J., Krajcik, J., & Soloway, E. (2000). Model-It: A design retrospective. In M. Jacobson & R. B. Kozma, (Eds.), *Innovations in science and mathematics education: Advanced designs for technologies of learning.* (pp. 77–116). Mahwah, NJ: Lawrence Erlbaum Associates, Inc.

Metz, K. E. (2004). Children's understanding of scientific inquiry: Their conceptualization of uncertainty in investigations of their own design. *Cognition and Instruction*, 22(2), 219–290.

Nersessian, N. J. (2002). The cognitive basis of model-based reasoning in science. In P. Carruthers, S. Stich, & M. Siegal (Eds.), *The cognitive basis of science.* (pp. 133–155). Cambridge: Cambridge University Press.

Nersessian, N. J., Kurz-Milcke, E., Newsletter, W. C., & Davies, J. (2003). Research laboratories as evolving distributed cognitive systems. In R. Alterman & D. Kirsh (Eds.), *Proceedings of the Twenty-Fifth Annual Conference of the Cognitive Science Society* (pp. 857–862). Mahwah, NJ: Erlbaum.

Olson, D. R. (1994). *The world on paper: The conceptual and cognitive implications of writing and reading.* New York: Cambridge University Press.

Penner, D. E. (2000). Explaining systems: Investigating middle school students' understanding of emergent phenomena. *Journal of Research in Science Teaching*, 37, 784–806.

Penner, D. E., Giles, N. D., Lehrer, R., & Schauble, L. (1997). Building functional models: Designing an elbow. *Journal of Research in Science Teaching*, 34(2), 125–143.

Penner, D. E., Lehrer, R., & Schauble, L. (1998). From physical models to biomechanics: A design-based modeling approach. *Journal of the Learning Sciences*, 7(3&4), 429–449.

Petrosino, A. J., Lehrer, R., & Schauble, L. (2003). Structuring error and experimental variation as distribution in the fourth grade. *Mathematical Thinking and Learning*, 5(2&3), 131–156.

Pickering, A. (1995). *The mangle of practice: Time, agency, and science.* Chicago: University of Chicago Press.

Resnick, M. (1994). *Turtles, termites, and traffic jams: Explorations in massively parallel microworlds.* Cambridge, MA: MIT Press.

Resnick, M. (1996). Beyond the centralized mindset. *The Journal for the Learning Sciences*, 5, 1–22.

Resnick, M., & Wilensky, U. (1998). Diving into complexity: developing probabilistic decentralized thinking through role-playing activities. *The Journal of the Learning Sciences*, 7, 153–172.

Schwartz, C. V., & White, B. Y. (2005). Metamodeling knowledge: Developing students' understanding of scientific modeling. *Cognition and Instruction*, 23, 165–205.

Shapin, S., & Schaffer, S. (1985). *Leviathan and the air pump.* Princeton: Princeton University Press.

Stenning, K., Greeno, J. G., Hall, R., Sommerfield, M., & Wiebe, M. (2002). Coordinating mathematical with biological multiplication: Conceptual learning as the development of heterogeneous reasoning systems. In P. Brna, M. Baker, K. Stenning, & A. Tiberghien (Ed.), *The role of communication in learning to model.* (pp 3–48). Mahwah, NJ: Lawrence Erlbaum Associates.

Stewart, I., & Golubitsky, M. (1992). *Fearful symmetry: Is God a geometer?* London: Penguin Books.

Stewart, J., Hafner, R., Johnson, S., & Finkel, E. (1992). Science as model building: Computers and high-school genetics. *Educational Psychologist*, 27, 317–336.

Stewart, S., Passmore, C., Cartier, J., Rudolph, J., & Donovan, S. (2005). Modeling for understanding in science education. In T. Romberg, T. Carpenter, and F. Dremock, (Eds.), *Understanding mathematics and science matters* (pp. 159–184). Mahwah, NJ: Lawrence Erlbaum Associates.

Troseth, G. L. (2003). Getting a clear picture: Young children's understanding of a televised image. *Developmental Science*, 6(3), 247–253.

Troseth, G. L., & DeLoache, J. S. (1998). The medium can obscure the message: Young children's understanding of video. *Child Development*, 69, 950–965.

Troseth, G. L., Pierroutsakos, S. L., & DeLoache, J. S. (2004). From the innocent to the intelligent eye: The early development of pictoral competence. In R. Kail (Ed.), *Advances in child development and behavior, Vol. 32* (pp. 1–35). New York: Academic Press.

White, B., & Frederiksen, J. (1998). Inquiry, modeling, and metacognition: Making science accessible to all students. *Cognition and Instruction*, 16, 3–118.

Wilensky, U. (1996). Modeling rugby: Kick first, generalize later? *International Journal of Computers for Mathematical Learning*, 1, 125–131.

Wilensky, U., & Resnick, M. (1999). Thinking in levels: A dynamic systems approach to making sense of the world. *Journal of Science Education and Technology*. 8(1): 3–19.

Wilensky, U., & Stroup, W. (1999). Learning through participatory simulations: Network-based design for systems learning in classrooms. *Computer Supported Collaborative Learning Conference*, Stanford University, California.

CHAPTER 23

Exploring Mathematics Through Construction and Collaboration

Richard Noss and Celia Hoyles

Introduction

All learning environments are designed based on a set of assumptions about what knowledge should be learned. For example, most mathematics classrooms are designed to teach a certain kind of mathematical knowledge that comprises procedures that solve isolated problems quickly, and this implicitly devalues the importance of structural understanding or of developing an appreciation of underlying mathematical models (see Lehrer & Schauble, this volume). This means that all too often, students do not see the need for consistency or rigor, do not notice conflicting strategies or solutions, and therefore cannot learn from them.

Based on our research in a variety of workplace situations, we are convinced that a crucial element of knowledge required by most, if not all, people, is precisely this appreciation of underlying models. A version of mathematics that emphasizes structures also has the potential to help students understand the computational systems that are increasingly critical in today's society, because computer systems *are* mathematical models – computer software is built out of variables and relationships. As technology becomes more and more advanced, and the underlying models more and more obscure and invisible, it becomes increasingly important that children learn awareness of models; how to build, revise, and evaluate them, and to develop some analytic understanding of how inputs relate to outputs.

In this chapter, we describe two learning environments that we have designed to further this agenda. Each of these environments is based on two principles. The first is *constructionism*: we should put learners in situations where they can construct and revise their own models (see Kafai, this volume; Lehrer & Schauble, this volume). The second is *collaboration*: if our concern is that students come to understand what is significant about models from a specifically mathematical point of view, then learning environments should foster discussion about and reflection upon these models.

Constructionist Design and Tool Mediation

Constructionism argues that students learn by building their own artifacts and sharing them within a community (see Harel & Papert, 1991). Given that the crucial constructionist insight is that learners build things and ideas simultaneously, and that building requires tools, this paradigm has focused on the design of tools and toolsets (see diSessa, 1997, for his discussion of open tools).

When computer tools become an integral part of a learning environment, the mathematical knowledge modeled by the tools and the students' conceptions of that knowledge will both change in the process. The tool shapes what the person can do, what she can think, what she can know, what becomes possible and what becomes impossible. In the opposite direction, the tool is shaped by the person: physically (or virtually) by adapting it, molding it for evolving purposes; or conceptually, by using the tool in ways unforeseen by its designers. Our preferred way of describing this interaction is that the learner builds *situated abstractions* in reciprocal relation with the symbolic tools of the environment; abstractions that are expressed within, and shaped by the tools, the activities and the context (see Noss & Hoyles, 1996; this relationship has also been described as one of "instrumental genesis," see Verillon & Rabardel, 1995, and Artigue, 2002).

This dialectic provides a useful way to think about tools as standing between the learner and the phenomenon being modeled. When tools are used in mathematics classrooms they are often naively assumed to be invisible or transparent: that is, it is assumed that there is a direct interaction between the learner and the mathematical knowledge. This is not the case. For example, a teacher using a simple graphing tool to demonstrate linear relations between variables might change the slope of the line to demonstrate a changing mathematical relationship. However, the students may simply

interpret the line to be rotating, focusing on the visible transformation and failing to see the underlying relationship that it models. As Balacheff (1993) has argued when discussing the idea of "computational transposition," computer tools introduce a new model of knowledge related to the functioning of the machine and the interface designed for the software: the knowledge instantiated in a computer system is not the same knowledge.[1] Alongside this epistemological and cognitive complexity, it is also important to recognize that tools act as mediators of social interaction through which shared expressions can be constructed. This suggests that we must not only analyse how tools shape and are shaped by individual learners' uses but also how they mediate the creation of a collaborative learning environment and the process of co-construction in a community of learners.[2]

This leads us to investigate the conditions under which collaborative learning might foster mathematical learning, and how this can be achieved within the constructionist paradigm. In each of the two learning environments we describe later, we designed ways in which students would interact actively with models, so that they would be encouraged to focus on structure rather than merely on surface-level features of the phenomena under consideration.

Collaboration

It is now generally accepted that descriptions of learning benefit from recognizing the importance of participation in communities of practice (see Lave & Wenger, 1991). Important progress in our understanding of how the community of practice paradigm works has come from studies of the way the scientific community produces knowledge. These studies have shown that, even more than individual or team efforts, the open process of publishing, critiquing, exchanging, and debating ideas significantly contributes to the growth of science (Latour, 1987; see also Roschelle, 1996). In the educational field, there have been attempts to model school learning on this paradigm of intellectual communities of practice (see, for example, Brown & Campione, 1990; Scardamalia & Bereiter, 1991).

Many learning scientists have argued that computers can support such collaborative discussion through specially designed Web-based environments (Stahl, Koschmann, & Suthers, this volume; Scardamalia & Bereiter, this volume). One approach is predicated on the belief that students learn best when they act like researchers: undertaking investigations, producing evidence and seeking contradictory evidence, interpreting outcomes on the basis of their theories, and discussing, explaining, and defending their emerging theories. A well-known example is Knowledge Forum, in which students are prompted toward scientific prediction and reflection by scaffolds that encourage them to articulate their theory, to express what they have learned, or to ask for an explanation (Scardamalia & Bereiter, this volume).

There is, however, evidence to suggest that knowledge building is only sometimes produced in quite the way envisaged by Scardamalia and Bereiter, because communication at a distance rarely continues long enough to produce significant learning (Stahl, 2001, p. 179). We believe that this may result from two tensions facing any classroom collaboration: the tension between the goals of the individual learner and the goals of the group (see Hoyles, Healy, & Pozzi, 1992), and the tension between the school's ethos of "getting the job done quickly" (the procedural approach in math classrooms), versus the sustained engagement needed for truly collaborative constructivist learning. In building the two collaborative learning environments described later, our focus is on "models-as-mathematical-expression." To achieve this, we designed activities that attempted to mesh the conflictual with the consensual, while taking account of the tool mediation of knowledge and of the interactions and discourse by which developing mathematical knowledge is shared.

The Playground Project

We first report an attempt at creating a collaborative and constructionist learning environment called the *Playground* project,[3] in which our overarching design criterion was to build a computational environment in which children could construct, modify, and share computer games using the formalization of rules (the underlying models for the games) as creative tools in the process. Children in different sites in several European countries engaged interactively in the iterative design and construction of games, which they would play together, and modify or rebuild from scratch. Playground provided a virtual world in which the construction and interpretation of formal rules through programming was a natural way to get things done: That is, by immersing the children in an environment in which they could program concretely visible events (e.g., when the ball hits the bat, make a sound), we intended that they would encounter the power of rigorous expression of relationships and model building. The rules had to be articulated explicitly and built externally before they would have any visible effect on the game; so this environment would contribute to model-based learning by allowing these forms of mathematical knowledge to become objects of reflection and discussion.

We worked with children aged six to eight, largely in informal out-of-school settings. Some of these children had only a basic ability to read and write, so requiring them to interact with the computer via text was not an option. We therefore designed and built two Playgrounds, each based on an existing visual programming environment for children: the first on *ToonTalk* (Kahn, 1996) and the second on *Imagine* (a powerful version of Logo: Kalas & Blaho, 2000).

The ToonTalk Playground

ToonTalk is a concurrent constraint-based programming language, in which the actions of animated cartoon-like characters are the source code of the language.[4] Instead of

Figure 23.1. A robot is trained to add the number 1 to a second number 1.

Figure 23.2. Beginning with Figure 1, the constraint that the initial number is 1 is removed by erasing the number 1 from the robot's "thought bubble" so that the robot will be less choosy: now it will add 1 to any number, and continue to do so indefinitely.

writing text-based programs, the ToonTalk programmer constructs programs by training an animated robot with an input, and by directly manipulating tools that tell the robot what to do with this input (see Cypher, 1993, for the idea of "programming by example"). Although robots are initially constrained to work only when the given inputs exactly match their training conditions, they can be generalized very simply without explicit resort to variables (see Figures 23.1 and 23.2). For more details concerning the principles of ToonTalk, together with its rationale and examples, see http://www.toontalk.com (accessed July 31, 2005).

Although it is possible in principle for children to build any desired program from scratch, we preferred to design a set of programs – or "behaviors" – that accomplished specific tasks that would assist in constructing games. A behavior is a ready-made collection of robots (that is, programs) that could be used as it stands, or could, if the learner preferred, be modified or combined with other programs. The design principles were twofold: that behaviors should be simultaneously *visible* and *functional*, so that both what they do and how they do it are easily understandable by children.[5]

Each object on the screen (typically a picture – a spaceship, say) is programmed how to behave by the behaviors attached to it (attaching a behavior to any object is a matter of dropping the robot(s)

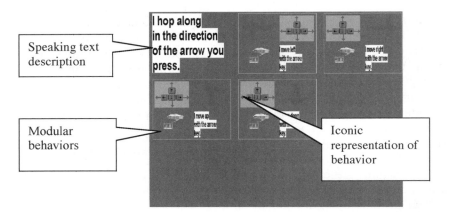

Figure 23.3. Four behaviors on the back of an object, showing the multimodal representation of their functionality.

Figure 23.4. Two examples of each of the three kinds of stones. From left to right: Control stones: *I am controlled by the mouse; I am controlled by the direction arrows.* Condition stones: *when I receive a message; when I touch an object.* Action stones: *I increase my speed (or direction or size); I play a sound.*

corresponding to that behavior onto the back of an object). Figure 23.3 shows the back of an object with four behaviors attached to it. Each one moves the object either right, left, up, or down when the user presses an arrow key; for example, the robot in the "moving left" behavior has in its thought bubble the condition "the left arrow key is pressed" and if that condition is satisfied, the robot moves the picture to the left. Any behavior can be removed directly from an object to disable that functionality (to prevent the object from moving up, for example); any behavior can be copied to another object (so that both objects do the same thing under the same conditions); and any robot within a behavior can be edited for reuse.

The Playground design team built a small set of ready-made games, including a Pong game and a simple adventure game, so that children could first play them and then take them apart or change the way they worked, rather than necessarily building games from scratch (examples of student work can be found in Hoyles, Noss, & Adamson, 2002).

The Imagine Playground

The second version of Playground was built in an icon-based environment called *Pathways.*[6] Instead of robots and thought bubbles, children defined objects' behaviors using collections of iconic rules, which could be viewed by opening a "scroll of paper" attached to the object. Each rule was expressed as a visible "sentence" or string of graphic icons which combined a condition and a series of actions to be executed whenever the condition was true. The icons rep-

resenting the conditions and actions were represented as "stones," small concrete manifestations of the concepts that could be strung together to constitute a rule (see Figure 23.4). Action stones had a convex left side so that conditions with their concave right sides could naturally fit to their left. Any object could accept any number of these iconic rules, all of which would be executed in parallel whenever the conditions for their execution were satisfied. Figure 23.5, for example, illustrates three rules for a "monster." Pathways provided thirteen conditions and twenty-five actions, together with a wide range of object parameters (such as speed and heading) that could be set by using sliders and other manipulable tools. Pathways also included predrawn objects, backgrounds, and – in the final version – a mobile phone icon that allowed players to send messages to each other. Objects could be edited (e.g., size and color changed), copied, deleted, and pasted.

We used the same design principles for both ToonTalk and Imagine, although how they were implemented was clearly shaped by the tool. In Imagine, just as in ToonTalk, we provided a set of premade games that could be taken apart and modified. Figure 23.6 shows one of these video games with a spacecraft, some space monsters, a couple of score displays (in the top corners), together with a set of controls along the bottom of the screen. Each object had its own set of iconic rules; in fact, the "monster" rules in Figure 23.5 are taken from this spaceship game, and any piece of the game could be modified or recycled. Examples of students' work can be found in Goldstein et al. (2001).

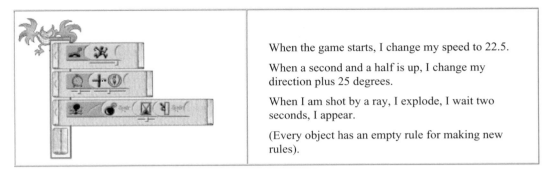

When the game starts, I change my speed to 22.5.

When a second and a half is up, I change my direction plus 25 degrees.

When I am shot by a ray, I explode, I wait two seconds, I appear.

(Every object has an empty rule for making new rules).

Figure 23.5. The stones combined into rules for a monster.

Findings of the Playground Project: Summary and Reflections

In this section we summarize the main outcomes of the Playground project and point to some of the challenges that emerged toward the end of the study.

MATHEMATICS AS MODELS

The Playground experience demonstrated that even very young children could learn about models, even without explicit instruction and in an after-school environment in which learning math and science were not the explicit agenda. By designing games, children learned several features of models: for example, they became aware that model rules could be invariant across different surface features – that is, games could be essentially the same despite changes in pictures, sounds, or spatial configuration of objects. We noted how children engaged with the models at different levels: by tweaking numerical parameters and observing visible results; or by changing part of a behavior or iconic rule to achieve a new effect. We observed some children making rather advanced mathematical discoveries for this age (recall that the oldest was eight) – for example, that two-dimensional motion could be decomposed into horizontal and vertical components (see Noss, 2001). Indeed, the idea of decomposition in general – that an object's behavior is the sum of its multiple underlying behaviors – was one of the important modeling ideas children grasped in the course of their game-building.

There were, however, some less positive outcomes. First, even if children had programmed a rule correctly, they could not necessarily express it precisely in spoken or written language. For example, instead of describing how a robot's rule controlled an object, they often tended to describe its visible behavior. Second, children were not always able to predict the consequences of a rule, even one they had programmed, particularly when that behavior did not make sense within the overall narrative of the game's play they had envisioned. We cannot therefore claim that the formal means of expression afforded by our Playgrounds were fully integrated with the children's verbal and written articulations. Third, the children seldom reached the point at which they could use the tools to build games from scratch without considerable help, although they did become proficient at taking apart and changing games built by others, and reusing and adapting the behaviors or iconic rules in their own games. Fourth, we had hoped children would focus on generalizing a behavior or adapting an iconic rule, but they often found it more interesting to change superficial features, like the colors of the backgrounds, or the shape of their object.

ENGAGING CHILDREN IN THE INSTRUMENTATION PROCESS

We have mentioned earlier how tools and conceptions develop in a dialectical relationship. One direction of this "tool to conception" process is the *instrumentation process*, one part of instrumental genesis mentioned

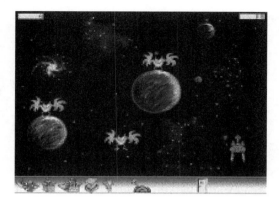

Figure 23.6. A space game.

earlier. This process encompasses the full extent of the new mathematical and technological demands placed on students when digital tools are introduced in mathematics classrooms. It represents a step toward theorising how to connect the standard mathematics curriculum to the changed body of student knowledge acquired by interacting with the new symbolic tools and their associated languages of expression (for an elaboration of these ideas see Hoyles, Noss, & Kent, 2004).

We noticed that the children in all the sites needed time to come to appreciate that there were models underlying their games, and also required time and assistance to engage with several aspects of the instrumentation process: first, how behaviors or iconic rules worked, that is, their syntactic requirements; second, to begin to master this syntax so that they were able to build or change the models on which the games were built; third, to understand that interpreting the models others had constructed for their games involved reading this new syntax; and fourth, to develop some appreciation of quite sophisticated ideas of computer science, such as concurrency and object-oriented programming.[7] However, we also noted that the time and energy necessary to create or modify games did not seem to be a problem: almost all the children became deeply engaged in their projects and were happy to return to them over and over again, throughout an extended period, without significant distraction. We also saw how chil-

dren gradually came to tune their expectations to the possibilities of the tools: and reciprocally, how their use of tools began to coalesce in novel and sometimes unexpected ways.

ENHANCING THE VISIBILITY OF THE RULES OF A GAME

In early interviews with children, we asked them to describe the rules of their favorite games, whether a computer game or a traditional playground or board game. Initially, children mostly described limiting rules (like "you mustn't hit other children") and not the generative rules or the structural constraints that underpinned them ("you have to pick up this object in order to get through that door"). This preference became less pronounced as the children developed familiarity with Playground. By making rules and models visible, the environment helped the children think about complex systems of rules, and how underlying and invisible models generate visible behavior.

FINDING THE RIGHT GRAIN SIZE

The children were able to build a range of games and could modify pre-built games by choosing different objects, behaviors, or iconic rules made by the Playground community as a whole, and take apart and combine them in different ways. Based on this observation, we conclude that we had built a manipulable user interface at about the right *grain size* – the appropriate level of complexity and functionality. We had designed each Playground so that children could make changes at three different grain sizes and classified their actions and game modifications accordingly, from surface to deep structure:

- the *game* grain size: where surface features such as color, sounds, background were modified but not the model underlying the game. We noted that these surface changes were easy to accomplish, but nonetheless could have a remarkable effect on the narrative of the game (see Littleton & Hoyles, 2002).

- the *behavior* or *iconic rule* grain size: swapping, adding, or taking away behaviors or stones, or making simple changes to them such as changing numerical parameters.
- the *model* grain size: where rules were built from scratch or the programs through which they were expressed were edited (only in ToonTalk; children were not offered access to this lower level in the Pathways system).

Children mainly worked at the game or behavior levels, making changes in ways that kept the underlying model essentially the same while achieving a range of different outcomes: for example, they would edit the sound made after a collision, or the picture in a list used for animation.

MOVING BETWEEN NARRATIVE AND MODEL RULES

When children built their games together, we noted that they adopted two types of rules:

> Player rules – *regulations that were agreed (possibly tacitly) among the players that should not be transgressed in the interests of the narrative of the game, but with nothing in the computer to force compliance.*

> Model rules – *programmed rules (at behavior or model levels) that specified the formal conditions and actions for the objects of the game and their relationships (e.g., if the ball hit the paddle then 1 is added to the score).*

When children first planned games, they often envisaged very complex rules; if a rule turned out to be too complex for them to program, they simply agreed to abide by those rules. We call these "player rules" to contrast them with the "model rules" that are explicitly programmed into the game. Over time, we saw how the children came to coordinate these two types of rules: If they wanted cats to *meow* when they drank milk, they recognized that they needed to program this to happen. In order to do this, they had to engage in the instrumentation process: What was the formal equivalent of "drinking milk"? Most defined it as "touching milk," not least because there was a sensor that made it easy to

detect two objects touching, so the rule was programmed as *when a cat touches milk it meows.*

EXPLOITING ONLINE COLLABORATION TO MOVE TOWARDS FORMALIZATION

When children shared games over the Web, we traced how they added complexity and innovative elements to their games in order to make them more challenging for their peers in other locations. They tended to achieve this by simply adding or taking away behaviors or iconic rules, copying objects and their functionality, or changing the appearances of games or the noises made. We noted in a couple of case studies (see Hoyles & Noss, 2004) that when the characters of a game had little or no functionality, the games received confused or lukewarm reactions: the players just did not know what to do. In one game, a dragon was supposed to guard a treasure, and two girls imagined that the dragon was fierce, although the actual image of the dragon looked quite benign (and static); in our terms, they had a player rule that it was fierce, but not a model rule. In a face-to-face setting, the girls would have been able to develop a shared enthusiasm for the narrative, and agree on both player and model rules to convey it. They sent their game to two boys in another country and, in the absence of any rules arising from an underlying model, the boys were unable to appreciate the rich narrative that the girls had constructed around their characters: the lack of a shared interpretation of the player rules made it impossible to appreciate the game in the way intended. Sharing games over the Web eventually pushed the children to formalize their rules, and helped them to articulate how these rules made things work in the way they did.

CONFLICTING RULES

We noted in the introduction to this chapter that in math classrooms children tend to be content with conflicting evidence or even conflicting solutions, because they do not necessarily expect consistency. In Playground, children often attached multiple behaviors or stone rules to a single screen object. We observed several cases in which two of these rules proved to be in conflict; a simple example would be the two rules "move left when you hit an object" and "move right when you hit an object." One example (see Noss et al., 2002) occurred when children built a Coffin game and did not predict the outcome of giving the following two behaviors to the coffin: a guarding behavior that blew up anything that it hit, and a bouncing behavior that made the coffin bounce between two barriers. When the game was played the effect was totally surprising to the children – the coffin, rather than bouncing off a barrier, blew it up. This meant the game could not be played as intended, and given the children's commitment to the game, rather than ignore the conflict – as they might be inclined to do in a math classroom – they worked hard to generate a solution.

WebLabs

Playground did not allow us sufficient time to design for the production of shared games through collaboration between different sites. Children did share their games, but there tended to be only brief dialogue about them and the rules underlying them. Because of limitations of time and resources, we were not able to build asynchronous communication and intersite group evaluation of games. We did come to realize the importance of developing an etiquette about how to make games and their components shareable – for example, by agreeing on a way to label objects, or deciding on a common filing system – but there was little opportunity to embed this etiquette across physical sites. Thus, we were largely unable to establish a community of game designers that spanned sites, or to develop appropriate tools to help children co-construct and reflect together at a distance on, for example, types of games, types of rules, or even problems they had encountered and different ways to overcome them.

A subsequent project, *WebLabs*,[8] started with an agenda similar to Playground, but focused more on developing sustained intersite collaboration. We tried to ensure that the potential of collaboration was exploited in all its forms, by including asynchronous discussion and evaluation as part of the design. We also aimed for a more explicit focus on learning mathematics through modeling, collaborating, and sharing.

We set out to build a system that allows students aged thirteen to fifteen to construct models of their emerging mathematical ideas, to share the models, and to focus students' attention on the process-based descriptions of the models. This agenda resulted in four design challenges:

1. to design a system through which students can share in the process of knowledge building – share their partial understandings through their evolving models of mathematical phenomena. The system needed to support the co-construction of models and also to provide a language of description for the community to talk and write about its developing knowledge of modeling.

2. to plan for constructive interaction of the individual and group agendas by designing activities that can engage a distributed community in modeling practices.

3. to construct an environment in which the etiquette and norms of the intrasite and intersite communities is to produce evidence on *why* a model is correct – why the model works based on *mathematical* reasoning.

4. to ensure that the complexity of the integration of the different technologies in the children's instrumentation process is built into both the design of the activities and into the evaluation of what is learned and how it is learned.

WebLabs comprises research teams in six different countries,[9] and focuses on concepts including Mathematical Sequences, Infinity, and Randomness. We introduce the *WebLabs* project with a sample activity sequence from Mathematical Sequences. Then we describe two technical responses to the design challenges: *transparent modules* and *WebReports*.

A Weblabs Activity Sequence

We have constructed activity sequences for each knowledge domain, designed iteratively with students, and tested against the reality of the curriculum in different countries. Each activity sequence within a given site follows a similar trajectory that includes provision for intersite commenting (see schematic illustratration in Figure 23.7).

The teacher (who is sometimes the researcher) has the crucial role of introducing and motivating the learning aims, the collaborative objectives, the goals of the activity and the different phases in the sequence. Following the motivation phase introduced by a question to explore, there is a class discussion, by the end of which we hope to have elicited more of what individuals know and – as it turns out, much more difficult – what the group collectively knows. Students move on to designing and modeling their ideas, using what we term *transparent modules*, open toolsets written in ToonTalk, and then share their models in WebReports, along with any reflections on the models. As the schematic diagram in Figure 23.7 indicates, modeling and sharing are an iterative cycle, including the writing of and commenting on individual WebReports. The cycle was planned to conclude with a collective intrasite group WebReport, written by the students (with teacher assistance), and including models, descriptions, and explanations.

Up to this point, most activities are assumed to take place within a given site (classroom, out-of-school club or small group); at the same time, students elsewhere will have worked through a similar cycle of activities. At convenient points of group activity, the students at one site are encouraged to read and comment on the WebReports from another student group. Finally, teachers orchestrate intersite exchanges about alternative models, eventually leading to a second round of intrasite group WebReports, and possibly a shared intersite WebReport.

We have trialed several activity sequences and we now present a small sample of student engagement in one of the sequences, which set out to explore the mathematical ideas of convergence and divergence. What happens to the sequence $1, 1/2, 1/4, 1/8, 1/16 \ldots$ and so on forever? Does the sequence $1, 1/2, 1/3, 1/4, 1/5 \ldots$ behave in the same way? What happens if we form the running totals ("partial sums") of these sequences, e.g. $1, 1 + 1/2, 1 + 1/2 + 1/3, \ldots$? There are many interesting mathematical ideas here that go beyond a superficial "spotting of pattern," and which require some structural appreciation of what happens and why. Until now, students would normally only learn about these ideas at or near university level, given the necessity to develop rather sophisticated algebraic competence to do so.

Students began by programming ToonTalk robots to generate simple sequences and the corresponding sequences of running totals. The aim was for the students to explore what happens to the terms of a sequence over time, and also conjecture and discuss what happens to the running totals as more and more terms are added. The students also used an EXCEL tool that we built that would automatically import data from a ToonTalk program into an EXCEL worksheet, with which the students were already familiar, so they could put graphs or charts into their WebReports to illustrate their arguments. Figure 23.8 shows schematically how the world of ToonTalk, in which process is made visible, is linked through a packaged tool, into data that is graphed in Excel. These activities led the students to ask questions such as: can the terms of a sequence get ever smaller yet never go below zero? (There was strong disagreement on this question!). Does the sum $1 + 1/2 + 1/3 + 1/4 + 1/5 + \ldots$ grow indefinitely, or is there a "limit" (the students' word)? After running the robot for thousands of terms (which can be achieved remarkably quickly), we found that most would think (correctly) that it would grow forever.

When the students repeated the activity to investigate the running totals of the sequence $1/2^n$, that is $1, 1 + 1/2, 1 + 1/2 + 1/4, 1 + 1/2 + 1/4 + 1/8 \ldots$, their first inclination

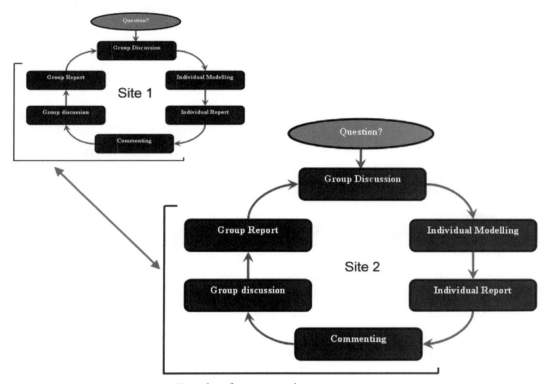

Figure 23.7. Template for intra- and intersite activity sequences.

was to remark that it would be like the reciprocals (as earlier).[10] On further investigation, one student felt that "It doesn't go over 2, because you're adding things that are getting small *really fast*" (see Figure 23.8): a good point for collective discussion.

During the activity sequence, several WebReports were published, and these suggested many opportunities for students to challenge each other's assertions that were taken up in the second iteration of the work. For example, what does a student mean by terms like "getting really small"? Can $1/n$ be *really* small? Other students felt that the long-term behavior of a sequence depended on the size of the starting number, so that, for example, $1/3^n$ would behave differently from $1000000/3^n$. On investigating this last sequence, and its associated series, one student commented on her WebReport: "In this task I found out that if you divide a million by 3 and carry on doing it, the number never drops below zero. I also found out that if you keep adding the previous numbers the numbers don't go above 1500000". Her

WebReport showed her packaged model, an Excel graph, and the explanations for her findings.

Transparent Modules

To support WebLab's collaborative activities, we built *transparent modules* (TMs), carefully packaged sets of tools with which students could construct working models of their evolving knowledge in the specific domains chosen. TMs are modules in the sense that each has embedded within it a set of mathematical ideas that are *operationalized*, that is, the ideas are made to do work by producing something useful or interesting enough to merit further exploration and discussion. They are transparent in the sense that it is relatively straightforward to inspect the underlying models, to manipulate and change them, and to rebuild them as necessary. We used ToonTalk as the platform, so the building of the TMs could benefit from our experiences of designing and building behaviors in Playground.

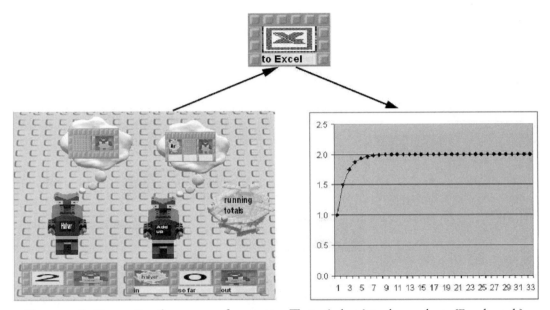

Figure 23.8. Connecting the process of generating $\sum 1/_{2n}$ (robots) to the products (Excel graph).

We encouraged the students to package their own models, and to include instructions on how to use them. Packaging a model made it easy to start up the model; upon clicking on a packaged model, the system would launch ToonTalk automatically, and the necessary robots and objects would appear on the screen to be run or inspected. Reversing the process, that is, uploading a new or revised model to the system, is equally straightforward: a student literally holds the ToonTalk object to be uploaded in her virtual "hand", pauses ToonTalk, and uploads the object to the WebReports clipboard. Once uploaded, the student can simply paste the ToonTalk object into a report as desired. Figure 23.9 illustrates an example of a WebReport showing a packaged model, an Excel graph generated by running the robots, and some comments by the students about the data produced from the activity.

WebReports

The second pillar of WebLabs was the design of the *WebReport* system, which we hoped would serve both as the collaboratively constructed, public record of the evolving understandings of a knowledge domain among the community, and as the final product of the community's work. On entering the WebReports section of the WebLabs Web site, students log in, accessing who is online, what messages they have received, a list of activities within each knowledge domain, and a description of the various tools available to explore them, including working models that can be uploaded for use in a project. There are also links to the students' personal homepages, and a range of other functionalities including the ability to view reports from other members of the group. There is a help section which includes a general teacher guide, a technical help facility, and a pedagogical guide for each activity sequence.

In one respect, our approach is similar to that of Knowledge Forum (Scardamalia & Bereiter, this volume), from whom we have drawn inspiration. But, as we suggested earlier, the challenge we face is somewhat different from Knowledge Forum: our focus is more specifically mathematical. This means that sharing the packaged models becomes the means to collaborate regarding mathematical ideas: the models are *themselves* the mathematical ideas we want

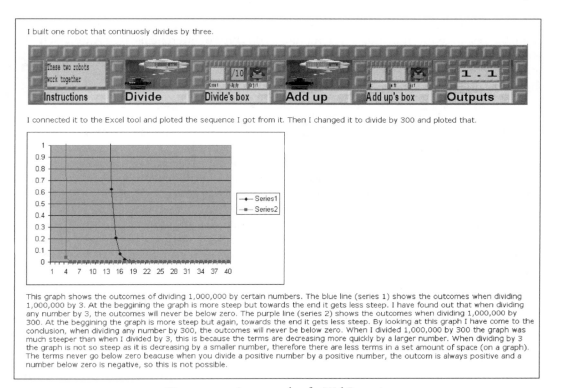

I built one robot that continuously divides by three.

These two robots work together

| Instructions | Divide | Divide's box | Add up | Add up's box | Outputs |

I connected it to the Excel tool and ploted the sequence I got from it. Then I changed it to divide by 300 and ploted that.

This graph shows the outcomes of dividing 1,000,000 by certain numbers. The blue line (series 1) shows the outcomes when dividing 1,000,000 by 3. At the beggining the graph is more steep but towards the end it gets less steep. I have found out that when dividing any number by 3, the outcomes will never be below zero. The purple line (series 2) shows the outcomes when dividing 1,000,000 by 300. At the beggining the graph is more steep but again, towards the end it gets less steep. By looking at this graph I have come to the conclusion, when dividing any number by 300, the outcomes will never be below zero. When I divided 1,000,000 by 300 the graph was much steeper than when I divided by 3, this is because the terms are decreasing more quickly by a larger number. When dividing by 3 the graph is not so steep as it is decreasing by a smaller number, therefore there are less terms in a set amount of space (on a graph). The terms never go below zero beacuse when you divide a positive number by a positive number, the outcom is always positive and a number below zero is negative, so this is not possible.

Figure 23.9. An example of a WebReport.

students to share and provide the language for sharing.

As well as describing work in progress, students can type a challenge for other students, again including a ToonTalk model. Borrowing from Knowledge Forum, we have added a range of scaffolds to the WebReports to encourage commenting, which include "Can you explain?", "What if...", "I have a conjecture...", and "This doesn't work because..." as well as a box to insert a new custom comment type or an unclassified comment. Comments also can be posted as replies to other comments so that threads of discussion can be created, in much the same way as in Internet newsgroups.

Our original plan was that students from different sites participating in the same activity sequence would produce their own group WebReports, and then two or more sites would collaborate to produce a final intersite report. However, this last step has proven to be much more difficult than we imagined. Many of the difficulties have been pragmatic; for example, the language barrier between students in different countries, differences in curricula, time differences, and the time-consuming nature of group report writing. More fundamentally, we have not yet managed to develop sufficiently the students' sense of ownership of these intersite group reports and a common understanding of their purpose. To address this challenge, we plan to enhance the intersite motivator phase and the WebReport system's support for viewing and comparing models.

WebLabs: Conclusions

Most students have been able to build models successfully with the TMs, and have become accustomed to the WebReport system, using it to upload their models and to insert reflective comments on them. WebReports have become part of classroom practice, and in some cases, have even proved to be a catalyst for developing an exploratory set of norms within the classroom. WebReports have also served as a valuable resource for individuals to remember and revisit their earlier work, sometimes producing new insights – a benefit that we had not anticipated. The technical tasks of learning about uploading models, commenting and adding graphs, and so on has been relatively straightforward; largely, we think, because students want to receive comments, and be part of this wider online community. This communication is greatly aided by the norms associated with packaging models, because students in remote sites can immediately know what to expect of a model and what to do with it. However, although a number of intrasite group reports were produced, there were few intersite group reports. Most reports received at most one comment, despite the fact that we know students enjoyed receiving comments, particularly from students in remote sites.

We have, however, achieved remarkable success in encouraging discussion of mathematical ideas in which the interchange was based around students challenging each other competitively rather than building a joint outcome. For example, one challenge, Guess My Robot, was to find the rule underlying a sequence, which was followed by the quest for more elegant solutions. This interchange was sustained over several weeks and increasingly sophisticated sequences and explanations were invoked (Mor et al., 2004). We adopted a similar approach, called Guess My Graph, in exploring motion, and that was equally successful in terms of sustained interactions between sites (see Simpson, Hoyles, & Noss, 2005). We have asked ourselves what characteristics of this type of activity might account for its success, in comparison to the relative failure of students to produce shared reports collaboratively. We believe that the "Guess My..." format taps into a game-like stance to achieve a "best" result, a competitive interaction based on a norm of achieving shared expression and understanding of different approaches. A competitive edge within a collaborative framework can be pedagogically effective, particularly in a distributed community, and we plan to

redesign other activity sequences to include this type of interchange (see Andriessen, this volume).

Concluding Comments

In both Playground and WebLabs, we have been addressing a general question facing the learning sciences: how individual learning, computational models, and community knowledge coevolve in activity. Our conception of mathematics learning – models-as-mathematical expression – can, with careful design, contribute to this general learning sciences endeavor. Even in the brief episodes reported earlier, we can begin to see how mathematical ideas expressed and shared as models can become the subject of reflection and discussion, and how this dialogue can begin to construct some rich understandings of mathematics that foreground its structure and the properties that follow from it.

One particularly salient feature of this "model-based reasoning" (see Lehrer & Schauble, this volume) suggests that we might wish to see reasoning as necessarily *layered*, and that this layering can be facilitated by the judicious design of tools and activities: sometimes it is only necessary to view a model, sometimes only to modify a model, and it may not always be possible or necessary to appreciate all the model's structural relationships. We would argue that a long-term goal is to design for appreciation of the existence of a model and then, over an extended time interval, dig deeper down the layers into how the model is made, how it can be modified, and how it can be combined with other models. These layers of activities and tools that facilitate appropriate interaction seem to open up a fruitful direction for developing corresponding layers of cognitive (and collective) knowledge building.

Getting students to share mathematical ideas is not straightforward. In our work we noticed a tendency for students to build new models rather than comment on those of others. We do not know to what degree this may be a result of the difficulty of "reading"

ToonTalk robots; reading them is difficult because it involves observing a narrative unfold over time, unlike reading a static text (although we noted a similar reluctance to reuse Logo programs some twenty-five years ago). However, we suspect that at least part of the challenge is learning sufficient fluency to express oneself in the language of the model.

Only teachers can ensure that discussions are about the group's evolving knowledge, even more so when discussions are about deep understanding rather than superficial facts and skills. This is, of course, a problem of establishing a sociomathematical norm in the classrooms of an expectation to uncover the layers of reasoning, and it is intimately tied not only to the actions of the teacher but also to the nature of the activity structures, tools, and other artifacts of the setting (such as the WebReports). We know from both Playground and WebLabs that students *are* able to manage their own learning; to listen to, challenge, and learn from others from diverse backgrounds; and to manage multiple technologies. Indeed, they enjoy engaging in this type of activity, but this type of classroom or interclassroom norm has to be developed over time, involving new roles for the teacher and student.

Although the teacher was not the focal point of our activity in either project, we observed that teaching was most successful when it was not merely motivational but, rather, more specific, encouraging high-level discussion of computational or mathematical ideas. Of course, this presupposes that teachers themselves have adequate knowledge of the content, of the tools, and of the benefits of developing a community of learners through such collaborative interchanges. Although the tools we have described here can facilitate this process, they could not hope to be successful until both the teacher and the school community recognize the benefits of sharing, ensure fluency of tool use, and incorporate cross-site collaboration into their practice – while recognizing at the same time how this fluency will shape students' reasoning and how this reasoning is expressed (Fishman & Davis, this volume).

All this will only happen when teachers have experienced the conceptual power of constructionist collaboration for themselves, a potential we have glimpsed in the two projects and that we hope has been conveyed in this chapter.

Footnotes

1. Colette Laborde has recently provided the following example (personal communication). Consider two parallelograms constructed by a dynamic geometry system. Version 1 takes a line segment AB, a second one BC, and then constructs parallel lines (and then line segments) to find the fourth vertex, D. Version 2 uses a well-known theorem concerning the midpoints of diagonals of a parallelogram, and finds the fourth vertex by constructing a "symmetrical point" of the midpoint of AC. Now a thought experiment: how do versions 1 and 2 behave as the parallelogram is reshaped by moving point A to be on the same line with B and C, so that it has zero area (i.e., is the degenerate parallelogram still a parallelogram?).

2. We do not here discuss the question of the legitimacy of the knowledge developed in different communities. From a sociocultural point of view, instrumentation can be regarded as part of the process of developing participation within a community of practice, a process that first must accept "nonstandard" ways of expressing mathematical ideas as legitimate contributions to collective activity (see Hoyles, Noss, & Kent, 2004).

3. The Playground Project was funded by the EU Experimental Schools Environments program, Grant #29329. We acknowledge the contribution of all the Playground team, and notably the UK team, R. Adamson, M. Graham, S. Lowe, and ToonTalk's designer K. Kahn.

4. The underlying computation model of ToonTalk consists of autonomous agents executing their programs concurrently. These agents coordinate and communicate by asynchronous passing of messages via ToonTalk "birds."

5. To account for the young age of the children, we designed behaviors with multimodal representations of their functionality: descriptive text that also spoke when pointed at, together with graphical (often animated) descriptions.

6. *Magic Forest* in its English version and *Floresta Magica* in Portuguese (Portugal and Brasil). See http://www.logo.com/cat/view/magicforest.html, accessed July 31, 2005.

7. Learners discussed for example issues such as "which object should have the behavior/rule" and how inheritance should work when behaviors/rules were swapped between objects.

8. Grant IST 2001–3220 of the Information Society Technologies Programme of the European Commission. We acknowledge the contribution of all the *WebLabs* team, and notably the UK researchers, Y. Mor and G. Simpson. See http://www.weblabs.eu.com, accessed July 31, 2005.

9. The Institute of Education, University of London; Logotron Ltd, Cambridge, UK; Royal Institute of Technology (KTH), Stockholm, Sweden; Institute for Educational Technology, Genoa, Italy; University of Lisbon, Lisbon, Portugal; University of Cyprus, Nicosia, Cyprus; Sofia University, Sofia, Bulgaria.

10. One student initialized the robot with 2 in the input box, equivalent to n = o.

References

Artigue, M. (2002). Learning mathematics in a CAS environment: The genesis of a reflection about instrumentation and the dialectics between technical and conceptual work. *International Journal of Computers for Mathematical Learning, 7*(3), 245–274.

Balacheff, N. (1993). Artificial intelligence and real teaching. In C. Keitel & K. Ruthven (Eds.), *Learning from computers: Mathematics education and technology* (pp. 131–158). Berlin: Springer-Verlag.

Brown, A. L., & Campione, J. C. (1990). Communities of learning and thinking, or a context by any other name. *Contributions to Human Development, 21*, 108–126.

Cypher, A. (Ed.). (1993). *Watch what I do: Programming by demonstration.* Cambridge, MA: MIT Press.

diSessa, A. A. (1997). Open toolsets: New ends and new means in learning mathematics and science with computers. In E. Pehkonen (Ed.), *Proceedings of the 21st Conference of the International Group for the Psychology of Mathematics Education*, Vol. 1, pp. 47–62. Lahti, Finland. (available at http://www.soe.berkeley.edu/boxer and www.pyxisystems.com, both accessed November 21, 2005)

Goldstein, R., Kalas, I., Noss, R., & Pratt D. (2001). Building rules. In M. Beynon, C. L. Nehaniv, & K. Dautenhahn (Eds.), *Proceedings of the 4th International Conference of Cognitive Technology CT2001* (pp. 267–281). Coventry, UK: University of Warwick.

Harel, I., & Papert, S. (Eds.). (1991). *Constructionism.* Norwood, NJ: Ablex Publishing Corporation.

Hoyles, C., Healy, L., & Pozzi, S. (1992). Interdependence and autonomy: Aspects of groupwork with computers. In H. Mandel, E. De Corte, S. N. Bennett, & H. F. Friedrich (eds.), *Learning and instruction: European research in international context* (Vol. 2, pp. 239–257).

Hoyles, C., & Noss, R. (2004). Making rules in collaborative game design. In J. Siraj-Blatchford (Ed.), *Developing new technologies for young children*, pp. 55–73. Stoke on Trent/Sterling: Trentham Books.

Hoyles, C., Noss, R., & Adamson, R. (2002). Rethinking the microworld idea. *Journal of Educational Computing Research, 27*(1&2), 29–53.

Hoyles, C., Noss, R., & Kent (2004). On the integration of digital technologies into mathematics classrooms. *International Journal of Computers for Mathematical Learning, 9*(3), 309–326.

Kahn, K. (1996). ToonTalk – An animated programming environment for children. *Journal of Visual Languages and Computing 7*(2), 197–217.

Kalas, I., & Blaho, A. (2000). Imagine... new generation of Logo: programmable pictures. In *Proceedings of conference on educational uses of information and communication technologies, IFIP 16th world computer conference* (pp. 427–430). ISBN 3-901882-07-3. Beijing, China.

Latour, B. (1987). *Science in action.* Milton Keynes, UK: Open University Press.

Lave, J., & Wenger, E. (1991). *Situated learning: Legitimate peripheral participation.* Cambridge: Cambridge University Press.

Littleton, K., & Hoyles, C. (2002). The gendering of information technology. In N. Yelland, & A. Rubin (Eds.), *Ghosts in the machine: Women's voices in research and technology* (pp. 3–32). New York: Peter Lang Publishing.

Mor, Y., Hoyles, C., Kahn, K., Noss, R., & Simpson, G. (2004). Thinking in progress. *Micromath*, 20(2), 17–23.

Noss, R. (2001). For a learnable mathematics in the digital culture. *Educational Studies in Mathematics*, 48, 21–46.

Noss, R., & Hoyles, C. (1996). *Windows on mathematical meanings: Learning cultures and computers*. Dordrecht: Kluwer Academic Press.

Noss, R., Hoyles, C., Gurtner J-L., Adamson R., & Lowe, S. (2002). Face-to-face and online collaboration: Appreciating rules and adding complexity. *International Journal of Continuing Engineering Education and Lifelong Learning* 12(5/6), 521–539.

Roschelle, J. (1996). Learning by collaborating: Convergent conceptual change. In T. Koschmann (Ed.), *CSCL: Theory and practice of an emerging paradigm* (pp. 209–248). Mahwah, NJ: Lawrence Erlbaum Asscociates.

Scardamalia. M. & Bereiter, C. (1991). Higher levels of agency for children in knowledge building: A challenge for the design of new knowledge media. *Journal of the Learning Sciences*, 1, 38–68.

Simpson, G., Hoyles, C., & Noss, R. (2005). Designing a programming-based approach for modelling scientific phenomena. *Journal of Computer Assisted Learning*, 21, pp. 143–158.

Stahl, G. (2001). Rediscovering CSCL. In T. Koschmann, R. Hall, N. Miyake (Eds.), *CSCL2: Carrying forward the conversation* (pp. 177–178). Mahwah, NJ: Lawrence Erlbaum Asscociates.

Verillon, P., & Rabardel, P. (1995). Cognition and Artifacts: a contribution to the study of thought in relation to instrumented activity, *European Journal of Psychology of Education*, 10(1), 77–101.

Part V

LEARNING TOGETHER

CHAPTER 24

Computer-Supported Collaborative Learning

Gerry Stahl, Timothy Koschmann, and Daniel D. Suthers

Computer-supported collaborative learning (CSCL) is an emerging branch of the learning sciences. It is concerned with studying how people can learn together with the help of computers.

As we will see in this chapter, such a simple statement conceals considerable complexity. The interplay of learning with technology turns out to be quite intricate. The inclusion of collaboration, computer mediation, and distance education has problematized the very notion of learning and called into question prevailing assumptions about how to study it.

Like many active fields of scientific research, CSCL has a complex relationship to established disciplines, it evolves in ways that are hard to pinpoint, and it includes important contributions that seem incompatible. The field of CSCL has a long history of controversy about its theory, methods, and definition. Furthermore, it is important to view CSCL as a vision of what may be possible with computers and of what kinds of research should be conducted, rather than as an established body of broadly accepted laboratory and classroom practices. We start from some popular understandings of the issues of CSCL and gradually reveal its more complex nature.

CSCL Within Education

As the study of particular forms of learning, CSCL is intimately concerned with education. It considers all levels of formal education from kindergarten through graduate study as well as informal education, such as in museums. Computers have become important at all levels of education, with school districts and politicians around the world setting goals of increasing student access to computers and the Internet. The idea of encouraging students to learn together in small groups has also become increasingly emphasized in the learning sciences, as seen in many of the other chapters of this handbook. However, the ability to combine these two ideas (computer support and collaborative learning, or technology and education) to effectively enhance learning remains a challenge – a challenge that CSCL is designed to address.

Computers and Education

Computers in the classroom are often viewed with skepticism. They are seen by critics as boring and antisocial, a haven for geeks, and a mechanical, inhumane form of training. CSCL is based on precisely the opposite vision: it proposes the development of new software and applications that bring learners together and that can offer creative activities of intellectual exploration and social interaction.

CSCL arose in the 1990s in reaction to software that forced students to learn as isolated individuals. The exciting potential of the Internet to connect people in innovative ways provided a stimulus for CSCL research. As CSCL developed, unforeseen barriers to designing, disseminating, and effectively taking advantage of innovative educational software became more and more apparent. A transformation of the whole concept of learning was required, including significant changes in schooling, teaching, and being a student. Many of the necessary changes are reflected in the educational approaches presented in Part 1 of this volume; for instance, adopting educational frameworks such as constructionism, knowledge building, and situativity.

E-Learning at a Distance

CSCL is often conflated with e-learning, the organization of instruction across computer networks. E-learning is too often motivated by a naïve belief that classroom content can be digitized and disseminated to large numbers of students with little continuing involvement of teachers and without the cost of buildings and transportation. There are a number of problems with this view.

First, it is simply not true that the posting of content, such as slides, texts, or videos, makes for compelling instruction. Such content may provide important resources for students, just as textbooks always have, but they can only be effective within a larger motivational and interactive context.

Second, online teaching requires at least as much effort by human teachers as classroom teaching. Not only must the teacher prepare materials and make them available by computer; the teacher must motivate and guide each student, through ongoing interaction and a sense of social presence. Whereas online teaching allows students from around the world to participate and allows teachers to work from any place with Internet connectivity, it generally significantly increases the teacher effort per student.

Third, CSCL stresses collaboration among the students, so that they are not simply reacting in isolation to posted materials. The learning takes place largely through interactions among students. Students learn by expressing their questions, pursuing lines of inquiry together, teaching each other, and seeing how others are learning. Computer support for such collaboration is central to a CSCL approach to e-learning. Stimulating and sustaining productive student interaction is difficult to achieve; it requires skillful planning, coordination, and implementation of curriculum, pedagogy, and technology.

Fourth, CSCL is also concerned with face-to-face (F2F) collaboration. Computer support of learning does not always take the form of an online communication medium; the computer support may involve, for instance, a computer simulation of a scientific model or a shared interactive representation. In this case, the collaboration focuses on the construction and exploration of the simulation or representation. Alternatively, a group of students might use a computer to browse through information on the Internet and to discuss, debate, gather, and present what they found collaboratively. Computer support can take the form of distant or F2F interaction, either synchronously or asynchronously.

Cooperative Learning in Groups

The study of group learning began long before CSCL. Since at least the 1960s, before the advent of networked personal computers, there was considerable investigation of cooperative learning by education researchers. Research on small groups has an even longer history within social psychology.

To distinguish CSCL from this earlier investigation of group learning, it is useful to draw a distinction between *cooperative* and *collaborative* learning. In a detailed discussion of this distinction, Dillenbourg (1999b) defined the distinction roughly as follows:

> In cooperation, partners split the work, solve sub-tasks individually and then assemble the partial results into the final output. In collaboration, partners do the work "together." (p. 8)

He then referred to Roschelle and Teasley's (1995) definition of collaboration:

> This chapter presents a case study intended to exemplify the use of a computer as a cognitive tool for learning that occurs socially. We investigate a particularly important kind of social activity, the collaborative construction of new problem solving knowledge. *Collaboration is a process by which individuals* negotiate and share meanings *relevant to the problem-solving task at hand.* ... *Collaboration is a coordinated, synchronous activity that is the result of a continued attempt to construct and maintain a shared conception of a problem. (p. 70, emphasis added)*

In cooperation, the learning is done by individuals, who then contribute their individual results and present the collection of individual results as their group product. Learning in cooperative groups is viewed as something that takes place individually – and can therefore be studied with the traditional conceptualizations and methods of educational and psychological research. By contrast, in the Roschelle and Teasley characterization of collaboration, learning occurs socially as the collaborative construction of knowledge. Of course, individuals are involved in this as members of the group, but the activities that they engage in are not individual-learning activities, but group interactions like negotiation and sharing. The participants do not go off to do things individually, but remain engaged with a shared task that is constructed and maintained by and for the group as such. The

collaborative negotiation and social sharing of *group meanings* – phenomena central to collaboration – cannot be studied with traditional psychological methods.

Collaboration and Individual Learning

As we have just seen, collaborative learning involves individuals as group members, but also involves phenomena like the negotiation and sharing of meanings – including the construction and maintenance of shared conceptions of tasks – that are accomplished interactively in group processes. Collaborative learning involves individual learning, but is not reducible to it. The relationship between viewing collaborative learning as a group process versus as an aggregation of individual change is a tension at the heart of CSCL.

Earlier studies of learning in groups treated learning as a fundamentally individual process. The fact that the individuals worked in groups was treated as a contextual variable that influenced the individual learning. In CSCL, by contrast, learning is also analyzed as a group process; analysis of learning at both the individual and the group unit of analysis is necessary.

To some extent, CSCL has emerged in reaction to previous attempts to use technology within education and to previous approaches to understand collaborative phenomena with the traditional methods of the learning sciences. The learning sciences as a whole have shifted from a narrow focus on individual learning to an incorporation of both individual and group learning, and the evolution of CSCL has paralleled this movement.

The Historical Evolution of CSCL

The Beginnings

Three early projects – the ENFI Project at Gallaudet University, the CSILE project at the University of Toronto, and the Fifth Dimension Project at the University of California San Diego – were forerunners for what was later to emerge as the field of

CSCL. All three involved explorations of the use of technology to improve learning related to literacy.

The ENFI Project produced some of the earliest examples of programs for computer-aided composition or "CSCWriting" (Bruce & Rubin, 1993; Gruber, Peyton, & Bruce, 1995). Students who attend Gallaudet are deaf or hearing impaired; many such students enter college with deficiencies in their written-communication skills. The goal of the ENFI Project was to engage students in writing in new ways: to introduce them to the idea of writing with a "voice" and writing with an audience in mind. The technologies developed, though advanced for the time, might seem rudimentary by today's standards. Special classrooms were constructed in which desks with computers were arranged in a circle. Software resembling today's chat programs was developed to enable the students and their instructor to conduct textually mediated discussions. The technology in the ENFI project was designed to support a new form of meaning-making by providing a new medium for textual communication.

Another early, influential project was undertaken by Bereiter and Scardamalia at the University of Toronto (see Scardamalia & Bereiter, this volume). They were concerned that learning in schools is often shallow and poorly motivated. They contrasted the learning that takes place in classrooms with the learning that occurs in "knowledge-building communities" (Bereiter, 2002; Scardamalia & Bereiter, 1996), like the communities of scholars that work on a shared research problem. In the CSILE Project (Computer Supported Intentional Learning Environment), later known as Knowledge Forum, they developed technologies and pedagogies to restructure classrooms as knowledge-building communities. Like the ENFI Project, CSILE sought to make writing more meaningful by engaging students in joint text production. The texts produced in each case were quite different, however. The ENFI texts were conversational; they were produced spontaneously and were generally not preserved beyond the completion of a class. CSILE texts, on the other hand, were archival, like conventional scholarly literatures.

As was the case for CSILE, the Fifth Dimension (5thD) Project began with an interest in improving reading skills (Cole, 1996). It started with an after-school program organized by Cole and colleagues at Rockefeller University. When the Laboratory of Comparative Human Cognition (LCHC) moved to the University of California at San Diego, the 5thD was elaborated into an integrated system of mostly computer-based activities selected to enhance students' skills for reading and problem solving. The "Maze," a board-game type layout with different rooms representing specific activities, was introduced as a mechanism for marking student progress and coordinating participation with the 5thD. Student work was supported by more-skilled peers and by undergraduate volunteers from the School of Education. The program was originally implemented at four sites in San Diego, but was eventually expanded to multiple sites around the world (Nicolopoulou & Cole, 1993).

All of these projects – ENFI, CSILE, and 5thD – shared a goal of making instruction more oriented toward meaning-making. All three turned to computer and information technologies as resources for achieving this goal, and all three introduced novel forms of organized social activity within instruction. In this way, they laid the groundwork for the subsequent emergence of CSCL.

From Conferences to a Global Community

In 1983, a workshop on the topic of "joint problem solving and microcomputers" was held in San Diego. Six years later, a NATO-sponsored workshop was held in Maratea, Italy. The 1989 Maratea workshop is considered by many to mark the birth of the field, as it was the first public and international gathering to use the term "computer-supported collaborative learning" in its title. The first full-fledged CSCL conference was organized at Indiana University in the fall of 1995. Subsequent international meetings have taken place at least biennially, with conferences at the University of Toronto in 1997, Stanford University in 1999, the University of Maastricht in the Netherlands in 2001, the University of Colorado in 2002, the University of Bergen in Norway in 2003, and the National Central University in Taiwan in 2005.

A specialized literature documenting theory and research in CSCL has developed since the NATO-sponsored workshop in Maratea. Four of the most influential monographs are Newman, Griffin, and Cole (1989); Bruffee (1993); Crook (1994); and Bereiter (2002). Additionally, there have been a number of edited collections specifically focusing on CSCL research, including O'Malley (1995); Koschmann (1996a); Dillenbourg (1999a); and Koschmann, Hall, and Miyake (2002). A book series on CSCL published by Kluwer (now Springer) includes five volumes to date. The CSCL conference proceedings have been the primary vehicle for publications in the field. A number of journals have also played a role, particularly the *Journal of the Learning Sciences*. The *International Journal of Computer-Supported Collaborative Learning* started publishing in 2006. Although the community was centered in Western Europe and Northern America in its early years, it has evolved into a rather well-balanced international presence (Hoadley, 2005; Kienle & Wessner, 2005). The 2005 conference in Taiwan and the establishment of the new international journal were planned to make the community truly global.

From Artificial Intelligence to Collaboration Support

The field of CSCL can be contrasted with earlier approaches to using computers in education. Koschmann (1996b) identified the following historical sequence of approaches: (a) computer-assisted instruction, (b) intelligent tutoring systems, (c) Logo as Latin, (d) CSCL.

The first use of computers in education was computer-assisted instruction. This was a behaviorist approach that dominated the early years of educational computer applications beginning in the 1960s. It conceived of learning as the memorization of facts. Domains of knowledge were broken down into elemental facts that were presented to students in a logical sequence through computerized drill and practice. Many commercial educational software products still take this approach.

The second use of computers in education was the intelligent tutoring system (e.g., Koedinger & Corbett, this volume). These systems were based on a cognitivist philosophy that analyzed student learning in terms of mental models and potentially faulty mental representations. They rejected the behaviorist view that learning could be supported without concern for how students represented and processed knowledge. Originating in the cognitive science of the 1970s, this approach created computer models of student understanding and then responded to student actions based on occurrences of typical errors identified in student mental models.

The third use of computers in education began in the 1980s, and was epitomized by the teaching of the Logo programming language. Logo took a constructivist approach, arguing that students must build their knowledge themselves. It provided stimulating environments for students to explore and to discover the power of reasoning, as illustrated in software programming constructs: functions, subroutines, loops, variables, recursion, and so on.

CSCL represents the fourth and most recent use of computers in education. CSCL approaches explore how computers could bring students together to learn collaboratively in small groups and in learning communities. Motivated by social constructivist and dialogical theories, these efforts seek to provide and support opportunities for students to learn together by directed discourse that would construct shared knowledge.

During the 1970s and 1980s, at a time when mainframe computers were becoming available to schools and microcomputers started to appear, artificial intelligence

(AI) was near the height of its popularity. So it was natural that computer scientists interested in educational applications of computer technology would be attracted by the exciting promises of AI. AI is computer software that closely mimics behaviors that might be considered intelligent if done by a human (e.g., to play chess by considering the pros and cons of alternative sequences of legal moves). Intelligent tutoring systems are a prime example of AI, because they replicate the actions of a human tutor – providing responses to student input (e.g., detailed steps in solving a math problem) by analyzing the student problem-solving strategy and offering advice by comparing student actions to programmed models of correct and erroneous understanding. This is still an active research area within the learning sciences (see Koedinger & Corbett, this volume), but it is limited to domains of knowledge where mental models can be algorithmically defined.

In its most ambitious form, the AI approach sought to have the computer handle certain teaching or guiding functions that would otherwise require a human teacher's time and intervention. Within CSCL, the focus is on learning through collaboration with other students rather than directly from the teacher. Therefore, the role of the computer shifts from providing instruction – either in the form of facts in computer-aided instruction or in the form of feedback from intelligent tutoring systems – to supporting collaboration by providing media of communication and scaffolding for productive student interaction.

The primary form of collaboration support is for a network of computers (typically connected over the Internet) to provide a medium of communication. This may take the form of e-mail, chat, discussion forums, videoconferencing, instant messaging, and so on. CSCL systems typically provide a combination of several media and add special functionality to them.

In addition, CSCL software environments provide various forms of pedagogical support or scaffolding for collaborative learning. These may be implemented with rather complex computational mechanisms, including AI techniques. They can offer alternative views on the ongoing student discussion and emerging shared information. They can provide feedback, possibly based on a model of group inquiry. They can support sociability by monitoring interaction patterns and providing feedback to the students. In most cases, the role of the computer is secondary to the interpersonal collaboration process among the students (and, often, the teacher, tutor, or mentor). The software is designed to support, not replace, these group processes.

The shift from mental models of individual cognition to support for collaborating groups had enormous implications for both the focus and the method of research on learning. The gradual acceptance and unfolding of these implications has defined the evolution of the field of CSCL.

From Individuals to Interacting Groups

At about the time of the first biannual CSCL conference in 1995, Dillenbourg et al. (1996) analyzed the state of evolution of research on collaborative learning as follows:

For many years, theories of collaborative learning tended to focus on how individuals function in a group. This reflected a position that was dominant both in cognitive psychology and in artificial intelligence in the 1970s and early 1980s, where cognition was seen as a product of individual information processors, and where the context of social interaction was seen more as a background for individual activity than as a focus of research. More recently, the group itself has become the unit of analysis and the focus has shifted to more emergent, socially constructed, properties of the interaction. In terms of empirical research, the initial goal was to establish whether and under what circumstances collaborative learning was more effective than learning alone. Researchers controlled several independent variables (size of the group, composition of the group, nature of the task, communication media, and so on). However, these variables interacted with one another in a way that made it almost impossible to establish causal links between the conditions and the effects of collaboration. Hence, empirical studies have more recently started to focus less on establishing parameters for effective collaboration *and more on trying to* understand the role that such variables play in mediating interaction. *This shift to a more process-oriented account requires* new tools for analyzing and modeling interactions. *(p. 189, emphasis added)*

The research reviewed by Dillenbourg et al. – which studied the effects of manipulating collaboration variables on the measures of individual learning – did not produce clear results. Effects of gender or group composition (i.e., heterogeneous or homogeneous competence levels) might be completely different at different ages, in different domains, with different teachers, and so on. This not only violated methodological assumptions of variable independence but also raised questions about how to understand what was behind the effects. To get behind the effects meant to understand in some detail what was going on in the group interactions that might cause the effects. This, in turn, required the development of methodologies for analyzing and interpreting group interactions as such. The focus was no longer on what might be taking place in the heads of individual learners, but what was taking place between them in their interactions.

From Mental Representations to Interactional Meaning-Making

The shift to the group unit of analysis coincided with a focus on the community as the agent of situated learning (Greeno, this volume; Lave, 1991) and on collaborative knowledge building (Scardamalia & Bereiter, 1991, this volume). But it also called for the elaboration of a social theory of mind, such as Vygotsky (1930/1978) had begun to outline, which could clarify the relation of individual learners to collaborative learning in groups or communities. According to Vygotsky, individual learners have different developmental capabilities in collaborative situations than when they are working

alone. His concept of the "zone of proximal development" is defined as a measure of the difference between these two capabilities. This means that one cannot measure the learning – even the individual learning – that takes place in collaborative situations with the use of pre- and posttests that measure capabilities of the individuals when they are working alone. To get at what takes place during collaborative learning, it does not help to theorize about mental models in the heads of individuals, because that does not capture the shared meaning-making that is going on during collaborative interactions.

Collaboration is primarily conceptualized as a process of shared meaning construction. The meaning-making is not assumed to be an expression of mental representations of the individual participants, but is an interactional achievement. Meaning-making can be analyzed as taking place across sequences of utterances or messages from multiple participants. The meaning is not attributable to individual utterances of individual students because the meaning typically depends upon indexical references to the shared situation, elliptical references to previous utterances, and projective references to future utterances (see Sawyer, this volume).

From Quantitative Comparisons to Micro Case Studies

To observe learning in collaborative situations is different from observing it for isolated learners. First, in situations of collaboration, participants necessarily visibly display their learning as part of the process of collaboration. Second, the observations take place across relatively short periods of group interaction, rather than across long periods between pre- and posttests.

Ironically, perhaps, it is in principle easier to study learning in groups than in individuals. That is because a necessary feature of collaboration is that the participants display for each other their understanding of the meaning that is being constructed in the interaction. Utterances, texts, and diagrams that are produced during collaboration are designed by the participants to display their understanding. That is the basis for successful collaboration. Researchers can take advantage of these displays (assuming that they share the participants' interpretive competencies and can capture an adequate record of the displays, e.g., on digital video). Researchers can then reconstruct the collaborative process through which group participants constructed shared meaning, which was learned as a group.

Methodologies such as conversation analysis (Sacks, 1992; ten Have, 1999) or video analysis (Koschmann, Stahl, & Zemel, in press) based on ethnomethodology (Garfinkel, 1967) produce detailed case studies of collaborative meaning-making (Sawyer, this volume). These case studies are not merely anecdotal. They can be based on rigorous scientific procedures with intersubjective validity even though they are interpretive in nature and are not quantitative. They also can represent generally applicable results, in that the methods that people use to interact are widely shared (at least within appropriately defined communities or cultures).

How can the analysis of interactional methods help to guide the design of CSCL technologies and pedagogies? This question points to the complex interplay between education and computers in CSCL.

The Interplay of Learning and Technology in CSCL

The Traditional Conception of Learning

Edwin Thorndike (1912), a founder of the behaviorist educational approach, once wrote:

> If, by a miracle of mechanical ingenuity, a book could be so arranged that only to him who had done what was directed on page one would two become visible, and so on, much that now requires personal instruction could be managed by print. ... Children [could] be taught, moreover to use materials in a manner that will be most useful in the long run. (p. 165).

This quotation is notable in two respects. For one, it suggests that the central idea of computer-aided instruction long preceded the actual development of computers; but, more important, it also shows how the goal of research in educational technology is closely tied, indeed indistinguishable from, the conventional goal of educational research, namely to enhance learning as it is operationally defined. Thorndike envisioned an educational science in which all learning is measurable and, on this basis, by which all educational innovations could be experimentally evaluated. Historically, research on educational technology has been tied to this tradition and represents a specialization within it (cf., Cuban, 1986).

In the past, educational researchers have treated learning as a purely psychological phenomenon that has three essential features. First, it represents a response to and recording of experience. Second, learning is always treated as a change that occurs over time. Finally, learning is generally seen as a process not available to direct inspection (Koschmann, 2002a). This formulation is so culturally entrenched that it is difficult to conceive of learning in any other way. It rests on established traditions in epistemology and philosophy of mind.

Contemporary philosophy has called these traditions into question, however. The so-called edifying philosophers (Rorty, 1974) – James, Dewey, Wittgenstein, and Heidegger – rebelled against the view of learning as an inaccessible event in which knowledge is inscribed in an individual mind. They aspired to construct a new view of learning and knowing, one that properly located it in the world of everyday affairs. CSCL embraces this more situated view of learning, thereby rejecting the foundations of conventional educational research. CSCL locates learning in meaning negotiation carried out in the social world rather than in individuals' heads. Of the various socially oriented theories of learning, social practice theory (Lave & Wenger, 1991) and dialogical theories of learning (e.g., Hicks, 1996) speak most directly to a view of learning as socially organized meaning construction. Social practice theory focuses on one aspect of meaning negotiation: the negotiation of social identity within a community. Dialogical theories locate learning in the emergent development of meaning within social interaction. Taken together, they provide a new way of thinking about and studying learning.

Designing Technology to Support Learner Meaning-Making

The goal for design in CSCL is to create artifacts, activities, and environments that enhance the practices of group meaning making. Rapid advances in computer and communication technologies in recent decades, like the Internet, have dramatically changed the ways in which we work, play, and learn. No form of technology, however – no matter how cleverly designed or sophisticated – has the capacity, in and of itself, to change practice. To create the possibility of an enhanced form of practice requires more multifaceted forms of design (bringing in expertise, theories, and practices from various disciplines): design that addresses curriculum (pedagogical and didactic design), resources (information sciences, communication sciences), participation structures (interaction design), tools (design studies), and surrounding space (architecture).

As the title of a commentary by LeBaron (2002) suggested, "Technology does not exist independent of its use." Substitute "activities, artifacts, and environments" for "technology" and the message remains the same – these elements themselves cannot define new forms of practice, but are instead constituted within practice. An environment for a desired form of practice is constructed by the organized actions of its inhabitants. Tools and artifacts are only tools and artifacts in the ways in which they are oriented to and made relevant by participants in directed practice. Even activities are only rendered recognizable as such in the ways that participants orient to them as ordered forms of joint action.

Design of software for CSCL, therefore, must be coupled with analysis of the meanings constructed within emergent practice. Meanings reflect past experience and are open to endless negotiation and re-

evaluation. Furthermore, neither analysts nor participants have privileged access to others' subjective interpretations. Despite these issues, participants routinely engage in coordinated activity and operate as if shared understanding was both possible and being achieved. A fundamental question, therefore, is: How is this done? In order to design technology to support collaborative learning and knowledge building, we must understand in more detail how small groups of learners construct shared meaning using various artifacts and media.

The question of how *intersubjectivity* is accomplished has been taken up in a variety of specialized disciplines such as pragmatics (Levinson, 2000; Sperber & Wilson, 1982), social psychology (Rommetveit, 1974), linguistic anthropology (Hanks, 1996), and sociology (cf. Goffman, 1974), especially sociological research in the ethnomethodological tradition (Garfinkel, 1967; Heritage, 1984). The problem of intersubjectivity is of particular relevance for those who wish to understand how learning is produced within interaction. Learning can be construed as the act of bringing divergent meanings into contact (Hicks, 1996), and instruction construed as the social and material arrangements that foster such negotiation. The analysis of meaning-making calls for the appropriation of the methods and concerns of psychology (especially the discursive and cultural varieties), sociology (especially the microsociological and ethnomethodologically informed traditions), anthropology (including linguistic anthropology and anthropologies of the built environment), pragmatics, communication studies, organizational science, and others.

CSCL research has both analytic and design components. Analysis of meaning making is inductive and indifferent to reform goals. It seeks only to discover what people are doing in moment-to-moment interaction, without prescription or assessment. Design, by contrast, is inherently prescriptive – any effort toward reform begins from the presumption that there are better and worse ways of doing things. To design for improved meaning-making, however, requires some means of rigorously studying practices of meaning-making. In this way, the relationship between analysis and design is a symbiotic one – design must be informed by analysis, but analysis also depends on design in its orientation to the analytic object (Koschmann et al., in press).

CSCL must continue with its work of self-invention. New sources of theory are introduced, analyses of learner practice are presented, and artifacts are produced accompanied by theories of how they might enhance meaning-making. The design of CSCL technology, which opens new possibilities for collaborative learning, must be founded on an analysis of the nature of collaborative learning.

The Analysis of Collaborative Learning

Koschmann (2002b) presented a programmatic description of CSCL in his keynote at the 2002 CSCL conference:

> CSCL is a field of study centrally concerned with meaning and the practices of meaning-making in the context of joint activity, and the ways in which these practices are mediated through designed artifacts. (p. 18)

The definition of CSCL as being concerned with the "practices of meaning-making in the context of joint activity" can be understood in multiple ways.

The aspect of collaborative learning that is perhaps hardest to understand in detail is what may be called *intersubjective learning* (Suthers, 2005) or *group cognition* (Stahl, in press). This is learning that is not merely accomplished interactionally, but is actually *constituted* of the interactions between participants. Following Garfinkel, Koschmann et al. (in press) argued for the study of "member's methods" of meaning-making: "how participants in such [instructional] settings actually go about *doing* learning" (emphasis in original). In addition to understanding how the cognitive processes of participants are influenced by social interaction, we need to understand how learning events themselves take place in the interactions between participants.

The study of joint meaning-making is not yet prominent within CSCL practice. Even where interaction processes (rather than individual learning outcomes) are examined in detail, the analysis is typically undertaken by assigning coding categories and counting predefined features. The codes, in effect, substitute preconceived categories of behavior for the phenomenon of interest rather than seeking to discover those phenomena in their unique situations (Stahl, 2002).

A few studies published in the CSCL literature have directly addressed this problem of describing the constituting of intersubjectivity in interaction (for example, Koschmann et al., 2003; Koschmann et al., in press; Roschelle, 1996; Stahl, in press). Roschelle's early study designed software especially to support meaning-making related to physics, defined student activities to engage learners in joint problem solving, and analyzed their collaborative practices in micro detail. Koschmann's work has generally focused on participants' methods of *problematization*: how groups of students collectively characterize a situation as problematic and as requiring further specific analysis.

Stahl (in press) argued that small groups are the most fruitful unit of study, for several reasons. Most simply, small groups are where members' methods for intersubjective learning can be observed. Groups of several members allow the full range of social interactions to play out, but are not so large that participants and researchers alike necessarily lose track of what is going on. The shared construction of meaning is most visible and available for research at the small-group unit of analysis, where it appears as *group cognition*. Moreover, small groups lie at the boundary of, and mediate between, individuals and a community. The knowledge building that takes place within small groups becomes "internalized by their members as individual learning and externalized in their communities as certifiable knowledge" (Stahl, in press). However, small groups should not be the only social granularity studied. Analysis of large-scale changes in communities and organizations may lead to an understanding of emergent social-learning phenomena as well as elucidate the role of embedded groups in driving these changes.

The study of the interactional accomplishment of intersubjective learning or group cognition gives rise to interesting questions that are among the most challenging facing any social-behavioral science, and even touch upon our nature as conscious beings: Do cognitive phenomena take place transpersonally in group discourse? How is it possible for learning, usually conceived of as a cognitive function, to be distributed across people and artifacts? How can we understand knowledge as accomplished practice rather than as a substance or even predisposition?

The Analysis of Computer Support

In CSCL contexts, interactions among individuals are mediated by computer environments. The second half of Koschmann's programmatic definition of the domain of CSCL is "the ways in which these practices [meaning-making in the context of joint activity] are mediated through designed artifacts" (2002b, p. 18). Computer support for intersubjective meaning-making is what makes the field unique.

The technology side of the CSCL agenda focuses on the design and study of fundamentally social technologies. To be fundamentally social means that the technology is designed specifically to mediate and encourage social acts that constitute group learning and lead to individual learning. Design should leverage the unique opportunities provided by the technology rather than replicate support for learning that could be done through other means, or (worse) try to force the technology to be something for which it is not well suited. What is unique to information technology that can potentially fill this role?

- Computational media are reconfigurable. Representations are dynamic: it is easy to move things around and undo actions. It is easy to replicate those actions elsewhere:

one can bridge time and space. These features make information technology attractive as a "communication channel," but we should exploit technology for its potential to make new interactions possible, not try to force it to replicate face-to-face interaction.

- Computer-mediated communication environments "turn communication into substance" (Dillenbourg, 2005). A record of activity as well as product can be kept, replayed, and even modified. We should explore the potential of the persistent record of interaction and collaboration as a resource for intersubjective learning.

- Computational media can analyze workspace state and interaction sequences, and reconfigure themselves or generate prompts according to features of either. We should explore the potential of adaptive media as an influence on the course of intersubjective processes, and take advantage of their ability to prompt, analyze, and selectively respond.

Human communication and the use of representational resources for this communication is highly flexible: we cannot "fix" meanings or even specify communicative functions (Dwyer & Suthers, 2005). Informed by this fact, CSCL research should identify the unique advantages of computational media, and explore how these are used by collaborators and how they influence the course of their meaning-making. This would enable the design of technologies that offer collections of features through which participants can interactionally engage in learning with flexible forms of guidance.

The Multidisciplinarity of CSCL

CSCL can presently be characterized as consisting of three methodological traditions: experimental, descriptive, and iterative design.

Many empirical studies follow the dominant *experimental* paradigm that compares an intervention to a control condition in terms of one or more variables (e.g., Baker & Lund, 1997; Rummel & Spada, 2005; Suthers & Hundhausen, 2003; Van Der Pol, Admiraal, & Simons, 2003; Weinberger et al., 2005). Data analysis in most of these studies is undertaken by "coding and counting": interactions are categorized and/or learning outcomes measured, and group means are compared through statistical methods in order to draw general conclusions about the effects of the manipulated variables on aggregate (average) group behavior. These studies do not directly analyze the accomplishment of intersubjective learning. Such an analysis must examine the structure and intention of unique cases of interaction rather than count and aggregate behavioral categories.

The ethnomethodological tradition (exemplified in CSCL by Koschmann et al., 2003; Koschmann et al., in press; Roschelle, 1996; Stahl, in press) is more suited for *descriptive* case analyses. Video or transcripts of learners or other members of the community are studied to uncover the methods by which groups of participants accomplish learning. This grounded approach is data-driven, seeking to discover patterns in the data rather than imposing theoretical categories. The analysis is often microanalytic, examining brief episodes in great detail. Descriptive methodologies are well suited to existentially quantified claims (e.g., that a community sometimes engages in a given practice). Yet, as scientists and designers we would like to make causal generalizations about the effects of design choices. Descriptive methodologies are less suited for claiming that a specific intervention causes an observed outcome; causal claims are the province of experimental methodology.

The traditional analytic methods of experimental psychology miss the "member methods" through which collaborative learning is accomplished – intersubjective meaning-making. But this does not imply that all CSCL research should be ethnomethodological. Rather, the foregoing considerations suggest that we explore hybrid research methodologies (Johnson & Onwuegbuzie, 2004). Experimental designs

can continue to compare interventions, but the comparisons would be made in terms of microanalyses of how the features of information technology influence and are appropriated for members' methods of joint meaning-making. Conceptually, the process analysis changes from "coding and counting" to "exploring and understanding" ways in which design variables influence support for meaning-making. Such analyses are time intensive: we should explore, as research aids, the development of instrumentation for learning environments and automated visualization and querying of interaction logs (as in Cakir et al., 2005; Donmez et al., 2005). Traditional analyses, especially measures of learning outcomes but also "coding and counting," also might be retained to obtain quick indicators of where more detailed analyses are merited, thereby focusing the detail work (as in Zemel, Xhafa, & Stahl, 2005).

The *iterative design* tradition is exemplified by Fischer and Ostwald (2005), Lingnau, Hoppe, and Mannhaupt (2003) and Guzdial et al. (1997) (also see Barab, this volume). Driven by the dialectic between theory and informal observations and by engaging stakeholders in the process, design-oriented researchers continuously improve artifacts intended to mediate learning and collaboration. Their research is not necessarily either qualitative or quantitative but also may be "quisitive" (Goldman, Crosby, & Shea, 2004). It is not enough just to observe people's behaviors when they use new software. We need to explore the space of possible designs, pushing into new areas and identifying promising features that should receive further study under the other methodological traditions. Designers also need to conduct microanalyses of collaborative learning with and through technology in order to identify the features of designed artifacts that seem to be correlated with effective learning. When a new technical intervention is tested, experimental methods can be used to document significant differences, whereas descriptive methods can document how the interventions mediated collaborative interactions differently. A conversation between the theoretical assumptions of ethnomethodology and those of design can lead to a "technomethodology" that changes the very objectives of design (Button & Dourish, 1996).

A potential limitation of descriptive methodologies should be noted. If we focus on finding examples of how members accomplish effective learning, we may miss abundant examples of how they also fail to do so. Yet in order to find that something is not there, we need to have an idea of what we are looking for. A purely data-driven approach that derives theory but never applies it won't be adequate. Descriptive methods can be modified to address this need. Common patterns found in successful learning episodes subsequently become the theoretical categories we look for elsewhere with analytic methods, and perhaps do not find in instances of unsuccessful collaboration. Having identified where the successful methods were *not* applied, we can then examine the situation to determine what contingency was missing or responsible. Unique and unreproducible instances where collaboration using technology breaks down in interesting ways can often provide the deepest insights into what is happening, and into what is normally taken for granted and invisible. Care should be taken, however, to make sure that in finding examples where the interactional accomplishment of learning is absent, we do not fail to notice where something else of value to the participants *is* being accomplished! For example, establishment and maintenance of individual and group identity are worthwhile accomplishments as far as the participants are concerned (Whitworth, Gallupe, & McQueen, 2000), and indeed are a form of situated learning, even though researchers may initially identify it as "off topic" social chatting.

CSCL Research in the Future

We have seen that research in CSCL must respond to multiple goals and constraints. The research community necessarily includes people from a variety of professional and disciplinary backgrounds and trainings. They bring with them different research paradigms, contrasting views of data, analysis methods, presentation formats, concepts of rigor, and technical vocabularies. They come from around the world with various cultures and native languages. CSCL is a rapidly evolving field, located at the intersection of other fields that are themselves undergoing continuous change. Community participants at any given time are operating within diverse conceptions of what CSCL is all about. For instance, Sfard (1998) defined two broad and irreconcilable metaphors of learning that are necessarily relevant to CSCL: the acquisition metaphor, in which learning consists of individuals acquiring knowledge stored in their minds, and the participation metaphor, in which learning consists of increasing participation in communities of practice. Lipponen, Hakkarainen, and Paavola (2004) added a third metaphor based on Bereiter (2002) and Engeström (1987): the knowledge creation metaphor, in which new knowledge objects or social practices are created in the world through collaboration. Consequently, it is hard to present a well-defined, consistent, and comprehensive definition of CSCL theory, methodology, findings, or best practices. Perhaps one must conclude that CSCL today necessarily pursues seemingly irreconcilable approaches – as Sfard argued. We have suggested that more integrated, hybrid approaches may be possible in the future.

Research methodology in CSCL is largely trichotomized between experimental, descriptive, and iterative design approaches. Although sometimes combined within a single research project, the methodologies are even then typically kept separate in companion studies or separate analyses of a single study. Different researchers sometimes wear different hats on the same project, representing different research interests and methodologies. This situation may still be productive: the experimentalists continue to identify variables that affect general parameters of collaborative behavior, the ethnomethodologists identify patterns of joint activity that are essential to the meaning-making, and designers innovate to creatively adapt new technological possibilities. Soon, however, experimentalists within CSCL may start to focus on the dependent variables that directly reflect the phenomenon of interest to the descriptive researchers (Fischer & Granoo, 1995), ethnomethodologists may look for predictive regularities in technology-mediated meaning making that can inform design, and the designers may generate and assess promising new technology affordances in terms of the meaning-making activities they enable. Mutual assistance and closer collaboration may be possible through hybrid methodologies – for example, by applying richer descriptive analytic methods to the problem of understanding the implications of experimental manipulations and new designs, or through computer support for our own meaning-making activities as researchers.

CSCL researchers form a community of inquiry that is actively constructing new ways to collaborate in the design, analysis, and implementation of computer support for collaborative learning. A broad range of research methods from the learning sciences may be useful in analyzing computer-supported collaborative learning. Having appropriated ideas, methods, and functionality from cognate fields, CSCL may in its next phase collaboratively construct new theories, methodologies, and technologies specific to the task of analyzing the social practices of intersubjective meaning-making in order to support collaborative learning. We have argued that CSCL requires a focus on the meaning-making practices of collaborating groups and on the design of technological artifacts to mediate interaction, rather than a focus on individual learning. Whether this focus can, will, or should lead to a coherent theoretical framework and research methodology for CSCL remains to be seen.

References

Baker, M., & Lund, K. (1997). Promoting reflective interactions in a CSCL environment. *Journal of Computer Assisted Learning, 13*, 175–193.

Bereiter, C. (2002). *Education and mind in the knowledge age*. Mahwah, NJ: Lawrence Erlbaum Associates.

Bruce, B. C., & Rubin, A. (1993). *Electronic quills: A situated evaluation of using computers for writing in classrooms*. Mahwah, NJ: Lawrence Erlbaum Associates.

Bruffee, K. (1993). *Collaborative learning*. Baltimore, MD: Johns Hopkins University Press.

Button, G. Y., & Dourish, P. (1996). *Technomethodology: Paradoxes and possibilities*. Paper presented at the ACM Conference on Human Factors in Computing Systems (CHI '96), Vancouver, Canada.

Cakir, M., Xhafa, F., Zhou, N., & Stahl, G. (2005). *Thread-based analysis of patterns of collaborative interaction in chat*. Paper presented at the international conference on AI in Education (AI-Ed 2005), Amsterdam, Netherlands.

Cole, M. (1996). *Cultural psychology: A once and future discipline*. Cambridge, MA: Harvard University Press.

Crook, C. (1994). *Computers and the collaborative experience of learning*. London, UK: Routledge.

Cuban, L. (1986). *Teachers and machines: The classroom use of technology since 1920*. New York: Teachers College Press.

Dillenbourg, P. (Ed.). (1999a). *Collaborative learning: Cognitive and computational approaches*. Amsterdam: Pergamon, Elsevier Science.

Dillenbourg, P. (1999b). What do you mean by "collaborative learning"? In P. Dillenbourg (Ed.), *Collaborative learning: Cognitive and computational approaches* (pp. 1–16). Amsterdam: Pergamon, Elsevier Science.

Dillenbourg, P. (2005). Designing biases that augment socio-cognitive interactions. In R. Bromme, F. Hesse, & H. Spada (Eds.), *Barriers and biases in computer-mediated knowledge communication – and how they may be overcome*. Dordrecht, Netherlands: Kluwer Academic Publisher.

Dillenbourg, P., Baker, M., Blaye, A., & O'Malley, C. (1996). The evolution of research on collaborative learning. In P. Reimann & H. Spada (Eds.), *Learning in humans and machines: Towards an interdisciplinary learning science* (pp. 189–211). Oxford: Elsevier.

Donmez, P., Rose, C., Stegmann, K., Weinberger, A., & Fischer, F. (2005). *Supporting CSCL with automatic corpus analysis technology*. Paper presented at the International Conference of

Computer Support for Collaborative Learning (CSCL 2005), Taipei, Taiwan.

Dwyer, N., & Suthers, D. (2005). *A study of the foundations of artifact-mediated collaboration.* Paper presented at the international conference of Computer-Supported Collaborative Learning (CSCL 2005), Taipei, Taiwan.

Engeström, Y. (1987). *Learning by expanding: An activity-theoretical approach to developmental research.* Helsinki, Finland: Orienta-Kosultit Oy.

Fischer, K., & Granoo, N. (1995). Beyond one-dimensional change: Parallel, concurrent, socially distributed processes in learning and development. *Human Development, 1995 (38),* 302–314.

Fischer, G., & Ostwald, J. (2005). Knowledge communication in design communities. In R. Bromme, F. Hesse & H. Spada (Eds.), *Barriers and biases in computer-mediated knowledge communication – and how they may be overcome.* Dordrecht, Netherlands: Kluwer Academic Publisher.

Garfinkel, H. (1967). *Studies in ethnomethodology.* Englewood Cliffs, NJ: Prentice Hall.

Goffman, E. (1974). *Frame analysis: An essay on the organization of experience.* New York: Harper & Row.

Goldman, R., Crosby, M., & Shea, P. (2004). Introducing quisitive research: Expanding qualitative methods for describing learning in ALN. In R. S. Hiltz & R. Goldman (Eds.), *Learning together online: Research on asynchronous learning networks* (pp. 103–121). Mahwah, NJ: Lawrence Erlbaum Associates.

Gruber, S., Peyton, J. K., & Bruce, B. C. (1995). Collaborative writing in multiple discourse contexts. *Computer-Supported Cooperative Work, 3,* 247–269.

Guzdial, M., Hmelo, C., Hubscher, R., Newstetter, W., Puntambekar, S., Shabo, A., et al. (1997). *Integrating and guiding collaboration: Lessons learned in computer-supported collaboration learning research at Georgia Tech.* Paper presented at the international conference on Computer-Supported Collaborative Learning (CSCL '97), Toronto, Canada.

Hanks, W. (1996). *Language and communicative practices.* Boulder, CO: Westview.

Heritage, J. (1984). *Garfinkel and ethnomethodology.* Cambridge, UK: Polity Press.

Hicks, D. (1996). Contextual inquiries: A discourse-oriented study of classroom learning. In D. Hicks (Ed.), *Discourse, learning and school-*ing (pp. 104–141). New York: Cambridge University Press.

Hoadley, C. (2005). *The shape of the elephant: Scope and membership of the CSCL community.* Paper presented at the international conference of Computer-Supported Collaborative Learning (CSCL 2005), Taipei, Taiwan.

Johnson, R. B., & Onwuegbuzie, A. J. (2004). Mixed methods research: A research paradigm whose time has come. *Educational Researcher, 33 (7),* 14–26.

Kienle, A., & Wessner, M. (2005). *Our way to Taipei: An analysis of the first ten years of the CSCL community.* Paper presented at the international conference of Computer-Supported Collaborative Learning (CSCL 2005), Taipei, Taiwan.

Koschmann, T. (Ed.). (1996a). *CSCL: Theory and practice of an emerging paradigm.* Mahwah, NJ: Lawrence Erlbaum Associates.

Koschmann, T. (1996b). Paradigm shifts and instructional technology. In T. Koschmann (Ed.), *CSCL: Theory and practice of an emerging paradigm* (pp. 1–23). Mahwah, NJ: Lawrence Erlbaum.

Koschmann, T. (2002a, April). *Dewey's critique of Thorndike's behaviorism.* Paper presented at the AERA 2002, New Orleans, LA.

Koschmann, T. (2002b). Dewey's contribution to the foundations of CSCL research. In G. Stahl (Ed.), *Computer support for collaborative learning: Foundations for a CSCL community: Proceedings of CSCL 2002* (pp. 17–22). Mahwah, NJ: Lawrence Erlbaum Associates.

Koschmann, T., Hall, R., & Miyake, N. (Eds.). (2002). *CSCL2: Carrying forward the conversation.* Mahwah, NJ: Lawrence Erlbaum Associates.

Koschmann, T., Stahl, G., & Zemel, A. (in press). The video analyst's manifesto (or the implications of Garfinkel's policies for the development of a program of video analytic research within the learning sciences). In R. Goldman, R. Pea, B. Barron, & S. Derry (Eds.), *Video research in the learning sciences.* Mahwah, NJ: Lowrence Erlbaum Associates.

Koschmann, T., Zemel, A., Conlee-Stevens, M., Young, N., Robbs, J., & Barnhart, A. (2003). Problematizing the problem: A single case analysis in a dPBL meeting. In B. Wasson, S. Ludvigsen & U. Hoppe (Eds.), *Designing for change in networked learning environments: Proceedings of the international conference on computer support for collaborative learning (CSCL '03)* (pp. 37–46). Bergen, Norway: Kluwer Publishers.

Lave, J. (1991). Situating learning in communities of practice. In L. Resnick, J. Levine, & S. Teasley (Eds.), *Perspectives on socially shared cognition* (pp. 63–83). Washington, DC: APA.

Lave, J., & Wenger, E. (1991). *Situated learning: Legitimate peripheral participation*. Cambridge: Cambridge University Press.

LeBaron, C. (2002). Technology does not exist independent of its use. In T. Koschmann, R. Hall, & N. Miyake (Eds.), *CSCL 2: Carrying forward the conversation* (pp. 433–439). Mahwah, NJ: Lawrence Erlbaum Associates.

Levinson, S. C. (2000). *Presumptive meanings: The theory of generalized conversational implicature*. Cambridge, MA: MIT Press.

Lingnau, A., Hoppe, H. U., & Mannhaupt, G. (2003). Computer supported collaborative writing in an early learning classroom. *Journal of Computer Assisted Learning, 19* (2), 186–194.

Lipponen, L., Hakkarainen, K., & Paavola, S. (2004). Practices and orientations of CSCL. In J.-W. Strijbos, P. Kirschner, & R. Martens (Eds.), *What we know about CSCL: And implementing it in higher education* (pp. 31–50). Dordrecht, Netherlands: Kluwer Academic Publishers.

Newman, D., Griffin, P., & Cole, M. (1989). *The construction zone: Working for cognitive change in schools*. Cambridge: Cambridge University Press.

Nicolopoulou, A., & Cole, M. (1993). Generation and transmission of shared knowledge in the culture of collaborative learning: The fifth dimension, its playworld and its institutional contexts. In E. Forman, N. Minnick, & C. A. Stone (Eds.), *Contexts for learning: Sociocultural dynamics in children's development*. New York: Oxford University Press.

O' Malley, C. (1995). *Computer supported collaborative learning*. Berlin, Germany: Springer Verlag.

Rommetveit, R. (1974). *On message structure: A framework for the study of language and communication*. New York: Wiley & Sons.

Rorty, R. (1974). *Philosophy and the mirror of nature*. Princeton, NJ: Princeton University Press.

Roschelle, J. (1996). Learning by collaborating: Convergent conceptual change. In T. Koschmann (Ed.), *CSCL: Theory and practice*

of an emerging paradigm (pp. 209–248). Mahwah, NJ: Lawrence Erlbaum Associates.

Roschelle, J., & Teasley, S. (1995). The construction of shared knowledge in collaborative problem solving. In C. O'Malley (Ed.), *Computer-supported collaborative learning* (pp. 69–197). Berlin, Germany: Springer Verlag.

Rummel, N., & Spada, H. (2005). Sustainable support for computer-mediated collaboration: How to achieve and how to assess it. In R. Bromme, F. Hesse, & H. Spada (Eds.), *Barriers and biases in computer-mediated knowledge communication – and how they may be overcome*. Dordrecht, Netherlands: Kluwer Academic Publisher.

Sacks, H. (1992). *Lectures on conversation*. Oxford: Blackwell.

Scardamalia, M., & Bereiter, C. (1991). Higher levels of agency in knowledge building: A challenge for the design of new knowledge media. *Journal of the Learning Sciences, 1,* 37–68.

Scardamalia, M., & Bereiter, C. (1996). Computer support for knowledge-building communities. In T. Koschmann (Ed.), *CSCL: Theory and practice of an emerging paradigm* (pp. 249–268). Mahwah, NJ: Lawrence Erlbaum Associates.

Sfard, A. (1998). On two metaphors for learning and the dangers of choosing just one. *Educational Researcher, 27* (2), 4–13.

Sperber, D., & Wilson, D. (1982). Mutual knowledge and relevance of theories of comprehension. In N. V. Smith (Ed.), *Mutual knowledge*. New York: Academic Press.

Stahl, G. (2002). Rediscovering CSCL. In T. Koschmann, R. Hall, & N. Miyake (Eds.), *CSCL 2: Carrying forward the conversation* (pp. 169–181). Mahwah, NJ: Lawrence Erlbaum Associates.

Stahl, G. (in press). *Group cognition: Computer support for building collaborative knowledge*. Cambridge, MA: MIT Press.

Suthers, D. (2005, May–June). *Technology affordances for intersubjective learning: A thematic agenda for CSCL*. Paper presented at the international conference of Computer Support for Collaborative Learning (CSCL 2005), Taipei, Taiwan.

Suthers, D., & Hundhausen, C. (2003, June). An empirical study of the effects of representational guidance on collaborative learning. *Journal of the Learning Sciences, 12* (2), 183–219.

ten Have, P. (1999). *Doing conversation analysis: A practical guide*. Thousand Oaks, CA: Sage.

Thorndike, E. L. (1912). *Education: A first book.* New York, NY: Macmillan.

Van Der Pol, J., Admiraal, W., & Simons, R.-J. (2003, June). *Grounding in electronic discussions: Standard (threaded) versus anchored discussion.* Paper presented at the international conference of Computer-Supported Collaborative Learning (CSCL 2003), Bergen, Norway. Proceedings pp. 77–81.

Vygotsky, L. (1930/1978). *Mind in society.* Cambridge, MA: Harvard University Press.

Weinberger, A., Reiserer, M., Ertl, B., Fischer, F., & Mandl, H. (2005). Facilitating collaborative knowledge construction in computer-mediated learning environments with cooperation scripts. In R. Bromme, F. Hesse, & H. Spada (Eds.), *Barriers and biases in computer-mediated knowledge communication – and how they may be overcome.* Dordrecht, Netherlands: Kluwer Academic Publisher.

Whitworth, B., Gallupe, B., & McQueen, R. (2000). A cognitive three-process model of computer-mediated group interaction. *Group Decision and Negotiation, 9,* 431–456.

Zemel, A., Xhafa, F., & Stahl, G. (2005, September). *Analyzing the organization of collaborative math problem-solving in online chats using statistics and conversation analysis.* Paper presented at the CRIWG International Workshop on Groupware, Recife, Brazil.

CHAPTER 25

WILD for Learning

Interacting Through New Computing Devices Anytime, Anywhere

Roy D. Pea and Heidy Maldonado

We use the acronym WILD to refer to Wireless Interactive Learning Devices.[1] WILD are powerful and small hand-held networked computing devices.[2] The smallest hand-held computers fit in one hand easily. The user interacts with the device either by touching the screen with a pen-shaped stylus, or by typing with both thumbs on a small keyboard known as a thumb-pad keyboard. The largest are the size of a paperback book and have a keyboard that is large enough to type on with all ten fingers. Their low price point and high usability have captured the imaginations of educators and learning scientists. The promise of harnessing computing where every student has his or her own computer, and where they are available everyday, anytime, anywhere – for equitable, personal, effective, and engaging learning – give WILD a greater transformative potential than desktop computers.

This chapter provides an account of the learning, education, social, policy, and technical contexts for these developments. We begin by establishing these contexts, and then survey available research on and commercial applications of WILD computing.

We focus on efforts where the "technology in the WILD" is being used to bring learners into activities previously unreachable – whether because of administrative, time, financial, demographic, previous knowledge, accessibility, or academic constraints. We emphasize the unique features that WILD add to classroom dynamics and to learning in the world, both in formal and informal contexts. In closing, we review the technical convergences and societal trends in WILD computing that will shape this field.

Motivation

As the costs of increasingly capable computers and of Internet access drops, and as the teaching force responds to the latest standards in certification and technological fluencies, we expect that teachers all over the world will increasingly incorporate computers into their classroom practices. Ever more prevalent, and presupposing at least a 1:1 ratio between students and computers, is the concept of "ubiquitous computing"

(Weiser, 1991), in which computers are embedded in everyday life activities to the point of invisibility, so that we unconsciously and effortlessly harness their digital abilities as effort-saving strategies for achieving the benefits of "distributed intelligence" (Pea, 1993).

Within the United States, several companies and districts (Edison Schools, Illinois' School District 203, and the State of Maine, among others) are already supplying every student within their middle- and high-school classrooms with laptops or hand-held computers. In a notable large-scale implementation in 2001, Henrico County Public Schools (HCPS) in the state of Virginia became the largest school district in the United States to give every student a computer in its middle and high schools, serving twenty-five thousand grade 6–12 students and teachers.

At a National Research Council workshop on improving learning with information technologies that brought together K–12 educators, learning scientists and technology industry leaders, Pea et al. (2003) characterized 1:1 computing as an essential "first transformation" for realizing the potential of computing to support learning and educational processes. Because the potential for each student to have a personalized Internet-enabled device with them at all times seems within grasp, the challenge now is to combine advances in the sciences of learning with information technology capabilities to dramatically improve student learning. New research groups and consortia have been formed to explore what the future may hold, and to recommend policies based on international research, such as the G1:1 – a global network of collaborative researchers studying one-on-one educational computing (http://www.g1on1.org/, accessed July 31, 2005).

Why Hand-Held Computers, or WILD Learning

Driving this trend for equitable, interactive, Internet-enabled, individualized distribution of technology in schools are hand-held computers. Hand-helds can cost less than the graphing calculators that math classes in high school typically require, and are quickly rising to prominence as affordable, personalized, portable devices (Roschelle & Pea, 2002; Soloway et al., 2001). More than 10 percent of U.S. public schools provide hand-held computers to students and teachers for instructional purposes (Parsad & Jones, 2005). The popularity of hand-helds reflects the desire of schools to make computing integral to the curriculum, rather than only occasionally used in labs, as evidenced by the success of the Palm Education Pioneers program that SRI administered (Vahey & Crawford, 2002): SRI received over fourteen hundred applications for the one hundred classroom awards available. In year-end evaluations, 96.5 percent of teachers indicated that hand-held computers were effective instructional tools, and 93 percent indicated that the use of hand-held computers contributed positively to the quality of the learning activities that their students completed.

Besides affordability, there are seven other device features contributing to the rise in hand-held use within schools and beyond: (1) size and portability; (2) small screen size; (3) computing power and modular platform; (4) communication ability through wireless and infrared beaming networks; (5) wide range of available multipurpose applications; (6) ready ability to synchronize and backup with other computers; and (7) stylus driven interface.

Small Size, Portability, and Ready-to-Hand

As their name implies, hand-helds are more portable than the slimmest laptops, allowing students to use them anytime, anywhere – whether they are taking data samples in the field with *probeware* – specially designed probes that can plug into a hand-held's data port, and can sense and measure environmental properties such as dissolved oxygen in water ecosystem projects (Tinker & Krajcik, 2001; Vahey & Crawford, 2002); being an environmental detective in a campus-based learning game (Klopfer,

Squire, & Jenkins, 2002); or Googling on hand-held Web browsers to answer questions that may arise while talking with friends. Using probes in the field is among the most popular uses for hand-held computers in middle-to-high school education – for example, students take their hand-held computers and probes to a stream and take measurements there, which are then collected by beaming to a teacher base machine, for later classroom graphing and pattern analyses.

The German philosopher Martin Heidegger first introduced the complex concept of *ready-to-hand* (*zuhanden*) to describe a condition of interacting with the world as mediated through the use of objects when we care about them, objects whose design allows us to remain *engaged* in the tasks to be accomplished, rather than to focus on the devices themselves (Heidegger, 1927/1973; Winograd & Flores, 1987). Hand-helds are ready-to-hand because of their size and features, and their software applications can provide guidance and augmentation of the activities we engage in as they encode, shape, and reorganize our everyday tasks (Pea, 1993).

Roschelle and Pea (2002) described how the hand-helds' small size allows teachers to break free from the contrastive teaching paradigms of "sage-on-the-stage" (teacher-centered instruction) and "guide-by-the-side" (teacher-guided discovery), a partial artifact of desktop technology, because that technology left little space pedagogically and physically for the teacher to occupy once several students were sharing the view and controls of the desktop computers. In classrooms populated by hand-held devices, teachers have the choice of conducting classes somewhat as an orchestra conductor: attending primarily to the group performance, to the ebbs and flows of classroom dynamics, while guiding particular students when the need arises. Several WILD applications use this new "conductor-of-performances" paradigm: the teachers' computer includes a birds-eye view of the classroom layout, such that every student is represented with respect to their location or group within the classroom, and information about each students' device activity is displayed (e.g., Goldman et al., 2004). The color of each student's device, as displayed on the teacher's screen, shows the teacher at a glance the relative proportion of students engaged in the activity, and those waiting to connect to the network or otherwise idle (see Figure 25.1). Teachers can thus determine which activities each group is engaged in – and even view the content of the students' screens to help guide their support.

Small Screen Size

The size of hand-helds allows them to share space comfortably on the student's desk, leaving room for books and notebooks, in contrast to laptop computers that occupy most of the desk surface. Of course, this ready-to-hand screen size makes them less effective for some types of learning activities: prolonged periods of reading long text segments may be better suited to wall-sized displays. Nonetheless, there are many collaborative applications for which these devices are ideal. Beyond merely shrinking the display and images, porting any software to a hand-held platform involves significant redesign, particularly for learning, because scaffolding support for complex tasks is integral (Luchini, Quintana, & Soloway, 2004). Among other considerations, text and graphics must be proportioned to maintain readability; the interface must be designed to maximize available screen real estate; and the organization of categories should follow scrolling principles, or divide tasks across several screen choice-points for options and menus.

Although hand-helds have small screens, their network connectivity permits sharing of the limited screen real state within a team, and across different symbolic representations such as a graph, an algebraic equation, and a data table (Goldman, Pea, & Maldonado, 2004). One may also increase the available visual field of the display for interactivity and learning by combining several hand-held displays (such as CILT's [1998] DataGotchi design concept for a low-cost hand-held mathematical collaborative

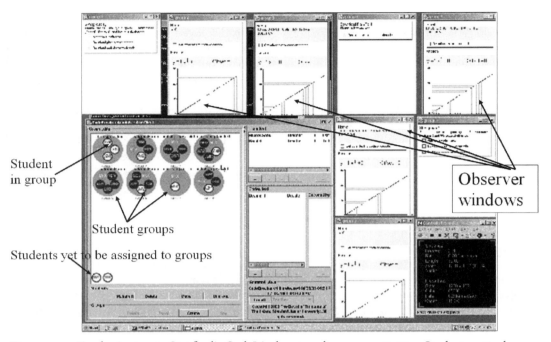

Figure 25.1. Teacher's view in Stanford's CodeIt!, showing classroom activities: Students actively connected to the system (by circle color), their assignment into groups (by circle's placement), and group's current processing (through observer windows).

learning tool, described in Roschelle and Mills [1999], or by using the tiled displays suggested by Mandryk et al. [2001]). Other researchers, such as Stanford's BuddyBuzz Project, are exploring how to best leverage rapid serial visual presentation (RSVP) techniques to present text by flashing on-screen in rapid succession the words of a document, one at a time, at a controllable speed that is as comprehensible and in some conditions several times faster than traditional text display methods.[3] While limiting the amount of information that can be simultaneously presented, smaller screens allow for greater sharing within small groups than bulky desktop displays; students can tilt their screens to share their content, and they can talk face-to-face at the same time, enabling perception of nonverbal behaviors that would be blocked by a large desktop monitor (see Figure 25.2).

Most students are already accustomed to viewing and manipulating information on small-sized screens from using popular portable entertainment and video game consoles. Nintendo has sold over 190

million portable GameBoy computers globally since its release in 1989,[4] and this platform has been used in recent educational interventions in schools (Rosas et al., 2003; http://hand-held.hice-dev.org/, accessed July 31, 2005). In one of the few studies using hand-held gaming computers to study school learning, Rosas et al. (2003) studied 1274 students from economically disadvantaged schools in Chile, using videogames specifically designed to support the educational goals of first to second grade for basic mathematics and reading comprehension, over thirty hours of intervention over three months. Although they found a significant difference between students in schools where the experimental tool was introduced and where it was not, they did not find any significant difference between the experimental and internal control groups within the school, which they interpreted in terms of a school-internal Hawthorne Effect, with control teachers competing with the game classrooms to improve learners' achievements.

Figure 25.2. Two groups of students working with WILD in the CodeIt! Project. Note the closeness of the exchanges, facilitated by device size, and their cohabitation with the multitude of papers students have on their desks.

Today, with the GameBoy Advance, Game Boy Dual Screen, Sony's Playstation Portable (PSP), Nokia N-Gage, and other mobile videogame consoles, 55 percent of U.S. children eight through eighteen own a hand-held videogame player (Kaiser Family Foundation, 2004). Few attempts have been made as yet to turn these gaming devices into educational platforms, although there are arguments that this would be beneficial (e.g., Gee, 2003). The new generation devices come enabled with Internet capabilities, hard drives, and many modular features of WILD educational applications.

Computing Power

In terms of computing power, the 2005 hand-helds are multipurpose devices already comparable to a 2000 desktop or 2001 laptop.[5] This CPU power means that the graphics processing capabilities that are familiar from many media-rich Web and desktop applications are now available in a hand-held. Moreover, hand-helds start up immediately, which contrasts sharply with the long seconds delay on starting a desktop or laptop computer.

Access to Diverse Communication Networks

Hand-helds allow collaboration and communication through their wireless Internet access and through their infrared "beaming" feature, which lets users exchange informa-

tion easily in either peer-to-peer or teacher-student designs (see Tatar et al., 2003, for summary of diverse use scenarios). Directed communication through infrared beaming or Wi-Fi networks has been used to control audiovisual equipment in the classroom, and to share applications, text messages, audio clips, contact information, drawings, and data (Batista, 2001; Myers et al., 2004; Pownell & Bailey, 2001) through the simple physical gesture of pointing the device at the intended recipient.

Wireless connectivity helps eliminates challenges in connecting to the Internet, a key feature for schools. In the most recent U.S. school survey, 32 percent of public schools in 2003 used wireless connections (Parsad & Jones, 2005), and 92 percent of these connections were high speed, a large jump from 23 percent in 2002 (Kleiner & Lewis, 2003). As school wireless connections and networks grow, they increase the ease for students' engagement in peer-peer collaboration and teacher hub-spoke learning scenarios within the classroom, and for student Internet access through their devices.

Access to a Broad Range of Applications

Hand-held computers are increasingly attractive to schools because they combine classic organizer and calendar functions with critical software applications: (1) desktop productivity applications, for example, smaller-screen versions of word processors; (2) the functions of application task-specific devices, for example, graphing calculators; (3) versatile modular hardware (e.g., scientific probes, cameras, keyboards, GPS); (4) desktop computers (e.g., participatory simulations software, e-mail readers, Web browsers); and (5) complex interactions with other networked computers.

Data Synchronization Across Computers

Hand-helds can be used as "thin clients" for accessing applications running on Web servers, and the satellite design of hand-helds makes data backup possible by regular synchronization with a desktop or laptop computer – essential for educational settings to coordinate the flow of teaching assignments and student work.

Stylus Input Device

Globally it is the *stylus* of hand-helds that is influencing purchase decision over desktop and laptop computers. For populations whose written language does not use Roman characters, such as Japanese *Kanji*, stylus-driven interaction is a critical feature, permitting text entry in the students' handwriting, rather than requiring complex key sequences for character entry. Taiwanese classrooms, for example, have been observed to use tablet computers primarily for this purpose, casting aside the tablets' keyboards.[6]

Learning Outside Schools

In the United States in 2004, 13 percent of students eight through eighteen years old reportedly already have a hand-held computer with Internet access and approximately 39 percent have a cell-phone (Roberts, Foehr, & Rideout, 2005); when broken down by age, the numbers grow faster as students move through high-school: 75 percent of teenagers between fifteen and seventeen years of age have cell-phones, up from 42 percent in 2002 (NOP World, 2005), and more than 20 percent of those devices have multimedia capabilities (NetDay, 2005). If those numbers are surprising, consider that the United States lags behind many other countries in cell- or mobile-phone penetration and the numbers of teenagers owning the devices. For example, 95 percent of the fifteen- to twenty-four-year-old population in Japan in 2001 already owned Web-enabled cell-phones (Thornton & Houser, 2004); and in New Zealand 73 percent of students twelve to nineteen years of age own their own devices (NetSafe, 2005).

Mobile phones prove a relevant case to consider for learning outside schools, as they often are equipped with organizational and media capabilities (Rasmusson et al., 2004), from photo- and videocameras to music players, and also meet each of the seven WILD characteristics earlier described. Often running the same operating system as hand-helds, mobile phones have continued to improve in terms of processor speed, memory, and screen size, even as they shrink in volume and weight (Lindholm, Keinonen, & Kiljander, 2003) so that many are becoming hand-held computers in addition to phones, even adapting keyboards and styluses to the interaction. Using mobile phones, students can interact with learning content anytime, anywhere they choose, and WILD projects have been under way since 2000 to capitalize on the devices' popularity by exploring opportunities for informal learning. For example, companies are providing "learning bites": small pieces of educational content that users can access while they are engaged in a different activity.

The first educational arena where cell-phone lessons are being developed and commercially available is language learning: from SAT vocabulary to foreign language learning, both through voice-only systems and through SMS text (short message service), phones are delivering content to users traveling on the subway, waiting in line, and sitting at home (Prensky, 2004; Thornton & Houser, 2004). For example, Thornton and Houser (2004) studied Japanese university students receiving brief English vocabulary lessons on their mobile phones, and found that they learned significantly more than students urged to study identical materials on paper or the Web.

WILD are also prime targets for gradual and timely health behavior modification programs, as they can potentially infer and leverage context information to deliver just-in-time advice or recommendations, at key decision points. Popular downloads of hand-held software include support for weight management (calorie calculators, exercise assistants), as well as for quitting smoking and controlling chronic diseases such as asthma, diabetes, and hypertension.

Small bite instruction and health behavior modification WILD interventions have several common design concerns, such as *interruptions* – determining when is it appropriate to interrupt the user with a suggestion, and how to detect when the learning intervention has been interrupted by real-world events requiring the user's attention – as well as *context*. "Context" refers to the hand-held's ability to use implicit information about its user's whereabouts and activities. Given the ease of adapting a global positioning system (GPS) module to hand-helds, and the availability of this information for cellular telephony services, several projects are exploring educational applications that respond to the wearer's current location, sometimes combined with records of previously visited spots. Examples of WILD context-aware applications include *tour guides* (Abowd et al., 1997) and *location-aware language learning applications* that adapt the content presented according to users' location (Ogata & Yano, 2002), *facilitating informal meetings* of study partners within college campuses (Griswold et al., 2002), and *digitally augmenting field trips* (Rogers et al., 2004; Williams et al., 2005).

Rheingold (2002, p. xv) observed how these additional capabilities of context-awareness mean that:

> [H]and-held devices can detect, within a few yards, where they are located on a continent, within a neighborhood, or inside a room. These separate upgrades in capabilities don't just add to each other; mobile, multimedia, location-sensitive characteristics multiply each other's usefulness. At the same time, their costs drop dramatically ... the driving factors of the mobile, context-sensitive, Internet-connected devices are Moore's Law (computer chips get cheaper as they grow more powerful), Metcalfe's Law (the useful power of a network multiplies rapidly as the number of nodes in the network increases), and Reed's Law (the power of a network, especially one that enhances social networks, multiplies even more rapidly as the number of different human groups that can use that network increases). Moore's Law drove the PC industry and the cultural changes that resulted, Metcalfe's Law drove the deployment of the Internet, and Reed's Law will drive the growth of the mobile and pervasive Net.

Other informal learning locales where hand-helds are becoming more commonplace are *museums* and *exhibitions*. Hand-helds can offer in-depth explanations for particular exhibits, additional reference materials, and may create a record of the visitors' museum path for subsequent online access, a WILD use that Roschelle and Pea (2002) categorized as "act becomes artifact." School and family groups can use this recording feature to later discuss their experiences, reflect on concepts learned, and share souvenir images with others. Hand-helds are also being shown to be effective teaching tools for museum guides, facilitating their access to relevant content as visitors' questions arise, controlling remote exhibits on cue, reporting problems, collecting relevant data, as well as incorporating on-the-job training through small bite instruction (Hsi, 2004).

Another example of how "act becomes artifact" through WILD is also taking shape in the form of weblogs, or as they are more commonly known, *blogs*, that permit posting online of multimedia accounts from any device, with little technology training.[7] Covering a wide range of interests, from topic-based to teenage diaries, blogs are growing at an explosive rate and democratizing the distribution of publishing globally accessible information: from revealing industry secrets to breaking news in war zones, they have become another information source for learners to evaluate, process, and contribute to. Blogs primarily accessed and updated through mobile devices have been termed *moblogs*, and carriers of cellular telephony are quickly incorporating services designed to cater to budding journalists.

Everyone and anyone can distribute content right from their phone to the world via the Web; mobile wireless interactive devices are democratizing media production. The embedded digital camera has been predicted to be one of the most common features on hand-helds and mobile phones, growing from 178 million units in 2004 to over 860 million units in 2009, or 89 percent of all mobile phone handsets shipped.[8] Several worldwide communities around these photo journalistic moblogs are available online (http://www.rabble.com and http://www.textamerica.com/, both accessed July 31, 2005), often leveraging social networking features to help readers find personally meaningful content, through collaborative filtering. Despite their popularity as forums for creative writing and collaborative critique, there are not yet published empirical studies of blogging for learning. However, we believe that these trends are likely to influence hand-held learning and education, as long as privacy and safety concerns are met, because blogs have been shown to be powerful tools for personal and political expression.

Schools and Classrooms

We have covered some of the existing state of the art applications of WILD technologies outside the classroom, implicit and explicit in their learning goals; yet many more await us inside the school walls. We can distinguish two foci within the space of WILD in classrooms: first are three common evaluation dimensions of applications for hand-helds that drive the decisions behind their introduction in school: *their lower costs* (already discussed), *the needs of the intended audience*, and *their ties to curricula*. After briefly describing needs and curriculum ties, we concentrate on the five key application-

level benefits of WILD that allow for innovation in classroom practices (Roschelle & Pea, 2002).

The second evaluative dimension is the target audience. Is the innovation catering primarily to teachers or administrators? Is it aimed at students, working individually or collaborating in groups? Commercial WILD applications make some school and class administration tasks more efficient and convenient. Several companies, including Media-X systems, GoKnow, Wireless Generation, ETS, and Houghton Mifflin, provide applications specifically meant for schools' administrative tasks – ranging from sharing agenda notes through the hand-helds' beaming feature, to accessing data during meetings, to quickly checking on any given students' schedule, record, photo, or parent contact information. Teachers are using tools that let them compare students' essays with available online sources, and tag potential plagiarisms for them to review.[9] Companies have developed software specifically for hand-helds and tailored for student assessment for almost all grades and subjects of instruction: from checklists and menus that make for easy diagnosis of reading difficulties in the early grades, to sharing students' progress across subjects and teachers, to student assessment and gradebook aides – particularly helpful for subjects where teachers are not always at a desk, such as physical education, labs, and field trips (COSN, 2004).

Many applications cater to individual students' needs in the classroom, and we focus on WILD applications that foster deep understanding, inquiry processes, and collaborative problem solving, whether in small groups or as a whole classroom. Within the realm of student applications, a evaluation dimension we have identified involves the closeness between the technological intervention and the curricula. Some applications are directly linked with specific publishers' curricula, providing teacher training and development materials as well as addressing specific units in a predetermined sequence matched with school district and state goals. At other times, the technology is much more loosely linked to academic purposes, and provided within the school setting for enrichment or extracurricular activities.

From organization tools, to portable course materials, to recording and archiving the content of blackboards, to recording and listening to audio-related class content, school and university faculty are increasingly supportive of providing hand-helds for their students. For example, in 2004 all incoming freshmen to Duke University received an iPod, a digital music player characterized by the additional capacity of a considerable hard drive, and teaching is slowly incorporating audio components across subjects beyond the music department: some courses are using this device to provide news feeds, language learning, interviews and field data collection, and signal analysis, among other uses.

We are particularly interested in applications that maintain an emphasis on inquiry processes, social constructivist theories, and distributed cognition designs; hence, although there are many applications designed for individual use, we concentrate on those that favor collaboration among students. Roschelle and Pea (2002) distinguished five application-level affordances of hand-held implementations in schools: (1) augmenting physical space with information exchanges, (2) leveraging topological space, (3) aggregating coherently across all students participating individually, (4) conducting classroom performances, and (5) enabling act becomes artifact.

Augmenting Physical Space with Information Exchanges

The first affordance, augmenting physical space with information exchanges, includes activities where information exchanges are overlaid on the physical movements of students. One such application domain is *participatory simulations* to promote learning about decentralized systems, where each student, through his or her device, represents an "agent" or conceptual entity in a simulation of a complex system: a car on the road of a traffic model, or a person coming in contact with a viral disease ecosystem (e.g., Colella, 2000; Wilensky & Stroup, 1999). In participatory simulations, students' memories of their path of data exchanges through close encounters with others drive the inquiry and analysis of the spread of the virus or emergent behavior. Other applications that find a niche within this category are probeware – enhancing the hand-helds' data collection possibilities through scientific probe modules (mentioned earlier) – and other uses of hand-helds in the field, such as photographing and wirelessly matching field specimens to an online database (e.g., Chen et al., 2004).

Leveraging Topological Space

Roschelle and Pea (2002) alluded to two ways of leveraging topological space: *geospatial mappings* between the hand-held and the real-world that facilitate navigation and context-aware applications, and *semiospatial representations*, in which the spatial attributes of the topological representation are not mappable to spatial attributes of the physical world (except to those of the inscription themselves). Semiospatial representations include Cartesian and other graphs, concept maps, flowcharts, and non-geo-gridded information visualizations generally. WILD applications that use semiospatial representations include concept map makers such as GoKnow's *PiCoMap* (Royer, 2004) and *Pocket Model-It* (Luchini, Quintana, & Soloway, 2004), Kaput and Roschelle's *SimCalc* software for learning about the mathematics of change (Roschelle, Penuel & Abrahamson, 2004), and *Chemation*, a chemistry modeling and animation tool (Scott et al., 2004).

One successful implementation of hand-helds within the semiospatial realm that is tightly coupled to curriculum and teacher development is the *CodeIt!* program (Goldman, Pea, & Maldonado, 2004; Goldman, Pea, Maldonado, Martin, & White, 2004) where students interact fluidly with multiple representations of mathematical functions (ordered pairs, graphs, equations, function and frequency tables) to develop rigorous algebra skills. *CodeIt!* is inspired by the curriculum unit *Codes, Inc*, developed by the Middle-school Mathematics through Applications Project (MMAP), which teachers found helpful for transitioning to the use of technology and more applications-based curriculum materials (Lichtenstein, Weisglass, & Erickan-Alper, 1998).

CodeIt! is set within the real-world context of cryptography, and students working in teams can observe and analyze as changes to any representation propagate across the other representations and the other students' devices. The results from the pilot evaluation of this program are promising, despite extremely heterogeneous groups in terms of age, previous knowledge of algebra, and students' socioeconomic background. In four of six of the groups studied, students made significant gains, in some cases raising their scores by 15 to 30 percent. Students showed significant gains on test items relating to evaluating exponents and the graphs of functions, validating the hand-held's use of semiospatial topographical space, and on one graphical item, 44 percent of students answered correctly on the posttest, as compared to only 13 percent on the pretest. Overall, researchers report a mean increase from pre- to posttests of eight percentage points.

Aggregating Across All Students

The third application-level affordance of WILD identified by Roschelle and Pea is supporting data aggregation across all students. For example, in *ClassTalk* (Roschelle, Penuel, & Abrahamson, 2004) students answer multiple-choice questions through their WILD. The answers are aggregated as a histogram, and projected onto a publicly shared display space for the class to discuss and reflect on common misconceptions. We have discussed earlier two evaluation dimensions – target audience and ties to curricula – and commercial applications that aggregate coherently across students offer a great example of the first evaluation dimension we mentioned, cost. Some hand-held solutions that aggregate students' input and partic-

ipation (sometimes preserving anonymity) are developed specifically to maximize cost-effectiveness, such as *ETS Discourse* and *eInstruction*. Called either classroom response systems, classroom performance systems, or classroom communication systems, these cost-effective solutions offer limited choices – through buttons on "clickers" that resemble television remote controls – but leverage the shared displays to make publicly available the classroom's level of consensus on concepts taught, information often missed in traditional instruction.

Such systems can help the teacher focus instructional attention on the issues most significant for the classroom-as-a-whole considered as the unit of learning. To the extent that such systems can provide the powerful learning intervention of formative assessment (Means, this volume) by providing more feedback than usual on learning-teaching interrelationships, they hold considerable promise for improving learning outcomes for both students and teachers (Davis, 2003). For example, the instructor of a large lecture class can receive real-time feedback on the speed and difficulty of the lecture, and adapt the presentation accordingly. And although answers may be shown anonymously on the shared aggregate display, each student's response can be recorded and linked to the relevant online content for that student to later review on the Internet, as in the Berkeley Digital Chemistry Project (Cuthbert et al., 2005).

Improvements in students' content knowledge, motivation, and engagement often result when this technology is introduced. However, students can interact with complex subject matter in richer ways with a full-fledged WILD, an activity researchers have labeled "CATAALYST" ("Classroom Aggregation Technology for Activating and Assessing Learning and Your Students' Thinking," Penuel et al., 2004), when it is deployed for class-wide aggregation and reflection. Classroom network technologies in math and science have been shown to augment classroom communication, students' engagement, and enjoyment, and to improve students' performance measures, primarily through the teachers' implementation of pedagogical practices that leverage the WILD application capabilities (Roschelle, Abrahamson, & Penuel, 2004, provide a review of the literature on these effects).

Beyond the improvements in equity and extent of participation, and the feelings of support experienced by students, the projection onto a publicly shared display offers a cognitive and conceptual focus of joint attention for each student in the class, rather than focusing on activity and materials in their individual workspaces. The joint display permits "viewing the classroom as a distributed system ... [which] can enable relatively simple mathematical behaviors at the individual student level to result in the emergence of more complex group-level mathematical or scientific constructions" (Penuel et al., 2004, p. 5; also see Hegedus & Kaput, 2004).

Conducting Classroom Performances

WILD allow teachers to take a conductor's role. However, negotiating and directing students' parallel contributions such that transformative learning conversations become the norm (Pea, 1994) requires masterful conducting efforts. Most of the CATAALYST interventions we have discussed start their cycle with a question designed and posed by the teacher to elicit significant responses. Some large college courses are letting their students give feedback to the lecturer, both student- and professor-initiated. Examples of student-initiated feedback include students posting questions during the lecture onto the aggregated display, and the lecturer can determine whether to pause and answer if sufficient students "vote" on it (Griswold et al., 2002), and also students giving continuous feedback with regard to the lecture's pace that the instructor can immediately observe in the aggregate display (Scheele et al., 2003).

Enabling Act Becomes Artifact

WILD can give users a grasp of their own learning progress, self-monitoring their performance for the purpose of improving teaching (as when instructors use the feedback mechanisms described earlier) and learning. In SRI's WHIRL (Wireless Handhelds for Improving Reflection on Learning), teachers are part of the design team, devoted to giving students the tools and scaffolding necessary to reflect and improve on their learning practices, gauge their understanding, and incorporate mindful data collection activities. WHIRL is currently taking place in disadvantaged districts in South Carolina (Penuel, Roschelle, & Tatar, 2003).

Questions and Directions: Transformative Innovations for Learning Futures

The field continues to experiment and discover new areas for expansion, yet we call on colleagues and researchers to ensure that the coming years see not only continued growth in novel ways to interact with the subject matter, but also see an emphasis on learning evaluations. Because of the enthusiasm surrounding its widespread adoption and egalitarian goals, few WILD researchers have developed the complex measurement instruments needed to show across contexts that activities and curriculum are helping students to learn. We need new metrics for assessing the roles of WILD in learning and performance, and in relation to the development of interests, motivation, and personal identity in the *learning ecologies* that they traverse with learners (home, school, community, virtual spaces: Barron, 2004).

The future of WILD learning provides an exciting frontier for the learning sciences. In our view, we need to leverage two kinds of convergences to advance WILD learning and teaching. There is a multidimensional convergence of rapid developments related to information technology hardware and services, largely driven by steady increases in processing power, memory, and connectivity, resulting in explosive growth in media richness, ubiquitous connectivity, and smart, personalized software services. From 1990 to 2003, there was exponential growth in hardware capabilities: increases in processor speed by a factor of 400, memory size by a factor of 120, wireless connection speed by a factor of 18, and fiber channel bandwidth by a factor of 10,000 (National Science Foundation, 2003). However, a third type of convergence would also be beneficial to societies worldwide: a convergence between the technical integration being pursued by industry, the research and development being advanced by the learning sciences, and the wisdom of practice from K–12 educators.

Consider what it will be like to have such learning interwoven into everyday activities and communications, whether in or out of school, across the boundaries of intentionally designed institutions of education to the home, community, workplace, and other organizations. Like Department of Defense DARPA agency-funded work in the 1960s that led to many of the core technology innovations we take for granted today (PITAC, 2000), the target should be radical improvements that aim for orders of magnitude improvements in learning and education. These test-beds would demonstrate feasibility and early stage potential of substantively new tools, content, and pedagogies that leverage technical advances and learning sciences knowledge at the cutting edge of what is possible. As researchers, we need to live in specifically created possible futures as pioneering scouts, and report back what life is like in such possible futures, where WILD technologies become ubiquitously woven in new ways into the fabric of tomorrow's societal learning systems (Pea & Lazowska, 2003). Such expeditions scouting out the future of ubiquitous computer-aided learning would require networking the communities and expertise of diverse stakeholders – K–20 educators and institutions, researchers in the sciences of learning and uses of educational technologies, subject matter experts, advanced telecommunications professionals, education schools, and industry – to plan, invent, explore, and support their design and continuous improvement. Changes in information and computing technologies are proceeding at such a rapid pace that it will take the talented engagements of the educational, research, and technology industries to forge the visions and innovations in tools, environments, and instructional practices that can build on as well as advance the sciences and contexts of learning, teaching, and education. Such partnerships would explore systemic approaches to educational change – aligning standards, curriculum, pedagogy, assessment, teacher development, school culture, and school-home connections, in addition to the use of educational technology. The partnerships would undertake a continuous innovation cycle for educational techniques and technology, where the design of new prototypes would be followed by observation of the use of those prototypes, which would immediately feed back into modifications in the prototype designs.

Footnotes

1. WILD is an acronym created at SRI International's Center for Technology in Learning in 2000 by Roy Pea and Jeremy Roschelle when they developed a research program and series of projects on hand-held computing for learning, with work together on this topic beginning in 1998. Preparation of this chapter was supported in part by funding from the Wallenberg Global Learning Network, and National Science Foundation grant number #0354453.

2. The first hand-held computers used broadly in education were calculators from Texas Instruments, HP, Casio, and others, although the Apple Newton had devoted advocates in its brief heyday (1993–97), as did the Psion Organizer (released in 1986).

3. BuddyBuzz at http://captology.stanford.edu/notebook/archives/000121.html, accessed July 31, 2005.

4. See http://newswww.bbc.net.uk/1/hi/technology/3754663.stm, accessed July 31, 2005.

5. This comparison pits reported clock speeds of the HP-Compaq iPaq hand-held against Apple Computer's Power Macintosh G4 desktop and Powerbook G4 laptop. In terms of Palm's hand-helds, a 2003 Tungsten T model is comparable to the Toshiba Libretto (70CT: Pentium MMX 120 Mhz), a 1997 PC laptop and the 1995 Apple Macintosh 7200, a desktop computer. This comparison is approximate because reported clockspeeds are imprecise measurements of a computer's performance due to differences in instruction sets and optimized code.

6. Tablet computers are not discussed here, for whereas they share stylus-driven input with hand-helds and add a larger screen, their relative lack of power and cost (often twice as much as comparable laptop computers) reduces their potential to equalize access to the technology for global 1:1 computing.

7. In March 2005, there were over 7.8 million weblogs, double the number of blogs from October 2004. Companies such as Google, AOL, SixApart, and MoveableType are facilitating the creation of about 30K–40K new blogs daily, increasing the collective size of blogs (often referred to as the "blogosphere") over sixteen times in the last twenty months (numbers tracked by http://www.technorati.com/ and reported in http://www.sifry.com/alerts/archives/000298.html, both pages accessed July 31, 2005).

8. InfoTrends/CAP Ventures (http://www.infotrends-rgi.com/home/Press/itPress/2005/1.11.05.html).

9. See *TurnItIn* (http://www.turnitin.com/), *Glatt Plagiarism Services* (http://www.plagiarism.com), or the *Moss* for programming classes – the Measure Of Software Similarity index (http://www.cs.berkeley.edu/~aiken/moss.html) (all pages accessed July 31, 2005).

References

Abowd, G., Atkeson, C., Hong, J., Long, S., Kooper, R., & Pinkerton, M. (1997). Cyberguide: a mobile context-aware tour guide. *Wireless Networks*, 3(5), 421–433.

Barron, B. (2004). Learning ecologies for technological fluency: Gender and experience differences. *Journal of Educational Computing Research*, 31(1), 1–36.

Batista, E. (2001). Debating the merits of palms in class. *Wired News*, Available at: http://www.wired.com/news/school/0,1383,45863,00.html. Accessed August 23, 2001.

Center for Innovative Learning Technologies (CILT). (1998). *DataGotchi Deep Dive*. SRI International. Available at: http://www.cilt.org/images/DataGotchi.pdf. Accessed April 2002.

Chen, Y., Kao, T., Yu, G., & Sheu, J. (2004). A mobile butterfly-watching learning system for supporting independent learning. In J. Roschelle, T. W. Chan, Kinshuk, S. Yang (Eds.), *Proceedings of the 2nd IEEE WMTE2004* (pp. 11–18). New York: IEEE Press.

Colella, V. (2000). Participatory simulations: Building collaborative understanding through immersive dynamic modeling. *Journal of the Learning Sciences*, 9(4), 471–500.

COSN (2004). *COSN's guide to hand-held computing in K–12 schools*. Washington, DC: Consortium for School Networking.

Cuthbert, A., Kubinec, M., Tanis, D., Ieong, F., Wei, L., & Schlossberg, D. (2005). Advanced technology for streamlining the creation of ePortfolio resources and dynamically-indexing digital library assets: A case study from the Digital Chemistry project. In *Conference Abstracts and Applications*, CHI 2005, p. 972–987. New York: ACM Press.

Davis, S. (2003). Observations in classrooms using a network of hand-held devices. *Journal of Computer Assisted Learning*, 19(3), 298–307.

Gee, J. P. (2003). *What video games have to teach us about learning and literacy*. New York: Palgrave Macmillan.

Goldman, S., Pea, R., & Maldonado, H. (2004). Emerging social engineering in the wireless classroom. In Y. Kafai, W. Saldoval, N. Enyedy, A. S. Nixon, & F. Herrera (Eds.), *Proceedings of the Sixth ICLS 2004* (pp. 222–230). Mahwah, NJ: Lowrence Erlbaum Associates.

Goldman, S., Pea, R., Maldonado, H., Martin, L., & White, T. (2004). Functioning in the wireless classroom. In J. Roschelle, T. W. Chan, Kinshuk, & S. Yang (Eds), *Proceedings of the 2nd IEEE WMTE2004*. (pp. 75–82). New York: IEEE Press.

Griswold, W., Shanahan, P., Brown, S., Boyer, R., Ratto, M., Shapiro, R. B., Truong, T. M. (2002). *ActiveCampus – Experiments in community-oriented ubiquitous computing*. Technical Report CS2003-0750, Computer Science and Engineering, UC San Diego, June 2002.

Hegedus, S., & Kaput, J. (2004). An introduction to the profound potential of connected algebra activities: issues of representation, engagement and pedagogy. In *Proceedings of the 28th Conference of the International Group for the Psychology of Mathematics Education* (Vol. 3, pp. 129–136). Bergen, Norway.

Heidegger, M. (1927/1973). *Being and time*. Trans. J. Macquarrie & E. Robinson. Oxford: Basil Blackwell.

Hsi, S. (2004). I-Guides in progress: Two prototype applications for museum educators and visitors. In J. Roschelle, T. W. Chan, Kinshuk, S.Yang (Eds.), *Proceedings of the 2nd IEEEWMTE2004* (pp. 187–192). New York: IEEE Press.

Kaiser Family Foundation. (2004). *Children, the digital divide, and federal policy.* September 2004 Issue Brief. Henry J. Kaiser Family Foundation.

Kleiner, A., & Lewis, L. (2003). *Internet access in U.S. public schools and classrooms: 1994–2002,* U.S. Department of Education, National Center for Education Statistics. NCES 2004-011.

Klopfer, E., Squire, K., & Jenkins, H. (2002). Environmental detectives: PDAs as a window into a virtual simulated world. In M. Milrad, U. Hoppe, & Kinshuk (Eds.), *WMTE2002* (pp. 95–98). Los Alamitos, CA: IEEE Computer Society.

Lichtenstein, G. Weisglass, J., & Erickan-Alper, K. (1998). *Final evaluation report: Middleschool Mathematics through Applications Project.* Denver, CO: Quality Evaluation Design.

Lindholm, C., Keinonen, T., & Kiljander, H. (2003). *How Nokia changed the face of the mobile phone.* McGraw-Hill.

Luchini, K., Quintana, C., & Soloway, E. (2004). Design guidelines for learner-centered handheld tools. In *Proceedings of CHI 2004* (pp. 135–142). New York: ACM Press.

Mandryk, R., Inkpen, K., Bilezikjian, M., Klemmer, S., & Landay, J. (2001). Supporting children's collaboration across hand-held computers. In *Extended Abstracts of CHI2001* (pp. 255–256). New York: ACM Press.

Myers, B. A., Nichols, J., Wobbrock, J. O., & Miller, R. C. (2004). Taking hand-held devices to the next level. *IEEE Computer,* 36(12), 36–43.

National Science Foundation. (2003). *Revolutionary science and engineering through cyberinfrastructure: Report of the National Science Foundation Blue-Ribbon Advisory Panel on Cyberinfrastructure.* Arlington, VA.

NetDay. (2005). *NetDay's 2004 survey results.* Available at: http://www.netday.org/news_2004_survey_results.htm (Accessed March 9, 2005).

NetSafe. (2005). *Text Generation survey.* Available at: http://www.netsafe.org.nz/isgnews/Text_Generation.aspx (Accessed February 8, 2005).

NOP World. (2005). *mKids Study.* United Business Media. Available from: http://www.nopworld.com/news.asp?go=news_item&key=151. (Accessed March 9, 2005)

Ogata, H., & Yano, Y. (2002). Context-aware support for computer supported ubiquitous learning. In J. Roschelle, T. W. Chan, Kinshuk, & S. Yang (Eds.), *Proceedings of the 2nd IEEEWMTE2004* (pp. 27–34). New York: IEEE Press.

Parsad, B., & Jones, J. (2005, February). *Internet access in U.S. public schools and classrooms: 1994–2003.* Washington, DC: US Department of Education, National Center for Education Statistics.

Pea, R. D. (1993). Practices of distributed intelligence and designs for education. In G. Salomon (Ed.) *Distributed cognitions: psychological and educational considerations* (pp. 47–87). New York: Cambridge University Press.

Pea, R. D. (1994). Seeing what we build together: Distributed multimedia learning environments for transformative communications. *Journal of the Learning Sciences,* 3(3), 283–298.

Pea, R. D., & Lazowska, E. (2003). A vision for LENS Centers: learning expeditions in network systems for the 21st century. In Pea, R. D., Wulf, W. A., Elliot, S. W., & Darling, M. A. (2003). (Eds.) *Planning for two transformations in education and learning technology: Report of a workshop* (pp. 84–89). Washington, DC: National Academies Press.

Pea, R. D., Wulf, W. A., Elliot, S. W., & Darling, M. A. (2003). (Eds.) *Planning for two transformations in education and learning technology: Report of a workshop.* Washington, DC: National Academies Press.

Penuel, W. R., Roschelle, J., Crawford, V., Shechtman, N., & Abrahamson, L. (2004). *Workshop report: Advancing research on the transformative potential of interactive pedagogies and classroom networks.* Menlo Park: SRI International.

Penuel, W. R., Roschelle, J., & Tatar, D. (2003). *The role of research on contexts of teaching practice in informing the design of learning technologies.* Available from: http://www.projectwhirl.org/Downloads/RoleResearch-ContextInforming.pdf (Accessed December 12, 2004).

Pownell, D., & Bailey, G. (2001). Getting a handle on hand-helds. *American School Board Journal,* 188(6), 18–21.

Prensky, Marc. (2004) *What can you learn from a cellphone?* Available at http://www.marcprensky.com/writing/Prensky-What_Can_You_Learn_From_a_Cell_Phone-FINAL.pdf. (Accessed 5 January 2005).

President's Information Technology Advisory Committee (PITAC) Report to the President. (2000, February). *Resolving the digital divide: Information, access, and opportunity conference report.* National Coordination Office for Information Technology Research and Development, Washington, DC.

Rasmusson, J., Dahlgren, F., Gustafsson, H., & Nilsson, T. (2004). Multimedia in mobile phones – The ongoing Revolution. *Ericsson Review, 2, 98–107.*

Rheingold, H. (2002). *Smart mobs: the next revolution.* Cambridge, MA: Perseus Publishing.

Roberts, D., Foehr, U. G., & Rideout, V. (2005, March). *Generation M: Media in the lives of 8–18 year-olds.* Henry J. Kaiser Family Foundation.

Rogers, Y., Price, S., Fitzpatrick, G., Fleck, R., Harris, E., Smith, H., Randell, C., Muller, H., O'Malley, C., Stanton, D., Thompson, M., & Wela, M. (2004). Ambient Wood: Designing new forms of digital augmentation for learning outdoors. In *Proceedings of the 2004 IDC Building a community* (pp. 3–10). New York: ACM Press.

Rosas, R., Nussbaum, M., Cumsille, P., Marianov, V., Correa, M., Flores, P., Grau, V, Lagos, F., López, X., López, V., Rodriguez, P., & Salinas, M. (2003). Beyond Nintendo: design and assessment of educational video games for first and second grade students. *Computers & Education, 40(1), 71–94.*

Roschelle, J., Abrahamson, L. A., & Penuel, W. R. (2004, April). *Integrating classroom network technology and learning theory to improve classroom science learning: A literature synthesis.* Paper presented at AERA, San Diego, CA.

Roschelle, J., & Mills, M. (1999, August). Toward low-cost, ubiquitous, collaborative computing for the math class. Communications of the ACM, 42(8), 24–25.

Roschelle, J., & Pea, R. (2002). A walk on the WILD side: How wireless hand-helds may change CSCL. *The International Journal of Cognition and Technology, 1(1), 145–168.*

Roschelle, J., Penuel, W. R., & Abrahamson, L. A. (2004). The networked classroom. *Educational Leadership, 61(5), 50–54.*

Royer, R. (2004, February) What a concept! Using concept mapping on hand-held computers. *Learning and leading with technology, 31(5),* 12.

Scheele, N., Mauve, M., Effelsberg, W., Wessels, A., Horz, H., & Fries, S. (2003). The interactive lecture: A new teaching paradigm based on ubiquitous computing. In *CSCL 2003 Poster Proceedings,* Bergen, Norway.

Scott, L., Zimmerman, R., Chang, H., Heitzman, M., Krajcik, J., McNeill, K., Quintana, C., & Soloway, E. (2004) Chemation: A hand-held chemistry modeling and animation tool. In *Proceedings of IDC2004y* (pp. 119–120). New York: ACM Press.

Soloway, E., Norris, C., Blumenfeld, P., Fishman, B. J. K., & Marx, R. (2001). Devices are ready-at-hand. *Communications of the ACM, 44(6),* 15–20.

Tatar, D., Roschelle, J., Vahey, P., & Penuel, W. R. (2003, September). Hand-helds go to school: Lessons learned. *IEEE Computer,* 30–37.

Thornton, P., & Houser, C. (2004). Using mobile phones in education. In J. Roschelle, T. W. Chan, Kinshuk, & S. Yang (Eds)., *Proceedings of the 2nd IEEE WMTE2004* (pp. 3–10). New York: IEEE Press.

Tinker, R. F., & Krajcik, J. S. (Eds.). (2001). *Portable technologies: science learning in context.* New York: Kluwer Academic.

Vahey, P., & Crawford, V. (2002). *Palm Education Pioneers Program: Final evaluation report.* Menlo Park, CA: SRI International.

Weiser, M. (1991). The computer for the twenty-first century. *Scientific American, 265(3),* 94–100.

Wilensky, U., & Stroup, W. (1999). Learning through participatory simulations: Network-based design for systems learning in classrooms. In C. Hoadley & J. Roschelle (Eds.), *Proceedings of the 3rd CSCL '99, Stanford University, CA.*

Williams, M., Jones, O., Fleuriot, C., & Wood, L. (2005). Children and emerging wireless technologies: Investigating the potential for spatial practices. In *Proceedings of the 2005 ACM Conference On Human Factors In Computing System* (CHI 2005) (pp. 819–828). Portland, OR. ACM Press.

Winograd, T., & Flores, F. (1987). *Understanding computers and cognition: A new foundation for design.* Reading, MA: Addison-Wesley.

CHAPTER 26

Arguing to Learn

Jerry Andriessen

Many people think that arguing interferes with learning. They link argumentation to a certain type of oppositional argument that is increasingly prevalent in our media culture. Tannen (1998) analyzed the aggressive types of argument that are frequently seen on talk shows and in the political sphere, where representatives of two opposed viewpoints spout talking points at each other. In these forms of argumentation, the goal is not to work together toward a common position, but simply to score points. All teachers and parents have seen children engaged in this type of argumentation, and most would probably agree that it has little to contribute to education.

The learning sciences are studying a different kind of argumentation, which I call *collaborative* argumentation. For example, collaborative argumentation plays a central role in science; science advances not by the accumulation of facts, but by debate and argumentation (Kuhn, 1962, 1970; Bell, 2004). Even when two scientists disagree, they still share the common values of science and both of them are interested in achieving the same goals. Argumentation in science is

not oppositional and aggressive; it is a form of collaborative discussion in which both parties are working together to resolve an issue, and in which both scientists expect to find agreement by the end of the argument. Exposure to collaborative argumentation can help students learn to think critically and independently about important issues and contested values.

When students collaborate in argumentation in the classroom, they are *arguing to learn*. When viewed as a collaborative practice, argumentation can help learners to accomplish a wide variety of important learning goals. First, argumentation involves elaboration, reasoning, and reflection. These activities have been shown to contribute to deeper conceptual learning (Bransford, Brown, & Cocking, 1999). Second, participating in argumentation helps students learn about argumentative structures (Kuhn, 2001). Third, because productive argumentation is a form of collaboration, it can help develop social awareness and collaborative ability more generally (Vygotsky, 1978; Wertsch, 1985). Fourth, groups of people – at work, at home, or in social contexts – often share a common tradition of argumentation, and effective participation in these groups requires knowing how to argue competently within them (Billig, 1987; Koschmann, 2003). This is particularly true of the knowledge-based communities that are so central to the knowledge society – groups of highly trained professionals such as scientists, doctors, lawyers, and executives.

Argumentation has been studied from many perspectives – philosophy, literature, public speaking – but there have been very few educational studies of argumentation. However, a few learning scientists have been studying the educational use of argumentation, and this chapter summarizes this research. Studies of arguing to learn have the potential to help learners, teachers, and researchers design learning environments that facilitate collaborative argumentation. I begin the chapter by discussing argumentation theory: its vocabulary and different viewpoints on argumentation. Then, I discuss the relation between argumentation and learning. Finally, I summarize learning in learning environments where argumentation is mediated by computer networks, such as chat rooms and Internet newsgroups.

Argumentation Theory

Argumentation theory (van Eemeren, Grootendorst, & Snoeck Henkemans, 2002) studies the production, analysis, and evaluation of argumentation. The goal is to develop criteria for judging the soundness of an argument. Describing and evaluating arguments are some of the oldest topics of scholarship; Aristotle distinguished several kinds of argumentation, including didactic, dialectical, examination, and eristic. For most of the last century, the study of argumentation has been dominated by scholars who focused on the sequential structure of an argument. In this tradition, a good argument was thought to have a certain type of structure, and scholars attempted to specify the "grammar" of argument, by analogy

with the syntax of a well-formed sentence. For example, Toulmin (1958) identified the following stages of sound argumentation:

- A *claim* states the standpoint or conclusion: "The Kyoto protocol to reduce global warming is necessary."
- The *data* are the facts or opinions that the claim is based on: "Over the last century, the earth's temperature has been rising as a result of greenhouse gas emissions."
- The *warrant* provides the justification for using the data as support for the claim: "Scientists agree that there is no other explanation for this rise in temperature."
- Optionally, the *backing* provides specific information supporting the warrant. "Scientists have identified the atmospheric mechanisms whereby greenhouse gases cause a warming of the earth's surface."
- A *qualifier* adds a measure of certainty to the conclusion, indicating the degree of force which the arguers attribute to a claim: "However, the earth's temperature has been found to fluctuate over geological time, in some cases without any obvious cause."
- Exceptions to the claim are expressed by a *rebuttal*: "The Kyoto protocol would not be necessary if the world's countries had already reduced their output of greenhouse gases."

This type of approach has been very influential, especially in the analysis of written argumentation. It is a concise description of what appears in a sound line of reasoning, or even in a productive line of inquiry. However, in recent years, the study of argumentation has become a more empirical and scientific study, and the grammatical approach does not correspond very well to the ways that arguments unfold in collaborative discourse. Van Eemeren and Grootendorst (1999) note that the model fails to consider both sides involved in (real-world) argumentation; it covers only the proponent, not the opponent. A related problem is that it fails to consider argumentation as a discourse phenomenon that is always embedded in a specific contextual and social environment. For the learning sciences, another serious problem is that the grammatical view ignores development (Leitão, 2001), as well as the higher level problem-solving nature of argumentative discourse (Voss, Tyler, & Yengo, 1983).

Instead of this grammatical concept of argument, the learning sciences draw on scholars who analyze argumentation as a type of dialogue. For example, *formal dialectics* (Barth & Krabbe, 1982) describes argumentation as a dialogue between a proponent and an opponent around a certain thesis. *Pragma-dialectics* (Van Eemeren & Grootendorst, 1992; 1999) explains the interaction between proponent and opponent by describing the necessary conditions for critical discussion rather than by describing the rules of logic for generating a debate. Van Eemeren and Grootendorst (1999) show how pragma-dialectics can be applied to the analysis of argumentative discourse. In *dialogue theory* (Walton, 2000), an argument is seen as a move made in a dialogue in which two parties attempt to reason together. Six types of dialogue are described – persuasion, inquiry, negotiation, information-seeking, deliberation, and eristic (personal conflict) – to be used as a normative model to provide the standards for how a given argument should be used collaboratively. A dialogue begins with an opening move, and then each pair of moves represents a so-called adjacency pair. Sequences of moves – formal dialectical structures – are meant to model argumentation, but also other speech acts. Table 26.1 provides an example of such a sequence, in which the first line illustrates the moves "why-question" (asks for justification) and "putting forward an argument" (supports a proposition by quoting another one).

Argumentation and Learning

Dialogue theory suggests that in arguing to learn, students are not primarily attempt-

Table 26.1. Moves in a Sample Dialogue (Adapted from Walton, 2000)

Proponent	Respondent
1. Why should I accept *A*?	Because *B*, and if *B* then *A*.
2. Why should I accept *B*?	Because you accepted it before.
3. All right, I accept *B*.	Do you accept "If *B* then *A*"?
4. Yes.	Do you accept *A*?
5. No.	You are inconsistent!

ing to convince each other; instead, they are engaged in *cooperative explorations of a dialogical space* of solutions (cf. Walton, 1989; Nonnon, 1996). An argument for learning should be evaluated on the basis of its collaborative value as a contribution to the conversation (Grice, 1975).

Baker (2004) identified four learning mechanisms that are potentially associated with effective arguing to learn. These mechanisms are based on general learning sciences findings that seem to apply broadly to a wide range of content knowledge (Sawyer introduction, this volume):

- *Making knowledge explicit*: Learners that provide explanations, or make explicit the reasoning underlying their problem solving behavior, show the most learning benefits (Chi & Van Lehn, 1991). Argumentation provides many opportunities for explanation, and preparing a justification or argumentative defense fosters reflection that often leads to deeper learning.
- *Conceptual change*: Debating a question may raise doubt about initial misconceptions. Conceptual transformation is supported by argumentation.
- *Co-elaboration of new knowledge*: In argumentation, learners work together to develop new knowledge. The interactive, interpersonal nature of verbal interaction helps to scaffold individual learning.

- *Increasing articulation*: Argumentation obliges learners to precisely formulate questions and statements, and articulation transforms and deepens during the argument.

The Development of Argumentative Skill

The ability to understand argumentation emerges early in development. It develops out of a desire to ensure that personally meaningful goals are attained. By the age of three, children generate and understand the principal components of an argument (Stein & Albro, 2001; Stein & Miller, 1993). The ability to construct detailed, coherent rationalities in defense of a favored position improves with age. This development, however, does not guarantee a deeper understanding of one's opponents, because argumentative knowledge is necessarily asymmetrical (Stein & Bernas, 1999). Individuals have more knowledge about the positive benefits of their own position than of those of their opponent's position. Also, they know more about the weaknesses of their enemies than about their own weaknesses. We can train people to understand the opposing position in a more accurate and complex fashion; but only when they begin to change their stance do learners start generating reasons that favor the opponent's position.

The mental structures used to understand arguments are related to those used to understand social conflict and goal-directed action. A conflict may exist between displaying good argument skills and participating in morally and socially responsible negotiations; it may be the case that good arguers have less knowledge about and poorer relationships with their opponents. The question then is how to teach skill in negotiation that leads to personal and interpersonal success rather than personal success at the expense of the other (Stein & Albro, 2001). This is of direct relevance to argumentation in learning contexts, because arguing contributes more effectively to learning when it is not competitive. If we want to use argumentation for learning, students need to balance an assertiveness in advancing their claims with a sensitivity to the social effects of their argument on their opponents.

Arguing to Learn Contributes to Reasoning Skills

During reasoning, individuals make inferences from given knowledge to reach a conclusion that was not given (Voss & Means, 1991). The inferences that support reasoning have a similar structure to an argument, and the same criteria are applied to evaluate the legitimacy of an inference as are applied to evaluate an informal argument. This is why Means and Voss (1996) concluded that informal reasoning skills develop through the learning of discourse structures like argumentation. Argumentation facilitates storage of and access to knowledge in memory, and the development of elaborate mental models, and both of these cognitive skills support inference generation, problem solving, and learning.

Kuhn (1991) studied argumentation and informal reasoning about issues of genuine importance: What causes prisoners to return to crime after they are released? What causes children to fail in school? Participants were 160 individuals in four age groups (teens, twenties, forties, and sixties) who were asked to prepare arguments and counterarguments. Kuhn interviewed the participants to determine their causal theories, the evidence they used to support their theories, their ability to generate an alternative theory on their own, and their ability to generate counterarguments to their theory and to rebut the counterarguments.

Most participants tended to provide ineffective arguments. Instead, they provided theories along with a list of unrelated causes. Only 16 percent of the participants could generate genuine evidence for their theories. Most evidence generated was of a type that Kuhn called *pseudoevidence*; there was a lack of separation between theory and evidence. Somewhat better scores were obtained for the ability to conceive of an alternative theory (33 percent). Equally crucial is the ability to produce counterarguments, and subjects showed similar scores: 34 percent were consistently able to generate a counterargument to either their own or an alternative theory that they had generated. Finally, the percentage of subjects that generated valid rebuttals to their own theories was between 21 percent and 32 percent across topics.

Kuhn related these findings about people's argumentative skills to their epistemological theories – that is, the view they held about the nature of knowledge and knowing. It appears there are two very different kinds of knowing. At one pole, knowing prevails in complete ignorance of alternative possibilities (the absolutist epistemology). At the other pole, knowing is an ongoing, effortful process of evaluating possibilities, one that is never completed (the evaluative epistemology). Only a minority of the subjects (between 9 percent and 22 percent of the subjects across topics) held to the evaluative epistemology. This means that most people do not hold to the appropriate epistemology to reason through argumentation. For such learners to progress to the more advanced understanding of argumentation, they have to be capable of reflection on their own thought.

Learning to Argue in Small Groups

The learning sciences have shown that collaborative classroom interaction can often contribute to individual learning (Greeno, this volume; Sawyer, this volume; Billig, 1987; Kuhn & Udell, 2003). This is particularly true of argumentative discourse. For example, Kuhn, Shaw, and Felton (1997) asked participants (students and adults) to write an essay about capital punishment, and then engaged these students in argumentation over this topic for a period of several weeks, following which an essay justifying their positions was elicited again. The argumentation was in pairs with multiple partners, with each argument lasting ten to fifteen minutes. The results showed that sustained engagement involving multiple dialogues with different partners over a period of weeks significantly enhanced the number of two-sided (as opposed to one-sided) and functional (as opposed to nonfunctional) arguments in the subjects' reasoning.

The approach of Reznitskaya et al. (2001) was based on a method called *collaborative reasoning*, an approach to discussion that aims to provide elementary school children with the opportunity to become skilled in argumentation. Collaborative reasoning helps students develop *argument schema*, abstract knowledge structures that represent extended stretches of argumentative discourse. Such schema enable the organization and retrieval of argument-relevant information, facilitate argument construction and repair, and provide the basis for anticipating objections and for finding flaws in one's arguments and the arguments of others (Anderson & Pearson, 1984; Reznitskaya et al., 2001).

Fifth graders in the experimental group participated twice a week during a period of five weeks, in discussions about controversial issues in small groups. Students were asked to take positions on an issue (on the basis of story information) and provide supporting reasons and evidence for their opinions. With coaching from their teacher, students challenged each other's viewpoints, offered counterarguments and rebuttals, and asked for clarifications. In addition, these students were exposed to the formal argument devices in teacher-led activities. Also, twice per week, students engaged in fifteen-minute discussions with other participating classrooms via the Internet.

Learning was assessed by analyzing an argumentative essay that was based on a realistic story dilemma. The essay was scored on relevant arguments, counterarguments, and rebuttals. Students who participated in the collaborative reasoning discussions wrote essays that contained a significantly greater number of arguments, counterarguments, rebuttals, and references to text information than the essays of students who did not experience collaborative reasoning (Reznitskaya et al., 2001).

Learning Through Collaborative Argumentation

Argumentation is one of the features of collaborative learning that make student groups so effective at promoting individual learning. Keefer, Zeitz, and Resnick (2000) studied argumentation during oral classroom peer discourse. Their point of departure was the idea that statements, assertions, and arguments can be understood as (tacitly agreed on) *commitments* that a participant in the dialogue is obliged to defend if challenged (Grice, 1975; Walton & Krabbe, 1995). An important contribution of this study is that it empirically attempts to identify different types of discussion (Walton & Krabbe, 1995). Each dialogue has an initial starting point, an assigned goal, the participants' goals, and the characteristic means of reaching the goal. Participants' goals may shift during discussion, possibly changing the dialogue type.

The most suitable type of dialogue for a peer-led discussion focusing on understanding literary content was called a *critical discussion*. The characteristics of critical discussion are (1) starting with a difference of opinion; (2) having a goal of accommodation and understanding of different viewpoints; (3) using a balance-of-considerations style, in which the most persuasive arguments prevail; (4) persuading others and sharing understanding are the participants' goals. A second type of dialogue was called *explanatory inquiry*, characterized by (1) a lack of knowledge as a starting point; (2) correct knowledge as the goal; (3) cumulative steps as the means by which knowledge is achieved; (4) a participants' goal of convergence to a solution or conclusion.

The assessment involved four minutes of conversational reasoning in twelve peer discussions (six groups at the beginning and at the end of the year) by fourth grade students. The researchers identified a number of features of argumentation that resulted in the most learning. The biggest influence was holding a sustained commitment to the pursuit of an issue. For issue-driven critical dialogues to be sustained, concessions in the course of argumentation (that is: one agrees to being convinced) were necessary to accommodate the differences in opinion that existed at the start of the dialogue. Sometimes this involved altering some commitment, either by attacking arguments that supported conclusions previously presented, or by building on arguments that attacked those previously presented conclusions. Dialogues with too many challenges (critical questions or attacks) were not necessarily productive, because the challenges were not always followed by serious consideration of their impact on some viewpoint. Dialogues where participants conceded their positions too easily were also unproductive; they built on the first claim presented, without seriously considering alternatives.

Summary: Argumentation and Learning

Many people have trouble arguing productively. They are not good at distinguishing evidence from theory, and do not tend to consider alternative positions. And because the social cost of threatening a good relationship is rather high, people are not inclined to argue in situations in which they do not feel at ease. There may be important cultural differences here; but in the western European context, students must be explicitly socialized into productive argumentation in school contexts.

Individual reasoning can benefit from arguing to learn, but argumentation must be scaffolded by the environment to support a gradual appropriation of collaborative argumentation. In collaborative learning, argumentative activities are grounded in other (shared) activities; they are not goals in themselves (or perhaps they are goals only during brief moments of reflection). Arguing to learn needs to be embedded in collaborative activity, and driven by a desire for understanding and sharing that understanding with others.

Collaborative Argumentation in Electronic Environments

The learning sciences are discovering that much knowledge is learned more effectively in collaboration. But in the above section, I reviewed research showing that most people have difficulty arguing collaboratively. Technology – especially computer-supported collaborative learning (CSCL) – has the potential to support productive argumentation, with the potential to lead to deeper understanding (see Stahl et al., this volume). In this section, I describe several software systems in which students type their arguments on the computer. These systems aim to *scaffold* student argumentation in some way – by providing structure to the roles of each student and the relationships between them in a dialogue, and by offering new and multiple ways of *representing* and manipulating the structure and content of argumentation. These systems aim to somehow guide and structure the way students argue, in order to raise awareness of argumentation, and ultimately, of argumentative learning. Because we are dealing with new forms of mediation of argumentative knowledge, learners may require considerable experience to appropriate these tools to their advantage.

The topics that I address in this section are (1) scaffolding argumentation with dialogue games; (2) scaffolding argumentation by assigning roles; (3) scaffolding negotiation in computer supported collaborative writing; (4) scaffolding arguments with argument maps; and (5) scaffolding scientific argumentation.

Scaffolding Argumentation as a Dialogue Game

Inspired by dialogue theory (Walton, 2000, see earlier), dialogue game theory attempts to structure participants' behavior in terms of roles and constraints made explicit by a list of ordered moves and parameters for the types of behavior the participants are supposed to be engaged in at each point in the argument (Levin & Moore, 1980). For example, Mackenzie (1979) developed an argumentation computer game called DC that allowed the user to select a move and type in its content. The moves that were provided included Question, Statement, Challenge, Resolution, and Withdraw. The system then evaluates the contribution according to a

preset list of rules. There are rules defining what happens as a result of a move, and there are rules defining when a move may be made. The rules prevent each player from evading a question, arguing in a circle, or failing to support a claim.

Also based on dialogue game theory, McAlister, Ravenscroft, and Scanlon (2004) developed a tool called AcademicTalk that supports synchronous debate between peers. The system requires a learner to choose a sentence opener for each new message (see Table 26.2), and then to complete the message (note similarities with the scaffolds in Knowledge Forum; Scardamalia & Bereiter, this volume). The openers were designed to support argumentation, and at each point in the argument certain openers are highlighted as suggestions to be considered. Students prepare for a debate by reading source materials, then they engage in the debate. Finally, there is a consolidation phase and a summary of key arguments is posted to the group.

The tool was compared with a tool which allowed online discussion but with no scaffolding. Preliminary results from a group of twenty-two students indicated that students using AcademicTalk engaged more directly with each other's positions and ideas (claims, challenges, and rebuttals), and produced more extended argumentation. In contrast, students in normal chat did not engage in as much argumentation and instead simply exchanged information.

Scaffolding Argumentation Through Role Play

In a postgraduate university course on computer-mediated communication, Pilkington and Walker (2003) asked their students to adopt one of three *argumentation roles*, based on research showing that when students are forced to adopt these roles, it leads to improved argumentative reasoning (Mercer, Wegerif, & Dawes, 1999). Role 1 students challenge others to provide evidence and point out alternatives or contradictions (e.g. "No, because...", or "Yes, but..."); Role 2 students ask for explanations and clarifications; and Role 3 students

Table 26.2. Sentence Openers in AcademicTalk (Adapted from McAlister et al., 2004)

Inform	Question	Challenge
I think...	Why do you think that...?	I disagree because...
Let me explain...	Why is it...?	I'm not so sure...
Let me elaborate...	Can you elaborate...?	How is that relevant...?
Because...	Can you give an example...?	A counter-argument is...
An example...	Is it the case that...?	An alternative view is...
My evidence...	Don't we need more evidence...?	Is there evidence...?
		How reliable is that evidence...?

Reason	Support	Maintain
Therefore...	I agree because...	Yes
What I think you are saying...	I see your point of view...	No
That is valid if...	Also...	OK
Is your assumption that...?	That's right	Thank you
Both are right in that...	Good point	Sorry...
To summarize...		Is this OK...?
Let's consult...		Would you please...
		OK. Let's move on.
		Can we...?
		Goodbye

provide information, either spontaneously or in answer to an inquiry. Students had regular electronic discussions throughout the course. At the beginning of the course, a teacher was heavily involved in the discussions; the teacher was responsible for a substantial number of argumentative contributions (between 27 percent and 42 percent of the challenges). Partway through the semester, the students participated in a role-playing exercise in which they were asked to assume one of the three roles; after this one role-playing session, there was no mention of roles anymore. Even so, after the role-playing session, the tutor's responsibility for scaffolding the students' argumentation declined to between 21 percent and 25 percent; students increasingly took over the responsibility for sustaining the debate. The level of content building (Role 3) decreased as the adoption of other roles increased. No one was explicitly assigned the content building role, and the authors took its drop as a positive sign because it led to fewer but deeper parallel discussion threads. The exercise showed that there is gain to be obtained by making students aware of roles in discussions and by providing them with role-play experiences in CMC.

Scaffolding Argumentation in Collaborative Writing

Andriessen et al. (2003) studied the role of argumentation in collaborative writing by university students. Students worked in pairs to write a letter to the local government about employment contracts – arguing for either steady contracts with infinite duration, or for flexible temporary job contracts – both from the point of view of the workers and that of the employers. They used both electronic communication and a shared text editor. Before the discussion, each participant received a (different) list of three arguments – called *given arguments* – as an incentive for a debate. The researchers examined in detail the relationship between the specific concepts that were discussed in the online dialogues and the concepts included in the collaborative text. For each concept, researchers examined when it was discussed (the protocol was divided into three phases), to what extent it was discussed, and if and when it was included in the text. This conceptual analysis revealed that the three phases of collaborative text production could be characterized as (1) content generation (many new

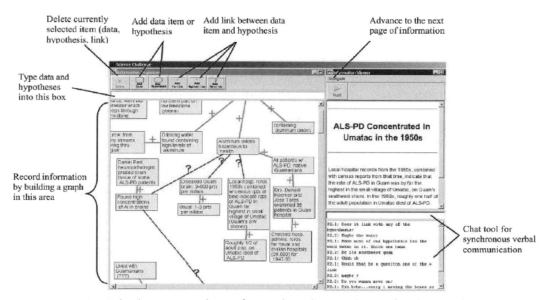

Figure 26.1. Belvedere 3.0. graph interface in the online condition of Suthers et al. (2003).

concepts proposed in the chat), (2) text generation (many concepts from earlier chat put in the text), and (3) text completion (less discussion, more text).

Negotiations were distinguished by their function (informative or argumentative) and their degree of elaboration (minimal, moderate, and elaborate). *Minimal negotiation* merely involved the proposition of one argument to include in the text; *moderate negotiation* implied that there was some elaboration, such as a short explanation or additional support by one of the participants. Only in *elaborate negotiation* was there two-sided argumentation, by each participant proposing and/or elaborating an argument.

Most negotiation (77.3 percent) did not involve explicit agreement. Given arguments were only part of minimal negotiation, even though each participant received different concepts. Most negotiation of any type involved defending the preferred position. Only 10.2 percent of the dialogue patterns were classified as elaborate negotiation, but when the arguments that were given beforehand are not included in the count, proportions of elaborated negotiation in the dialogue were between 37 percent and 52 percent, depending on the argumentative orientation (in favor of or against the main claim) of the dialogue pattern. Finally, nego-

tiations were different in each of the three phases, indicating that argumentation during complex learning tasks serves different functions, and may require different scaffolds.

Scaffolding Argumentation with Argument Maps

Many systems use the graphical power of today's personal computers to graphically display the relations between moves in an argument. Systems that use visual argument maps to scaffold argumentation include CHENE (Chaines ENErgetiques; Tiberghien & De Vries, 1997), which was designed to be used by two students who were collaborating to build an electronic circuit; C-CHENE (Baker & Lund, 1997), which provided dialogue buttons for each of about ten different dialogue moves, as well as dialogue buttons for agreeing, disagreeing, and managing the ongoing argument; and CONNECT (Baker, 2004), which displayed every statement made by each of the two students, and provided buttons for each student to agree or disagree with each statement.

Figure 26.1 shows a screen display of the argument map system Belvedere 3.0. Belvedere is intended to support secondary school children's learning of critical inquiry skills in the context of science (Suthers, 2003). The diagrams were designed to engage students in complex scientific argumentation. The boxes represent hypotheses and data, and the lines show relations of support and disagreement. An earlier version allowed propositions to be categorized as *Principal, Theory, Hypothesis, Claim,* or *Report*. Research with this early version showed that most interesting argumentation was not within the diagrams, but was the oral discussion between students who were working together at a single computer (Suthers, 2003). As a result, the diagrams were later simplified to focus on evidential relations between data and hypotheses, and this is the version in Figure 26.1.

In a study of their VCRI tool (Virtual Collaborative Research Institute; Jaspers & Erkens, 2002), Munneke, van Amelsvoort and Andriessen (2003) analyzed argumentative interactions and the possible roles of argumentative diagrams in supporting them. The variables of interest were *broadening* and *deepening* the space of debate. Broadening referred to students using different epistemological and societal views with the associated arguments, and deepening referred to students using many related concepts and modes of reasoning while exploring. Graphical representations support these activities in many ways: by forcing students to make their ideas explicit and complete (van Bruggen, Boshuizen, & Kirschner, 2003; Suthers & Hundhausen, 2003), by helping students to share focus (Veerman, 2000, 2003), by providing aids for organizing and maintaining coherence during problem solving (Suthers, 2001), and by serving as resources for conversation and reasoning (Baker, 2003; Suthers, 2003).

In their study, Munneke et al. (2003) compared the effect of constructing diagrams (individually) *before* or (together) *during* an electronic discussion, on argumentative interactions in the dialogues. The assignment was the construction of a collaborative text on genetically modified organisms, using the VCRI tool (see Figure 26.2). In the first condition, diagrams were individually constructed as a preparation for debate.

Subjects were instructed to represent their own opinion, supported by arguments and by refutation of counterarguments, in a diagram. After that, subjects were paired, and individual diagrams were available to be consulted during the collaboration phase, where participants discussed and produced a collaborative text on the topic. In the collaborative diagram condition, students discussed the topic, also after a reading phase, while collaboratively constructing a diagram which had to reflect their discussion.

All content-related episodes were scored using an ordinal score system of increasing depth: (1) stating an argument; (2) giving an example or explanation; (4) presenting support or rebuttal; (8) explaining a relation between several arguments. A total score of depth could be calculated for every pair and for every individual, as well as for every subtask. In addition, individual utterances were coded for dialogue function: social relation, interaction management, task management, or content elaboration. Some findings were:

1. Most chat activities were task management, especially in the collaborative diagram condition (67.5 percent vs. 76.9 percent).

2. Conversely, in the individual diagram condition there was somewhat more argumentation (8.6 percent vs. 13.8 percent).

3. The diagrams constructed individually differed widely in the number of boxes, and, as always, there were more arguments in favor of than against the claim (56 vs. 137).

4. It seemed that the individually prepared diagrams were used as information sources during the debate most of the time, to find (and copy) arguments for the discussion or to find the text to write.

5. In the collaborative diagram condition there were instances of diagrams being used to summarize the discussion.

6. Discussions in the individual condition were somewhat broader (more different topics).

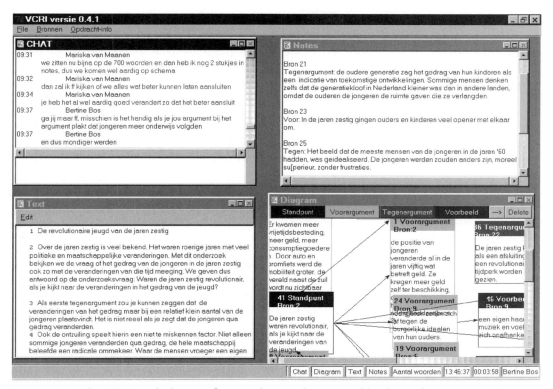

Figure 26.2. The VCRI-tool, showing four windows, to be arranged by the students, serving (1) synchronous chat; (2) individual notes (not used in the experiment described here); (3) a collaborative text editor; and (4) a collaborative diagram.

7. Diagrams and discussions were similar in depth in both conditions.
8. The texts produced were deeper than the diagrams in both experiments, showing more rebuttals, supports, and relations between arguments.

Overall, students did not really discuss each other's arguments; they simply took proposed arguments for granted. Short fragments of argumentation were followed by rapid reconciliation. Hence, it seems that the role of diagrams in directly forcing students to make their ideas explicit was very limited. The second role of the diagram, maintaining focus, was confirmed by the task and content focus of most of the utterances, but it seemed that the goal of writing a collaborative text (simultaneously) distracted the students from discussing the content in depth.

Scaffolding Argumentation in Scientific Inquiry

In everyday issues we are often skillful in challenging, counterchallenging, justifying, or agreeing during conversation, but the arguments we hold are generally mediocre according to analytical criteria (Pontecorvo, 1993). In contrast, in scientific domains we simply accept expert arguments, but we generally do not use them in further activities to convince, challenge, or justify our viewpoints (Schwarz & Glassner, 2003).

Good argumentation depends on knowing the facts of a field, but knowing the facts does not predict good argumentation (Goldman et al., 2003). Goldman et al.'s intervention program, using Knowledge Forum (see Scardamalia & Bereiter, this volume), takes the private knowledge claims of individual students and small groups of students and makes them public. This form of argument is then taken as a starting point to develop more complex argumentation skills. Students are provided with tools that address the construction, coordination, and evaluation of scientific knowledge claims, which include claims about theory (what knowledge is important), method (strategies for obtaining and analyzing data), and goals (outcomes and how they are attained). The role of the teacher in whole-class and small-group discussions is to actively process the reasoning of the students, and to intervene with questions, comments, and prompts for additional student input, always oriented toward evidence-based consensus building. This is no easy task, and it is still uncertain how and if this kind of teacher role gives the desired results.

Argumentation and debate are the motors of progress in the natural sciences (Bell, 2002). Argumentation serves the exploration of theoretical controversy, involving the explicit coordination of evidence with theoretical ideas. Linn and her team designed the Web-based Integrated Science Environment (WISE; formerly known as the Knowledge Integration Environment or KIE; see Linn, this volume) to scaffold students in these activities. Knowledge integration is a dynamic process through which students connect their conceptual ideas, link ideas to explain phenomena, add more experiences from the world to their mix of ideas, and restructure ideas with a more coherent view (Linn, this volume; Bell & Linn, 2000).

Some research on WISE has focused on how argument construction and collaborative debate could be promoted in the science classroom for the dual purpose of having students learn science content while also learning about scientific practice. In these studies, middle school students engage in forms of scientific inquiry as they simultaneously develop scientific knowledge that is grounded in and relevant to scientific and personal life situations (Linn, Bell & Hsi, 1998; Bell & Linn, 2000). For example, after a five-week curriculum sequence, a debate was started on the topic "How far does light go?," during which students

explored multimedia evidence items, constructed explanations and arguments about how the evidence relates to the debate topic, and then engaged in a whole-class debate about the issues, claims, and evidence. This was a design-based research project, during which the research design was adapted as a function of the observed learning activities (Barab, this volume). The cycle involved iterative refinement of the collaborative activity, spanning several years of teaching. I describe a total of five iterative phases of this research project.

For the first phase the teacher selected two competing theories to frame the debate: students indicated their initial positions and then explored twelve multimedia evidence items. Analysis of the second phase revealed that students were overly focused on particular evidence items, instead of considering the entire corpus of evidence. Perhaps unsurprisingly, they focused on one or two pieces of evidence they believed would strongly support their perspective, and ignored counterevidence. In addition, the arguments they produced were not very elaborated. This led Linn's colleague Philip Bell to develop a tool called SenseMaker (Bell, 1997), which supported the coordination of claims (the boxes in Figure 26.3) and evidence (the lists in each box) to create argument maps. SenseMaker is an argument editor; it supports development of an argument that makes sense of the collected evidence (Bell, 1997).

In the third phase, students were told to organize evidence with claims after having explored all of the evidence. There was evidence showing that in this phase, students did consider the entire corpus of evidence. However, they needed still more experience with the use of argument maps, because students did not categorize the claims in the manner originally intended by the researchers.

The fourth phase started with a two-day curriculum project to better introduce the concept of argumentative map representations and to more systematically support students in using the argumentation tool. The students created more elaborated arguments within an activity structure

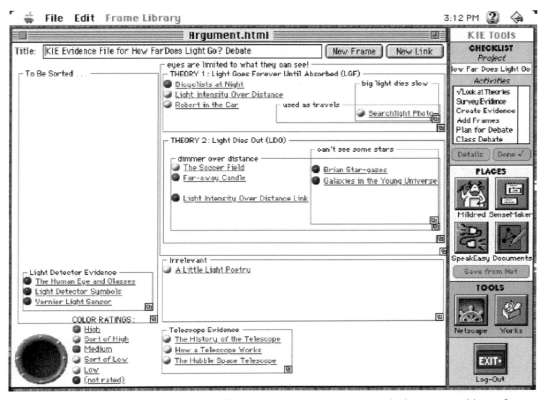

Figure 26.3. SenseMaker, with a display of two claim boxes (Theory 1 and Theory 2) and lists of supporting evidence in each. From Bell (1997).

where the knowledge representation tool was integrated into their interpretation and theorizing about evidence. Evidence and claims were central and visible features of the user interface, so as to scaffold students' inquiry processes. But students were still generally confused about the argument map representation and the manner of working with it to produce a synthesis rather than an ongoing product.

In the fifth phase, a historical debate between actual scientists was represented in an argument map prepared in advance by the researchers. This allowed students to understand aspects of scientific argumentation and the creativity involved in theorizing and coordinating with evidence, as well as how individual ideas can shape one's interpretation of evidence and constructed arguments.

When students debated in class without the argument maps, they presented their strongest pieces of evidence to make their points. When the argument maps were incorporated into the debates, the discourse patterns shifted. Students still highlighted the strongest forms of evidence, but now questions from students in the audience focused on evidence not presented. The argument maps became collectively shared scaffolds that allowed students to compare interpretations of evidence. Audience members used the maps to hold presenters more accountable to the total corpus of evidence involved with the project. The maps provided a social mechanism for articulating and externalizing student thinking.

Final evaluations showed that students developed greater understanding of the evidentiary basis of scientific argumentation, the general connection between argumentation and learning, and the social refinement of their own integrated understanding during the debate activity (Bell & Linn, 2000).

Conclusion

Some researchers believe that all teaching is in some sense an argumentative activity, because the task facing the teacher is to persuade learners to assume a novel point of view (Laurillard, 1993). Petraglia (1998) proposed the rhetorical tradition as a framework for education, emphasizing the essentially dialogic nature of learning. When learning is conceived of as a process of active construction, of collaborative knowledge building, then it can be thought of as an outcome of argumentative processes.

Based on the research summarized in this chapter, I draw six conclusions.

1. Students cannot simply be told to learn by arguing; arguing to learn requires significant scaffolding. In order to show why and how argumentation is good for learning we first have to create appropriate learning contexts (Andriessen, 2005) in a kind of design experiment (Confrey, this volume). I suggest constructing complex task sequences, incorporating many argumentative activities over an extended period.

2. Students should be scaffolded in supporting each other's argumentation. This approach is at odds with the traditional view of argumentation as oppositional, and of knowledge and expertise as absolute. Arguing to learn is a collaborative process of collective knowledge building.

3. The type of medium has a major impact on arguing to learn. We have seen some examples of tool use which, on the one hand, lead to results similar to argumentation in oral communication contexts, but, on the other hand, we find possibilities for scaffolding that result in more advanced argumentation than simple oral communication. Researchers are working to find the appropriate conditions of instructions and tool design for adequate support.

4. Students are more efficient at managing their ongoing collaboration through face-to-face conversation than when mediated by the computer. The educational quality of argumentation decreases if students have to spend a lot of time working with the software tool. The challenge for developers is to make the user interface as learner-centered as possible (Quintana et al., this volume).

5. How a tool is used depends in part on what other tools and activities are in focus at the same time. The role and nature of argumentation differs between phases of a complex task sequence such as collaborative writing or a project-based science class. However, sometimes it seems that transfer between such phases is very limited; students tend to approach each phase as a separate activity. When a complex task sequence is designed, we need to know more about what transfers from one phase of the sequence to the next and what conditions facilitate the most transfer.

6. Most studies report great individual differences in using tools. Understanding why participants use these tools differently may allow us to discover how tool appropriation may develop; I think we must be careful not to fall into the trap of deciding too early which use is correct and which one is not. An argumentation tool is not like a hammer; rather, it is like a toolkit with many possible solutions and uses, including new ones.

Currently, many learners feel argumentation is a waste of time; they simply want their teachers to give them the answers. Piaget argued that learners should be allowed to discover as much as possible on their own, and that each decision that the teacher makes for them deprives them of a potentially more powerful learning experience. The question seems to be who should bridge that gap: the teacher or the learner. If argumentation in learning situations can be detached in some way from competition, losing face, and hollow rhetoric, and adequate support for argumentation can be designed – so that focusing on understanding, explanation and reasoning, and interpersonal success, is the rule rather than the exception – the promises of arguing to learn and of computer support for learning may become reality. In that case, students will not want to be provided with answers any more; they will want to argue for them, because then they will experience autonomy, and powerful learning.

References

Anderson, R. C., & Pearson, P. D. (1984). A schema-theoretic view of basic processes in reading comprehension. In P. D. Pearson, R. Barr, M. L. Kamil, & P. Mosenthal (Eds.), *Handbook of reading research* (pp. 255–291). New York: Longman.

Andriessen, J. (2005). Collaboration in computer conferencing. In A. O'Donnell, C. Hmelo, & G. Erkens (Eds.), *Collaboration, reasoning, and technology* (pp. 277–321). Mahwah, NJ: Lawrence Erlbaum Associates.

Andriessen, J., Erkens, G., van de Laak, C. M., Peters, N., & Coirier, P. (2003). Argumentation as negotiation in electronic collaborative writing. In J. Andriessen, M. Baker, & D. Suthers (Eds.), *Arguing to learn: Confronting cognitions in computer-supported collaborative learning environments* (pp. 79–116). Dordrecht: Kluwer.

Baker, M. J. (2003). Computer-mediated argumentative interactions for the co-elaboration of scientific notions. In J. Andriessen, M. Baker, & D. Suthers (Eds.), *Arguing to learn: Confronting cognitions in computer-supported collaborative learning environments* (pp. 47–78). Dordrecht: Kluwer.

Baker, M. J. (2004). Recherches sur l'élaboration de connaissances dans le dialogue [Research on knowledge elaboration in dialogues]. Synthèse pour l'habilitation à diriger les recherches. Université Nancy 2.

Baker, M., & Lund, K. (1997). Promoting reflective interactions in a computer-supported collaborative learning environment. *Journal of Computer Assisted Learning, 13*, 175–193.

Barth, E. M., & Krabbe, E. C. W. (1982). *From axiom to dialogue: A philosophical study of logics and argumentation*. Berlin: Walter de Gruyter.

Bell, P. (1997). Using argument representations to make thinking visible for individuals and groups. In R. Hall, N. Miyake, & N. Enyedy (Eds.), *Proceedings of CSCL '97* (pp. 10–19). Mahwah, NJ: Lawrence Erlbaum Associates.

Bell, P. (2002). Science *is* argument: Developing sociocognitive supports for disciplinary argumentation. In T. Koschmann, R. Hall, & N. Miyake (Eds.), *CSCL 2: Carrying forward the conversation* (pp. 449–455). Mahwah, NJ: Lawrence Erlbaum Associates.

Bell, P. (2004). Promoting students' argument construction and collaborative debate in the science classroom. In M. C. Linn, E. A. Davis, & P. Bell (Eds.), *Internet environments for science education* (pp. 115–143). Mahwah, NJ: Lawrence Erlbaum Associates.

Bell, P., & Linn, M. C. (2000). Scientific arguments as learning artifacts: Designing for learning from the web with KIE. *International Journal of Science Education, 22*(8), 797–817.

Billig, M. (1987). *Arguing and thinking: A rhetorical approach to social psychology*. Cambridge: Cambridge University Press.

Bransford, J. D., Brown, A. L., & Cocking, R., (1999). *How people learn: Brain, mind, experience and school*. Washington, DC: National Academy Press.

Chi, M. T. H., & Van Lehn, K. A. (1991). The content of physics self-explanations. *Journal of the Learning Sciences, 1*(1), 69–105.

Goldman, S. R., Duschl, R. A., Ellenbogen, K., Williams, S., & Tzou, C. T. (2003). Science inquiry in a digital age: Possibilities for making thinking visible. In H. van Oostendorp (Ed.), *Cognition in a digital world* (pp. 253–283). Mahwah, NJ: Lawrence Erlbaum Associates.

Grice, H. P. (1975). Logic and conversation. In P. Cole & J. L. Morgan (Eds.), *Syntax & semantics 3: Speech acts* (pp. 41–58). London: Academic Press.

Jaspers, J., & Erkens, G. (2002, September). *VCRI. Virtual Collaborative Research Institute* (Version 1.0) [Computer software]. Utrecht, The Netherlands: Utrecht University.

Keefer, M. W., Zeitz, C. L., & Resnick, L. B. (2000). Judging the quality of peer-led student dialogues. *Cognition and Instruction, 18*(1), 53–81.

Koschmann, T. (2003). CSCL, argumentation, and Deweyan inquiry: argumentation *is* learning, In J. Andriessen, M. Baker & D. Suthers (Eds.), *Arguing to learn: Confronting cognitions in computer-supported collaborative learning environments* (pp. 259–265). Dordrecht: Kluwer.

Kuhn, D. (1991). *The skills of argument*. Cambridge, MA: Cambridge University Press.

Kuhn, D. (2001). How do people know? *Psychological Science, 12*(1), 1–8.

Kuhn, D., Shaw, V., & Felton, M. (1997). Effects of dyadic interaction on argumentative reasoning. *Cognition and Instruction, 15*(3), 287–315.

Kuhn, D., & Udell, W. (2003). The development of argument skills. *Child Development 74*(5), 1245–1260.

Kuhn, T. (1962, 1970). *The structure of scientific revolutions.* Chicago: University of Chicago Press.

Laurillard, D. (1993). *Rethinking university teaching: A framework for the effective use of educational technology.* London: Routledge.

Leitão, S. (2001). Analyzing changes in view during argumentation: A quest for method. *Forum Qualitative Social Research, 2*, 2.

Levin & Moore (1980). Dialogue-games: Meta-communication structure for natural language interaction. *Cognitive Science, 1*(4), 395–420.

Linn, M. C., Bell, P., & Hsi, S. (1998). Using the internet to enhance student understanding of science: The knowledge integration environment. *Interactive Learning Environments, 6*(1–2), 4–38.

Mackenzie, J. D. (1979). Question-begging in noncumulative systems. *Journal of Philosophical Logic, 8*, 117–133.

McAlister, S., Ravenscroft, A., & Scanlon, E. (2004). Combining interaction and context design to support collaborative argumentation using a tool for synchronous CMC. *Journal of Computer Assisted Learning, 20*(3), 194–204.

Means, M. L., & Voss, J. F. (1996). Who reasons well? Two studies of informal reasoning among children of different grade, ability, and knowledge levels. *Cognition and Instruction, 14*(2), 139–178.

Mercer, N., Wegerif, R., & Dawes, L. (1999). Children's talk and the development of reasoning in the classroom. *British Educational Research Journal, 25*(1), 95–111.

Munneke, L. van Amelsvoort, M., & Andriessen, J.,(2003). The role of diagrams in collaborative argumentation-based learning. *International Journal of Educational Research, 39*, 113–131.

Nonnon, E. (1996). Activités argumentatives et élaboration de connaissances nouvelles: Le dialogue comme espace d'exploration. *Langue Francaise, 112*, 67–87.

Petraglia, J. (1998). *The rhetoric and technology of authenticity in education.* Mahwah, NJ: Lawrence Erlbaum Associates.

Pilkington, R., & Walker, A., (2003). Facilitating debate in networked learning: Reflecting on online synchronous discussion in higher education. *Instructional Science, 31*, 41–63.

Pontecorvo, C. (ed.) (1993). *Cognition and Instruction, 11*(3 & 4). Special issue: Discourse and Shared Reasoning.

Reznitskaya, A., Anderson, R. C., McNurlen, B., Nguyen-Jahiel, K., Archodidou, A., & Kim, S. (2001). Influence of oral discussion on written argument. *Discourse Processes, 32*(2–3), 155–175.

Schwarz, B., & Glassner, A. (2003). The blind and the paralytic: Supporting argumentation in everyday and scientific issues. In J. Andriessen, M. Baker, & D. Suthers (Eds.). *Arguing to learn: Confronting cognitions in computer-supported collaborative learning environments* (pp. 227–260). Dordrecht: Kluwer.

Stein, N. L., & Albro, E. R. (2001). The origins and nature of arguments: Studies in conflict understanding, emotion, and negotiation. *Discourse Processes, 32*(2–3), 113–133.

Stein, N. L., & Bernas, R. (1999). The early emergence of argumentative knowledge and skill. In J. Andriessen & P. Coirier (Eds.). *Foundations of argumentative text processing* (pp. 97–116). Amsterdam: Amsterdam University Press.

Stein, N. L., & Miller, C. A. (1993). The development of memory and reasoning skill in argumentative contexts: evaluating, explaining, and generating evidence. In R. Glaser (Ed.), *Advances in instructional psychology* (pp. 285–335). Hillsdale, NJ: Lawrence Erlbaum Associates.

Suthers, D. D. (2001). Towards a systematic study of representational guidance for collaborative learning discourse. *Journal of Universal Computer Science, 7*(3), 254–277.

Suthers, D. D. (2003). Representational guidance for collaborative inquiry. In J. Andriessen, M. Baker & D. Suthers (Eds.), *Arguing to learn: Confronting cognitions in computer-supported collaborative learning environments* (pp. 27–46). Dordrecht: Kluwer.

Suthers, D. D., & Hundhausen, C. D. (2003). An experimental study of the effects of representational guidance on collaborative learning processes. *The Journal of the Learning Sciences,* 12(2), 183–218.

Suthers, D. D., Hundhausen, C. D., & Girardeau, L. E. (2003). Comparing the roles of representations in face-to-face and online computer supported collaborative learning. *Computers & Education, 41,* 335–351.

Tannen, D. (1998). *The argument culture: Moving from debate to dialogue.* New York: Random House Trade.

Tiberghien, A., & De Vries, E. (1997). Relating characteristics of learning situations to learner activities. *Journal of Computer Assisted Learning, 13,* 163–174.

Toulmin, S. E. (1958). *The uses of argument.* Cambridge: Cambridge University Press.

Van Bruggen, J. M., Boshuizen, H. P. A., & Kirschner, P. A. (2003). A cognitive framework for cooperative problem solving with argument visualization. In P. A. Kirschner, S. J. Buckingham Shum, & C. S. Carr (Eds.), *Visualizing argumentation: Software tools for collaborative and educational sense-making* (pp. 25–47). London: Springer.

Van Eemeren, F., & Grootendorst, R., (1992). *Argumentation, communication, and fallacies: a pragma-dialectical perspective.* Hillsdale, NJ: Lawrence Erlbaum Associates.

Van Eemeren, F., & Grootendorst, R. (1999). Developments in argumentation theory. In J. Andriessen & P. Coirier (Eds.). *Foundations of argumentative text processing* (pp. 43–57). Amsterdam: Amsterdam University Press.

Van Eemeren, F., Grootendorst, R., & Snoeck Henkemans, F. (2002). *Argumentation: Analysis, Evaluation, Presentation.* Mahwah, NJ: Lawrence Erlbaum Associates.

Veerman, A. L. (2000). Computer-supported collaborative learning through argumentation. [Doctoral dissertation]. Enschede: Print Partners Ipskamp.

Veerman, A. L. (2003). Constructive discussions through electronic dialogue. In J. Andriessen, M. Baker, & D. Suthers (Eds.) *Arguing to learn: Confronting cognitions in computer-supported collaborative learning environments* (pp. 117–143). Dordrecht: Kluwer.

Voss, J., & Means, M. (1991). Learning to reason via instruction in argumentation. *Learning & instruction, 1,* 337–350.

Voss, J. F., Tyler, S. W., & Yengo, L. A. (1983). Individual differences in the solving of social science problems. In R. F. Dillon & R. R. Schmeck (Eds.) *Individual differences in cognition* (pp. 204–232). New York, Academic Press.

Vygotsky, L. (1978). *Mind in society: The development of higher psychological processes.* (M. Cole, V. John-Steiner, S. Scribner, & E. Souberman, Eds.). Cambridge, MA: Harvard University Press.

Walton, D. (2000). The place of dialogue theory in logic, computer science and communication studies. *Synthese, 123,* 327–346.

Walton, D. N. (1989). *Question-reply argumentation.* New York: Greenwood Press.

Walton, D. N., & Krabbe, E. C. W. (1995). *Commitment in dialogue.* Albany, New York: Suny Press.

Wertsch, J. V. (1985). *Vygotsky and the social formation of mind.* Cambridge, MA: Harvard University Press.

CHAPTER 27

Learning in Online Communities

Amy Bruckman

John Dewey wrote that "Education is not preparation for life; education is life itself" (Dewey, 1938). Dewey argued that learning communities should not be a world apart, but instead integrated with the rest of society. Students should be encouraged to be a part of civil society, pursuing interests in collaboration with others. More than fifty years later, Scardamalia and Bereiter (1994) articulated a similar vision, and noted that computer-mediated communication (CMC) creates new possibilities for building learning communities that are deeply integrated with society. "Computer-mediated communication" refers to communication between people that occurs through the medium of the computer, and includes email, instant messages, chat rooms, newsgroups, and blogs. Learning sciences researchers have made great progress in understanding how CMC can be used to connect learners together, and to allow learners to connect with society at large.

Learning takes place especially felicitously as part of a knowledge-building community (Scardamalia & Bereiter, 1994) that brings together people of all ages and diverse social roles. Scardamalia and Bereiter comment,

> [I]t is fanciful (but nonetheless exciting) to contemplate advantages of having communal structures that span the whole of the school years and that also profitably engage those in research institutes and other knowledge-creation enterprises. The fancifulness is not with the technology – recent developments make that by far the easy part. The problems to be solved are educational. (Scardamalia & Bereiter, 1994, p. 276)

With the help of computer-mediated communication, students can learn while engaged in authentic activities with real consequences. The Internet connects groups of people, information, and institutions in new ways, creating new opportunities to realize this vision.

This is just one vision of how learning might be different on the Internet. Ann Renninger and Wesley Shumar comment that "the Internet has altered our sense of boundaries, participation, and identity. It allows for the recasting of both self and community, meaning that through the Internet a person or group can revise his or her sense of possibilities" (Shumar & Renninger, 2002, p. 14).

The Internet is particularly effective at supporting the kinds of learning that learning sciences research is discovering to be most effective: project-based learning (Barron et al., 1998), constructionist learning (Papert, 1991), and Learning by Design (Kolodner et al., 2003). In project-based learning, groups of students work collaboratively to solve the problem posed by a driving question (Krajcik & Blumenfeld, this volume). In constructionist learning, learners construct their own knowledge while working in communities of learners who share discoveries and build on each other's ideas (Kafai, this volume). In Learning by Design students share design ideas, ask for advice, constructively criticize other students' solution procedures, and build on other students' ideas in their own projects (Kolodner, this volume). Particularly successful examples of online learning communities based on learning sciences principles include The Math Forum (Renninger & Shumar, 2002), CoVis (Edelson & O'Neill, 1994), SCOPE/KIE/WISE (Linn, Davis, & Bell, 2004), CSILE/Knowledge Forum (Scardamalia & Bereiter, 1994), One Sky Many Voices (Songer, 1996), and Quest Atlantis (Barab, this volume; Barab et al., 2005).

All of these learning environments are based on discoveries from the learning sciences that reveal the important role of social context, situativity, collaboration, and argumentation in learning (Andriessen, this volume; Greeno, this volume; Sawyer, this volume). In this chapter, I focus on one key feature shared by all of these learning environments: they are designed to help students to create *learning communities*, collaborative communities of learners who work together to support everyone's learning.

This chapter is organized around four main points.

- First, I will define what I mean by a "community."

- Second, I will describe what is meant by the term "learning community," as a subcategory of community. Learning sciences researchers have identified several different kinds of effective learning communities. I will summarize three significant kinds: knowledge-building communities, communities of practice, and samba schools.

- Third, I will discuss two unique features of CMC that help to support effective learning communities: the types of social interaction and support they provide, and the ways that they support the creation of authentic learning tasks.

- Fourth, I give an example of the kind of learning community that becomes possible when CMC is used: the MOOSE crossing project (Bruckman, 1998).

When we select pedagogically sound models for "learning community" and combine these with appropriately chosen technologies, new kinds of learning become possible. The intriguing potential of the Internet is that the technology could be used to bring students together in new types of learning communities, communities that support all students in more effective learning and deeper understanding of material. Researchers are still at an early stage in exploring this potential. As researchers in the learning sciences come to better understand this medium, new forms of online learning communities will emerge.

A Prototype View of "Community"

For many people, the word "community" evokes images of an idyllic small-town, middle-class, 1950s world. "Learning community" evokes images of a small school within that town, with a young female teacher leading a lesson while writing on a blackboard. Or, learning community may evoke earlier images of the nineteenth-century little red school house. But today's classrooms are not much like those stereotypes. To better understand online learning communities, it's important to begin by examining three examples of existing learning communities: Lave and Wenger's (1991) tailor shops, groups of scientists debating new ideas, and Brazilian samba schools. These examples of learning communities help better focus our attention on some key features of learning communities and why they matter.

Much ink has been spilled on the topic of whether online communities are really communities. On one end of the spectrum, writers like Howard Rheingold chronicle the benefits that online communication can bring to participants, from daily camaraderie to emotional support and real aid in times of crisis (Rheingold, 1993). On the other side, some writers argue that although so-called Internet "communities" are of course "groups," the quality of the interaction is nowhere near that of a real community. For example, Rob Kling and Christina Courtwright argue that "the casual use of the term community to characterize groups that are engaged in learning, or groups that participate in e-forums, is seriously misguided" (Kling & Courtwright, 2004, p. 91). For Kling and Courtwright, creating a successful learning community is a rare and substantial accomplishment, and using the word "community" casually risks trivializing that accomplishment. They set a high standard for what counts as a community. Discussing whether groups on USENET are communities, Teresa Roberts argues that "the word 'community' has been used in a metaphorical sense for long enough that it doesn't have a precise meaning" (Roberts, 1998, p. 361).

It's not surprising that what constitutes an online community is contested, given that the underlying notion of community has always been hotly debated by sociologists (Hillery, 1955; Wellman & Leighton, 1979). The sociologists Barry Wellman and Milena Gulia caution us that our more idealistic notions of community may be overblown. They write that "pundits worry that virtual community may not truly be community. These worriers are confusing the pastoralist myth of community for reality. Community ties are already geographically dispersed, sparsely knit, connected heavily by telecommunications (phone and fax), and specialized in content" (Wellman & Gulia, 1999, p. 187).

I propose to explore the notion of community by using theories from cognitive science about how categories are defined. Eleanor Rosch (summarized in Lakoff, 1987) argued that each category has one or more exemplary members that she called the *prototypes* for the category. For example, a robin or sparrow is a better example of a bird than an emu or penguin, so robins and sparrows are better prototypes of the category *bird* than emus and penguins. If categories are defined by their prototype members, then they can have fuzzy boundaries; instead of a black-and-white decision about whether or not an object is a member of the category, each item in the category has a degree of membership, depending on its similarities and differences from the prototypes (Lakoff, 1987). Thus, when Wellman and Gulia argue that the worriers are confusing a pastoralist myth for the reality of community, they are saying in effect that our prototypes for the category *community* are not realistic, but are ahistorical and idealized.

In this light, asking whether a group is a community is a poorly formed question unlikely to yield deep insights, because the category *community* has fuzzy boundaries. Instead, the question becomes: how similar is a particular group to the prototype of community? This is a more productive line of inquiry, because it challenges us to reflect on the nature of our prototypical model of community, and explore in detail its specific features and why they might or might not matter.

Prototypes of Learning Communities

From this perspective, *learning community* is a subcategory of community, with its own prototypical members. What then are its focal members? The most common prototype, of course, is the classroom in a traditional school. However, this model is somewhat disputed – the enterprise of learning sciences research is largely about trying to improve that type of learning community, in either incremental or more radical ways.

If we are to rethink the nature of learning communities, there are alternate prototypical learning communities to draw from. Here I summarize three of these prototypes: Lave and Wenger's *communities of practice*, Scardamalia and Bereiter's *knowledge building*, and Papert's *samba schools*.

Lave and Wenger's work on *communities of practice* (CoPs) is the first alternate prototype. Lave and Wenger studied traditional craft work such as the Vai and Gola tailors of West Africa, and proposed a model of learning as *legitimate peripheral participation* (LPP) (Lave & Wenger, 1991). An apprentice tailor begins by doing an unskilled task like sweeping the floor. This first activity, although unskilled, is *legitimate* because the floor really needs to be swept. It is *peripheral*, because he/she begins with an easy task that is related to the core activity. In the process of sweeping, the apprentice is *participating* in the overall activity of the tailor's shop; she sees the activity going on around her, and learns through observation. When the time arrives for the apprentice to try cutting fabric for a pair of pants, she will have observed the activity many times. LPP involves participation as a way of learning – of both absorbing and being absorbed in the culture of practice. The community of tailors and apprentices forms what Lave and Wenger referred to as a "community of practice," and this concept is a useful alternate prototype of a learning community – very different from the stereotype of traditional classroom instruction.

Tailoring is a physical activity. What would it mean to translate this approach to learning to an intellectual domain, like learning to read and write? Collins (this volume) calls this approach *cognitive apprenticeship*. The transformation from traditional to cognitive apprenticeship presents educational challenges. Craft activities like tailoring are visible and easily observable by a novice. When we try to translate traditional apprenticeship into cognitive apprenticeship, the challenge arises of how we make thinking visible. Additionally, as we move from a community of practice where members have clear, shared goals (like creating garments and selling them) to a more artificial context like school, the question of legitimacy arises. The new apprentice tailor knows that the floor really needs to be swept, but it may be less clear to the elementary school student exactly why the word problem needs to be solved. Barbara Rogoff pointed out that "schooling is by nature a specialized setting devised by adults which focuses self-consciously on learning, and thus differs importantly from a community of learners in which children learn in an unselfconscious way by being involved in the mature activities of the group with the support of their elders" (Rogoff, 1994, p. 217). Collins (this volume) observes that the learning process is divided into phases of *modeling* (expert demonstrates behavior desired), *coaching* (expert assists learner, providing scaffolding in the learner's zone of proximal development), and *fading* (external support for learning is slowly removed as the learner grows in independence).

The second alternate prototype is a community of scientists working in a specialized discipline. Marlene Scardamalia and Carl Bereiter (this volume) suggest that schools should create groups of students that work like adult communities of scientists. They call this approach "knowledge-building communities." Drawing on research in sociology of science such as work by Bruno Latour (Latour, Woolgar, & Salk, 1986), Scardamalia and Bereiter highlight how groups of scientists critique one another's ideas and as a group come to a deeper understanding. Their Knowledge Forum software environment (formerly called CSILE) is based on this idea.

In a community of scientists, the processes of publication and peer review create a public discourse in which ideas are critiqued and only become generally accepted after close scrutiny by many individuals. For professionals, the goal of this process is to advance the state of accepted knowledge. When knowledge building is used as an approach to education, the goal is for students to learn through the process of engaging in this collaborative, critical dialog about ideas. The Knowledge Forum (KF) software is a good example of the knowledge-building approach to creating learning communities. KF creates this process in miniature, using a bulletin-board-type system. The software scaffolds this process in a variety of ways, such as asking students to label each online contribution with a tag describing what the contribution adds to the discourse. For example, students must decide whether their post is *theory building* or *opinion*. If it is *theory building*, they must select from these subcategories: *my theory, I need to understand, new information, this theory cannot explain, a better theory,* or *putting our knowledge together* (Learning-in-Motion, 2005). This added structure can help students engage in metacognition – helping them to think not just about the science content, but more importantly, about scientific method and the nature of critical inquiry. Ideally, in a Knowledge Forum classroom the object of classroom activity shifts from completing a teacher-assigned task to gaining deeper personal knowledge of the phenomenon under investigation through knowledge-building discourse (Hewitt, 2004).

The third new prototype of a learning community is the samba schools of Brazil. Samba schools are a kind of Brazilian social club, in which members work together to prepare a presentation for Carnival (also see Kafai, this volume). Seymour Papert (1980) wrote:

> During the year each samba school chooses its theme for the next carnival, the stars are selected, the lyrics are written and re-written, the dance is choreographed and practiced. Members of the school range in age from children to grandparents and in ability from novice to professional. But they dance together and as they dance everyone is learning and teaching as well as dancing. Even the stars are there to learn their difficult parts. (p. 178)

Papert was attracted to many features of samba schools as learning environments. Activity in samba schools is self-motivated,

richly connected to popular culture, creative, and intellectual, and it engages people across age and class boundaries. He suggested that perhaps we could try to create a kind of "technological samba school," a place where a community of people come together to engage in creative projects mediated by technology.

Expanding on Papert's suggestion that we use samba school as a prototype for a learning community, José Zagal and I analyzed the characteristics of real samba schools that support learning, and noted these features:

- *Flexibility to outsiders:* It is possible to participate in the core activity of the samba school by simply buying a costume and dancing with the group at Carnival. This provides an easy route for people to become involved, and possibly choose to become members later.

- *Existence of a public event:* All activity of the school is focused on an annual, high profile event. This helps create rhythms of life within the school, and motivates participation.

- *Pluralism of membership:* Members of samba schools are diverse in terms of age, race, and socioeconomic status. This stands in contrast to the extreme segregation of traditional Western schooling – mandated segregation by age, and often de facto by race and class as well. Richer kinds of collaboration can take place with a more diverse group of participants in a learning community (Zagal & Bruckman, 2005).

As we come to better understand the characteristics of alternative prototypes of learning communities like the three described here, we can better leverage what we have learned, in order to create new kinds of learning communities supported by computer-mediated communication.

Authenticity

Computer-mediated communication (CMC) has unique affordances that can help support the formation of learning communities.

At first pass, we might simply divide these affordances into the ability to transmit information and the ability to connect people. Computer networks have the unique ability to move information rapidly from many people to many others. However, sociologists of science like Bruno Latour have argued that facts are socially constructed (Latour et al., 1986). In their model, something becomes a scientific fact when a group of people – the community of scientists working in that area – come to accept it as true. Processes like peer review function to support the creation of new facts, in this social sense. As a result, these seemingly separate functions of connecting people and moving information are really intimately intertwined. Information ultimately always comes from a human source, either directly or indirectly. The credibility of the source directly affects the credibility of the information. Thus we can see the Internet's two key functions – distributing information and connecting people – as really one richer function: distributing situated information. The Internet can be used to help create a rich web of interconnections among people and ideas.

How can this new medium be used to foster learning? An unusual example makes a compelling case: the Web sites Company-Command.com and PlatoonLeader.org, created by and for young officers in the United States Army (described in Baum, 2005). Military officers in the field often find themselves facing challenges that their formal training did not prepare them for. In a standard military situation, if an individual has an insight they want to share with others, they might report it to their superiors. The information would then move slowly up the chain of command. If it is vetted, it will be formally presented to fit within the structures of official policy, and reappear weeks or months later as a pamphlet distributed to other officers. The process is slow and bureaucratic. Two young officers, Majors Nate Allen and Tony Burgess, found that during their evening informal chats, they often shared valuable information. Wanting to share this with others, at their own expense they began a Web site

on a civilian Internet service provider called CompanyCommand.com. On the site, army captains can share experiences and advice in real time, without intervening bureaucracy. The site proved so popular and helpful that they soon created PlatoonLeader.org for platoon leaders, and the army itself later created Cavnet for cavalry officers.

Consider this dramatic example: one officer in the field discovered grenades being placed behind posters the army had been told to tear down. The information was posted online in time for the next patrol. Follow-up posts confirmed that numerous grenades were found behind posters just hours later. In this instance, the rapid peer-to-peer sharing of information via computer-mediated communications saved lives. More generally, junior army officers represent a group with an urgent need to learn, and forming a knowledge-building community mediated by a computer network has proved startlingly successful – so successful that the army has sent Allen, Burgess, and two other organizers of the Web sites to get Ph.D.s, and later continue work on these sites and teach at West Point (Baum, 2005). In this example, we see aspects of both communities of practice and knowledge-building communities facilitated by CMC with spectacular results.

Authenticity in the Classroom

Young army officers have a real and urgent need to learn to be better at their jobs. Students in classes often do not feel a real personal desire to learn the assigned material, much less an urgent one. Computer networks can help address this problem. By connecting learners to the real world, they can connect students to real problems, creating a more authentic context for learning. Learning sciences researchers have found that when learning is situated in real-world settings, and focused on authentic problems that have meaning for students, then students develop a much deeper understanding of the material.

Shaffer and Resnick (1999) reviewed the educational literature on "authenticity" and noted that the word is used in four distinct ways:

- Activities aligned with the outside world
- Assessment aligned with instruction
- Topics aligned with what learners want to know
- Methods of inquiry aligned with a discipline.

In each of these senses, Company-Command and PlatoonLeader contribute to creating an authentic learning environment – much more so than the training the officers received before going into the field.

A host of research projects in computer-supported collaborative learning (CSCL) explore how to make classroom learning environments more authentic (Stahl et al., this volume). This has been explored particularly well in the domain of science learning (Linn et al., 2004; Songer, 1996).

A noteworthy early example is the National Geographic Kids Network (Tinker, 1991). Each of the curriculum units created by Tinker's team gets students actively involved in scientific practice by requiring students to make measurements and share them online with other students and scientists. In the acid rain unit, students design their own rain collectors, and measure the pH of the rainwater collected. Before taking measurements, the students learn the background information needed to give the measurement activity a meaningful context. The teacher then scaffolds the students as they interpret their data and address its implications. At the end of the week, each student group sends its data values to a central computer where they are analyzed by an expert scientist and returned to the students. Tinker commented that

The unit regularly generates excitement and serious participation among its student-scientists. The kids sense that what they do matters; that this is not just another silly exercise or cookbook lab. The act of sending off the data is taken seriously because they understand that someone – other classes and the participating scientist – will look at their work and that this work will con-

tribute to a pattern that they will all have a chance to analyze. The effect on the class is palpable: kids come in on weekends if there was rain because it is important to measure the pH soon after the storm; sometimes learning disabled kids shine; teachers report students exhibit talents they never knew lay dormant; other teachers revise their whole instructional strategy as a result of what they learn about student learning in this unit. (Tinker, 1991)

Sharing real data with other students helps create a more authentic science-learning environment. The affordances of online communication help us to create a situation in which, in Tinker's words, "the kids sense that what they do matters." Our electronic webs of connections among people and ideas can help move students beyond textbooks and lab manuals written years ago, and into the context of contemporary ideas and adults professionally engaged with those ideas.

To take a second example, in the SCOPE (Science Controversies On-line: Partnerships in Education) project, students learn about real, contemporary scientific controversies. SCOPE units explore contemporary topics like why there are so many deformed frogs in North America, and whether genetically modified foods carry health risks. In the deformed frogs curriculum, students begin by watching video about the controversy. They review background information available on the Internet, and use the Sense-Maker online discussion tool (Bell, 2004) to critique that information. Finally, they choose between the two, current competing hypotheses, and the project culminates in an in-class debate. Philip Bell (2004) noted that by learning about current controversies, students not only are more motivated to learn science content, but they also learn about how scientific knowledge is constructed.

In this section, I've described three different learning communities in which the design emphasizes authenticity – Company-Command, National Geographic Kids Network, and SCOPE. These share many characteristics with both the community of practice and knowledge-building community prototypes of learning community.

Social Support for Design-Based Learning Online: The MOOSE Crossing Project

In my own work, I have built on the three prototypes of learning communities that I described earlier, with the goal of designing effective learning communities via the Internet. I created the MOOSE Crossing project with Papert's idea of a technological samba school as an inspiration. My goal was to create a playful environment, closely connected to popular culture, where people of diverse ages learn together in a self-motivated fashion by working on creative projects scaffolded by technology.

MOOSE Crossing is a text-based virtual reality environment (or MUD – a Multi-User Domain) in which kids ages eight to thirteen learn object-oriented programming and practice their creative writing by creating new objects and places in a shared online world. The online world is created by its members, and kids interacting in the world are immersed in projects created by their peers. The specially designed programming language (MOOSE) and environment (MacMOOSE and WinMOOSE) make it easy for young kids to learn to program. Members don't just experience the virtual world – they construct it collaboratively. For example, Carrot[1] (girl, age nine) created a swimming pool complex, and she created a computer representation of various objects in the complex, including in particular the swimming pool itself. Using lists that are stored along with the representation of the swimming pool, she kept track of who was in the pool, sauna, or Jacuzzi, and who had changed into a bathing suit. You obviously can't jump into the pool if you're already in the water...you need to get out first! (See Figure 27.1.) This gave Carrot opportunities for comic writing as well as programming. The text-based nature of the environment is not a technical limitation, but a deliberate design choice: it gives kids a context for using language playfully and imaginatively. Carrot enjoyed inviting other kids over to the pool. They in turn learned about programming and writing, using her work as a model. The environment attracts a diverse population of kids, not just those who you would normally think would want to learn to program.

The online community provides a ready source of peer support for learning. Kids learn from one another, and from one another's projects. Students working on design and construction activities sometimes need help understanding what kinds of projects are possible. In online environments such as MOOSE Crossing, kids are continually surrounded by projects made by their peers. These project models not only serve as inspiration but also can be a concrete jumping-off point: you can start a project by building on work done by others (Bruckman, 1998).

Peers in the environment not only can help answer technical questions but also can reassure learners that they have faced similar challenges in their own projects. Peer support is often not just technical but also emotional. In answering a question, one child may tell another, "I got confused by that at first too."

The online community provides a ready source of role models. If, for example, girls are inclined to worry that programming might not be a cool thing for a girl to do, they are surrounded by girls and women engaging in this activity successfully and enjoying it. Finally, the online community provides an appreciative audience for completed work. Kids get excited about being creative in order to share their work with their peers. One thirteen-year-old girl commented,

Another thing about moose-crossing is that I feel as if I can really help someone. I like learning and doing stuff on my own, but the real reason I come to moose-crossing is that I feel needed, and wanted. While programming is a lot of fun, I don't think I'd do it, if there wasn't anyone who would appreciate it.

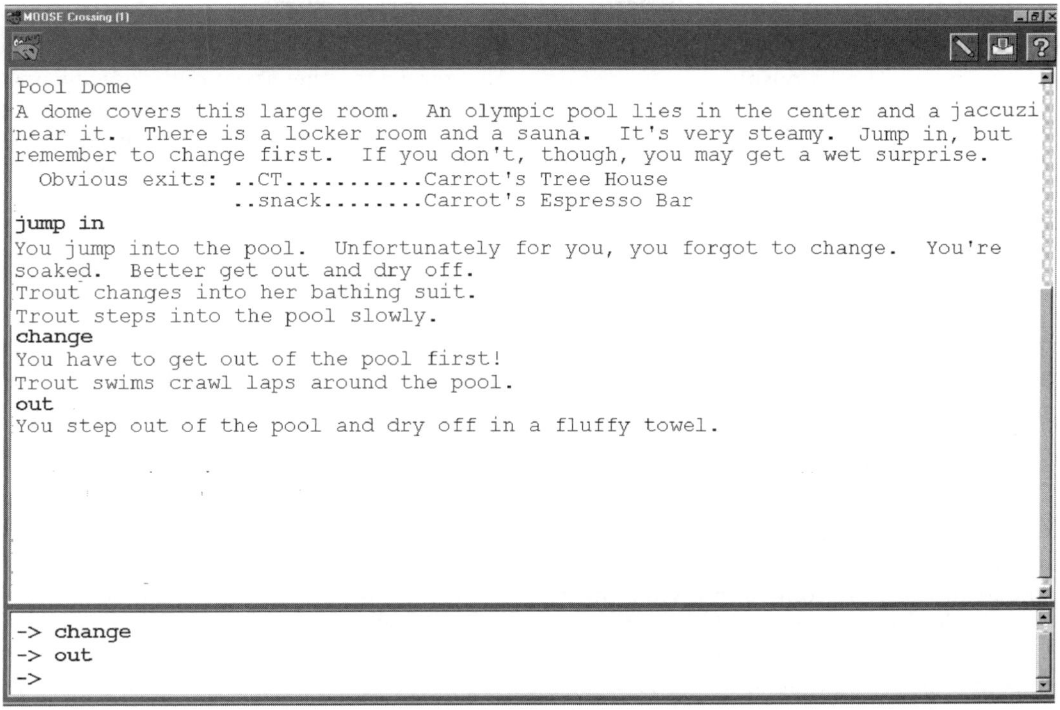

```
MOOSE Crossing (1)
Pool Dome
A dome covers this large room.  An olympic pool lies in the center and a jaccuzi
near it.  There is a locker room and a sauna.  It's very steamy.  Jump in, but
remember to change first.  If you don't, though, you may get a wet surprise.
   Obvious exits: ..CT.........Carrot's Tree House
                  ..snack.......Carrot's Espresso Bar
jump in
You jump into the pool.  Unfortunately for you, you forgot to change.  You're
soaked.  Better get out and dry off.
Trout changes into her bathing suit.
Trout steps into the pool slowly.
change
You have to get out of the pool first!
Trout swims crawl laps around the pool.
out
You step out of the pool and dry off in a fluffy towel.




-> change
-> out
->
```

Figure 27.1. Carrot's swimming pool on MOOSE Crossing.

From this work, I found that online communities can provide students with ready access to

- Role models,
- Project models,
- Technical support,
- Emotional support, and
- An appreciative audience. (Bruckman, 1998)

Projects on MOOSE Crossing are quite different from, for example, the "samples folder" that comes with many computer applications. First, the author of each project is clearly marked. These are not created by some disembodied, unreachable adult authority, but by peers. This sends the message to kids that they could do something similar. Furthermore, in many cases contacting the actual author of an admired project is possible. Many successful learning conversations begin with a statement like, "I love your pet dragon! How'd you make it?"

The exact same dragon in a "samples folder" would have much less impact. Thus, it is not just the content of support for learning that matters, but also its *context* and *connectedness* to other aspects of the learning environment.

Online learning communities can provide support for learners who sometimes feel afraid to attempt intellectual activity (Pintrich & Schunk, 1996). If a student worries that someone like them (for example because of their gender, race, or age) isn't good at a particular type of intellectual activity (like math or computers), it helps if other people just like them are visible within the online environment. For example, you can't worry that "girls just aren't good at math" when you are surrounded by positive role models such as girls and women doing math successfully on The Math Forum (Renninger & Shumar, 2002).

Analysis of learning on MOOSE Crossing suggests that support for learning is more valuable when it is:

- From a source (either human or computational) with whom the learner has a positive personal relationship,
- Ubiquitously available,
- Richly connected to other sources of support, and
- Richly connected to everyday activities. (Bruckman, 2000)

Computer-mediated communication has unique affordances that can help designers of learning communities to foster situated support for learning.

MOOSE Crossing is a somewhat extreme example of relying on a samba school metaphor. Scaffolding for learning on the site is predominantly social. The environment is playful and open – students are free to choose to become immersed in making wonderful creations, dabble a little in a few small projects, simply be social, or perhaps not participate at all. This is similar to an open cultural institution like a samba school – individuals may become amazing dancers, choreographers, or costume designers, may simply hang out, or may not come at all. In some cases, MOOSE Crossing's open nature encourages individuals to become inspired to care about their projects in a new way. For other students, this does not happen. For a free-time, voluntary activity, this outcome is expected and acceptable. Not everyone chooses to excel at piano lessons – some people prefer Little League baseball, or some other group or individual activity. However, for an in-school activity, this is problematic – we generally expect a least common denominator of achievement from all students as an outcome of mandatory educational activity, even if this effectively lowers the achievement on the high end (Bruckman et al., 2000).

Radical thinkers like Seymour Papert advocate a fundamental rethinking of the basic nature of school to embrace this freedom to learn. Moderates such as myself see uneven learning outcomes as problematic, but struggle to find ways to preserve aspects of the vitality of open learning environments in more formal contexts. The broader lesson is that any given model for learning community depends for its success on many specific details of the situation, and translating that model to other situations is not always a straightforward process. Nevertheless, as we come to better understand our models, we develop a richer vocabulary of design elements that we can leverage.

Conclusion

While much of the richest work in online communities has been done in the domains of math (Renninger & Shumar, 2002) and science (Linn et al., 2004; Songer, 1996), Scardamalia and Bereiter note that a knowledge-building community can be built around almost any domain we might wish students to understand (Scardamalia & Bereiter, this volume). For example, in writing workshops (Lensmire, 1994) students create a learning community surrounding creative writing; in reciprocal teaching (Palincsar & Brown, 1984), teams of students work together to help scaffold each other's developing ability to understand text. Palincsar and Ladewski (this volume) shows how significant the Internet has become to literacy, by creating an authentic, motivating context for students to engage in written communication.

Future research should explore how to make learning communities more effective, and that research will always be guided by one or more prototypes of learning communities. The specific prototypes that the researcher chooses guide which characteristics of the learning environment are emphasized. Research will be more valuable if the researchers are explicit about which prototypes of learning community are guiding their research.

As we come to better understand the unique features of CMC, new possibilities for learning community will emerge. The primary challenge in realizing that potential is in cultivating a deep, nuanced, and detailed understanding of a wide variety of existing learning communities, and leveraging that understanding to guide our exploration of new kinds of online learning communities. Eventually, we will move beyond those prototypes that are based on existing learning communities, and new genres of online learning community will emerge that have no direct analog in anything that has come before. Understanding and learning from existing learning communities is essential to realizing this vision.

Footnote

1. All real names and online pseudonyms of participants have been changed to protect their confidentiality.

References

Barab, S., Thomas, M., Dodge, T., Carteaux, R., & Tuzun, H. (2005). Making learning fun: Quest Atlantis, a game without guns. *Educational Technology Research and Development*, 53(1), 86–107.

Barron, B., Schwartz, D., Vye, N., Moore, A., Petrosino, A., & Zech, L. (1998). Doing with understanding: Lessons from research on problem- and project-based learning. *Journal of the Learning Sciences*, 7(3&4), 271–312.

Baum, D. (2005, January 17, 2005). Battle lessons: What the generals don't know. *The New Yorker*, 42–48.

Bell, P. (2004). Promoting students' argument construction and collaborative debate in the science classroom. In M. C. Linn, E. A. Davis, & P. Bell (Eds.), *Internet environments for science education* (pp. 115–143). Mahwah, NJ: Lawrence Erlbaum Associates.

Bruckman, A. (1998). Community support for constructionist learning. *Computer Supported Cooperative Work*, 7, 47–86.

Bruckman, A. (2000). Situated support for learning: Storm's weekend with Rachael. *Journal of the Learning Sciences*, 9(3), 329–372.

Bruckman, A., Edwards, E., Elliott, J., & Jensen, C. (2000, June). *Uneven achievement in a constructionist learning environment*. Paper presented at the International Conference on the Learning Sciences, Ann Arbor, MI.

Dewey, J. (1938). *Experience and education*. New York: Macmillan Publishing Company.

Edelson, D., & O'Neill, K. (1994, June). *The Covis collaboratory notebook: Supporting collaborative scientific inquiry*. Paper presented at the National Educational Computing Conference (NECC), Boston, MA.

Hewitt, J. (2004). An exploration of community in a knowledge forum classroom, an activity system analysis. In S. Barab, R. Kling, & J. Gray (Eds.), *Designing for virtual communities in the service of learning* (pp. 210–238). New York: Cambridge University Press.

Hillery, G. A. (1955, June). Definitions of community: Areas of agreement. *Rural Sociology*, 20, 111–123.

Kling, R., & Courtwright, C. (2004). Group behavior and learning in electronic forums, a socio-technical approach. In S. Barab, R. Kling, & J. Gray (Eds.), *Designing for virtual communities in the service of learning* (pp. 91–119). New York: Cambridge University Press.

Kolodner, J., Camp, P., Crismond, D., Fasse, B., Gray, J., Holbrook, J., Puntambekar, S., & Ryan, M. (2003). Problem-based learning meets case-based reasoning in the middle-school science classroom: Putting learning by design into practice. *Journal of the Learning Sciences*, 12(4), 495–547.

Lakoff, G. (1987). *Women, fire, and dangerous things; what categories reveal about the mind*. Chicago: University of Chicago Press.

Latour, B., Woolgar, S., & Salk, J. (1986). *Laboratory life*. Princeton, NJ: Princeton University Press.

Lave, J., & Wenger, E. (1991). *Situated learning: Legitimate peripheral participation*. Cambridge: Cambridge University Press.

Learning-in-Motion. (2005). *Knowledge forum*. Santa Cruz, CA: Learning in Motion.

Lensmire, T. J. (1994). Writing workshop as carnival: Reflections on an alternative learning environment. *Harvard Educational Review*, 64(4), 371–391.

Linn, M. C., Davis, E. A., & Bell, P. (Eds.). (2004). *Internet environments for science education*. Mahwah, NJ: Lawrence Erlbaum Associates.

Palincsar, A. S., & Brown, A. L. (1984). Reciprocal teaching of comprehension fostering and comprehension monitoring. *Cognition and Instruction*, 1(2), 117–175.

Papert, S. (1980). *Mindstorms: Children, computers, and powerful ideas*. New York: Basic Books.

Papert, S. (1991). Situating constructionism. In I. Harel & S. Papert (Eds.), *Constructionism*. Norwood, NJ: Ablex Publishing.

Pintrich, P. R., & Schunk, D. H. (1996). *Motivation in education*. Englewood Cliffs, NJ: Prentice Hall.

Renninger, K. A., & Shumar, W. (2002). Community building with and for teachers at the math forum. In K. A. Renninger & W. Shumar (Eds.), *Building virtual communities* (pp. 60–95). New York: Cambridge University Press.

Rheingold, H. (1993). *The virtual community: Homesteading on the electronic frontier*. Reading, MA: Addison-Wesley Publishing Company.

Roberts, T. (1998, April). *Are newsgroups virtual communities?* Paper presented at the CHI, Los Angeles, CA.

Rogoff, B. (1994). Developing understanding of the idea of communities of learners. *Mind, Culture, and Activity, 1*(4), 209–229.

Scardamalia, M., & Bereiter, C. (1994). Computer support for knowledge-building communities. *The Journal of the Learning Sciences, 3*(3), 265–283.

Shaffer, D. W., & M. Resnick (1999). "Thick" authenticity: New media and authentic learning. *Journal of Interactive Learning Research, 10*(2), 195–215.

Shumar, W., & Renninger, K. A. (2002). On conceptualizing community. In K. A. Renninger & W. Shumar (Eds.), *Building virtual communities* (pp. 1–17). New York: Cambridge University Press.

Songer, N. (1996). Exploring learning opportunities in coordinated network-enhanced classrooms: A case of kids as global scientists. *The Journal of the Learning Sciences, 5*(4), 297–327.

Tinker, R. F. (1991, July). *Science for kids: The promise of technology*. Paper presented at the AAAS Forum: Technology for Teaching and Learning, Washington, DC. Available at http://archive.concord.org/publications/sci4kids.html, accessed November 22, 2005.

Wellman, B., & Gulia, M. (1999). Virtual communities are communities: Net surfers don't ride alone. In M. A. Smith & P. Kollock (Eds.), *Communities in cyberspace*. New York: Routledge.

Wellman, B., & Leighton, B. (1979). Networks, neighborhoods, and communities: Approaches to the study of the community question. *Urban Affairs Quarterly, 14*(3), 363–390.

Zagal, J., & Bruckman, A. (2005). From samba schools to computer clubhouses: Cultural institutions as learning environments. *Convergence, 11*(1), 88–105.

Part VI

LEARNING ENVIRONMENTS

CHAPTER 28

Motivation and Cognitive Engagement in Learning Environments

Phyllis C. Blumenfeld, Toni M. Kempler, and Joseph S. Krajcik

When learning environments are based on learning sciences principles (e.g. project, problem, and design approaches), they are more likely to be motivating for students. The principles – such as authenticity, inquiry, collaboration, and technology – engage learners so that they will think deeply about the content and construct an understanding that entails integration and application of the key ideas of the discipline. For a learning sciences approach to work, students must invest considerable mental effort and must persist in the search for solutions to problems. In many ways, newly designed environments based on learning sciences principles require students to be more motivated than do traditional environments (Blumenfeld et al., 1991). Although there is evidence that students respond positively to these learning environments (Hickey, Moore, & Pellegrino, 2001; Mistler-Jackson & Songer, 2000), it remains unclear whether students are willing to invest the time and energy necessary for gaining the desired level of understanding. Many classroom activities in which students enthusiastically participate

do not necessarily get students cognitively engaged.

The concept of *cognitive engagement* couples ideas from motivation research with ideas regarding learning strategy use. It includes students' willingness to invest and exert effort in learning, while employing the necessary cognitive, metacognitive, and volitional strategies that promote understanding (Fredricks, Blumenfeld, & Paris, 2004). The use of strategies can be superficial or deep. Superficial cognitive engagement involves the use of memory and elaboration strategies. Deep level engagement involves the use of elaboration and organization strategies as students try to connect new ideas to old. Metacognitive strategies include setting goals, planning, monitoring, evaluating progress, and making necessary adjustments when accomplishing a task. Volitional strategies regulate attention, affect, and effort in the face of distractions.

Although past research has investigated the relation between positive attitudes (liking and interest), participation, and achievement, this work has been primarily conducted in traditional settings. Such research likely reflects the fact that, within traditional classrooms, tests mainly contain factual questions or simple applications. Students can do well on these tests even if their motivation is to simply pay attention, and they can use low-level learning strategies to memorize information. Some students may not be willing to delve more deeply into the material – to relate new material to prior knowledge, to reconsider their ideas, to critique and revise their work, and to self-regulate – as required by learning-sciences based environments. The challenge for designers and teachers is to maximize the motivational benefits of learning sciences principles so that students are cognitively engaged.

In this chapter we briefly review the literature on motivation and cognitive engagement, and discuss how the key features of learning sciences-based environments are likely to influence them. We indicate some challenges posed by each of these features, for students and for teachers, which may have negative effects on motivation. We describe strategies for meeting these challenges, and argue that the challenges should be taken into account when designing learning environments and when enacting them in the classroom.

Determinants of Motivation and Cognitive Engagement

Motivation sets the stage for cognitive engagement. Motivation leads to achievement by increasing the quality of cognitive engagement. That is, content understanding and skill capabilities are enhanced when students are committed to building knowledge and employing deeper learning strategies.

We are guided by three underlying assumptions. First, although there are individual differences in motivation, classroom contexts and instructional practices affect the degree to which students simply participate or are willing to invest in learning and understanding. Second, these aspects of

motivation are correlated and affect each other; consequently, changing one classroom feature in an effort to improve an aspect of motivation may have repercussions on other classroom features. Third, motivation is iterative. That is, interest may lead to deeper engagement with the material, which results in increased skills and knowledge. This increase may encourage interest and sustain cognitive engagement. Similarly, success in creating an artifact or mastering an idea or skill can lead to greater feelings of competence and greater perceived value of the endeavor, and result in higher levels of engagement.

We discuss four determinants of motivation and cognitive engagement and indicate features of learning environments that are likely to impact them. For each determinant of motivation, we discuss definitions, outcomes, and the impact of classroom practices.

Value

There are several ways in which students can value subject matter. *Intrinsic* value is influenced by interest for the topic and enjoyment experienced when performing the task. *Instrumental* value refers to students' perceptions of how tasks are related to their future goals and everyday life. *Attainment* value refers to the personal importance that students place on accomplishing the task.

The most researched aspect of value is intrinsic value, and a separate literature has developed specifically on student interest. The interest literature makes a further distinction between situational interest, which is short-lived, and a more enduring form of personal interest, which is conceptually similar to intrinsic value. Situational interest can be enhanced by features of the task like variety, novelty, and incongruity or challenge that can "hook" interest by grabbing student attention (Mitchell, 1993). Although some students come to the learning environment with a well-developed personal interest in subject areas or specific topics, for other students, features of the context are important for fostering situational interest.

Situational interest may transition into what Mitchell and Renninger term "hold," when student interest is sustained (Mitchell, 1993; Renninger, 2000). More enduring interest and investment in learning the subject matter can lead to deeper cognitive engagement (Hidi & Harackiewicz, 2000).

Drawing connections to students' personal lives, embedding the introduction of new concepts and skills within meaningful tasks, and emphasizing the instrumental value of mastering a skill or doing well in a subject matter enhances value. For example, teachers can bring in speakers and experts from the local community to more authentically draw connections with life outside of school. A second way to enhance value is by incorporating topics that students find interesting (e.g. space travel, dinosaurs). Finally, value may be enhanced by having students work on questions and use practices similar to those used by members of the discipline (e.g. scientists and mathematicians).

However, attempts to enhance interest can backfire and decrease learning. Brophy (1999) cautioned against using "bells and whistles" to obtain interest. Evidence from the interest literature specifically cautions against using seductive details in text (Schraw & Lehman, 2001). Seductive details are highly interesting for students, but may draw attention toward issues that are less relevant, potentially deflecting attention away from key ideas. Using classroom demonstrations in science that include explosions or other attention getting devices has similar effects.

Competence

Students' feeling of competence or of efficacy regarding their ability to succeed in a particular class or on a specific task has a positive influence on their effort, persistence, use of higher-level learning strategies, and choice of challenging activities. Alternatively, students with lower self-efficacy may choose easier tasks, or tasks that they feel more confident about, to ensure success and avoid working on difficult tasks. Students' sense of competence is enhanced when

teachers provide support through instruction in strategies, skills, and concept development. In addition, scaffolding encourages self-efficacy as teachers model thinking and break down tasks to prepare students for activities. Finally, encouragement, recognition of student progress, and constructive feedback on student work also enhances perceptions of efficacy (see Schunk & Pajares, 2002; Wigfield & Eccles, 2000, for a review).

Relatedness

Students' needs for relatedness or belonging are met when they have positive interactions with their peers and teachers. Feelings of belonging are satisfied by teachers and peers through expressions of respect, caring, and interest for a student's well-being (Battistich et al., 1997; Davis, 2003; Wentzel, 1997). In addition, opportunities for collaboration with peers encourage feelings of relatedness (Cohen, 1994). Satisfaction of relatedness needs enhances student interest, participation, and academic effort (Wentzel, 1997).

Autonomy

Autonomy refers to perception of a sense of agency, which occurs when students have the opportunity for choices and for playing a significant role in directing their own activity. Teachers can support autonomy by allowing students to make decisions about topics, selection and planning of activities, and artifact development. When teacher practices are autonomy-supportive, students respond with increased interest and willingly approach challenges (Ryan & Grolnick, 1986).

Challenges to Motivation and Cognitive Engagement

Motivation alone is not sufficient for ensuring achievement. Cognitive engagement mediates the ways in which values and needs, as discussed above, relate to learning and achievement. Students who value the subject matter and/or perceive that their needs have been met are more likely to be invested in learning, to expend effort, and to employ deep level learning, metacognitive, and volitional strategies.

Researchers often assume that learning sciences-based classrooms will sufficiently motivate and cognitively engage students as they collaborate on meaningful problems, engage in active learning, use technology, and create artifacts. This assumption may not be well founded. Although constructivist-based learning environments incorporate features that may enhance cognitive engagement far more than traditional classrooms, these environments also introduce difficulties that may interfere with students' willingness to engage.

Several characteristics of these learning environments may threaten the quality with which students engage, even if they are initially motivated. Students must become accustomed to new rules and new classroom norms. They need to adjust to new relationships with their teacher, who becomes a facilitator rather than the primary source of information. Students must be self-regulating as their responsibility for constructing understanding and for directing learning increases. Moreover, students must be committed to collaborating and enhancing the community's knowledge, meaning that students must participate actively during small group collaboration and whole class discussion. There is ample evidence that this higher quality of engagement is hard to achieve. Often, students approach schoolwork with what Scardamalia, Bereiter, & Lamon (1994) call a "schoolwork module." They focus on completing work with minimal effort. Scardamalia et al. contrast this lower quality of commitment with being an "intentional learner." These students strive to expand their knowledge and skills, and hold a long-term view of enriching their understanding.

New classroom norms require that students' ideas and artifacts be critiqued during work on activities. Students may not respond well to the idea of reflecting on and revising their work. First, there are individual differences in students' dispositions toward challenge, with some responding positively while others avoiding doing difficult work (Meyer, Turner, & Spencer, 1997). Moreover, there are also within-student individual differences in terms of how a student may respond to a given task across an inquiry unit (Patrick & Middleton, 2002). Second, the expectation for revision and reflection requires considerable self-efficacy on the part of students, and students may be unwilling to confront their ideas or explore inconsistencies (Pintrich, Marx, & Boyle, 1993). Students may resist doing more work because they perceive that they have already done enough work and have completed the assignment. When the amount of effort required to succeed exceeds what they are willing to do, students resist, complain, and try to renegotiate requirements (Doyle, 1983). Students may view critiques and mistakes not as opportunities to learn, but as reflecting poorly on their abilities. They may not view learning as a process in which artifacts reflect current thinking and in which revision can be a route to greater understanding. Martin (2000) describes how teachers gave up on a constructivist middle school math program when students refused to turn in homework, did not redo assignments, and were generally uncooperative because they thought the work was too hard and too much.

A related problem is that classrooms are evaluative. Although many new programs attempt to decrease emphasis on performance, and to highlight improvement and the value of learning, there are still statewide tests to take and grades to be given. Therefore, students may resist engaging in long-term tasks and ambiguous tasks because they worry about not doing well.

Finally, and most problematic, even if these features of learning environments prove motivating and students are willing to cognitively engage, they may lack the requisite skills for this engagement to lead to increased understanding. Lack of prior knowledge or unorganized bits of facts make it difficult to link new to existing knowledge and thus to build deep understanding. Also, students need to be strategic about long-term planning for various activities and about accomplishing immediate tasks. In addition, they need to be able to regulate and sustain their on-task behavior and thinking during complex and long-term tasks. Students need skills for collaborating with others and learning to participate productively in discussions. Finally, this type of learning requires that students use all of these skills simultaneously.

Given the challenges introduced by learning-sciences based environments, it is important to examine whether meaningful tasks, collaboration, and technology are cognitively engaging. It may be the case that these features work to promote motivation, but may only serve to "hook" but not sustain student interest. If so, designers and teachers will need to explore what steps can be taken to sustain motivation in the face of presented challenges and translate interest into the high-quality cognitive engagement required for meaning making. It is critical that designers and teachers consider ways to help scaffold the development of these skills and ways to support and encourage the use of such skills over time.

Influence of Specific Features of Learning Environments on Motivation and Cognitive Engagement

In this section, we point out challenges to motivation posed by each feature of learning-sciences based environments. The features that we discuss include authenticity, inquiry, collaboration, and technology. Although we discuss each feature separately for clarity, they are intertwined with each other and with instruction in influencing motivation and cognitive engagement. The goal is to point out what needs to be considered in design and instruction to address these challenges. Here, we discuss challenges for students and teachers based on our own

and others' experiences, and detail various strategies used to meet those challenges.

Authenticity

Authenticity is achieved by drawing connections to the real world, to students' everyday lives, and to practice in the discipline, and by requiring transformation of knowledge (Newmann, Marks, & Gamoran, 1996). Content is often situated in questions, problems, designs, or anchoring events that encompass important subject matter concepts so that students learn ideas, processes, and skills as they go about working. For example, students learn about ecosystems and natural selection while investigating changes in populations of plants and animals within the BGuILE learning environment Galapagos Finches (Edelson & Reiser, this volume; Reiser et al., 2001).

These meaningful problems create a "need-to-know situation" to learn specific ideas and concepts, and provide a reason to understand. They provide students with multiple opportunities to work with concepts as the class keeps coming back around to the driving question, the real-world problem under study. The creation of a final product or artifact enables students to apply content and skills learned in class. In addition to motivating students through stimulating real-world value, these artifacts provide a venue for cognitive engagement and knowledge transformation.

One instructional challenge is to determine what students find meaningful. Our experiences in classrooms show differences in the effectiveness of driving questions in urban middle schools. Students considered some questions more "real world" than others. Those that focused on ecology, such as "What is the quality of air in my community?" were considered more relevant than ones focused on physical science, such as "How can we build big things?" Second, it is difficult to choose questions, problems, or designs that are meaningful, represent the discipline, and match standards and learning goals. A second challenge is feasibility. Developing units for classroom use that are meaningful and mirror the world outside of school is a huge challenge. Time, resources, accessibility of technology, and rules about students taking trips or working in the surrounding community constrict options. A third challenge is ensuring that the variety and novelty of driving questions and anchoring events heighten student interest without a cost to cognitive engagement (Brophy, 1999). Barron et al. (1998) describe one instance in which students were so captivated by testing rockets and competing over whose rocket flew the furthest, that they failed to consider the principles underlying effective designs.

One obvious way to enhance motivation would be to let students choose their own driving questions. This strategy may not always be productive because the question, problem, or designs they select have to align with district, state, and national standards. Teachers cannot help every child select worthwhile questions and create accompanying individual plans, especially when they are responsible for many sections. Moreover, teachers must also collect necessary resources and materials to support student generated questions. Finally, when questions change each term, teachers are unable to use their experience with a particular question to improve subsequent classroom enactment. One compromise solution for promoting interest is to allow students to raise subquestions or issues to investigate within the framework of the overall question.

The cultural backgrounds of students and school settings also affect perceptions of authenticity. Moje et al. (2004) discuss the problem of the disconnect between inside and outside of school for many youngsters. Their intensive case studies show that students can discuss what they are learning in class but make little attempt to relate it to anything beyond the classroom. Making this connection between students' everyday lives and what they are learning in school is what Moje et al. call working in the "third space." They suggest that teachers contrast cultural or everyday explanations with how scientists go about understanding phenomena. Some driving questions may work across populations, but others may not. Suggestions for enhancing meaning for students from diverse backgrounds also include drawing on community funds of knowledge (Moll et al., 1992). Moll et al. describe academic projects organized around gardening and auto mechanics, where parents and other relatives participate by sharing their experiences and knowledge.

A driving question that initially does not seem motivating can be redesigned to make it more effective. Edelson, Gordon, and Pea (1999) reported that in early instantiations of WorldWatcher there was a mismatch between what the researchers thought would interest the students, and the ways in which students reacted. The authors found that student interest and level of engagement were enhanced by adding consideration of implications for people and the environment, and by including discussion of the social and political implications of controversies surrounding global warming.

Inquiry

Inquiry includes a variety of components that have the potential to be motivating by influencing value and perceived autonomy. Students' sense of autonomy is enhanced when they have opportunities to decide on ways to collect, analyze, and interpret information. Choice of artifacts and of presentation format also enhances perceived autonomy and cognitive engagement. Exploring real-world topics, sharing results and conclusions with others inside and outside the classroom, and taking on the role of scientists, mathematicians, or historians can augment feelings of value and enhance commitment. Cognitive engagement is necessary for each of these phases of investigation. As students synthesize, plan, make decisions, and transform information and data into a variety of forms, higher-level learning strategies and self-regulation are required.

Each of these features of inquiry poses difficulties in achieving their motivational potential. In the following two sections, we address collaboration and technology during inquiry. In this section, we focus on the motivational challenges introduced by complexity and difficulty. Complexity means that the task has many different steps or parts. Difficulty means that each of those parts are cognitively challenging as they require knowledge of content and process, use of multiple skills, and synthesis or problem solving.

Inquiry is complex; to succeed, students need to engage in multiple steps and do multiple things. Students raise questions and decide on what information is needed to create a plan for obtaining the information. This might include designing an experiment or a Web search, determining a way to systematically collect and organize information, analyzing data correctly, drawing appropriate conclusions, and sharing these conclusions with others. Each of these steps requires that students have process skills, literacy skills, and numeracy skills. Process skills include knowledge of how to pose questions that are feasible to answer and that also encompass important content, knowledge of experimental design or how to do literature searches, the ability to carry out data collection procedures or mathematical operations, and the organizational skills to keep track of what has been done. Literacy and numeracy skills include the ability to understand text, graphs, or other representations.

In addition to these inquiry skills, students must be capable of metacognition as they decide on goals, monitor progress, and evaluate whether they are achieving those goals. They also must employ learning strategies to relate new information to prior knowledge and to organize ideas. Moreover, the fact that these learning and metacognitive strategies and inquiry process skills must be used simultaneously necessitates that students coordinate their use and makes inquiry even more complex and difficult.

Motivational research suggests that students like tasks that are moderate in challenge (Ryan & Deci, 2000). Many descriptive studies show that merely presenting high-level tasks is not enough to insure greater involvement or high-level thinking among students (Blumenfeld & Meece,

1988). If the task is too difficult or time consuming, students may not remain invested with the necessary effort to accomplish the learning goals. One reason may be that the perceived value of the task may not be high enough to merit this quality of involvement. Second, students may not feel competent to accomplish the work given the overlapping complexities presented. Third, even if students are interested, they may become overwhelmed and quickly discouraged as difficulties mount over the course of the inquiry event or during artifact construction. Finally, individual differences in dispositions toward learning mean that some students may focus more on completion or grades at the expense of learning goals. When faced with challenge, students may respond by trying to simplify the cognitive demands of the situation through negotiation with the teacher. Accordingly, although the opportunity to engage in inquiry has motivating features, these may not be enough to sustain motivation and cognitive engagement in the face of challenge.

Descriptions of how students engage in initial experiences with inquiry suggest that another motivational challenge is that students are often interested in surface features of the investigation, not in the underlying content (Krajcik et al., 1998). Students often get excited about what they are seeing and doing during inquiry. However, students who lack the skills cited above can appear interested and excited about what they are doing, even though this does not necessarily translate into cognitive engagement with the content. For instance, in a project on trash, students observed mold growing in test tubes when studying conditions that affect decomposition. Students focused on surface features as they exclaimed about how "gross" the mold was. Yet, when the teacher suggested that they try to find out more about the mold, students only went so far as to identify its type; they failed to consider the scientific implications or to relate their observation to the question under study. Similarly, during data analysis, students may fail to include all the pertinent information and only focus on the parts they find interesting. In this manner, excitement and interest may sufficiently sustain participation in the investigation, but may not lead to deeper levels of cognitive engagement.

Another challenge is that those students who possess necessary skills and knowledge may not use these appropriately to foster conceptual understanding. One reason students may not become cognitively engaged is that they do not realize which skills are necessary. A second may be that they are not able to coordinate many different types of knowledge, skills, and strategies simultaneously. A third may be that students can become bored if a unit extends over time when they are used to short-term activities. As they attempt to follow procedures and complete steps during long-term inquiry, they may lose sight of overarching goals.

In order to support students' motivation during inquiry, teachers need to employ practices that both stimulate motivation and support students' cognitive engagement. Designers and teachers can break tasks down into smaller more manageable chunks when students are being introduced to inquiry. Short, highly structured inquiry activities, like launcher units (Holbrook & Kolodner, 2000), can be used first to mirror steps, skills, and strategies that will be needed during long-term efforts. Also, teachers can support students' self-efficacy by providing them with feedback that focuses on their progress and on their developing skills and knowledge over the course of an inquiry unit. Teachers can help students to sustain their interest by continuing to highlight the value and the importance of their driving question, so that students stay focused on the bigger issues as they engage in complex and difficult activities. In an effort to augment cognitive engagement, teachers need to scaffold both the use of specific skills and the coordination of multiple skills. Also, teachers should couple the above scaffolding of inquiry skills with instructional practices that encourage students to extend beyond surface features of the task. Here, scaffolding has the potential to support students' use

of process skills and learning strategies, but can also support students' perceived competence as their capabilities are improved. Finally, through the use of prompts, press, and feedback, teachers can encourage student synthesis and meaning making. Teachers press students by asking them to explain and justify answers during discussions, on assignments, and during artifact construction and presentation. Case studies show that student inquiry skills grow over time, but that they must be carefully nurtured and supported (Roth & Roychoudhury, 1993).

Collaboration

Collaboration with peers encourages motivation and cognitive engagement. Collaboration involves working with others both inside and outside of the classroom to obtain information, to share and discuss ideas, to exchange data and interpretations, and to receive feedback on work. Numerous studies show that students have positive attitudes toward these opportunities for collaboration (Cohen, 1994). First, collaboration enhances motivation because it meets students' needs for relatedness as they work with peers and other adults. As students work toward a shared goal and feel jointly responsible for their success, efficacy and social goals are enhanced (Wentzel, 1997). Second, because some members of the group may be more proficient in skills, or have more prior knowledge or different talents than others, the shared effort can diminish feelings of inadequacy (Hickey, 1997). Third, collaboration can benefit cognitive engagement as students are encouraged to explain, clarify, debate, and critique their ideas (Yackel, Cobb, & Wood, 1991).

Holbrook and Kolodner (2000) note that the small-group work feature of the Learning by Design unit served as a "hook" that engaged students who did not consider themselves to be scientists or to value science. Collaboration allowed students to interact with peers and to contribute where they had strengths. Group work served as a hook for sustaining interest; observations suggested that as a result of collaboration, students began to see science as an explanation of their everyday experiences.

Opportunities for collaboration are provided by interacting in small group contexts during investigations, when using technology, and during artifact creation. Collaboration can also be fostered through building a community of learners. Here, the goal is to develop an "intersubjective attitude" (Palincsar, 1998), or a joint commitment to building understanding. Becoming a community member can motivate students to participate, to internalize the values of the community, and to learn shared practices and norms (Hickey, 1997). For example, community knowledge building and collaboration is promoted by Knowledge Forum (Scardamalia & Bereiter, this volume), in which classes share knowledge by working together on a common topic, and posting information and comments on the multimedia community knowledge space.

Beyond the classroom, collaboration with other students, experts, and neighborhood members enhances student motivation. Students are excited when they have the chance to communicate with other students outside of the classroom via the World Wide Web. Opportunities for sharing work with their peers and community members beyond the classroom enhance feelings of ownership and value. Finally, telementoring enhances students' perceptions of authenticity and cognitive engagement as they collaborate with scientists and mathematicians who support their efforts, provide feedback, and model scientific rigor (O'Neill, 2001).

Above and beyond the complexity and difficulty related to inquiry, there are additional challenges posed by collaboration which may diminish the potential motivational benefits for cognitive engagement and learning. First, characteristics of the group's composition, such as ability level, gender, and cultural background, can affect group productivity (Webb, 1991). For example, whereas girls often play an active role in groups, because of their commitment to the group's success, they may be primarily involved with procedures or interpersonal issues rather than the content of the activity. Second, students from backgrounds where debate or questioning of authority are not valued may find collaboration difficult. Third, students may feel threatened making comments during class discussion if they are not proficient in English (Lee, 2003). Fourth, status differences based on student background and achievement level may result in stigmatization of students who are weaker academically, differ from others in some way, or have poor social skills (Cohen, 1994). For instance, high achieving students may feel that working with less knowledgeable classmates slows down their progress. Finally, there are individual differences in response to collaboration, with some students preferring to work alone and some focusing on looking smart rather than working with their peers.

There are additional problems arising from group members' tendency toward "social loafing." Group work can create interest but diminish thoughtfulness by encouraging reliance on others. Similarly, cognitive engagement can suffer when students are off-task having social conversations. These problems are exacerbated when the accountability structure does not hold students responsible for contributing to the group and there is group-level but not individual evaluation (Slavin, 1996).

Another serious challenge in trying to sustain interest and participation during group work is that students may not have the skills needed to collaborate productively. Collaboration requires that students know how to engage in productive discussions and how to sustain participation. Students may not be skilled at explaining their ideas or evaluating the ideas of others (Webb & Palincsar, 1996). These challenges may threaten students' perceived competence if they fail to complete work and to achieve the expected level of understanding.

There are several strategies for group work that encourage students' cognitive engagement and offer a structure of accountability. First, there are programs for improving students' collaboration skills so that they learn to listen to fellow group members, share ideas, and offer explanations (see Cohen, 1994; Webb, 1991). Interactions among students can be structured through group roles and through prompts that improve the quality of questions and discussion (King, 1997; Cohen, 1994). One such program, reciprocal teaching, uses a cycle of prompts to encourage participation and strategy use among students around text (Palincsar & Brown, 1984). King's (1997) work employs a set of questions and prompts that improve student explanations. Another strategy involves using the participation structure of the group in order to enhance active contributions of all students. For instance, Jigsaw creates interdependence among group members by having each student become an expert on information that others in the group need (Brown & Campione, 1994).

In order to enhance student accountability, group researchers sometimes use competition among groups to promote effort, participation, and cohesion (Slavin, 1996). In contrast, some motivational theorists argue that the addition of between-group competition and the use of group rewards create the risk of having students focus on winning rather than on the inherent value of learning and developing understanding (Ryan & Deci, 2000; Kempler & Linnenbrink, 2004). It is important to note that competition may be less effective at promoting motivation on tasks that are complex and ill-structured, which characterizes many of the activities in constructivist-based learning environments (Cohen, 1994).

Technology

Technology has motivational benefits as a "hook" that gets students to participate. It also can help sustain interest and promote cognitive engagement. Student interest is heightened by access to resources, real-time information, input from others, and data that bears on controversial issues and unresolved questions (e.g., global warming; Edelson et al., 1999). Interest may stem from the variety of activities technology affords; students can build and represent knowledge in different ways, such as using visualization and multimedia capabilities. Students' feelings of autonomy and cognitive engagement are likely to be increased because they have greater choice in what topics to study, in how to explore the topic, and in how to represent their understanding.

Some software, such as cognitive tutors, diagnoses student difficulties and provides immediate feedback about their progress on the task and their skill development, thereby promoting perceptions of efficacy (Koedinger & Corbett, this volume). Competence can be heightened as the technology enables students to progress at their own rates. Being proficient in technology use is seen as a valuable skill outside of school, so students are motivated to become competent in its use. This competence in technology use may increase the engagement of students who know less about the subject matter (Mistler-Jackson & Songer, 2000). Youngsters with poor literacy skills and second language learners may similarly benefit.

More mental effort can be devoted to deeper understanding when more procedural work like drawing on graph paper, making calculations, and accessing information is offloaded onto the software (Reiser, 2004). This can increase interest because students may become engaged by the content rather than worrying about procedures. Simplifying tasks, breaking them into smaller pieces, helping students organize, and providing prompts are common in software designed for students – scaffolding student thinking and increasing perceived competence. Software can also encourage students to revise and improve their work by making it easier for them to make changes to documents and virtual artifacts.

However, technology adds complexity and difficulty to students' experiences because students need to both learn how to use the technology and learn to use the tool in a way that enhances learning. Technology poses challenges for schools; access, maintenance, and technical support are essential. When students face maintenance issues, cannot get access to machines, or encounter bugs, they are likely to become frustrated. Second, students need time to learn to use the machines; if they are not experienced, they need to learn to type, and to create, save, and integrate files. The cost of learning new software and new uses of technology is often high for students and this may diminish interest in both the technology and the subject matter. Third, the time needed to become proficient with different software programs takes away from cognitive engagement and may decrease student efficacy. Many software applications are tailored for a particular program; the features contained in any one piece of software may not appear in another or the affordances may work differently. Finally, if the technology is not used again in different units or programs, then students may not experience the benefits of becoming proficient, and the perceived value of learning to use technology may diminish.

Students' prior knowledge will affect whether technology has the desired impact on cognitive engagement. If students have not encountered complex tasks that require taking several steps, keeping track of different sources of information, and synthesizing ideas, then scaffolds in the technology that support these processes may not have the intended benefit. Students may have to go through the whole process of inquiry several times to become familiar with the different aspects of tasks that need to be accomplished and with how the software can be helpful. There are many examples of how students ignore prompts to plan or explain their answers; sometimes they even disable scaffolding features in order to avoid going through some steps. If students have trouble benefiting from the opportunities for learning afforded by the technology, the result may be a decreased level of participation and cognitive engagement.

Conclusions

In 1991, faculty at the University of Michigan published a paper on motivating project based learning (Blumenfeld et al., 1991). In that article we pointed out that the two challenges facing these learning environments were both to support the learning and to sustain the doing. We thought that many of the features of the new learning environments had potential for motivation; however, given the complexity, difficulty, and ambiguity of the tasks, and the required use of strategic and metacognitive skills, this potential would not be easily achieved unless these challenges were addressed.

Fourteen years later, we still struggle with the same issues. The learning sciences has matured, and design experiments have resulted in design principles, instructional task scaffolding techniques, and professional development programs that begin to address these problems. We have found that environments based on the learning sciences can create situational interest and participation. However, there is less evidence for how to hold and sustain this interest and transform it into cognitive engagement, so that students willingly invest in learning and exert the mental effort necessary for understanding the academic content, even in the face of difficulty and complexity. Most research has focused on issues of learning, not on motivation. We argue that the field would profit from making motivation an explicit concern. This chapter summarizes what the field has learned and what challenges we still face in promoting motivation and enhancing cognitive engagement.

Effective enactment involves deliberately highlighting motivational aspects of the features throughout a unit: discussing the value of the content and using many opportunities to point to real-world relevance; consistently relating the material to the larger question, problem, or design; demonstrating the positive aspects of collaboration and community knowledge building; and allowing choice and decision making in selection of topics, design of inquiry, and creation of artifacts. Teachers can support student competence by pointing out progress in conceptual understanding and skill development, and by helping students view mistakes as a natural part of the learning process. These instructional scaffolds serve to support and sustain students' motivation by encouraging perceptions of value and meaningfulness of the work (Brophy, 1999; Turner et al., 2002).

Another challenge for teachers is to anticipate learner difficulties during enactment. Enactment of the features and overcoming their challenges is difficult for students; it takes time and experience for teachers to become proficient at sustaining motivation, supporting learning, and promoting cognitive engagement. This is made more complicated because teachers are themselves encountering challenges enacting learning sciences–based programs. One challenge is management of multiple activities to maximize productive time use and to consistently monitor student progress in activities that continue for long time periods. Another challenge is to create positive climates in which students are respectful of one another and become a community of learners. Teachers must also tailor instruction to individual differences. Additionally, teachers are developing the content, pedagogical content, and pedagogical skills to enact inquiry, promote collaboration, use technology for learning, and help students learn to critique and revise their work. Teachers also need to gain an understanding of the underlying learning sciences principles in order to make adaptations in designs that are responsive to situations and student needs, but that remain true to the underlying principles. Finally, to meet the instructional challenges of motivating students and promoting cognitive engagement, teachers must be motivated and invested in improving their own knowledge and enactment skills.

Teachers must provide pervasive scaffolding and support (Mergendoller et al., in press) so that students are not discouraged by the complexity and difficulty of completing activities and learning content and skills. Otherwise, students are likely to be confused or frustrated, to feel less competent, and consequently to be less cognitively engaged. One critical focus is the teaching of learning and metacognitive strategies, which are essential for cognitive engagement. A second is breaking down tasks so that students can tackle manageable pieces of complex activities. A third is gradually transferring responsibility for learning to students as they develop the requisite process, organizational, and metacognitive skills. A final critical challenge for teachers is finding ways to hold students accountable for doing and understanding work, while at the same time supporting learning. The failure to press for understanding will negatively impact cognitive engagement because students will not perceive the need to invest in learning or to exert the necessary effort to gain deep level understanding.

References

Barron, B. J. S., Schwartz, D. L., Vye, N. J., Moore, A., Petrosino, A., Zech, L., Bransford, J. D., & The Cognition and Technology Group at Vanderbilt (1998). Doing with understanding: Lessons from research on problem and project-based learning. *The Journal of the Learning Sciences*, 7(3&4), 271–311.

Battistich, V., Solomon, D., Watson, M., & Schaps, E. (1997). Caring school communities. *Educational Psychologist*, 32(3), 137–151.

Blumenfeld, P. C., & Meece, J. L. (1988). Task factors, teacher behavior, and students' involvement and use of learning strategies in science. *Elementary School Journal*, 88(3), 235–250.

Blumenfeld, P. C., Soloway, E., Marx, R. W., Krajcik, J. S., Guzdial, M., & Palincsar, A. (1991). Motivating project-based learning: Sustaining the doing, supporting the learning. *Educational Psychologist*, 26(3 & 4), 369–398.

Brophy, J. (1999). Toward a model of the value aspects of motivation in education: Developing appreciation for particular learning domains and activities. *Educational Psychologist*, 34(2), 75–85.

Brown, A. L., & Campione, J. C. (1994). Guided discovery in a community of learners. In K. McGilly (Ed.), *Classroom lessons: Integrating cognitive theory and classroom practice* (pp. 229–270). Cambridge, MA: MIT Press.

Cohen, E. G. (1994). Restructuring the classroom: Conditions for productive small groups. *Review of Educational Research*, 64(1), 1–35.

Davis, H. A. (2003). Conceptualizing the role and influence of student-teacher relationships in children's social and cognitive development. *Educational Psychologist, 38*(4), 207–234.

Doyle, W. (1983). Academic work. *Review of Educational Research, 53*(2), 159–199.

Edelson, D. C., Gordin, D. N., & Pea, R. D. (1999). Addressing the challenges of inquiry-based learning through technology and curriculum design. *The Journal of the Learning Sciences, 8*(3&4), 391–450.

Fredricks, J. A., Blumenfeld, P. C., & Paris, A. H. (2004). School engagement: Potential of the concept, state of the evidence. *Review of Educational Research, 74*(1), 59–109.

Hickey, D. T. (1997). Motivation and contemporary socio-constructivist instructional perspectives. *Educational Psychologist, 32 (3)*, 175–193.

Hickey, D. T., Moore, A. L., & Pellegrino, J. W. (2001). The motivational and academic consequences of elementary mathematics environments: Do constructivist innovations and reforms make a difference? *American Educational Research Journal, 38*(3), 611–652.

Hidi, S., & Harackiewicz, J. M. (2000). Motivating the academically unmotivated: A critical issue for the 21st century. *Review of Educational Research, 70*, 151–179.

Holbrook, J., & Kolodner, J. L. (2000). Scaffolding the development of an inquiry-based (science) classroom. In B. Fishman & S. O'Connor-Divelbiss (Eds.), *Proceedings of the fourth international conference of the learning sciences* (pp. 221–227). Mahwah, NJ: Lawrence Erlbaum Associates.

Kempler, T. M., & Linnenbrink, E. A. (2004, April). *Re-examining the influence of competition structures in group contexts: Implications for social and cognitive interactions in small groups.* Paper presented at the Annual Convention of the American Educational Research Association, San Diego.

King, A. (1997). ASK to THINK-TEL WHY: A model of transactive peer tutoring for scaffolding higher level complex learning. *Educational Psychologist, 32*(4), 221–235.

Krajcik, J., Blumenfeld, P. C., Marx, R. W., Bass, K. M., Fredricks, J., & Soloway, E. (1998). Inquiry in project-based science classrooms: Initial attempts by middle school students. *The Journal of the Learning Sciences, 7*(3 & 4), 313–350.

Lee, O. (2003). Equity for linguistically and culturally diverse students in science education:

A research agenda. *Teachers College Record, 105*(3), 465–489.

Martin, D. B. (2000). *Mathematics success and failure among African-American youth.* Mahwah, NJ: Lawrence Erlbaum Associates.

Mergendoller, J. R., Markham, T., Ravitz, J., & Larmer, J. (in press). Pervasive management of project based learning: Teachers as guides and facilitators. In C. M. Evertson & C. S. Weinstein (Eds.), *Handbook of classroom management: Research, practice, and contemporary issues.* Mahwah, NJ: Lawrence Erlbaum Associates.

Meyer, D. K., Turner, J. C., & Spencer, C. A. (1997). Challenge in a mathematics classroom: Students' motivation and strategies in project-based learning. *Elementary School Journal, 97*(5), 501–521.

Mistler-Jackson, M., & Songer, N. B. (2000). Student motivation and Internet technology: Are students empowered to learn science? *Journal of Research in Science Teaching, 37*(5), 459–479.

Mitchell, M. (1993). Situational interest: Its multifaceted structure in the secondary school mathematics classroom. *Journal of Educational Psychology, 85*, 424–436.

Moje, E. B., Ciechanowski, K. M., Kramer, K., Ellis, L., Carrillo, R., & Collazo, T. (2004). Working toward third space in content area literacy: An examination of everyday funds of knowledge and discourse. *Reading Research Quarterly, 39*(1), 38–70.

Moll, L. C., Amanti, C., Neff, D., & Gonzalez, N. (1992). Funds of knowledge for teaching: Using a qualitative approach to connect homes and classrooms. *Theory into Practice, 31*, 132–141.

Newmann, F. M., Marks, H. M., & Gamoran, A. (1996). Authentic pedagogy and student performance. *American Journal of Education, 104*, 280–312.

O'Neill, D. K. (2001). Knowing when you've brought them in: Scientific genre knowledge and communities of practice. *The Journal of the Learning Sciences, 10*(3), 223–264.

Palincsar, A. S. (1998). Social constructivist perspectives on teaching and learning. *Annual Review of Psychology, 49*, 345–375.

Palincsar, A. S., & Brown, A. L. (1984). Reciprocal teaching of comprehension-fostering and comprehension-monitoring activities. *Cognition and Instruction, 1*(2), 117–175.

Patrick, H., & Middleton, M. J. (2002). Turning the kaleidoscope: What we see when self-regulated learning is viewed with a qualitative lens. *Educational Psychologist*, 37(1), 27–39.

Pintrich, P. R., Marx, R. W., & Boyle, R. A. (1993). Beyond cold conceptual change: The role of motivational beliefs and classroom contextual factors in the process of conceptual change. *Review of Educational Research*, 63(2), 167–199.

Reiser, B. J. (2004). Scaffolding complex learning: The mechanisms of structuring and problematizing student work. *The Journal of the Learning Sciences*, 13(3), 273–304.

Reiser, B. J., Tabak, I., Sandoval, W. A., Smith, B. K., Steinmuller, F., & Leone, A. J. (2001). BGuILE: Strategic and conceptual scaffolds for scientific inquiry in biology classrooms. In S. M. Carver & D. Klahr (Eds.), *Cognition and instruction: Twenty-five years of progress* (pp. 263–305). Mahwah, NJ: Lawrence Erlbaum Associates.

Renninger, K. A. (2000). Individual interest and its implications for understanding intrinsic motivation. In C. Sansone & J. M. Harackiewicz (Eds.), *Intrinsic and extrinsic motivation: The search for optimal motivation and performance* (pp. 373–404). New York: Academic Press.

Roth, W. M., & Roychoudhury, A. (1993). The development of science process skills in authentic contexts. *Journal of Research in Science Teaching*, 30, 127–152.

Ryan, R. M., & Deci, E. L. (2000). Intrinsic and extrinsic motivations: Classic definitions and new directions. *Contemporary Educational Psychology*, 25(1), 54–67.

Ryan, R. M., & Grolnick, W. S. (1986). Origins and pawns in the classroom: Self-report and projective assessments of individual differences in children's perceptions. *Journal of Personality and Social Psychology*, 50(3), 550–558.

Scardamalia, M., Bereiter, C., & Lamon, M. (1994). CSILE: Trying to bring students into world 3. In K. McGilly (Ed.), *Classroom lessons: Integrating cognitive theory and classroom practice* (pp. 201–228). Cambridge, MA: MIT Press.

Schraw, G., & Lehman, S. (2001). Situational interest: A review of the literature and directions for future research. *Educational Psychology Review*, 13, 23–52.

Schunk, D. H., & Pajares, F. (2002). The development of academic self-efficacy. In A. Wigfield & J. S. Eccles (Eds.), *Development of achievement motivation* (pp. 15–31). San Diego: Academic Press.

Slavin, R. E. (1996). Research for the future: Research on cooperative learning and achievement: What we know, what we need to know. *Contemporary Educational Psychology*, 21, 43–69.

Turner, J. C., Midgley, C., Meyer, D. K., Gheen, M., Anderman, E. M., Kang, Y., & Patrick, H. (2002). The classroom environment and students' reports of avoidance strategies in mathematics: A multimethod study. *Journal of Educational Psychology*, 94(1), 88–106.

Webb, N. M. (1991). Task-related verbal interaction and mathematics learning in small groups. *Journal for Research in Mathematics Education*, 22, 366–389.

Webb, N. M., & Palincsar, A. S. (1996). Group processes in the classroom. In D. Berliner & R. Calfee (Eds.), *Handbook of educational psychology* (pp. 841–873). New York: Macmillan.

Wentzel, K. R. (1997). Student motivation in middle school: The role of perceived pedagogical caring. *Journal of Educational Psychology*, 89(3), 411–419.

Wigfield, A., & Eccles, J. S. (2000). Expectancy-value theory of achievement motivation. *Contemporary Educational Psychology*, 25, 68–81.

Yackel, E., Cobb, P., & Wood, T. (1991). Small-group interactions as a source of learning opportunities in second-grade mathematics. *Journal for Research in Mathematics Education*, 22, 390–408.

CHAPTER 29

Learning as a Cultural Process

Achieving Equity Through Diversity

Na'ilah Suad Nasir, Ann S. Rosebery, Beth Warren, and Carol D. Lee

In this chapter, we argue that learning and teaching are fundamentally cultural processes (Cole, 1996; Erickson, 2002; Lee, Spencer, & Harpalani, 2003; Rogoff, 2003). The learning sciences have not yet adequately addressed the ways that culture is integral to learning. By "culture," we mean the constellations of practices historically developed and dynamically shaped by communities in order to accomplish the purposes they value. Such practices are constituted by the tools they use, the social networks with which they are connected, the ways they organize joint activity, the discourses they use and value (i.e., specific ways of conceptualizing, representing, evaluating and engaging with the world). On this view, learning and development can be seen as the acquisition throughout the life course of diverse repertoires of overlapping, complementary, or even conflicting cultural practices.

Through participation in varied communities of practice, individuals appropriate, over time, varied repertoires of cultural practices. As youth make their rounds through the varied settings of their everyday lives – from home to school, mathematics class to English literature class, basketball team to workplace or church youth group – they encounter, engage, and negotiate various situated repertoires of practices. Each repertoire represents a particular point of view on the world, characterized by its own objects, meanings, purposes, symbols, and values (Bakhtin, 1981; Gee, 1990). Navigation among these repertoires can be problematic at any time in any place for any human being. However, for youth from non-dominant groups (i.e., students of color, students who speak national or language varieties other than standard English, and students from low income communities), this navigation is exacerbated by asymmetrical relationships of power that inevitably come into play around matters of race, ethnicity, class, gender, and language. Thus these youth must learn to manage multiple developmental tasks: both the ordinary tasks of life course development, as well as tasks that involve managing sources of stress rooted in particular forms of institutional stigmatization due to assumptions regarding race, poverty, language variation, gender, and disability (Burton, Allison, & Obeidallah, 1995; Spencer, 1987, 1999). Such stigmatization limits access to opportunities (e.g., schooling, work, etc.) across the life course for certain groups of youth.

Historically, studies of culture have often viewed nondominant students and communities as the "other" and have assumed a singular pathway of development based on American middle class norms. For the last century, culture has for the most part been viewed in static terms – as well-integrated, cohesive sets of neatly bounded traditions that are used to distinguish groups of people (González, 2004; Moll, 2000). Rogoff and Angelillo (2002) referred to this treatment of culture as the "box" problem. It leads to statements such as, "Mexicans do this; Anglos do that," as if culture is a fixed, holistic configuration of traits (an "essence") carried by the collection of individuals that comprise these groups (Gutiérrez & Rogoff, 2003). The tendency to "essentialize" groups has obscured the heterogeneity of practice within both dominant and nondominant groups.

Although we argue against essentializing, we acknowledge that there are historically-rooted continuities that connect individuals across generations (Boykin & Bailey, 2000; Lee, 2003b). Erickson (2002) used the example of the piñata in Mexican American culture to make the point that while not every Mexican American family has a piñata at birthday parties 100 percent of the time, the piñata is a practice that is common and an aspect of continuity of time and space in Mexican American culture. We argue that culture at once involves diverse developmental pathways across communities and historical continuities within them, but that such continuities are flexible. What makes essentializing so dangerous is not the attention to perceived continuities, but the implied assumption that those who differ from American middle class norms are somehow deficient.

In this chapter, we draw on empirical research into the cultural nature of learning. The research we discuss includes studies of (a) learning in and out of school settings; (b) relationships between everyday and academic knowledge and discourse, with particular reference to youth from nondominant groups; and (c) classroom-based design research that explores linkages among the varied repertoires of practice of youth and those of academic disciplines. These bodies of research address multiple dimensions of learning, including cognition, discourse, affect, motivation, and identity. We argue that a cultural view of learning encompasses *adaptive expertise* (Bransford et al., this volume; Hatano & Inagaki, 1986; Spiro et al., 1991), that is, the development of flexible knowledge and dispositions that facilitate effective navigation across varied settings and tasks. Adaptive expertise is crucial for youth from nondominant groups who typically face and must be able to address extreme societal challenges.

A cultural view of learning challenges the normative view that tends to dominate educational thinking and practice. Rather than privileging a restricted set of practices as fundamental to learning, this view expands the research lens to include three critical, related questions:

- What characterizes learning in the varied repertoires of practice in which people routinely participate as they go about their everyday lives?
- In what specific ways do these varied repertoires of practice connect with academic disciplinary practices?
- In what ways can these varied repertoires of practice be recruited to create meaningful opportunities for academic learning for all students? What principles of design emerge from this expanded inquiry into learning?

In this chapter, we discuss the significance of each of these questions for a cultural view of learning, and we illustrate each with examples from the research literature on science, literacy, and mathematics learning and teaching.

Question 1: What Characterizes Learning in the Varied Repertoires of Practice in Which People Routinely Participate as They Go About Their Everyday Lives?

One way to explore issues of equity in the learning sciences is to pay close attention to the nature and organization of settings where students are learning successfully. In this section, we review research on the out-of-school learning of children from non-dominant groups with the point of illuminating what such learning looks like and how it happens. Consider the following vignette from a study of learning in the game of dominoes (Nasir & Stone, 2003, p. 17).

> *Four 10-year-old African American boys are playing a game of dominoes. In their version of the game, the goal is to score points by creating a sum of the end pieces that is a multiple of five. A novice player in the group puts a play on the board, then uses his finger to count the number of points on the board, but does not know if it is a score. An expert player notices his confusion and says, "It's not nothing!" Later, at the end of this hand of play, the expert player suggests pieces that the novice could have played to create a score.*

In this vignette, the expert player served as an important resource for supporting the sense-making of the novice player, both through the feedback he offered directly, and as an example of what more advanced play looks like. Through interactions like these, domino players come to learn both more competent play and concepts of multiples and serial addition.

As this vignette illustrates, learning happens in a wide range of activities outside of school, including carpet-laying (Masingila, 1994), dairy factory work (Scribner, 1985), plumbing (Rose, 2004), hair-dressing (Majors, 2003), candy-selling (Saxe, 1991), basketball (Nasir, 2000), gardening (Civil, 2005), and everyday language use (Ball, 1992, 1995; Heath, 1983; Lee, 1993). Several studies have pointed

to the context-specificity of the skills and knowledge learned in informal settings (Cole et al., 1971; Lave, 1988). Often, people can competently perform complex cognitive tasks outside of school, but may not display these skills on school-type tasks. This finding indicates the importance of understanding the nature of learning in out-of-school settings, and how to build on this learning to support learning in school.

As we discuss selected studies of successful out-of-school learning environments, we argue that scaffolding plays a critical role in the development of adaptive expertise. Scaffolding involves (1) organizing participation in activities in ways that address basic human needs for a sense of safety as well as belonging; (2) making the structure of the domain visible and socializing participants for dispositions and habits of mind necessary for expert-like practice; (3) helping novices understand possible trajectories for competence as well as the relevance of the domain to the learners; and (4) providing timely and flexible feedback.

Participation that Addresses Basic Needs

A key part of scaffolding in out-of-school learning involves organizing participation in ways that address basic human needs for safety, belonging and identification, self-esteem and respect (Maslow, 1962). The need for safety (both physical and psychological) is central to the creation of a learning environment. Although it seems fairly obvious that learning requires a sense of physical safety, psychological safety is less often acknowledged. Psychological safety can be defined as a sense of comfort, willingness to take risks and be oneself, and a feeling of acceptance. Steele's work documenting stereotype threat demonstrates the profound influence that a *lack* of psychological safety has on learning (Steele, 1997). This work has demonstrated that when the climate was psychologically unsafe (i.e., African American students were made to think that their performance on a test was diagnostic, triggering fears of fitting into a stereotype about their race), performance suffered. In other learning settings, including community-based programs for youth (Heath & McLaughlin, 1993; Rosenfeld, 2005), adult organizers recognized the importance of creating safe spaces for activity.

Successful learning contexts also attend to students' need for a sense of belonging and identification (Hirsch, 2005). This occurs through both the organization of the practice itself and through the social interaction that occurs within these contexts. For instance, in a study of high school track and field (Nasir, Cooks, & Coffey, 2005), this sense of belonging was explicitly attended to by the coaches, such that they viewed a sense of belonging to the team as an important outcome. The athletes discussed this feeling of belonging and identification as one reason they persisted in the sport, and they continued to work to improve their performance, even through difficult races.

Making Visible the Structure of the Domain

Effective out-of-school settings also make visible a deep structural knowledge of the domain. For example, in dominoes (Nasir, 2002), not only do more expert players make their thinking about game strategies (involving multiplication and probability) available to novices, but they do this in a developmental fashion; that is, as players become more skillful, they are given feedback that pushes them to the next level of understanding the game. Language practices are critical to this scaffolding, because it is through language that novices are given access to the structure of the domain.

Language practices also play an important role in the Investigators Club (I-Club), an after-school science program for middle school students who are not experiencing academic success in school (Sohmer & Michaels, 2005). In I-Club, dynamic metaphors that bridge actual situations in the world and scientific concepts are used to scaffold student investigators

toward scientific discourses. Participants also talk about talk, that is, how scientific talk differs from everyday talk. In these ways, I-Club practices help make visible to participants how particular scientific discourses work.

A number of studies have documented the literacy practices that are embedded in a variety of out-of-school settings, including church (Baquedano-Lopez, 1997), blue collar work settings (Rose, 2004), sports (Mahiri, 1998), and the arts (Ball, 1995). Fisher (2003) documented how a number of nontraditional community-based organizations create multigenerational spaces where African American and Latino/a adolescents gather to create written and oral poetry called "spoken word" (see also Morgan, 2002). In spoken word communities, as in domino communities, public discussions of criteria for quality writing or play are routine.

Trajectories for Competence

Providing novices a clear view of more expert practice is another form of scaffolding. This allows newcomers to see how experts participate and provides them with a sense of possible learning trajectories. This form of scaffolding has been observed across many kinds of practice. This research has documented how novices work in apprentice roles while performing tasks in conjunction with experts. Rogoff (2003) has described such learning as "intent participation," highlighting the ways participants learn by observing the flow of an activity. Within after-school environments such as I-Club and the Computer Clubhouse at the Museum of Science in Boston, youth also have access to each others' experience and practice. At the Computer Clubhouse, youth work closely with one another and with support and inspiration from adult mentors to learn to use leading-edge software to create their own artwork, animations, simulations, multimedia presentations, virtual worlds, musical creations, Web sites, and robotic constructions (Resnick & Rusk, 1996).

Timely and Flexible Feedback

Timely and flexible feedback takes many forms in out-of-school practices and often involves evaluation and on-the-spot correction. In candy-selling among Brazilian children, evaluation and correction occur when sellers are pricing candy, or when they are counting their profits. Saxe (1991) described sellers who correct the pricing conventions of others during the course of activity. In dominoes (Nasir 2000; 2005), not only does correction occur in the midst of game play (usually with more competent players advising and correcting less sophisticated players), but evaluation is a part of the regular game structure in the form of a post-game analysis, where players discuss the strengths and weaknesses of the plays in the previous round of the game. In track, a similar process occurs between the coach and the runners (Nasir et al., 2005). After each race the coach and runner deconstruct each leg together – evaluating performance, techniques, and setting goals for the next race. This focus on evaluation and correction is a formative and routine part of the practice, rather than an assessment to judge one's competence or worthiness.

It is important to note that these four features are often coordinated, and this coordination can be very powerful for learning. Such coordination is evident in 5th Dimension afterschool clubs (Nicolopoulou & Cole, 1993) where youth have access to a variety of resources to support their developing expertise with computer games, including college-age tutors, peers, information cards, and the now famous virtual wizard to whom youth and adults can write for advice. In addition, Gutierrez et al. (1999) asserted that the participation structure of play invites engagement, and – in conjunction with multiple forms and layers of support – facilitates persistence and identification of personal goals. Whereas we have focused on out-of-school settings, the forms of scaffolding that we have highlighted may also be enacted in school learning settings.

Question 2: In What Specific Ways Do These Varied Repertoires of Practice Connect with Academic Disciplinary Practices?

In this section, we examine research that explores intersections between everyday practices and important disciplinary knowledge. This work expands what we know about both everyday practice and disciplinary practice, and fundamentally entails rethinking what counts as disciplinary practice. We believe that educators can use the varied and productive resources youth develop in their out-of-school lives to help them understand content-related ideas.

Intersections with Science

The following vignette (described in greater detail in Ballenger, 2003), illustrates differences in students' sense-making practices in elementary school science.

While discussing the question, "Do plants grow everyday?", third grade children in a two-way Spanish-English bilingual program debated the pattern of growth and whether you can see it. One girl, Serena, the child of highly educated parents who was considered an excellent student, approached these matters from a stance outside the phenomenon, through the logic of measurement. She argued that growth can be seen through the evidence of measurement on a chart of a plant's daily growth. Another girl, Elena, approached the question differently. The child of immigrant, working class parents, Elena was repeating third grade. She took up the question of how one can see a plant's growth by imagining her own growth through "the crinkly feeling" she has when her feet are starting to outgrow her socks.

This vignette illustrates two important scientific practices, one commonly recognized and one not. Serena's approach is valued in the classroom; it conforms to widely held conceptions of scientific reasoning. While undoubtedly important, it represents one tool in what ought to be a wide-ranging repertoire of sense-making practices in science. In contrast, Elena's approach is undervalued, sometimes even dismissed by teachers and researchers as confused, which can have profound implications for her learning and sense of herself as a thinker. In fact, Elena's move to imagine her own growth and, through this, the growth of a plant, reflects scientific practice. Scientists regularly use visual and narrative resources to place themselves inside physical events and processes in order to explore how these may behave (Keller, 1983; Ochs, Jacoby, & Gonzales, 1996; Wolpert & Richards, 1997).

Studies of scientific practice have described the fundamental heterogeneity of science-in-action as an intricate intertwining of conceptual, imaginative, material, discursive, symbolic, emotional, and experiential resources (Biagioli, 1999; Galison, 1997). These analyses of the everyday work of scientists challenge a stereotype of science as largely hypotheticodeductive in nature, discontinuous with everyday experience of the physical world, and represented in thinking practices distinct from those used to make sense of everyday life. Dominant understandings like these have shaped traditional science education in ways that privilege certain ways of displaying understanding (e.g., Serena's) over others (e.g., Elena's).

Classroom-based studies have documented intersections between the sense-making practices of scientists and those of youth from nondominant groups. One result is an expanded view of what counts as scientific thinking and activity – including, among other things, use of embodied imagining (as noted above), argumentation, and metaphor for the purposes of theorizing and knowledge-building. Let us look at argumentation as one example.

In *Laboratory Life*, Latour and Woolgar (1986) argued that scientists transform their observations into findings through argumentation and persuasion, rather than through measurement and discovery. They portrayed the activity of laboratory scientists as a constant struggle for the generation and acceptance of fact-like statements. Similarly, researchers working in bilingual classroom settings found that Haitian youth use a common Haitian discourse practice, *bay odyans*, to argue claims and evidence in biology and physics (Hudicourt-Barnes, 2003). *Bay odyans* takes several forms, one of which is argument. In everyday life, this form of *bay odyans* centers around religion, soccer, or politics; is highly animated; and can seem like a fight to outsiders. But to participants, this is a form of theatre in which one speaker asserts a claim, which is then immediately challenged by others. Participants express, defend, and dispute divergent points of view with evidence or logic, often forcing one another to narrow their claims, in a manner similar to disagreement sequences documented by Lynch (1985) in studies of professional scientific activity. *Bay odyans* has been shown to support students' learning in science by helping students specify meanings for crucial terms, explore potential explanatory models, and develop norms of scientific accountability (Ballenger, 1997; Warren & Rosebery, 1996). Other studies have documented how practices of narrative sequencing and metaphor are used by youth from nondominant groups to express arguments and explanations in science (Gee & Clinton, 2000; Warren, Ogonowski, & Pothier, 2005). Although these discourse practices look and sound different from those valued in school science, they connect no less deeply with discourse practices routinely used in scientific communities.

Intersections with Literacy

Historically, the language of so-called nonmainstream dialect speakers (such as African American English [AAE] or Appalachian English) and of English language learners has been positioned as inadequate when compared to academic forms of learning. However, much research indicates that nonmainstream dialects are complex in their own right with features relevant to learning academic reading and writing. For example, Gee (1989) documented complex literary features of what Michaels (1981) called an AAE topic associative narrative style. Ball (1995) illustrated preferred expository patterns among African American adolescents reflecting rhetorically powerful patterns used by great African American orators, but not typically taught in high schools. Lee (Lee et al., 1999) scaffolded everyday knowledge of narrative conventions among child AAE speakers to produce high quality written narratives. These everyday conventions include what Smitherman (1977) called the African American Rhetorical Tradition as well as event scripts from African American cultural life. Smitherman (2000) conducted post hoc analyses of African American writing samples from the 1984 and 1988/1989 National Assessment of Educational Progress (NAEP) writing assessments. She found these African American rhetorical features were highly correlated with high quality of writing as determined by NAEP examiners.

Other studies document how bilingual speakers use competencies in their first language in reading, writing and speaking in a second language, at the level of vocabulary, syntax, and discourse (Garcia, 2000; Jimenez, Garcia, & Pearson, 1996; Langer et al., 1990; Moll & González, 2004). Literacy in the first language can scaffold reading and writing in the second, particularly with respect to content area learning, making technical distinctions in science (Warren et al., 2001), and reasoning in mathematics (Moschkovich, 1999). Others (Orellana et al., 2003; Valdes, 2002) have documented the metalinguistic competencies of bilingual youth who translate for their parents in consequential settings, including adapting speech registers to the setting, comprehending complex technical texts, and managing complex power relations.

Intersections with Mathematics

In mathematics, studies have shown how sophisticated mathematical thinking has occurred across multiple repertoires of practice for nondominant students. For instance, Nasir (2000) showed how African American high school basketball players learned concepts of average and percent as a part of calculating their own and others' game statistics. Other work has documented how Latino students work with principles of spacing and geometric design in the context of sewing and gardening with their families (Civil, 2005; Moll & González, 2004) as well as how families involve adolescents in budgeting practices and using standard algorithms to find batting averages (Goldman, 2001). Research on younger children has documented Brazilian and African American students' participation in buying (Taylor, 2004) and selling (Saxe, 1991) activities.

This work is striking because the participants rarely view what they are doing as mathematics and often claim to be very poor at math. This poses a challenge for teachers and researchers: how do researchers, teachers, and participants learn to see the math in what they are doing? On one hand, recognizing mathematics is simple, if we view math as calculations. However, this becomes more difficult when we are dealing with more sophisticated mathematics, such as geometry or probabilistic thinking. Furthermore, even when the mathematics involves simple calculations, in practices outside of school such problems are often solved by estimating. Estimating strategies can result in a deeper understanding of mathematical relationships even as they fail to yield precise mathematical answers of the sort valued in school.

Our point here is that in order to see robust, authentic connections between the everyday knowledge and practices of youth from nondominant groups and those of academic disciplines, we must look beyond the typical connections made in school curricula and identify important continuities of practice. By identifying and then using practices such as imagining, *bay odyans*, or AAE discursive forms, we not only create spaces in which students can participate in academic disciplinary practices, but we also put ourselves in a position to better understand the role such practices play in learning (Lee, 1993, 1995; Rosebery et al., 2005; Warren et al., 2001).

Question 3: In What Ways Can These Varied Repertoires of Practice be Recruited to Create Meaningful Opportunities for Academic Learning for All Students? What Principles of Design Emerge from This Expanded Inquiry into Learning?

Learning to see heterogeneous – and often unfamiliar – meaning-making practices as being intellectually related to those in academic domains entails two related moves: expanding conventional views of these domains and deepening understanding of the intellectual power inherent in varied discursive and reasoning practices that youth from nondominant groups bring to school. To do this, teachers and researchers must work continually to make sense of youth's varied ideas, ways with words, and experiences (Lee, 2001; Ballenger & Rosebery, 2003; Warren et al., 2001), coming to grips with the limiting assumptions of one's own knowledge, perspectives and values with regard to academic discourses, learning and teaching, language, culture, and race (Ball, 2000; Ballenger, 1999; Foster, 1997; Ladson-Billings, 2001; Lee, 2005; Rosebery & Warren, in press).

To take up the intellectual resources embedded in youth's everyday practices requires us to reorganize school practices in ways that actually make explicit the linkages between everyday and school-based knowledge and discourse. This act of design requires principles for

1. making the structure of the domain visible;
2. engaging youth in actively populating academic discourses with meaning and intention, through participation structures that create roles and relationships through which youth can identify with the practices of the domain;
3. structuring occasions for metalevel analysis (e.g., talk about thinking and language) that help youth see relationships between usually tacit everyday knowledge and discourse and academic knowledge and discourse.

Such design work also requires that researchers, curriculum designers, and teachers recognize that learning in academic disciplines includes more than mastery of a body of conceptual knowledge. Crucially, it also involves critical engagement with epistemological assumptions, points of view, values, and dispositions (Collins & Ferguson, 1993; Lee, 2001; Perkins, 1992; Warren et al., 2005). It also brings to the forefront the many issues of affect and emotion that attend academic risk-taking, especially for youth who have not experienced academic success in school (Heath, 2004).

A number of school-based interventions have taken up these design challenges. These include the Algebra Project (Moses & Cobb, 2001), Chèche Konnen (Conant et al., 2001; Rosebery, 2005; Warren et al., 2001, 2005), the Cultural Modeling Project (Lee, 1993, 1995, 2001), the Funds of Knowledge Project (González, Amanti, & Moll, in press), the Kamehameha Early Education Project (Au, 1980; Tharp & Gallimore, 1988), the Migrant Student Summer Program at UCLA (Gutierrez, 2005), and the Talent Development Project at Howard University (Boykin, 2000; Boykin & Bailey, 2000), among others. We discuss three of these as an illustration of attempts to design the kinds of classrooms that support deep learning of important disciplinary ideas and practices for nondominant students.

Cultural Modeling (Lee, 1993, 1995, 2001, 2003a; Lee & Majors, 2005) is a framework for the design of learning environments that leverage knowledge constructed out of everyday experience to support subject matter learning. Studies in Cultural Modeling have focused on literature and narrative writing with African American youth (Lee et al., 1999). In this work, a detailed analysis of the structure of these domains determined the cultural practices and forms of everyday knowledge that would provide the most leverage. Types of generative problems, strategies, and general heuristics for identifying and tackling such problems and necessary habits of mind or intellective dispositions were identified. This called for a different orientation to the idea of genre in literature, and to the genre's usefulness in helping novice readers make sense of texts. Interpretive problems such as symbolism, irony, satire, and use of unreliable narration were identified as crucial for literary readings across national and other traditions. All of these interpretive tasks require an ability to deal with problems of figuration and often require analogical reasoning. For example, Lee found that AAE speakers' knowledge of *signifying* (Mitchell-Kernan, 1981; Smitherman, 1977) – a form of ritual insult requiring analogical reasoning, appreciation of language play, and comprehension of figurative language – could be leveraged effectively to teach literary reasoning.

The following vignette illustrates such design principles at work:

> *Beginning a literature unit on symbolism, a class of African American high school students critique the Hip Hop lyrics "The Mask" by The Fugees. Jonetha offers this explication of the second stanza: "I'm saying I think he had a mask on when he was fighting, when he beat him up, because in order for him to have the mask on – he was spying on that person. He was spying on somebody. I don't know who he was spying on. But in order for him to realize that the man was spying on him, he had to take off his mask. In order to realize that the man was saying . . . I don't know – shoot. (laughter from class). I'm saying that the man, in order for him to realize that the other man was spying on him, that he had to take off his mask." (Lee, 2005b)*

In this example, design principles involved using rap lyrics (see also Mahiri, 2000/01; Morrell, 2002) as what Lee called "cultural data sets" where students make public how they understand that the mask is not literal, but symbolic. They went on to apply what are now public (through class discussion) strategies for interpreting symbolism to the analysis of the canonical text *Beloved* by Toni Morrison. Jonetha's explication demonstrated analogical reasoning, appreciation of language play, close textual analysis without direct instruction from the teacher, and intellectual risk-taking.

By drawing on models of competence students already have (for example, knowing the features that distinguish a good rap

from a bad one, recognizing when a signifying retort is not sufficiently creative, missing the tenor of the previous metaphor), the talk that surrounds these cultural data sets privileges reflection about the structure of particular problems in the domain, strategies for tackling such problems, criteria for evaluating the goodness of fit of explanations – in short, for making the practices of the domain public and the trajectories for competence within it visible. The examination of such cultural data sets provides models of generative domain problems rooted in everyday experience that facilitate analogical reasoning, a powerful problem solving strategy used both by novices and historically used by scientists and mathematicians at the edges of new discoveries. From a design perspective, the challenge is to locate analogies that are sufficiently rooted in students' everyday experiences to bring both relevant knowledge and interest to the task, and that connect to crucial features of the target learning. Second, the relationship between teacher and students is fundamentally restructured when the discussion is about texts that students know a lot about. This reorganization of relationships between experts and novices – in Lee's study, students and teachers are both functioning simultaneously as expert and novice – facilitates a sense of identification with the practice, and as a consequence a greater sense of belonging to a community of learners.

Chèche Konnen Center teachers and researchers have developed an inquiry practice they call *Science Workshop* (Warren & Rosebery, 2004). Science Workshop is designed to engage children in exploring possible meanings and functions of their own and others' diverse "ways with words" in the science classroom. It explicitly features language as an object of inquiry, by focusing students' attention on a repertoire of discursive practices broader than that typically featured in school science and more representative of the practices that children from nondominant groups bring to the classroom. In Science Workshop, the potential meanings and functions of varied ways with words – whether those of child, a scientist or a text – are explored. For example, while discussing possible titles for a student-made mural depicting the life cycle of a pumpkin plant, a second grade African American boy felt a need to enlarge the scope of the discussion (described in greater detail in Warren & Rosebery, 2004). Drawing on metaphoric practices known to be prevalent within African American discourse communities, he likened the life cycle of pumpkin seeds to a spider, "because when the mom dies it lays eggs before it dies." Later, as the class probed his analogy, they made visible various relationships implied in it (e.g., the pumpkin forms seeds before it rots just as a spider lays eggs before it dies). This kind of expansive inquiry into possible meaning for diverse ways of conceptualizing, representing and evaluating scientific phenomena has several effects. First, it takes children deeper into the scientific terrain (e.g., in what ways are eggs and seeds alike or different and how does each gives rise to new life?). Second, it engages them with varied ways with words, which they explore as tools for their own thinking. Third, by positioning learners as analysts of their own and others' ways with words, it engages them in thinking through both the affordances and limits of ways with words (e.g., what does this analogy *not* explain?), which helps make explicit how such practices function as meaning-making tools in the sciences. Finally, as in Cultural Modeling, talk in Science Workshop is hybrid – combining serious analytic work and playful engagement with language and other symbol systems (e.g., models, tables, graphs). To help students build a sense of the structure of and ways of knowing in academic science, teachers need to have respect for and to pay explicit attention to: the heterogeneity of students' thinking and discourse and that of scientific disciplines; the construction of a community of learners; and their own scaffolding.

The Algebra Project (AP) is another intervention that takes up the design challenges we have identified. Operating in twenty-eight cities and serving ten thousand children annually, the AP includes curriculum,

professional development, and an out-of-school organization – the Young People's Project – in which youth actively assume the banner of mathematics as the civil right of the twenty-first century. Dr. Robert Moses, founder of the AP, identified the conceptual shift from arithmetic to algebraic thinking as a major stumbling block to higher mathematics. He asked what in the everyday practices of urban adolescents, particularly African American youth, embodied mathematical problems such as displacement and equivalence. He came up with travel on an urban transit system as an anchor for examining such problems. The AP has since developed units on ratio and proportion – one of which uses African drumming traditions. In linking mathematics learning and social justice (Brantlinger, in preparation; Gutierrez, 2002; Gutstein, 2003; Tate, 1995), the AP explicitly engages important developmental relationships between youth and adults both within and outside the school community. Related to many of our earlier examples, the AP takes seriously the challenges of translating from students' everyday language to the symbolic inscriptions that characterize the discourse of mathematics. Similar to Cultural Modeling and Chèche Konnen, the AP supports an understanding of mathematics that is rooted in the everyday cultural practices of students. In doing so, students are positioned as competent members of both their home communities and the academic community of "doers of mathematics."

Concluding Remarks

We have argued that culture and diversity are not external to understanding fundamental processes of learning, but rather that to understand learning it is crucial to view it as a cultural process of engagement in repertoires of practices (Gutiérrez & Rogoff, 2003; Lee, 2005a; Rogoff, 2003). In doing so, we move toward transforming "diversity" into a pedagogical asset, rather than a problem to be solved (Gutiérrez et al., 2000; Warren et al., 2001). This is particularly important in rethinking how we view and address issues of race, culture, ethnicity, class, and gender in the learning sciences. Our perspective encompasses much more than a naïve notion that all types of diversity matter, and we are not simply arguing that prior knowledge matters. Rather, we contend that particular configurations of race, ethnicity, and class require that youth wrestle with pervasive challenges (Spencer, 1999) and that designing learning environments for these students must address multiple (and often neglected) elements of learning, including identity and affect.

This argument has important implications both for the practice of designing learning environments and for the development of learning theory. With regard to practice, the perspective that we describe argues for a radical restructuring of the way we organize learning in school and of the assumptions that we make about learners and relevant knowledge. The restructuring involves, on the one hand, changing our collective understanding of the routine language and social practices of daily life and their relation to the practices of academic disciplines, and on the other hand, designing classrooms to accommodate the myriad pathways along which learning can proceed. With regard to theory, we put forth the assertion that learning is a cultural process for *everyone* regardless of racial or ethnic group membership, class, or gender. Moreover, we view learning not merely as a cognitive process, but as intertwined with multiple aspects of development – including identity and emotion. This lens on learning requires the research community to ask a broader and deeper set of questions about what learning looks like and how it can best be supported.

Our hope is that this chapter will contribute to moving discussions of equity and diversity in the learning sciences away from a sole focus on increasing the numbers of nondominant students who "survive" school, and towards a concern with how we can draw on multiple repertoires of practice in schools to better support learning of core academic disciplines and learners' basic needs for belonging and identification. Moving toward equity will occur as we create learning environments that connect in deep ways to the life experiences of all students. Fundamental to this perspective is the view that in the end, equity is not about offering or producing sameness, but about enabling youth to appropriate the repertoires they need in order to live the richest life possible and reach their full academic potential.

A Note About Authorship

Na'ilah Suad Nasir served as lead author in organizing this chapter. All authors have made equal contributions to its content.

References

Au, K. (1980). Participation structures in a reading lesson with Hawaiian children: Analysis of a culturally appropriate instructional event. *Anthropology Education Quarterly, 11*(2), 91–115.

Bakhtin, M. M. (1981). *The dialogic imagination: Four essays.* Austin: University of Texas Press.

Ball, A. F. (1992). Cultural preferences and the expository writing of African-American adolescents. *Written Communication, 9*(4), 501–532.

Ball, A. F. (1995). Community based learning in an urban setting as a model for educational reform. *Applied Behavioral Science Review, 3*, 127–146.

Ball, A. (2000). Teachers developing philosophies in literacy and their use in urban schools. In C. D. Lee & P. Smagorinsky (Eds.), *Vygotskian perspectives on literacy research: Constructing meaning through collaborative inquiry.* New York: Cambridge University Press.

Ballenger, C. (1997). Social identities, moral narratives, scientific argumentation: Science talk in a bilingual classroom. *Language and Education, 11*(1), 1–14.

Ballenger, C. (1999). *Teaching other people's children: literacy and learning in a bilingual classroom.* New York: Teachers College.

Ballenger, C. (2003). The puzzling child: Challenging assumptions about participation and meaning in talking science. *Language Arts*, 81(4), pp. 303–311.

Ballenger, C., & Rosebery, A. (2003). What counts as teacher research? Continuing the conversation. *Teachers College Record*, 105(2), 297–314.

Baquedano-Lopez, P. (1997). Creating social identities through Doctrina narratives. *Issues in Applied Linguistics*, 8(1), 27–45.

Biagioli, M. (1999). Aporias of scientific authorship: credit and responsibility in contemporary biomedicine. In M. Biagioli (Ed.). *The science studies reader*. New York: Routledge.

Boykin, A. W. (2000). The talent development model of schooling: Placing students at promise for academic success. *Journal of Education for Students Placed At Risk*, 5, 3–25.

Boykin, A. W., & Bailey, C. (2000). *Experimental research on the role of cultural factors in school relevant cognitive functioning: Synthesis of findings on cultural contexts, cultural operations and individual differences*. (Center for Research on the Education of Students Placed At Risk (CRESPAR) Technical Report #42 ed.). Washington, DC, and Baltimore, MD: Howard University and John Hopkins University.

Brantlinger, A. (in preparation). *Designing and Implementing a Socially Relevant Geometry Curriculum: The Complications of Teaching Math for Social Justice*. Unpublished doctoral dissertation: Northwestern University.

Burton, L., Allison, K., & Obeidallah, D. (1995). Social context and adolescents: Perspectives on development among inner-city African-American teens. In L. Crockett & A. Crouter (Eds.), *Pathways through adolescence: Individual development in social contexts* (pp. 119–138). Hillsdale, NJ: Lawrence Erlbaum Associates.

Civil, M. (2005, October). *Building on Community Knowledge: Challenges and Possibilities for Mathematics Education*. Talk presented at Investigations in Number, Data, and Space, Boston, MA.

Cole, M. (1996). *Cultural psychology, A once and future discipline*. Cambridge, MA: The Belknap Press of Harvard University Press.

Cole, M., Gay, J., Glick, J., & Sharp, D. (1971). *The cultural context of learning and thinking*. New York: Basic Books.

Collins, A., & Ferguson, W. (1993). Epistemic forms and epistemic games: Structures and strategies to guide inquiry. *Educational Psychologist*, 28(1), 25–42.

Conant, F., Rosebery, A., Warren, B., & Hudicourt-Barnes, J. (2001). The sound of drums. In E. McIntyre, A. Rosebery, and N. González, (Eds.), *Classroom diversity: Connecting curriculum to students' lives*, pp 51–60. Portsmouth: Heinemann.

Erickson, F. (2002). Culture and human development. *Human Development*, 45(4), 299–306.

Fisher, M. T. (2003). Open mics and Open minds: Spoken word poetry in African diaspora participatory literacy communities. *Harvard Education Review*, 73(3), 362–389.

Foster, M. (1997). *Black teachers on teaching*. New York: The New Press.

Galison, P. (1997). *Image and logic: A material culture of microphysics*. Chicago: University of Chicago Press.

Garcia, G. E. (2000). Bilingual children's reading. In M. Kamil, P. Mosenthal, P. D. Pearson, & R. Barr (Eds.), *Handbook of reading research* (Vol. 3, pp. 813–834). Mahwah, NJ: Lawrence Erlbaum Associates.

Gee, J. P. (1989). The narrativization of experience in the oral style. *Journal of Education*, 171(1), 75–96.

Gee, J. P. (1990). *Social linguistics and literacies: Ideology in discourses*. London: Falmer.

Gee, J. P., & Clinton, K. (2000). An African-American child's "science talk": Co-construction of meaning from the perspective of multiple discourses. In M. Gallego & S. Hollingsworth (Eds.), *What counts as literacy: Challenging the school standard* (pp. 118–135). New York: Teachers College Press.

Goldman, S. (2001). *Factoring families into math success*. Unpublished manuscript.

González, N. (2004) Disciplining the discipline: Anthropology and the pursuit of quality education. *Educational Researcher*, 33(5), 17–25.

González, N., Amanti, C., & Moll, L. (in press). About culture: Using students' lived experience to build curriculum. In A. Rosebery & B. Warren (Eds.). *Teaching science to English language learners*. Washington, DC: National Science Foundation.

Gutiérrez, R. (2002). Enabling the practice of mathematics teachers in context: Toward a new equity research agenda. *Mathematical Thinking and Learning*, 4, 145–187.

Gutierrez, K. (2005, April). *Intersubjectivity and grammar in the third space*. Talk presented at the annual meeting of the American Educational Research Association.

Gutierrez, K., Baquedano-Lopez, P., Alvarez, H., & Chiu, M. (1999). Building a culture of collaborating through hybrid language practices. *Theory into Practice*, 38(2), 87–95.

Gutiérrez, K. D., Baquedano-López, P., & Tejada, C. (2000). Rethinking diversity: Hybridity and hybrid language practices in the third space. *Mind, Culture, and Activity*, 6, 286–303.

Gutiérrez, K., & Rogoff, B. (2003). Cultural ways of learning: Individual traits or repertoires of practice. *Educational Researcher*, 32(5), 19–25.

Gutstein, E. (2003). Teaching and learning mathematic for social justice in an urban, Latino school. *Journal for Research in Mathematics Education*, 34, 37–73.

Hatano, G., & Inagaki, K. (1986). Two courses of expertise. In H. W. Stevenson, H. Azuma, & Hakuta (Eds.), *Child development and education in Japan* (pp. 262–172). New York: Freeman.

Heath, S. B. (1983). *Ways with words: Language, life, and work in communities and classrooms*. Cambridge: Cambridge University Press.

Heath, S. B. (2004). Risks, rules, and roles: Youth perspectives on the work of learning for community development. In A. N. Perret-Clemont, C. Pontecorvo, L. B. Resnick, T. Zittoun, & B. Burge (Eds.), *Joining society: Social interaction and learning in adolescence and youth* (pp. 41–70). New York: Cambridge University Press.

Heath, S. B., & McLaughlin, M. (1993). *Identity and inner-city Youth*. New York: Teachers' College.

Hirsch, B. (2005). *A place to call home: After-school programs for urban youth*. New York: Teachers College Press.

Hudicourt-Barnes, J. (2003). The use of argumentation in Hatian Creole science classrooms. *Harvard Educational Review*, 73(1), 73–93.

Jimenez, R. T., Garcia, G. E., & Pearson, P. D. (1996). The reading strategies of Latina/o students who are successful English readers: Opportunities and obstacles. *Reading Research Quarterly*, 31(1), 90–112.

Keller, E. F. (1983). *A feeling for the organism: The life and work of Barbara McClintock*. New York: W. H. Freeman.

Ladson-Billings, G. (2001). *Crossing over to Canaan: The journey of new teachers in diverse classrooms*. San Francisco, CA: Jossey-Bass.

Langer, J., Bartolome, L., Vasquez, O., & Lucas, T. (1990). Meaning construction in school literacy tasks: A study of bilingual students. *American Educational Research Journal*, 27(3), 427–471.

Latour, B., & Woolgar, S. (1986). *Laboratory life: The social construction of scientific facts. 2nd Ed.* Princeton: Princeton University Press.

Lave, J. (1988). *Cognition in practice*. New York: Cambridge.

Lee, C. D. (1993). *Signifying as a scaffold for literary interpretation: The pedagogical implications of an African American discourse genre*. Urbana, IL: National Council of Teachers of English.

Lee, C. D. (1995). A culturally based cognitive apprenticeship: Teaching African American high school students' skills in literary interpretation. *Reading Research Quarterly*, 30(4), 608–631.

Lee, C. D. (2001). Is October Brown Chinese: A cultural modeling activity system for underachieving students. *American Educational Research Journal*, 38(1), 97–142.

Lee, C. D. (2003a). Cultural modeling: CHAT as a lens for understanding instructional discourse based on African American English discourse patterns. In A. Kozulin, B. Gindis, V. Ageyev, & S. Miller (Eds.), *Vygotsky's educational theory in cultural context* (pp. 393–410). New York: Cambridge University Press.

Lee, C. D. (2003b). Why we need to re-think race and ethnicity in educational research. *Educational Researcher*, 32(5), 3–5.

Lee, C. D. (2005). Double voiced discourse: African American vernacular English as resource in cultural modeling classrooms. In A. Ball & S. W. Freedman (Eds.), *New literacies for new times: Bakhtinian perspectives on language, literacy, and learning for the 21st century* (pp. 129–147). NY: Cambridge University Press.

Lee, C. D. (2005a). Intervention research based on current views of cognition & learning. In J. King (Ed.), *Black education: A transformative research and action agenda for the new century* (pp. 73–114). Mahwah, NJ: Lawrence Erlbaum (joint publication with the American Educational Research Association).

Lee, C. D. (2005b). The state of knowledge about the education of african americans. In

J. King (Ed.), *Black education: A transformative research and action agenda for the new century* (pp. 45–72). Mahwah, NJ: Lawrence Erlbaum (joint publication with the American Educational Research Association).

Lee, C. D., & Majors, Y. J. (2005). *Cultural modeling's response to Rogoff's challenge: Understanding apprenticeship, guided participation and participatory appropriation in a culturally responsive, subject matter specific context.* Unpublished manuscript.

Lee, C. D., Mendenhall, R., Rivers, A., & Tynes, B. (1999). *Cultural modeling: A framework for scaffolding oral narrative repertoires for academic narrative writing:* Paper presented at the Multicultural Narrative Analysis Conference at the University of South Florida.

Lee, C. D., Spencer, M. B., & Harpalani, V. (2003). Every shut eye ain't sleep: Studying how people live culturally. *Educational Researcher, 32*(5), 6–13.

Lynch, M. (1985). *Art and artifact in laboratory science: A study of shop work and shop talk in a research laboratory.* Boston: Routledge and Kegan Paul.

Mahiri, J. (1998). *Shooting for excellence: African American and youth culture in new century schools.* New York: Teachers College Press and National Council of Teachers of English.

Mahiri, J. (2000/2001). Pop culture pedagogy and the end(s) of school. *Journal of Adolescent & Adult Literacy, 44*(4), 382–386.

Majors, Y. (2003). Shoptalk: Teaching and learning in an African American hair salon. *Mind, Culture and Activity, 10*(4), 289–310.

Masingila, J. (1994). Mathematics practice in carpet laying. *Anthropology & Education Quarterly, 25*(4), 430–462.

Maslow, A. (1962). *Toward a psychology of being.* Princeton, NJ: Von Nostrand.

Michaels, S. (1981). "Sharing time," Children's narrative styles and differential access to literacy. *Language in Society, 10,* 423–442.

Mitchell-Kernan, C. (1981). Signifying, loud-talking and marking. In A. Dundes (Ed.), *Mother wit from the laughing barrel* (pp. 310–328). Englewood, Cliffs, NJ: Prentice Hall.

Moll, L. (2000). Inspired by Vygotsky: Ethnographic experiments in education. In C. D. Lee & P. Smagorinsky (Eds.), *Vygotskian perspectives on literacy research: Constructing meaning through collaborative inquiry* (pp. 256–268). Cambridge: Cambridge University Press.

Moll, L., & González, N. (2004). Engaging life: a funds of knowledge approach to multicultural education. In J. Banks & C. McGee Banks (Eds.). *Handbook of research on multicultural education (2nd edition)*, pp. 699–715. New York: Jossey-Bass.

Morgan, M. (2002). *Language, discourse and power in African American culture.* New York: Cambridge University Press.

Morrell, E. (2002). Toward a critical pedagogy of popular culture: Literacy development among urban youth. *Journal of Adolescent & Adult Literacy, 46*(1), 72–78.

Moschkovich, J. N. (1999) Supporting the participation of English language learners in mathematical discussions. *For the Learning of Mathematics, 19*(1), 11–19.

Moses, R. P., & Cobb, C. E. (2001). *Radical equations: Math literacy and civil rights.* Boston: Beacon Press.

Nasir, N. (2000). "Points Ain't Everything": Emergent goals and average and percent understandings in the play of basketball among African-American students. *Anthropology and Education Quarterly, 31*(3), 283–305.

Nasir, N. (2002). Identity, goals, and learning: Mathematics in cultural practice. In N. Nasir & P. Cobb (Eds.) *Mathematical thinking and learning*, Special issue on Diversity, Equity, and Mathematics Learning, vol. 4 (nos. 2 & 3), 211–247.

Nasir, N. (2005). Individual cognitive structuring and the sociocultural context: Strategy shifts in the game of dominoes. *Journal of the Learning Sciences, 14,* 5–34.

Nasir, N., Cooks, J., & Coffey, J. (2005). *Track literacy: Becoming a runner and learning to run.* Unpublished manuscript.

Nasir, N., & Stone, L. (2003). *"Mo' money, no problem": Learning to talk and play dominoes.* Unpublished manuscript, Stanford University.

Nicolopoulou, A., & Cole, M. (1993). Generation and transmission of shared knowledge in the culture of collaborative learning: The Fifth Dimension, its play-world, and its institutional contexts. In E. Forman, N. Minnick, & C. A. Stone (Eds.). *Contexts for learning: Sociocultural dynamics in children's development* (pp. 283–314). New York: Oxford University.

Ochs, E., Gonzales, P., & Jacoby, S. (1996). "When I come down I'm in the domain state":

Grammar and graphic representation in the interpretive activity of physicists. In E. Ochs, E. A. Schegloff, & S. A. Thompson (Eds.), *Interaction and grammar* (pp. 328–369). Cambridge: Cambridge University Press.

Orellana, M., Reynolds, J., Dorner, L., & Meza, M. (2003). In other words: Translating or "paraphrasing" as a family literacy practice in immigrant households. *Reading Research Quarterly*, 38(1), 12–34.

Perkins, D. (1992). *Smart schools: Better thinking and learning for every child*. New York: The Free Press.

Resnick, M., and Rusk, N. (1996). Access is not enough: Computer clubhouses in the inner city. *American Prospect*, 27, 60–68.

Rogoff, B. (2003). *The cultural nature of human development*. New York: Oxford University Press.

Rogoff, B., & Angelillo, C. (2002). Investigating the coordinated functioning of multifaceted cultural practices in human development. *Human Development*, 45(4), 211–225.

Rose, M. (2004). *The mind at work*. New York: Viking.

Rosebery, A. (2005). "What are we going to do next?" A case study of lesson planning. In R. Nemirovsky, A. Rosebery, B. Warren, B., & J. Solomon (Eds.), *Everyday matters in mathematics and science: Studies of complex classroom events* (pp. 299–328). Mahwah, NJ: Erlbaum Lawrence/Associates.

Rosebery, A., & Warren, B. (Eds.). (in press). *Teaching science to English language learners*. Washington, DC: The National Science Foundation.

Rosebery, A. Warren, B., Ballenger, C., & Ogonowski, M. (2005). The generative potential of students' everyday knowledge in learning science. In T. Romberg, T. Carpenter, & F. Dremock (Eds.). *Understanding mathematics and science matters* (pp. 55–80). Mahwah, NJ: Lawrence Erlbaum Associates.

Rosenfeld, E. (2005). *Telling, adapting, and performing personal stories: Understanding identity development and literacy learning for stigmatized youth*. Unpublished doctoral dissertation, Northwestern University.

Saxe, G. B. (1991). *Culture & cognitive development: Studies in mathematical understanding*. Hillsdale, NJ: Lawrence Erlbaum Associates.

Scribner, S. (1985). Knowledge at work. *Anthropology and Education Quarterly*, 16(3), 199–206.

Smitherman, G. (1977). *Talkin and testifyin: The language of Black America*. Boston: Houghton Mifflin.

Smitherman, G. (2000). African American student writers in the NAEP, 1969–1988/89 and "The Blacker the berry, the sweeter the juice." In G. Smitherman (Ed.), *Talkin that talk: Language, culture and education in African America* (pp. 163–194). New York: Routledge.

Sohmer, R., & Michaels, S. (2005). The "two puppies" story: The role of narrative in teaching and learning science. In U. Quasthoff & T. Becker, (Eds.). *Narrative interaction* (pp. 57–91). Philadelphia: John Benjamins Publishing Company.

Spencer, M. B. (1987). Black children's ethnic identity formation: Risk and resilience in caste-like minorities. In J. Phinney & M. Rotheram (Eds.), *Children's ethnic socialization: Pluralism and development* (pp. 103–116). Newbury Park, CA: Sage.

Spencer, M. B. (1999). Social and cultural influences on school adjustment: The application of an identity-focused cultural ecological perspective. *Educational Psychologist*, 34(1), 43–57.

Spiro, R., Feltovich, P. L., Jackson, M. J., & Coulson, R. L. (1991). Cognitive flexibility, constructivism, and hypertext: Random access instruction for advanced technology acquisition to ill-structured domains. *Educational Technology*, 31(5), 24–33.

Steele, C. M. (1997). A threat in the air: How stereotypes shape intellectual identity and performance. *American Psychologist*, 52, 613–629.

Tate, W. F. (1995). Returning to the root: A culturally relevant approach to mathematics pedagogy. *Theory into Practice*, 34, 166–173.

Taylor, E. (2004, April). *Low-income African-American second grade students' engagement in currency exchange: The relationship to mathematical development*. American Educational Research Association Annual Meeting, San Diego, CA.

Tharp, R., & Gallimore, R. (1988). *Rousing minds to life: teaching, learning, and schooling in social context*. New York: Cambridge University.

Valdes, G. (2002). *Expanding the definitions of giftedness: The case of young interpreters from immigrant countries*. Mahwah, NJ: Lawrence Erlbaum Associates.

Warren, B., Ballenger, C., Ogonowski, M., Rosebery, A., & Hudicourt-Barnes, J. (2001). Rethinking diversity in learning science: The logic of everyday sensemaking. *Journal of Research in Science Teaching, 38*, 529–552.

Warren, B., Ogonowski, M., & Pothier, S. (2005). "Everyday" and "scientific": Rethinking dichotomies in modes of thinking in science learning. 2005. In R. Nemirovsky, A. Rosebery, J. Solomon, & B. Warren (Eds.), *Everyday matters in mathematics and science: Studies of complex classroom events* (pp. 119–148). Mahwah, NJ: Lawrence Erlbaum Associates.

Warren, B., & Rosebery, A. (1996). "This question is just too, too easy!": Perspectives from the classroom on accountability in science. In L. Schauble & R. Glaser (Eds.), *Innovations in learning: New environments for education* (pp. 97–125). Mahwah, NJ: Lawrence Erlbaum Associates.

Warren, B., & Rosebery, A. (2004, February). *"What do you think Hassan means?" Exploring possible meanings of explicitness in the science classroom*. Invited talk at the Center for the Scholarship of Teaching, Michigan State University.

Wolpert, L., & Richards, A. (1997). *Passionate minds: The inner world of scientists*. Oxford: Oxford University Press.

CHAPTER 30

Prospects for Transforming Schools with Technology-Supported Assessment

Barbara Means

The last two decades have been marked by great expectations – and some important progress – in bringing technology to bear on the process of schooling. True, the more dramatic predictions of two decades ago concerning the impact of Information Age technology on schooling (see for example, Milken Family Foundation, 1999; Office of Technology Assessment, 1995) have not come to pass. But even so, the cup is half full. Today the average student:computer ratio is 5:1 in American schools (National Center for Education Statistics, 2003), and the use of technology for student research and report preparation has become commonplace. But arguably the biggest "buzz" in the educational technology community today is around the use of technology to improve assessment. School reformers, technology enthusiasts, and business interests have all identified assessment as an area with great potential for increased classroom use of technology (Bennett, 2002; CEO Forum on Education and Technology, 2001; CoSN, 2005; Education Week, 2003).

Although enthusiasm for a marriage of classroom assessment and technology is widespread, there are two competing visions of the purpose and nature of effective classroom assessments, each with different implications for the role of technology. One vision calls for connecting classroom assessment practices more closely to state-mandated content standards and accountability systems. The other vision, which draws heavily on recent advances in the learning sciences, calls for using technology to develop and deliver assessments that are integrated into day-to-day instruction and that enable teachers to gain deeper insights into their students' thinking and to adapt their instruction accordingly. Proponents of both visions claim the term "formative assessment," but it means quite different things in the two visions.

In this chapter, I first introduce the vision of technology-supported assessment as an adjunct to standards-based accountability systems. I then discuss the concept of formative assessment and the weakness of accountability-based classroom assessments for formative purposes from a learning sciences perspective. Next, I turn to the main focus of the chapter – the second vision of technology-supported assessments, with its roots in recent learning sciences research, and I discuss the more deeply diagnostic formative function of this vision. The remainder of the chapter provides descriptions of some notable examples of prototype and research-based systems implementing this second vision.

Technology-Based Classroom Assessment in Support of Accountability

One vision of the transforming role that technology-based assessment could have on schools involves tighter linkage between classroom practice and the standards set by district and state education offices, as embodied in accountability systems. If teachers are regularly and efficiently testing students on state standards, the reasoning goes, they will be able to use these test results to see where they need to focus instruction, both for a class as a whole and for individual students. By making it easy for teachers to assess students on the standards applicable to the subject and grade they teach, technology-based systems can encourage an appropriate focusing of instruction (and greater standardization across classrooms, schools, and districts within a state).

This vision precedes, but was certainly given strong impetus by the No Child Left Behind (NCLB) legislation. Since the passage of No Child Left Behind, the (1) heightened emphasis on tying instruction to specific content standards and (2) increasing stakes tied to students' performance on statewide tests (i.e., the requirement that schools demonstrate Adequate Yearly Progress on test scores for all student subgroups) have created a demand for assessment tools that teachers can use to gauge their students' progress, and that administrators can use to identify potential trouble spots early on. Commercial entities have been quick to see the market potential offered by school, district, and state administrators who are nervous about their students' likely performance vis-à-vis NCLB-required

Adequate Yearly Progress. Market trend analysts note that there has been stagnation in recent years in the market for instructional software, but dramatic growth in sales of computer-based assessment systems (Dyson, 2004). Accountability-related testing systems have been part of what the 2003 special issue of *Education Week* – devoted to technology – referred to as "the greatest precollegiate testing boom in history" (Education Week, 2003, p. 10).

In some cases, states and districts themselves are developing computer-based assessments that students can take to practice for the state's tests. An *Education Week* survey of state departments of education in 2003 found that twelve states offered such practice exams. Notable among the state systems are those of Texas, with its online Texas Math Diagnostic System, and Florida, where the FCAT Explorer provides test items and skills practice keyed to the Florida Comprehensive Assessment Test (Borja, 2003; Olson, 2003). Among the available commercial products is Pearson's Progress Assessment Series. A February 2005 ad for this product (Pearson Education, 2005, p. 9) opened with the headline, "Measure Their Success Before They Achieve It." The advertisement explains that formative assessments, taken throughout the year, forecast performance on state-specific proficiency standards.

Pinnacle Plus, from Excelsior Software, offers computer-based "real-time assessment feedback for truly informed instruction" (eSchool News, September 2004, p. 31). HOST Learning claims that its LearnerLink product "simplifies standards-based instruction in the classroom" by providing "formative assessments and prescriptive lesson planning" that are "aligned with state and local standards as well as large-scale standardized assessments" (http://www.hosts.com/products/learnerlink.html, accessed 7/31/05). Students take the computer-based assessments, and the LearnerLink System presents the teacher with a list of instructional resources geared to the standards that the students have not yet mastered. SOLAR

System offers pre-assessments that pin-point achievement gaps. PLATO's *eduTest* (formerly distributed by Lightspan) offers online assessments linked to state standards for classroom use. The PLATO eduTest Brochure, available at (http://www.plato. com/products.asp?cat = Assessment&ID = 83, accessed 7/31/05) describes the product as "a comprehensive standards-based online assessment program for classroom formative and district benchmark assessments and reporting." A selling point used for these products is that they enable a principal or district administrator to obtain midyear information on how well students are doing with respect to the requirements for annual improvement in the state's standards for NCLB.

The primary advantage touted in pro-moting these systems is the ability to iden-tify specific standards a student has not yet attained at a point during the school year when there is still time to provide addi-tional instruction. Some of the systems, like the FCAT Explorer, include an instructional component; others provide teachers and administrators with the assessment results and leave it to them to provide appropriate instruction.

A technology-enabled advantage of these systems is the capability for customization. Commercial vendors have large banks of test items mapped to specific skills and content areas. One can use the system to develop tests that fit a specific state's or district's standards for a particular grade level. Many of the systems offer teachers the option of reviewing test items keyed to standards and then selecting a subset of items that they deem most appropriate. Some systems allow teachers to modify test items or add their own. The testing formats used in these sys-tems are mostly multiple choice and short answer.

Although marketing materials often describe such systems as formative assess-ment – a type of assessment that is conducted during an instructional unit or sequence with the purpose of making instruction more effective – it should be noted that they provide limited (though important) information to guide instruction. The reports typically provide information on those standards on which the student performs at a level commensurate with state or district expectations, and those standards on which the student falls below the criterion level. The systems reflect a *mastery learning* approach to instruction (Bloom, 1976; Keller, 1983): the content to be learned is subdivided into discrete topics or skills, and individual students work on a topic or skill until it is "mastered." Instruction and learning are characterized in terms of exposure or "time on task" rather than in terms of the quality or nature of interaction with the material. A student failing to meet a standard typically receives more instruction of the same type received before, or even repetition of the very same practice exercises. This view of learning is very different from that underlying modern work in the learning sciences (see Sawyer introduction, this volume).

Rising Interest in Formative Assessment

While the increased emphasis on account-ability testing is undoubtedly the most obvi-ous assessment trend in recent years, there has been a concurrent rising interest in the concept of genuinely formative assess-ment. Formative assessment is contrasted with *summative assessment*, the testing that occurs at the end of a unit of instruction to document or certify what has been learned. An influential review of over 250 studies by Black and Wiliam (1998) concluded that the use of formative assessment techniques was one of the most powerful classroom-level interventions documented in the research literature:

> *There is a body of firm evidence that for-mative assessment is an essential feature of classroom work and that development of it can raise standards. We know of no other way of raising standards for which such a strong* prima facie *case can be made on the basis of evidence of such large learning gains. (p. 19)*

Formative assessment may be receiving more lip service than serious adoption. Its use is widely advocated by researchers (National Research Council, 2001; Pellegrino, Chudowsky, & Glaser, 2001; Shepard, 2000) and it is finding its way into professional development activities (Black & Harrison, 2001; Koch & Sackman, 2004; McTighe & Seif, 2003; Shepard, 1997). As described earlier, commercial entities distributing test preparation software tout their products as tools for formative assessment. However, the activities they call formative assessments are often simply the same end-of-year summative assessments administered before the end of the school year, not assessments that are designed specifically to inform future instruction.

This critical component – that the assessment provide information that shapes further instruction – was emphasized by Black and Wiliam (1998). If an assessment is used merely to assign grades, and there are no further learning opportunities on the content, the assessment is not really formative. Only if the assessment reveals specifics about students' thinking in ways that can inform further instruction, *and* additional learning opportunities are provided that make use of that diagnostic information, is the assessment "formative" in the sense that Black and Wiliam applied the concept in reviewing classroom studies. (See also the concept of "informative assessment" in Bass & Glaser, 2004.) *The formative nature of an assessment thus lies not in the assessment per se but rather in the intersection between the assessment and its role in the classroom.* (This is similar to a recent shift in the concept of test validity – validity should be evaluated based on how a test's results are used, rather than being inherent to the test instrument itself independent of the context of use.)

Many of the systems that are designed to support classroom assessments that are linked to standards and accountability systems lack this ability to inform instructional decisions. They tend to provide information on whether a student has achieved mastery, but not to provide insights into the way the student is thinking. The items in these systems tend to stress facts, name recognition, and discrete procedures, rather than deeper understanding or the relationships among concepts. Although nearly every curriculum standard–setting body makes statements about the importance of emphasizing depth in key content areas rather than mere breadth of coverage, the proliferation of standards across multiple content areas has produced the notorious "mile wide–inch deep" approach to content in American classrooms (Schmidt et al., 1997). A concrete illustration of how this works was provided by the comments of a math teacher whom I interviewed recently. The teacher showed me the pages of math standards that his large, urban district has stipulated need to be taught in each quarter of the academic year. This requirement is given teeth through district testing on the standards every nine weeks. When I asked the teacher what he did about students who needed more time to attain a standard, he reported that he had to follow the district's guidance, which he characterized as "touch upon it and move on." Technology can make this process more efficient, but when used to generate tests focusing on standards coverage rather than on student understanding, technology will only reinforce a bureaucratic approach to education.

Assessment in the Service of Cognitive Diagnosis

Genuinely formative assessment is an integral part of the vision of researchers who are trying to bring insights from the learning sciences to bear on classroom practice. In drawing educational implications from the body of research summarized in *How People Learn* (Bransford, Brown, & Cocking, 1999), a committee established by the National Research Council (Donovan, Bransford, & Pellegrino, 1999) concluded, "Teachers must draw out and work with the preexisting understandings that their students bring with them" (p. 15) and "Formative assessments – ongoing assessments designed to make students' thinking visible to both teachers and students – are essential" (p. 21).

Cognitive research on how people learn and acquire expertise in various content areas has given rise to new perspectives on assessment. From this standpoint, the purpose of a formative assessment is to provide insight not so much into a student's level of performance as into the nature of the student's understanding and reasoning in the domain being assessed. Mastery learning approaches decompose learning goals into discrete skills or bits of knowledge, and seek to assess whether each of these is in a state of mastery or nonmastery. In contrast, cognitive learning theorists put greater emphasis on assessing the way in which knowledge and skills are organized in the minds of students. These theorists describe knowledge as a hierarchically organized conceptual framework that predisposes the individual to see problems in terms of meaningful patterns, and to apply approaches that have been successful in dealing with these patterns to new situations. Furthermore, there is a tradition of cognitive research conducted within specific subject domains – contrasting the thinking and problem solving behaviors of novices and experts, or of students at different stages of development. These studies suggest that there are often different ways of "not knowing" something. The younger student's thinking is described not as random guesses produced in the absence of knowledge, but rather as consistently off the mark in a predictable way that makes sense given a particular misconception (diSessa, this volume). Common misconceptions have been identified for numerous science topics, including classical mechanics (Champagne, Klopfer, & Anderson, 1980), motion (Carmazza, McCloskey & Green, 1981; McCloskey, 1983; McCloskey & Kohl, 1983), and understanding of seasons and the movement of the earth (Sadler, 1987). Often students have models of some aspect of a subject area that are partially correct and that lead to correct answers or adaptive responses in some situations but not others (Linn, this volume). In some cases, there is a fairly typical developmental sequence

of ways of thinking. For example, most young children can answer questions about "more" and "less" and can reliably count a set of objects before they can integrate these two competencies to answer questions about whether one number is more or less than another (Griffin & Case, 1997). In other cases, there are different common misconceptions and no known dominant sequence (Chi & Slotta, 1993). Learning theorists stress the need for teachers to understand how individual students think about the phenomenon being studied:

> Students come to the classroom with preconceptions about how the world works. If their initial understanding is not engaged, they may fail to grasp new concepts and information presented in the classroom, or they may learn them for purposes of a test but revert to their preconceptions outside the classroom. (Donovan, Bransford, & Pellegrino, 1999, p. 2)

In this view, the goal of formative assessment is not so much to ascertain whether a student "has got it" as it is to reveal the way in which the student is thinking about the topic or problem. Two students may both lack a scientifically correct understanding of some phenomenon, for example, but may think about it in very different ways. If a teacher is to focus teaching at each student's level of prior understandings, the teacher needs to know the nature of individual students' thinking. In those curricular areas where research has uncovered detailed models of cognition, those models provide a basis for the development of formative assessments that can inform instruction.

Using Cognitive Research to Design Assessment Items

Phil Sadler's work on students' understanding of the movements of the earth and the solar system provides a good example of how assessments can provide a diagnosis of student understanding. Earlier research in which students of various ages were questioned about the earth's orbit and the reason why temperatures vary with the season revealed that many students think that the earth's orbit is shaped in such a way that the earth is physically closer to the sun in summer (Sadler, 1987). Other students retain the notion that distance from the sun is the critical factor, but describe differences in distance caused because the earth "leans" toward the sun in summer and away from it in winter (from a Northern Hemisphere perspective). Only a minority of students ever attains the understanding that the earth's spherical shape coupled with the earth's tilt means that the angle at which the sun's rays strike the earth is larger in summer, resulting in longer days and the sun being higher in the sky. Sadler used this research on misconceptions and the development of understanding of seasons as the basis for developing a series of test items (Sadler, 1998). In addition to a correct answer option, each item had incorrect choices ("distractors") which were the answers one would give on the basis of the various misconceptions found in the research literature. Similarly, items were developed to probe students' reasoning about what causes night and day, about the relative distance of stars outside our solar system, about the phases of the moon, and so on. Sadler's astronomy assessment is used to identify the ways in which students think about each of these areas, not just whether or not they give scientifically correct accounts. By giving his assessment to large numbers of students, Sadler was able to demonstrate several instances in which the proportion of students choosing the correct answer appeared to fall off as student age increased, until it began to rise among the oldest grade levels tested. Sadler used these data to argue that in these cases a decrease in "correct" answers to some kinds of questions is in fact a marker of cognitive development. An immature conceptual framework often produces correct answers to some questions for the wrong reasons; as students' concepts mature, they may start giving wrong answers to questions they previously answered correctly for some period, until a new, more comprehensive understanding has solidified.

This description of Sadler's work shows that building an assessment based upon

empirical research on how students think about a complex topic is a labor-intensive undertaking. Learning sciences research provides us with a foundation for this work in the form of cognitive studies of reasoning in areas such as early mathematics, biology, calculus, economics, physics, and history (Bransford, Brown, & Cocking, 1999; Donovan & Bransford, 2005). Even so, the systematic development of assessments that are sensitive to important differences in understanding within a domain requires not only careful crafting of assessment tasks but also trying them out with examinees and determining their technical characteristics (e.g., the distribution of examinee responses and the interrelationships among responses to different assessment tasks or portions of tasks). Creating research-based assessments for all areas of the K–12 curriculum would require a huge effort. Certainly, developing research-based assessment items is not something that we would expect every teacher, or even every school district, to take on independently. Although this task is too big for an individual teacher or district, it can be tractable if we pool our efforts, and technology supports make this kind of pooling possible. By developing Web-accessible versions of assessments capable of cognitive diagnosis, researchers are starting to provide resources for an increasing number of classroom teachers.

Using the Web to Make Diagnostic Assessments Widely Available

Jim Minstrell, Earl Hunt, and their colleagues have developed of technology-based diagnostic assessment items in a content area, and have disseminated them over the Web. A former high school physics teacher himself, Minstrell began compiling a set of student conceptions about force and motion based upon both the research literature and the observations of teachers. Some of these ideas, or "facets" in Minstrell's terminology, are considered scientifically correct (or at least correct to the degree one would expect at the stage of introductory physics). Others are partially incorrect, and still others are seriously flawed. The goal of assessment in this work is to elicit student responses that reveal the underlying thinking, or *knowledge facets*, of each student. Having developed an inventory of knowledge facets, Minstrell and his colleagues proceeded to develop assessment items that would elicit different responses depending on which facets a student held (Minstrell, 1999). For example, when asked to reason about the weight of objects totally or partially submerged in a liquid, one set of facets concerns separating the effect of a fluid or other medium from the effect of gravity. A student might think that surrounding forces don't exert any pressure on objects. Alternatively, he might think that fluid mediums produce an upward pressure only or that the weight of an object is directly proportional to the medium's pressure on it. Some students may have memorized the mathematical formula for net buoyant pressure and may be able to apply it to some problems in order to obtain a correct answer, but might nonetheless lack the facet for a qualitative conceptual understanding (net upward push is a result of differences in pressure gradients).

Minstrell and his colleagues (see http://www.facetinnovations.com, accessed 7/31/05) have developed a computer-based assessment system to get at students' facets. The student is presented with a problem situation (e.g., a solid cylinder is hung by a long string from a spring scale. The reading on the scale shows that the cylinder weighs 1.0 lb. About how much will the scale read if the cylinder which weighs 1.0 lb. is submerged just below the surface of the water?) and a set of multiple-choice answers, each of which is associated with a specific facet. After choosing an answer to the original question, the student is asked to provide the reasoning behind the original answer. The system compares the facet associated with the student's explanation to that associated with the original answer choice. Over multiple problems, the system diagnoses the student's probable facets and the consistency between student predictions and explanations. The system presents the teacher with reports of this diagnosis and with an instruc-

tional prescription appropriate for the diagnosed facets.

The first technology-based version of the system, called DIAGNOSER, was developed using Apple's HyperCard environment. More recently, the FACETS system offers teachers Web access to diagnostic assessments in a variety of content areas in middle school science and mathematics. The system also provides guidance to teachers on how to analyze their students' open-ended explanations in terms of facets. After student misconceptions are identified through the FACETS assessments, "benchmark lessons" are suggested to challenge student beliefs. Their purpose is to encourage students to apply their beliefs to new situations, examine their own reasoning, and see where their expectations are confirmed and where there are discrepancies between their beliefs and what they observe actually happening.

Using Technology to Perform Complex Diagnoses

The FACETS assessments illustrate technology's contribution to formative assessment in providing readily accessible banks of research-based diagnostic assessment items and associated instructional strategies and materials. Technology also has the potential to perform complex analyses of patterns of student responses that would be time-consuming and difficult for teachers to perform. An example of the use of technology to analyze student performance with complex problems in ways that would be difficult or impossible for a human teacher is provided by the IMMEX (Interactive Multimedia Exercises) system at UCLA (Vendlinski & Stevens, 2000). The system was originally developed to teach diagnostic skills to medical students, but has been extended to teach problem solving in grades kindergarten through twelve in topics in earth science, chemistry, social studies, mathematics, and language (see http://www.immex.ucla.edu, accessed 7/31/05).

The IMMEX system presents students with a dramatic, complex problem scenario such as spilling of a chemical in a stock room after an earthquake, or identification of a child's true parents after a potential incident of baby switching at the hospital. The learner is challenged to investigate the problem, and is given both background information and the option to perform various simulated tests (such as submitting the mystery chemical to a flame test) and to receive the results of the tests before proposing a solution. The system maps out the information that each student examined, the sequence in which it was examined, and the amount of time spent in each portion of the problem (Underdahl, Palacio-Cayetano, & Stevens, 2001). Using neural network technology, the IMMEX system compares the sequence of steps taken by a learner to the problem-solving steps of more and less skilled learners working with the same type of problem. The teacher receives a search path map showing each student's problem-solving strategy. Student solutions can be classified in terms of problem-solving strategies which vary in the kinds of information examined, the incorporation of strategic elements (such as choosing information most likely to rule out alternatives), and the likelihood of reaching a correct solution for a given problem set (Stevens et al., 2004).

The IMMEX team has developed additional supports for teachers to implement IMMEX problem solving units in their classrooms. An authoring system allows teachers to author their own IMMEX problems. Professional development around the use of IMMEX provides teachers with suggestions on when and how to provide additional instruction on problem solving strategies, based on students' performance on IMMEX problems (Underdahl, Palacio-Cayetano, & Stevens, 2001).

Technology Supports for Student Self-Assessment

The ThinkerTools Inquiry Project of Barbara White and John Frederiksen has developed technology-supported classroom assessment practices that involve students in assessing their own understanding. ThinkerTools is a middle school curriculum that helps students learn the concepts of force and motion, as well as the processes of scientific inquiry. Each "inquiry cycle" begins with the identification of a question about a set of phenomena (e.g., how a puck moves on surfaces with different amounts of friction) that students do not yet understand. The class is subdivided into small research groups to discuss their intuitions about these situations and to develop hypotheses or models. Students then test their models, using both computer-based simulations and real-world materials, and record their observations. Each group reasons about what they have learned from testing their predictions and models, and then all the groups reassemble in a research symposium to present their models, findings, and interpretations. The class discusses the various groups' models and findings, coming to consensus on the best model, and then tries to apply that model to new situations. White and Frederiksen (2000) tested the effects of adding a formative assessment component to ThinkerTools in which the students themselves engaged in what the researchers called "reflective assessment." A computer-based system provides students with a set of criteria characterizing good scientific inquiry, and asks them to evaluate their own and each other's work according to those criteria. The inclusion of this formative assessment component led to greater gains on a science inquiry test, especially for those students who began the project with lower scores on a standardized achievement test. Thus, the incorporation of reflective assessment appeared to reduce the achievement gap in the area of science inquiry.

White and Frederiksen argued that such self-assessment activities address an important goal for instruction: Students need strong models of good performance and also need help internalizing the criteria for high-quality performance. The ThinkerTools work exemplifies the way in which students can be actively involved in classroom assessment practices – not just responding to examination questions, but rather applying assessment criteria themselves. This kind of involvement highlights both the essential qualities of the performance or product students are expected to achieve and the process whereby such products are created (Frederiksen & Collins, 1989).

Combining Technology Supports and Human Judgment

While the IMMEX system described above illustrates the capability of neural net software to perform pattern diagnoses that would be difficult and time consuming for humans, there are many scholars in the learning sciences community who would argue that in most cases, human observers can do better instructional diagnoses than can today's artificial intelligence software. Even if that were true, technology could still play an important role by delivering problems that elicit a systematic set of student responses for the human observer to use in instructional diagnosis.

In ThinkerTools, for example, the technology-based environment provides simulations for use in testing students' ideas, and a structure reflecting the inquiry cycle, which can both be related to assessment activities. The reflective assessment itself, however, is done not by the system but by the learners themselves and their peers. In a similar vein, research on an intelligent tutoring system for high school geometry (Schofield, Eurich-Fulcer, & Britt, 1994) found that teachers could use students' interactions with computer-based geometry problems as a basis for providing feedback and assistance that was better tuned to student needs, according to the students. Schofield et al. concluded that teacher assistance was more articulate and relevant to student needs than the feedback provided by the computer-based tutoring system, but the tutor was able to reveal areas of individual need in ways that normal whole-class instruction was not. Hence, the tutoring system and the teacher together provided formative assessment in a way that neither could do alone.

Integrating Technology-Based Assessment with the Act of Teaching

In contrast to the approaches described earlier, which have stressed the diagnosis of individual students' thinking, are a set of emerging technology-supported practices that provide instructors with a nearly real-time snapshot of the thinking of entire classes (Means et al., 2004). The challenge of teaching large college classes triggered the development of classroom communication systems (CCS). A CCS consists of a networked set of computers, personal digital assistants, or small wireless input devices that look like TV remote control. Every student in the class can answer the question using their personal device, and the wireless network aggregates and presents their responses on a screen (usually as a histogram).

Eric Mazur, a Harvard physics professor, has been one of the major proponents of using classroom communication systems to support teaching for conceptual understanding (Crouch & Mazur, 2001; Fagen, Crouch, & Mazur, 2002; Mazur, 1997). After finding that many of his students still did not understand basic physics concepts at the end of his course, Mazur switched from his accustomed practice of delivering content through lecture alone to using formative assessment and a technique he called "peer instruction." Using this new approach, Mazur would lecture for a short while and then pose a conceptual question (e.g., "Imagine holding two bricks below water. Brick A is just below the surface, while Brick B is at a greater depth. How does the force needed to hold Brick B in place differ from that needed for Brick A?"). Students used the classroom's communication system to register their responses to the question, and then Mazur would invite them to work with one or two other students, discussing their answers and providing explanations to try to convince each other. After these discussions among small groups, Mazur would had the class answer the same question a second time. Typically, the proportion of correct responses rose dramatically. At this point, after the students had been actively engaged via the initial visible clash of opinions, Mazur then explored the topic more deeply, for example, by challenging students to think about the limits of the rule or explanation they had converged on, or the relationship of that explanation to underlying principles.

Mazur (1997) offered concrete advice on the strategic planning and classroom practice required for a teacher to implement peer instruction. He made it clear that there is an art to designing good tasks and questions; in particular, the task must get to the heart of the conceptual matter and be neither too easy (or there is no need for discussion) nor too hard (which would result in an insufficient distribution of the correct answer among the class population). Mazur believed that technology's contribution resides in prompting students to think deeply enough about the question initially to commit to a response to the question, and in making students feel comfortable in arguing for their response by making it clear that the class as a whole holds a range of opinions (as reflected in the projected histogram of student responses). Students' initial thinking is made visible, both through their responses to the instructor's question and through the arguments and explanations they offer to their peers.

Classroom communication systems are starting to be applied in K-12 settings as well. Hartline (1997) described the practices of an elementary reading teacher who used a classroom communication system to check students' comprehension of reading passages. After having the fifth graders in her inner-city school read text passages, the teacher had them use the classroom communication system to answer comprehension and inference questions about the passages. When the students finished, she would open up discussion around conceptual issues by projecting a histogram of class responses to the first

question. If students had different responses, she asked students to volunteer "clues" from the reading passage that could help explain or justify their particular answer choices. As students called out clues, she would write them on the blackboard next to the answer. Then students were invited to talk about which was the best set of clues and why one set of clues was more persuasive than another. After discussion, students could change their answers, and then the teacher projected a new histogram and introduced another cycle of discussion.

Both the college physics class and the elementary reading class illustrate ways in which a classroom communication system provides a means of eliciting student understandings so that rich classroom discussions that connect with and build on that initial understanding can occur (also see Pea & Maldonado, this volume). Although students do not think of these experiences as tests, they do have all the earmarks of formative assessments.

System Supports for Assessment Design

Developing formative assessments based on cognitive research in specific domains is a resource-intensive activity. How could we possibly develop enough of the kinds of cognitive formative assessments described here to have a significant impact on K–12 education? Fortunately, technology, when coupled with advances in cognitive research and assessment theory, holds potential for supporting the development of formative assessments with cognitive diagnostic value (Pellegrino, Chudowsky, & Glaser, 2001). The ongoing Performance Assessment Designs for Inquiry (PADI) Project, led by Geneva Haertel and Bob Mislevy, is attempting to bring together advances in cognitive science – which provide insights into how students reason in particular content domains – with advances in psychometric models, which can now handle more complex, multipart items than was possible in conventional psychometric models. PADI is implementing a process of evidence-centered design (Mislevy, Steinberg, et al., 2003) in which assessment items are constructed systematically, beginning with a *student model* of proficient performance in the area to be assessed, then moving to a *task model*, which specifies the assessment situation to be presented to the learner, and an *evidence model*, which specifies the evidence needed to support the inferences that can be made from various possible elements of task performance. This approach is being applied in the development of *design patterns* that characterize learning goals common in middle school science curricula (e.g., using data to support a scientific argument, designing and conducting a scientific experiment, evaluating the quality of scientific data) in a narrative form that lays out the logic chain linking the conclusions one wants to make about student thinking to the observable behaviors that would support or refute those conclusions and the situations that could elicit those behaviors.

The assessment developer using the computer-based PADI tools has a structure for laying out the logic that leads from specific student responses on an assessment task to inferences about the student's understanding and skill. The design patterns lay the groundwork for the more technical specification required for the design of particular assessments (Mislevy, Hamel, et al., 2003). The design patterns apply across different science specialties (i.e., they are applicable to genetics, chemistry, and physics); currently, the PADI design patterns are being used by science curriculum development projects at the University of Michigan and the University of California, Berkeley's Lawrence Hall of Science. Because assessments built on the PADI framework are designed around a cognitive model of proficient task performance, they are capable of supporting both formative and summative assessment practices, with teachers using assessment findings to draw inferences about their students' thinking and about the specific kinds of learning opportunities their students need.

Shall the Twain Ever Meet?

This chapter has described two very different visions of technology supported assessment. Both visions call for frequent assessment and a closer connection between instruction and assessment, but they have very different views of the nature of good assessments and of what teachers and students should learn from the assessment activities. The first vision in essence makes the standards-driven accountability system part of day-to-day classroom activity – practice tests pinpoint areas where an individual student is likely to fare poorly on the end-of-year test that is used for accountability purposes, so that classroom instruction can focus on those topics or skills. The second vision arises out of concern with understanding the preconceptions and problem solving strategies that students bring to the classroom. The notion here is that teachers must address not only students' mastery of content, but also their preconceptions and problem-solving strategies, to bring about deep and lasting changes in student thinking.

The two visions reflect very different learning theories. The first is closely associated with large-scale testing, and thus inherits testing's relationship to the goal of differentiating among students with varying levels of achievement or "potential," and reflects behavioristic theories of learning (Shepard, 2000). The second derives from modern conceptions in the learning sciences (Bransford, Brown, & Cocking, 1999) and the goal of understanding human intellectual performance as a precursor to enhancing it. Interestingly, proponents of both visions borrow some formative assessment arguments and jargon from the other, but the two remain quite different at their core.

Two questions remain:

- Are the visions really in conflict?
- Does either or both have the potential to transform schools?

The two visions are not necessarily mutually exclusive. A given classroom could exercise both types of technology-supported assessment at different times. Adoption of one approach does not preclude adoption of the other, and the two could, in fact, share the same technology infrastructure. But even so, classrooms always face a trade-off between covering a small number of important concepts in depth versus covering a large amount of content with less time per topic, and the two assessment visions come down on two different sides of the depth versus breadth trade-off. One could also characterize this trade-off in terms of focus: Assessment practices geared to the school's accountability system will tend to focus teaching and learning on the content covered in the state or district test; practitioners, researchers, and the general public differ in whether they view this focus as a positive or a negative result. Each combination of school system and classroom teacher will resolve this trade-off somewhat differently.

The two visions also suggest somewhat different roles for the teacher. Accountability-oriented assessments provide the teacher with a set of data designed to predict performance relative to state or district standards. But the data teachers receive from these assessments are typically either at a level of aggregation that is too gross to provide instructional insights beyond a focus topic (e.g., spend more time on fractions).[1] This situation is a natural consequence of the fact that these assessments link to standards rather than to students' thinking. The learning sciences approach, in contrast seeks to provide insight into how students actually think about the area being assessed. Cognitively oriented formative assessments provide teachers with more information concerning a starting point for instruction, but by themselves do not tell teachers how to help their students move from that starting point to a more complete understanding. Either approach to formative assessment, then, depends on teachers bringing considerable pedagogical content knowledge to the task of designing instruction to support further learning (Shulman, 1987).

With respect to the potential for significant change, the two visions have rather different prospects. Technology-supported accountability-focused classroom assessment is an increasing reality. Many districts are purchasing or considering systems that integrate classroom testing with their larger student information systems. One market analyst (Dyson, 2004) estimated the sales at $645 million and growing. In addition to giving teachers earlier feedback about areas where students need more instruction if they are to achieve state standards, these assessment systems, because of their linkage to student data systems, provide more detailed, inspectable information for administrators at higher levels of the education system (U.S. Department of Education, 2004). A principal or district curriculum specialist can direct a teacher to spend additional time teaching fractions or to give more emphasis to spelling. For this reason, individuals at higher levels of the education system are promoting use of these computer-based assessments. Widespread implementation of these systems is just beginning. We know that districts are buying them, but we do not know how and to what extent teachers are using the assessment features of the systems with their students. To the extent that districts adopting accountability-related assessment systems experience increases in test scores, this trend is likely to gather momentum.

The alternative – the cognitive diagnosis vision of technology-supported assessment – faces longer odds for having a real impact on schooling. The vision has the potential to bring about the blurring of the distinction between assessment and instructional practices – as many researchers advocate (Bransford, Brown, & Cocking, 1999; Pellegrino, Chudowsky, & Glaser, 2001; Shepard, 2000). It has strong appeal within the learning science research community and among some teachers. The challenges of producing research-based assessments for cognitive diagnosis is much higher than that of producing practice versions of standardized reading and mathematics tests, however. Without the commercial interests and policy imperatives that are propelling the accountability-oriented classroom assessment systems, these research-based systems face many more barriers to adoption. Moreover, such approaches make heavy demands on teachers to develop deep expertise, both in the subjects they teach and in the ways students think about and problem solve in those content areas. If the theory underlying this approach is correct, though, instruction with cognitively diagnostic formative assessment should produce learning that is more long lasting and more likely to be brought to bear in new learning or problem solving situations (Bransford & Schwartz, 1999). Research demonstrating these advantages could well be a critical enabler of acceptance of technology-supported cognitively diagnostic assessments.

Acknowledgments

I am indebted to my Center for Technology in Learning colleagues Geneva Haertel and Bill Penuel for their advice and suggestions provided in response to an earlier draft.

Footnote

1. It could be argued that these systems do provide detailed information since many of them are capable of generating performance reports at the individual item level. When assessment items are developed and sampled simply as exemplars from the larger topic covered by a subtest, however, item-level performance information adds little except the temptation to teach the correct answers to missed items (rather than addressing a conceptual misunderstanding).

References

Bass, K. M., & Glaser, R. (2004). *Developing assessments to inform teaching and learning.* CSE Report 628. Los Angeles: National Center for Research on Evaluation Standards, and Student Testing, University of California, Los Angeles.

Bennett, R. E. (2002). Inexorable and inevitable: The continuing story of technology and assessment. *Journal of Technology, Learning, and Assessment, 1*(1). Available from http://www.jtla.org, accessed November 22, 2005.

Black, P., & Harrison, C. (2001). Feedback in questioning and marking: The science teacher's role in formative assessment. *School Science Review, 82*(301), 55–61.

Black, P., & Wiliam, D. (1998). Assessment and classroom learning. *Assessment and Education, 5*(1), 7–74.

Bloom, B. S. (1976). *Human characteristics and school learning.* New York: McGraw-Hill.

Borja, R. R. (2003). Prepping for the big test. *Technology Counts 2003, 22*(35), 23–24, 26.

Bransford, J. D., Brown, A. L., & Cocking, R. R. (1999). *How people learn: Brain, mind, and experience.* Washington, DC: National Academy Press.

Bransford, J. D., & Schwartz, D. L. (1999). Rethinking transfer: A simple proposal with multiple implications. In A. Iran-Nejad & P. D. Pearson (Eds.), *Review of research in education* (Vol. 24, pp. 61–100). Washington, DC: American Educational Research Association.

Carmazza, A., McCloskey, M., & Green. B. (1981). Naïve beliefs in "sophisticated" subjects: Misconceptions about trajectories of objects. *Cognition, 9,* 117–123.

CEO Forum on Education and Technology. (2001). *School technology and readiness – Key building blocks for achievement in the 21st century: Assessment, alignment, access, analysis.* Available at www.ceoforum.org/downloads/report4.pdf, accessed November 22, 2005.

Champagne, A. B., Klopfer, L. E., & Anderson, J. H. (1980). Factors influencing the learning of classical mechanics. *American Journal of Physics, 8,* 1074–1075.

Chi, M. T. H., & Slotta, J. D. (1993). Ontological coherence of intuitive physics. *Cognition and Instruction, 10*(2&3), 249–260.

CoSN (Consortium for School Networking). (2005). *From vision to action: How school districts use data to improve performance.* Washington, DC: Author.

Crouch, C. H., & Mazur, E. (2001). Peer instruction: Ten years of experience and results. *The Physics Teacher*, 69, 970–977.

Donovan, M. S., & Bransford, J. D. (2005). *How students learn history, mathematics, and science in the classroom*. Washington, DC: National Academy Press.

Donovan, M. S., Bransford, J. D., & Pellegrino, J. W. (1999). *How people learn: Bridging research and practice*. Washington, DC: National Academy Press.

Dyson, E. (2004, October). Held back: The market for software in our schools. *Release 1.0. Esther Dyson's Monthly Report*. Available at http://www.release1-0.com, accessed November 22, 2005.

Education Week. (2003). Pencils down: Technology's answer to testing. *Technology Counts 2003*, 22(35), 8, 10.

Excelsior Software. (2004, September). Advertisement for Pinnacle Plus Assessment Management System. *eSchool News*, p. 31.

Fagen, A. P., Crouch, C. H., & Mazur, E. (2002). Peer instruction: Results from a range of classrooms. *The Physics Teacher*, 40, 206–207.

Frederiksen, J. R., & Collins, A. (1989). A systems approach to educational testing. *Educational Researcher*, 18, 27–32.

Griffin, S., & Case, R. (1997). Re-thinking the primary school math curriculum: An approach based on cognitive science. *Issues in Education*, 3(1), 1–49.

Hartline, F. (1997). *Analysis of 1st semester of Classtalk use at McIntosh Elementary School*. Yorktown, VA: Better Education.

Keller, J. M. (1983). Motivational design of instruction. In C. Reigeluth (Ed.), *Instructional-design theories and models: An overview of their current status*. Hillsdale, NJ: Lawrence Erlbaum Associates.

Koch, M., & Sackman, M. (2004). Assessment in the palm of your hand. *Science and Children*, 33(9), 33–37.

Mazur, E. (1997). *Peer instruction: A user's manual*. Upper Saddle River, NJ: Prentice Hall.

McCloskey, M. (1983). Naïve theories of motion. In D. Genuner & A. I. Stevens (Eds.), *Mental models* (pp. 299–324). Hillsdale, NJ: Lawrence Erlbaum Associates.

McCloskey, M., & Kohl, D. (1983). Naïve physics: The curvilinear impetus principle and its role in interactions with moving objects. *Journal of Experimental Psychology Learning, Memory, and Cognition*, 9, 146–156.

McTighe, J., & Seif, E. (2003). *A summary of underlying theory and research base for understanding by design*. Unpublished manuscript.

Means, B., Roschelle, J., Penuel, W., Sabelli, N., & Haertel, G. (2004). Technology's contribution to teaching and policy: Efficiency, standardization, or transformation? In R. E. Floden (Ed.), *Review of Research in Education* (Vol. 27, pp. 159–181). Washington, DC: American Educational Research Association.

Milken Family Foundation. (1999). *Transforming learning through technology: Policy roadmaps for the nation's governors*. Santa Monica, CA: Author.

Minstrell, J. (1999). Facets of student understanding and assessment development. In J. W. Pellegrino, L. R. Jones, & K. Mitchell (Eds.), *Grading the nation's report card: Research from the evaluation of NAEP*. Washington, DC: National Academy Press.

Mislevy, R. J., Hamel, L., Fried, R., Gaffney, T., Haertel, G., Hafter, A., et al. (2003). *Design patterns for assessing science inquiry*. PADI Technical Report 1. Menlo Park, CA: SRI International.

Mislevy, R. J., Steinberg, L. S., Almond, R. G., Haertel, G. D., & Penuel, W. (2003). Improving educational assessment. In G. D. Haertel & B. Means (Eds.), *Evaluating educational technology: Effective research designs for improving learning* (pp. 149–180). New York: Teachers College Press.

National Center for Education Statistics (NCES), U.S. Department of Education. (2003). *Internet access in U.S. public schools and classrooms, 1994–2002*. Washington, DC: Author.

National Research Council (2001). *Classroom Assessment and the National Science Education Standards*. Washington, DC: National Academy Press.

Office of Technology Assessment, U.S. Congress. (1995). *Education and Technology: Future Visions*. OTA-BP-HER-169. Washington, DC: U.S. Government Printing Office.

Olson, L. (2003). Legal twists, digital turns. *Technology Counts 2003*, 22(35), 11–14, 16.

Pearson Education. (2005, February). Advertisement for Progress Assessment Series. *ESchool News*, p. 9.

Pellegrino, J. W., Chudowsky, N., & Glaser, R. (Eds.) (2001). *Knowing what students know: The science and design of educational assessment*. Washington, DC: National Academy Press.

Sadler, P. M. (1987). Alternative conceptions in astronomy. In J. D. Novak (Ed.), *Second international seminar on misconception and educational strategies in science and mathematics* (Vol. 3, pp. 422–425). Ithaca, NY: Cornell University Press.

Sadler, P. M. (1998). Psychometric models of student conceptions in science: Reconciling qualitative studies and distractor-driven assessment instruments. *Journal of Research in Science Teaching*, 35(3), 265–296.

Schmidt, W. H., Raizen, S., Britton, E. D., Bianchi, L. J., & Wolfe, R. G. (1997). *Many visions, many aims: Volume II: A cross-national investigation of curricular intentions in school science*. London: Kluwer.

Schofield, J. W., Eurich-Fulcer, R., & Britt, C. L. (1994). Teachers, computer tutors, and teaching: The artificially intelligent tutor as an agent of classroom change. *American Educational Research Journal*, 31 (3), 579–607.

Shepard, L. (1997). *Insights gained from a classroom-based assessment project*. CSE Technical Report 451. Los Angeles, CA: National Center for Research on Evaluation, Standards, and Student Testing.

Shepard, L. A. (2000). The role of assessment in a learning culture. Presidential address at the annual meeting of the American Educational Research Association, New Orleans, April 26. Available at aera.net/pubs/er/arts/29–07/shep02.htm.

Shulman, L. (1987). Knowledge and teaching: Foundations of the new reform. *Harvard Education Review*, 57, 1–22.

Stevens, R., Soller, A., Cooper, M., and Sprang, M. (2004). Modeling the development of problem solving skills in chemistry with a web-based tutor. In Lester, J. C., Vicari, R. M., & Paraguaca, F. (Eds.), *Intelligent Tutoring Systems*. (pp. 580–591). Heidelberg, Germany: Springer-Verlag.

Underdahl, J., Palacio-Cayetano, J., & Stevens, R. (2001). Practice makes perfect: Assessing and enhancing knowledge and problem solving skills with IMMEX software. *Learning and Leading with Technology*, 28, 26–31.

U.S. Department of Education, Office of Educational Technology. (2004). *Toward a new golden age in american education: How the internet, the law and today's students are revolutionizing expectations*. Washington, DC: U.S. Department of Education.

Vendlinski, T., & Stevens, R. (2000). The use of artificial neural nets (ANN) to help evaluate student problem-solving strategies. In B. Fishman & S. O'Connor-Divelbiss (Eds.), *Proceedings of the fourth international conference of the learning sciences* (pp. 108–114). Mahwah, NJ: Lawrence Erlbaum Associates.

White, B., & Frederiksen, J. (2000). Metacognitive facilitation: An approach to making scientific inquiry accessible to all. In J. Minstrell and E. van Zee (Eds.), *Inquiring into inquiry learning and teaching in science*. (pp. 331–370). Washington, DC: American Association for the Advancement of Science.

CHAPTER 31

Internet Use in Schools

Promise and Problems

Janet Ward Schofield

Schools in the United States are often characterized as bastions of stability, as institutions still strongly shaped by the early twentieth century, whose mission, rather ironically, is to prepare students to function effectively in the twenty-first century (Molenda, 1992). Yet, schools have changed quite dramatically in at least one way during the last twenty-five years. Specifically, in the 1980s school districts in the United States, as well as in many other developed countries, began to purchase large numbers of computers for instructional use, and in the mid-1990s they built on this trend by very rapidly connecting classrooms to the Internet. Furthermore, many school districts adopted computer technology with the specific goal of changing students' educational experiences in ways that would improve their education.

This chapter explores the introduction of the Internet into schools for instructional purposes, examining the Internet's potential to improve education and the factors that appear to impede full realization of this potential. This chapter focuses on

Internet use, rather than on the use of computer technology more generally, because different kinds of computer use have somewhat different kinds of potential to change education (Levin & Bruce, 2003; Means, 1994; Salomon, 1993) and they do not face exactly the same set of impediments to the realization of their potential. For example, cognitive tutors are designed specifically to help students learn particular cognitive skills. Their success is measured in terms of whether students learn specific subject matter better and/or faster than otherwise, and they function on self-contained personal computers (Anderson et al., 1995; Koedinger & Corbett, this volume). In contrast, Internet use is often intended to help students gather information or to communicate with others. Success in such cases is a function of whether the appropriate amount and kind of information can be located or whether the communication enhances the attainment of the educational goals it was intended to further. In addition, the fact that the Internet provides access to information and individuals outside of the school raises a set of important issues not raised by the use of stand-alone software like cognitive tutors.

The Internet's Potential for Changing Education

The Internet is seen by many as having the potential to change education dramatically. Some, like Mambretti (1999, p. 17), believe that the Internet "is a revolutionary technology. . . . bound to change every aspect of society and, in particular, the education system," and are convinced that Internet use has the potential not just to enrich current approaches to teaching and learning but also to fundamentally transform educational systems.

Indeed, the Internet has the potential to challenge the very notion of a school as a physical location in which teachers and students interact with each other face to face (Berman & Tinker, 2000; Bushweller, 2002; Orange & Hobbs, 2000; Trotter, 2002; Virtual Schools Forum Report, 2002; Zehr, 1997; Zucker et al., 2003). For example, some states in the United States now have virtual schools, and distance education opportunities have expanded dramatically in the past decade. The trend toward home schooling also seems likely to be stimulated by the Internet, because the Internet provides ready access to so many educational resources that would not be available from home otherwise. In addition, the fact that some school districts have began to replace textbooks – long an item around which much classroom activity has been structured – with laptop computers with Internet connections that allow students to connect with teachers, peers, and informational resources from wherever they happen to be also highlights the potential for major structural change in our educational system inherent in Internet use (also see Sawyer conclusion, this volume).

However, it seems very unlikely that schools as physical places will disappear, at least anytime soon. Furthermore, it is certainly debatable whether this would be desirable. Thus, the Internet's main potential for improving K–12 education in the foreseeable future depends on how fully educational institutions find ways to make good use of the unique benefits that the Internet provides. The Internet's merging of computing and telecommunications provides tremendously enhanced access to information and to other individuals and groups. However, mere access to information and to other people, in and of itself, does not necessarily lead to improved education. The crucial question determining whether Internet access enhances students' education is how this access is used to change their educational experiences.

Importantly, Internet use has the potential to greatly facilitate changes in education in ways that current theory and research in the learning sciences suggest will improve it. The changes that this body of work suggests are important include:

- organizing learning around active work on real world problems and projects rather than around more passive assimilation of information about predetermined topics (Krajcik & Blumenfeld, this volume; Savin-Baden, 2000).
- providing students with more authentic learning experiences (Means, 1994; Shaffer & Resnick, 1999)
- harnessing the power of well-structured collaborative work to foster learning (Scardamalia & Bereiter, this volume)
- allowing students more latitude to pursue topics of personal interest and importance (Shaffer & Resnick, 1999)

The unique benefits provided by the Internet seem capable of facilitating such changes, and Becker's (1998) research documents a connection between Internet use and teachers changing their practices towards more constructivist approaches (e.g., having students involved in long and complex projects, giving students more choice regarding tasks and the resources used to complete them, and so on), although the data are only correlational. Because the

Internet merges computing and telecommunications, it has great potential to foster and support authentic project-based learning in real-world contexts: it facilitates access to experiences, information, and project partners not available within the confines of the school. The Internet also provides access to virtual worlds that let students actively explore real-world phenomena that would be too dangerous, time-consuming, expensive, or logistically difficult to explore otherwise. The Internet's ubiquity, the rapidity of the communication it fosters, and the fact that many people have worked to create collaborative opportunities for students that make use of these characteristics, opens up many opportunities for learning through collaborative work that would not be possible otherwise. In addition, the range of information, experiences, and communicative opportunities available via the Internet makes it possible for students to follow their own individual interests in various subject areas that it would be difficult or impossible to pursue within the school's walls otherwise. Finally, Internet use also often seems to nudge schools and classrooms toward changes in school roles and relationships that lead to increased student autonomy, because of factors including increased student access to external resources and the reversal of the usual knowledge disparity between teachers and students in the numerous cases in which students know more about the Internet than their teachers (Schofield & Davidson, 2002).

A cross-national study of innovative technology use in twenty-eight countries on five continents demonstrates how Internet use can fulfill its potential to improve learning by leading to the kinds of changes just discussed (Anderson, 2003). For example, students in Israel undertook a major Web development project featuring information about the salt flats surrounding their school. Work toward this goal led to collaboration with Jordanian students, substantial technical training for older students who took responsibility for much of the work required to develop the Web site, and to a variety of student projects producing some of the materials posted on the Web site. Such a project embodies many of the changes discussed above. In producing and posting information about their local area for others to use, students undertook an authentic real-world project-based activity. In doing so, they collaborated with students from a neighboring country, something unlikely to have been possible otherwise. Furthermore, the fact that successful completion of the project required both an array of technical skills and the production of many kinds of products for posting provided the opportunity for students with varying skills and interests to develop them in a way that would be unlikely if they were all working on the same predetermined curricular material, as is often the case in traditional classrooms.

There are many other readily available examples of the ways in which the Internet can facilitate the kind of learning experiences that the learning sciences suggest are beneficial. For example, in the GLOBE program and Global Lab Curriculum project, students in schools around the world learn about science by gathering data from their local environment to contribute to databases used by scientists, and by interacting with those scientists (Roschelle et al., 2000; Songer, 1998). Chapters in this handbook (Bruckman; Fishman & Davis; Scardamalia & Bereiter; Stahl, Koschman, & Suthers) and elsewhere (Jonassen & Howland, 2003) discuss numerous others. However, as I discuss later, barriers often arise that limit or shape Internet use so that its potential to enhance students' learning is not realized.

The Realities of Internet Use for Instruction

Three things seem clear from research regarding Internet use for instructional purposes. First, Internet access for instructional purposes is common in many countries and appears to be increasing rapidly. Second, in spite of the increasing availability of the Internet in schools, students often do not use the Internet for instructional purposes as much as one might expect. Third, although there are many cases in which the Internet is used in ways that research in the learning sciences suggests is likely to be productive, the Internet is more often used in rather pedestrian ways that do not fully capitalize on its potential to enrich education. Before turning to a discussion of why this is, I briefly discuss the evidence for these three assertions.

The Rapid Growth of Internet Access in Schools

Internet access is exceedingly widespread in schools in many countries. For example, a study of fourteen countries, mainly in Europe, found that in the year 2000, 94 percent of upper secondary students attended schools in which Internet access was available, compared to only 24 percent in 1995 (OECD, 2003, table D3.1). Similarly, 99 percent of all public schools in the United States in 2002 had Internet access, up from 35 percent in 1994 (NCES, 2004) and the percent of their instructional rooms with Internet access rose from 3 percent to 92 percent in that same time period (NCES, 2004). Indeed, by 2002 the ratio of students to instructional computers with Internet access in public schools in the United States was less than 5 to 1, and the difference between this ratio in schools serving the most and least affluent students was quite small (NCES, 2004). Internet access in schools is, of course, not the exclusive province of highly developed western countries. Numerous countries in other parts of the world, including Korea, Thailand, Hong Kong, and Chinese Taipei, also have substantial Internet access (OECD, 2003; Pelgrum & Anderson, 2001).

The Limited Amount of Internet Use in Schools

Although access to the Internet for instructional purposes is extremely widespread in many countries, it appears that students do not use it as much as one might expect, given its ubiquity. For example, Süss (2001) found that only 13 percent of over four thousand European students using comput-

ers in school reported using the Internet there, although a very large proportion of schools in Europe had Internet connections at the time of Süss's study. Similarly, a large national survey in the United States (Becker, 1999) concluded that only about one quarter of teachers whose situation included those elements conducive to Internet use (such as a good educational background, good Internet access, school support of technology use, and some expertise with computers) used cross-school Internet collaboration with their students or posted their students' work on the Internet. Teachers whose situation did not include many of those elements were extremely unlikely to make such uses of the Internet.

A more recent study of students selected because of high self-reported levels of Internet use, including home use, found that they perceived numerous serious barriers to their productive use of the Internet at school (Levin & Arafeh, 2002). This finding is consistent with much case study and qualitative research, as well as with reports from those working in schools. For example, a study of the implementation of Kids Network, an innovative curriculum for grades 4–6 designed to allow students to engage with scientific problems and to use telecommunications to collaborate with other students doing similar work, found that students themselves rarely used the telecommunications tools, contrary to the designers' intention (Karlan, Huberman, & Middlebrook, 1997). Rather, their teachers typically used those tools, often before or after class when participating students were not even around. Love & McVey (2000, p. 1) reported that students in their preservice education courses find that "many of the experienced teachers with whom they work do not use the Internet as a part of their classroom instruction."

The Peripheral and Pedestrian Nature of Much Student Internet Use

Although the Internet appears to hold great potential for improving students' learning, this potential is unlikely to be realized when

Internet use is peripheral in the classroom. At least two factors are important in making Internet use peripheral – minimal use or devoting use to activities that are not intended to foster central and valued outcomes of schooling. It seems reasonable to expect that the impact of Internet use, like that of a great many educational activities, is likely to be limited if students' involvement in that activity is very brief, although important exceptions to this rule undoubtedly exist. Project-based and collaborative activities – which can make excellent use of the Internet's potential to enrich students' learning – often require quite intensive interaction over extended periods of time. These factors severely limit Internet use and undermine its potential.

However, time allocated to an activity does not determine in and of itself how central or peripheral that activity is in the classroom. The second factor determining centrality is the degree to which the activity is perceived to be linked to the accomplishment of important learning goals. Activities that are seen as unrelated to teachers' and schools' core objectives are peripheral in the sense that they are likely not to be taken as seriously as others, as suggested by the common observation that in these days of high stakes testing teachers often feel obliged to focus strongly on teaching to the test.

Internet use by students in classrooms is often quite peripheral (Cuban, 2001). For example, Schofield and Davidson's (2004) intensive study of a project designed to foster Internet use in numerous schools in a large urban school district found that Internet use was commonly viewed as an enrichment activity, rather than as a way to accomplish core curricular objectives, even in an environment that provided substantial assistance to teachers in integrating Internet use into classroom activities. Consistent with this, Zhao and Frank (2003) reported that the most common purpose for student computer use, reported by teachers in four U.S. school districts that had spent considerable sums on instructional technology, was its use as a reward for completed work or other classroom management purposes.

Interestingly, teacher use seems to be considerably more common than student use. For example, although almost 60 percent of the teachers surveyed by Zhao and Frank (2003) reported using computers weekly or daily themselves to do things such as download materials (which implies Internet use), under 15 percent reported using computers with similar frequency for student inquiry (such as database searching) and fewer than 8 percent reported weekly or more frequent student use of the Internet to contact other students, an activity central to many of the kinds of collaborative activities that the learning sciences suggest can be especially valuable.

There is no doubt that the Internet can be a valuable resource in schools even if it is peripheral to students' own classroom activities. It can provide teachers with extraordinary resources for lesson planning as well as with a wealth of professional development opportunities (Schofield & Davidson, 2002). In addition, educators have begun to make use of the Internet to increase communication with parents and the broader community in which their school is embedded, although such activities are not as common as many others (Kozma, 2003). However, the fact that so many schools currently have or are working toward a relatively low ratio of students per Internet-connected computer makes it clear that both student and teacher use is envisioned by the policy makers and administrators making decisions about technology expenditures as well as by many of the parents and community organizations that have worked to bring Internet connections to schools through "Net Days" and other efforts. Thus, no matter how useful the changes are that stem from the Internet's role in providing professional development experiences and communication with the broader community, the Internet's full potential to improve education will not be realized without student use.

Not only is student use of the Internet often peripheral; it is often quite pedestrian, by which I mean that the Internet is often used in simple and obvious ways that do little to change the basic nature of students' learning experiences. For example, a survey of Internet-using students found that they complain about rote Internet assignments that are like traditional classroom activities, such as filling out worksheets, and that they perceive the quality of their Internet-based assignments in school to be poor (Levin & Arafeh, 2002). There is little reason to expect such pedestrian uses to significantly improve students' learning, compared to similar activities that do not make use of the Internet. Interestingly, and consistent with this assertion, a survey of nearly six thousand Canadian students (Environics Research Group, 2001) found that fewer than a quarter of them reported that the Internet's biggest benefit to them was academic. More commonly highlighted were its social benefits (36 percent), its convenience (31 percent), and its entertainment value (27 percent). Indeed, another study concluded "Whereas teachers felt they are making dramatic leads in their ability to harness the power of technology to create stimulating, engaging, and challenging learning experiences for students, the students themselves have seen few changes in classroom instruction" (Power to Teach, 2003, p. 1).

Why Is Student Internet Use Often Relatively Limited and Structured in Ways That Do Not Make Full Use of Its Educational Potential?

To some extent the factors that limit student Internet use in schools and that often shape it in ways that lead to pedestrian uses are similar to those that limit and shape other kinds of computer use in schools. Important among these are lack of adequate or dependable technical infrastructure; lack of adequate technical training and support for teachers; lack of professional development focused on helping teachers see how technology can be used to achieve their curricular goals; lack of time in the school day for teachers to develop their technology skills; and lack of fit between common classroom and school structures and practices – such as

whole class instruction and relatively short class periods – and those practices needed for students to make optimal use of such technology (Schofield & Davidson, 2002; Schofield, in press; Zhao et al., 2002).

Although considerable progress has been made on these fronts during the past two decades, these issues still impede effective use of many kinds of computer technology in many schools. For example, lack of sufficient teacher training for productive technology use is still a significant problem even in developed countries that have made large investments in computer technology (Ansell & Park, 2003; Pelgrum & Anderson, 2001).

The Internet Is a Gateway to the World Beyond the School

There are other factors shaping the amount and nature of student Internet use in schools that are unique to Internet use, or at least are especially pronounced with regard to it. The potential to link the school to the world beyond its walls is often cited as among the chief virtues of the Internet (Cummins & Sayers, 1995; Garner & Gillingham, 1996; Koizumi et al., 2000; Starkey, 1998). This capability opens up an extraordinary variety of potentially useful educational possibilities, as mentioned earlier. However, it also raises some serious issues that can impede student Internet use and shape it in ways that make realization of its full potential difficult.

Concerns About the Nature of the Information Available on the Internet Limit Use

The Internet provides access to a vast array of information more varied and more current than the best school library could ever hope to provide otherwise (Pelgrum & Anderson, 2001). Teachers value this capability; they list getting information and ideas more frequently than any other goal when asked their primary objectives for computer use (Becker, 2000). However, whether students have access to the Internet in the context of traditional school tasks, such as the preparation of research papers, or in the context of the more complex kinds of collaborations and real-world projects that the Internet facilitates, school districts, and teachers are often concerned that students can use the Internet to access material that the teacher or other community members might find inappropriate, especially relating to sexuality or violence (Thornburgh & Lin, 2002). These concerns are sometimes heightened by worries about legal liability if students access certain kinds of objectionable materials, ranging from explicit sexual information to information on suicide and bomb construction (Schofield & Davidson, 2002). Thus, many teachers do not let students, especially young ones, use the Internet unless an adult can observe what they are doing. Because many classes have a small number of computers in the back of the room and it is difficult for the teacher to both teach other students and to simultaneously closely supervise the subset of students using the Internet, such concerns can curtail Internet use dramatically (Schofield & Davidson, 2002).

In addition to limiting Internet use itself, concerns about the kinds of information available to students via the Internet can circumscribe the materials that students are allowed to access when they do use the Internet, undermining at least some of its potential educational value and the extent to which students can pursue their own interests. The most obvious example is the use of filters designed to block materials pertaining to sexuality, violence, and other controversial topics, a practice found in roughly 90 percent of the school districts in the United States (National School Boards Foundation, 2002). Much of the material blocked by filters is of questionable educational value and some might indeed be harmful. However, the institutional needs of educational organizations to maintain public support and to avoid political problems are often given priority over the educational needs of students when decisions are made regarding the amount and kind of filtering that is desirable (Thornburgh & Lin, 2002). Not surprisingly then, students frequently complain about

the blocking of access to Internet materials for which they believe they have a legitimate educational need, suggesting that overblocking is more than a theoretical possibility (Levin & Arafeh, 2002; Thornburgh & Lin, 2002).

Numerous other practices stemming from concern about the nature of materials available on the Internet can also severely constrain students' ability to use the Internet efficiently and effectively. For example, Schofield and Davidson's (2002) study of a large urban school district found that some teachers allowed students to visit only preapproved Web sites, which dramatically reduced the resources students could access as well as undermined the development of many kinds of Internet-related skills. They also found that sometimes students were not permitted to use the Internet in the school library until the librarian had approved the search terms they planned to use, a procedure that markedly discouraged student searches and constrained students from making useful changes in search terms in response to initial search results. These or similar practices are common, as suggested by the fact that 48 percent of U.S. school districts report using some sort of restriction of access to online communication above and beyond filtering to deal with concerns about security, privacy, and safety (National School Boards Foundation, 2002).

Concerns Raised by the Internet's Facilitation of Interaction with Those Outside the School Limit Use

The Internet has the potential to link students to the world outside the school, and one of the most highly touted opportunities of the Internet is the potential for students to interact with others with whom they would otherwise be unable or very unlikely to be in contact. Although communicating electronically was selected as a primary objective for computer use by under 10 percent of U.S. teachers in a large survey (Becker, 2000), many teachers do have their students communicate with others, even if only to engage in the equivalent of electronic pen pal exchanges. Others have their students engage in more complex communicative and collaborative Internet activities described in other chapters of this volume (Bruckman, this volume; Scardamalia & Bereiter, this volume; Andriessen, this volume).

However, the use of the Internet as a vehicle for communication with others carries with it inherent risks that limit and shape its use in schools. Specifically, concerns about student safety stemming from the fact that students can use the Internet to interact with those they do not know limit its use in a variety of ways (Lankshear, Snyder, & Green, 2000; Süss, 2001). For example, in one district, some elementary school teachers monitored all the e-mail their students sent, partly to ensure that students did not give out personal information (such as their home addresses) that might compromise their safety if the person with whom they were communicating intended to exploit or otherwise harm them (Schofield & Davidson, 2002). This undercut the rapidity with which messages were exchanged, which is significant in light of the fact that speed is often cited as one of the primary advantages of using the Internet for correspondence. Furthermore, it created a disincentive for e-mail projects because of the amount of work the monitoring created for teachers. Monitoring student e-mail also allowed teachers to control the content of the messages, which they occasionally did even when safety was not a primary concern. For example, in one case a teacher changed the content of an e-mail that was part of an exchange designed to foster understanding between white and African American elementary students in nearby but very different communities. An invitation from one student to another to meet to go the movies was transformed, without the students' knowledge, into a general observation about how nice it would be to meet, due to the teacher's concern that parents might object to the proposed outing.

Student Web page development projects provide a public platform that students can use to convey their ideas and their work to others as well as to get broad feedback on them. These projects can provide students with the kind of authentic real world tasks that learning sciences suggests can provide excellent learning opportunities. However, such projects can create conflict regarding who controls students' communications when they are at odds with the public image the school wishes to convey, and can create concerns for teachers about how to regulate communication content. For example, student critiques of their school or of school staff posted on a Web site have the potential to embarrass the school and its staff, even if the critiques are well founded. Thus, teachers may insist on reviewing and approving such postings and on requiring students to delete materials critical of the school or its staff or otherwise deemed inappropriate (Schofield & Davidson, 2002). Of course, school control over the dissemination of student work products is not unique to the Internet. Traditionally, teachers have had the power to select the materials they put up on their classroom walls, and faculty advisors approve materials in yearbooks, student newspapers, and the like. However, the size of the public potentially reached via the Internet is very large, and norms on the Internet accept and even encourage "flaming." Thus, activities involving the Internet are likely to make the issue of control of student communications especially salient. This tends to lead to the creation of mechanisms to limit and control such communication and can even lead to avoidance of Internet-based activities.

Logistical and Other Issues Impede Collaborative Internet Projects

The Internet's capacity to connect students to the world outside of the school opens up not only the potential for communication with an audience via Web pages, e-mails, or other mechanisms. It also provides the potential for ongoing collaborations between students and others, ranging from peers in other locales, to mentors, to scientists engaged in ongoing research. However, such uses of the Internet are typically quite limited, in spite of their intriguing potential, perhaps partly because learning to collaborate with others is not high on teachers' list of objectives for computer use (Becker, 2001; Hunter, 2002). Indeed, a large international study of technology and educational change concluded, "We saw few cases in which teachers and students connected and collaborated with others outside the classroom. . . . Very few innovations involved collaboration with scientists, professors, and business people. Far fewer cases connected parents to the classroom. It is still rare that ICT (Information and Communication Technology) is being used to break down schoolhouse walls, even in these innovative classrooms around the world" (Kozma, 2003, p. 221).

In addition to concerns regarding the nature of the information available on the Internet, and concerns raised by having students interact with people neither they nor their teachers know, several other factors conspire to limit such collaborative uses. First, logistical issues related to different school schedules, different holidays, and even the fact that vacations in different hemispheres and nations come at different times, are more complex and disruptive than might be expected. Second, schools in different cities, states, and countries do not have perfectly overlapping curricula, and finding content that multiple schools can center a project around is not easy – a problem that is exacerbated if the collaboration includes scientists or other professionals who have their own particular interests and areas of expertise. Related to this problem are differences in the tests that are used in various locales to judge student progress (and by inference, teacher competence and success). To the extent that teachers work in school systems that stress different knowledge and skills in their standardized testing programs, disincentives to major collaborative projects are strong. Third, as happens in e-mail exchange projects as well, collaborative enterprises put teachers and students in any given location at the mercy of others who may or may not make their joint activity a high priority. This often causes problems, as suggested by the fact that a survey of teachers

participating in the second Global Exchange program, in which students and scientists from around the world worked together on a meteorology project, found that teachers' major complaint was that those at other sites were not sending back replies as often as desired (Songer, 1998). These logistical and other issues impede Internet use all the more because time is at such a premium in schools (Bacharach, Bauer, & Shedd, 1986), and teachers are used to working quite independently without having to learn how to anticipate and deal with such issues on a daily basis (Lieberman & Miller, 1990; Little, 1990).

Furthermore, there is reason to think that face-to-face interaction is important in making learning communities work (Malarney, 2000), which limits the potential of far-flung collaborations. For example, a major study of classrooms using the Internet for collaborative science projects ended up concluding that students were not using the Internet to carry on scientific discussions as intended (Feldman et al., 2000, p. 97). Indeed, that study concluded that "on-line discussions are a poor substitute" for classroom discussions because of difficulties related to timing, monitoring, and nonverbal communication that impede the development of reflective online discussions.

The Internet, and Much of the Content Accessible Through It, Were Not Designed for Educational Purposes

The origins of the Internet lie in the Cold War and the U.S. Department of Defense's interest in ensuring electronic communications in the event of a nuclear attack, its desire to provide defense researchers with long-distance access to powerful computers, and the National Science Foundation's belief that electronic communication could importantly facilitate other scientific research as well. Thus the Internet's technical infrastructure was not constructed with education in mind. For example, some Web sites get overwhelmed if large numbers of students try to use them simultaneously, especially at an already busy time of day, and teachers may have little choice about when they schedule such activities because of constraints placed on them by class schedules (Schofield & Davidson, 2002). Also, the Internet's culture, which stresses freedom of expression, change, and individuality, reflects in many ways the culture of the research communities involved in its creation, and the broader public which has adopted the Internet with such enthusiasm, more than that of primary and secondary schools (Schofield & Davidson, 2002).

Nevertheless, the Internet's origins help to account for the potential it currently holds for primary and secondary education. Early on, its perceived utility for defense purposes and for "big science" provided a level of federal involvement and funding hard to imagine had the Internet been conceived of primarily as an educational enterprise. Furthermore, the Internet's foundations in the adult university-based world of research provided the impetus for a culture which values producing and sharing information, whether or not that information has a specific practical purpose, which has undoubtedly contributed to the Internet's educational potential. However, the fact that the Internet was not developed primarily as a resource or tool for teachers and their students also gives rise to issues that impede its use in school by primary and secondary school students.

Information Type and Quality Can Pose Problems in Educational Contexts

Reflecting the Internet's origins, the vast majority of the information it makes accessible and many of the activities made possible by it are not intended for specific educational purposes. This poses a real challenge to teachers and students who wish to use the Internet for educational purposes, whether they be pedestrian and peripheral, or whether they seem more likely to realize the Internet's full potential for improving education. First, of course, it raises the issue discussed previously – that information readily available on the Internet may be considered objectionable and inappropriate for

students to access from schools – with the limiting consequences already mentioned.

Second, even if the topic of the information students access is seen as appropriate, the information produced by Web search tools is often not well suited for educational purposes. For example, it may not match well with students' reading ability, their preexisting knowledge, or the level of detail they need for a given purpose. Mismatches in any of these domains can frustrate students and significantly impede their learning. In addition, there is no reason to assume that the information students obtain from the Internet is valid. Anyone with access to a computer and minimal knowledge can post whatever they wish on the Internet. Although there is certainly controversy regarding the extent to which textbooks reflect specific worldviews, the information in textbooks and other materials typically found in school libraries has usually gone through a more rigorous review for accuracy than the information available on the Internet. Because teachers are used to having their students use textbooks and other relatively dependable sources for their research, they sometimes do not recognize the need to provide students with instruction regarding how to determine whether the information students find there is credible. Furthermore, even when they do recognize the need for such training, they may not feel they have space in their curriculum to add it (Schofield & Davidson, 2002).

In contrast, many non-Internet kinds of computer-based educational applications, ranging from software for computer-assisted instruction to intelligent tutors to educational games, come ready to use in particular subjects for students at given grade levels. In addition, they tend to be relatively self-contained and many are specifically designed to provide students with experiences carefully structured to foster their learning, and so that they do not require a great deal of teacher involvement. Of course, teachers need to develop some familiarity with such software, but that task is relatively well defined. And once the teacher has invested that time little additional time is necessary because, unlike the Internet, such applications typically do not change rapidly or unexpectedly.

As the Internet has moved from being an exciting innovation to being an integral part of everyday life for many people, as well as a tool widely available in schools, increasing attention has been paid to creating a wide variety of resources to help avoid or mitigate such problems. For example, Web sites created just for students of various ages and for the study of various specific topics now abound. However, it takes both time and various kinds of knowledge for teachers to locate such resources and to discover how to make productive use of them with their students.

The Internet's Flexibility and Richness Create Challenges for Teachers

The very flexibility that makes possible varied and creative uses of the Internet can make the Internet less attractive and more difficult for teachers to use than software designed for a specific educational purpose, because the link between the technology and educational outcomes is less straightforward and apparent (Zhao, 2003). The options for ways to use the Internet are so many and so varied that they can be overwhelming to teachers, who typically feel pressed for time (Bacharach, Bauer, & Shedd, 1986; Cuban, 2001; Schofield & Davidson, 2002). Teachers may hardly know where to start in choosing between having their students engage in e-mail exchanges, produce Web sites, search for information, interact with mentors, explore microworlds, or engage in extended collaborations, each of which can take somewhat different skills for the teacher to discover and implement. Books and Web sites providing guidance for teachers facing this challenge have proliferated rapidly in recent years. However, finding and exploring Web sites and other Internet activities suitable for a wide range of students, topics, and purposes still is likely to require substantial time and effort, which undercuts usage. Furthermore, in contrast to most computer applications used for instruction in schools, the Internet is constantly changing. Web sites, search mechanisms, and Internet-based educational projects and opportunities appear, disappear, and evolve. Thus, not only are locating and exploring the options that best suit one's students potentially time-consuming and daunting tasks, but teachers cannot be sure whether the investment will produce lasting rather than ephemeral opportunities.

The Internet's richness and flexibility create yet another potential problem in schools. Students working on the Internet are only a mouse click or two away from entertainment and recreational sites that exert a very strong pull on many of them. Although there may be nothing inherently objectionable about most of these sites, their ready availability in the classroom, combined with the fact that monitoring student Internet use takes time and resources, creates a potential problem. Students do often find working on the Internet enjoyable and motivating (Neilsen, 1998; Schofield & Davidson, 2002; Songer, 1996). Yet, there is also reason to think that when working on the Internet they may drift or dart away from prescribed educational activities, and be drawn to competing materials that they find enthralling. Although students have traditionally had the opportunity to daydream or chat with peers in class when they were supposed to be working, they have never before had instant and quite private access to a tremendous array of enticing entertainment. Thus, the same resource that holds the very real possibility of increasing students' motivation to work in school also presents an unparalleled temptation to play (Schofield & Davidson, 2002).

Conclusion

The Internet is a remarkably rich resource for education. It provides the opportunity for teachers to access an astonishing array of information and to build their professional skills. Similarly, it provides affordances that hold the potential to help teachers change students' educational experiences in ways that research in the learning sciences suggests can significantly improve students' learning.

There are clearly cases in which the potential of the Internet to reshape and improve education has begun to be been realized (Anderson, 2003). Yet often, in spite of large expenditures on technology and professional development for teachers, Internet use is more sporadic, peripheral to the core curriculum, and pedestrian in nature than its proponents initially envisioned it would be. To some extent, this situation reflects the fact that change in large and loosely coupled organizations takes a lot of time (Feldman et al., 2000), and Internet use in schools is still relatively new. However, two factors intrinsic to the Internet – that it is a gateway to the world beyond the school and that its structure and content have not generally been developed with education in mind – pose major obstacles to Internet use in schools, at the same time that they may ironically have been advantageous in other regards. Finding creative ways to take advantage of these factors, as well as to deal effectively with the problems they pose, is the key to realizing the Internet's potential for teachers and students alike.

References

Anderson, J. R., Corbett, A. T., Koedinger, K. R., & Pelletier, R. (1995). Cognitive tutors: Lessons learned. *The Journal of the Learning Sciences*, 4(2), 167–207.

Anderson, R. E. (2003). Stellar cases of technology-supported pedagogical innovations. In R. B. Kozma (Ed.), *Technology, innovation, and educational change: A global perspective* (pp. 195–215). Eugene, OR: International Society for Technology in Education (ISTE).

Ansell, S. E., & Park, J. (2003, May). Tracking tech trends: Student computer use grows, but teachers need training, *Education Week*, 22, 43–49.

Bacharach, S. B., Bauer, S. C., & Shedd, J. B. (1986). Education and reform. *Teachers College Record*, 88, 241–256.

Becker, H. J. (1998, April). *The influence of computer and Internet use on teachers' pedagogical practices and perceptions*. Paper presented at the annual meeting of the American Educational Research Association, Irvine, CA.

Becker, H. J. (1999). *Internet use by teachers: Conditions of professional use and teacher-directed student use*. (Report No. 1). University of California, Irvine and University of Minnesota [Online]. Retrieved March 26, 2003, from http://www.crito.uci.edu/TLC/findings/Internet-Use/startpage.htm

Becker, H. J. (2000, July). *Findings from the teaching, learning, and computing survey: Is Larry Cuban right?* Revision of a paper written for the School Technology Leadership Conference of the Council of Chief State School Officers, Washington, DC.

Becker, H. J. (2001, April). *How are teachers using computers in instruction?* Paper presented at the meeting of the American Educational Research Association, Irving, TX.

Berman, S., & Tinker, R. (2000). The world's the limit in the virtual high school. In Pea, R. D. (Intro.), *Technology and learning* (pp. 192–196). San Francisco: Jossey-Bass.

Bushweller, K. (2002). Cyber schools, online teaching and testing, and other e-learning initiatives are changing how schools operate. *Education Week*, 21(35), 8–11.

Cuban, L. (2001). *Oversold and underused: Computers in the classroom*. Cambridge, MA: Harvard University Press.

Cummins, J., & Sayers, D. (1995). *Brave new schools: Challenging cultural illiteracy through global learning networks*. New York: St. Martin's Press.

Environics Research Group (2001). *Young Canadians in a wired world: The students' view: What are youth doing online, and what do their parents need to know?* Retrieved April 7, 2003, from http://www.media-awareness.ca/eng/ webaware/netsurvey/index.htm

Feldman, A., Konold, C., & Coulter, B. with Conroy, B., Hutchison, C., & Londo, N. (2000). *Network science, a decade later: The Internet and classroom learning*. Mahwah, NJ: Lawrence Erlbaum Associates.

Garner, R., & Gillingham, M. G. (1996). *Internet communication in six classrooms: Conversations across time, space, and culture*. Mahwah, NJ: Lawrence Erlbaum Associates.

Hunter, B (2002). Learning in the virtual community depends upon changes in local communities. In K. A. Renninger and W. Shumar (Eds.) *Building virtual communities*. New York: Cambridge.

Jonassen, D. H., & Howland, J. (2003). *Learning to solve problems with technology: A constructivist perspective* (2nd ed.). Upper Saddle River, NJ: Merrill Prentice Hall.

Karlan, J. W., Huberman, M., & Middlebrooks, S. H. (1997). Challenges of bringing the kids network to the classroom. In S. Raizen & E. O. Britton (Eds.), *Bold ventures: Vol. 2. Case studies of U.S. innovations in science education* (pp. 304–393). Dordrecht: Kluwer Academic Publishers.

Koizumi, H., Dasai, T., Graf, K. D., Yokochi, K., & Moriya, S. (2000). Interactive distance learning between Japan and Germany. In D. M. Watson & T. Downes (Eds.), *Communications and networking in education: Learning in a networked society* (pp. 39–50). Norwell, MA: Kluwer Academic Publishers.

Kozma, R. B. (2003). Summary and implications: For ICT-based educational change. In *Technology, innovation, and educational change: A global perspective. A report of the second information technology in education study: Module 2*. Eugene, OR: ISTE (International Society for Technology in Education).

Lankshear, C., Snyder, I., & Green, B. (2000). *Teachers and technoliteracy: Managing literacy, technology and learning in schools*. St. Leonards, NSW, Australia: Allen & Unwin.

Levin, D., & Arafeh, S. (2002, August). *The digital disconnect: The widening gap between internet-savvy students and their schools*. Prepared for the Pew Internet & American Life Project. Retrieved March 26, 2003, from http://www.pewinternet.org/reports/toc.asp?Report=67

Levin, J. A., & Bruce, B. C. (2003). Technology as media: A learner-centered perspective. In Y. Zhao (Ed.), *What should teachers know about technology: Perspectives and practices* (pp. 45–51). Greenwich, CT: Information Age Publishing.

Lieberman, A., & Miller, L. (1990). The social realities of teaching. In A. Lieberman (Ed.), *Schools as collaborative cultures: Creating the future now* (pp. 165–193). Bristol, PA: Falmer Press.

Little, J. W. (1990). The persistence of privacy: Autonomy and initiative in teachers' professional relations. *Teachers College Record, 91*, 509–536.

Love, R., & McVey, M. (2000). *Teachers' use of the Internet*. Retrieved July 18, 2000, from http://www.tcrecord.org/PrinterText.asp?@ID Number=10538

Malarney, M. (2000). *Learning communities and on-line technologies: The classroom at sea experience*. Ph.D. Dissertation, College of Education, University of Washington, Seattle.

Mambretti, C. (1999). *Internet technology for schools*. Jefferson, NC: McFarland.

Means, B. (1994). Introduction: Using technology to advance educational goals. In B. Means (Ed.), *Technology and education reform* (pp. 1–21). San Francisco: Jossey-Bass.

Molenda, M. (1992). Technology and school restructuring: Some clarifying propositions. In D. Ely & B. Minor (Eds.), *Educational media and technology yearbook* (pp. 77–90). Englewood, CO: Libraries Unlimited.

National Center for Education Statistics (NCES) (2004). *Internet access in U.S. public schools and classrooms: 1994–2002*. Retrieved November 15, 2004, from http://nces.ed.gov/surveys/frss/publications/2004011/.

National School Boards Foundation (2002). *Are we there yet?: Research and guidelines on schools' use of the Internet*. Retrieved April 18, 2003, from http://www.nsbf.org/thereyet/fulltext.htm.

Neilsen, L. (1998). Coding the light: Rethinking generational authority in a rural high school telecommunications project. In D. Reinking, M. C. McKenna, L. D. Labbo, & R. D. Kieffer (Eds.), *Handbook of literacy and technology: Transformations in a post-typographic world* (pp. 129–143). Mawah, NJ: Lawrence Erlbaum Associates.

OECD (2003). Table D3.1. *Introduction of basic computer applications in upper secondary education (1980–2000)*. Retrieved November 15, 2004, from oecd.org/dataoecd/2/14/14558779.

Orange, G., & Hobbs, D. (2000). *International perspectives on tele-education and virtual learning environments*. Berlington, VT: Ashgate.

Pelgrum, W. J., & Anderson, R. E. (2001). *ICT and the emerging paradigm for life-long learning: An IEA educational assessment of infrastructure, goals, and practices in twenty-six countries*. Amsterdam: IEA.

Power to Teach (2003). *The growing technology gap between schools and students: Findings* from the BellSouth Foundation power to teach program. Retrieved April 9, 2003, from http://www.bellsouthfoundation.org/pdfs/pttreport03.pdf.

Roschelle, J. M., Pea, R. D., Hoadley, C. M., Gordin, D. N., & Means, B. M. (2000). Changing how and what children learn in school with computer-based technologies. *The Future of Children*, 10(2), 76–101.

Salomon, G. (1993). On the nature of pedagogic computer tools: The case of the writing partner. In S. P. Lajoie & S. J. Derry (Eds.), *Computers as cognitive tools* (pp. 179–196). Hillsdale, NJ: Lawrence Erlbaum Associates.

Savin-Baden, M. (2000). *Problem-based learning in higher education: Untold stories*. Buckingham, UK: Open University Press.

Schofield, J. W. (in press). Realizing the Internet's educational potential. To appear in Weiss, J., Nolan, J., Hunsinger, J., & Trifonas, P. (Eds.), *The international handbook of virtual learning environments*. Dordrecht, The Netherlands: Kluwer Academic Publishers.

Schofield, J. W., & Davidson, A. L. (2002). *Bringing the Internet to school: Lessons from an urban district*. San Francisco, CA: Jossey-Bass.

Schofield, J. W., & Davidson, A. L. (2004). Achieving equality of student Internet access within schools. In A. H. Eagly, R. M. Baron, & V. L. Hamilton (Eds.), *The social psychology of group identity and social conflict: Theory, application, and practice* (pp. 97–109). Washington, DC: American Psychological Association.

Shaffer, D. W., & Resnick, M. (1999). "Thick" authenticity: New media and authentic learning. *Journal of Interactive Learning Research*, 10(2), 195–215.

Songer, N. B. (1996). Exploring learning opportunities in coordinated network-enhanced classrooms: A case of kids as global scientists. *The Journal of Learning Sciences*, 5, 297–328.

Songer, N. B. (1998). Can technology bring students closer to science? In B. J. Fraser & K. G. Tobin (Eds.), *International handbook of science education* (Vol. 1, pp. 333–347). Dordrecht, The Netherlands: Kluwer Academic.

Starkey, B. A. (1998). Using computers to connect across cultural divides. In H. Bromley & M. W. Apple (Eds.), *Education/technology/power* (pp. 175–185). Albany: State University of New York Press.

Süss, D. (2001). Computers and the Internet in school: Closing the knowledge gap? In S. Livingstone & M. Bovill (Eds.), *Children and their changing media environment: A European comparative study* (pp. 221–241). Mahwah, NJ: Erlbaum.

Thornburgh, D., & Lin, H. S. (2002). *Youth, pornography, and the Internet*. Washington, DC: National Academy Press.

Trotter, A. (2002). E-learning goes to school. *Education Week*, 21(35), 13–18.

Virtual Schools Forum Report, Virtual Schools Forum held October 21–22, 2002 in Denver, Colorado. Retrieved March 26, 2003, from http://www.centerdigitaled.com/highlightstory.phtml?docid=40235.

Zehr, M. A. (1997). Partnering with the public. *Education Week*, 17(11), 36–39.

Zhao, Y. (2003). What teachers need to know about technology? Framing the question. In Y. Zhao (Ed.), *What should teachers know about technology: Perspectives and practices* (pp. 1–14). Greenwich, CT: Information Age Publishing.

Zhao, Y., & Frank, K. (2003). Technology uses in schools: An ecological perspective. *American Educational Research Journal*, 40(4), 808–840.

Zhao, Y., Pugh, K., Sheldon, S., & Byers, J. L. (2002). Conditions for classroom technology innovations. *Teachers College Record*, 104(3), 482–515.

Zucker, A, Kozma, R, with Yarnall, L, Marder, C. & Associates (2003). *The virtual high school: Teaching generation V*. New York: Teachers College Press.

CHAPTER 32

Teacher Learning Research and the Learning Sciences

Barry J. Fishman and Elizabeth A. Davis

Teacher learning is an active area for research in education, and although the learning sciences have not been primarily focused on teacher learning, teacher education, or professional development, we argue that the perspectives our field brings to the study of teachers' learning offer great promise. Learning sciences researchers – guided by the cognitive, sociocognitive, sociocultural, and systems-oriented perspectives that are prevalent in our field – have made contributions to and extended research on teacher learning in new and significant directions.

Fostering change in classroom learning and teaching is a central concern of the learning sciences, and teachers are a cornerstone of nearly all formal instructional systems. Teachers are the ultimate interpreters of any classroom-based intervention, and are responsible for a large amount of variance in the effects of instructional interventions – this is known as the "teacher effect" (Nye, Konstantopoulos, & Hedges, 2004). If learning sciences researchers are interested in translating research into practice to effect change at the classroom level – and we

believe that they are – it is imperative that the field pay careful attention to how teachers learn their craft and learn to effectively enact the innovations (technologies, curricula, etc.) that emerge from learning sciences research (Fishman et al., 2004).

The learning sciences have developed a focus on teacher learning only recently. Much learning sciences research focuses on teaching and learning in classroom contexts (e.g., Bransford et al., 1990; Brown, Collins, & Duguid, 1989), but this foundational research focuses on how teachers should or might teach, as opposed to how teachers might *learn how to teach* in these new ways. In this chapter, we examine major theoretical and methodological contributions that the learning sciences offer to research on teacher learning, and provide examples of how those contributions are realized in both research and practice. We begin with a brief look at major trends in the study of teacher learning in the broader educational research community, as a pointer into literature that might inform the work of learning scientists in this area.

Current Knowledge About Teacher Learning

Since the 1970s, cognitivism has been the dominant paradigm in psychology and also in educational psychology. Cognitively-oriented studies of teacher learning sometimes focus on teacher beliefs and attitudes, but most of all they focus on what knowledge teachers have to have to be effective (see Richardson, 1996, for a review of this topic). For example, Shulman (1986) argued that teachers draw on three major types of knowledge. The first two, knowledge of the content area and knowledge of pedagogy, were traditional foci of teacher learning. Shulman argued that teachers also needed a third type of knowledge, *pedagogical content knowledge*. Content knowledge is not enough; teachers have to organize content knowledge in a uniquely transformed way, so that it can effectively support teaching specific content. More recently, Hiebert, Gallimore, and Stigler (2002) proposed that there are two broad categories of knowledge involved in teaching: *professional knowledge for teaching*, which is public, community-generated, and subject to continuous evaluation and appraisal, and *practitioner knowledge*, which is often personal, local, and hard to verify, but equally important. These views of teacher knowledge are consistent with learning sciences perspectives on the sociocultural and situated nature of knowledge and learning (e.g., Brown et al., 1989).

When learning how to teach, teachers pass through a developmental trajectory called the *teachers' professional continuum*. This continuum identifies at least three major phases of teachers' careers: preservice education, induction into teaching, and continuing mastery of the profession (Feiman-Nemser, 2001). Preservice teachers develop new visions about teaching, and gain increasing understanding of learners and the learning process as they expand their teaching repertoires. During induction – the first few years on the job – teachers develop increased knowledge about their students and the broader context of their school and community, as well as how to teach within that context. They might, for example, recognize a need to adapt curriculum materials that are responsive to the needs of their students. New teachers also continue to develop their professional identities. Once teachers become more experienced, but before their practice stabilizes, they continue to expand their knowledge base, and begin to strengthen their dispositions toward self-improvement and toward taking on leadership roles in their schools. Teacher learning research in the learning sciences touches on all phases of this continuum, from preservice teachers to veterans.

The term "teacher education" usually refers to teachers' formal learning in schools of education or in alternative certification programs. Teacher education programs differ greatly, with programs focusing on teaching diverse learners, incorporating constructivist approaches to teaching, or promoting reflection, to name just a few. In contrast, the term "professional development" refers to teacher learning after teachers are working full-time – often referred to as "in-service" education, to contrast it with "preservice" teacher education. Professional development includes mentoring, curriculum materials, workshops, and conferences. Research has found that the most effective professional development is of extended duration, emphasizes content knowledge, and is coherent with other learning activities (Garet et al., 2001; Kennedy, 1999). The most effective professional development also requires teachers to examine their own practice (Putnam & Borko, 2000; Richardson & Anders, 1994), promotes reflection, provides opportunities for social supports (Putnam & Borko, 2000) and is closely coupled to what is expected to be taught in the classroom (Cohen & Hill, 1998). Indeed, much research on teacher learning in the learning sciences is set in the context of classroom practice and teachers' use of curriculum materials. The goal is to take advantage of the in-class, on-the-job setting to make teacher learning more effective.

How do teacher education and professional development improve the quality of teaching? Researchers typically assume that engagement in high-quality teacher education or professional development experiences leads to changes in teachers' beliefs and knowledge, changes in subsequent classroom enactment, and ultimately improved student learning. However, relatively few studies of teacher learning have gathered convincing data at each of the points in this chain; it is difficult to connect student outcomes directly to professional development in a single study (Loucks-Horsley & Matsumoto, 1999). One study emerging from the learning sciences serves as an example of how these connections can be made using more direct measures (Fishman et al., 2003). This is a critical area for future research.

What Does the Learning Sciences Bring to Teacher Learning Research?

Teacher learning is an active area of education research, with scholars from many perspectives contributing to the construction of a robust knowledge base. The American Educational Research Association's Division K, "Teaching and Teacher Education," is second in size only to Division C, "Learning and Instruction." What can the learning sciences uniquely contribute to this vast scholarly enterprise? The answer lies in a shift in research on teacher learning over the past decade to include a "situative perspective" (Greeno, this volume; Greeno, Collins, & Resnick, 1996), that Putnam and Borko (2000) describe as comprising three themes: that cognition is situated in particular contexts (Brown et al., 1989), is social (Wenger, 1998), and is distributed across people and tools (Pea, 1993). The situative perspective is at the core of the learning sciences, and as teacher learning research moves toward this perspective, the learning sciences are ideally positioned to make vital contributions.

Though methodology and theory are usually treated as discrete aspects of scholarly work, in the learning sciences there is a valuable synchrony between the two.

For example, the learning sciences field has become strongly associated with the use of design experiments (Barab, this volume; Confrey, this volume; Brown 1992; Cobb et al., 2003; The Design-Based Research Collective, 2003) to develop theory-based innovations in learning and teaching. Design experiments have become widely used in the learning sciences because this methodology is ideally suited to research which is rooted in real-world contexts of practice. When situativity is central to research, controlled laboratory experiments are not appropriate.

As learning sciences researchers develop curriculum materials, technologies, and new teaching designs, they often concurrently conduct professional development for participating teachers. This professional development ranges from the highly informal, such as participation in design sessions or "work circles" (Reiser et al., 2000), to highly structured workshops or online materials for broad distribution. Rarely, however, is professional development seen as the focus of research. More frequently, it is viewed as an incidental step in the deployment of an innovation. But the situated contexts in which learning scientists conduct research represent ideal opportunities for the study of teacher learning.

The learning sciences have an advantage in conducting teacher learning research in situated contexts: by nature and even by name, the learning sciences combine many different disciplines, and these projects are often conducted in teams that include multiple perspectives. A common critique of teacher education research is that it usually does not include disciplinary perspectives such as those of science educators or educational psychologists. This is a problem because research in cognitive development has shown that knowledge and learning are domain-specific, and the learning sciences incorporate these perspectives to help us understand content-specific changes in teacher knowledge. More general treatments of teacher learning tend to miss out on the domain-specific aspects of teacher knowledge. Because the learning sciences combine the perspectives of multiple fields, its approach can readily address these concerns. One example of such research is the work of the Center for Highly Interactive Classrooms, Curricula, and Computing in Education (hi-ce), which brings together researchers in science education, psychology, computer science, learning technologies, and literacy with K–12 teachers in a collaborative team to develop inquiry-oriented and technology-rich materials and tools. Because the hi-ce group includes researchers from these distinct perspectives, they are able to see highly specific aspects of teacher learning that might be overlooked by any single individual coming from just one perspective.

Although hi-ce's original work focused on promoting student learning, the group recognized the opportunity for studying teachers' learning through the design and evaluation of a broad set of professional development activities (Fishman et al., 2003), including an online professional development environment (Fishman, 2003) and educative curriculum materials for teachers (Schneider & Krajcik, 2002) connected to their larger reform goals. A similar expansion of focus has taken place in other learning sciences research groups (e.g., Linn, Davis, & Bell, 2004). The lesson is that once you start implementing innovations in real-world school contexts, teacher learning becomes increasingly central to the research.

Teacher learning research is sometimes decontextualized from practice because of the methodological demands of large scale experimental, quasi-experimental, or cross-sectional research (e.g., Garet et al., 2001). Such large-scale designs allow researchers to aggregate results over large numbers of teachers, but to do so, the designs must look across many different innovations and settings. The result is that we begin to learn what kinds of professional development are effective *in general*, but not in conjunction with specific innovations, which might have widely varying demands. This research can, however, yield critical policy-informing data about the impact of innovations when used in concert with other approaches in a con-tinuum of methodologies. Learning sciences research, by contrast, tends to occur on relatively small scales, allowing for much deeper understandings of the specifics of a single context. But learning scientists must take up the challenge of scale in order to translate findings from design-based and case-study research into larger-scale studies that more readily inform policy-making with respect to teacher professional development and preparation. The teacher learning research projects that we describe later employ the full range of these methodologies, typically leveraging contexts that allow even large-scale projects to be situated in real-world practice.

Examples of Learning Sciences Research on Teacher Learning

Teacher learning research has not been prominent within the learning sciences community to date. However, in the following we review projects that show how the learning sciences can contribute to our understanding of teacher learning. These projects provide both theoretical and methodological insights. We group our examples into two types: research that foregrounds social supports for teacher learning and the distributed nature of knowledge, and research that foregrounds the situated nature of teacher learning within practice.

In this review we have chosen to focus on examples that use technology to mediate teachers' learning. Much learning sciences research on teacher learning involves the development and study of online environments, in which teacher learning takes place using computer mediation, often (but not always) over a distance using a network such as the Internet (Vrasidas & Glass, 2004). These environments are particularly attractive for their potential to scale teacher learning by making learning opportunities available more flexibly and by reaching more teachers with less expense. Online teacher learning environments also have the potential to sustain teacher learning by reifying practice within a delivery mechanism that leverages research-based knowledge on teacher cognition and learning to ensure consistency and quality of content beyond the initial efforts of the designers.

Foregrounding Social Supports and Distributed Expertise

The learning sciences are unified by a belief that learning is social and distributed (e.g., Cobb, 1994; Linn, Davis, & Eylon, 2004; Pea, 1993). As learning scientists, we likewise believe that the most effective teacher learning is social and distributed. We begin our review by exploring examples of programs that emphasize social supports for teacher learning that aid teachers in distributing and sharing expertise.

BUILDING ONLINE COMMUNITIES OF PRACTICE

Teacher learning research has found that teachers need to be brought together in ways that allow them to learn productively from each other (Grossman, Wineburg, & Woolworth, 2001; Putnam & Borko, 2000). Unfortunately, teachers are typically isolated from one another in their work (Lortie, 1975). Learning sciences research on teacher learning has emphasized that "community" is essential to effective teacher learning (see Bruckman, this volume, and Shumar & Renninger, 2002, for discussions of the multiple meanings of this term). Many of the software tools developed by learning sciences researchers create communities by providing online communication tools, such as email and bulletin or discussion boards, that support open exchange of ideas and communication among teachers. These online communities have the potential to break teachers out of their usual isolation, and support productive collaboration.

The situated approach of the learning sciences makes it a natural paradigm for the scientific study of the role(s) that communities of teachers – both face-to-face and electronic – play in enhancing teacher learning. The concept of a *community of practice* (Wenger, 1998) has often been applied in the learning sciences, as researchers strive to design environments that support teachers

in the sharing of diverse expertise, in the construction of professional knowledge bases, and in supporting newcomers as they are apprenticed into increasingly expert practice (Collins, this volume). These ideas have particular relevance to the induction phase, when newly trained teachers are just beginning their first teaching jobs; many studies have explored the value of electronic networks for novice teachers (Riel & Levin, 1990).

An early effort to create a teacher community of practice was LabNet (Ruopp et al., 1993). LabNet was designed to support teachers as they began to use project-based methods (see Krajcik & Blumenfeld, this volume) in their science classrooms. Although it was before the Internet was widely available, LabNet used text-based e-mail and bulletin boards to create a community of practice among secondary science teachers. Eventually LabNet grew to more than 550 teachers. LabNet attributes its success to the development of peer leaders within its membership. These leaders were able to encourage and mentor newer participants through the challenges of using projects in their classrooms.

There were many efforts to reduce teacher isolation through formal online course offerings, such as the Bank Street College/EDC Mathematics Learning Forums (Honey et al., 1994) and the PBS Mathline Project (Rockman et al., 1996). In her research with teachers participating in both of these efforts, McMahon (1996) found that actual online participation (such as posting responses to messages) was much lower than the course designers had anticipated, and was related to the amount and location of access teachers had to the network (home access was related to greater use of the electronic tools). The amount of use was also inversely related to the strength of teachers' local support environments. These findings echo the caveats to success reported by the LabNet researchers (Ruopp et al., 1993).

Another project with a long history is the Math Forum (http://mathforum.org/; Renninger & Shumar, 2004), which was founded in 1992 as a "community center" for students, hobbyists, and math educators to provide access to high quality materials, activities, and person-to-person interactions. The Math Forum contains an interactive library of mathematics resources. But in addition to serving as a repository of classroom resources, it gives teachers access to a growing and active community of peers with whom they can discuss issues, share ideas, and ask questions. One of the key innovations of the Math Forum was to build its resource library by archiving the best interactions from site services such as the "Problem of the Week," which provides a non-routine challenge problem that teachers can use in their classes, and "Ask Dr. Math," which is a question-and-answer service for both teachers and students. This latter service operates using a scalable form of online mentoring that depends on a growing cadre of volunteers who provide guidance on finding solutions as opposed to simply answering questions. The Math Forum has developed its community of teachers by combining face-to-face workshops with online activities that allow teachers to become leaders on the site and contribute resources and expertise.

The Inquiry Learning Forum (ILF, http://ilf.crlt.indiana.edu/) is also based on a community of practice model (Barab, this volume; Barab et al., 2001). The ILF is designed to support teachers in mathematics and science (primarily in Indiana) who are working to improve their use of inquiry-based practice, and is based on four primary principles: (1) foster ownership and participation among users, (2) focus on inquiry, (3) enable virtual classroom "visits," and (4) support communities with shared purposes (Barab, MaKinster, & Scheckler, 2004). The user base of ILF is unusual in that it includes both preservice teachers who are required to use ILF as part of their teacher education coursework, as well as inservice teachers whose participation is completely voluntary. By studying interaction patterns within and among these groups, the researchers were able to deduce inherent tensions that, potentially, have design implications for other such environments (Barab et al., 2004). These include balancing between predetermined and emergent designs that meet the changing needs of the community, opportunities for users to create new meanings for themselves and for ideas to become reified for others, and the local and immediate needs of users and the more global interests of designers. Two more tensions include appealing to the broadest possible set of interests while still maintaining an identifiable core for the environment, and differentiating between online and face-to-face components of professional development.

The final online learning community we highlight here is Tapped In (http://www.tappedin.org/), developed by SRI International in 1997. Envisioned as a teacher professional development "institute," Tapped In uses a place and space metaphor in a Web-based multiuser virtual environment that encourages users to imagine themselves on a virtual campus with buildings that house classrooms, meeting rooms, and personal offices. Users can communicate via threaded discussion and text chat and can share files and resources such as Web links (Schank et al., 1999). Tapped In is unique in that it is not in and of itself a teacher learning program, but rather a platform that others can adopt to extend their programs and expand their capacity using Tapped In's community-building tools and services. For example, the Math Forum has used Tapped In as a place where visitors can meet with "Dr. Math," and school districts have established spaces in Tapped In to provide professional development and support for new teachers; Pepperdine University was the first of several universities to use Tapped In extensively to support online graduate programs in educational technology (Riel & Polin, 2004). Tapped In has seen continuous growth in its membership (currently at more than twenty-one thousand). On average, 15 to 20 percent of Tapped In community members log in each month and stay more than forty-five minutes per visit.

SRI researchers specifically designed Tapped In to support the formation of online communities of practice (Schlager, Fusco, & Schank, 2002). Recently, these researchers have turned their attention to the same online versus face-to-face problem described by the ILF team; both teams have noted that it's harder to establish communities of practice online than face-to-face. Schlager and Fusco (2004) suggest that it would be valuable to turn our attention to using technology to strengthen local (not distance-based) efforts in teacher learning. For example, these researchers recently replicated the Tapped In online framework to build a sustainable network for the support of new teachers in the Milwaukee Public Schools (Schlager et al., 2003).

These learning sciences projects have contributed to our understanding of how to design online environments that foster teacher community formation and support. This research shows that these communities go a long way toward alleviating the isolation teachers feel. These environments work especially well in providing the social supports teachers need and in providing a tool for expert teachers to share their knowledge with others.

MENTORING AND COACHING

Coaching is an important component of cognitive apprenticeship (Collins, this volume) and cognitive tutoring (Koedinger & Corbett, this volume). Coaching can be especially productive for teachers, who benefit from regular, sustained, and personalized interactions with others around their practice (Schaverien & Cosgrove, 1997). Providing access to mentors and coaches – potentially online – is one way of providing social supports at a smaller, more personalized scale than is typically the case in an online community. This access can then focus on teacher learning in addition to providing the social support teachers need. Mentors and coaches represent an important way of distributing the expertise of teachers; more experienced and expert teachers can scaffold newer or less expert teachers in developing new knowledge, beliefs, and practices.

For example, the Learning to Teach with Technology Studio (LTTS; http://ltts. indiana.edu) is a Web-based environment where practicing and preservice teachers can take self-paced courses on the topics of technology integration and learner-centered teaching. A key feature of LTTS is mentoring, with all students receiving one-on-one feedback from mentors who are experienced teachers well versed with the pedagogical philosophy of the system. In an experimental study of the effect of social presence – defined in terms of how friendly, trustworthy, and personable mentors appeared to students – it was found that though social presence affected students' perception of mentors, it had no effect on students' perceived learning or satisfaction or the actual quality of their course products (Wise et al., 2004). Another example of online coaching for teachers, called Wide-scale Interactive Development for Educators (WIDE World; http://wideworld.pz.harvard.edu/), is an online course environment designed to help teachers connect research-based pedagogies to the improvement of practice. A significant feature of WIDE World is that for every ten participants in a course there is a peer coach who is responsible for giving feedback on assignments and engaging teachers in multiple cycles of online exchange and dialogue. In formative evaluations that led to its current design, WIDE World developers tried and rejected as ineffective an initial approach that incorporated little or no human interaction around online resources (Wiske & Perkins, 2005).

The Web-based Inquiry Science Environment (WISE; http://wise.berkeley.edu) is a technology-mediated learning environment for students (Linn, this volume; Linn, Clark, & Slotta, 2003) with face-to-face and online supports for teachers learning to use the environment in their classrooms (Slotta, 2004). The WISE model of mentored professional development differs from LTTS and WIDE World in that teachers are connected to a personal mentor who interacts with them mostly face-to-face, as opposed to online. WISE mentored professional development employs the same pedagogical principles for teachers as WISE does for students. For example, WISE makes inquiry visible through visits to a mentor's classroom and through workshops where videotapes of WISE master teachers are discussed. A mentor also works with teachers one-on-one. As teachers become more proficient in using WISE in their classrooms, the nature of the mentor's role in supporting each teacher changes, first becoming more substantive rather than logistical, and then fading as appropriate. The mentored professional development is complemented by online supports such as discussion spaces for teachers, assessment and feedback tools teachers can use with students, and an authoring environment for adapting existing curriculum units or creating new ones. Research on the WISE mentored professional development model indicates that in whole-school implementations of the model, the professional development approach successfully supports even teachers with very different teaching styles (Slotta, 2004).

These studies, as with the studies of teacher communities described above, demonstrate the critical role social supports can play for teachers. These social supports provide a mechanism for distributing teacher expertise, giving teachers access to a far wider range of ideas than they have available to them otherwise. Another interesting side-effect of these systems is that they provide a potential way to measure teacher learning, by evaluating the artifacts that teachers produce for online courses, or through carefully documenting teachers' online interactions with a mentor when they begin to use new innovations with their students.

Foregrounding Situativity by Focusing on Practice

One of the central ideas in the learning sciences is that learning is more effective when it is situated in authentic contexts (Greeno, this volume; Brown et al., 1989). Situated learning is the foundation of learning sciences approaches including case-based learning (Kolodner, this volume) and problem-based learning (PBL; Koschmann et al., 1996). Cognitive flexibility theory goes further by suggesting that by visiting and revisiting the same information indexed from multiple perspectives ("crisscrossing" the domain), learners can broaden and deepen their perception of the complexity of cases and enhance their ability to transfer learning to new situations, eventually learning to make meaningful connections between concepts that seem disparate on the surface (Spiro et al., 1988). Situated learning, cognitive apprenticeship, case-based reasoning, PBL, and cognitive flexibility theory are all approaches for drawing on prior experience to facilitate conceptual change (diSessa, this volume). Each of these constructs, to varying degrees, informs the examples we discuss here. These examples foreground the role that situating learning within the practice of teaching can play in promoting teacher learning. We turn first to ways in which designers have situated teachers' learning by exposing them to carefully selected video images of classroom teaching.

USING VIDEO AS A VEHICLE FOR TEACHERS' LEARNING

Teachers frequently request to see other teachers' classrooms in action, as they feel that is the best way for them to understand how ideas related to teaching translate into practice (Fishman & Duffy, 1992). But it is difficult and inconvenient to leave one's own classroom and enter another's, so this desire is often addressed using video. Several researchers have explored, for example, the use of video clubs or study groups as a way to foster teacher learning (Frederiksen et al., 1998; Sherin, 2004; Thomas et al., 1998). One face-to-face video club involved videotaping the classroom practice of two of the participating middle school mathematics teachers (two others opted not to be videotaped) and then discussing an excerpt from the videotape once a month in the video club with the four teachers and two researchers (Sherin, 2004). This experience, spread over an entire school year, helped these teachers develop "professional vision," that is, "the ability to see and interpret critical features of classroom events" (Sherin, 2004, p. 179). Specifically, teachers became more likely to consider student ideas and the relationships between student thinking and pedagogical decisions, rather than focusing exclusively on evaluating the pedagogy of the video-taped teacher. Sherin further suggests that teachers learn in these ways even when they do not review their *own* practice in the context of the club; each of the four teachers seemed to develop in similar ways and extents.

Video cases embedded in online or computer-based materials have also proven to be a popular way to bring images of classroom practice into teacher learning. For example, Strategic Teaching Frameworks (STF; Chaney-Cullen & Duffy, 1998; Fishman & Duffy, 1992) was designed to embody cognitive apprenticeship (Collins, this volume) by modeling teaching practice and the reflective critique of teaching. STF took a single lesson as its unit of analysis. Commentary tracks approached the subject matter from multiple perspectives – including those of the classroom teacher, a subject matter expert, and a pedagogical expert from outside of the classroom. The video was also linked to a reference library with readings about the techniques being employed. Evaluations showed that STF promoted reflection about teaching among inservice (Chaney-Cullen & Duffy, 1998) and preservice teachers (Lambdin, Duffy, & Moore, 1997). Many of the key ideas from the stand-alone STF environment were incorporated into its Web-based successor, the ILF (described earlier). A similar early example of incorporating ideas of situated learning into support for teacher learning is the Casebook of Project Practices (CaPPs; Krajcik et al., 1996; Marx et al., 1998), developed to support teachers learning about project-based science.

Learning sciences researchers at the University of Wisconsin and Rutgers University have collaborated on eSTEP (the Elementary and Secondary Teacher Education Program), which has developed tools to enable the creation of online courses and activities for preservice teachers that systematically integrate collaborative instructional planning with text and video study (Derry & Hmelo-Silver, 2002). eSTEP courses taught at both universities include a hypermedia library of learning sciences concepts applied to teaching, linked to a video database of classroom-based teaching examples. Researchers describe a range of challenges in this work, including that of striking a balance between teacher expectations and the goals of the learning environment. In this case, preservice teachers often desire a great deal of specificity in their preparation, hoping to be told answers to pressing concerns about teaching and to gain access to specific activities to use in their imagined classrooms. eSTEP designers hope to help the preservice teachers develop a rich theoretical understanding of learning and gain access to tools to help them relate that knowledge to situations they may encounter (Derry et al., 2004).

Palincsar and Spiro draw on cognitive flexibility theory and the use of video to frame a project aimed at scaling up the knowledge base on text comprehension (Palincsar, Spiro, & Magnusson, 2004). Working with a large corpus of data that features two approaches to text comprehension instruction, they have created a Web-based tool called Experience Acceleration Support Environment – Comprehension (EASE-C) in which ten themes specific to struggling readers, features of informational text, and teachers' practices, can be searched according to the needs and interests of the user. Palincsar and Spiro are comparing the learning and teaching practices of fourth and fifth grade teachers using EASE-C with that of teachers in a comparison condition who have access to the same video content, but presented in linear video cases without the searchability of EASE-C. The researchers hypothesize that there will be treatment-by-aptitude effects across the two conditions as a function of teachers' prior knowledge, current practices, and experience within the condition.

The Generative Virtual Classroom (GVC; Schaverien, 2000) incorporates similar features to some of the systems described earlier – examples of video plus commentary on the video from experts – but the GVC video focuses mainly on students, providing teachers with improved access to, and thus insight about, students and the ways in which they make sense of concepts. Framed by a generative perspective on learning, the GVC allows teachers to learn generatively – exploring ideas, testing those ideas, and then explaining and, eventually, understanding those ideas (Schaverien, 2003). Studies using the GVC demonstrate that teachers learn when they perceive that their learning mirrors the generative character of students' learning. The designers emphasize the importance of users' organic movement through the video examples and through e-learning environments in general, as opposed to imposing a lockstep route.

Lampert and Ball (1998) took a different approach to employing video in teacher education; they gathered video of their *own* teaching as part of their Multimedia and Teaching through Hypermedia (M.A.T.H.) Project (which encompasses several efforts that go by different names, including the Space for Learning and Teaching Explorations (SLATE)). Lampert and Ball taught mathematics in a public elementary school as part of their research, and collected comprehensive records of their teaching through the use of video, daily diaries, lesson plans, and student work. This database is used in elementary teacher education courses to give preservice teachers a view of teaching in all its complexity. Preservice teachers can use an electronic notebook to create multimedia documents using video and other artifacts from the system as representations of their own developing understanding of the classroom environment. Gathering, indexing, and storing video on this time scale is a massive undertaking, and it is not surprising that no other projects (to our knowledge) have attempted a similar enterprise.

By situating teachers' learning in representations of practice, these projects go a long way toward promoting teacher learning. The highly contextualized nature of learning sciences research lends itself to models of teacher education and professional development that are highly contextualized as well. We find particular merit in what is coming to be called *practice-based professional development* (Krajcik & Reiser, 2003), in which inservice teachers' learning is structured around materials and activities that they employ directly in their own classroom practice. This is in contrast to more generalized professional development that might focus on broad concepts, such as "constructivist teaching," "inquiry," or "collaborative learning," but leaves it up to teachers to translate the ideas to their own classrooms.

USING EDUCATIVE CURRICULUM MATERIALS
TO SUPPORT TEACHER LEARNING

The concept of *educative curriculum materials* is a core component of some practice-based approaches. Since curriculum materials are a primary source of guidance for what teachers teach, Ball and Cohen (1996) suggest that the process-related ideas of reform should be embedded directly into the materials teachers use to teach, thus serving to distribute some of the expertise necessary for reform-oriented teaching to one of the key tools used by teachers at the same time as situating that expertise within the teachers' daily practice. Davis and Krajcik (2005) extend these ideas and describe how educative curriculum materials can promote particular teacher learning processes. Educative curriculum materials provide an ideal context for practice-based professional development, because not only do they represent effective approaches to teaching, but they also provide ongoing supports for specific aspects of teachers' learning.

We explore three examples of learning sciences projects that embrace these perspectives. These projects are each framed by the basic notion that a limitation of print-based materials is that space constraints require curriculum developers to make editorial decisions about how best to present any given activity, including any surrounding educative information about pedagogy or content knowledge. By providing an online extension to the curriculum, one can extend the print materials with multiple variations of any given lesson, as well as provide multimedia materials to present information difficult to convey in text.

Knowledge Networks On the Web (KNOW; http://know.umich.edu/; Fishman, 2003) is an online professional development environment developed specifically as an extension to the inquiry-oriented curriculum materials developed for the Center for Learning Technologies in Urban Schools (LeTUS); in particular, for print-based educative curriculum materials developed with the Detroit Public Schools (Singer et al., 2000). KNOW designers opted to provide two primary types of video: *images of practice* videos that provide windows onto classroom practice, and *how to* videos that give step-by-step visual instruction about how to set up and use scientific apparatuses or software. In addition, KNOW provides a broad range of student work samples as well as a discussion environment linked to each of the curriculum units. Though it could be used as the sole source of professional development, KNOW functions best in conjunction with other professional development activities, including face-to-face workshops. (This integrated professional development approach provides one solution for the online versus face-to-face problem considered earlier.) The integrated professional development approach results in strong gains in student learning (Geier et al., 2004; Marx et al., 2004). Furthermore, the integrated professional development approach can be directly (and empirically) connected to changes in classroom practice and to student learning (Fishman et al., 2003; Kubitskey, Fishman, & Marx, 2004).

The Living Curriculum (Shrader & Gomez, 1999), developed as part of LeTUS activities in Chicago, is also designed around curriculum materials. In addition, the Living Curriculum is case-based, following two teachers through a complete enactment of the curriculum. A central goal here is to increase teacher reflection about their enactment of the curriculum. Because the Living Curriculum and KNOW are both designed for use in the context of systemic reform efforts, and thus are intended to be used by any teacher in the system as opposed to self-selected or volunteer teachers, the potential user base for these systems is quite different than that of systems such as CaPPS, the ILF, and STF. These differences have implications for the kinds of knowledge support teachers are likely to need.

Building on many of the successful design features of KNOW and the Living Curriculum, as well as print-based educative curriculum materials such as those developed by hi-ce (Schneider & Krajcik, 2002; Singer et al., 2000), Kids as Global Scientists (Songer, 1996), and others, the Curriculum Access System for Elementary Science (CASES; http://cases.soe.umich.edu; Davis, Smithey, & Petish, 2004) environment is aimed specifically at preservice and new elementary science teachers. CASES research and development emphasize both educative elements targeted for these beginning teachers and particular challenges they face. For example, each CASES lesson includes one or more short narratives describing issues arising for a new teacher, thus contextualizing pedagogical concepts such as inquiry-oriented science teaching in the lessons themselves as well as in the narratives (Davis et al., 2004; Smithey & Davis, 2004). This example illustrates how a single design feature can serve to provide social support, to distribute expertise, and to situate learning all at the same time. Research indicates that preservice teachers relate strongly to the teachers in the narratives and see them as resources to help them envision how lessons will play out in the classroom (Smithey & Davis, 2004). Other research on new inservice teachers' use of CASES similarly indicates that teachers benefit from features that help them envision their use of lessons and units (Petish, 2004). This emphasis on how teachers use and learn from specific educative elements, combined with a recognition that all the elements necessarily function together, builds on another strength typical of learning sciences research (e.g., Linn, Davis, & Bell, 2004).

Whether grounded in teachers' own practice or in the practice of others, the examples reviewed in this section illustrate the power of situativity in designing supports for teacher learning. Teachers, like students, benefit from the contextualization of what they are learning.

Looking Forward

Learning sciences researchers have developed new environments that support teacher learning, and learning sciences research increasingly incorporates a study of teacher learning as part of the larger research project. The situated approach of the learning sciences is a natural fit with the increasing realization, within the broader teacher learning community, that cognition and communities of learners are central to teacher learning. The future will undoubtedly bring technological advances which will extend our ability to both study and advance teacher learning. For example, new video technologies will make it simpler for teachers to be in control of video capture, editing, and sharing, facilitating the development of rich media bases of classroom practice. Advances in student assessment will make it easier for connections to be made between teacher learning and student learning, enabling a stronger focus on key reform outcomes of professional development.

We believe that future research needs to increase its focus in several areas. The most important need is to study the cognitive and conceptual change that occurs during teacher learning within school contexts. In addition, we need a better understanding of how teacher education and professional development result in changes in teachers' classroom practice, and ultimately, changes in student learning. These causal links are notoriously difficult to study (Loucks-Horsley & Matsumoto, 1999), but learning sciences projects offer rich contexts that are ideal for this study. For example, earlier we described work within the LeTUS collaboration that links student learning data to design-based research on professional development (Fishman et al., 2003). This research produces information on teacher learning that has high internal and external validity, shaping the design of future teacher learning activities around LeTUS curricula in ways that are both scalable and sustainable.

The learning sciences will benefit from paying closer attention to teacher learning. The better able we are to help teachers learn to teach with the pedagogical ideas and technological tools that we create, the more likely that our research-based innovations will succeed and ultimately impact student learning.

Acknowledgments

The authors' work described in this chapter was supported by the W. K. Kellogg Foundation, the Hewlett Packard Corporation, and the National Science Foundation under grant numbers REC-9720383, REC-9725927, REC-9876150 and REC-0092610. We also thank the following people for their feedback on this chapter: Sasha Barab, Sharon Derry, Tom Duffy, Magdalene Lampert, Marcia Linn, Annemarie Palincsar, Lynnette Schaverien, Mark Schlager, Wes Shumar, Jim Slotta, Stone Wiske, and especially Chris Quintana. The views expressed are those of the authors and do not necessarily represent the views of the funding agencies or the University of Michigan.

References

Ball, D. L., & Cohen, D. K. (1996). Reform by the book: What is – or might be – the role of curriculum materials in teacher learning and instructional reform? *Educational Researcher,* 25(9), 6–8.

Barab, S. A., MaKinster, J., Moore, J. A., Cunningham, D. J., & The ILF Design Team. (2001). Designing and building an on-line community: The struggle to support sociability in the Inquiry Learning Forum. *Educational Technology Research and Development, 49*(4), 71–96.

Barab, S. A., MaKinster, J., & Scheckler, R. (2004). Designing system dualities: Characterizing an online professional development community. In S. A. Barab, R. Kling, & J. H. Gray (Eds.), *Designing for virtual communities in the service of learning* (pp. 53–90). Cambridge, MA: Cambridge University Press.

Bransford, J. D., Sherwood, R. D., Hasselbring, T. S., Kinzer, C. K., & Williams, S. M. (1990). Anchored instruction: Why we need it and how technology can help. In D. Nix & R. Spiro (Eds.), *Cognition, education, and multimedia: Exploring ideas in high technology* (pp. 115–141). Hillsdale, NJ: Lawrence Erlbaum Associates.

Brown, A. L. (1992). Design experiments: Theoretical and methodological challenges in creating complex interventions in classroom settings. *The Journal of the Learning Sciences, 2*(2), 141–178.

Brown, J. S., Collins, A., & Duguid, P. (1989). Situated cognition and the culture of learning. *Educational Researcher, 18*(1), 32–42.

Chaney-Cullen, T., & Duffy, T. M. (1998). Strategic teaching frameworks: Multimedia to support teacher change. *The Journal of the Learning Sciences, 8*, 1–40.

Cobb, P. (1994). Where is the mind? Constructivist and sociocultural perspectives on mathematical development. *Educational Researcher, 23*(7), 13–20.

Cobb, P., Confrey, J., diSessa, A., Lehrer, R., & Schauble, L. (2003). Design experiments in educational research. *Educational Researcher, 32*(1), 9–13.

Cohen, D. K., & Hill, H., C. (1998). *State policy and classroom performance: Mathematics reform in California* (CPRE Policy Brief No. RB-23). Philadelphia, PA: Consortium for Policy Research in Education.

Davis, E. A., & Krajcik, J. (2005). Designing educative curriculum materials to promote teacher learning. *Educational Researcher, 34*, 3–14.

Davis, E. A., Smithey, J., & Petish, D. (2004). Designing an online learning environment for new elementary science teachers: Supports for learning to teach. In Y. B. Kafai, W. A. Sandoval, N. Enyedy, A. S. Nixon, & F. Herrera (Eds.), *Proceedings of the 6th International Conference of the Learning Sciences* (pp. 594). San Diego: Lawrence Erlbaum Associates.

Derry, S. J., & Hmelo-Silver, C. (2002). Addressing teacher education as a complex science: Theory-based studies within the STEP project. In P. Bell, R. Stevens, & T. Satwicz (Eds.), *International Conference of the Learning Sciences (ICLS)* (pp. 611–615). Mahwah, NJ: Lawrence Erlbaum Associates.

Derry, S. J., Seymour, J., Steinkuehler, C., Lee, J., & Siegel, M. A. (2004). From ambitious vision to partially satisfying reality: An evolving socio-technical design supporting community and collaborative learning in teacher education. In S. A. Barab, R. Kling, & J. H. Gray (Eds.), *Designing for virtual communities in the service of learning* (pp. 256–295). Cambridge: Cambridge University Press.

Feiman-Nemser, S. (2001). From preparation to practice: Designing a continuum to strengthen and sustain teaching. *Teachers College Record, 103*(6), 1013–1055.

Fishman, B. (2003). Linking on-line video and curriculum to leverage community knowledge. In J. Brophy (Ed.), *Advances in research on teaching: Using video in teacher education* (Vol. 10, pp. 201–234). New York: Elsevier.

Fishman, B., & Duffy, T. M. (1992). Classroom restructuring: What do teachers really need? *Educational Technology Research and Development, 40*(3), 95–111.

Fishman, B., Marx, R., Best, S., & Tal, R. (2003). Linking teacher and student learning to improve professional development in systemic reform. *Teaching and Teacher Education, 19*(6), 643–658.

Fishman, B., Marx, R., Blumenfeld, P., Krajcik, J. S., & Soloway, E. (2004). Creating a framework for research on systemic technology innovations. *The Journal of the Learning Sciences, 13*(1), 43–76.

Frederiksen, J. R., Sipusic, M., Sherin, M., & Wolfe, E. (1998). Video portfolio assessment: Creating a framework for viewing the functions of teaching. *Educational Assessment, 5*(4), 225–297.

Garet, M. S., Porter, A. C., Desimone, L., Birman, B. F., & Yoon, K. S. (2001). What makes professional development effective? Results from a national sample of teachers. *American Educational Research Journal, 38*(4), 915–945.

Geier, B., Blumenfeld, P., Marx, R., Krajcik, J. S., Fishman, B., & Soloway, E. (2004). Standardized test outcomes of urban students participating in standards and project-based science curricula. In Y. B. Kafai, W. A. Sandoval, N. Enyedy, A. S. Nixon, & H. Francisco (Eds.), *Proceedings of the Sixth International Conference of the Learning Sciences* (pp. 206–213). Santa Monica, CA: Lawrence Erlbaum Associates.

Greeno, J. G., Collins, A., & Resnick, L. B. (1996). Cognition and learning. In D. Berliner & R. Calfee (Eds.), *Handbook of educational psychology* (pp. 15–46). New York: Macmillan.

Grossman, P., Wineburg, S., & Woolworth, S. (2001). Toward a theory of teacher community. *Teachers College Record, 103* (6), 942–1012.

Hiebert, J., Gallimore, R., & Stigler, J. W. (2002). A knowledge base for the teaching profession: What would it look like and how can we get one? *Educational Researcher, 31* (5), 3–15.

Honey, M., Bennett, D., Hupert, N., Kanze, B., Meade, T., Panush, E. M., et al. (1994). The mathematics learning forums online: Using telecommunications as a tool for reflective practice. *Machine-Mediated Learning, 4* (2–3), 163–176.

Kennedy, M. (1999). *Form and substance in mathematics and science professional development* (NISE Brief No. 3 (2)). Madison, WI: National Center for Improving Science Education. Retrieved, from http://www.wcer.wisc.edu/nise/Publications/Briefs/Vol_3_No_2/Vol.3, No.2.pdf, Accessed November 23, 2005.

Koschmann, T., Kelson, A. C., Feltovich, P. J., & Barrows, H. S. (1996). Computer-supported problem-based learning: A principled approach to the use of computers in collaborative learning. In T. Koschmann (Ed.), *CSCL: Theory and practice of an emerging paradigm* (pp. 83–124). Mahwah, NJ: Lawrence Erlbaum Associates.

Krajcik, J. S., & Reiser, B. J. (2003, April). *Design principles for developing inquiry materials with embedded technologies.* Paper presented at the Annual Meeting of the American Educational Research Association, Chicago, IL.

Krajcik, J. S., Soloway, E., Blumenfeld, P., Marx, R. W., Ladewski, B., Bos, N., et al. (1996). The Casebook of Project Practices: An example of an interactive multimedia system for professional development. *Journal of Computers in Mathematics and Science Teaching, 15*, 119–135.

Kubitskey, B., Fishman, B., & Marx, R. (2004, April). *Teacher learning from reform-based pro-*

fessional development and its impact on student learning: A case study. Paper presented at the Annual Meeting of the National Association of Research on Science Teaching, Vancouver, Canada.

Lambdin, D., Duffy, T. M., & Moore, J. A. (1997). Using an interactive information system to expand preservice teachers' visions of effective mathematics teaching. *Journal of Technology and Teacher Education, 5*, 171–202.

Lampert, M., & Ball, D. L. (1998). *Teaching, multimedia, and mathematics: Investigations of real practice.* New York: Teachers College Press.

Linn, M. C., Clark, D., & Slotta, J. D. (2003). WISE design for knowledge integration. *Science Education, 87* (4), 517–538.

Linn, M. C., Davis, E. A., & Bell, P. (2004). *Internet environments for science education.* Mahwah, NJ: Lawrence Erlbaum Associates.

Linn, M. C., Davis, E. A., & Eylon, B.-S. (2004). The scaffolded knowledge integration framework for instruction. In M. C. Linn, E. A. Davis, & P. Bell (Eds.), *Internet environments for science education* (pp. 47–72). Mahwah, NJ: Lawrence Erlbaum Associates.

Lortie, D. (1975). *Schoolteacher: A sociological study.* Chicago: University of Chicago Press.

Loucks-Horsley, S., & Matsumoto, C. (1999). Research on professional development for teachers of mathematics and science: The state of the scene. *School Science and Mathematics, 99* (5), 258–271.

Marx, R. W., Blumenfeld, P., Krajcik, J. S., Fishman, B., Soloway, E., Geier, B., et al. (2004). Inquiry-based science in the middle grades: Assessment of learning in urban systemic reform. *Journal of Research in Science Teaching, 41* (10), 1063–1080.

Marx, R. W., Blumenfeld, P., Krajcik, J. S., & Soloway, E. (1998). New technologies for teacher professional development. *Teaching and Teacher Education, 14* (1), 33–52.

McMahon, T. A. (1996). *From isolation to interaction? Computer-mediated communications and teacher professional development.* Unpublished doctoral dissertation, Indiana University, Bloomington, IN.

Nye, B., Konstantopoulos, S., & Hedges, L. V. (2004). How large are teacher effects? *Educational Evaluation and Policy Analysis, 26* (3), 237–257.

Palincsar, A. S., Spiro, R. J., & Magnusson, S. J. (2004). *Investigating the feasibility of scaling* up effective reading comprehension instruction using innovative case-based hypermedia (IERI Proposal No. REC-0343578). Arlington, VA: National Science Foundation. Retrieved October 20, 2004, from http://www.nsf.gov/awardsearch/showAward.do?AwardNumber=0343578.

Pea, R. D. (1993). Practices of distributed intelligence and designs for education. In G. Salomon (Ed.), Distributed cognitions: Psychological and educational considerations (pp. 47–87). New York: Cambridge University Press.

Petish, D. (2004). Using educative curriculum materials to support new elementary science teachers' learning and practice. Unpublished doctoral dissertation, University of Michigan, Ann Arbor, MI.

Putnam, R., & Borko, H. (2000). What do new views of knowledge and thinking have to say about research on teacher learning? Educational Researcher, 29(1), 4–15.

Reiser, B. J., Spillane, J. P., Steinmuller, F., Sorsa, D., Carney, K., & Kyza, E. (2000). Investigating the mutual adaptation process in teachers' design of technology-infused curricula. In B. Fishman & S. O'Connor-Divelbiss (Eds.), Proceedings of the Fourth International Conference of the Learning Sciences (pp. 342–349). Mahwah, NJ: Lawrence Erlbaum Associates.

Renninger, K. A., & Shumar, W. (2004). The centrality of culture and community to participant learning at and with The Math Forum. In S. A. Barab, R. Kling, & J. H. Gray (Eds.), Designing for virtual communities in the service of learning (pp. 181–209). Cambridge: Cambridge University Press.

Richardson, V. (1996). The role of attitudes and beliefs in learning to teach. In J. Sikula, T. Buttery, & E. Guyton (Eds.), Handbook of research on teacher education (pp. 102–119). New York: Simon & Schuster Macmillan.

Richardson, V., & Anders, P. L. (1994). The study of teacher change. In V. Richardson (Ed.), Teacher change and the staff development process: A case in reading instruction (pp. 159–180). New York: Teachers College Press.

Riel, M., & Levin, J. A. (1990). Building electronic communities: Success and failure in computer networking. Instructional Science, 19, 145–169.

Riel, M., & Polin, L. (2004). Online learning communities: Common ground and critical differences in designing technical environments. In S. A. Barab, R. Kling, & J. H. Gray (Eds.), Designing for virtual communities in the service of learning (pp. 16–50). Cambridge: Cambridge University Press.

Rockman et al. (1996). Evaluation of PBS Mathline middle school mathematics project 1995–1996: The Second Year. San Francisco, CA: Rockman et al. Retrieved October 15, 2004, from http://rockman.com/projects/pbs/Mathline.pdf.

Ruopp, R. R., Gal, S., Drayton, B., & Pfister, M. (1993). LabNet: Toward a community of practice. Hillsdale, NJ: Lawrence Erlbaum Associate.

Schank, P., Fenton, J., Schlager, M. S., & Fusco, J. (1999). From MOO to MEOW: Domesticating technology for online communities. In C. M. Hoadley & J. M. Roschelle (Eds.), Proceedings of the Conference on Computer Support for Collaborative Learning (pp. 518–526). Palo Alto, CA: Stanford University.

Schaverien, L. (2000). Towards research-based designing for understanding functional concepts: The case of the web-delivered Generative Virtual Classroom for teacher education. Australian Journal of Educational Technology, 16(1), 1–12.

Schaverien, L. (2003). Teacher education in the Generative Virtual Classroom: Developing learning theories through a web-delivered, technology-and-science education context. International Journal of Science Education, 25(12), 1451–1469.

Schaverien, L., & Cosgrove, M. (1997). Learning to teach generatively: Mentor-supported professional development and research in technology-and-science. The Journal of the Learning Sciences, 6(3), 317–346.

Schlager, M. S., & Fusco, J. (2004). Teacher professional development, technology, and communities of practice: Are we putting the cart before the horse? In S. A. Barab, R. Kling, & J. H. Gray (Eds.), Designing for virtual communities in the service of learning (pp. 120–153). Cambridge: Cambridge University Press.

Schlager, M. S., Fusco, J., Koch, M., Crawford, B., & Phillips, M. (2003, July). Designing equity and diversity into online strategies to support new teachers. Paper presented at the National Educational Computing Conference, Seattle, WA.

Schlager, M. S., Fusco, J., & Schank, P. (2002). Evolution of an online education community of practice. In K. A. Renninger & W. Shumar (Eds.), Building virtual communities: Learning and change in cyberspace (pp. 129–158). Cambridge: Cambridge University Press.

Schneider, R. M., & Krajcik, J. S. (2002). Supporting science teacher learning: The role of educative curriculum materials. *Journal of Science Teacher Education, 13*(3), 221–245.

Sherin, M. G. (2004). Teacher learning in the context of a video club. *Teaching and Teacher Education, 20*, 163–183.

Shrader, G., & Gomez, L. (1999). Design research for the Living Curriculum. In C. M. Hoadley & J. M. Roschelle (Eds.), *Proceedings of the Conference on Computer Support for Collaborative Learning* (pp. 527–537). Palo Alto, CA: Stanford University.

Shulman, L. S. (1986). Those who understand: Knowledge growth in teaching. *Educational Researcher, 15*(2), 4–14.

Shumar, W., & Renninger, K. A. (2002). On conceptualizing community. In K. A. Renninger & W. Shumar (Eds.), *Building virtual communities: Learning and change in cyberspace* (pp. 1–17). Cambridge: Cambridge University Press.

Singer, J., Marx, R. W., Krajcik, J. S., & Clay-Chambers, J. (2000). Constructing extended inquiry projects: Curriculum materials for science education reform. *Educational Psychologist, 35*(3), 165–178.

Slotta, J. D. (2004). The Web-based Inquiry Science Environment (WISE): Scaffolding knowledge integration in the science classroom. In M. C. Linn, E. A. Davis, & P. Bell (Eds.), *Internet environments for science education* (pp. 203–231). Mahwah, NJ: Lawrence Erlbaum Associates.

Smithey, J., & Davis, E. A. (2004). Preservice elementary teachers' identity development: Identifying with particular images of inquiry. In Y. B. Kafai, W. A. Sandoval, N. Enyedy, A. S. Nixon, & F. Herrera (Eds.), *Proceedings of the 6th International Conference of the Learning Sciences* (pp. 635). San Diego: Lawrence Erlbaum Associates.

Songer, N. B. (1996). Exploring learning opportunities in coordinated network-enhanced classrooms: A case of kids as global scientists. *The Journal of the Learning Sciences, 5*(4), 297–327.

Spiro, R. J., Coulson, R. L., Feltovich, P. J., & Anderson, D. (1988). Cognitive flexibility theory: Advanced knowledge acquisition in ill-structured domains. In *Proceedings of the Tenth Annual Conference of the Cognitive Science Society* (pp. 375–383). Hillsdale, NJ: Lawrence Erlbaum Associates.

The Design-Based Research Collective. (2003). Design-based research: An emerging paradigm for educational inquiry. *Educational Researcher, 32*(1), 5–8.

Thomas, G., Wineburg, S., Grossman, P., Myhre, O., & Woolworth, S. (1998). In the company of colleagues: An interim report on the development of a community of teacher learners. *Teaching and Teacher Education, 14*(1), 21–32.

Vrasidas, C., & Glass, G. V. (2004). Teacher professional development: Issues and trends. In C. Vrasidas & G. V. Glass (Eds.), *Online professional development for teachers* (pp. 1–11). Greenwich, CT: Information Age Publishing.

Wenger, E. (1998). *Communities of practice: Learning, meaning, and identity.* Cambridge: Cambridge University Press.

Wise, A., Chang, J.-Y., Duffy, T. M., & del Valle, R. (2004). The effects of teacher social presence on student satisfaction, engagement, and learning. *Journal of Educational Computing Research, 31*(3), 247–271.

Wiske, M. S., & Perkins, D. N. (2005). Dewey goes digital: Scaling up constructivist pedagogies and the promise of new technologies. In C. Dede, J. Honan, & L. Peters (Eds.), *Scaling up success: Lessons learned from technology-based educational improvement* (pp. 27–47). New York: Jossey-Bass.

CHAPTER 33

Scaling Up

Evolving Innovations Beyond Ideal Settings to Challenging Contexts of Practice

Chris Dede

"Scaling up" involves adapting an innovation that is successful in one setting to be effectively used in a wide range of contexts. In contrast to experiences in other sectors of society, scaling up successful programs has proved very difficult in education (Dede, Honan, & Peters, 2005). Innovations at one fast-food location may easily transfer to every store in that franchise and perhaps to any comparable type of restaurant. However, a new type of teaching strategy that is successful with one practitioner often is difficult to generalize even to other instructors in the same school, let alone to a broad range of practitioners. In general, the more complex the innovation and the wider the range of contexts, the more likely a new practice is to fail the attempt to cross the chasm from its original setting to other sites where its implementation could potentially prove valuable (Moore, 1999). In other words, scalable designs for educational transformation must avoid what Wiske and Perkins (2005) term the "replica trap": the erroneous strategy of trying to repeat everywhere what worked locally, without taking account of local variations in needs and envi-

ronments. This involves resolving problems of magnitude (fostering the necessary conditions for change in large numbers of settings with average resources at considerable distances from one another) and variation (diverse and often unfavorable conditions across settings).

In the context of innovations in teaching and curriculum, Coburn (2003) defines scale as encompassing four interrelated dimensions: depth, sustainability, spread, and shift in reform ownership. *Depth* refers to deep and consequential change in classroom practice – altering teachers' beliefs, norms of social interaction, and pedagogical principles as enacted in the curriculum. *Sustainability* involves maintaining these consequential changes over substantial periods of time, and *spread* is based on the diffusion of the innovation to large numbers of classrooms and schools. *Shift* requires districts, schools, and teachers to assume ownership of the innovation, deepening, sustaining, and spreading its impacts. A fifth possible dimension to extend Coburn's framework is *evolution*, in which the innovation as revised by its adapters is influential in reshaping the thinking of its designers, creating a community of practice that evolves the innovation.

This chapter defines scaling up individual educational innovations as different from systemic reform. An extensive scholarly literature documents the challenges of systemic reform, which involves implementing suites of innovations that collectively transform the mission, goals, processes, personnel, and products of an educational institution (Berends, Bodilly, & Kirby, 2002). Scaling up a suite of innovations through systemic reforms that assure their incorporation and effectiveness by changing the entire context of their implementation to embed their conditions for success is less frequent and more challenging than the more typical situation of scaling up a single innovation through implementation in a potentially resistant educational setting that lacks some conditions related to the innovation's prior successes. I discuss both types of scaling up in this chapter.

An Analogical Conceptual Framework for Scaling Up in Educational Settings

Adaptation of an organism, innovation, or organization to local conditions is a fundamental phenomenon in both natural and human settings. Analogies related to various types of adaptation are helpful for understanding the special case of scaling up in educational settings. This section draws on insights about adaptation from studies in both the biological and social sciences to construct an analogical conceptual framework for the adaptation of educational innovations.

The adaptation of biological species is distinct from human adaptation in both its rate and its degree of intentionality. Over long periods of time, shifts in an ecosystem can induce the adaptation of species that inhabit that specific context (Moya & Font, 2004). As one illustration, changes in a natural environment may mean that particular forms of coloration for a type of insect provide better camouflage, enhancing the chances

of its survival. As a result, through natural selection over time, that coloration becomes more prevalent in that insect species. In contrast, the changes in the dinosaur's environment were evidently too great for random mutations to generate the necessary adaptive changes in time to save many types of dinosaurs. In ecosystems, adaptation is a non-purposive, slow process driven by natural selection; a change in a species is emergent rather than deliberately designed and implemented.

In human settings, a somewhat analogous process of adaptation to contextual conditions occurs. For example, in the rapidly shifting context of modern economies, many businesses must frequently alter their products and processes to stay competitive or even viable. In turn, employees of these businesses find that various types of skills or knowledge wax or wane in importance. Some workers intentionally adjust their mix of capabilities to adapt to this shift; others unwilling or unable to change may lose their jobs. In contrast to the slow and non-purposive process of natural selection in ecosystems, the human progression of contextual change, organizational response, and individual adaptation is sometimes deliberate, sometimes inadvertent, and has accelerated markedly over the past few decades (Levy & Murnane, 2004).

For both natural and human settings, the context itself is shaped by successes and failures of adaptation. Through systemic processes, the interactions among various flora and fauna in an ecosystem are altered by the prevalence of each species. For example, pine trees lose needles that, on the forest floor, inhibit some other types of trees from growing. Similarly, the characteristics of a society are affected by the types of businesses that prosper or fail. As an illustration, the success of a factory creates regional conditions (e.g., economic prosperity, a skilled workforce, rail transport) conducive to opening other factories. These reciprocal interactions between the context and its organisms or organizations create complex longitudinal processes of mutual adaptation (Midgley, 2003).

Altering suites of internal institutional policies and practices in response to a change in organizational context may require complex forms of adaptation. If the shifts in setting are small, many institutions can readily make relatively minor alterations in subsets of their standard procedures and human resource capabilities. For example, to reduce costs, a manufacturing plant might shift from keeping large inventories of parts to using a just-in-time logistical system based on sophisticated tracking mechanisms and constant communication with suppliers. The products the plant builds remain the same, as do the roles of many employees outside of the operational sector that has altered. However, larger changes in context may demand purposive, transformational adaptations in objectives, products, policies, practices, and personnel throughout an organization. As an illustration, the manufacturing enterprise may decide to alter its entire product line in response to changing market conditions, affecting almost every role within the company. Such transformational shifts are quite difficult to accomplish for any enterprise; the challenges of rapid, discontinuous institutional changes are well documented in the scholarly literature on organizational innovation (Agyris, 2004).

Despite their differences, both biological and social adaptation have fundamental similarities. Systems models of organisms, of people's cognitive and affective processes, of organizations, and of contexts are all based on nested, interrelated, longitudinal dynamic interactions that reinforce change (positive feedback loops) or resist change (negative feedback loops). Both types of feedback are important, but change-resisting mechanisms tend to predominate, to preserve the entity's integrity and to enhance survival. Such conservative responses to change are particularly evident in educational settings (Senge et al., 2000). For example, local communities in the United States historically have exerted a high degree of control over public schools through politically volatile vehicles such as school boards. As a result, attaining the coherent, sustained will and resources to achieve a nationwide transformational shift has been extremely difficult (Tyack & Cuban, 1996), even though innovation within individual districts is easier than in countries dominated by national education policies. Other countries with educational systems historically more strongly shaped by national policies have experienced fewer barriers to transformational change.

Although this preponderance of preservational processes is valuable for many reasons, resistance to change is often a liability at times of rapid shifts in individual and organizational context. For example, economists and high-tech businesses believe that the emergence of a global, knowledge-based economy demands that education provide its graduates with different skills and knowledge than were optimal for industrial civilization (Levy & Murnane, 2004; Partnership for 21st Century Skills, 2003). Yet current educational reform initiatives in many countries are regressively emphasizing basic skills and broad, shallow content, rather than stressing higher order skills based on deep knowledge of a few core principles (Dede, 2003; Sawyer, 2004; Sawyer conclusion, this volume). Transcending change-resisting processes to enable the evolution of new types of behaviors is challenging for individuals, but even more difficult for organizations, since their institutional policies and practices as well as the employees who carry them out must alter. Not surprisingly, given the rapid rate of societal change in modern times, organizations have a higher rate of extinction than species do (Klein, 2000).

In response to the threats to identity and viability that shifts in context pose, both individuals and organizations seek to gain the power to shape their settings. Kings and dictators impose national policies and induce cultural beliefs that increase their personal power over their countries. Businesses may seek monopoly status for their products and services, may try to alter the governmental policies that govern their activities, or may attempt to influence the culture of societies in which they function in ways favorable to their interests.

In turn, human settings also shape which types of individuals and organizations prosper within societies through cultural and economic mechanisms. For example, the characteristics and capabilities of successful people and thriving organizations differ within capitalist and socialist economies. Also, a country may seek to shape its larger global context to reduce threats to its identity and survival. Thus, whether a particular entity is seen as a context to which other entities adapt (e.g., a nation to which its organizations adapt) or an entity adapting to its context (for example, a nation shaped by its role in the larger setting of global civilization) depends on the analytic perspective utilized.

In summary, this analogical conceptual framework is based on the assumption that coupled, cyclic, hierarchically nested, longitudinal, change-reinforcing and change-resisting processes can model the behaviors of individuals, innovations, and organizations in ways that lead to insights about their interrelationships and their ability to evolve (Morecraft & Sterman, 2000). In applying this modeling strategy to adaptation in a variety of natural and social systems, the following high-level observations emerge:

- Contexts shape the entities that inhabit them (organisms, people, organizations) through rewarding or inhibiting various types of behaviors. As an illustration, knowledge based economies provide financial incentives for individuals to attain twenty-first century skills, which in turn influences the mission of schools (Partnership for 21st Century Skills, 2003).
- Entities influence their setting by changing its characteristics in ways that alter the behaviors that context reinforces or suppresses. For example, parents who have attained high levels of education tend to value quality schools for their children and to act in ways that encourage their society to invest in education, a self-reinforcing feedback loop.
- In social settings, the rate of innovation has accelerated in recent decades through

mutually reinforcing feedback loops augmenting shifts in context, organizations, and individuals (e.g., the rapid evolution of knowledge economies relative to the comparable development of industrial or agricultural economies). Tyack and Cuban (1996) delineate the many change-resisting processes characteristic of educational institutions, and Cuban (2001) further documents the particular challenges educational innovations based on information technology entail. Because of these factors, the general acceleration of innovations over recent decades has affected schooling less than other sectors of society.

- People can respond to environmental feedback by deliberately altering their individual knowledge and skills. However, for people to rapidly modify these in a major way is difficult because of various change-resisting mechanisms, such as cognitive and affective limits on how quickly and thoroughly teachers can unlearn behaviors that were successful in their schools before an innovation changed their context (Spillane, 2002).
- Institutions can respond to environmental feedback by modifying their practices and by shifting capacity-building strategies for their employees. However, for organizations to rapidly modify these processes in a major way is difficult because of various change-resisting mechanisms. For example, many school districts have multiple layers of review and approval that make changing operational practices difficult, as well as affiliated institutions (e.g., teacher unions) that can retard changes in human resources, policies, and roles.

How does this analogical conceptual framework inform studies of scaling up innovations in education? The challenges involved in adapting an intervention successful in some local educational setting to effective usage in wide range of other contexts draw on all of these observations. Studies in both the biological and social sciences provide examples of successful strategies that could be adapted to scale up educational innovation.

The remainder of this chapter applies this high level-framework in describing and contrasting the analytic strategies used by scholars to study various educational cases in which success was achieved in scaling up. The cases considered are drawn from presentations at an invitational research conference on scaling up technology-based educational innovations held at Harvard in 2003 (http://www.gse.harvard.edu/scalingup/) and papers in the book that resulted from that meeting (Dede, Honan, & Peters, 2005).

Scaling Up a Set of Exemplary Instructional Practices and Curricula

As part of an National Science Foundation grant to create a Center for Learning Technologies in Urban Schools (http://www.letus.org), in 1997 the University of Michigan and Northwestern University partnered with the Detroit Public Schools and the Chicago Public Schools to improve urban science education. The LeTUS initiative developed hands-on, project-based, technology-intensive curricula (Krajcik et al., 2000), then worked to scale up the implementation of those curricula beyond those teachers who participated in designing this innovation, into classrooms throughout these districts and potentially to other districts as well. In Detroit, the scaling up strategy involved both broad-based professional development and close collaboration with school and district administrators, including a high-level champion in the district's central office.

In particular, the professional development activities included extended summer workshops, monthly Saturday work sessions, in-classroom consultations, and online professional development environments (Fishman et al., 2003). In addition, the curriculum itself was designed to be educative for teachers (Schneider & Krajcik, 2000) and to meet community needs (Moje et al., 2001). The LeTUS team also worked to incorporate this professional development initiative into the larger context of a systemic reform movement in the Detroit Public Schools.

Through these combined efforts, approximately sixty-five teachers, representing 26 percent of all middle-grade science teachers in Detroit, are now using these innovative curricula and pedagogies (eighty-five teachers in Detroit have worked with LeTUS over the years, but due to promotion and attrition, roughly twenty no longer directly teach science; there are approximately 250 middle-grade science teachers in Detroit.) This is certainly a success in scaling up relative to many other curricular and pedagogical innovations, but it also indicates the difficulties of persuading the majority of an educational innovation's potential users to adapt it.

The LeTUS team developed a framework for evaluating the fit between innovations and intended contexts of use (Blumenfeld et al., 2000). The underlying model for this framework is *usability*, the extent to which people can use tools or innovations to accomplish work (Nielsen, 1993). Three dimensions of usability (capability, policy and management, and school culture) are arrayed as three axes originating from a common point (the origin, which represents the current capacity of the district to use the innovation) to form a three-dimensional space. The innovation is mapped into this space, and its distance from the origin represents a gap between the capacity required to successfully use the innovation and the current capacity of the school district.

Conceptualized in this manner, scaling up involves closing gaps that exist between the innovation's demands and an organization's capacity. Closing a gap on the culture axis (the extent to which an innovation adheres to or diverges from the existing norms, beliefs, values, and expectations for practice at different levels of the system) may entail providing opportunities for teachers and administrators to gain new visions of practice and policy consistent with features of the innovation. Closing a gap on the capability

Table 33.1. A Taxonomy of Potential Factors Influencing the Scalability of Effective Instructional Usage of Technology (from Russell, Bebell, & O'Dwyer, 2003)

District	Community Attitudes about Educational Technology
	District Vision for Technology
	Leadership of Technology Initiatives
	Resources for Technology Initiatives
	Support Services for Technology Initiatives
	Infrastructure of Computers and Telecommunications
	Professional Development Related to Technology
	Relationship Between Technology and Equity
	Technology-Related Policies and Standards
School	Leadership of Technology Initiatives
	Principal's Pedagogical Beliefs
	Principal's Technology Beliefs
	Principal's Technology Preparedness
	School Culture
Classroom	Teacher's Pedagogical Beliefs
	Teacher's Technology Beliefs
	Teacher's Technology Preparedness
	Teacher Demographic Characteristics
	Technology Resources
	Students' Home Access
	Students' Home Usage
	Students' Comfort with Technology
	Students' Demographic Characteristics

dimension may involve providing professional development for teachers or modifying activities and redesigning technology to reduce new knowledge and skills required for effective implementation. Closing a gap on the policy and management dimension may require changing school and district policies and procedures, as well as adapting the innovation to improve its fit with current practices. In close collaboration with the Detroit Public Schools, the university's design team made all these types of adaptations to close the usability gap (Blumenfeld et al., 2000).

Applying the analogical conceptual framework sketched earlier to this case study, or to similar initiatives of scaling up educational innovations, requires the use of a structural category system that maps the parts of the innovation's organizational context. Structural issues are not important in non-purposive change (such as biological evolution or inadvertent institutional shifts), but are central to deliberate organizational

innovation. As an example, Russell, Bebell, and O'Dwyer (2003) studied a variety of factors thought to influence the conditions for success of the implementation of instructional technology in school districts (Table 33.1). In any given situation, various factors might assume greater or lesser importance.

Reasons of space preclude mapping all the interventions involved in the scaling up strategy used by the University of Michigan and the Detroit Public Schools onto this hierarchically nested structure of factors. Such a mapping can provide insights as to which types of interventions from the full range of possibilities this group's adaptation strategies emphasized. In this case study, the partnership particularly focused on influencing teachers' beliefs about pedagogy, providing teachers with technology support services and professional development about technology usage, and adapting the innovation in various ways to reduce the size of the gap teachers and administrators faced along the three usability dimensions (Fishman, 2005).

Such a strategy emphasizes the key role of *alignment* (coherence and mutual reinforcement among shifts in policies and practices) in scaling up innovations. Cohen and Hill's study of effective state educational reform approaches (2001) shows the importance of coherence among curriculum, professional development, and student assessment. Striking a chord of mutually reinforcing innovations is important in enabling each to have the conditions for success required for scaling up (Dede & Nelson, 2005). The effective use of antibiotics illustrates this concept: Antibiotics are a powerful technology but worshiping the vial that holds them or rubbing the ground-up pills all over one's body or taking all the pills at once are ineffective strategies for usage – only administering pills at specified intervals works as an implementation strategy. A huge challenge educators face, and one of the reasons this field makes slower progress than venues like medicine, is the complexity of conditions for success, and the sophistication of the processes necessary to achieve these conditions. Powerful educational innovations are not as simple or as easily administered as an inoculation in medicine. Fostering coherence and alignment among a suite of innovations that is less comprehensive than a full-scale systemic reform effort, but simultaneously is implemented to provide each other's conditions for success, is an effective approach to scaling up.

Beyond delineating the nested, hierarchical interrelationships among various conditions for success, analysis using the structural category system of Table 33.1 helps to show how adapting innovations is shaped by both change-resisting and change-reinforcing processes (as described earlier in the high-level observations on the analogical framework). For example, providing technology support services involved overcoming various types of concerns from the Detroit Public School's management information systems department, which is responsible for its technology infrastructure. Linking the innovation to the larger context of the systemic

reform initiative under way in the district provided a change-reinforcing mechanism to help resolve these concerns.

Part of the goal of LeTUS is to influence participating districts not only via direct effects of implementing technology-intensive, inquiry-based curricular units, but also through shaping schools' policies and culture to build capacity for usability, enabling the ready adaptation of future, similar innovations. As the high-level observations on the analogical conceptual framework suggest, two substantial factors in this evolution are teachers' ability to reconceptualize their professional roles, and the district's capability to alter its policies for both practice and human resources management. The emphasis in the usability framework on policies and culture reflects the importance the University of Michigan Detroit Public Schools partnership places on altering underlying systemic dynamics, rather than focusing primarily on superficial changes in policy and practice targeted just to this specific innovation. Such a strategy for adapting innovations is a stepping-stone toward the systemic reform type of scaling up – which I discuss next.

Comparing Scaling Up Innovations via Systemic Reform Initiatives

I stated at the start of the chapter that scaling up a single innovation into a school or district is different than conducting a full-scale systemic reform of that educational organization. Contrasting the endpoints of the continuum between, on the one hand, adaptation of an isolated intervention into a single setting lacking some of its conditions for success and, on the other hand, transforming the entire context of a school district through a suite of innovations that embed their conditions for success, highlights similarities and differences in strategy between these two types of educational improvement. Union City, New Jersey, is a well-studied instance of systemic reform based on adapting suites of innovations.

As Carrigg, Honey, and Thorpe (2005, p. 7) describe:

In 1989, the Union City school district was the second-worst-performing district in New Jersey. It had failed forty-four of fifty-two indicators that the state uses to determine the efficacy of school systems; in fact, the state had threatened to take over governance unless radical and successful restructuring was implemented within five years.... The transformation in academic achievement that the district experienced during the 1990s and has sustained into the current decade constitutes a surprising success story. By 1995, Union City's average scores on the state's eighth-grade readiness test surpassed those of its urban counterparts by as much as 20 percentage points.... By 2002, Union City's test scores ranked highest among New Jersey cities with populations of 50,000 or more.

What suites of innovations led to these dramatic advances, and what systemic reform processes were used to scale these across the district?

The reform efforts initially emphasized literacy, seeing this as a prerequisite for many other forms of learning. Particularly in the early grades, district leadership implemented a variety of pedagogical and curricular innovations in teaching reading. Also, teachers began to infuse language and reading into all areas of the curriculum, using a long-range strategy for gradual implementation of innovations; a decade was required for full implementation of shifts in literacy instruction from grades K–12. Details on the specifics of the literacy innovations are available on the Union City district Web site (http://www.union-city.k12.nj.us/curr/k12curr/escurr/1-4humanities/index.html, Accessed November 22, 2005).

In part because improvements in student outcomes came rapidly and were well publicized, the district benefited from stable political leadership and community support over this entire time period. To promote this, school leaders regularly solicited community feedback during the process and encouraged parent buy-in and collabora-

tion. To aid teachers as they worked toward proficiency in the innovations, the district shifted to a five stage model of professional development: awareness, practice, sharing, peer coaching, and mentoring.

Basing systemic reforms on strong, stable leadership; teacher ownership; and community support is a pattern commonly seen in successful systemic reform. Snipes, Doolittle, and Herlihy (2002) focused on determining which large urban districts have improved on a system-wide scale and what common factors across these district initiatives seem responsible for successful reforms. Their major findings on district characteristics that promote success in systemic reform are:

- Urban school districts that have improved performance on a broad scale share certain preconditions for reform, such as political and organizational stability over a prolonged period, and agreement among school board members, the superintendent, and community leaders that student achievement is the top priority.

- District leadership can play a key role in scaling up improvements through strategies such as setting district-wide goals, holding district- and building-level administrators personally accountable for results, adopting uniform curriculum and instructional approaches that apply to every school, and redefining the main role of the central office as one of guiding, supporting, and improving instruction at the school level.

- Faster-improving urban school districts provide principals and teachers with early and ongoing assessment data, along with training and support to help them use these data to improve teaching and learning.

Although Union City is smaller than many of the urban districts participating in this study, its case study affirms these conditions for success in adapting innovations. Beyond the factors already discussed, to monitor students' growth and achievement in literacy over time, Union City utilized both formal and informal assessment methods (Carrigg et al., 2005). The objective was to focus on students as individuals, evaluating their progress based on their abilities and learning styles. The district implemented a mix of diagnostic, formative, and summative assessments. In part because the diagnostic and formative measures were used to improve and individualize instruction, students' test scores improved substantially without basing the curriculum around high-stakes testing.

These and other aspects of the Union City case study resonate with a key design principle Goldman (2005) describes as underlying successful systemic reforms: Conducting a process of a continuous inquiry – based on access to information, analysis of information, and actions aimed at supporting what is going well and improving what is not – is important in making sustainable progress toward educational improvement. In that respect, scaling up is like biological evolution – but more purposive: One watches to see what emergent innovations occur (mutations), then allocates resources for those that are successful. Means and Penuel (2005) support this principle of data-based decision making, indicating that the research base needed for scaling up goes beyond the question, "What works?" to a more complex question, "What works when, and how?" They state

> Rather than an average effect size, local decision makers need research findings that shed light on the expected effects under different circumstances and on the contextual and implementation factors that are likely to influence success. An emphasis on average effects can be counterproductive if it results in inattention to these critical factors in efforts to move interventions to new settings and to scale. (p. 216)

Findings that link gains in student achievement to detailed, practical strategies for implementation also help practitioners and policymakers make the case for further innovation.

How does the Union City example of systemic reform illustrate differences in strategy between scaling up a single innovation and conducting a systemic reform? Systemic reforms tend to utilize an entire suite of mutually reinforcing innovations, a broader range of adaptations to provide the conditions for success for those innovations, and a longer time-frame to enable the full institutionalization of transformation change. Systemic reforms also use district-wide, data-based decision making to develop strategies that increase investment in promising innovations, decrease support for innovations not successfully adapted to this context, and identify change-reinforcing processes to aid in institutional transformation.

Scaling Up Innovations Without Partnering with Local Contexts

What about scaling up in settings that not only are unwilling to undertake full-scale systemic reform, but also are largely uninterested in implementing even isolated innovations? Some educational innovations must be designed to function effectively across a range of relatively inhospitable settings (Dede, 2004). This is in contrast to the models presented thus far for effective transfer of an innovation to another context, which involve partnering with a particular school or district to make that setting a conducive site for adapting a particular design. Scalability into typical school sites that are not partners in innovation requires developing interventions that are effective even when the usual conditions for success (e.g., supportive administration, qualified and enthusiastic teachers, a well maintained technology infrastructure, a student population consistently present) may be absent or attenuated. Under these circumstances, major intended aspects of an innovation's design may not be enacted as intended by its developers, who can anticipate that parts of their design will be "defenestrated" (thrown out the window).

Evolving a design for scalability even into contexts in which its conditions for success are attenuated or lacking requires enhancing the robustness of its effectiveness when parts of its intended enactment are defenestrated. Such "design-for-defenestration" is exemplified in studies the author and his colleagues are conducting. With National Science Foundation funding, we are creating and studying graphical multiuser virtual environments (MUVEs) that enhance middle school students' motivation and learning about science and society (Dede et al., 2004).

Our "River City" MUVE is centered on higher order inquiry skills such as hypothesis formation and experimental design, as well as on content related to national standards and assessments in biology and ecology (http:/muve.gse.harvard.edu/muvees2003/). Through design-based research (Barab, this volume; Dede, 2005), we are documenting how students can gain this knowledge through immersive simulations, interaction with digitized museum artifacts, and participatory historical situations. Students learn to behave as scientists by collaboratively identifying problems through observation and inference, forming and testing hypotheses, and deducing evidence-based conclusions about underlying causes. The goal is to promote learning for all students, particularly those who are unengaged or low performing.

Design-for-defenestration involves identifying conditions for success likely to be attenuated in many contexts, then evolving the design to retain substantial effectiveness under those circumstances. For example, in some implementations of the MUVE, a few teachers ignored all or most of the professional development made available online. These teachers then typically encountered problems in implementation, such as not understanding the purpose and process of the curricular intervention, lacking knowledge about the higher order inquiry skills and standards-based scientific content the intervention helps students to learn, and missing skills in leading the small group and whole class interpretive discussions important for students' understanding of both their MUVE experiences and the data collected. Although this list sounds quite grim, in practice the curricular intervention

worked fairly well in these situations. The MUVE is designed for scalability, creating curricular interventions so compelling for students and with sufficient internal guidance that they have a fulfilling, self-directed learning experience – albeit with reduced educational outcomes – even with a confused teacher.

In response to attenuation of the teacher-preparation condition for success, we evolved the professional development portion of the design to increase its scalability. For example, we produced a summary version of the online professional development that an overwhelmed teacher can skim for ten minutes per day during the unit, providing essential information needed to guide students for that stage of the learning experience. We are also designing variants of the MUVE that simplify the teacher's role without substantially compromising the effectiveness of the innovation.

However, some aspects of any educational innovation are difficult to resolve through robust designs. For example, for MUVE implementations in urban sites, student attendance rates for class averaged about 50 percent (although this improved during the implementation of the learning experience, an encouraging measure of its effectiveness). Also, in the shadow of high stakes testing and accountability measures mandated by the federal No Child Left Behind legislation, persuading schools to make available two weeks of curricular time is difficult for any design that does not use traditional pedagogy to inculcate students with basic skills and factual content.

These pose challenges difficult to overcome for even the best, most robust designs. However, innovators can still attempt to get leverage on these factors. For example, the MUVE curriculum is very engaging for students and teachers, uses standards-based content and skills linked to the high stakes tests, and shows strong outcomes with subpopulations of concern to many schools worried about making adequate yearly progress across all their types of students.

Reasons of space preclude mapping design-for-defenestration strategies onto the analogical conceptual framework described earlier. However, the pattern of investments in scalability that such an analysis generates is different than for strategies that involve partnering with implementation sites to enhance their capabilities. In robust designs, more resources are invested in developing variants of the innovation adapted to special circumstances, less in building capacity at implementation sites. Overall, design-for-defenestration may represent a more effective strategy for moving to very large scale across many sites, but is likely to be less effective in developing high levels of usage at a particular site than the alternative scaling up strategy of working with that particular context to build its capacity.

Scaling Up a Context-Independent Strategy for Teacher Professional Development

Thus far, this discussion of scalability has centered on curricular and pedagogical innovations in precollege schooling. How do effective scaling up strategies differ with various types of innovations and different audiences served? The case study that follows exemplifies the challenges of scaling up innovations in teacher professional development not linked to any particular local context, but disseminated worldwide. Operating through the Internet, WIDE (Wide-scale Interactive Development of Educators) World focuses on professional development of constructivist teaching practices for schools and other settings (Fishman & Davis, this volume; Wiske & Perkins, 2005). Participants include practicing teachers, professors, teacher developers, administrators, and others actively engaged in education. WIDE World courses emphasize active experimentation with various pedagogical frameworks in one's professional context (http://wideworld.pz.harvard.edu/, accessed November 22, 2005). A part of WIDE World's research program is studying how this initiative encounters and resolves challenges to using the World Wide Web for scaling up educational improvement.

This innovation was designed in response to the realization that even well constructed education-oriented Web sites do not provide the kind of sustained guidance and support most teachers need in order to make sustained, significant changes in their practice. This shortfall is not surprising in a passive, largely presentational medium like Web sites. In contrast, WIDE World offers semester-long professional development courses in which participants learn about research-based pedagogies, apply these principles in designing and enacting new approaches with their own students, receive frequent support and feedback from a coach, and engage in regular reflective exchanges with fellow participants in the course. The courses focus on the development of new practices, in contrast to on-site or online university courses that foreground academic learning. In the fall of 2004, WIDE courses involved approximately 773 participants representing 40 countries throughout the world. Since WIDE World's inception, WIDE has worked with more than three thousand participants representing eighty-two countries.

WIDE World is designed so that its professional development takes into account the many dimensions of context that affect attempts to implement organizational innovations. Consistent with other typologies summarized in this chapter, Bolman and Deal (1997) developed a taxonomy of four dimensions that need attention and coordination when fostering change in organizations: *human resources* (knowledge, skills, and beliefs of people), *structural* (roles, relationships, schedules, and other forms of organizational structures), *cultural-symbolic* (norms, values, symbols, rituals, and rewards that affect perceptions of meaning and well-being), and *political* (the allocation of authority and responsibility, and commitment from stakeholders). To this, Wiske and Perkins (2005) add a fifth dimension, *technical* (tools, technologies, materials, and other tangible resources).

Given this framework, the design of WIDE World is based on two central assumptions (Wiske & Perkins, 2005). First, improving education requires bridging the knowledge-action gap: the gulf between current understandings of best practice and actual practice (Perkins, 2003; Pfeffer & Sutton, 2000). One strategy is to cultivate research-based pedagogical craft while adapting to or adjusting the context to support wide-scale change. This requires investments in the human resources and technical dimensions of the Bolman-Deal taxonomy as augmented by Wiske and Perkins (2005), as well as shifts in the structural, cultural-symbolic, and political dimensions. Second, designs should be based on explicit scaling models: causal theories about how the designs address some, if not all, aspects of craft and context as they are complicated at scale by problems of magnitude and variation.

The scalability model for WIDE World that emerges from these assumptions relies on human interaction rather than prepared materials to build teachers' capacity for innovation. WIDE World utilizes expert coaches to provide tailored support and suggestions and to promote interaction among peers as teachers change their practice, to manage mutual adaptation of WIDE innovations and local context, and to augment the support provided by materials.

Learning occurs through presentations of ideas by the instructor, short assignments of reading or examination of online models, activities in which participants try new practices and post designs or reflections online, feedback from coach and peers, and participation in reflective on-line discussions. WIDE World courses guide participants in designing, applying, critiquing, and revising new practices, through multiple cycles of exchange with peers and coaches, with an emphasis on changing participants' practice as well as their minds.

Challenges to this scalability model include:

- Financial issues (will a sufficient number of participants pay for WIDE World services to sustain the enterprise?)

- The availability of coaches (will a sufficient fraction of WIDE World participants choose to serve as coaches for future participants?)
- Effectiveness issues (to what extent can the learning model described above resolve across distance the problems of adaptation to context discussed throughout this chapter?).

Similar challenges of scalability are intrinsic to other initiatives that provide online teacher professional development services, such PBS's TeacherLine (http://teacherline. pbs.org/teacherline/), EDC's Ed Tech Leaders Online (http://www.edtechleaders. org/), and TERC's collaboration with Lesley University, Science Online (http:// scienceonline. terc.edu, all pages accessed November 22, 2005).

Like the design-for-defenestration approach, WIDE World does not focus on a particular site like Detroit or Union City. Such decontextualized strategies for scaling up have the strength of potentially influencing a much broader audience, but the challenge of generating a substantial impact on practice when all the support mechanisms rely on mediated communication, rather than face-to-face interactions. In these models for scaling up, more responsibility falls on the remote participant to accomplish successful adaptation of both the innovation and that setting. This involves both selecting which aspects of the Bolman-Deal structural category system are most important to modify, and devising implementation strategies that use change-reinforcing processes to overcome change-resisting mechanisms.

Developing New Analytic Methods for Studying Adaptation and Scalability

Conducting research on innovation processes this complex is quite challenging. Developing new methods of analysis for studying adaptability and scalability, then examining their validity and value, is an important frontier for research. For example, researchers, policymakers, and practitioners would all benefit from the creation of a generalizable metric for assessing the scalability of an educational intervention or design (Dede, 2004). Such an index would measure the degree to which the educational effectiveness of the design is robust despite attenuation of its conditions for success. By identifying factors within the intervention's context that represent important conditions for success, and summarizing the extent to which the effect of the intervention is sensitive to variation in each, this index could provide prospective adopters of the innovation a better sense of what its likely effectiveness would be in their own particular circumstances.

Such an index must include a limited taxonomy of important contextual factors that can serve as viable conditions for success across many types of educational interventions. The structural category system in Table 33.1 is one example. The conditions for success exist at several nested levels of the educational hierarchy. This nesting not only complicates the creation of a scalability index, but also increases the challenge of estimating the precision of this measure at each level.

Fortunately, for many types of innovations, a relatively small set of contextual factors are often very influential in determining effectiveness. Potential influential factors in this subset may include teachers' knowledge of content and pedagogy, students' socioeconomic and linguistic backgrounds, students' mobility and absenteeism, and (for technology-based innovations) the extent and reliability of the computer/networking infrastructure. Examining scalability in the context of this subset of powerful conditions for success may still yield a workable index, but only investigating its feasibility by using real data can determine the potential validity and value of such a measure.

At its core, the evaluation of the sensitivity of an intervention's impact to specific contextual conditions is a question of statistical interactions. In evaluating the sensitivity to the conditions for success, one asks:

Is the effect of the intervention dependent on the selected contextual conditions? For example, is the intervention more effective for children of lower SES, or higher? Does the impact of the intervention depend on specific teacher capabilities? On features of the classroom and school infrastructure?

An accurate scalability index must ensure that such interactions are included in the statistical models that underpin the data analyses conducted to assess the implementation of educational interventions. If the interactions have a statistically significant effect, then we know that the effect of the treatment is sensitive to the conditions that participated in the interaction. Estimating the various effect sizes anticipated for the intervention under each of the interacting conditions may enable pooling these into a global index of scalability that captures the extent to which the intervention's effect size is sensitive to variation in the conditions for success.

Several important technical challenges to implementing this approach in practice make the validity of this measure uncertain. First, how one should pool the several effect sizes – representing variation in the intervention's impact across levels of a particular contextual factor – into a single index of sensitivity or scalability, is uncertain. Second, as conditions for success are drawn from higher levels of the organizational hierarchy (classrooms, schools, districts), mustering the statistical power necessary to detect interactions between these conditions and the intervention being studied is increasingly difficult. As a result, for conditions of success lying at higher levels of the organizational hierarchy, it may not be possible to estimate the sensitivity of the treatment effect to these conditions in a single study. However, a synthesis of findings across many studies, in the manner of meta-analysis, might suffice. Overall, examining the feasibility of new methods of analysis – such as a scalability index – is an important frontier for research on scaling up, and may generate strategies for quantifying various aspects of the analogical conceptual framework for scaling up described earlier.

Summary

In their summary of participant discussions at the Scaling Up Success conference referenced earlier, Dede and Honan (2005) identify four key themes in adapting an educational innovation successful in one setting to be used in wide range of contexts:

- *Coping with change*: context, leadership, and funding
- *Promoting ownership*: building constituent support; institutionalizing innovations
- *Building human capacity*: working with collaborators and partners; providing professional development
- *Effective decision making*: interpreting data; creating and applying usable knowledge

This chapter describes how these themes are articulated in four types of scaling up strategies.

To study these and related issues, an important next step is to develop mechanisms to provide funding and build capacity in research, practice, and policy. At present, U.S. resources for scholarship are focused on clinical intervention studies involving random assignment, a model for evolving educational effectiveness that captures only part of the research needed to effectively enable the scaling up approaches discussed earlier. Clinical trials can aid in determining what to scale, but not how to effectively adapt that innovation to various local situations. Hopefully, this synthesis and related work will inspire public and private sources who realize the crucial nature of adaptation-oriented research to provide the substantial, sustained support required to undertake these types of sophisticated studies.

References

Agyris, C. (2004). *Reasons and rationalizations: The limits to organizational knowledge*. Oxford: Oxford University Press.

Berends, M., Bodilly, S. J., & Kirby, S. (2002). *Facing the challenges of whole-school reform: New American Schools after a decade*. Santa Monica, CA: RAND Corporation.

Blumenfeld, P., Fishman, B. J., Krajcik, J. S., Marx, R. W., & Soloway, E. (2000). Creating usable innovations in systemic reform: Scaling up technology-embedded project-based science in urban schools. *Educational Psychologist, 35*(3), 149–164.

Bolman, L. G., & Deal, T. E. (1997). *Reframing organizations: Artistry, choice, and leadership (2nd ed.)*. San Francisco: Jossey-Bass.

Carrigg, F., Honey, M., & Thorpe, R. (2005). Moving from successful local practice to effective state policy: Lessons from Union City. In C. Dede, J. Honan, & L. Peters (Eds.), *Scaling up success: Lessons learned from technology-based educational improvement* (pp. 1–26). New York: Jossey-Bass.

Coburn, C. (2003). Rethinking scale: Moving beyond numbers to deep and lasting change. *Educational Researcher 32*(6): 3–12.

Cohen, D. K., & Hill, H. C. (2001). *Learning policy: When state education reform works*. New Haven, CT: Yale University Press.

Cuban, L. (2001). *Oversold and underused: Computers in classrooms*. Cambridge, MA: Harvard University Press.

Dede, C. (2003). No cliché left behind: Why education policy is not like the Movies. *Educational Technology 43* (March–April), 5–10.

Dede, C. (2004). *Design for defenestration: A strategy for scaling up promising research-based Innovations*. Chicago, IL: NORC.

Dede, C. (2005). Why design-based research is both important and difficult. *Educational Technology, 45*, 5–8.

Dede. C., & Honan, J. (2005). Scaling up success: A synthesis of themes and insights. In C. Dede, J. Honan, & L. Peters (Eds.), *Scaling up success: Lessons learned from technology-based educational improvement* (pp. 227–239). New York: Jossey-Bass.

Dede, C., Honan, J., Peters, L. (Eds.). (2005). *Scaling up success: Lessons learned from technology-based educational improvement*. New York: Jossey-Bass.

Dede, C., & Nelson, R. (2005). Technology as Proteus: Digital infrastructures that empower scaling up. In C. Dede, J. Honan, & L. Peters

(Eds.), *Scaling up success: Lessons learned from technology-based educational improvement* (pp. 110–132). New York: Jossey-Bass.

Dede, C., Nelson, B., Ketelhut, D., Clarke, J., & Bowman, C. (2004). Design-based research strategies for studying situated learning in a multi-user virtual environment. *Proceedings of the 2004 International Conference on Learning Sciences*, pp. 158–165. Mahweh, NJ: Lawrence Erlbaum Associates.

Fishman, B. (2005). Adapting innovations to particular contexts of use: A collaborative framework. In C. Dede, J. Honan, & L. Peters (Eds.), *Scaling up success: Lessons learned from technology-based educational improvement* (pp. 48–66). New York: Jossey-Bass.

Fishman, B., Marx, R., Best, S., & Tal, R. (2003). Linking teacher and student learning to improve professional development in systemic reform. *Teaching and Teacher Education*, 19(6), 643–658.

Goldman, S. B. (2005). Designing for scalable educational improvement: Processes of inquiry in practice. In C. Dede, J. Honan, & L. Peters (Eds.), *Scaling up success: Lessons learned from technology-based educational improvement* (pp. 67–96). New York: Jossey-Bass.

Klein, J. (2000). *Corporate failure by design: Why organizations are built to fail*. New York: Quorum Books.

Krajcik, J. S., Blumenfeld, P., Marx, R. W., & Soloway, E. (2000). Instructional, curricular, and technological supports for inquiry in science classrooms. In J. Minstrell & E. H. V. Zee (Eds.), *Inquiring into inquiry learning and teaching in science* (pp. 283–315). Washington, DC: American Association for the Advancement of Science.

Levy, F., & Murnane, R. J. (2004). *The new division of labor: How computers are creating the next job market*. Princeton, NJ: Princeton University Press.

Means, B., & Penuel, W. R. (2005). Research to support scaling up technology-based educational innovations. In C. Dede, J. Honan, & L. Peters, Eds, *Scaling up success: Lessons learned from technology-based educational improvement* (pp. 176–197). New York: Jossey-Bass.

Midgley, G. (Ed.). (2003). *Systems theories and modeling (Volume II of Systems thinking)*. New York: Sage.

Moje, E. B., Collazo, T., Carrillo, R., & Marx, R. W. (2001). "Maestro, what is 'quality'?": Language, literacy, and discourse in project-based science. *Journal of Research in Science Teaching*, 38(4), 469–498.

Moore, G. A. (1999). *Crossing the chasm (Rev. ed.)*. New York: HarperPerennial.

Morecraft, J. D. W., & Sterman, J. D. (Eds.). (2000). *Modeling for learning organizations*. New York: Productivity Press.

Moya, A., & Font, E. (Eds.). (2004). *Evolution: From molecules to ecosystems*. Oxford: Oxford University Press.

Nielsen, J. (1993). *Usability engineering*. San Francisco: Morgan Kaufmann.

Partnership for 21st Century Skills. (2003). *Learning for the 21st century*. Washington, DC: Partnership for 21st Century Skills. Retrieved November 20, 2004, from http://www.21stcenturyskills.org/downloads/P21_Report.pdf.

Perkins, D. N. (2003). *King Arthur's round table: How collaborative conversations create smart organizations*. Hoboken, NJ: Wiley.

Pfeffer, J., & Sutton, R. (2000). *The knowing-doing gap*. Boston: Harvard Business School Press.

Russell, M., Bebell, D., & O'Dwyer, L. (2003) *Use, support, and effect of instructional technology study: An overview of the USEIT study and the participating districts*. Boston, MA: Technology and Assessment Study Collaborative. Retrieved August 29, 2004, from http://www.bc.edu/research/intasc/studies/USEIT/description.shtml.

Sawyer, R. K. (2004). Creative teaching: Collaborative discussion as disciplined improvisation. *Educational Researcher*, 33(2), 12–20.

Schneider, R. M., & Krajcik, J. S. (2000, April). *The role of educative curriculum materials in reforming science education*. Paper presented at the annual meeting of the American Educational Research Association, New Orleans, LA.

Senge, P. M., Cambron-McCabe, N. H., Lucas, T., Kleiner, A., Dutton, J., & Smith, B. (2000). *Schools that learn: A fifth discipline fieldbook for educators, parents, and everyone who cares about education*. New York: Currency Press.

Snipes, J., Doolittle, F., & Herlihy, C. (2002). *Foundations for success: Case studies of how urban school districts improve student achievement*. Washington, DC: Council of the Great City Schools. Retrieved on November 27, 2004, from http://www.cgcs.org/reports/Foundations.html.

Spillane, J. P. (2002). Local theories of teacher change: The pedagogy of district policies and programs. *Teachers College Record*, 104(3), 377–420.

Tyack, D., & Cuban, L. (1996). *Tinkering toward utopia: A century of public school reform*. Cambridge, MA: Harvard University Press.

Wiske, M. S., & Perkins, D. (2005). Dewey goes digital: Scaling up constructivist pedagogies and the promise of new technologies. In C. Dede, J. Honan, & L. Peters, Eds, *Scaling up success: Lessons learned from technology-based educational improvement* (pp. 27–47). New York: Jossey-Bass.

CHAPTER 34

Conclusion

The Schools of the Future

R. Keith Sawyer

The schools of today were largely designed in the nineteenth and twentieth centuries to provide workers for the industrial economy. In the 1970s, economists and other social scientists began to realize that the world's economies were shifting from an industrial economy to a knowledge economy (Bell, 1973; Drucker, 1993; Toffler, 1980). By the 1990s, educators had begun to realize that if the economy was no longer the 1920s-era factory economy, then our schools were designed for a quickly vanishing world (Bereiter, 2002; Hargreaves, 2003; Sawyer, in press). Leading thinkers in business, politics, and education are now in consensus that schools have to be redesigned for the new economy, and that the learning sciences are pointing the way to this new kind of school – a school that teaches the deep knowledge required in a knowledge society. This consensus led major governmental and international bodies to commission reports summarizing learning sciences research; these reports include the U.S. National Research Council's *How People Learn* (Bransford, Brown, & Cocking, 2000), the OECD's *Innovation in the Knowledge Economy: Implications for Education and Learning* (2004), and a study of twenty-eight countries conducted by the International Society for Technology in Education, called *Technology, Innovation, and Educational Change: A Global Perspective* (Kozma, 2003).

Those societies that can effectively restructure their schools on the learning sciences will be the leaders in the twenty-first century (OECD, 2000, 2004). The issues addressed by the learning sciences have been recognized as critical in all twenty-eight of the countries studied by the ISTE (Kozma, 2003). The leaders of these countries agree that the world economy has changed to an innovation- and knowledge-based economy, and that education must change for a society to make this transition successfully. For example, the Ministry of Education in Finland has created a vision of the Finnish Information Society that stresses collaborative teaching and learning, networking, and team work (Ministry of Education, Finland, 1999). Singapore's "Master Plan for IT in Education" integrates computers into all aspects of education, with the goals of helping students to think flexibly, creatively, and collabora-tively – a vision known as "Thinking Schools, Learning Nation" (Ministry of Education, Singapore, 2002). Unlike most other coun-tries, the U.S. educational system is not centralized under federal government con-trol and it is not possible to implement a new vision nationwide; but various influ-ential national entities are taking action. The National Research Council funded the preparation of *How People Learn* in 1999, and the National Science Foundation announced competitions in 2003 and 2005, each total-ing about $20,000,000, to create a network of Science of Learning Centers to extend learning sciences research; many of the U.S. authors of this handbook conduct research that is now funded by these grants.

The NRC, ISTE, and OECD reports helped to build a consensus around the learning sciences, but they were necessarily preliminary. They did not provide specific details about how learning sciences research could be used to build the schools of the future. This handbook begins the important work recommended by these reports; the chapters collected here describe the build-ing blocks of the schools of the future. If you closely read all of these chapters, various visions of the schools of the future begin to take shape – but the outlines remain fuzzy. The key issue facing the learning sciences in the next ten to twenty years will be to outline an increasingly specific vision for the schools of the future. In this conclusion, I begin by presenting some possible visions of the schools of the future. I then discuss some unresolved issues that will face the learning sciences as its findings begin to be used to build the schools of the future.

Schools and Beyond

The learning sciences have enormous poten-tial to transform schools so that students learn better and more deeply, are more pre-pared to function in the knowledge econ-omy, and are able to participate actively in an open, democratic society. Although these chapters don't tell us what schools will look like, they take the first step in that direction by telling us how learning environ-ments should be designed. It's telling that these chapters talk about "learning environ-ments" rather than "schools" or "classrooms." Learning environments include schools and classrooms but also the many informal learn-ing situations that have existed through history and continue to exist alongside formal schooling. A true science of learn-ing has to bring together understandings of both informal and formal learning environ-ments, drawing on the best features of all known learning environments to build the schools of the future (Bransford et al., this volume). Instead of studying small incre-mental changes to today's schools, learning scientists ask a more profound question: are today's schools really the right schools for the knowledge society?

Most learning sciences researchers are committed to improving schools, and they believe that school reform should involve working together with teachers, engag-ing in professional development, and inte-grating new software into classrooms. A new research methodology developed by learning scientists – the design experi-ment – is conducted in classrooms, and requires that researchers work closely with teachers as they participate in curriculum development, teacher professional develop-ment, and assessment (Barab, this volume; Confrey, this volume).

But learning sciences research might also lead to more radical alternatives that would make schools as we know them obsolete, leaving today's big high schools as empty as the shuttered steel factories of the faded industrial economy. Roger Schank (1999) and Seymour Papert (1980) have argued that computer technology is so radically trans-formative that schools as we know them will have to fade away before the full ben-efits can be realized. Everything is subject to change: schools may not be physical loca-tions where everyone goes, students may not be grouped by age or grade, students could learn anywhere at any time. As of 2005, twenty-two states had established online virtual schools; during the 2003–2004 school year, the Florida Virtual School became the state's seventy-third school district, and now receives per-student funding from the state just like any other district. In the 2004–2005 school year, twenty-one thousand students enrolled in at least one of its courses (Borja, 2005).

Imagine a nation of online home-based activities organized around small neighborhood learning clubs, all connected through high-bandwidth Internet software. There would be no textbooks, few lectures, and no curriculum as we know it today. "Teachers" would operate as independent consultants who work from home most of the time, and occasionally meet with ad-hoc groups of students at a learning club. Each meeting would be radically different in nature, depending on the project-based and self-directed learning that those students were engaged in. In fact, each type of learning session might involve a different learning specialist. The teaching profession could become multitiered, with master teachers developing curriculum in collaboration with software developers and acting as consultants to schools, and learning centers staffed by a variety of independent contractors whose job no longer involves lesson preparation or grading, but instead involves mostly assisting students as they work at the computer or gather data in the field (Stallard & Cocker, 2001).

Educational software gives us the opportunity to provide a customized learning experience to each student to a degree not possible when one teacher is responsible for six classrooms of twenty-five students each. Well-designed software could sense each learner's unique learning style and developmental level, and tailor the presentation of material appropriately (see Koedinger & Corbett, this volume, for an example). Some students could take longer to master a subject, while others would be faster, because the computer can provide information to each student at his or her own pace. And each student could learn each subject at different rates; for example, learning what we think of today as "fifth grade" reading and "third grade" math at the same time. In age-graded classrooms this would be impossible,

but in the schools of the future there may be no educational need to age-grade classrooms, no need to hold back the more advanced children or to leave behind those who need more help, and no reason for a child to learn all subjects at the same rate. Of course, age-graded classrooms also serve to socialize children, providing opportunities to make friends, to form peer groups, and to participate in team sports. If learning and schooling were no longer age-graded, other institutions would have to emerge to provide these opportunities.

In 1980, Seymour Papert famously predicted that when the total twelve-year cost of personal computers was $1000 per student, they would begin to transform education (Papert, 1980, p. 17); this prediction is finally on the horizon. In 2005, the MIT Media Lab launched a new research initiative with the goal of releasing a $100 laptop computer for students by 2007; a prototype was unveiled in November, 2005 (http://laptop.media.mit.edu, accessed November 22, 2005). In 2005, Advanced Micro Devices Inc. released a $200 "personal internet communicator" to bring networked computing to classrooms in the third world. When a laptop computer becomes available for $100, it can store all of a student's textbooks and curriculum materials; as the technology is gradually refined and improved, paper textbooks may eventually become obsolete.

Conservative critics of schools see the future emerging through an open market system of competition, in which local property tax dollars can be used by parents to choose from a wide range of learning environments. To take just one hypothetical possibility, tutoring centers like Sylvan Learning Centers might begin to offer a three-hour intensive workday, structured around tutors and individualized educational software, with each student taking home his or her laptop to complete the remainder of the day at home. Because each tutor could schedule two three-hour shifts in one day, class size could be halved with no increase in cost. Because curriculum and software would be designed centrally, and the software does the grading automatically, these future tutors could actually leave their work at the office – unlike today's teachers, who stay up late every night and spend all weekend preparing lesson plans and grading. For those parents who need an all-day option for their children due to their work schedule, for-profit charter schools could proliferate, each based on a slightly different curriculum or a slightly different software package. Particularly skilled teachers could develop reputations that would allow them to create their own "start-up schools," taking ten or twenty students into their home for some or all of the school day – the best of them providing serious competition for today's elite private schools, and earning as much as other knowledge workers such as lawyers, doctors, and executives.

Museums and public libraries might play an increasingly larger role in education. They could receive increased funding to support their evolution into learning resource centers, perhaps even receiving a portion of the property tax revenue stream. They could participate in several ways: for example, by developing curriculum and lesson plans and making these available to students anywhere over the Internet, and by providing physical learning environments as they redesign their buildings to support schooling. Science centers have taken the lead in this area, developing inquiry-based curricula and conducting teacher professional development, but art and history museums may soon follow suit.

The boundary between formal schooling and continuing education will increasingly blur. The milestone of a high school diploma could gradually decrease in importance, as the nature of learning in school begins to look more and more like on-the-job apprenticeship and adult distance education. The $100 computer and the inexpensive handheld allow for learning to take place anywhere, anytime; sixteen-year-olds could work their part-time jobs during the day and take their classes at night, just like adults do now. Many types of knowledge are better learned in workplace environments; this kind of learning will be radically transformed by the availability of anywhere,

anytime learning, as new employees take their laptops or handhelds on the job with them, with software specially designed to provide apprenticeship support in the workplace. Professional schools could be radically affected; new forms of portable just-in-time learning could increasingly put their campus-based educational models at risk.

The above scenarios are all hypothetical; it isn't yet clear how schools will change in response to the new research emerging from the learning sciences, and to the computer technology that makes these new learning environments possible. But if schools do not redesign themselves on a foundation in the learning sciences, alternative learning environments that do so could gradually draw more and more students – particularly if charter schools and vouchers become widespread. And even if schools do not face competition from charters and vouchers, learning will increasingly take place both inside and outside the school walls – in libraries, museums, after-school clubs, online virtual schools, and at home.

Computers and the Schools of the Future

Learning scientists build learning environments that are based on scientific principles. As we've seen throughout this handbook, carefully designed computer software can play a critical role in these learning environments. However, learning scientists know that for fifty years, reformers have been claiming that computers will change schools – and these predictions have never come to pass. The first was in the 1950s, when B. F. Skinner claimed that his "teaching machines" made the teacher "out of date" (1954/1968, p. 22). Then, Papert's 1980 book *Mindstorms* argued that giving every child a computer would allow students to actively construct their own learning, leaving teachers with an uncertain role: "schools as we know them today will have no place in the future" (p. 9). Nonetheless, two decades later, Larry Cuban famously documented the failure of computers and the Internet to improve U.S. schools in his 2001 book *Oversold and Underused*. How is the software being developed by learning scientists any different?

The fundamental differences are that learning scientists begin by first developing a foundation in the basic sciences of learning, their computer software is designed with the participation of practicing teachers, and is *learner centered* (Quintana, Shin, Norris, & Soloway, this volume), unlike most of the software currently in use in classrooms, which is generic productivity software like Microsoft Office, and is not designed for learning. One example of the potential is Virginia Tech's *Math Emporium*, a former five-and-dime store that has been outfitted with five hundred personal computers, each running specially designed software to teach calculus, linear algebra, and other subjects (http://www.emporium.vt.edu, accessed August 6, 2005). The emporium is open twenty-four hours a day, is accessible from off-site via the Internet, and has professor and graduate student help on staff fourteen hours a day. It serves nearly seven thousand math students each year, at less than half the cost of the lecture courses it replaced, and with higher student math scores and student satisfaction.

Learning scientists work closely in schools; part of the reason that the design research methodology (Barab, this volume; Confrey, this volume) is so central to research practice is that this methodology allows computers and programs to be embedded in a complex and integrated curriculum. Learning scientists realize that computers will never realize their full potential if they are merely add-ons to the existing instructionist classroom; that's why they are engaged in the hard work of designing entire learning environments – not just stand-alone computer applications, as previous generations of educational software designers did.

Curriculum

What should be taught in second grade math, or in sixth grade social studies? Learning scientists have discovered that what seems more simple to an adult professional is not necessarily more simple to a learner. The most effective sequencing of activities is not always a sequence from what experts consider to be more simple to more complex. Children arrive at school with naïve theories and misconceptions; and during the school years, children pass through a series of cognitive developmental stages. Instructionist textbooks and curricula were designed before learning scientists began to map out the educational relevance of cognitive development.

In the next ten to twenty years, new curricula for K–12 education will emerge that are based in the learning sciences. Major funding should be directed at identifying the specific sequences of activities and concepts that are most effective in each subject. For example, the chapter by Cobb and McClain demonstrates a short unit that teaches children the key features of using a coordinate system to represent distributions. But of course, that is only one tiny piece of what we want students to learn from twelve years of math instruction. Developing these new curricula will require an army of researchers – distributed across all grades and all subjects – to identify the most appropriate sequences of material, and the most effective learning activities, based on research into children's developing cognitive competencies and how children construct their own deep knowledge while engaged in situated practices.

Federal agencies and private foundations will need to coordinate their efforts to make sure that each subject and each grade level is being studied, and to avoid duplication of effort. For example, rather than fund five large centers studying tenth grade biology, funding should be spread across five different grades or five different subjects. In their funding of education research, the NSF and the Department of Education have traditionally been field-driven – responding to the important ideas emerging from a loose national network of scholars. But they are both becoming more focused, guiding the nation's research efforts to ensure that all grades and subject areas are covered.

Related to the issue of curriculum is the sensitive topic of coverage – how much material, and how many topics, should students learn about at each age? In instructionism, the debate about curriculum is almost exclusively a debate about topic coverage – what should be included at each grade, and how much. But this focus on breadth is misguided. According to the Trends in International Mathematics and Science Study (TIMSS), which compares student achievement in math and science in fifty countries every four years, U.S. science and math curricula contain much more content than other countries as a result of their survey approaches to material – but rather than strengthening students' abilities, this survey approach weakens U.S. achievement relative to other countries (Schmidt & McKnight, 1997). Compared to other countries, U.S. science curricula are "a mile wide and an inch deep" (Vogel, 1996, p. 335). Each topic is taught as its own distinct unit – and the new knowledge is often forgotten as soon as the students turn to the next topic. Studies of the TIMSS data show that children in nations that pursue a more focused, coherent, and deep strategy do substantially better on the mathematics assessment than do U.S. children (Schmidt & McKnight, 1997). This is consistent with the learning sciences finding that students learn better when they learn deep knowledge that allows them to think and to solve problems with the content that they are learning.

A near-term task facing the learning sciences is to identify the content of the curriculum for each subject and each grade, and then to design an integrated, coherent, unified curriculum to replace existing textbooks. Learning sciences research could be directed toward identifying which deep knowledge should be the outcome of each grade. These curricula are likely to contain fewer units and fewer overall line items, with more time spent on each item. This will be a political challenge, because some will view it as removing material from the curriculum, "dumbing down" or reducing expectations of students. In the United States, politicians and school boards have frequently responded to concerns about education by adding content requirements to the curriculum – contributing to the "mile wide, inch deep" phenomenon. It will take a paradigm change to shift the terms of this policy debate, and learning scientists could make valuable contributions.

The Teachers of the Future

The learning sciences focus on learning and learners. Many education researchers are instead focused on teachers and teaching, and these readers may observe that the classroom activities described in these chapters seem very challenging for teachers. How are we going to find enough qualified professionals to staff the schools of the future? The teachers of the future will be knowledge workers, with equivalent skills to other knowledge workers such as lawyers, doctors, engineers, managers, and consultants. They will deeply understand the theoretical principles and the latest knowledge about how children learn. They will be deeply familiar with the authentic practices of professional scientists, historians, mathematics, or literary critics. They will have to receive salaries comparable to other knowledge workers, or else the profession will have difficulty attracting new teachers with the potential to teach for deep knowledge. The classrooms of the future will require more autonomy, more creativity, and more content knowledge.

Over a wide variety of international schools, a set of best practices surrounding educational technology is emerging (Kozma, 2003; Schofield & Davidson, 2002). Instead of instructionism – with the teacher lecturing in a transmission-and-acquisition style – these classrooms engage in authentic and situated problem-based activities. If you looked into such a classroom, you'd see the teacher advising students, creating structures to scaffold student activities, and monitoring student progress. You'd see the students actively engaged in projects, managing and guiding their own activities, collaborating with other students, and occasionally asking the teacher for help.

The teachers of the future will be highly trained professionals, comfortable with technology, with a deep pedagogical understanding of the subject matter, able to respond improvisationally to the uniquely emerging flow of each classroom (Sawyer, 2004). They will lead teams of students, much like a manager of a business or the master in a workshop, preparing students to fully participate in the knowledge society.

Scaling Up

Learning scientists generally believe that learning cannot be studied apart from its contexts. But this results in a difficult problem: if learning is always unique to a specific context, then how can research ever result in sustainable products that can be disseminated and adopted in a wide range of schools? A design experiment transforms one learning environment or classroom, or sometimes an entire school, with a huge investment of highly paid university researchers and assistants. But systemic change can only occur if a design experiment results in curricula and software that can be transferred to many other schools with a relatively minor additional investment.

As a body of research knowledge accumulates, the learning sciences will eventually result in new curriculum materials, software products, teacher professional development courses, and assessments focused on deep knowledge and authentic reasoning abilities. A few of the more established learning sciences laboratories have already developed widely used curricula that are summarized in this handbook: Krajcik's project-based learning, Linn's knowledge integration, Kolodner's Learning By Design, and Koedinger's cognitive tutors.

Speed Bumps in the Road to the Future

It is too early to predict exactly what the schools of the future will look like. Two things are certain: first, that schools will eventually have to change to meet the needs of the modern knowledge society; and second, that schools are complex institutions that have proven to be amazingly resistant to change. The road from instructionism to the schools of the future will be long and unpredictable, but some of the speed bumps can be predicted.

Incompatibilities Between Schools and the Learning Sciences

In a forthcoming book, Collins and Halverson (in preparation) identify several entrenched features of today's public schools that might make them resist the necessary changes emerging from the learning sciences:

Uniform learning versus customization. Schools are based on the assumption that everyone learns the same thing at the same time. Courses are structured so that everyone reads the same pages of the text at the same time, and everyone takes the same test on the same day. But in the schools of the future, each learner will receive a customized learning experience.

Teacher as expert versus diverse knowledge sources. In the constructivist and project-based learning advocated by the learning sciences, students gain expertise from a variety of sources – from the Internet, at the library, or through e-mail exchange with a working professional – and the teacher will no longer be the only source of expertise in the classroom. But today's schools are based on the notion that teachers are all-knowing experts, and their job is to transmit their expertise to the students.

Standardized assessment versus individualized assessment. Today's assessments require that every student learn the same thing at the same time. The standards movement and the resulting high-stakes testing are increasing standardization, at the same time that learning sciences and technology are making it possible for individual students to have customized learning experiences. Customization combined with diverse knowledge sources enable students to learn different things. Schools will still need to measure learning for accountability purposes, but we don't yet know how to reconcile accountability with customized learning.

Knowledge in the head versus distributed knowledge. In the real world, people act intelligently by making frequent use of books, papers, and technology. And in most professions, knowledge work occurs in teams and organizations, so that several times every hour, a person is interacting with others. But in today's schools, there is a belief that a student only knows something when that student can do it on his or her own, without any use of outside resources. There is a mismatch between today's school culture and the situated knowledge required in the knowledge society.

Connecting Individual and Group Knowledge

Learning scientists emphasize the importance of learning in groups, in part because most knowledge work takes place in complexly organized teams. But this leads to a tension between group work and individual learning. Many psychologists focus on individual learning and assume that all knowledge is individual knowledge. For these researchers, the basic science of learning must be the science of how individuals learn, and social context is only of secondary importance – as a potential influence on these basically mental processes. But some learning scientists reject this individualist view, and argue that all knowledge is in some sense group knowledge, because it is always used in social and cultural contexts (e.g., Rogoff, 1998).

The learning sciences combine a diverse range of positions on this issue, from cognitive psychologists who focus on the mental structures that underlie knowledge, to sociologists who believe that it may be impossible to identify the mental structures corresponding to situated social practice. Most learning scientists reside in the center of this debate, believing that a full understanding of learning requires a combination of individual cognitive analysis and social interactional analysis – the synthesis that Greeno (this volume) refers to as "situative." But there is disagreement among learning scientists about where the emphasis should be placed, and how important it is to focus on individual learning.

Individual learning is always going to be an important goal of schooling. Individuals learn some knowledge better in social and collaborative settings than they do in isolation, but schools will continue to be judged on how well individual graduates perform on some form of individualized assessment. The learning sciences strongly suggest that today's assessments are misguided in design, in part because they isolate individuals from meaningful contexts. New assessments could include components that evaluate the individual's ability to work in a group, to manage diversity of backgrounds, or to communicate in complex, rapidly changing environments. But although new forms of assessment may place individuals in groups, we will still need to tease out the individual learning of each group participant.

Assessment and Accountability

In today's high-stakes testing environment, learning sciences researchers need to demonstrate that their methods result in better student outcomes. The learning sciences suggest that today's standardized tests are deeply flawed, because they assess only the surface knowledge emphasized by instructionism, and do not assess the deep knowledge required by the knowledge society. Standardized tests, almost by their very nature, evaluate decontextualized and compartmentalized knowledge. For example, mathematics tests do not assess model-based reasoning (Lehrer & Schauble, this volume); science tests do not assess whether preexisting misconceptions have indeed been left behind (diSessa, this volume; Linn, this volume) nor do they assess problem-solving or inquiry skills (Krajcik & Blumenfeld, this volume). As long as schools are evaluated on how well their students do on such tests, it will be difficult for them to leave instructionist methods behind.

One of the key issues facing the learning sciences is how to design new kinds of assessment that correspond to the deep knowledge required in today's knowledge society (Carver, this volume; Means, this volume). Several learning sciences researchers are developing new assessments that focus on deeper conceptual understanding. For example, Lehrer and Schauble (this volume) have developed a test of model-based reasoning – a form of deeper understanding that is emphasized in their curriculum, but that does not appear on traditional standardized mathematics tests. The VNOS (Views of the Nature of Science) questionnaire assesses deeper understanding of scientific practice rather than content knowledge (Lederman et al., 2002).

In classrooms that make day-to-day use of computer software, installed on each student's own personal computer, there is an interesting new opportunity for assessment – the assessment could be built into the software itself. After all, the learning sciences has found that effective educational software has to closely track the student's developing knowledge structures to be effective; since that tracking is being done anyway, it would be a rather straightforward extension to make summary versions of it available to teachers. New learning sciences software is exploring how to track deep learning during the learning process, in some cases inferring student learning from such subtle cues as where the learner moves and clicks the mouse – providing an opportunity for assessment during the learning itself, not in a separate multiple-choice quiz (e.g., Gobert, Buckley, & Dede, 2005).

These new forms of assessment represent the cutting edge of learning sciences research. A critical issue for the future is to continue this work, both in the research setting but also in the policy arena – working with developers of standardized tests and working with state boards of education to develop broad-scale standardized tests. Test construction is complex, involving field tests of reliability and validity for example, and will require learning scientists to work with psychometricians and policy experts.

New Methodologies

Experimental studies that randomly assign students to either a new educational intervention or a traditional classroom remain the gold standard for evaluating what works best to improve learning. Many educators and politicians have recently applied the medical model of research to education (Shavelson & Towne, 2002). But the medical model does not imply that all research consists of controlled experiments. Medical research proceeds in roughly five phases:

> Preclinical: basic scientific research. A wide range of methodologies is used.
>
> Phase 1: Feasibility. How to administer the treatment; how much is appropriate. Again, a wide range of methodologies is used.
>
> Phase 2: Initial efficacy. How well does it work? Quasi-experimental methodologies are typically used.
>
> Phase 3: Randomized controlled experiment. The gold standard, the controlled experiment is necessary to prove efficacy of the treatment.
>
> Phase 4: Continuing evaluation and follow-on research.

The learning sciences are still in the Preclinical and Phase 1 stages of research, with a few of the more well-established efforts entering Phase 2. Anderson and Koedinger's cognitive tutors (Koedinger & Corbett, this volume) have entered Phase 3 – but their research has been under way for over twenty years (Cherniavsky, 2005). Experimental studies are not sufficient to create the schools of the future, for several reasons (cf. Raudenbush, 2005):

1. Learning sciences researchers are still in a preclinical phase of identifying the goals of schools: the cognitive and social outcomes that we expect our students to attain. Experimental methodologies alone cannot help us to rigorously and clearly identify the knowledge that we want students to learn.

2. Experimental methodologies are premature at the preclinical and first phases, when learning scientists are still developing the learning environments of the future. At these early phases, hybrid methodologies and design experiments

are more appropriate. Conducting experimental research is expensive, and it wouldn't be practical to do an experiment at every iterative stage of a design experiment. Once well-conceived and solidly researched new curricula are in place, then experimental methodologies can appropriately be used to compare them.

3. Experimental methodologies identify causal relations between inputs and outcomes, but they cannot explain the causal mechanisms that result in those relations – the step-by-step processes of learning – and as a result, these methodologies are not able to provide specific and detailed suggestions for how to improve curricula and student performance.

A typical learning sciences research project involves at least a year in the classroom; sometimes a year or more in advance to design new software and learner-centered interfaces; and a year or more afterwards, to analyze the huge volumes of videotape data, interviews, and assessments gathered from the classroom. Many learning scientists have developed new technological tools to help with analyzing large masses of complex data. Several such examples were presented in a special issue of the *Journal of the Learning Sciences* edited by Barab and Kirshner (2001). Roth created a database that organizes text, photos, written notes, and copies of student work; Barab et al. developed a graphing tool to represent the classroom's network of activity; Kulikowich and Young developed a computer interface that generated time-stamped records of each student's problem solving process. Many researchers now use the Transana tool for transcribing and analyzing digital video data (freeware downloadable from http://www.transana.org, accessed August 6, 2005). New tools for digital video ethnography are being developed (Goldman et al., in press).

The studies reported in this handbook typically took at least three years to complete – and the research behind each chapter

has resulted in many books, scientific articles, and research reports. This is complex, difficult, and expensive work. It's almost impossible for any one scholar to do alone; most learning sciences research is conducted by collaborative teams of researchers – software developers, teacher educators, research assistants to hold the video cameras and transcribe the tapes, and scholars to sift through the data, each using different methodologies, to try to understand the learning processes that occurred, and how the learning environment could be improved for the next round. Because it requires such a massive human effort, learning sciences work has tended to occur at a small number of universities where there is a critical mass of faculty and graduate students, and has tended to cluster around collaborative projects supported by large NSF grants at those universities. The NSF recognized this in 2003 and 2005 by creating a few large Science of Learning Centers. This trend will continue, and the learning sciences, to a certain extent, will become more like "big science."

To create the schools of the future, we will need more research sites, and the government will have to increase its funding dramatically. Fortunately, a necessary first step is occurring: training the next generation of scholars in doctoral programs to prepare them to take faculty positions and start their own research projects. These doctoral students are being trained in interdisciplinary learning sciences programs; they are learning to draw on a wide range of theoretical frameworks and research methodologies, and learning to combine the basic sciences of learning with hands-on issues like classroom organization, curriculum and software design, teacher education, and assessment.

The Goals of Education and the Nature of Knowledge

The shift away from the industrial economy makes the facts and procedures emphasized by instructionism insufficient. In addition, students need deep knowledge: the ability to think and reason, the ability to use knowledge in the authentic practices of their everyday lives, and the ability to deeply understand the scientific and technological systems that are increasingly important in society. The theory of knowledge that forms the basis of the learning sciences is taken from the cognitive sciences and from studies of knowledge work, and involves theories of representation, knowledge structures, expert practices, concepts, and understanding.

Most of the chapters in this handbook focus on math and science learning. Learning scientists may have focused on science and math simply because there is more government funding for such research (Kolodner, personal communication). But this raises an important question: Does the same kind of knowledge underlie subjects like history, literature, and the arts? Learning sciences researchers tend to believe that the general principles emerging from their work in math and science classrooms are relevant to all content areas (e.g., Bransford, Brown, & Cocking, 2000). But we have not yet done the research to determine whether this is true. After all, knowledge in science and math shares characteristics that are not likely to hold true of softer disciplines: it is rigorously articulated, it has attained a high degree of consensus, and detailed representational formalisms exist to represent such knowledge. Disciplinary knowledge in history, art, and literary criticism is different, and it may turn out that these forms of knowledge are learned in fundamentally different ways than science and math.

Building the Community

The learning sciences approach is relatively new – the name was coined in 1989, and the research tradition extends only back to the 1970s. There are several groups of scholars engaged in learning sciences research who do not necessarily use that term for their research; the learning sciences community should actively engage with these groups to grow the field:

The large community of *educational technologists* and *instructional system designers* who develop computer software for instructional purposes. This community includes university researchers but also for-profit software companies developing training systems for corporations and "integrated learning systems" for schools.

The large community of *cognitive psychologists* and *cognitive neuroscientists* who are studying basic brain functions that are related to learning. One of the most significant research topics in cognitive psychology today is *memory*, and memory research has obvious potential implications for education (e.g., Roedinger & Karpicke, in press).

The large community of *educational psychologists* that are studying a wide range of psychological functions related to learning. A subset of this group that will be particularly important to bring into the learning sciences will be assessment researchers, both in universities and at institutions like the Educational Testing Service (the developer of many widely used tests including the SAT, AP, and GRE).

The task facing society today is to design the schools of the future, and that is a massive undertaking that will involve many different communities of practice.

Education: The Hardest Science

We usually refer to natural sciences like physics and biology as the "hard" sciences, and social sciences like psychology, education, and sociology as the "soft" sciences. But the biologist Edmund Wilson pointed out that in fact, the social sciences are much harder than the natural sciences, because the systems they study are infinitely more complex (1998). The social systems studied by learning scientists are some of the most complex systems in the modern world – they contain students, teachers, administrators, parents, and politicians, networked in complex overlapping patterns; they contain complex products like textbooks, worksheets, experimental apparatuses, maps, and classroom posters; they contain assessments and criteria for success like grades and standardized tests; and they contain education researchers, trying to ensure that the whole system is grounded in the sciences of learning. Given this complexity, it should not be surprising that only a few decades of research have not completely revealed the deepest secrets of how learning works. But we have started down the road and the schools of the future are slowly taking shape.

In the next ten to twenty years, the task facing all knowledge societies will be to translate learning sciences research into educational practice. Perhaps the most solid finding to emerge from the learning sciences is that significant change can't be done by fiddling around at the edges of a system that remains instructionist at the core. Instead, the entire instructionist system will have to be replaced with new learning environments that are based on the learning sciences. Many tasks have to be accomplished:

Parents, politicians, and school boards must be convinced that change is necessary. The shift will require an initial investment in computers, software, and network infrastructure – perhaps even new buildings with as-yet-undetermined architectural designs – but once the shift is in place the annual costs will not necessarily be any more than current expenditures on textbooks and curricular materials.

Textbooks must be rewritten (or even reconceived as laptop-based software packages), to present knowledge in the developmentally appropriate sequence suggested by the learning sciences, and to present knowledge as a coherent, integrated whole, rather than as a disconnected series of decontextualized facts.

The shift to customized, just-in-time learning will result in a radical restructuring of the school day, and will make many features of today's schools obsolete: schools years will no longer be grouped by age, school days will no longer be organized into class periods, standardized tests will no longer be administered en masse to an auditorium of students, not everyone will graduate high school or start college at the same age. Many of the socially entrenched aspects of schools that are not directly related to education will change as a result: organized sports, extracurricular activities, class parties that function as rites of passage.

The relationship between the institution of school and the rest of society may need to change, as network technologies allow learners to interact with adult professionals outside the school walls, and as classroom activities become increasingly authentic and embedded in real-world practice.

Standardized tests must be rewritten to assess deep knowledge instead of surface knowledge, and to take into account the fact that due to customization, different learners might learn different subject matter.

Teacher education programs must prepare teachers for the schools of the future.

We are at an exciting time in the study of learning. This handbook was created by a dedicated group of scholars committed to uncovering the mysteries of learning. These researchers have been working since the 1970s, developing the basic sciences of learning – beginning in psychology, cognitive science, sociology, and other disciplinary traditions, and in the 1980s and 1990s, increasingly working closely with educators and in schools. Since the 1990s, the brain research of cognitive neuroscience has made rapid progress that may soon allow it to join with the learning sciences (Bransford et al., this volume). As these scholars continue to work together in a spirit of interdisciplinary collaboration, the end result will be an increasingly detailed understanding of how people learn. And once that understanding is available, the final step to transform schools must be taken by our whole society: parents and teachers, and the administrators and politicians who we entrust with our schools.

Acknowledgment

I would like to thank John Cherniavsky, Allan Collins, Stacy DeZutter, Janet Kolodner, and Barbara Olds for their helpful comments on earlier drafts of this chapter.

References

Barab, S., & Kirshner, D. (Eds.). (2001). *Rethinking methodology in the learning sciences.* Special issue of *Journal of the Learning Sciences,* Volume 10, Issues 1 and 2. Mahwah, NJ: Lawrence Erlbaum Associates.

Bell, D. (1973). *The coming of the post-industrial society: A venture in social forecasting.* New York: Basic Books.

Bereiter, C. (2002). *Education and mind in the knowledge age.* Mahwah, NJ: Lawrence Erlbaum Associates.

Borja, R. J. (2005, May 5). Cyber schools' status. *Education Week, 24,* 22–23.

Bransford, J. D., Brown, A. L., & Cocking, R. R. (Eds.). (2000). *How people learn: Brain, mind, experience, and school.* Washington, DC: National Academy Press.

Cherniavsky, J. C. (2005). *Research on cognitive tutors.* Paper presented at the American Educational Research Association, Montreal, Canada.

Collins, A., & Halverson, R. (in preparation). *The second educational revolution: From apprenticeship to schooling to lifelong learning.*

Drucker, P. F. (1993). *Post-capitalist society.* New York: HarperBusiness.

Gobert, J., Buckley, B. C., & Dede, C. J. (2005). *Logging students' learning with hypermodels in BioLogica and Dynamica.* Paper presented at the American Educational Research Association, Montreal, Canada.

Goldman, R., Pea, R., Barron, B., & Derry, S. (Eds.). (in press). *Video research in the learning sciences.* Mahwah, NJ: Lawrence Erlbaum Associates.

Hargreaves, A. (2003). *Teaching in the knowledge society: Education in the age of insecurity.* New York: Teacher's College Press.

Kozma, R. B. (Ed.). (2003). *Technology, innovation, and educational change: A global perspective.* Eugene, OR: International Society for Technology in Education.

Lederman, N. G., Adb-El-Khalick, F., Bell, R. L., & Schwartz, R. S. (2002). Views of Nature of Science Questionnaire (VNOS): Toward valid and meaningful assessment of learners' conceptions of nature of science. *Journal of Research in Science Teaching, 39*(6), 497–521.

Ministry of Education, Finland. (1999). *Education, training, and research in the information society: A national strategy for 2000–2004* (ISBN 952-442-228-X). Helsinki, Finland: Ministry of Education.

Ministry of Education, Singapore. (2002). *Masterplan 2.* Available at http://www.moe.gov.sg/edumall/mp2/mp2.htm. Accessed August 5, 2005.

OECD. (2000). *Knowledge management in the learning society.* Paris: OECD Publications.

OECD. (2004). *Innovation in the knowledge economy: Implications for education and learning.* Paris: OECD Publications.

Papert, S. (1980). *Mindstorms: Children, computers, and powerful ideas.* New York: Basic Books.

Raudenbush, S. W. (2005). Learning from attempts to improve schooling: The contribution of methodological diversity. *Educational Researcher, 34*(5), 25–31.

Roediger, H. L., & Karpicke, J. D. (in press). Test-enhanced learning: Taking memory tests improves long-term retention. *Psychological Science.*

Rogoff, B. (1998). Cognition as a collaborative process. In D. Kuhn & R. S. Siegler (Eds.), *Handbook of child psychology, 5th edition, Volume 2: Cognition, perception, and language* (pp. 679–744). New York: Wiley.

Sawyer, R. K. (2004). Creative teaching: Collaborative discussion as disciplined improvisation. *Educational Researcher, 33*(2), 12–20.

Sawyer, R. K. (in press). Educating for innovation. *The Journal of Thinking Skills and Creativity.*

Schank, R. C. (1999). The disrespected student, or, the need for the virtual university: A talk with Roger Schank (interview with John Brockman, 8/16/1999), http://www.edge.org/3rd/culture/schank/schank/index.html, accessed August 1, 2005.

Schmidt, W. A., & McKnight, C. C. (1997). *A splintered vision: An investigation of U.S. science and mathematics education.* Dordrecht, The Netherlands: Kluwer Academic.

Schofield, J. W., & Davidson, A. L. (2002). *Bringing the Internet to school: Lessons from an urban district.* San Francisco, CA: Jossey-Bass.

Shavelson, R. J., & Towne, L. (2002). *Scientific research in education*. Washington, DC: National Academy Press.

Skinner, B. F. (1954/1968). The science of learning and the art of teaching. In B. F. Skinner (Ed.), *The technology of teaching* (pp. 9–28). New York: Appleton-Century-Crofts. (Original work published in 1954 in the *Harvard Educational Review* [Vol. 24, No. 2, pp. 86–97]).

Stallard, C. K., & Cocker, J. S. (2001). *The promise of technology in schools: The next 20 years*. Lanham, MD: Scarecrow Press.

Toffler, A. (1980). *The third wave*. New York: Morrow.

Vogel, G. (1996). Global review faults U.S. curricula. *Science, 274*(5286), 335.

Wilson, E. O. (1998). *Consilience: The unity of knowledge*. New York: Alfred A. Knopf.

Afterword: After How Comes What

Seymour Papert

In a conversation about social science, Marvin Minsky – who was famous for his caustically insightful witticisms – once said: "Anything that calls itself science isn't." Socratically stung by this remark, over the years I have built up a collection of features a would-be new science might borrow from disciplines that do not proclaim their science-ness in their names. Keith Sawyer positions this volume as number two after *How People Learn* in the evolution of a new science, the learning sciences (see Preface, this volume). Perhaps a sample from my collection, presented as an afterword to number two, might prefigure a foreword to number three.

A Sense of the Fundamental

Consider the speeds of light, of sound, and of the bullet train. Each is *important* in its context but physicists would agree that the first has the special status of being *fundamental*. This volume treats many *important* ideas about learning. But our still embryonic science has not yet developed a consensus about which ideas are *fundamental*.

At critical times the mature sciences have identified critical problems whose solutions would spawn theories with fundamental consequences: Is light a particle or a wave? Is there a universal decision procedure for mathematics? What is the genetic code? From time to time one or another theory of learning has enjoyed a heady period of seeming to have a similarly fundamental status – examples include behaviorism, Piaget's theories, and information processing models. But so far all have failed to generate either lasting consensus or transformational advances in practice. The learning sciences will escape Minsky's sting when new contenders for fundamental status emerge.

This essay is guided by a perception that this emergence is inhibited by the narrowness of the boundaries that learning sciences has set for itself. My title expresses one facet of this perception: educational psychology has often focused on how people learn knowledge entities that are given independently of it, while the deepest source of new ideas may be the exercise of inventing new entities. As this possibility becomes apparent in our community, I anticipate a widening of focus from *how* people learn to include more study of *what* they learn. The importance of this issue to the learning sciences is reflected in the title of Part 3 of this handbook, "The Nature of Knowledge" (also see Sawyer's introduction). Could there be a scientific basis for deciding what children should know? What properties of knowledge make it more or less learnable or more or less able to facilitate other learning?

A Thought Experiment

Einstein's famous thought experiment of being in an elevator whose cable had snapped made its point as solidly as equations or experimental observation. I illustrate my belief that a more developed culture of *properly disciplined* thought experiments would enrich thinking about learning by using a thought experiment.

Imagine that learning scientists existed in the days when numbers were manipulated using Roman numerals. Imagine that because only a small number of people could do multiplication, economic progress was very slow, and that learning scientists were funded to mobilize all the great ideas in *How People Learn* to remedy the situation. Undoubtedly better teaching would increase the number of people capable of performing the complex art of multiplication. But something else did this far more effectively: the invention of Arabic arithmetic, which turned the formerly esoteric skill of multiplication into one of the basics.

The question to ponder is how the invention of Arabic arithmetic is related to learning sciences. A simplistic answer is: *not at all, it belongs to mathematics*. Indeed, historically, Arabic numerals were not invented with a educational intent. *But they could have been.* And would that bring it within the scope of our science? Or ponder this: Even if learning scientists considered that the invention of representations for numbers belonged to another discipline, was it not their duty –

before accepting funding to study how to teach Roman numerals better – to perform due diligence to determine whether another way existed? And how could they do this without making part of their science the study of alternative structures of disciplinary knowledge?

Liberating Mathematics from Math[1]

These questions are relevant to thinking about the boundaries of the learning sciences but they barely touch the surface. To go deeper, consider the opinion of Steve Pinker about why language is easier to learn than mathematics:

> On evolutionary grounds it would be surprising if children were mentally equipped for school mathematics. These tools were invented recently in history and in only a few cultures, too late and too local to stamp the human genome.

Stated simplistically, Pinker's Chomskian position is that language learning has become innate because language is old enough to influence the emergence of genes that support it, whereas algebra has not been around long enough. I propose an alternative theory which allows a more constructive role for learning sciences: Language did not stamp the genome, the genome stamped language. Language molded itself, as it developed, to genetic tools already there. The reason algebra is less well aligned with genetic tools is that it was *not allowed* to align itself: it was *made* by mathematicians for their own purposes while language *developed* without the intervention of linguists.

This theory suggests how one might make an entity that would stand to algebra as Arabic arithmetic to Roman arithmetic: a different way (possibly only useful to learners) of achieving the same functional ends. *Creating such entities would be doing artificially for elementary mathematics what a natural process did for language.*[2]

This idea would not long ago have been of only very abstract interest. It is brought down to earth by the presence of digital technologies, combined with theoretical observations – such as noting that computer programming languages share functions and structures with both algebra and natural language. Their language-like side enters in two ways. The first is the now-well-established fact that programming languages such as Logo, Squeak, Boxer, and ToonTalk (Kafai, this volume; Noss & Hoyles, this volume) permit very young concrete-minded children to command computers to perform actions of personal interest. The second, which is more often missed, is seen in the design criterion for Logo to make its version of "variable" also be a version of "pronoun," thus reducing the cognitive distance between algebra and language and making it plausible that both could draw on the same genetic tools. Thus, in what might be a theoretically important sense, saying the word "it" is doing prealgebra and the so-called language instinct is also a mathematics instinct.

Environmentalism as Model

When I was growing up the concepts of "the environment" and "environmentalism" did not exist. Of course we had problems that are addressed today by environmentalists. There was pollution of rivers and soil erosion and deforestation and even an accumulation of hothouse gasses in the atmosphere. But these problems were small enough, and changed slowly enough, to be handled in piecemeal fashion. There were professionals for each of them. There was nobody whose job and professional competence was to deal with the whole of which they are parts, until events such as the 1962 publication of Rachel Carson's *Silent Spring* precipitated a movement that would soon give rise to a truly fundamental idea: thinking in a holistic way about everything that affects the waters, the airs, and the lands of our planet.

I believe that the time has come for an educational concept similar in its holistic nature to "the environment," an entity one might call the Mathetic Environment – everything that affects learning in all its forms. I use the words "mathetic" and "learn-

ing" almost interchangeably. By "mathetic," I mean related to learning; the Greek stem "math-" originally referred to learning as in "polymath," which refers to a person with multiple learnings, not to a mathematician.

Until recently little harm was done by the circumstance that there are specialists on innumerable aspects of learning but nobody whose job and competence are concerned with this whole. As a first step towards explaining what I mean by this, I extend the Roman-Arabic thought experiment as a parable to pinpoint one of the consequences of fragmentation in the field of learning.

Elementary school math specialists are hard at work on very specific problems like undoing misconceptions such as "since LX is ten more than L, LIX should be ten more than LI." The idea of abandoning Roman numerals had occurred to one of them but was immediately dropped: the children would not be able to manage the higher grades. The NCTM had tried to issue standards for all grades based on the new system. But the universities complained and the parents screamed that the kids aren't learning the "real math" they had learned – moreover, all the money they had spent on buying software to prepare the toddlers for school would be wasted. And, besides, the NSF reviewers . . . well enough, the point is clear.

I use a parable to make my point because it is easier to get a consensus that Arabic arithmetic is better for society than it is to get a consensus on any of the many real examples of change that are impeded by similarly antiscientific reasons. The main point I want to make is that significant change in what children learn may require thinking outside the fragmented boxes of the education system. It is a challenge to the learning sciences to find ways to do so.

Love and Fear in the Mathetic Environment

The rapid formation of environmentalism cannot be understood in affectively neutral terms. Carson and others made people aware of frightening dangers; I suspect we may have been lucky that this happened at a time when so many people were in love with such ideas as "holistic" and "nature." In the case of the mathetic environment, my belief in the possibility of a tipping point is fueled by the existence of causes for fear and potentials for love. I begin with the negative side and mention two reasons for alarm.

The biggest effect of computers on school comes from computers out of school and is deeply negative. Every child can see that the school's ways of using computers are not how the increasingly digital society does things. To my mind there is no doubt, and certainly it is a plausible conjecture for scientists of learning to examine, that the growing disaffection with school comes largely from awareness of this gap. I see disaffection most directly in statistics that show a yearly increase in the number of high school students in the United States who declare that what they learn in school is irrelevant to their lives. I see it also in the growing epidemic of "learning disabilities," a name that is belied by noting how often they somehow do not impede the learning of complex computer games. I believe that this growing trend cannot be reversed by "better" teaching of what the children correctly see as obsolete knowledge; it can only be reversed by changing what is learned and taught.

I mention my second promised reason for alarm before hinting at the principles that might guide the selection of new content. There are a billion children in the world who have access to global information, including a direct view on TV screens of a better life than theirs, but do not have the learning opportunities that might enable them to be part of that life. I am not sure whether it is up to the learning sciences to understand more deeply how this deprivation of learning contributes to hatred, violence, and instability. Perhaps this is in any case quite obvious. What I do know for sure is that it has to be on the agenda of the learning sciences to find ways to bring modern learning to these billion people and to do it fast.

It seems obvious to me that the scale of these two alarming situations is such that the means to deal with them will have to be based on mobilizing the same powerful technologies that have caused them. But of course technology alone will not do it. Finding the right ways to use technology is a serious – perhaps the most urgent – challenge facing the learning sciences. But it is easy to find a starting point.

Across the globe there is a love affair between children and the digital technologies. They love the computers, they love the phones, they love the game machines, and – most relevantly here – their love translates into a willingness to do a prodigious quantity of learning. The idea that this love might be mobilized in the service of the goals of educators has escaped no one. Unfortunately, it is so tempting that great energy and money has been poured into doing it in superficial and self-defeating ways – such as trying to trick children into learning what they have rejected by embedding it in a game. Nobody is fooled. The goal should not be to sugar coat the math they hate but offer them a math they can love.

The Mathetic Cupid's Arrow

I became a mathematician by falling in love with mathematics. The passage in my own writing that has been most often quoted and reprinted is a description in my book *Mindstorms* of how I fell in love with mathematics by first becoming attached to a "transitional object" – as it happens, mechanisms involving wheels and gears – which was more meaningful for a young child. The idea which is critical to my present theme has been made more so by two very recent shifts in my thinking.

Until recently, I used the language of "falling in love" quite loosely, as meaning metaphorically nothing more than an intensive form of "like." The first shift consists of exploring the possibility of a more literal meaning and so opening a whole branch of study for the learning sciences. Recent brain studies offer hope of identifying a neural basis for falling in love and for monogamous mating. I have suggested ways in which these studies could be modified to explore the possibility that falling in love with an intellectual topic or an idea could be neurologically as well as metaphorically related to falling in love with a person and that the kind of devotion to a subject that many people develop could be related to the phenomenon of monogamous attachment to a person. If these conjectures have any truth, what we do at school in the name of motivation would be exactly wrong. Teachers try to make every child enjoy the mathematics we have chosen to teach. But when a person falls in love with another this is very different from falling in love with people in general – indeed, almost the very opposite.

My second shift, related to this last remark, modifies what I have long taken as my guiding principle for research in mathematics education: *Instead of making children learn the math they hate let's make a mathematics they will love.* The idea that one could make a mathematics that all children would love now makes me uncomfortable. Instead, I would now set as my guiding goal to give children the means to find unique ways to create a personal mathematics of their own to love.

This might seem like a copout: surely society decides what its citizens should know; and the job of the learning sciences is to facilitate their knowing it. But recall the parable of the shift from Roman to Arabic arithmetic. What "society wants" is not for people to have the ability to manipulate particular symbols whether they are C, X, V, and I or 3, 2, 1, and 0; society wants people to be able to think about numbers and to use them to think about other things. And this is equally true of all mathematics and indeed of all areas of thinking.

There is, of course, a more serious objection: even if the goal is desirable surely it is not attainable; making a mathematics means building a formal system and this is something that only a few highly educated adults have ever done. My answer

approaches the crux of my essay: the objection *was* valid until quite recently, but we see it becoming unraveled by looking at another successful new science – computer science. Today, every one of several million programmers is engaged, although not necessarily in a self-conscious or even useful way, in building formal systems. The deep meaning for children of giving them the ability to program computers is to provide the tools for them to do the same. In my vision, whatever they know intuitively, implicitly, innately, and whatever they care about passionately, could be expressed in the creation of a formal system that is entirely theirs. The deep meaning for the learning sciences of allowing children from the earliest ages to learn an appropriate form of programming is to create for the first time the possibility of freely exploring the infinitely open-ended variety that forms of knowledge and their learning can take.

Making Drugs, Genes, Elements, and Knowledge

Before history, we were scouring nature to find plants that would heal. Later we extracted the compounds responsible. Still later we synthesized them. But in this we were still using what existed independently of us. Recently we are beginning to do something very different: develop substances that never existed in order to produce an effect we understand. One can see a similar progression from a type of breeding that acts indirectly on genes that exist, to modifying them directly, to making them. Alchemists tried in vain to turn one element into another. Today we do it routinely and even make elements that never existed.

Educators in the past have taught knowledge structures that existed independently of them. I have been suggesting that the learning sciences might follow the chemists, the biotechnologists, and the physicists by purposefully making *with a mathetic intent* knowledge structures that never existed. Curriculum designers may protest they have always been doing this. The distinction might be blurry, but I believe that it is worth making and worth studying how to make it better. I do not think one should describe the shift from Roman to Arabic numerals as "making a new curriculum" for arithmetic. That kind of shift is something very different. I began this afterword by suggesting that it might be the exercise ground for seeking the mathetic fundamental. I close by suggesting that finding the conceptual framework for that shift might be the critical fundamental problem our science needs. What does it mean to have mathetically different forms for knowledge? What makes some more learnable? What makes some more lovable?

Footnotes

1. Throughout this essay I use the word "mathematics" as a stand in for all disciplines. I use the word "math" to refer to the largely obsolete stuff they teach in schools.
2. A theoretical framework for this kind of relationship between mathematical structures will be the subject of a projected paper by Uri Wilensky and myself.

Epilogue: The Fundamental Issue in the Learning Sciences

Roger C. Schank

The problem with the learning sciences is that as we learn more about learning, it still remains difficult to act in any important way. Although I am more concerned with K–12 than I am with universities, I write here about universities. Universities should be the easiest educational institutions to change. There are many good reasons to start there, but it is still more or less impossible to make meaningful change in university education. Why? A few reasons (some of which also apply to K–12 schooling):

1. Universities Insist on Admissions Requirements

Gee, this doesn't seem like such a big issue in fixing education, does it? Let me explain.

The fundamental assumption behind university admission requirements is part of what hinders change. Why are there admissions requirements for top universities? Basically there are three arguments for these requirements:

a. There Is Only So Much Space

This argument is sometimes actually true. You can always stuff a few more into a lecture hall, but dorm rooms are expensive to build, and seminars need to be kept small in order to make them work. But, of course, space is not an issue in an online curriculum, so surely this reason wouldn't apply there. So, an online curriculum, the most likely venue for real change based on ideas in the learning sciences, wouldn't have admissions rules then, right?

Well no.

When I worked with Carnegie-Mellon University to build their online curriculum in Computer Science, I proposed admitting anyone who applied. This idea was rejected because of the next number:

b. If Everyone Had a Degree from an Elite School, Then It Would No Longer Be an Elite School, Would It?

Well, maybe not. But why should that matter? A good online university might give out thousands of degrees in a given field. The relevant question to ask would be: *Are the graduates of this program capable of doing something in the real world for which they have been trained by the school?*

Ah, so that is the real reason. Colleges don't typically train anyone to do anything real, so there would be no way to judge. This is why you will never see Yale online. Yale would cease to be seen as "Yale" if suddenly there were hundreds of thousands of graduates. There is no way to judge if Yale graduates can do anything in the real world. That isn't a measure that Yale uses. It was one I introduced in the CMU program I designed but, shall we say, the faculty weren't quite ready for that new model.

And then there is the most commonly cited argument:

c. It Is Difficult to Teach Students Who Are Not Well Prepared

I really love this argument. It says, in essence, that if it is hard to teach certain students, they shouldn't be taught. No idea of taking it as a challenge to get students ready to learn whatever it is you think they should know. Let's just not let them in.

No. Let's let everyone in. Let's design schools that have no space issues (one good reason for online schools.) Let's design schools that do not dwell on their elite name, ones that simply prepare people to do stuff. And, if students aren't ready to learn what is taught at these schools, let's make sure we have a program that meets them where they are and gets them ready.

It can be done. "Anyone can go to a high quality university" is an important idea. A university that teaches real-world skills is an important idea. Space must cease to be an issue to enable the death of the elitism that stifles change. Students would need to understand that if they can't do the work they will be left behind. This makes sense if the work is real.

2. Universities Allow Their Faculties to Determine the Curriculum

Well, why not? Faculty are the experts. Wouldn't they know what students who are studying in their field should learn?

This is indeed an interesting question and one that strikes at the heart of what is wrong with today's universities. The average student goes to college intending to graduate and get a job in a field relevant to what he studied in school. Not a radical thought really? Seems right, no?

However, a professor who teaches the field that the student has decided to study has a number of problems with this pretty straightforward idea; the first problem the professor has with this idea is that he cannot relate to it. In general, professors have not actually worked in the real-world versions of the disciplines they profess. A computer science professor, for example (this was my primary field when I was professor), probably last wrote a computer program when he was a student in school. His specialty in computer science (mine was artificial intelligence) is what he wants to teach. Unfortunately, the average student needs to learn this specialty like he needs a hole in his head. But the professor really doesn't care about this. The professor wants to teach what he knows best, what he loves to think about, and what is the least work for him. So he makes up a dozen rationalizations about why his esoteric field is really very important for any computer science major to know.

Bear in mind that there are a lot of professors in any given department in a large university. And they each want to teach their own specialty. And very few of them have real-world experience. So, when all is said and done, the curriculum is a compromise hodgepodge of specialty subjects that are surely "very important for every student to know" which when taken as a whole will not even come close to getting a student started in his profession in the real world.

Think this is just true of computer science? I was also a psychology professor. Students in that field typically want to work in psychological services, health, counseling, social work, and such. But the professor's specialties are again driving what is required. So everyone has to take cognitive psychology (my specialty in psychology) even if it no way will help them counsel people. Well, it might help them. How could it hurt them? This reasoning is a cover for the fact that many psychology departments don't have any faculty at all in clinical psychology because they do not consider it to be an academic subject. There is no idea at all, in most departments, of allowing students to be preclinical. They typically refuse to teach such practical subjects – often because they really don't know all that much about them.

Developmental psychology, for example, a subject that teaches about how children develop, is often filled with students who want to know about the children they expect to have some day. Will their professors accommodate them? No way. Their professors don't necessarily know much about child raising. (I have met their children.) What they do know about is how to do research in developmental psychology. They know how to conduct research and feel that they should therefore teach students to conduct research even though their students have no intention whatever of ever doing research in real life.

Wait. It gets worse. Remember those introductory courses you took in psychology? Didn't they seem dull? A mindless survey of everything anyone ever thought in psychology. And there was no way to get out them if you wanted to study anything else in psychology. Want to know why that was the case? In any research university psychology department, the faculty need subjects for experiments. They get them from the intro course; remember the experiments you had to sit through in order to get credit? So all students are funneled into that course in order to provide fodder to the experimental mill going on in the laboratories next door.

Do you see why you can't trust faculty to teach anyone who is not preparing to be exactly the kind of professional that they are – namely, a researcher in a particular specialty within a given field? Professors are enamored with theories and ideas precisely because that is what they deal with all day. If you want practical real-world skills, you won't learn them from them. But why should this be the case? Why shouldn't an undergraduate with no intention of becoming a researcher be unable to pursue a more pragmatic education?

This is simple to explain. Practitioners are looked down upon by researchers. Professors at top universities do not want to think they are training practitioners. That is just training and they don't like it. They rationalize the irrelevant education they provide by saying it is about ideas and that they are teaching you to think. This is a wonderful rationalization that allows them to keep on teaching their own specialties and then be able to go quickly back to doing their research. Lesser universities want desperately to be like the big boys, so even when their professors are not themselves researchers they aspire to be like the heroes of their field. So they teach the same courses they took when they were getting their Ph.D. It doesn't get any better at universities that do not emphasize research.

In general, students and their real-world needs and expectations are ignored by the faculty. Someone other than faculty needs to determine their course of study. Professors have proven that they don't really care about this issue over and over again.

All this happens at any university that exists today but would not happen at a well-planned online university. Why not? Because any new online university would ask advice about what to teach from professionals who did not have a vested interest in the answer. In other words, no online university would have to employ a permanent faculty, so there would be no one to press for their own special needs. In this way, students' needs could actually be served by professionals whose only interest was making sure that students were well-educated in their chosen field.

3. Courses Have Fixed Time Lengths and Are Taken in Parallel

The crux of the issue in teaching students is whether teaching them entails making them memorize information in order to pass tests, or whether it entails creating experiences for students from which they can learn through participation.

Since students typically take courses when they are in school, let's put this issue another way. How long should a course last?

The university's answer: fourteen weeks (plus or minus a few weeks).

And how often should a course meet?

The university's answer: three hours a week (more or less).

One would be right in assuming then, that a course should, for some reason always be about forty-two hours long. I wonder how that number was arrived at and how it happens that all courses are exactly the same length.

Do you think the answer might have anything to do with the needs of students? Or might it be more reasonable to assume that it has to do with the needs of the faculty?

When I was at Northwestern, I was expected to teach one course every two years. This course lasted twelve weeks and met for three hours a week. I was lured to Northwestern from Yale in part by this arrangement; at Yale I had to teach one course every year. (And it lasted sixteen weeks!)

Boy. That sure is weird, huh?

No. It isn't. The more important you are, the less you teach. Teaching, for professors at the top universities, is considered a burden that one is always trying to get out of. Bad professors (those that don't publish or bring in research funds for example) are punished with more teaching.

Now that you know this, and believe me what I am describing is quite normal at top universities, ask yourself why courses are structured the way they are. Whose interests are served by fixed course lengths and minimal course hours per week? You might think that having a student take four or five courses in a semester that are unrelated to each other serves the interests of student breadth and choice. But its actual purpose is helping professors not let teaching get in the way of more important matters. If courses are only going to meet three hours a week, then students will need to take lots of them to keep occupied. The fact that this sometimes leads to students not being able to focus at all on some of their courses does not bother the faculty (unless theirs is the course being blown off).

Courses that are structured in this way do not really allow instruction that is anything other than lecture and test. Designing real experiences for students – ones that allow them to thoroughly investigate something, or build something, or design something – would take more than forty-two hours and would require students to focus on only one or two courses at a time. This would in turn require professors to be available to help students whenever they needed help in pursuing whatever project they were involved in. So while an intensive course might be good for students by letting them get really involved in something, it would be bad for professors since it would not allow them to continue to treat teaching as the least important aspect of their job.

And how long should a course last? As long as it takes to learn whatever it is the student is trying to learn how to do. But how would that work exactly? Students would have to be allowed the freedom to pursue a project in the right time period for them (and for the project). This would mean that professors would have a life that was very unstructured – an unacceptable state of affairs for someone who has more important things on his agenda.

Courses as they exist today probably shouldn't exist at all. They exist to make life easy for faculty. Real teaching would require real experiences. Designing and monitoring those experiences should be what faculty do. It would be what faculty would do in an online university. This kind of apprenticeship-type teaching only happens at the end of Ph.D. programs in today's universities. Professors get serious about Ph.D. students. Perhaps they should get serious about everyone else.

4. Teaching Does Not Occur Just in Time

In an online, learning-by-doing, experience-based, learning environment, teaching occurs on an as-needed basis. Need help in what you are doing? Ask for it. Available to help: mentors, other students, and faculty. Teaching in an as-needed environment is not all that difficult really, especially since those faculty who do it do not have to lecture, meet classes, or grade tests. We did this in the online Master's programs we designed at Carnegie Mellon West and it is working just fine. The CMU West model should be the model for online universities for years to come.

Who should teach? Whoever is capable of mentoring a student through a particular issue. The idea of one teacher, one course is a classroom-based idea. In an online curriculum, there can be math mentors, physics mentors, computer mentors, writing mentors, and teamwork mentors all available as part of the same course.

The idea that the experts who teach must be Ph.D.s who are top-ranked researchers makes little sense in a project-oriented environment. When building a Web site as part of a project on medical information, for example, the best mentor might be a professional Web site builder, not the medical school staff.

5. Courses Are Dominated by Lectures, Not Projects

Many professors have recognized the value of project-based learning and it is not unusual to find this type of course in a university. One is more likely to encounter such courses in engineering or computer science or journalism. In other words, projects work well in courses in which the end result is a student who has learned to actually do something. This should be true of all fields, not just ones that are obviously about doing.

But more important is the placement of those projects in the curriculum. Typically, one finds the project course at the end of a curriculum – perhaps in the senior year in college. Why is that?

This again comes down to curriculum committees that have determined that one must know this or that before embarking on any real-world experience. They are inter-

ested, as I said, in filling seats in introductory courses. If they let people do project courses first, it would not be possible to make the economics of the department work. Project courses are expensive to run. You have to have a small student–teacher ratio to make them work. The 500–1 ratio that works so well (in terms of money to a department) in a lecture course is replaced by 20–1 or, worse, 10–1. The faculty gets paid the same one way or the other, so departments hate this. Never mind that, at least since Plato, scholars have been pointing out that we really only learn by doing. Students know this too, which is why they all prefer project course to lecture courses. (That is, those who want to learn prefer them.)

Starting with a project makes a lot more sense in terms of deciding whether you like a field as well. Listening to someone talk about a field tells you much less than actually trying to do work in that field will ever teach you. Universities encourage summer internships for this sort of thing. Or, to put this another way, they leave the real teaching to companies that students can get to take them on for free. Unfortunately, the teaching there is hit or miss, as the people in that company are unlikely to be teachers or care much about teaching.

Starting with projects – and, to be honest, continuing with projects (ones that relate one to the other would be nice) – works best for students, but the economics of the university prevent that. Once again, the online university can take care of this issue quiet effectively. The reason: just-in-time teaching is required for project-based learning and just in time teaching works exceedingly well in an online environment. Teachers can be available on demand in an online environment and suddenly the numbers start to work.

6. Success in School Is Still a Competitive Event

There is someone who works for me who is a graduate of a very respectable academic institution. I often need him to write things, but I keep having to remind myself not to ask him because he simply cannot write a coherent English sentence. The other day I asked him how it was possible that he could be a graduate of this esteemed institution and yet not be able to write at all. He responded that he was a math major in college and that he had chosen math precisely because there would be no papers to write. He knew he could not write. He therefore avoided writing courses. Now this may seem – and of course it is – the exact opposite of what college is supposed to be about. Shouldn't one focus on what is hard and learn that? How naïve!

This man was on a scholarship. He did not want to do anything to jeopardize the scholarship and that would include taking a course that might result in a bad grade. I remember a friend of my son who majored in psychology because it was full of multiple choice tests and he said he was very good at those tests. What a reason to study

something! I remember a French kid in one of my French classes when I was in college. When I asked him what he was doing there, he said it was an easy "A."

As long as education produces winners and losers, we will not be able to make meaningful change. As long as school is viewed as a competition, we will have players of the game who are good at the game but learn very little.

To various degrees, what I've said holds true of K–12 education as well. Semesters, courses, tests, and school-day schedules aren't designed for students but for teachers, administrators, politicians, and the buildings and rooms that classes are held in. Success in K – 12 schooling is also treated as a competitive event. Until all of this changes, the learning sciences will have only a limited impact on education. Real change in education requires more than research in education. There is a battle to be waged out there. Go to it!

Author Index

Subject Index